Female Entrepreneurship and the New Venture Creation

Women represent the fastest growing group of entrepreneurs today. Despite the enormous economic contributions of this group, female entrepreneurship remains under-explored and inadequately covered in academic literature.

Female Entrepreneurship and the New Venture Creation aims to address this gap by shedding light on the unique aspects of female entrepreneurship. Tracing women's journey along the venture creation process, Kariv's book:

- highlights the creatively different ways in which women approach the entrepreneurial enterprise;
- takes into account different environmental and cultural constraints that impact female entrepreneurship;
- provides a theoretical framework for the venture creation process that is practical and broadly applicable;
- includes in-depth case studies drawn from contributors around the world.

This book captures the diversity of female entrepreneurship and provides a valuable synthesis of the insights that emerge from the stories of women entrepreneurs around the world. It will be valuable for students of entrepreneurship, as well as professionals.

Dafna Kariv is a senior lecturer, researcher and the director of the TempusBiz project and "Young Entrepreneurs" at the College of Management, Academic Studies, Rishon LeZion, Israel. She is also a member of the Chair of Entrepreneurship at HEC, Montréal, Canada. Her research interests include entrepreneurship, gender and cross-national research.

Female Entrepreneurship and the New Venture Creation

An International Overview

Dafna Kariv

 Routledge
Taylor & Francis Group

NEW YORK AND LONDON

First published 2013
by Routledge
711 Third Avenue, New York, NY 10017

Simultaneously published in the UK
by Routledge
2 Park Square, Milton Park, Abingdon, Oxon OX14 4RN

Routledge is an imprint of the Taylor & Francis Group, an informa business

© 2013 Taylor & Francis

The right of Dafna Kariv to be identified as editor of this work
has been asserted by her in accordance with sections 77 and 78 of
the Copyright, Designs and Patents Act 1988.

Library of Congress Cataloging in Publication Data
Kariv, Dafna.
  Female entrepreneurship and the new venture creation :
    an international overview / Dafna Kariv.
    p. cm.
  1. Businesswomen.   2. Self-employed women.   3. Women-
  owned business enterprises.   4. Entrepreneurship.
  5. Businesswomen–Case studies.   6. Self-employed
  women–Case studies.   7. Women-owned business
  enterprises–Case studies. I. Title.
  HD6072.5.K37 2012
  338'.04082—dc23

                                              2012001446

ISBN: 978-0-415-89686-3 (hbk)
ISBN: 978-0-415-89687-0 (pbk)
ISBN: 978-0-203-14098-7 (ebk)

Typeset in Garamond
by RefineCatch Limited, Bungay, Suffolk, UK

This book is dedicated to the memory of Mr Dan David

Dan was an inspirational figure, a visionary leader, a creative and yet very practical man; he was the best role model for entrepreneurial spirit and action.

His thoughts and insights regarding this book were most valuable, and are reflected throughout the manuscript.

Dan passed away in September, 2011.

Contents

Figures   xiv
Tables   xvi
Acknowledgments   xviii
Preface   xx
Personal Outlook   xxii
Contributors   xxiv

**Introduction: The Area of Female Entrepreneurship
in the Initial Phases of the New Venture Creation**   1
   *The Entrepreneurial Revolution and the Contributions of
     Female Entrepreneurship 6*
   The Area of Female Entrepreneurship 7
   Female Entrepreneurship and Diversity 13
   The Global Sphere in the Female Entrepreneurial Realm 16
   The Book's Rationale 18
   The Theoretical Framework of this Book 18
   The Organization of the Book 21
   The Book's Model 24
   What Does the Book Not Entail? 24
   The Book's Contribution 25

   ***Case Study** 26*
   Marie-Louise Roy: True Freedom through Entrepreneurship 27
   JOËLLE PIFFAULT AND LOUIS JACQUES FILION

**PART 1
Female Entrepreneurship: What Makes this
Area Unique?**   39

  1 **Female Entrepreneurship: Constraints and
     Opportunities—A General Overview**   41

An International View 43
Directions in Female Entrepreneurship 46
Macro and Micro Perspectives on Female Venture Creation 52
Summary 57

Case Study 57
Female Entrepreneurship in France: Fighting against Socio-cultural
Heritage 58
KATHERINE GUNDOLF AND ANNABELLE JAOUEN

At a Glance 63
Comparing Paradoxes: The Cases of Norway and Thailand 63
ELIN M. OFTEDAL AND LENE FOSS

2 Motivations for Becoming Entrepreneurs:
A Woman's Perspective   72
Motivation to Start a Business: A Female Outlook 73
Opportunity and Necessity Motivations 76
The Female Entrepreneurial Mindset 79
Work–Family Topics 84
Summary 90

Case Studies 92
Marketing Women: A Sector Experience 93
CLARE BRINDLEY, CARLEY FOSTER AND DAN WHEATLEY
Necessity Entrepreneurs in France: Women and Business
Support Services 99
JANICE M. BYRNE AND ALAIN FAYOLLE

3 Female Venture Creation Process in Emerging
Markets: BRIC and MENA   115
The Emerging BRIC Markets 120
The Emerging BRIC Markets and the Female Perspective 122
The MENA Countries 124
Women's Entrepreneurial Perspective 125
Summary 126

Case Studies 127
China: The Rise of Select Female Entrepreneurs in the
Economic Reformation 128
WENXIAN ZHANG, ILAN ALON AND SHIRLEY ZE YU
Russia: Marina Kretova and Deonis: Entrepreneurial
Growth in the Russian Context 133
TATIANA IAKOVLEVA, JILL R. KICKUL AND LISA K. GUNDRY

*India: The Profits of Non-profits: Women Entrepreneurship
of NGOs 139*
MEENAZ KASSAM, BHAGYASHREE RANADE AND
FEMIDA HANDY
*Brazil: Balancing Work, Family and Social Entrepreneurship:
A Woman Entrepreneur in Action 144*
MARIA FREITAG AND CÂNDIDO BORGES

PART 2
The Venture Creation Process   153

4 **The Pre-venture Stages**   155
   A General Look into the Pre-launching Stages 156
   The Woman's View 159
   Communicating the Idea 169
   Summary 174

   Case Studies 174
   Supply Chain Management in Sri Lanka 175
   MARTHA E. REEVES
   Inuit Women Entrepreneurs Recognizing Opportunities 180
   ALDENE MEIS MASON, LEO-PAUL DANA AND ROBERT
      B. ANDERSON

   At a Glance 188
   Madame Vongpackdy Sithonh 188
   LEO-PAUL DANA

5 **Personal Core Competencies in Starting a
   New Venture**   196
   Core Competencies and the Quest for Capability 197
   *The Competitive Advantage Brought by Women
      Entrepreneurs "To the Table" 199*
   Networking and Social Capital 202
   The "Flip Side" of Social Capital in the Female Realm 205
   *The Function/Malfunction of Support Systems in the
      Woman Entrepreneur's Realm 206*
   *Mapping the Fuzzy Zone of Ethics in Female
      Entrepreneurship 210*
   Summary 213
   Case Study 214

Cristina Marques and the Instituto Evoluir*: Start-up and Innovation in the Third Sector 214*
EDMILSON LIMA

At a Glance 221
Women's Empowerment and Poverty Reduction through Mobile Phone Micro-enterprise: A Follow-up Study of the Village Pay Phone Program of the Grameen Bank in Bangladesh 221
LINDA HULTBERG AND MOHAMMAD SAHID ULLAH

PART 3
Women's Ride across the River: From Creativity, Innovation and Vision to Implementation   231

6 **Celebrating Creativity in the Female Entrepreneurial Realm**   233
Creativity among Women Entrepreneurs 234
Creativity and Gender 236
Managing Creativity in Women-led Businesses 238
The "Idea" 243
Taking Practical Action 246
Summary 247

Case Study 248
Bushra Ahmed: The Legendary Joe Bloggs 248
SPINDER DHALIWAL

At a Glance 253
Alice Goh: A Female Entrepreneur in Singapore 253
ROSALIND CHEW

7 **Innovation in the Context of Female Entrepreneurship**   258
The Role of Innovation in the Female Venture Creation Process 259
The Resource-based View on the Quest for Innovation 263
Innovation/Adaptation 265
Inventions and Breakthroughs among Women Entrepreneurs 272
Risk-taking: The Enigma of Innovation—A Female View 273
Summary 275

Case Studies 276
Sweden: Women's Entrepreneurship in a Scandinavian Welfare State 276
ELISABETH SUNDIN AND CARIN HOLMQUIST

8 The Vision: The Foundation of Entrepreneurship   282
   Vision in the Venture Creation Process 283
   Vision and Gender 286
   The Feminine Vision and Women Visionaries 289
   Vision and Mental Models 291
   Communicating the Vision 292
   Vision as the Driving Force 293
   Summary 296

   Case Study 297
   Chantale Robinson and Kilookas: Barking up the Right Tree! 297
   GENEVIÈVE GUINDON AND LOUIS JACQUES FILION

PART 4
The First Steps in Venture Creation   313

9 "In the Midst of Difficulty Lies Opportunity":
   A Woman's View   315
   The Process of Opportunity Exploitation 316
   Is There a Gendered Style in Opportunity Exploitation? 319
   Opportunities and the Business Life Cycle 321
   Networking and Social Capital 325
   Learning and Innovating in Shaping New Opportunities 328
   Hurdles Typical to Venture Creation of Women-led Businesses 332
   Planning through a Female Perspective 336
   Breaking Down the Risk Barriers 337
   Woman-related Strategies 340
   Summary 342

   Case Studies 343
   Coronilla of Bolivia: Leading Change in the Family Business 343
   BENOÎT LELEUX AND ANOUK LAVOIE ORLICK
   *Ines in Germany: From Cleaning Lady toward Holding a
      World Patent 352*
   KERSTIN ETTL AND FRIEDERIKE WELTER

10 Financing the New Venture: The Untapped
    Perspective in Female Entrepreneurship   358
    What Does the Financial Process Entail? 359
    Seeking Capital: Is There a Woman's Way? 361
    Women and Capital Acquisition 364

*The Reasons that Women and Men Use Different Strategies
   to Raise Initial Capital 370*
*Networks Genius: The Role of Networking in Capital
   Acquisition 374*
Women and the Investors' Community 382
Summary 383

Case Studies *384*
Smith Whiley & Company 385
SUSAN COLEMAN AND ALICIA ROBB

*Women Investment Portfolio Holding (WIPHOLD) of South Africa:
   Empowerment through Private Equity 390*
BENOÎT LELEUX

At a Glance *400*
Bliss Soy Cheese 400
RAMACHANDRAN KAVIL AND ERIN ROGALSKI

11 Entrepreneurial Paths of Women Entrepreneurs   405
New Career Patterns and Female Entrepreneurship 406
Home-based Entrepreneurship 410
Virtual Entrepreneurship 411
Multiplicity in Entrepreneurial Avenues 412
The Preferred Entrepreneurial Avenue 417
Social Entrepreneurship 420
Entrepreneurial Career Changes 424
Generations and Female Entrepreneurship 425
Summary 427

Case Studies *427*
Corinne: A Social Entrepreneur from Réunion Island 428
PATRICK VALÉAU
Women Entrepreneurs in Russia 433
ANN-MARI SÄTRE

PART 5
The Future of Female Entrepreneurship   441

12 Leadership in Female Entrepreneurship   443
Entrepreneurs Are Leaders 444
Leadership Styles and Gender in a Nutshell 445
Women Entrepreneurs and Leaders 446

Vision—The Linking Chain 450
Leaders and Investors in Their Fields 452
The Key Roles of the Leader-founder 454
Emotional Skills and Leadership—The Female Entrepreneurship
  Context 457
The Diva Phenomenon 458
Summary 461

Case Studies *462*
Personal History, Passion and the Entrepreneurial Project: Maria
  Montessori and Her Schools 462
VERONIKA KISFALVI AND FRANCINE RICHER
Born Green and Global: The Case of MADARA Cosmetics 469
ARNIS SAUKA AND FRIEDERIKE WELTER

13 **Breaking through the Barriers**   476
Understanding the Meaning of Business Growth 477
Promoting Female Entrepreneurship—Growth Strategies 478
The Dilemma of Growth in the Female Realm 482
Grow or Die? The Constraining Factors in Women's
  Business Growth Processes 483
Factors Contributing to Achieving Growth 487
Toward Overcoming Female-related Hurdles 488
Women in the High-tech Sector 492
Going Global 495
Summary 497

Case Studies *498*
An Israeli High-tech Woman Entrepreneur: "I Would Have
  Done the Same Things Again" 499
GILAT KAPLAN AND AYALA MALACH-PINES
Growth Strategies of Women Entrepreneurs in Technology-based Firms 504
BARBARA J. ORSER

Concluding Remarks: The Fortitude of Women
Entrepreneurs   519
Proactivity 520
Empowerment 522

References   530
Index   566

Figures

I.1   Angles in Female Entrepreneurial Research   5
I.2   Distinctiveness of Female Entrepreneurship   8
I.3   An Illustration of the Entrepreneurial Cycle   15
I.4   The Ecosystem: New Venture Creation and Women Entrepreneurs   17
I.5   The Theoretical Framework   21
I.6   The Book Model   24
1.1   An International Look at Female Entrepreneurship and Attitudes   44
1.2   Directions in Feminist Theory   48
1.3   The Main Themes in Female Entrepreneurship Research from Macro and Micro Perspectives   54
1.4   The Two Forces in the Female Entrepreneurship Realm   56
2.1   Motivations and the New Venture Creation   74
2.2   The Push–Pull Tradeoff for Women Entrepreneurs   77
2.3   Work–Life Conflict   85
3.1   Necessity–Opportunity Demonstrations at the Country Level: The Case of Female Entrepreneurship   119
3.2   BRIC vs. G7: Gender Participation in Entrepreneurial Activity   122
4.1   The Unexploited Area of the Pre-venture Creation Process: The Female Outlook   163
4.2   The Pre-launch Steps in the New Venture Creation Process   166
5.1   Core Competencies.   199
5.2   Social Capital Avenues   203
5.3   Female Entrepreneurial Needs   207
5.4   Support Means for Women Entrepreneurs   209
6.1   The Factors Involved in Creativity   235
6.2   Managing Creativity in the Business   240
6.3   Creativity and its Functions in the Female Venture Creation Process   242
6.4   The Idea in Venture Creation: Its Distinctiveness in the Woman's Realm   245

7.1	The Innovation Process: A Macro Perspective	261
7.2	Innovation Flow: A Woman-led Perspective	262
7.3	Women as Innovators	269
7.4	Barriers to Innovation: The Female View	270
8.1	The Vision: A Core Component in the Venture Creation Process	285
8.2	A Look into the Vision as Embedded in Feminist Theories	288
8.3	Vision: A Communication-based View	293
9.1	Opportunity Exploitation and Gender	320
9.2	Barriers and Hurdles Faced by Women Entrepreneurs: The Main Research Findings	335
9.3	Overcoming Women-related Barriers: Best Practices Offered by Successful Women Entrepreneurs	338
10.1	The Origins and Impact of Capital Acquisition	360
10.2	Sources of Financing the Venture: Women's Outlook	367
10.3	Different Classifications for Financing the New Venture	369
10.4	The Spiral Dynamics of Female Capital Raising and (lack of) Networking	377
11.1	Focusing and Leveraging	418
11.2	A Step-by-step Technique: Example of Angelina's Case of Starting a Publishing House for Children's Books in Buenos Aires, Argentina	419
11.3	The Common Ground of Female and Social Entrepreneurship	422
11.4	Career Transition and the New Venture's Life Cycle	425
13.1	Predominant Frameworks for Growth in the New Venture Creation Stages	481
13.2	Gender Comparisons in some Parameters of Business Growth	483
13.3	Key Factors in Female-led Business Growth	484
13.4	Two Approaches to Overcoming Hurdles	490
C.1	The New Ground for Female Entrepreneurship	520

Tables

I.1	The Entrepreneurial Realm	7
I.2	Main Hurdles Reported at Work by Women	10
1.1	Female Entrepreneurship around the Globe	45
1.2	Micro and Macro Perspectives and Female Entrepreneurship	46
1.3	Female Entrepreneurship in Research	47
1.4	Profiling Women Entrepreneurs in the New Venture Creation Process	52
2.1	Opportunity and Necessity Entrepreneurship—Micro Perspective	78
2.2	The Leading Work–Family Perspectives and their Implications for Entrepreneurship	87
2.3	Benefits of Work–Family Balance	90
2.4	What Women Entrepreneurs Need to do to Cope with the Work–Family Conflict	91
2.5	Breakdown of Marketing Occupations by Gender	94
2.6	An Overview of the SMEs	95
2.7	Motivation Factors	104
2.8	Profiling the Necessity Entrepreneur	105
2.9	Reflections on the Business Support Process	106
2.A1	Necessity and Opportunity Entrepreneurship Explained	108
2.A2	Coaching/Mentoring and Business Support Provision	109
2.A3	Overview of Interviews: Consultant and Entrepreneur Profiles	110
4.1	Leading Models of the Business Life Cycle: The New Venture Creation Outlook	157
4.2	Models Introduced to Facilitate Women's Decision-making Processes	170
5.1	Categories of Relevant Female/Male Traits	201
5.2	Main Ethical Concepts in Entrepreneurship	212
7.1	Innovation/Adaptation: Leading Research	266
8.A1	A Typical Working Week For Chantale	309
9.1	The Opportunity Exploitation Process in the New Venture Creation	318

9.2   The New Venture's Life Cycle, Resources Needed and the
      Female View   322
9.3   Networks; Locating Investors; Financial Approach   326
9.4   Main Hurdles Reported by Women Entrepreneurs   333
10.1 Gender Differences in Raising Capital in the New Venture
      Creation Stages   370
10.2 Best Practices Obtained from Women Entrepreneurs on
      how to Raise Capital for Entrepreneurial Ventures   379
12.1 Leadership and Entrepreneurship in the Female Context   448
12.2 The Leader-Founder and Female New Venture Creation   456
13.1 The Main Factors Associated with Businesses that Go Global   495

Acknowledgments

This book stemmed from my enthusiasm to learn more about women entrepreneurs' paths in the process of new venture creation, and to gain a deeper understanding of the role of gender in their fascinating entrepreneurial journey. I am personally intrigued by the experiences of women entrepreneurs from different ecosystems, and my aim with this book is to inspire women to embark on entrepreneurship and realize their dreams.

The creation of this book has been a fascinating journey, both in developing the framework and concept of the main theme, and in locating inspirational stories of women entrepreneurs around the world, contributed by leading researchers in the field. Publication of this book could not have been possible but for the vital support and encouragement provided by a number of people. I acknowledge with grateful thanks the assistance of Sharon Golan, editor of Routledge, New York, for her faith in me. Sharon and her team were at my side throughout the process of writing and publication. Her valuable feedback, practical outlook, thoughtful suggestions and highly professional approach provided me with most significant professional and practical support, freeing me to develop this book and bring it to fruition. Special thanks also to Sara Werden, Routledge, New York, for her strong and consistent support.

My heartfelt thanks go to the contributors of this book, the authors of the case studies and at-a-glance cases introduced in each chapter. My collaborators have added substantial value to this book by providing different angles and insights into the fascinating realm of female entrepreneurship. I am so fortunate to have encountered these extremely professional and dedicated researchers: at some point, academic relationships evolved into a real community of interest where different undertakings have since been initiated and promoted. Their vibrant spirit is echoed throughout the book, to the great benefit of its readers.

I wish to record my great debt to my beloved family; I owe them my deepest appreciation for being the prime and most meaningful source of my inspiration, dedication and strength throughout the writing process. To Raanan, my husband, and to Tomer, Ofir and Shir, my children, whose unconditional belief in me and enthusiasm for my work are my anchor and my drive to pursue my passion for entrepreneurship. Special thanks are due to my mother, Bianca Barel, for guiding me toward implementing my own vision and dreams; for her unflagging moral support, faith in me and constant encouragement. It is a notable asset to have parents that one can be proud of.

My deepest thanks and appreciation go to Professor Louis Jacques Filion, Director of the Rogers—J.A. Bombardier Chair of Entrepreneurship, HEC, Montréal, Canada; so much of my knowledge, curiosity and great interest in entrepreneurship emerged from my valuable interactions with Professor Filion. His support in me in so many aspects imbued me with the entrepreneurial spirit and the tenacity to pursue my dream. His valuable comments and suggestions have greatly expanded my reflections on the essence and dynamics of the entrepreneurial process and have accelerated my pursuit in the entrepreneurial field.

I would like to offer special thanks to Professor Lisa Gundry for her insightful and valuable contributions to this book, and for writing its preface.

I am grateful to the College of Management, Academic Studies, Rishon LeZion, Israel and to their School of Business Administration, which provided the financial support and technical input for the work on which this book is based.

I would like to acknowledge my indebtedness to Ms. Camille Vainstein for her valuable assistance in the copy-editing of this manuscript, and for substantially contributing to shaping my writing into the final form of this book.

Dafna Kariv
December, 2011

Preface

As we enter the second decade of the 21st century, women-owned enterprises have made a substantial and profound impact on the global economy and the sustainability of regional and local communities. In ever-increasing numbers, women are founding new ventures across industries and sectors, and their businesses are contributing to the well-being of their families, communities and even countries. Women are changing the fabric of the workplace, as their firms provide employment and their leadership shapes organizational cultures, work arrangements and performance.

Female Entrepreneurship and the New Venture Creation presents a multi-faceted exploration of women's entrepreneurship across cultures and economies. The book offers contemporary perspectives and practices of women entrepreneurs that deepen our understanding of women's roles as business leaders, employers, mentors, visionaries and champions of change. The chapters are organized within several major themes in the entrepreneurship arena. The book opens with an overview of the discipline, and the constraints and opportunities confronted by women as they found and grow ventures. Part 1 continues with chapters on the motives that drive women to choose entrepreneurship, and new venture creation in emerging markets. Part 2 focuses on the stages of preparation for launching a new venture, and includes the core competencies of entrepreneurs that lead to success. Part 3, creativity, innovation and the role of vision within the female entrepreneurial context, presents the most significant behaviors in business today that enable reinvention and change. Part 4 offers a look at entrepreneurial paths forged by women business owners, and the book concludes in Part 5 with a discussion of leadership issues and the future of female entrepreneurship.

For entrepreneurs and educators, the book showcases the achievements of women entrepreneurs across cultures and industries, and their stories resonate with the experience of millions of women worldwide that have courageously and determinedly created a business venture. These case studies reveal the strategies and practices of women business owners: their motivations and core competencies that drive their businesses, the strategies they deploy to create and grow their firms, the struggles they face in difficult economic and political contexts, and the ways in which they envision the future for their organizations and their communities.

For researchers, the book contains a concise and comprehensive review of the literature on women's entrepreneurship from both macro and micro perspectives. Key topics, levels of analyses and organizing factors are outlined, presenting a thorough view of research on women entrepreneurs across several decades that will prove indispensible to scholars engaged in this field.

A significant feature of this book is its coverage of women entrepreneurs in areas of the world that have not been the focus of entrepreneurship scholarship in the past. This provides new and important insights into the growing economic activity outside North America and Western Europe. The book contains a contemporary analysis of new venture creation in emerging economies, including BRIC (Brazil, Russia, India and China) and MENA (Middle East and North Africa), and the former Soviet Bloc that are of increasing significance to global economic growth. The success of women's ventures in transitional and emerging economies contributes strongly to the health and well-being of communities and families around the world. Women face unique challenges and opportunities in these regions, many of which are discussed in detail along with policy implications for the support of business development and growth in these same regions.

Dafna Kariv is a proven and prolific scholar of entrepreneurship and new venture creation. She has drawn together a group of contributors who provide a wide variety of perspectives on women business owners—their motivations and aspirations, the challenges confronting them, the opportunities they pursue, their strategies for growth, and their contributions to family, community, and greater society. The evolution of women's entrepreneurship has led to a substantive body of knowledge and information that has influenced scholars, teachers, and business founders. With its contribution to research and casework on successful women leaders in new ventures, this book takes its significant place in the field. It will inspire new generations of women entrepreneurs to find the courage and determination to create a new enterprise—and in so doing, better their lives and their families and communities around the world.

Lisa K. Gundry
Professor of Management
Director, Center for Creativity and Innovation
DePaul University
November, 2011

Personal Outlook

As a researcher interested in international entrepreneurship and gender, I have often wondered what makes female entrepreneurship a unique phenomenon; specifically, I am intrigued by the question of whether entrepreneurship might also be a gender-based phenomenon. In the course of my work, I meet with many entrepreneurs around the world, and I can easily identify their entrepreneurial characteristics. Gender-based characteristics are obviously easy to detect, yet female entrepreneurship can take on different forms: a combination of entrepreneurial and gender-based characteristics, an entrepreneurial form in which women exhibit unique, yet not necessarily feminine-based characteristics, a general entrepreneurial form in which gender-based characteristics are concealed, or a gender-based form of initiating a business, where entrepreneurial characteristics are uniquely exhibited.

Female entrepreneurship can be a perceptible, gender-based presentation of the venture creation process, i.e., women exhibit a set of activities by using a feminine style (intuition, better communication skills than men, engaging in social activities), or a latent phenomenon drawing on perceptions and attitudes regarding the venture creation's needs and best practices, which may be differently perceived by the genders. Such perceptions may result in either performing accordingly, or alternatively, performing as "expected" in entrepreneurship, even if such actions do not harmonize with the perceptions; for example, women may assess the validity of some financial sources in a certain way, yet ignore their intuition and perform a structured business plan to assess these financial sources' relevance to their business.

Concurrently, I am fascinated by the ecosystems surrounding female entrepreneurship: specifically, what are the main situations and conditions encountered by women-led ventures, and how do such situations differ from others faced by entrepreneurial businesses? Do the opportunities available to women and men differ? Are different networks used by women and men for their ventures' needs? Are there differences in the challenges and threats imposed on businesses led by women vs. men?

These interests and concerns triggered the journey taken with this book to delve into female entrepreneurship, led by a desire to decipher women's ways of initiating and starting new ventures. This book is not about comparing women to men, but rather about disproving some of the myths and stereotypes about the processes to which women entrepreneurs are subjected, in light of continual evidence showing that women-led businesses, compared to men's, are at a disadvantage in different business measures.

Contributors

Ilan Alon, PhD, is the George D. and Harriet W. Cornell Chair of International Business at Rollins College, Executive Director of the Rollins China Center, and Visiting Scholar and Asia Fellow of the Kennedy School of Government at Harvard University. He has published numerous books, peer-reviewed articles, and chapters on China, and is a regular featured keynoter in many professional organizations. Besides co-editing the mini case studies included in this book with Wenxian Zhang, some of his recent books include *China Rules: Globalization and Political Transformation* (Palgrave-Macmillan, 2009), *The Globalization of Chinese Enterprises* (Palgrave-Macmillan, 2008), *Business and Management Education in China: Transition, Pedagogy and Training* (World Scientific, 2005), *Chinese Culture, Organizational Behavior and International Business Management* (Greenwood, 2003), and *Chinese Economic Transition and International Marketing Strategy* (Greenwood, 2003).

Robert B. Anderson, PhD, is a Professor with the Faculty of Business of the University of Regina and an Adjunct/Visiting Professor at Simon Fraser University. Dr. Anderson has authored or co-authored more than 140 peer-reviewed articles (more than 40 of these are refereed journal articles) on economic development and entrepreneurship. He is the author of two books on the subject, co-author of a third and co-editor of a handbook on research in indigenous entrepreneurship. Bob is past editor of the *Journal of Small Business and Entrepreneurship* and a founding editor of the *Journal of Enterprising Communities* along with Leo-Paul Dana. He served as President of the Canadian Council for Small Business and Entrepreneurship and the Administrative Sciences Association of Canada, and as a Senior Vice-President (Programs) of the International Council for Small Business.

Cândido Borges has a PhD in Management from HEC Montréal, Canada, an MSc in Business Administration from Université du Québec à Trois-Rivieres, Canada, and graduated in business administration from Universidade Católica de Goiás, Brazil. He is adjoint professor at Faculdade de Administração, Ciências Contábeis e Ciências Econômicas

(FACE) Universidade Federal de Goiás (UFG). His areas of interest are entrepreneurship and innovation. His research focuses mainly on issues of new venture creation, technological entrepreneurship, spin-offs and social capital. He teaches courses on Entrepreneurship, Management of Innovation, Business Plan and Fundamentals of Management.

Clare Brindley, PhD, FRSA, is Professor of Marketing and Entrepreneurship at Nottingham Trent University. She is a Director at the Institute of Small Business and Entrepreneurship, founder of the International Supply Chain Risk Management (ISCRIM) network and a member of the Association of Business Schools Third Stream Committee. Her research is focused on women who work in the small business sector and on the impact of marketing on supply chain risk. She has published widely in journals such as the *International Journal of Entrepreneurial Behaviour and Research*, *New Technology Work and Employment*, and the *Journal of Small Business and Enterprise Development*. Her work has been presented at international conferences, including the Institute of Small Business and Entrepreneurship, British Academy of Management and the Academy of Marketing.

Janice M. Byrne is a PhD candidate (ABD) at EM Lyon Business School, France. She received her master's degree from Dublin City University, Ireland in Ecommerce in 2002 and her bachelor's degree in Business and International Marketing at Trinity College, Dublin. She is now in the final year of her doctoral studies at EM Lyon. Her thesis looks at objectives, methods and outcomes of entrepreneurship education and training. Her research reflects her particular interest in training and support, program evaluation and gender. She has published in *Academy of Management Learning and Education* and the *Journal of Industry and Higher Education*.

Rosalind Chew obtained her MA in Economics from the University of Western Ontario, Canada, and PhD in Economics from the National University of Singapore. She is the author of, inter alia, *Workers' Perception of Wage Determination* (Times Academic Press, 1990), *The Singapore Worker: A Profile* (Oxford University Press, 1991), *Employment-driven Industrial Relations Regimes: The Singapore Experience* (Avebury, 1995), and *Wage Policies in Singapore: A Key to Competitiveness* (International Labour Organization, 1996). She was awarded the Singapore Book Prize in 1996. A recognized specialist in the areas of Labor Economics and Industrial Relations, she has served as consultant to the International Labour Organization, the United Nations Industrial Development Organization, National Computer Board and the Ministry of Trade and Industry (Singapore).

Susan Coleman, PhD, is a Professor of Finance at the University of Hartford located in West Hartford, Connecticut. She teaches courses in entrepreneurial and corporate finance at both the undergraduate and graduate levels. Dr. Coleman's research interests include entrepreneurial and small business finance. She has published extensively on the topic of financing women-owned firms and is frequently quoted in the business press. Dr. Coleman is currently writing a book (with Alicia Robb) entitled *A Rising Tide: Financing Strategies for Women-owned Firms.*

Leo-Paul Dana is at GSCM Montpellier, France, on leave from the University of Canterbury in New Zealand, where he has been tenured since 1999. He also holds the honorary title of Adjunct Professor at the University of Regina, in Canada. He has served on the faculties of McGill University and INSEAD. He earned his BA and MBA degrees at McGill University, and a PhD from the Ecole des Hautes Etudes Commerciales. He has published extensively in a variety of leading journals including the *British Food Journal*, *Cornell Quarterly*, *Entrepreneurship Theory & Practice*, *Journal of Small Business Management*, *Journal of World Business*, and *Small Business Economics*.

Spinder Dhaliwal, PhD, academician and author, is a recognized leading expert in her field. She has written extensively about the Asian business community and compiled *Britain's Richest Asians*, reflecting her long-held interest in the field. Her book, *Making a Fortune: Learning from the Asian Phenomenon* (Capstone) has had wide notice. She wrote the influential study *Silent Contributors: Asian Female Entrepreneurs and Women in Business*, which highlighted this important, yet often neglected, issue. Her report for Barclays Bank entitled, "Asian entrepreneurs in the UK" received much attention. Spinder avoids the insularity of many in her profession, and her work targets (and hits) a much wider audience than just students and other academicians. She has been a regular contributor to the Asian media and, in the past few years, has become an increasingly influential figure in more mainstream circles. She was also the Education Editor for *Prospects* magazine and on the editorial panel of PROWESS (promoting women's enterprise), and was Vice President of the Institute of Small Business and Enterprise (ISBE). Spinder is invited to address audiences as a speaker, is a freelance writer, and helps major organizations target and understand the Asian community.

Kerstin Ettl is a Postdoctoral Researcher at the University of Siegen, Germany. Her research interests are entrepreneurship in general, and women's entrepreneurship, particularly with regard to the success of women entrepreneurs.

Alain Fayolle is Professor and Director of the Entrepreneurship Research Centre at EM Lyon Business School (France). His current research is focused on the dynamics of entrepreneurial processes, necessity entrepreneurship and poverty, critical studies in entrepreneurship, the influences of cultural factors on organizations' entrepreneurial orientation and the evaluation of entrepreneurship education. His last published research has appeared in

Academy of Management Learning & Education, Entrepreneurship and Regional Development, International Journal of Entrepreneurship and *Innovation, Frontiers of Entrepreneurship Research.*

Dr. Louis Jacques Filion, BA, BSS, MA, MBA, PhD, is the Rogers–J.A. Bombardier Professor of Entrepreneurship at HEC Montréal. He has broad professional experience in entrepreneurship and management and has created and managed small businesses. He has more than 200 publications, including 15 books. His research is concerned with the activity systems of entrepreneurs and intra-preneurs, the visionary process and new venture creation.

Lene Foss, PhD, is a full Professor at the Tromsø University Business School where she teaches and studies entrepreneurship, innovation and enterprise development. Dr. Foss has 70 publications, including refereed articles, books, book chapters, and research reports. Her international experience includes being a visiting scholar twice at the University of North Carolina at Chapel Hill, USA and at the University of Exeter, UK. She has been on the editorial board of *AMJ* and is now on the board of *IJGE.*

Carley Foster, PhD, is Reader in Retail Management at Nottingham Business School. Carley's main research interests explore employer branding and diversity issues associated with retail careers and retail service encounters. Her work has been funded by the ESRC, the British Academy, the DTI, the Academy of Marketing and the European Social Fund. She has published widely in journals such as the *International Journal of Retail & Distribution Management*, the *International Review of Retail, Distribution and Consumer Research* and the *Human Resource Management Journal.* Her work has been presented at international conferences including the British Academy of Management, EURAM, the Academy of Marketing, EAERCD and EIRASS.

Maria Freitag graduated in Business Administration from Universidade Estacio de Sa, Brazil, has an MSc in Business Administration from Universidade Federal do Rio Grande do Norte, a Doctor in Education from Universidade Federal do Rio Grande do Norte, Brazil, with a doctoral stage at the University of Aveiro, and an MBA from Universidade de São Paulo (FIA/USP). She is adjoint professor at Faculdade de Administração, Ciências Contábeis e Ciências Econômicas (FACE) Universidade Federal de Goiás (UFG). Her research projects are in the areas of organizational learning, skills, knowledge management and entrepreneurship. She teaches courses on human resources management and organizational theory. Her professional experience in human resources management includes several years at Petrobras, the Brazilian oil company.

Geneviève Guindon has a Bachelor's degree in Agro-food Economics and Management from Laval University, as well as a Certificate in Financial

Management from HEC Montréal. She has been an accountant for Desjardins Venture Capital since 2007, and is a member of Québec's order of CMA (Certified Management Accountants). She is the daughter of Dr. Paul Guindon, and has known Chantale Robinson for several years.

Katherine Gundolf, Associate Professor Dr., has been working at Groupe Sup de Co Montpellier Business School since 2006. Her research is published in top-tier French and international journals. Author of several books, her research activities focus on the field of entrepreneurship and particularly on microfirms. Recently, she has worked on alliances between microfirms, mergers between size-unequal partners, collective entrepreneurship and social networks.

Lisa K. Gundry is Professor of Management in the Kellstadt Graduate School of Business and Director of The Center for Creativity and Innovation at DePaul University, where she teaches courses in creativity and innovation in business, and entrepreneurship strategy. She conducts research, consults and is a frequent speaker to business on issues related to innovation processes in organizations and entrepreneurial growth strategies. She has authored several books, including the recently published *Women in Business: The Changing Face of Leadership*, and *Entrepreneurship Strategy: Changing Patterns in New Venture Creation, Growth, and Reinvention*, as well as numerous articles in academic and business publications. She received her PhD from Northwestern University.

Femida Handy received her PhD from York University in Canada, where she previously taught in the Department of Economics and Faculty of Environmental Studies. Dr. Handy now teaches economics of the nonprofit sector at the University of Pennsylvania's School of Social Policy & Practice. Her research interests include economics of the nonprofit sector, entrepreneurship, volunteerism and women's empowerment. She is currently chief editor of *Nonprofit and Voluntary Sector Quarterly*. Dr. Handy has published many papers and several books, including award-winning research articles. Her recent co-authored books include: *From Seva to Cyberspace: The Many Faces of Volunteering in India* in 2011 and a children's book, *Sandy's Incredible Shrinking Footprint*.

Carin Holmquist, PhD and Professor in Business Administration, holds the Family Stefan Persson Chair of Entrepreneurship and Business Creation at Stockholm School of Economics. Together with her former colleague Professor Elisabeth Sundin, now professor at Linköping University, she did pioneering work on women as entrepreneurs in Sweden. In 1989, they had already presented their first book (in Swedish *Kvinnor som företagare, Osynlighet, Mångfald anpassning*) and in 2003, a second. In addition, they have written many articles, both together and as solo writers, and with others on the topic. An example of the last is "Women's Entrepreneurship: Issues and Policies" (OECD 2004), co-author Frédéric Delmar.

Linda Hultberg is studying Media and Communication Studies at Jönköping University in Sweden. She got an MFS scholarship from Swedish International Development Assistance (SIDA). Her research interests include Development Communication and Communication Technologies. She has presented her research at academic conferences, including the International Association for Media and Communication Research (IAMCR) congress in Stockholm.

Tatiana Iakovleva received her Master of Science in Business in Norway (1998) and in Russia (1999), and a PhD in management from Bode Graduate School of Business, Norway (2007). From 2006 to 2008, she was a Senior Researcher in the Nordland Research Institute (Bodø, Norway). In 2008 she joined the Business School at Stavanger University (Norway) as an associate professor, and since 2009 she has been working in the Centre for Innovation Research within the Business School. Dr. Iakovleva's research interests include personal and organizational antecedents leading to innovation and superior entrepreneurial performance, female entrepreneurship, entrepreneurship in transitional economies, as well as factors affecting entrepreneurial intentions. She has several publications in international journals, including *Education and Training*, *International Journal of Entrepreneurship and Small Business*, *International Journal of Business and Globalization*, and the *International Journal of Entrepreneurship and Innovation*.

Annabelle Jaouen, Associate Professor Dr., is an Associate Professor at Montpellier Business School, France. She specializes in SMEs and microfirm strategies. She is the author (or co-author) of several books on the subject and regularly advises entrepreneurs on the creation or development of their projects. Her research has been published in French and international peer-reviewed journals, and concerns entrepreneurial types, territorialized cooperative strategies, alliances and networks, human resources management, as well as information systems in very small businesses.

Gilat Kaplan, PhD, is a certified clinical psychologist and clinical supervisor in psychotherapy and psycho-diagnostics. Dr. Kaplan's research focuses on psychological profiles of high-technology entrepreneurs and managers from a psychoanalytic point of view. She has published several articles, book chapters and lectures on this topic. She is the head of a mental health clinic for executives in governmental service and holds a private psychotherapy, selection and career guidance practice. Dr. Kaplan's current interest lies in the interrelationships between the individual's inner world and the culture and outer world that surrounds him/her.

Dafna Kariv, PhD, is tenured at the School of Business Administration, the College of Management, Rishon LeZion, Israel, and a member of the Chair of Entrepreneurship at HEC, Montréal, Canada. She teaches entrepreneurship; her research and publications focus on the areas of multinational entrepreneurship and gender. She is the author of the book: *Entrepreneurship: An International Introduction* (Routledge, 2011). Dr. Kariv is the recipient of several awarded funds, including the European Commission Grant on the topic "fostering entrepreneurship in higher education." Dr. Kariv is active in practical programs for entrepreneurs, such as consultant of the Ministry of Education in entrepreneurship, initiator of an incubator-workshop for students and representative of the Dan David foundation for entrepreneurship.

Meenaz Kassam received her PhD in Sociology from the University of Toronto, Canada where she previously taught. Dr. Kassam now teaches sociology at the American University of Sharjah, UAE. Her research interests include nonprofit entrepreneurship, volunteerism and women's empowerment. Her teaching interests include environmental issues, the sociology of human behavior and sociological theory. Dr. Kassam works with NGOs in India and co-authored *Grass Roots NGOs: The Driving Force of Development in India* (2006), and more recently, *From Seva to Cyberspace: The Many Faces of Volunteering in India* (Sage Publishers). She has also published several award-winning journal articles and book chapters.

Ramachandran Kavil is the Thomas Schmidheiny Chair Professor of Family Business and Wealth Management at the Indian School of Business. He has specialized in family business, entrepreneurship and strategy and has over 33 years of experience in academia. He obtained a PhD from the Cranfield School of Management, UK in 1986 on a comparative study of the small enterprise policies of Japan, UK and India. He has done research on family business, entrepreneurship and strategy, and has authored/edited six books and published extensively in reputed Indian and overseas journals. He has written several management cases, and has conducted training programs for family businesses on governance, professionalization, strategic management and entrepreneurship.

Jill R. Kickul, PhD, is the Director of the New York University Stern School of Business Social Entrepreneurship Program in the Berkeley Center for Entrepreneurship and Innovation. As a scholar, she has been awarded the Cason Hall & Company Publishers Best Paper Award, Michael J. Driver Best Careers Paper, the Coleman Foundation Best Empirical Paper, "John Jack" Award for Entrepreneurship Education, and the IntEnt Best Paper. She has more than 80 publications in entrepreneurship and management journals, including *Entrepreneurship Theory and Practice*, *Small Business Economics*, *Journal of Operations Management*, *Journal of Management*, *Journal of Small Business Management*, *Journal of Organizational Behavior*, and the *Academy of Management Learning and Education Journal*.

Veronika Kisfalvi, MBA, HEC Montréal; PhD, McGill University, is professor of management at HEC Montréal, where she teaches courses on leadership, management skills and decision-making. Her research focuses on leaders and their development, the relationships between personality, emotions and strategic decision-making, top management team dynamics and reflexivity in qualitative research. Her work has appeared in *Journal of Business Venturing, Journal of Management Inquiry, Organization Studies, Strategic Management Journal* and the online journal *M@n@gement*. She is a member of the Strategy-As-Practice Study Group at HEC Montréal, and was Director of the Graduate Diploma Program at HEC from 2004 to 2007. Prior to her academic career, Professor Kisfalvi held management positions in both private sector and not-for-profit organizations.

Benoît Leleux, PhD, is Stephan Schmidheiny Professor of Entrepreneurship and Finance at IMD, where he was director of the MBA program and of Research and Development. He was previously Visiting Professor at INSEAD and Associate Professor and Zubillaga Chair in Finance and Entrepreneurship at Babson College, Wellesley, MA (USA) from 1994 to 1999. He obtained his PhD at INSEAD, specializing in Corporate Finance and Venture Capital. His latest books include *Investing Private Capital in Emerging and Frontier Market SMEs* (IFC, 2009) and *Nurturing Science-based Startups: An International Case Perspective* (Springer, 2008). His teaching cases have earned a dozen European case-writing awards and he has run executive education programs for more than 50 leading global corporations.

Edmilson Lima is an Associate Professor in the Master and Doctoral Program in Business Management at Universidade Nove de Julho, São Paulo, Brazil, and member of the Rogers–J.A. Bombardier Chair of Entrepreneurship at HEC Montréal, Canada. He has a PhD in Administration from this same Canadian school and is a member of the board of the International Association of Research on Entrepreneurship and SME (Association Internationale de Recherche en Entrepreneuriat et PME, AIREPME). His teaching and research fields are SME administration, entrepreneurship and qualitative research. Dr. Lima has numerous academic publications that include articles in journals, book chapters and a book, written alone or in cooperation with other researchers in Brazil and abroad.

Ayala Malach-Pines is a clinical, social, and organizational psychologist who is the Dean of the Faculty of Management at Ben-Gurion University of the Negev. Professor Pines has published ten books, thirty book chapters and over one hundred research articles. Among her books: *Career Burnout: Causes and Cures* co-authored with Elliot Aronson; *Couple Burnout: Causes and Cures, Experiencing Social Psychology* co-authored with Christina Maslach; and *Career Choice in Management and Entrepreneurship* and *Handbook of Research on High-technology Entrepreneurs* co-edited with Mustafa Özbilgin. The books have been translated into many languages including French,

German, Spanish, Greek, Polish, Turkish, Chinese, Korean and Japanese. Her research interests include: Job and couple burnout; Psychological and cultural aspects of entrepreneurship; and Psychological determinants of career choice.

Aldene Meis Mason is an Assistant Professor in Business Administration at the University of Regina. She teaches entrepreneurship, strategy, human resources and business policy. Because there is a shortage of material and role models on sustainable indigenous entrepreneurship and business development, Aldene has chosen to do research and case writing in this area. She completed a BSc Science at Simon Fraser University, an MBA at the Richard Ivey Business School (UWO) and is a PhD Candidate at the University of Canterbury in New Zealand. Aldene is a Fellow Certified Management Consultant and Certified Human Resources Professional. Prior to joining the university, she was a manager and consultant for more than twenty years.

Michael A. Moodian is a Writer and Assistant Professor of Social Science at Chapman University in Orange, CA. He has authored two books and written numerous journal articles, book chapters and commentaries on a variety of topics. He has presented his research at various national and international conferences, and has served as an expert commentator on several television and radio programs. Michael holds a doctorate degree in organizational leadership from Pepperdine University.

Elin M. Oftedal, PhD, is employed as an Associate Professor at Tromsø University Business School (TUBS). She teaches management, innovation and entrepreneurship. Her research interests are innovation, high-tech entrepreneurship, social entrepreneurship, CSR and legitimacy processes. She has international experience from her stay as a visiting scholar in Austin Texas where she focused on innovation and entrepreneurship. She also taught management and did research on innovation and CSR at Asian University in Thailand.

Anouk Lavoie Orlick, Research Associate at IMD, performs research on leadership, executive development and family business. She was an editor of the book *Investing Private Capital in Emerging and Frontier Market Small and Medium Businesses*. Anouk is also a Learning Manager for several distance-learning programs in leadership for IMD clients. Anouk's industry background is in marketing and communications. In Paris, she managed operational marketing for a B2B software editor that provides business rules, resource optimization and visualization software.

Barbara J. Orser, MBA, PhD, is the Deloitte Professor in the Management of Growth Enterprises at the University of Ottawa Telfer School of Management. Her research focuses on the dynamics of enterprise growth and women's entrepreneurship. She also serves as consultant to government and not-for-profit agencies on women's financial engagement in the economy. She has co-authored over 100 academic publications and technical reports and two books. Barbara is a member of Canadian Women in Technology National Advisory Board, Editorial Board of the *Journal of Small Business and Entrepreneurship* and past board member of the International Council for Small Business and Entrepreneurship. Dr. Orser has won numerous academic and industry awards, including the 2010 International Alliance of Women, World of Difference 100 Award and 2010 Women's Executive Network Most Powerful Women in Canada, Champion Award.

Joëlle Piffault, PhD, has been a research assistant at HEC Montréal for more than twenty years. She specializes in case writing, mainly in the fields of Business Policy, Leadership and Entrepreneurship. She regularly gives workshops on case writing in French, English, and Spanish in a wide variety of countries.

Bhagyashree Ranade is the founder and President of the Institute for Women Entrepreneurial Development in Pune, India.

Martha E. Reeves is a Visiting Professor in the Markets and Management Studies Program and the Women Studies Department at Duke University. Previously, she served as a Program Director in Executive Education at the Kenan Flagler Business School at the University of North Carolina and taught marketing, management, and women's studies courses at the University of Georgia. Dr. Reeves has had corporate experience in both the UK and the US. She was Manager of Management Development for United Friendly Assurance (UK) and Director of Management Development for Acuma, an American Express Company. Professor Reeves continues to consult with businesses, local government and social service organizations on a number of issues and projects including women's development, leadership and gender issues in the workplace.

Francine Richer, research professional, analyst and case writer, holds a Masters degree in psycho-education from the Université de Montréal. She is interested in the trajectories of men and women who become leaders in their field or who have chosen entrepreneurship as a career by creating a business, taking over a family business or acquiring an existing business. The case study is her preferred research tool. At Presses de l'Université de Montréal (PUM), she has published two books in collaboration with Louise St-Cyr, extensively illustrated by case studies: *Préparer la relève—Neuf études de cas sur l'entreprise au Québec* (which won the Business Book Award in 2004) and *L'entrepreneuriat féminin au Québec—Dix études de cas* (which won the Business Book Award in 2008).

Alicia Robb, PhD, is a Senior Research Fellow with the Kauffman Foundation and a Research Associate with the University of California,

Santa Cruz. Her research focuses on firm dynamics, innovation, entrepreneurial finance, and entrepreneurship by women and minorities. In addition to numerous journal articles and book chapters, she is the co-author of *Race and Entrepreneurial Success* (with Robert Fairlie), published by MIT Press and *A Rising Tide: Financing Strategies for Women-owned Firms* (with Susan Coleman), published by Stanford University Press.

Erin Rogalski, freelancer, hails from a corporate finance background, working for seven years in the US in banking and mergers and acquisitions. Erin is now applying those skills to the development of projects in India and Africa. She has experience in the areas of access to financial services/financial literacy, improving the capacity of small businesses and associations, and livelihood development. Erin holds a Masters Degree in Business Administration from Northwestern University's Kellogg School of Management and spent one year as a post-graduate global fellow working in the Wadhwani Center for Entrepreneurship Development at the Indian School of Business. Erin received her BS in Management/Finance from Case Western Reserve University.

Ann-Mari Sätre, Associate Professor, is an economist specializing in the structure and performance of the Soviet/Russian economy. She is a senior lecturer at UCRS, the Centre of Russian and Eurasian Studies at Uppsala University. Her PhD from 1993 dealt with the transition of the Soviet economic system. Her current research focuses on gender issues, entrepreneurship, poverty and local development in Russia. Her most recent publications include articles, a book and book chapters on women's work in contemporary Russia. Since 2002 she has conducted field work in the Archangelsk region where she is following the development, mainly through interviews with local actors. Since March 2010, she has been engaged in a Russian research project on poverty in Nizhny Novgorod.

Arnis Sauka has been a Research Fellow at the Stockholm School of Economics in Riga since 2005, and since October 2011 has been the academic pro-rector at Ventspils University College. At the beginning of 2008, Arnis earned a PhD in Business Administration (magna cum laude) from the University of Siegen (Germany). Prior to that, he was a visiting PhD candidate at Jönköping International Business School (Sweden) and a teaching fellow at SSEES/University College London (UK). He also has extensive practical experience in business management and consultancy, including working as a senior consultant for PricewaterhouseCoopers. Arnis's main research interests include productive and unproductive entrepreneurship; business start-ups, growth and exits; entrepreneurship policy-making; and entrepreneurship in a transition context.

Elisabeth Sundin is PhD and Professor in Business Administration at the Department of Economic and Industrial Development (IE) and also one of the research leaders for Helix Vinn Excellence Centre, both at Linköping University. Together with her former college professor Carin Holmquist, now professor at Stockholm School of Economics, she performed pioneering work on women as entrepreneurs in Sweden. In 1989 they had already presented their first book (in Swedish *Kvinnor som företagare, Osynlighet, Mångfald anpassning*) and in 2003, a second. In addition, they have written many articles, both together and as solo writers, and with others on the topic. An example of the latter is "Masculinisation of the public sector: Local-level studies of public sector outsourcing in elder care" in the *International Journal of Gender and Entrepreneurship* (2010, 2(1): 49–67), co-author Malin Tillmar.

Mohammad Sahid Ullah is an Associate Professor in Communication and Journalism at Chittagong University, Bangladesh. He is one of the founding faculty members and served as Chair of the department from 1999 to 2002, and has been teaching since 1996. His research interests are Broadcast Journalism, Development Communication, Media Laws and Global Media Policy and Planning. He was winner of the best paper at the First World Journalism Education Congress (WJEC) in 2007. He serves as Co-Vice Chair of the Law Section of the International Association for Media and Communication Research (IAMCR) and is currently working as a SAGE–Tejeshwar Singh Memorial Fellow on "De-westernization of Media and Journalism Education in South Asia: In search of new strategies."

Patrick Valéau is a Lecturer and Researcher at Réunion University in France. He is director of the Master in Human Resources Management and has also created a Degree in Entrepreneurship and Management in the Non-Profit Sector. He was awarded a PhD from Lille University where he has also taught and is qualified to supervise PhD students. His research covers commitment, entrepreneurship and nonprofit organizations. He has written books and articles for different academic journals, in French and English, and has done consulting work for private companies, public administrations and nonprofit organizations. In 2005, he set up and became president of the ESE, a nonprofit community organization with 60 employees, providing educational, cultural and sporting activities for more than a thousand beneficiaries.

Friederike Welter is Professor and Associate Dean for Research at Jönköping International Business School, Sweden, which she joined in October 2008. From 1993 to 2006, she worked in the Rhine-Westphalia Institute for Economic Research; from 2005 to 2008 at the University of Siegen, Germany. She is affiliated to the Small Business Research Centre at Kingston University, UK, and holds the TeliaSonera Professorship for Entrepreneurship at SSE Riga, Latvia. Her main research interests are entrepreneurial behavior in different contexts, women's entrepreneurship, and support policies. She is on the review board of several leading entrepreneurship journals and associate editor of *Entrepreneurship Theory and Practice*. She is also a board member of the European Council of Small Business and Entrepreneurship (ECSB), which she headed as President from 2007 to 2009.

Dan Wheatley is a senior lecturer in economics at Nottingham Trent University. He completed his PhD entitled: "Working 9 to 5? Complex Patterns of Time Allocation among Managers and Professionals in Dual Career Households" in December 2009. His particular areas of interest are work-time, work–life balance, travel-to-work, and dual career households, and he has published both peer-reviewed journal articles and book chapters in these areas.

Shirley Ze Yu is an English news anchor for China Central Television (CCTV) and a former Mirrill Lynch financial consultant.

Wenxian Zhang is a recipient of the Cornell Distinguished Faculty Service Award and is Research Associate of the Rollins China Center, Arthur Vining Davis Fellow and Professor of Rollins College in Winter Park, Florida, where he joined the ranks of the Arts and Sciences faculty in 1995. In addition to *The Biographical Dictionary of New Chinese Entrepreneurs and Business Leaders* (with Ilan Alon, published by Edward Elgar, 2009), *A Guide to the Top 100 Companies in China* (with Ilan Alon, published by World Scientific, 2010), and *The Entrepreneurial and Business Elites of China: The Chinese Returnees Who Have Shaped Modern China* (with Huiyao Wang and Ilan Alon, published by Emerald, 2011), he has published many articles on information studies, international librarianship, historical research, and Chinese business management.

Introduction

The Area of Female Entrepreneurship in the Initial Phases of the New Venture Creation

---

Chapter Objectives

- Identifying the unique aspects of female entrepreneurship along the venture creation process;
- Understanding the key features of the new venture creation stage and differentiating this stage from the more advanced stages of the business;
- Delving deeper into the roles of external factors in women's planning and implementation of their ideas;
- Demarcating women's position, status and social roles in different cultures by their reflection in the entrepreneurial realm;
- Emphasizing the contribution of understanding female entrepreneurship to the contemporary reality of the entrepreneurial field;
- Outlining the main features of the entrepreneurial revolution, and understanding women's role as leading players in this revolution;
- Recognizing the hurdles and challenges faced by women in the new venture creation phases in the context of the dynamic entrepreneurial market;
- Moving the debate over women entrepreneurs to center stage by respecting their uniqueness and valuing their contribution to entrepreneurship—rather than attempting to "adjust" women entrepreneurs to the "male" way.

New venture creation is a separate and distinct phenomenon in the entrepreneurial sphere, which also includes the established business, mergers and acquisitions, and boosting the business, among others. The creation of a new venture is a complex, multidimensional and crucial process that shapes the future venture's building blocks; specifically, it includes the actions, activities, thoughts, and processes exhibited by entrepreneurs toward materializing their ideas and visions into a functioning business. Some researchers conceptualize new venture creation as a process based on the effort–performance–outcome model; in this framework, the effort expended to start a business (performance) leads to certain desired outcomes. Others address it as a phase, or stage, in the business's development that typifies the preparation and planning in starting a business. As such, this stage may provide solid ground to nurture the future venture into a successful, sustainable business, or alternatively, be a "broken reed,"[1] i.e., ground that appears promising, but is unable to support the business's competitive advantage in the long run. Due to its consequent effects, the new venture creation is critical, and as a field of research it has attracted much attention among scholars and practitioners.

Most of the practices typifying the new venture creation process are latent and difficult to expose, as attention is given to generating ideas, refining them, and then visualizing, preparing and organizing the venture-to-be. Thus, in contrast to the subsequent stages, the new venture creation stage occurs mainly in the entrepreneur's mind, through interactions and on the computer, while the "real" selling activities have not yet begun.

The major perspectives introduced in the new venture creation process are:

- types of opportunity recognition;
- ideas to be implemented as future businesses;
- visions;
- distinct activities and strategies that are typically employed in the first stages of the new venture;
- preparation—critical factors that enable materializing the ideas into a real venture;
- the quest for financing the future business;
- the meaning of planning and its subsequent effects on the entrepreneur and the business;
- typologies of the entrepreneurial profile of individuals exhibiting a new venture creation process;
- environment, which has a major role in influencing the new venture's processes.

(Alsos & Ljunggren, 1998; Bhave, 1994; Brush, Carter, Gatewood, Greene, & Hart, 2004; Carter, Gartner, & Shaver, 2004; Gartner, 1985, 1988; Mullins & Forlani, 2005; Orhan & Scott, 2001; Reynolds, Carter, Gartner, Greene, & Cox, 2002b; Timmons & Spinelli, 2004; Wennekers, Van Stel, Thurik, & Reynolds, 2005)

While the pursuits of women entrepreneurs draw continual attention in both research and practice, their contribution and impact in the area of new venture creation is still limited and underdebated. Moreover, although the number of women entrepreneurs has increased significantly in the last three decades in most countries, inducing more vibrant and dynamic economies, the phenomenon of female entrepreneurship also remains both underexplored and inadequately dealt with in the theoretical and practical academic literature.

This book sheds light on the unique aspects of female entrepreneurship by tracing women's journey through the venture creation process. Embedded within specific environmental constraints, which vary among different national and ethnic cultures, women entrepreneurs exploit opportunities and implement ideas for their business ventures in creatively dissimilar ways and through different avenues as compared to men.

The first decade of the present century has seen a marked increase in academic interest in the area of female entrepreneurship, in both research and education. Yet, despite the fact that women represent the fastest-rising group of entrepreneurs, and that women entrepreneurs contribute significantly to national economies by providing employment, creating value, introducing innovations, and stimulating the market to initiate even more entrepreneurial undertakings, female entrepreneurship is largely understudied (Aldrich, Carter, & Ruef, 2002; Aldrich & Wiedenmayer, 1993; Birley, 1989; Brush, 1992; Brush, Carter, Gatewood, Greene, & Hart, 2002a; Gatewood, Brush, Carter, Greene, & Hart, 2009; Greene, Brush, & Gatewood, 2006; Harper, 2007; Moore, 1990; Stevenson, 1986, 1990; Taniguchi, 2002; Verheul, Uhlaner, & Thurik, 2005). In part, this is the result of a number of shortcomings in research on female entrepreneurship, particularly the lack of theoretical grounding that drives the scholar into the "comfort zone" of the already known, male-gendered measuring instruments to assess female entrepreneurship (Baron, Markman, & Hirsa, 2001; Bird & Brush, 2002; Bruni, Gherardi, & Poggio, 2004a, 2005; Marlow & Strange, 1994).

At the center of the 21st century's turbulent evolution and revolution, entrepreneurship has become a promising path for women, enabling them to accomplish their personal goals, maintain a high quality of life, fulfill their needs and employ their capabilities and competencies in a productive, satisfactory and fair way.

In research, the entrepreneurship field is structured according to male-gendered norms and the ideal type of entrepreneur is always represented by men, e.g., Bill Gates, founder of Microsoft; Steve Jobs, founder of Apple; Mark Zuckerberg, founder of Facebook; or William Edward Boeing, founder of The Boeing Company. In this sense, research is bewildering, as entrepreneurial traits are debated and studied based on gender-neutral criteria; however, a high need for achievement, autonomy, dominance, aggressiveness, task orientation and proactiveness, among others

(McClelland, 1961; Shane & Venkataraman, 2000), represent characteristics that are mainly attributed to men. The implication is that entrepreneurship "suits" men more than women, as the former "naturally" possess the personal characteristics required for successful entrepreneurship. Yet, overwhelming empirical evidence on the growing participation of women in entrepreneurship cannot be ignored; female entrepreneurship should be studied as a respected, separate feature in the entrepreneurship field, and consequently, in research on the pursuit of women in the new venture creation process.

This book makes a contribution to the contemporary reality of women entrepreneurs by delineating the female entrepreneurial field in research and in practice, and demarcating aspects of the realm of female entrepreneurship in this configuration. In doing so, it exposes some questions for the readers (see Figure I.1) in order to stimulate their thinking on the meaning of female entrepreneurship in its different contexts, and to allow a flexible, tolerant definition of this area.

Figure I.1 offers an holistic illustration of the different roles in which gender is embedded in the entrepreneurial research; each angle responds to some concerns regarding female entrepreneurship, yet raises some others; for example, the upper arrow signifies gender effect on entrepreneurship; this angle may be valid in explaining topics such as females' lower motivation to become entrepreneurs and lower participation rate in entrepreneurship, yet, it also implies that women may be less entrepreneurial than men. Thus, the suggested model is about stimulating creative and outside-the-box ways of addressing women's new venture creation in the global context.

To capture the introduced challenges, this book offers case studies developed by renowned scholars who are active and involved in the area of female entrepreneurship in academic institutions in different countries, thus introducing and embracing the diversity in female entrepreneurship. These cases give the readers a glimpse of the experiences of women entrepreneurs from different countries, cultures, sectors, professions, social strata, educational levels, age and family status, as well as of women who embarked on entrepreneurship from different starting points. This book's message is that visions and success are loosely coupled because of women's lack of confidence in their abilities to start a business. This book bridges between the two by discussing the new venture creation process through women's eyes and making room for this unique form of entrepreneurship—female entrepreneurship.

This book is about learning from female role models, becoming familiar with women entrepreneurs' entrepreneurial ways, discovering the complexities and tracking the means employed by women entrepreneurs in different countries and cultures—so that the discourse of future generations on entrepreneurial role models will encompass examples of both women and men.

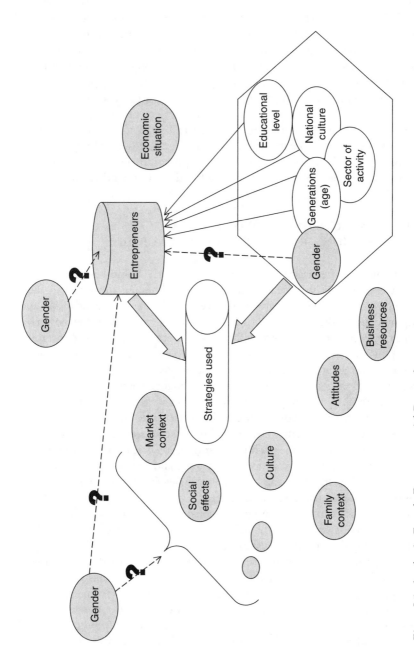

Figure I.1 Angles in Female Entrepreneurial Research.

The book is unique in several ways: it traces the routes taken by women entrepreneurs in the venture creation process, thus giving potential entrepreneurs a better understanding of the steps required to start a business. The chapters are based on leading research studies and the predominant theoretical frameworks in female entrepreneurship, which are practical and broadly applicable. In addition, the book offers various inspirational case studies of women entrepreneurs that incidentally present some best practices for a successful venture creation process. The book embraces the diversity among women entrepreneurs and between men and women entrepreneurs, and calls for discarding the perception of an ultimate model for success. Its main message is that any woman who harbors an idea or has a zeal for starting a business will find the described practices insightful and useful for facilitating the accomplishment of her goals and the fulfillment of her dreams.

THE ENTREPRENEURIAL REVOLUTION AND THE CONTRIBUTIONS OF FEMALE ENTREPRENEURSHIP

In the midst of the largest entrepreneurial surge the world has ever known, with the evolution of "mega-trends" such as technology and internet, local and global crises that repeatedly surface, instability in the financial and employment markets that coerce many countries to harness the power to boost competitiveness and productivity in order to cope with these instabilities, political and customer revolutions initiated and managed through Facebook and Twitter, and new technological inventions on a daily basis—under such conditions, *stability* appears to no longer be pertinent, a term taken from the distant past. Accordingly, there seems to be intense pursuit of the "right" path that will bridge between the hectic times and the basic, human propensity for some stability and control over the situations being tackled.

Entrepreneurship is one such promising path, as it provides individuals with the freedom to craft their own business and personal roads based on their own needs, interests and capabilities. They can control the conditions imposed on their businesses, as they are the ones responsible for their businesses; yet, they can easily change their businesses' processes and follow the changing trends, to optimally adjust their business concepts to the challenges imposed by their ecosystems (Table I.1).

Entrepreneurs have thus been regarded as role models of success combined with control and independence, and research has emphasized entrepreneurial characteristics, strategies and straightforward performance. Entrepreneurs have been sought by corporate and entrepreneurial businesses. However, delving into the "ideal type" of entrepreneur, both research and practice reveal the profile of a male entrepreneur: any random sample of respondents would probably think of Bill Gates, Mark Zuckerberg or Henry Ford, rather than Estee Lauder, Coco Chanel or Maria Montessori when asked about leading entrepreneurs.

Table I.1 The Entrepreneurial Realm

The entrepreneur
- Ambitious
- Non-conformist
- Find it difficult to adjust to the "regular" corporate system
- Adventurous
- Risk-takers
- Innovative
- Creative
- Proactive
- Passionate about their projects
- They may be very competitive in order to break into their market segment

The entrepreneurial business
- Innovative
- Uncertain
- Takes many forms
- Focused on expertise and specialties more than on the business set
- Vulnerable
- More sophisticated than the "general" market
- Inventing itself

The entrepreneurial environment
- Dynamic
- Vigorous
- Very competitive
- Risky
- Innovative
- Updated on a daily basis
- Imitative (businesses imitate each other)
- Using unique processes
- Sometimes associated with boom times

THE AREA OF FEMALE ENTREPRENEURSHIP

Female entrepreneurship is treated in research as a particular feature of entrepreneurship, focusing on the business level, i.e., businesses initiated, founded, managed or headed by women, and the individual level—women's entrepreneurial characteristics, motivations to start a business, strategies used and performance. Both of these angles are typically discussed in the context of female-related hurdles encountered by women entrepreneurs that are echoed in their consequent entrepreneurial performance. Female entrepreneurship is embedded in a specific ecosystem that encompasses constraints and opportunities that shape its uniqueness; its input, processes and outputs are thus female-oriented, as shown in Figure I.2 (Baughn, Chua, & Neupert, 2006; Brush *et al.*, 2004; Brush, Carter, Gatewood, Greene, & Hart, 2006a; de Bruin, Brush, & Welter, 2007; Verheul, Van Stel, & Thurik, 2006).

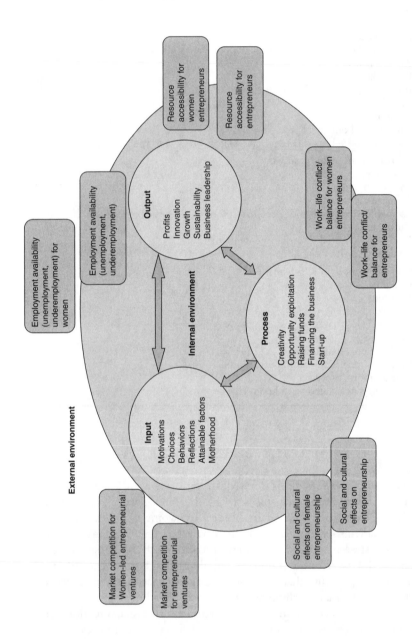

Figure I.2 Distinctiveness of Female Entrepeneurship.

Not only are we facing a relative scarcity in female entrepreneurship research today, but academic debate on female entrepreneurship is lacking in a conceptual, rigorous theory, and this area thus remains underexploited in both research and practice. Concurrently, there is a dearth of cross-country research on female entrepreneurship, leaving this area isolated and locally based. Cross-cultural exchanges have the potential to produce significant contributions in fostering the articulation of synergetic concepts and ideas in the female entrepreneurial realm.

Along their entrepreneurial course, entrepreneurs generally encounter various hurdles and challenges that are unique and typical to entrepreneurship, while women entrepreneurs face additional and more pronounced hurdles related to their gender and social role (Table I.2). Yet, women entrepreneurs must develop and maintain a competitive advantage in the market, regardless of these gender-based hurdles, in order to survive. Thus a deep look into the crafting of strategies is required to avoid or overcome the gender-related hurdles and to ascertain women's success in their entrepreneurial businesses (Barney, 1986a, 1991; Hitt & Ireland, 2000; Ireland, Hitt, & Sirmon, 2003; Teece, Pisano, & Shuen, 2007).

The Meaning of Entrepreneurship in the Female Realm

Entrepreneurship provides the individual with the freedom to craft a career and a personal path based on her or his own needs, interests, capabilities and dreams. For women, many of whom have experienced underemployment due to environmental constraints, such as the need to sacrifice professional or job-related aspirations to fulfill traditional social and domestic roles, as well as barriers in the labor market, entrepreneurship opens a door to a venture that allows women entrepreneurs to fulfill their needs and employ their job-related and professional experiences, knowledge and capabilities. More specifically, the independence of entrepreneurship allows women to decide on and control their time schedule, tasks, work pace and workload relative to their family and personal time.

Gender Differences

Several lines of research have contributed to our understanding of the differences between women and men in the venture creation path. Existing research considers several units of analysis—women founders, the venture teams in women-led businesses, the community and external environments of women-led businesses.

There are a number of studies that have explored issues unique to women business owners and then adapted their findings to the entrepreneurial process; some others have focused on the entrepreneurial process and then molded their findings into aspects relevant to women entrepreneurs.

Table 1.2 Main Hurdles Reported at Work by Women

Requisite skills	Sectors of activity	Motivation	Management styles	Strategies	Business unit
Limited business skills	Women's choice of smaller, traditional businesses in retail, service and caring	Different socialization experiences: home and children are the first priority	"Relational strategy" when working with clients, partners	Limited strategies developed to access to resources	Fewer resources at start-up
Limited managerial experience	Women's avoidance of high tech, manufacturing or non-traditional and "too" innovative sectors	To cope with the work–family conflict by working independently	Focus on development of teams, employees, empowering, perseverance	Limited strategic and tactical decisions	Focusing on industry-specific experience
Limited entrepreneurial experience	Choices of educational professional tracks that are less rewarding in the labor market	Turning a hobby into a business	"Feminine" management style, i.e., informally structured	Development of strategies emphasizing product quality; neglecting strategies addressing cost efficiency	Smaller businesses relative to men's
Limited employment of negotiation skills		"... just to make a living"; "I do not necessarily have to be profitable"		More risk-averse	More work from home thus less exposure of the business's products or services
Limited employment of financial-management skills					Discrimination – lenders discriminate against women; prefer to lend to established firms, which are usually male-dominated

The existing fields of research can be categorized as follows:

Individual level:

- Research on Gender—harnessed to fit into entrepreneurship research
- Research on Entrepreneurship—harnessed the fit into gender research
- Including the areas of: human capital; personal and demographic characteristics; motivations; aspirations; the meaning of success; values and psychological profiles

New venture level:

- Founding strategies and management routines
- Finance-related topics: initial capital resources (debt, equity, financing); investment process
- Networks

Community and external environment level:

- Expectations and stereotypes
- Challenging and inhibiting factors
- Global issues
- Public policy

Individual Level

At the individual level, two main lines of research are identified: that stemming from gender and feminist theories, harnessed to entrepreneurship to provide a deeper understanding of women who have started their own businesses, and that drawing on the leading models in entrepreneurship harnessed to the woman's world, to expand our understanding of women in the entrepreneurial world.

Women and men have traditionally been allocated different roles in society, family, labor market, politics, etc. Accordingly, some occupations, employment preferences and jobs have been considered more appropriate for women and others more appropriate for men. Thus, gender roles have been established and these reflect social and cultural conditioning and the socialization of women and men. Research discusses women entrepreneurs' human capital, mainly, their education level, prior experience in entrepreneurship, business ownership and management; their personal and demographic characteristics, such as family status, age, nationality, ethnicity; and their motivations to start a business, echoing their gendered priorities in life. For example, women are generally more focused on balancing work and family, and are thus attracted to entrepreneurship to control their time and assignments; men are more motivated to gain wealth through business ownership (Barrett, 1995; Buttner & Moore,

1997; DeMartino & Barbato, 2003; Sexton & Bowman, 1986; Sexton & Bowman-Upton, 1990).

Researchers in this field have also developed models on sex-role socialization, and occupational segregation. Studies on the values and psychological profiles of women and men entrepreneurs have also been reported (Bellu, 1993; Fagenson, 1993; Fagenson & Marcus, 1991; Shaver, Gartner, Gatewood, & Vos, 1996).

The New Venture Level

Women-led businesses' performance, growth, sustainability and success are the main areas of exploration in this category. Topics such as the new venture's founding strategies and management routines are explored and discussed, including opportunity exploitation, initial finance, social capital and networks, and communication and development of the concept in the initial founding stages of the business. A large body of research has addressed women-led businesses' financial state, financial growth patterns, business profitability, financial sources and investment-related aspects; networking and networks have attracted many studies, emphasizing gender-related patterns of their use for business growth and success. Different issues introduced under the business-level category can also be categorized under the individual level; for example, women-led businesses have been identified as underperforming in terms of growth prospects and profitability relative to men's; such important differences reflect the genders' different strategies for managing their businesses, i.e., the business level, but may also reflect the genders' aspirations to grow, i.e., the individual level (Aldrich, 1989; Anna, Chandler, Jansen, & Mero, 2000; Carter, 2003; Carter & Rosa, 1998; Chaganti, 1986; Du Reitz and Henrekson 2000; Rosa, Hamilton, Carter, & Burns, 1994). Such spillover is manifested with the community and environment level as well.

The Community and External Environment Level

The unique ecosystem in which women entrepreneurs start and manage their ventures appears in research through various lenses: studies on the ecosystem stemming from models on gender roles and extending beyond the entrepreneurial venture into other areas of female roles in society, which shape the expectations regarding women's careers, including the quest for entrepreneurship as a "favorable" career path for women, focusing on how women integrate ownership of a business with their roles—or socially-attributed roles—in their families (Holliday & Letherby, 1993; Loscocco, Robinson, Hall, & Allen, 1991). The effect of the ecosystem is then mirrored in research focusing on the conflict experienced by women between their work and family roles, as factors inhibiting entrepreneurship. Other factors that have attracted research refer to barriers imposed by the community and environment on women-led businesses with respect to obtaining investments, financing their businesses and competing with other businesses in the local or international arena, among others, and thus again a spillover into various categories is found (Brush, 1992; Greenhaus & Beutell, 1985; Parasuraman & Simmers, 2001).

Studies on public policies also prevail in the area of female entrepreneurship, aimed at contributing by raising female entrepreneurship and promoting it to center stage, as well as establishing assistance programs, e.g., training, empowerment, mentorship, networking and governmental rules and regulations that will stimulate, facilitate, foster and support female entrepreneurship (Birley, Moss, & Saunders, 1987; Chrisman, Carsrud, DeCastro, & Heron, 1990; Dumas, 2001; Walker & Joyner, 1999).

FEMALE ENTREPRENEURSHIP AND DIVERSITY

In an era when diversity and multiculturalism embrace the "unique" and "different," female entrepreneurship is making a significant contribution to diversity in entrepreneurship. Women entrepreneurs present specific entrepreneurial profiles: they start their businesses in specific sectors, develop specific products and services, pursue business goals that reflect their worlds and structure their businesses in a way that differs significantly from men. Female entrepreneurship introduces diversity in entrepreneurship by offering a unique culture, ways of thinking, development of products, services, and forms of organization that differ from men's. Female entrepreneurship, like any other segment in entrepreneurship, e.g., ethnic entrepreneurship, rural entrepreneurship, social entrepreneurship or entrepreneurship of and for people with disabilities, expands the customers' and employees' freedom to choose, deepens opportunities for learning and sharing, and expands the freedom to develop our knowledge on others' perceptions, preferences and attitudes with regard to entrepreneurial-related topics (Brush, 1992; Chaganti & Parasuraman, 1996; Verheul & Thurik, 2001).

Female entrepreneurship is thus a platform for animated academic and practical discourse aimed at exposing, accepting and managing the genders' differences and using them to leverage innovation, creations and inventions to higher levels, by the synergetic effect derived from the different views and experiences of men and women entrepreneurs.

Female entrepreneurship, however, is not universal, and it takes on different forms in different cultures. Entrepreneurial activities, including those performed by women, do not occur in a vacuum. The environmental context shapes the entrepreneur's initial motivation, processes, strategies and eventual success (Brush, de Bruin, & Welter, 2009; Covin & Slevin, 1991; Covin, 1994; Mitchell *et al.*, 2002; Wright & Zahra, 2011). In particular, the ways in which women entrepreneurs create and manage new ventures vary substantially among countries and cultures: such variation reflects the external environment's effects on women in their respective country contexts. At the same time, the accelerated pace, extent and variety of female entrepreneurship in different countries are stimulating national and international initiatives and policies in the face of these effects and are having a significant impact on the attitudes toward female entrepreneurship which might encourage and facilitate it. The American culture and spirit encourage stimulation, problem-solving, mastery and discovery; this has a significant impact on the country's dynamics and consequently, on its diversity in entrepreneurship. In contrast, the European culture is more reluctant toward entrepreneurship.[2] Sir Ronald Cohen[3] has affirmed that

> . . . there are many fewer entrepreneurs[4] than there are in a country such as the United States. In decades past, this was partly a problem of mindset—the idea of launching a business was not embedded into European culture or education. That's changed, but now the big obstacle is a dearth of opportunities for early-stage growth companies to raise capital through the public markets.
>
> (Gannon, 1994; Hiebert & Ley, 2003;
> Hofstede, 1980, 1991; Hofstede & Bond, 1988)

Figure I.3 illustrates a model giving the dynamic, cyclical sequence that affects, and is affected by, both national and international contexts. The model stresses that women entrepreneurs need to continually exploit the three cycles that will lead to their venture's success:

(a) The entrepreneur cycle—refers to entrepreneurs' knowing themselves deeply and truly, and being able to identify their real motivations, drivers, resources and barriers. By truly understanding their motivations to start a business, i.e. those derived from their own interests and needs rather than stemming from social pressures and trends, a better fit will emerge between their vision and their subsequent venture; accordingly, understanding their resources and strengths, as well as courageously facing their deficiencies and weaknesses, will enable women to prepare for the venture creation process.

(b) The entrepreneurial business cycle—an objective and realistic analysis of the business's concept, processes, structure, resources and capabilities is critical to any business; in the case of female entrepreneurship, their typically relatively limited relevant experience or knowledge in entrepreneurship may result in inadequate assessment of their businesses. An accurate acquaintance with their business enables women to confront its limitations as well as embrace its strengths. In addition, it is only by engaging in an objective perspective that women can be confident in starting and running their businesses in their

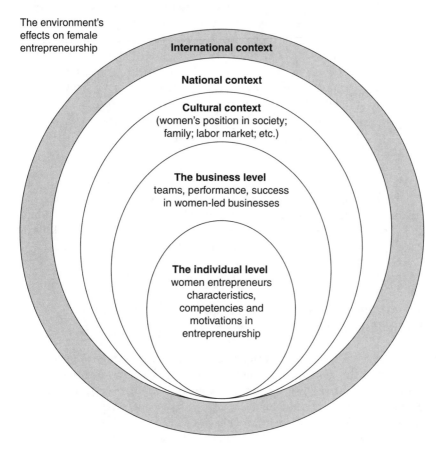

The environment's
effects on female
entrepreneurship

International context

National context

Cultural context
(women's position in society;
family; labor market; etc.)

The business level
teams, performance, success
in women-led businesses

The individual level
women entrepreneurs
characteristics,
competencies and
motivations in
entrepreneurship

Figure I.3   An Illustration of the Entrepreneurial Cycle.

own way, rather than automatically engaging in the "accepted" or
male-dominated way.

(c) The environment cycle—familiarity with their specific ecosystem is a
critical factor in the female venture creation process and success; such
familiarity is obtained by continually learning about and exploring
the environments that affect their business's success, in both the
short and long term. Female entrepreneurship exists in a context;
e.g., economic, political, social, cultural, etc. The transitions and
changes occurring around the world influence each of these contexts;
in turn, these transitions affect and shape female entrepreneurship.
For example, events, such as the Fukushima Daiichi nuclear crisis in
Japan in 2011,[5] which affected Japan's industrial and economic environments, clearly had after-effects on entrepreneurs at the business

level. Ms. Hikari Sasaki, an artist-entrepreneur from Nagoya, Japan who started a web-based business of "imaginary avatars" a year before the crisis, has been vastly affected. "As a 'nice-to-have' gaming-based initiative, my business collapsed due to the nuclear crisis . . . people were so terrified during these long months, and treated gaming as the 'forbidden city', as it may have symbolized a careless, neglectful attitude towards the nuclear crisis . . . I am looking for different web-based initiatives today," says Hikari. The environmental cycle effects have an impact at both the macro and micro levels.

Merging these three circles is essential in female entrepreneurship as they link the individual level, through the business level to the local and international levels. Maintaining and developing both an understanding and a capacity for pursuit of the best entrepreneurial strategies and skills in widely different contexts are key factors for women entrepreneurs to promote and benefit from the national and international arenas.

THE GLOBAL SPHERE IN THE FEMALE ENTREPRENEURIAL REALM

Many researchers in female entrepreneurship agree that more knowledge is required of the global entrepreneurial landscapes of female entrepreneurship. Comparative assessments of women entrepreneurs in different countries are necessary resources for any academic and practical attempt to track women's entrepreneurial behavior on a global scale. Research shows that among the published papers on female entrepreneurship, more than 80 percent are based on the Anglo-Saxon culture, with more than 60 percent of the publications on entrepreneurship in general based on the US (Ahl, 2002; Aidis, Welter, Smallbone, & Isakova, 2006; Lee & Peterson, 2000; Sexton & Bowman-Upton, 1990), thus biasing perceptions of female entrepreneurship as occurring only in environments that are well-developed and structured, and where property rights are protected, where entrepreneurs have substantial discretion over allocation of resources, and support systems are available. New empirical evidence and authentic experiences are needed to show female entrepreneurs ways to start their businesses in different contexts, and this book addresses this gap by offering case studies of women in different environments who are in the process of new venture creation.

Female entrepreneurship and its manifestations in different ecosystems expand our understanding of women-led businesses in both the local and global spheres, as presented in Figure I.4.

The case studies and narratives introduced in this book act as shared ground, where women entrepreneurs, nascent women entrepreneurs,

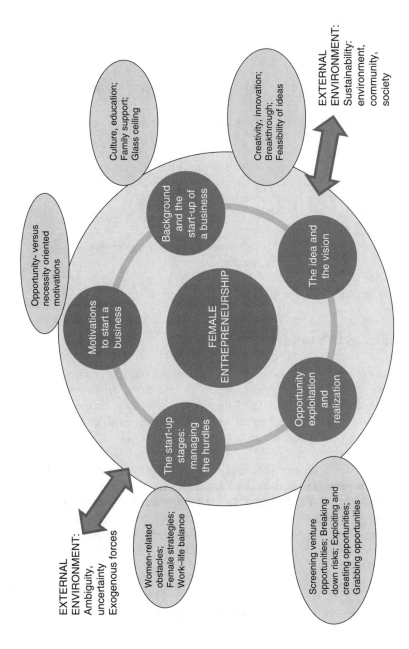

Figure I.4 The Ecosystem: New Venture Creation and Women Entrepreneurs.

novice women entrepreneurs and students in entrepreneurship programs can get a glimpse into this world, to deepen their familiarity with it, strengthen their self-confidence and empower them to try, experience, interact, share and learn from their local and global counterparts.

This book seeks to:

- Deepen our current understanding of the important issues in female entrepreneurship.
- Foster new research on female entrepreneurship.
- Develop a relevant, updated link between emerging topics in female entrepreneurship and the existing research.
- Understand female entrepreneurship through women's perspective, and subsequently develop and establish a robust theory of female entrepreneurship built on women's outlook.
- Facilitate cross-national collaborations in both research and practice between women entrepreneurs.
- Stimulate entrepreneurship among female entrepreneurs, women wishing to become entrepreneurs and students.
- Create a living document that can be the backbone for future research and best practices for women entrepreneurs.

THE BOOK'S RATIONALE

This book aims to trace women's paths in their venture creation process by introducing female entrepreneurship as an independent phenomenon. The book draws upon the emerging topics in female entrepreneurship research, and introduces case studies representing the experiences of female entrepreneurs' endeavors across national, cultural, social and economic contexts.

The readers will be given the opportunity to familiarize themselves with female entrepreneurship from its various angles, disclose its uniqueness and unleash it from the chains of the existing, male-dominated context, by accepting the distinctiveness of female entrepreneurship and founding female entrepreneurship as a research area to encourage researchers and practitioners to push the frontiers of research, governmental policy and practice further.

THE THEORETICAL FRAMEWORK OF THIS BOOK

This book combines resource-based theory, the dynamic capabilities approach and feminist perspectives to address the life cycle of the business.

The Resource-based View (RBV) and the Female New Venture Creation

This assists in understanding the generation of competitive advantages by women entrepreneurs at the early stages of the new venture creation. Businesses need to acquire relevant and varied tangible and nontangible resources which competitors, or potential competitors, will find difficult to create, replace or imitate. Only this can guarantee high levels of performance and a sustained competitive advantage. Researchers have characterized these required resources as valuable, rare, inimitable, and nonsubstitutable (the so-called VRIN attributes). The RBV articulates that, under market imperfection, there exists a diversity of businesses in terms of product diversity, specialization, level of innovation and technology introduced, which provokes a limited transfer of resources. Thus businesses must introduce superior resources and capabilities, and implement fresh value-creating strategies to build a basis for gaining and sustaining competitive advantage. The challenges tackled by women under such conditions are intriguing and call for more research, debate and development of implications (Amit & Schoemaker, 1993; Barney, 1986a, 1991; Conner & Prahalad, 1996; Hitt, Bierman, Shimizu, & Kochhar, 2001; Mahoney & Pandian, 1992; Penrose, 1952, 1953, 1959; Wernerfelt, 1984).

Dynamic Capabilities (DC) Approach

The concept of DC is most relevant to women entrepreneurs in the new venture creation phase. It stems from a key shortcoming of the RBV of businesses, criticized as giving marginal attention to the mechanisms by which resources actually contribute to competitive advantage, as well as ignoring the debate on questions focusing more on the dynamic processes occurring the business, such as how resources are developed, how they are integrated into the business and how they are introduced into the market. Due to the inherent diversity between the genders and its effects on their businesses' processes and practices, such an approach is most interesting in the female realm. Furthermore, the DC approach stresses that while the resources and capabilities generated by the business may not result in an immediate superior position in the market relative to competitors, they may nonetheless be critical to the business's longer-term competitiveness in unstable environments if the business's resources and capabilities are adjusted over time to optimally fit their ecosystem. Research continually reveals figures from countries around the world showing women's lower participation in entrepreneurship, and the lower pace and extent of their businesses' growth. These figures are mainly interpreted as reflecting women's lower capabilities to manage successful businesses. Drawing on the DC premise, however, women entrepreneurs can be understood by their different ways of reaching goals, and an optimistic look at women's long-term success can be proposed, even if it does not show immediately when certain entrepreneurial processes or strategies are implemented (Eisenhardt & Martin, 2000; Helfat *et al.*, 2007a; Hitt, Clifford, Nixon, & Coyne, 1999; Teece, 2007; Teece *et al.*, 1997; Winter, 2003).

Feminist Theories

Different feminist theory angles are discussed in Chapter 1, to introduce the readers to the key concepts through which female entrepreneurship can be understood. The extent to which these models consider female entrepreneurship to be a unique phenomenon varies, but the implications are to embrace female entrepreneurship. Theories such as feminist empiricism and liberal feminist theory assert that men and women are similar; the implications for entrepreneurship are that entrepreneurs should be treated as a group that encounters different difficulties and challenges typical to them, regardless of their gender. The social feminist, radical feminist and psychological feminist theories, on the other hand, advocate the essential difference between women and men and base their conceptions on females' and males' different experiences and socialization, which result in differences in their respective views and interpretations of the same situations; such views might have implications for entrepreneurship that will facilitate the female entrepreneurial path, as they are forced to follow a male-based approach. Theories such as social constructionism state that gender refers to the meaning of femininity and masculinity; as such, the implication for this book's scope would be to educate people to see beyond the stereotyped approaches to female entrepreneurship, to enable women entrepreneurs to craft their own entrepreneurial businesses (Ahl, 1997, 2002; Ahl & Samuelsson, 2000; de Bruin *et al.*, 2007; Du Reitz & Henrekson, 2000; Fischer, Reuber, & Dyke, 1993; Harding, 1987).

The Business Life Cycle Models and Women Entrepreneurs

This book focuses on the early stages of the new venture creation process. Many scholars and practitioners advocate that the new venture creation process never ceases, as new processes, niches, customers, product development, among others, implemented at different stages of the business, present new challenges to respond to in the context of the environment's demands and the business's goals. Nevertheless, this book focuses on the very early stages of the business, prior to its being registered and formalized—the stages at which ideas arise, and the entrepreneur is stimulated by these ideas and feels the urge to create a venture, to make a change. Many women entrepreneurs who are driven and enthused by innovation, action and creation ignore their inner feelings toward entrepreneurship, due to social expectations, family-related constraints and personal values and

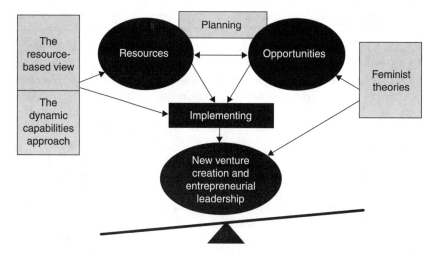

Figure I.5 The Theoretical Framework.

attitudes regarding women's role in society, including their potential competition with their male counterparts in the labor market, a territory that is embedded in the latter's culture. As such, this book endeavors to encourage such women to create their own entrepreneurial undertaking, in ways and with structures that suit their desires and their ecosystems. It is critical that we understand the early stages of the new venture creation in female entrepreneurship (Figure I.5), and these are thus the focus of this book.

THE ORGANIZATION OF THE BOOK

This book focuses on the venture creation process and covers a wide range of typically exhibited processes, strategies and behaviors taken by women to reach businesses success and fulfill their personal goals.

To capture a larger representation of entrepreneurial businesses initiated, founded, and/or headed by women in different countries, sectors and business stages, I invited scholars from around the world to contribute case studies that tell the stories of women entrepreneurs, addressing one or more topics associated with the venture creation process.

Each chapter is devoted to a different topic in the venture creation process and includes an overview of its main themes, drawing from existing research and developing new concepts and models; 27 case studies were reviewed and selected for this book out of 40 that were submitted, and these cases are introduced at the end of each chapter to illustrate that chapter's themes through women's experiences in different countries around the world. The cases can be used as learning tools, and therefore questions are included at the end of each to stimulate deep discussion and enable reflection and insights on the meeting points between academy and practice.

The book's model is prefigured in the introduction. Part 1, "Female Entrepreneurship: What Makes this Area Unique?" attempts to portray entrepreneurship through the lenses of women entrepreneurs, nascent women entrepreneurs, and women considering embarking on entrepreneurship. It includes an overview of the constraints and hurdles encountered by women, as well as the opportunities they create and the challenges they face, from macro and micro perspectives. This part of the book refers to the pre-stages of the business, and focuses largely on the main themes that have been found in the literature to affect women's decisions to become entrepreneurs.

A macro perspective on female's new venture creation is introduced: the main themes discussed in this section are the social and cultural forces and pressures that women encounter and that affect their decisions to become entrepreneurs, and the external forces that influence women's aspirations. It includes a global view on women's roles in their respective societies and labor markets, and discusses how such roles may affect their entrepreneurial paths.

The micro perspective on female venture creation offers an overview of women's motivations to embark on entrepreneurship: the psychological profiles of women entrepreneurs, the home–life conflict/balance among women in the venture creation process, and the role of education and prior experiences in starting new ventures among women.

Part 2 addresses the pre-venture stage, and thus discusses the pre-stages of the new venture by emphasizing this stage in women's experiences in their ecosystems. Women initially face social and cultural barriers, along with their personal deficiencies e.g., limited relevant education and experience, work–home conflict, self-navigation to specific business sectors and their interpretation of "success." This part presents the capabilities and competencies that are required to start a new venture and the different entrepreneurial avenues that can be considered by women. In it, one chapter is devoted to a quest for women entrepreneurs' motivations to start a new venture, including necessity–opportunity motivations. This latter topic is discussed in light of different approaches and includes examples of women whose enterprises began as necessity entrepreneurships but, by their use of relevant strategies and assistance measures, turned into successful entrepreneurs. Another chapter focuses on women's core competencies to start a new venture and their role in the success of women-led businesses.

Part 3 is devoted to the preparation process and focuses on the idea and the vision. The preparation constitutes the most significant step for an individual who has come up with a bright idea, as it is the practical course of action that requires practical preparations as well as strengthening and honing of the idea, including adjusting it to the needs and expectations of potential clients. This part includes a chapter on creativity among women entrepreneurs, and another on innovation in the context of female new venture creation, including examples of women innovators; it deals with innovations that can be transformed into businesses, and imparts the message that innovation is an important element in establishing a venture, as long as it serves the needs of potential clients. A chapter on the vision and new venture creation in the female context includes practical aspects emanating from the vision and discusses how these affect the preparation process prior to starting and establishing the venture. The vision is discussed in this chapter in the context of women in the business world and, by analyzing the biographies of several well-known women entrepreneurs, presents a "pragmatization" of the vision into practice.

Part 4 traces the first steps in the venture creation. One widespread explanation for women's lesser engagement in entrepreneurship is rooted in the start-up phase, i.e., the first steps as a real business. The entrepreneurship literature has highlighted gender differences in conceiving an idea and actually establishing a business, and concludes that women appear to be at a disadvantage. This part includes chapters on opportunity exploitation, creation and shaping as key entrepreneurial capabilities for women entrepreneurs. The research discussing ways in which women exploit opportunities is scarce: most of the empirical material on this topic is based on male models. This chapter discusses the pursuit of opportunities and proposes different ways to exploit them, as well as models of women who have exploited opportunities. Another chapter focuses on the process of financing the new venture as experienced by women, including the financing patterns and habits of women entrepreneurs, women's access to start-up financing, women's preferred types of initially generated capital, topics associated with their financing sources and possibilities, and women investors. A chapter is devoted to women's networking patterns and their role in their new venture creation, including financing the business. Women's entrepreneurial path wraps up this part, presenting different avenues to create a new venture and choose the route that is most convenient to women, i.e., that empowers them and reduces the encountered hurdles and barriers.

Part 5 is about the future of female entrepreneurship. This part of the book has a proactive slant and reflects upon the past achievements of female entrepreneurship and on how the subject can be developed in research, teaching and practice in the future. Different aspects of promoting female entrepreneurship are developed by tracing the steps of well-known and successful entrepreneurs. A chapter on leadership in female entrepreneurship is presented, introducing some strategies that well-known, successful women leader-entrepreneurs have taken. The concluding chapter discusses policy and breaking down the risk barriers; it focuses on the most promising ways to overcome female-related hurdles: through developing best practices for the new venture creation by incorporating innovation, choosing sectors, learning from successful women entrepreneurs, and developing a rigorous policy to empower women entrepreneurs and facilitate their process of new venture creation.

THE BOOK'S MODEL

The scope of this book is the first stages of the business life cycle, when the motivation to start a business emerges and the first steps toward realizing this motivation are taken. The model of this book, illustrated in Figure I.6, is built on the five salient building blocks of the start-up process in the female entrepreneurial realm: the motivation to start a business; the background of the founder; the idea for a business; the processes of starting a business, especially opportunity exploitation; and the management of eventual start-up stages. Each of these blocks encompasses facets that are treated or perceived differently by women vs. men entrepreneurs, e.g., spending more time with the children as a major motivation for flexibility and an entrepreneurial career path; traditional views on the role of women in the labor market and their effects on the probability of women choosing entrepreneurship; a social—rather than practical—orientation toward the use of networks for the business start-up; different choices of business sectors, and others.

WHAT DOES THE BOOK NOT ENTAIL?

This book focuses on the stages prior to establishing a business and discusses the very first stages of the business's life cycle. It does not cover topics related to managing an active and functioning business, including themes such as marketing, managing people, human resources, financing an

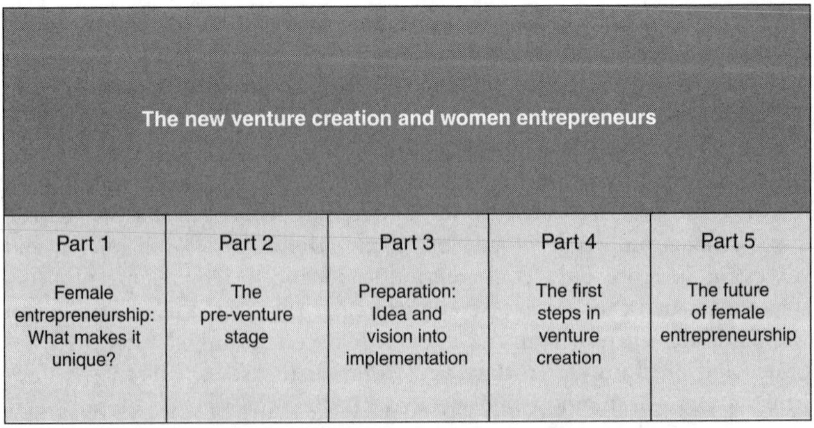

The new venture creation and women entrepreneurs				
Part 1	Part 2	Part 3	Part 4	Part 5
Female entrepreneurship: What makes it unique?	The pre-venture stage	Preparation: Idea and vision into implementation	The first steps in venture creation	The future of female entrepreneurship

Figure I.6 The Book Model.

existing business, business operation, client service and bootstrapping, among others. The main target of this book is to familiarize potential and existing entrepreneurs with the multifaceted preparation process, which is also the most risky and frustrating phase, and encourage entrepreneurship by providing more knowledge and information relevant to this phase.

THE BOOK'S CONTRIBUTION

Material for courses on female entrepreneurship is sorely lacking. This book contributes to filling this void in the following aspects:

1   It focuses exclusively on female entrepreneurship, thus responding to the need for books in this specific area.
2   It includes case studies of women entrepreneurs from different national cultures and ethnic groups, thus promoting knowledge of and familiarity with their diversity, rather than being restricted to American-oriented experiences; empathy and greater understanding of different experiences—some similar to their own lives and encounters, others very different—may enable students, women entrepreneurs, nascent women entrepreneurs, and women in general to consider initiating an entrepreneurial undertaking.
3   This book includes case studies developed by contributors from different countries and cultures, all of whom are known scholars involved in the area of female entrepreneurship. One of the book's main strengths lies in its having attracted the participation of many scholars interested in this emerging field of study.
4   The book's case studies, structured by contributors from different countries, provide exposure to different aspects of female entrepreneurship in varied environments, as well as to new directions for presenting this subject matter.
5   The book's contributors also disseminate the knowledge and information they present in this book in their own countries and impart it to their colleagues and students, as well as to their countries' entrepreneurial markets; in doing so, they increase the number of scholars who may consider developing courses in female entrepreneurship.
6   The exposure of the book's content and up-to-date message of diversity constitutes additional reasons for its hoped-for widespread use and popularity.
7   This book is a graphical, user-friendly yet professional academic book; its target audience, both students and teachers, will find extensive examples, detailed case studies and at-a-glance cases, links to video clips, questions for discussion in class, and more.
8   Entrepreneurship research's interest in social responsibility and diversity has evolved into a promising topic. The present book fits itself to

this budding interest by actually "doing" rather than just discussing this subject. It includes descriptions of widely varied entrepreneurship cases: a female member of a Canadian Inuit community, a private equity investment vehicle developed by a black woman in a South African township to create empowerment in a non-traditional manner, an ethnic Hawaiian woman entrepreneur, an ethnic Asian woman in the UK—these along with successful Canadian, Israeli, American and French women entrepreneurs, and many more.

9   The message of social responsibility and diversity is delivered by emphasizing that very diversity and including accounts of dissimilar women, rather than basing the subject matter on opportunity-driven entrepreneurial experiences. Addressing problems of necessity-driven entrepreneurship along with those of opportunity-driven entrepreneurship in a single book can bring together students, teachers, scholars and entrepreneurs around the topics of women and diversity, and it may enhance women entrepreneurs' well-being and lead to a sustainable future.

10   At-a-glance descriptions of women entrepreneurs in different countries and cultures are presented within the chapters of each part of the book. This is designed to expand the readers' acquaintance with an awareness of different types of female entrepreneurship and the varied avenues by which it can be pursued. These descriptions are not discussed but are offered for simple reading and the personal impact they will have on the readers.

CASE STUDY[6]

The case of Marie-Louise Roy illustrates an exciting journey toward the "true freedom" achieved through entrepreneurship, by tracing Ms. Roy's entrepreneurial path from a turbulent childhood in Canada's eastern provinces, through a stint in an haute couture workshop, a part-time job in a local department store, a position as a research assistant in a laboratory, an architect with environmental ethics values, yet, always opting for entrepreneurship; toward harmonically and spiritually assisting people, writing books, delivering workshops, producing CDs, among others.

Piffault and Filion delicately and sensitively intertwine the pieces of Roy's story together, describing the role of a woman, a mother and a determined creative entrepreneur, to craft an inspiring case study that demonstrates the power of determination and the entrepreneurial path as a route to achieve self-fulfillment and actualization.

Marie-Louise Roy: True Freedom through Entrepreneurship[7]

Joëlle Piffault[a] and Louis Jacques Filion[b]
[a]HEC Montréal, Quebec, Canada; [b]Chair of Entrepreneurship, HEC, Quebec, Canada

Marie-Louise Roy's[8] journey to become who she "really is" was a long and difficult one. As a child growing up in Canada's eastern provinces, she first experienced freedom through education. Later, as an adult in a male-dominated profession, she found it through her job in her chosen field of architecture. In recent years she has also been involved in her own personal quest for inner well-being, a task that has involved delving into her own roots. As a result of this long and difficult process, she has eventually been able to achieve what she refers to as "true freedom"in other words, a harmonious balance between her professional and spiritual lives. This case study describes the path taken by Marie-Louise Roy to achieve balance and well-being.[9]

A Turbulent Childhood

Marie-Louise Roy was born in 1953, in northwestern New Brunswick, Canada, and spent the first four years of her life in a small French-speaking community. However, her father, an intellectual and a practical man with interests that included meditation and yoga, heard about a vacancy for a technician with the Radio-Canada television station in Moncton. He applied, and was hired. The family moved to the city.

Marie-Louise was four years old at the time. She had to deal with a lot of changes, not the least of which was a change of language; in 1957, 75 percent of Moncton's population was English-speaking, whereas the family was French-speaking and had always lived in French-speaking communities. She still remembers the images, flavors and sensations from these early years:

> We loved to play with the other kids. We spoke Québec French at home, and English outside the home. We also spoke *Frenglish—J'aime ta* skirt—but we couldn't use it at home . . . We often went sledding in winter. I loved it. And we had our ritual activities on summer Sundays. We'd go to the beach in Shediac, about an hour's drive from Moncton, to swim and ride the ponies, and then for a fresh lobster supper.

Marie-Louise began to discover new things about herself. Her mother was the first to observe that five-year-old Marie-Louise "was a difficult child . . . hyperactive, but not the kind that needed Ritalin . . . she just had too much electricity in her body." Her father introduced her to meditation and yoga, and also tried to hypnotize her to calm her down.

In 1959, Marie-Louise started school. Although the family lived in an English-speaking community, she was able to attend a French-language school. The following year, however, the family moved to an Italian district in Montreal. This meant a new community and a new school, although linguistically speaking the change was less challenging than the first move. Two years later, they finally went to live in what would become their permanent home in the suburbs.

Architecture and Fashion: Two Abiding Features

Our house in the suburbs was one of the first to be finished on our street, which was at the end of a housing estate. The other houses were under construction. We weren't allowed near them, but there was nobody around when the workmen went home at 4:30 in the afternoon. Between the ages of 8 and 12, I used to go to different empty houses after school, with my dolls, and I'd gather up 2" × 4" planks to build dolls' houses. I'd copy the layout of the "real" house.

Even before her wooden dolls' houses, Marie-Louise would play at building houses, but her Lego constructions were too small for her dolls. The wooden structures allowed her to stretch her emerging imagination. She would also make clothes for her dolls, which she stored in tiny sets of drawers made from cardboard:

Basically, they were Barbie accessories. I made them on my bed in my room at home. We also had a playroom in the basement, but I don't remember making doll stuff there. My brother's electric train was set up on a 4' × 8' board 18" above floor level in the basement. I drew a whole cluster of houses on it . . .

By the time she was 12 years old, Marie-Louise knew she wanted to be an architect or a fashion designer, since these had been her two passions since early childhood. In the end it was her father who tipped the scales in favor of architecture, believing that "fashion design may be too unstable for a career." Enrolled in an experimental class, she crammed the last three grades into two years and was ready for college at 16 years of age.

The First Taste of Freedom: Education

Marie-Louise was 16 years old when she started college. It marked a new phase of her life, since it involved leaving home for a student residence. She enrolled in a science major, in preparation for her architecture degree, and arranged to take all her classes on Mondays to Thursdays. For the first year, she spent her Fridays and Saturdays working in an haute couture workshop in Montreal. On Sundays she studied, did her coursework and went back to the residence in the evening. It was a busy life, one she loved. Being away from home, although she continued to experience her spirituality, she missed practising yoga as her father had taught her. In her own words:

> I used to watch him do yoga, and really got into his energy. I realized I'd been having out-of-body experiences at home, and I was suddenly terrified of going through something like that without my father. He brought me back into my body. In many ways he was my anchor. Of course, all this went unspoken.

When she started university in 1972, Marie-Louise was still not prepared to fully accept her own spirituality—she poured all her energy into her courses. She was spoiled for choice, having been accepted by both McGill University and the University of Montreal. In the end she opted for the latter, because of its much lower tuition fees. The three hundred dollar saving "made all the difference"; even though her father was helping her financially, she still had to pay her share.

After her stint in the haute couture workshop, she found another part-time job in the menswear section of a local department store, as a cashier and seamstress, and later obtained a position as a research assistant in a concrete laboratory.

Her architecture program was a basic four-year degree course. Like the other nine or ten girls in her group, she quickly adjusted to an essentially male universe and enjoyed her years at university:

> As a member of the inception committee, I was as friendly with the older students as with those in my year. I was involved in projects with students from the other years. I moved around a lot; there was a real spirit of community. We used to organize wine and cheese evenings.

She obtained her degree in architecture in April 1976, and turned her attention to the job market.

Woman and Architect—Working in a Male-dominated Profession

Marie-Louise would have liked to continue working in the concrete laboratory where she had been a research assistant, but she was not an engineer and sadly she had to leave. However, she was advised to apply to its parent company, which had a planning department. After an initial five-month probationary contract, Marie-Louise was hired on a permanent basis and remained with the firm for five years.

She was busy both in the office and in the field:

Planning by-laws, residential estate planning, cycle paths, historical sites like old Boucherville. I travelled extensively throughout Québec. Most of my time was spent on land use planning, but I also did some urban planning and just enough architecture to become a qualified architect through the firm of architects with which the company worked.

Marie-Louise worked as part of a multidisciplinary team and was given many interesting projects. She was comfortable with her co-workers and loved her job. There was only one snag: her boss, whom she describes as a "womanizer." Even though she was married, Marie-Louise was still a target, and her boss became so insistent and unpleasant that she eventually chose to leave her job. Her release came in the form of an offer from a planning firm that also employed architects. During the year she spent with them, her career literally took over her life as she worked on several major federal building redevelopment projects in Canada's capital city, Ottawa.

In 1982, Marie-Louise went to work for another company. It turned out she was expecting her first child, although she had not known she was pregnant when she was first interviewed. Her new employers nevertheless felt betrayed and sacked her at the end of her maternity leave.

She then went to work for an interior design firm. Although she liked her job, she still found it was taking too much of her family time:

> I worked for the firm full-time for a year, and often went a full week without seeing my daughter. I really was torn between my career and my role as a mother. In addition, I didn't want to be sacked again because I was pregnant. The only solution was to work from home.

Her daughter was just starting to walk, but Marie-Louise could not enjoy the moment because she was constantly on the road, moving from one project to the next. So she opted for self-employment. As an extra measure of security she presented a plan of action to the employment insurance office, which agreed to help if her income proved to be insufficient. In the end, though, she never needed their help because other contracts began to pour in. "We had lift-off!", she says.

Discovering Self-employment

> When I chose to work from home, it certainly wasn't because I wanted more creative projects—I'd always had them. The word "creativity" must have been imprinted on my forehead, because I always got them without asking. And still do.

At long last, Marie-Louise found she was able to balance her work and family life. Between 1983 and 1990, she obtained contracts from several cities, including by-laws, land use plans and cycle trails. She was almost never without work. "The more I did, the more money I made, and the better it was!", she says.

From 1986 onwards, she began to take a much more community-oriented approach to her work, both in her own region (a suburb of Montreal) and further afield:

> I realized that if someone wanted to change my ideas for purely mercantile reasons, with no community justification, the project always ended up being blocked and would eventually come back to what I'd originally proposed.

Architecture and Urban Planning—Hand-in-hand with Environment and Land Use Management

After obtaining her bachelor's degree in architecture, Marie-Louise went on to study for a Master's degree in Environmental Studies at Montreal's engineering school, Polytechnique. In 1978, however, when the time came to write her Master's dissertation, she did not feel she was ready and asked to postpone submission, convinced that her experience in the field would lead her to a suitable subject.

Nearly ten years later, in 1985, she was pregnant with her second child and needed to cut down her workload. She took advantage of the time available to complete her Master's degree, which was finally awarded in 1988.

By opting for self-employment and focusing on ethical issues, Marie-Louise became more than just an architect. Everyone with whom she worked agreed that her strength was to find solutions and devise scenarios that suited everyone. Over time, the concept of "well-being"—her own and that of her clients—became her keyword when choosing her projects.

From 1990 onwards Marie-Louise felt strong enough in her convictions to abandon the city sector, concentrating instead on projects for large contractors in the high-end construction sector (houses and condominiums). She also worked on development projects as a consultant, with engineers, surveyors and lawyers, where there was a need for her particular expertise.

Having worked almost exclusively as a town planner throughout her career, Marie-Louise had acquired plenty of experience with housing developments. She was good at building design, but had never really been involved in the technical and production aspects. However, as she focused more on the human aspect of town planning, she gradually began to work as part of "consortiums" and less as a "freelancer." By 2002, she had negotiated several agreements with residential construction specialists working on sustainable urban developments using ecological materials—in other words, firms whose philosophies were consistent with her own. She was convinced this was the way of the future.

She built her own highly efficient, passive solar home, and also became a consultant for other homeowners. In particular, she loved designing solar homes:

> *Small is beautiful!* A big house would detract from my quality of life because I'd have to take care of it. I'd rather have a small house and more time for myself. Before the emergence of my spiritual journey, my "wealth" was in my bank account. Now it's elsewhere. I can take it with me, wherever I go.

Gradually, the type of work she was offered began to diverge from what she had done before, and she began to shift away from architecture and toward something else altogether:

> I enjoy [the type of planning and architectural work] I'm offered because it involves ecology, health and sacred geometry. Building something that resonates with the body to help it heal is an extension of my energy therapy activities. I see it as being the same thing.

Marie-Louise is also convinced that certain outside influences have had a major impact on her ability to combine the various factions of her life. "Life is a mirror of our inner state," she says, adding, "I used to dream of working on ecovillages. It was part of my need to work as a healer in a much more material way." Her dream became reality when a youth group came to her for help in designing an ecovillage based on agriculture and alternative medicine. As the group's coach, it was her job to help them build their own ecovillage with government subsidies.

More recently, she was involved in a legal case involving two sides of a local dispute:

> My job, beyond my official role, was to understand the whole psychological aspect underlying the case, to help the lawyer settle it quickly. Life seems to send me cases like this, where I can apply my whole experience. But the client doesn't know it. I'm something of a secret agent of the conscience, operating as an ordinary person. I can't always advertise my conscience in the commercial sense.

Discovering the World behind the Door of Her Spirituality: Living beyond the Family Karma

Over the years, Marie-Louise also worked hard on her spirituality.

> As the years went by I tried to find out what was tainting my life. Why did I always seem to find myself in uncomfortable situations? Why did the things I really wanted never happen? And why did the other things

I didn't want often happen? I suppose I was looking for change. I went back over my family tree, not in the historical sense of finding my ancestors, but rather to uncover the family secrets that might have made me what I was without my knowing . . .

"It's very subtle," she says. "I was living in a model where the men needed strong women to manage their lives." It was here that her long process of self-examination began. To use her own words:

How can you get rid of a suit of armour that's been handed down over the generations? I had to peel off a great many emotional onionskins before I realized they were an inherent family trait . . .

In 1988, her journey into her own past led her to a rebirthing workshop. "I went down some extraordinary avenues, trying to understand my family," she says. "We all develop our own outer shields to protect ourselves, but the suffering and potential is the same. I discovered an interesting mirror image." In their very first workshop, the shock was brutal for both Marie-Louise and her husband, as they discovered their own personal wounds:

All the wounds from my own childhood were present in my husband's family, but in different forms. His musical potential had never been developed, partly out of fear and partly because it required an effort . . . His parents hoped he'd choose a "real" profession . . . He wasn't from a background where he could do what he wanted; they wanted him to be something he wasn't . . . He saw the musical potential in me, and I saw it in him, but we didn't see it in ourselves. (. . .) We realized just how automated we'd become, how we weren't really ourselves any more, locked into the social shackles imposed on us by our parents and society. We'd let ourselves be defined by others, believing that's how it was in life. I really thought I'd never be able to get out of it. For my husband, the discovery was too much. He abandoned the workshops.

As the process of self-discovery moved forward, Marie-Louise and her husband began to feel uncomfortable in their marriage, and although they consulted therapists, they ultimately divorced in 1992.

Marie-Louise persevered with her self-exploration, attending nine weekend rebirthing sessions, digging deeper into her subconscious and gradually peeling away her "emotional onionskins." At one of the sessions, she confided in the facilitator about the physical sensation she experienced in her hands as she tried to physically calm the racing heartbeat of one of her friends. The facilitator suggested she might have "healing hands." This gave Marie-Louise the impetus she needed, and in 1990 she enrolled at the Mind and Body Therapy School. Over the next three years, while still working as an architect, she took 500 hours of Polarity Therapy courses.

As she looked more closely at her own spiritual powers, her barriers and limitations were gradually removed. At the same time, though, she felt as though she was literally falling apart, appearing to live in more than one world at once. She felt torn. For almost three years, "I really wanted to close the door, but it kept opening again," she says. "Part of me wanted to go forward, and the other part didn't. I lived with this ambiguity from the fall of 1992 right through to 1995. It took that long for me to feel safe."

> The channeling phenomenon has existed since time immemorial. The Tibetans referred to channelers as oracles, people who predicted the future. In the Middle Ages, the Catholics would burn you if you were even remotely like that without papal authorization. My fear of chan-neling, probably a result of all this hidden background, meant that I felt uncomfortable with it . . .

Thanks to the help she received during her three-year learning period, she was able to overcome her discomfort and began to give public confer-ences. In the process, she discovered that her spiritual goal was to assimi-late the fact of being a channeler, rather than the channeling itself. This is how she describes her choice:

> My six years as a practising channeler—from 1995 to 2000—were a springboard for me. Life asks us quite simply to become what we preach. Ultimately, I understood that I had to become everything I'd said . . .

In fact, Marie-Louise had been practising Polarity Therapy since she had graduated in 1993, and had been attending regular training sessions since 1995, including some given by Ron Young, an American healer. Between 1995 and 1999, she took three high-level sessions and one pilgrimage workshop to Assisi in Italy. At the time of the interview, she was waiting impatiently for the fifth and last Ron Young workshop, a rare occurrence.

Apart from the workshops, she uses intense meditation to regenerate her energies:

> On average, I meditate for between an hour and a half and two hours a day. I also regenerate through singing and musical creation, my daily hobby. I usually work from 9 a.m. to 4.30 p.m., two to four days a week, that is, no more than 30 hours a week. (My regeneration time) is essential, otherwise I couldn't be a conscience any more!

Spiritual Fulfilment through Self-employment

In her Polarity practice, Marie-Louise attracts two types of customers: people going through a career change and people dealing with difficult family dynamics. She also works occasionally with people who want to develop their creativity. She describes her work as follows:

> What I do is offer awareness to those who want it. You can't fill a glass that's already full, you have to empty it first. I take people into another dynamic, which involves unlearning their preconceived ideas of what humans, life, society and things should be . . . It's very important to realize that when you offer awareness, you have to deal first with any obstructions in its way.

And obstructions are always in plentiful supply. Marie-Louise encourages her clients to talk about their problems for about half-an-hour before asking them to lie down for an energy reading. She then delves into their subconscious:

> . . . to see what's stopping them from achieving fulfilment . . . It's not up to me to tell them what they should be, it's up to them to find out. I take away the bars that are preventing them from being who they are. I help them understand how the bars got there, why they might have put them there to protect themselves, and how that "protection" is no longer needed at that specific time in their lives.

Marie-Louise does not advertise her services, on the basis that "awareness, in its most basic sense, can't be sold." If awareness were to become a commodity, it would no longer be awareness. Where, then, does she get her clients? Some are referrals from existing clients, while others come to her because they have read her books and want to know more. Word-of-mouth is her best form of publicity.

At the same time, Marie-Louise had also been developing her meditative and musical abilities. In 2001, with the help of a friend, she produced a meditation CD in French, a kind of anti-depressive reviver that takes listeners on a voyage through the human body. In 2003, she produced a musical CD in English on which she "lovingly" sings her own compositions dedicated to healing the planet. In 2009, a second music CD was launched, honoring the "Sacred Feminine." In 2010, she produced a second meditation CD (in English) honoring Tibetan mantras. In addition, she has just finished writing a book about her professional journey as a woman in a man's job. She is also the author of several self-awareness books.

How, then, is this hard-won harmony between spiritual awareness and physical reality reflected in Marie-Louise's everyday life? Architecture is

still a major component, accounting for about 75 percent of her professional activity, followed by her awareness practice and her writing, at
25 percent. Music is her principal activity outside her professional life. She
is now perfectly comfortable with all these facets of herself (this was not
always the case), and describes her feelings as follows:

> I feel a lot less torn into three now. I found it hard to accept the feeling
> of being divided. Architecture and planning are spiritual too, by
> extension; otherwise they would have been evacuated from my life. I
> feel as comfortable with this aspect of my life as with my personal and
> musical growth. They overlap, make me feel safe, and fuel my
> progress.

She adds:

> In its most subtle element, music is sound. In its densest application,
> sound becomes matter. Architecture can therefore be very close to
> music. A building is crystallized music. It's a question of structuring
> matter or the material world to become as musical as possible.

When asked what advice she would give to people considering self-
employment, she has this to say:

> They should believe in their values and have faith that they will be
> able to bring their dreams to fruition, whatever they are. There's
> nothing silly about dreaming. It's a valuable faculty of human
> creativity. In some cases intellect can get in the way of dreams. Dreams
> and intellect often conflict with one another—not to mention outside
> forces. If you're capable of dreaming about something, you're capable
> of doing it. If you come across obstacles, you need to work on your
> awareness to remove them . . .

By fulfilling her dreams and overcoming the mercantile aspects of
life, Marie-Louise has achieved harmony between her body, soul and
environment. What will she become? What does the future hold for her?

Questions for Discussion

1   What are the leading factors that paved Ms. Roy's entrepreneurial
    path?
2   Identify the different influences that shaped Ms. Roy's current career.
3   What makes Ms. Roy's career path entrepreneurial?
4   How do you see the link between Ms. Roy's current activities and the
    journey she took? Explain.

5 Why does Ms. Roy's journey illustrate a female venture creation process? Identify and discuss the different factors and conditions that make this story a female-based exposé of the venture creation process.

Notes

1 From the Bible: Isaiah, chapter 43, verse 24.
2 Mr. Edmund Phelps, a professor at Columbia University, is the 2006 Nobel Laureate in economics.
3 From: The Kauffman Foundation. The State of Entrepreneurship in Europe— An Investor's View. An interview with Sir Ronald Cohen: Cofounder and former Chairman, Apax Partners; Author, *The Second Bounce of the Ball: Turning Risk into Opportunity*. Available at: http://www.kauffman.org/entrepreneurship/ state-of-entrepreneurship-in-europe.aspxhttp://www.kauffman.org/entrepre- neurship/state-of-entrepreneurship-in-europe.aspx
4 Refereeing to entrepreneurship in European countries.
5 Japan—Earthquake, Tsunami and Nuclear Crisis (2011); *The New York Times*, June 20, 2011; available at: http://topics.nytimes.com/top/news/international/ countriesandterritories/japan/index.htmlhttp://topics.nytimes.com/top/news/ international/countriesandterritories/japan/index.html
6 The author(s) of the case studies and at-a-glance cases are fully and solely responsible for their content, phrasing consistency and flow, terminology, English proofing and reference lists.
7 This case is a short version of the case entitled "Marie-Louise Roy: in tune with the inner self," presented at the 22nd International WACRA (World Association for Case Research and Application) Conference in Brno, Czech Republic, July 3–6, 2005, and published in the proceedings of that conference.
8 Copyright © 2005 HEC Montréal. All rights reserved for all countries. Any translation or alteration in any form whatsoever is prohibited. This case is intended to be used as the framework for an educational discussion and does not imply any judgment on the administrative situation presented. Deposited with the HEC Montréal Centre for Case Studies, 3000, chemin de la Côte-Sainte-Catherine, Montréal (Québec) Canada H3T 2A7.
9 Marie-Louise Roy's remarks in this case study are drawn from an interview with the authors on April 29, 2002, in her home office in Boisbriand, on the outskirts of Montreal. The interview followed on from an earlier case study. Ms. Roy has been a guest speaker at HEC on numerous occasions, in our courses and conferences.

Part 1

Female Entrepreneurship

What Makes this Area Unique?

Part 1 focuses on:

- Recognizing the main themes from the literature on female entrepreneurship;
- Understanding the roles of social and cultural forces in women's decision to become entrepreneurs;
- Drawing on the unique characteristics of women entrepreneurs, including human capital, social capital and family status, among others;
- Outlining women's entrepreneurial motivations, aspirations and choices with respect to entrepreneurship;
- A familiarization with female entrepreneurship in emerging markets, established markets, and in the context of necessity- and opportunity-driven economies;
- This part includes chapters and case studies illustrating the female entrepreneurial realm, including the constraints and opportunities it encompasses, women's motivations to embark on entrepreneurship, and a glimpse into female entrepreneurship in emerging economies such as those of the BRIC and MENA countries.

Part 1 of the book draws upon important themes from the literature on female entrepreneurship, which are presented via a practical, "down-to-earth" approach that includes examples of, and quotations from women entrepreneurs, followed by detailed case studies. The main themes discussed in this section are the social and cultural forces and pressures encountered by women that affect their decision to become entrepreneurs. These include, for example, the stereotyping of women entrepreneurs, discrimination against women in the labor market and a lack of relevant experience in entrepreneurship, but also women's greater participation in the higher education system, a factor that fosters their participation in the entrepreneurial realm. The external forces that influence women's entrepreneurial aspirations are considered, as is a global view of women's roles in their respective societies and labor markets.

Another aspect addressed herein is women's experiences in the labor market as a premise for their entrepreneurial choices: motivations, including a thorough look into the emerging BRIC markets in the context of necessity- and opportunity-driven economies, and push-vs.-pull external factors.

1   Female Entrepreneurship

Constraints and Opportunities—A General Overview

Chapter Objectives

- Discussing the roles of country, culture, policies, and services in crafting and reflecting women's and men's attitudes toward female entrepreneurship;
- Detailing the micro-level and macro-level effects on women's motivations to become entrepreneurs and on their aspirations to grow their new ventures;
- Learning and discussing the relevance of the feminist theories in female entrepreneurship; assessing the added value of each theory for an understanding of female entrepreneurship;
- Creating the drive to develop practical angles stemming from the feminist theories for female entrepreneurship;
- Understanding the differences between "sex" and "gender" and recognizing the contexts in which these have evolved;
- Exhibiting themes such as stereotyping, discrimination, inequality and regulations in the context of women in general, and women entrepreneurs in particular.

The different roles of men and women in society—in both the home and the labor market—and their changing nature in the past few decades, are presented and discussed, to familiarize the reader with the state of female employment around the world and the respective state of entrepreneurship.

In seeking explanations that account for these differences, both theoretical and practical examples are offered, and the macro and micro perspectives are introduced. Themes such as personal attributes relevant to entrepreneurship and family status (micro perspective) are presented along with social and cultural pressures (macro perspective), to demonstrate the complex situation that women entrepreneurs must tackle in their entrepreneurial course.

The theoretical, organizational framework of this chapter is based on theoretical approaches to feminism, which are broadly discussed, and several angles emerging from the feminist perspective are introduced.

The process of new venture creation originates from entrepreneurial activity; the way in which women handle new venture creation echoes the female-oriented motivations, activities and strategies that typify the new venture creation phase. While the area of female new venture creation has scarcely been studied, female entrepreneurship has been recognized as an important budding research area, albeit a largely untapped source of economic growth. Women entrepreneurs create new jobs, promote national and international economies, and provide society with inventive solutions that emerge from their entrepreneurial ventures and innovations. More importantly, women entrepreneurs introduce new and unique ways of tackling unexploited entrepreneurial opportunities and overcoming obstacles in the venture creation process, and implement their vision in a set of unique business practices. This distinctiveness, however, is somehow overlooked in research and practice; of the fields that have attracted entrepreneurship scholars over time, e.g., opportunity exploitation, sources of financing, venture capitalists' practices and social networks, gender in the women entrepreneur's quest has been, for the most part, treated as a component of "personal characteristics," similar to age and educational attainment. By offering a general look into the venture creation process, the male perspective dominates the area of entrepreneurship, leaving the female perspective essentially unexploited (Ahl, 2006; Moore, 1990; Stevenson, 1990).

Female entrepreneurship, however, deserves special attention since a woman's background is distinct and unique: the socialization path and social expectations faced by women, their distinct routines, i.e., the challenges and obstacles tackled by women entrepreneurs, have shaped their attitudes, thoughts and performance in their new venture creation process.

By disregarding women's perspective, women's performance remains blurred. The entrepreneurial paths which are more commonly followed by women to pursue opportunities, develop their ideas for a business or finance their ventures, for example, may appear ineffective to the male or "general" market. Women are not taken seriously as entrepreneurs, and any success in woman-led businesses is treated as the exception rather than the rule. The outcome is mirrored in the general approach toward female entrepreneurship, while entrepreneurship as a career path is considered more appropriate for men than for women.

Yet, the significant number of women entrepreneurs—inventors, founders, innovators and pioneers, among them Nobel Prize winners—

proves that the creative, innovative, entrepreneurial path is diversified and can suit anyone, regardless of gender. By embracing the woman-oriented, entrepreneurial path, maintaining an open mind and accepting that there are different entrepreneurial paths, including female-oriented and male-oriented ones, the entrepreneurial field will benefit and be promoted (Boden & Nucci, 2000; Brush, 1992; Scheinberg & MacMillan, 1988; Shane, Kolvereid, & Westhead, 1991).

AN INTERNATIONAL VIEW

Scholars in female entrepreneurship and international entrepreneurship continue to disagree on the prevalence of gender or national culture in the new venture creation process. Most studies tackle gender by examining differences between female and male entrepreneurs. However, more evidence of country-level influences on the practices exhibited by women within the new venture creation process is required to deepen our understanding in this field.

Different questions addressing the underlying effects of the ecosystem's intricacies on new venture creation processes spring to mind, e.g., social expectations of women in different societies, cultural norms regarding women's independence in the labor market, including entrepreneurship, national policies, strategies, cultural and economic influences, regional support, policies supporting women entrepreneurs, and services developed to facilitate their entrepreneurial path and empower them, and corollary basic public policies, e.g., government support of more business training and initiatives for women. To date, research into female entrepreneurship has failed to thoroughly explore these questions.

Obviously, encouragement, positive attitudes and higher confidence in women's abilities to succeed in entrepreneurship will lead women to embark on the new venture creation process. However, there is no one key to women's fundamental characteristics, and women in different countries are driven by different national and cultural codes. It is only by becoming familiar with different local contexts that the avenues to reaching the essence of such keys can be explored. This exploration will delineate the broader common ground of entrepreneurial activity among women entrepreneurs in different countries, while sketching the uniqueness of female entrepreneurship in each.

For example, while in the broad context women are more reluctant than men to start entrepreneurial ventures, in the local context, American women consider education and training to be driving forces for embarking on entrepreneurship, western European women appreciate other women entrepreneurs as role models, while women in the Middle East may find their family's consent to be the driver in starting a new venture. Thus, variations exist across women entrepreneurs in various countries,

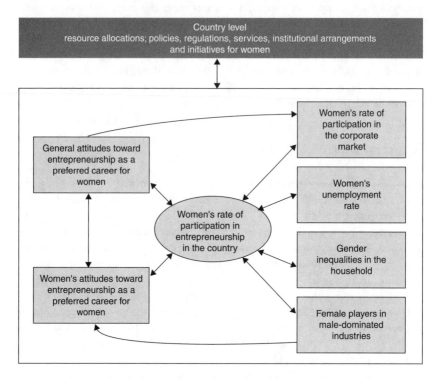

Figure 1.1   An International Look at Female Entrepreneurship and Attitudes.

and such distinctness has significant implications at both the macro and micro levels (Buttner & Rosen, 1989; Fagenson, 1993; Kalleberg & Leicht, 1991; Minniti, Arenius, & Langowitz, 2005b; Sexton & Bowman-Upton, 1990).

Figure 1.1 shows the relations and dynamic effects of the local context on prevalence of female entrepreneurship, and its consequent dual-faceted effects on different aspects of the labor market and life.

The roles of country, culture, policies, and services are all salient in both crafting and reflecting upon the attitudes toward female entrepreneurship, following women's distinctiveness in the new venture creation process (Hofstede, Hofstede, & Minkov, 2010; Minkov & Hofstede, 2011; Singh, Reynolds, & Muhammad, 2001).

Female Entrepreneurship around the Globe

Higher levels of entrepreneurial activity are associated with increasing involvement of women. Research and empirical reports (e.g., Global Entrepreneurship Monitor (GEM), OECD[1]) yield a clear picture of female

Table 1.1 Female Entrepreneurship around the Globe

Main themes	Main findings
Entrepreneurial activity	The level and type of entrepreneurial activity vary across countries
	Countries with similar levels of per capita GDP tend to exhibit broadly similar gender gaps
	Women entrepreneurs, similar to men, create and run businesses across all of the broad industrial sectors, but there are a significantly higher percentage of women's ventures in the consumer-oriented sector
	The gender gap in business survival rates varies; in high-income countries there is no gender difference
Motivation: necessity opportunity	Across all countries, the rate of male opportunity entrepreneurship is higher than that of women
	There is no gender gap with respect to necessity entrepreneurship, irrespective of country group
	Women (and men) in households with the highest incomes are more likely to be involved in entrepreneurial activity
Main characteristics	Female and male entrepreneurs have similar growth potentials in all countries (sector, innovation)
	Age distribution is similar for men and Women entrepreneurs
	The likelihood of being involved in entrepreneurial activity is significantly higher for employed vs. unemployed women

entrepreneurship as a distinctive phenomenon in different countries. Table 1.1 summarizes the empirical evidence from different sources in three categories, to emphasize the genders' similarities and differences in the global entrepreneurial realm in recent years.

In seeking explanations for these differences, the existing research has examined environmental factors that affect women's participation in entrepreneurship, such as women's traditional social roles, unemployment, underemployment, discrimination in the labor market (macro perspective), and entrepreneurial attitudes, motivations and behavior (micro perspective). Both perspectives can either prompt or restrict women's entrepreneurial activity and success. The main topics organizing the existing research in female entrepreneurship can be aggregated as in Table 1.2.[2]

Understanding the context of female entrepreneurship enables capturing its essence and respecting its uniqueness. Obtaining a context-driven picture of female entrepreneurship may provide a springboard for future research and policy decisions that will assist in mitigating the existing

Table 1.2 Micro and Macro Perspectives and Female Entrepreneurship

The MICRO perspective:	*The MACRO perspective*
The entrepreneur Personal attributes Entrepreneurial characteristics Motivations	**The context** Women's role in society Inhibiting factors Social networks and social capital
Identity and behavior Prior experience in the labor market Personal and family status Female-related hurdles and barriers	**International setting** Perception of female entrepreneurship Cultural effect on women's employment Necessity- vs. opportunity-driven environments
Networking	**Public policy issues**
The business unit Choice of industry Initial capital resources Founding strategies Investment process	Rules, norms and regulations for female participation in the labor market Regulations for mothers; ethnic women entrepreneurs; single mothers, etc. Lobby for women entrepreneurs

gender gap by eliminating gender stereotyping and other generalizations about women entrepreneurs (Ahl, 2006; Fagenson & Marcus, 1991; Gupta, Turban, Wasti, & Sikdar, 2009; Kepler & Shane, 2007).

DIRECTIONS IN FEMALE ENTREPRENEURSHIP

The directions emerging from research on female entrepreneurship can be categorized as in Table 1.3, which demonstrates some of the leading studies in areas that have been pertinent in research on female entrepreneurship. These research directions can be organized into two paths: (a) a simple process model: input–process–output of the entrepreneurial realm, and (b) a micro, i.e., individual perspective, and a macro, i.e., business and environment perspective.

The table illustrates the extensive work conducted on female entrepreneurship and on gender. Relative to the empirical work conducted on male entrepreneurship, the work on female entrepreneurship is still limited. However, collectively, the research reveals that the ways in which women and men tackle new venture creation vary substantially across industrial sectors, countries and business stages (Achtenhagen & Welter, 2007; Bruni, Gherardi, & Poggio, 2004b; Brush, Carter, Gatewood, Greene, & Hart, 2003; Brush, de Bruin, & Welter, 2009; Campbell, 2005; Carter, Gartner, Shaver, & Gatewood, 2003; Petterson, 2005).

Table 1.3 Female Entrepreneurship in Research

Organizing factor	Level of analysis	Topic	Description
Input	MICRO	Human capital	Women are portrayed as possessing lower education and prior work experience than men, while their education and experience are less relevant to their entrepreneurial undertakings
		Motivations Attitudes Perceptions	Women's motivations to start a business are opportunity-driven, yet, relative to men, more necessity-driven entrepreneurship is found among women
		Dual role: home and work	Women are engaged in childcare and domestic responsibilities that hinder their ability to start and maintain successful ventures
	MACRO	Business sector	Women tend to found their ventures in specific sectors, typified as more "feminine," e.g., service-oriented, care-giving, while avoiding high-tech and "masculine" based sectors
		Initial business resources	Women start their businesses with limited resources relative to men

For more reading on this topic, see: Brush, Carter, Gatewood, Greene, & Hart (2006); Du Reitz & Henrekson (2000); Kangasharju (2000); Kariv, Menzies, Brenner, & Filion (2009); Manolova, Carter, Manev, & Gyoshev (2007); Unger, Rauch, Frese, & Rosenbusch (2011). Despite the seemingly massive body of research in female entrepreneurship and the new venture creation, robust, explicit theoretical grounding is still needed to advance this field from its marginal position in research and practice to center stage in the entrepreneurial arena.

Theoretical Feminist Perspectives for Female Entrepreneurship

The research in female entrepreneurship lacks a rigorous theoretical foundation; thus, the organizing concepts herein draw from models and theories of either "general" entrepreneurship or the feminist trends.

While the leading models in entrepreneurship are frequently debated in female entrepreneurship research, relatively fewer studies engage the feminist theories in their explorations. Feminism is a comprehensive, wide-ranging theory that assists in understanding many situations relevant to women, through the female prism. It is broadly defined as the recognition of men's and women's unequal conditions and the desire to change these in order to achieve conditions that fit both genders' needs, rather than enforcing conditions and attitudes favored by men, as the leading, dominant ones. Feminism is about promoting a world in which women enjoy equal opportunities, while considering the vibrant and changing ecosystems that require reinventing and transforming the processes and regulations across time and place to enable an equitable world. Figure 1.2 shows the main directions developed within feminist theory.[3]

The classical aspects in feminist thought are helpful in organizing various female themes and combining them with entrepreneurship. These aspects are delineated here.

Women and Men are Essentially Similar

Feminist empiricism considers sex a category, such as age or education, and as relevant as any other attribute, making it an unbiased category in the context of entrepreneurship.

Liberal feminist theory emphasizes the similarities between women and men. It considers any disadvantage of women relative to men as temporal and dependent on objective factors that do not reflect any differences between the genders; in addition, it is presumed that any disadvantage can

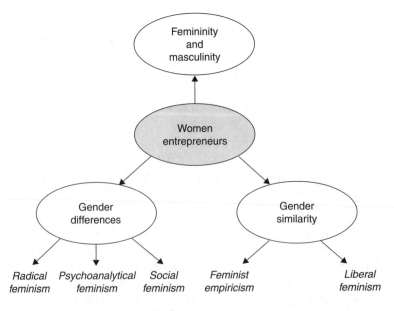

Figure 1.2 Directions in Feminist Theory.

be easily eliminated. The theory also stresses that women's disadvantage in the labor market is a result of the evident discrimination they encounter (e.g., in recruitment, income and career path, acquisition of the relevant human capital, especially education and job experience). Liberal feminists work toward an egalitarian society which will uphold the right of each individual to fulfill his or her potential, and therefore urge dramatic social reform to give women the same status and opportunities as men.

Women and Men are Essentially Different

Social feminist theory is founded on the theoretical concepts of inequality and "class"; i.e., women as a class are marginalized and are not recognized in the production system because of their attributed responsibility to the home, rather than to work. The differences between the genders are attributed to male and female experiences through deliberate socialization which produces differences in their respective views and interpretations of the same situations and conditions encountered. Social feminism focuses on the unique needs, experiences, competencies, and values of women, as women.

Psychoanalytical feminist theory maintains that the psychological reality of sex has to be distinguished from the anatomical reality: men and women are not physically or socially "made" to be male or female but become such. Feminist scholars perceive psychoanalysis as reproducing patriarchal inequalities by emphasizing the function of mothering, thereby creating an asymmetrical relationship between boys and girls. Women's attributes of relatedness, empathy and nurturance are devalued in the male-dominated culture; this also prevents females from having any "desires of their own." Issues of power and submission are located in the sphere of relationships. This area of feminism calls to move toward a view of masculinity and femininity in a contingent, relationally constructed context.

Radical feminist theory founds its basic concepts on the principle that women and men are innately different, i.e., biologically, psychologically and emotionally, while women's bodily experiences (pregnancy, breast feeding) induce characteristics that are typical to women, such as tenderness, benignity, caring for others and lack of aggressiveness. Such conceptions about women's characteristics not only separate them from the "mainstream" but also, in a male-dominated context, marginalize women as well as "women-based" characteristics. Women are thus treated as "less" or "having less" with respect to business or personal success, growth, and productivity in the labor market. Men maintain the power in many, if not all, spheres of the labor market and life, such as politics, finance, employment and social status, and oppress women's personal growth. Men explain this oppression by women's innate capability—childbearing—which places them "in the home." Subsequently, women are oppressed by men and by social structures through socialization. The call is to liberate women as solely responsible for childcare by either sharing the domestic and childcare responsibilities in the family or developing technological means to liberate women from childbearing.

Construction of Femininity and Masculinity

Social constructionism states that gender refers to the meaning of femininity and masculinity. Gender is treated as the result of background and culture, thus making it dependent on time and place. Gender is a dynamic, rather than static entity, which is reflected in the performance of gender. For more reading on feminist theories and implications for the labor market, see: Beasley (1999); Bristor & Fischer (1993); Butler (1990); Carter & Cannon (1992).

Despite the differences reflected in these categories of feminism, feminist theory postulates that women and men cannot perform as they choose, in a gender-free way, as each gender's culture dictates its norms and provides the constraints of proper gender behavior. Such behavior both affects and is affected by society. One such affected/affecting presentation is entrepreneurship, and entrepreneurship is therefore gendered.

Another core theme in feminism that is most relevant to entrepreneurship is the constant drive to develop a practical, accepted feminist theory, by pointing out that men and women start and manage businesses in essentially the same way. The main task of feminist research and policies is to facilitate women's path to reaching a state of equality with men by removing the obvious discrimination and male-dominated barriers that go against women; no special privileges for women are demanded. In addition, feminism calls for education and relevant experience, and urges women to obtain the relevant human and social capital to establish their position in the entrepreneurial market.

Calls for proactiveness and a "go-getter" spirit are found among feminist scholars, urging women to take full responsibility for their own choices and actions, and to craft equality by believing in it and advocating it in the labor market (Archer & Lloyd, 2002; Barnett & Hyde, 2001; Calás, Smircich, & Bourne, 2009; Stanford Encyclopedia of Philosophy[4]).

In summary, feminist theories posit that women's social disadvantage stems from society's male-dominated structure. Home is not just a place of consumption, but of production as well, as this form of production contributes to society at large. Women's work within the home permits men to work outside the home; yet, work at home is not measured in money, but rather in social worth, and women working at home are not adequately compensated for their work.

Socialist feminists strive to reshape the labor market's traditional stereotyping, because they see the gender division of labor that locks men and women into stereotypical occupational categories as preventing women from aiming for all types of occupational fields. The labor market should be freed of gender-specific constraints, even if it means reorganizing the family structure to share in child-rearing responsibilities. Accordingly, entrepreneurship may function as an effective career path, by enabling women to use their own abilities to accomplish their desires, while managing both work and home duties. Feminism calls for women to take responsibility and make changes in the existing structure by, e.g., eliminating the barriers to accessing public life, including the labor market, recognizing women's different experiences as valuable contributions to society, and even compensating women working at home. Home-based entrepreneurship, accordingly, may provide an acceptable social restructuring of the female realm in this aspect.

An inspiring undertaking is the Diana Project, which was established in 1999 by Candida Brush (Babson College), Nancy M. Carter (Catalyst, Inc.), Elizabeth J. Gatewood (Wake Forest University), Patricia G. Greene (Babson College) and Myra M. Hart (Harvard Business School), aimed at being the impetus for the implementation of policy, training, and resources that will advance the state of practice of women entrepreneurs, with two primary goals:

1   to assist women entrepreneurs seeking financing by educating them and providing them with the relevant information about the characteristics of equity-funded businesses;
2   to raise awareness and educate equity capitalists about the benefits gained through investment in women-owned businesses.

Currently, more than thirty researchers from twenty countries are involved in Diana International (to read more about it and the research outcomes, see: http://www.esbri.se/dianae.asp?link=research_outcomes).

Issues of Sex and Gender in Entrepreneurship

Sex is a biological variable that is determined at birth, while gender is a socially constructed and contested characteristic, which is accepted during life, and thus has different interpretations across countries and cultures. Gender refers to the psychosocial implications of being male or female; consequently, a human being of the "female" sex might adapt to a "male" gender by accepting lifestyles categorized as belonging to the male gender. In the entrepreneurial realm, sex is not the relevant explanatory attribute in identifying or explaining the differences between the genders in motivations to embark upon entrepreneurship, their managerial styles or the ways in which they generate financing for their ventures. Sex is the main source but not the cause of such differences; it represents the culture within which entrepreneurs are rooted and determines its meaning through the socialization process. Individuals develop a set of beliefs, or stereotypes, consisting of a multifaceted, internally consistent set of ideas that they have about gender, including gender roles, labeling traits as "feminine" or "masculine," and attributing gender-related capabilities in, for example, finance, technology, and entrepreneurial success.

MACRO AND MICRO PERSPECTIVES ON FEMALE VENTURE CREATION

Female entrepreneurship is one of the fastest growing types of entrepreneurship in today's world, comprising between one-quarter and one-third of businesses in the formal economy and likely to play an even greater role in informal sectors. As discussed earlier, the distinctive feature of entrepreneurship led by women is that it is still considered an "exception" and has not reached the position of a leading model for successful entrepreneurship.

Scholars often bring up the dividing line between female and male processes in new venture creation, in a continual attempt to theorize the essence of each feature. It appears that an individual engaged in new venture creation is envisioned as a man, and not a woman, and most of the developed definitions of entrepreneurship are gendered concepts. The profiles of women entrepreneurs as portrayed in research are summarized in Table 1.4.[5]

Table 1.4 Profiling Women Entrepreneurs in the New Venture Creation Process

Businesses started by women as compared to men	
Differences	*Similarities*
On average, participation rates for women tend to be 50% lower	Overall, opportunity is the dominant motivation for women's entrepreneurship, similar to men
Women entrepreneurs have a smaller amount of start-up capital, a smaller proportion of equity, and a higher proportion of bank loans	Similar to men, women entrepreneurs rely on role models and social networks for both information and access to resources
Women entrepreneurs tend to target existing markets and use known technology	Similar to men, most of the women involved in starting a new business hold other jobs
Women entrepreneurs start consumer-oriented businesses while men start service-oriented enterprises	
More women entrepreneurs are involved in necessity-oriented entrepreneurship	

The macro level of analysis introduces broad topics in many cultures, such as external effects, modernization and high technology—developments that shape the female new venture creation process, while outlining the common ground and differences between women in different countries. For example, in most countries women are still considered responsible for familial duties, although this role manifests differently in different countries and cultures. Most interesting are ethnic groups' behaviors in their enclaves in host countries. Under such conditions, ethnic women may either adapt to the host country's culture or maintain their ethnic norms with respect to employment choices.

Macro effects are manifested in social, economic, political and cultural effects, in local regulations, government rules and assistance systems. Cultural norms and values regarding the behaviors required for starting a business, e.g., risk-taking, hard work, and delayed gratification, and the outcomes related to owning a business, e.g., financial independence, being "one's own boss," expanding networks—also have a significant effect on women's propensity for the pursuit of creating a new venture. Accordingly, women in some cultures adhere to norms and values that are unfavorable to entrepreneurship and economic success in general, leading them to renounce entrepreneurship.

Research has also been dedicated to an unwieldy debate on new venture creation as an alternative found by women to survive unemployment or underemployment, i.e., some women receive unfair salaries or job evaluations, or are measured as employees against irrelevant criteria. They encounter horizontal career moves into positions with less promotion potential, are discriminated against or are dismissed from their positions on grounds that are not achievement-based. Under such circumstances, women often embrace entrepreneurship as an economic and social survival strategy.

The predominant areas in female entrepreneurship discussed from macro and micro perspectives are presented in Figure 1.3.

For further reading on the main themes in female entrepreneurship research from macro and micro perspectives, the following are suggested:

MACRO LEVEL

Social and cultural expectations and norms
Push factors; necessity entrepreneurship; dissatisfaction
Stereotyping; discrimination (e.g., financing, investment, networks, partnership)
Inequality in household responsibility
Regulations, local and institutional arrangements; services for women entrepreneurs

For further reading: Alsos, Isaksen, & Ljunggren (2006); Babcock, Laschever, Gelfand, & Small (2003); Bird & Brush (2002); Marlow & Patton (2005); Orser, Riding, & Manley (2006).

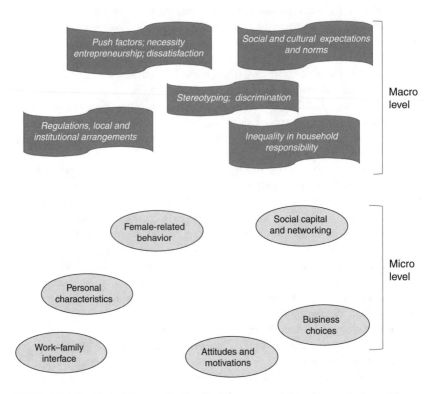

Figure 1.3 The Main Themes in Female Entrepreneurship Research from Macro and Micro Perspectives.

MICRO LEVEL

Attitudes, motivations
Work–life interface
Business choices: sectors, industries and types of entrepreneurial businesses
Female-related behavior
Education and prior experience
Personal characteristics, demographic characteristics, family-related factors
Social capital and networking

For further reading: Aldrich (1989); Chaganti & Parasuraman (1996); Carter, Williams, & Reynolds (1997); DeMartino & Barbato (2003); DeTienne & Chandler (2007); Greve & Salaff (2003); Gundry & Welsch (2001); Verheul & Thurik (2001).

The micro perspective is mainly dedicated to discovering the reasons why women start new business ventures, what steers them toward one type of business or another, and how "big" they think about their business, among others. The motivations to choose entrepreneurship as a career path are considered to be embedded in women's related attitudes, aspirations, traits and capabilities. A large bulk of research on motivations, aspirations and attitudes toward entrepreneurship focus on the "why" rather than the "how," i.e., why do some women choose entrepreneurship while others do not? Women's attitudes, motivations and behaviors lead to a unique entrepreneurial process, including more reluctance to take risks, exploiting opportunities in unique ways and embarking on less skeptical undertakings, depicted in their business's unique activities and procedures. Consequently, the process elicits outputs typical of female-headed businesses, based on their expectations of their business's profits, growth rates and leadership in the market/sector.

Studies have continually proven that the nature of women's attitudes toward entrepreneurship predicts their subsequent entrepreneurial behavior, which is then reflected in the new venture creation course and its success measures.

Most research in female entrepreneurship coalesces around the concept that the traditional socialization of women influences their motivation to start a business. However, some studies show that women differ in their interpretations of the experiences and attitudes embedded in their social-ization. Consequently, they are attracted to entrepreneurship for different reasons, e.g., to be their own boss, to make full use of their skills, to be financially independent, to have flexible working hours, to be able to manage the duality of work and home demands.

Pressures and conflicting demands emanating from a social role—being a mother, being responsible for household duties—that are incompatible with those from another role—being an employee, being responsible for work-related duties, may produce a work–family conflict that women, more than men, report as being inherent in their lives.

Many women "live with the conflict," i.e., they manage their lives in both places, work and home, without holding back from experiencing work-related challenges or neglecting their families. Yet, "living with a conflict" is a heavy load, in terms of emotions, energy, time, and effort devoted to internally managing or dealing with this conflict. This, in turn, may affect the methods and styles chosen by women entrepreneurs along their career path, including embarking upon entrepreneurship, financing their start-ups, setting the success goals for their businesses. Women around the world encounter the dual message of allocating time and energy to childcare and household duties, and exploiting their professional and job-related capabilities and accomplishing their personal dreams. These forces are illustrated in Figure 1.4.

Women's choice of sector in which to start their businesses, specifically, the woman-related, traditional areas, such as providing personal services which are often extensions of women's roles in the home, and shying away from nontraditional areas that are associated with higher risk, demand for more capital, and higher technical expertise, have been pinpointed in research.

Women-related forces:
The meaning of business success
The meaning of self-fulfillment
Work–life balance approach
Personal ROI (return on investment)
Interpretation of work-related situations
Past successful/unsuccessful
work-related experiences

Environment-related forces:
Social forces/pressures
Cultural forces/pressures
Glass ceiling experiences
Push versus pull factors
Stereotyping and discrimination
at the labor market

Figure 1.4 The Two Forces in the Female Entrepreneurship Realm.

A large number of studies argue that women's entrepreneurial activities are shaped by their unique experiences; and as females and males have been subjected to fundamentally different socialization experiences, their business-related behaviors will reflect this. In addition, the research identifies gender differences in psychological profiles, such as risk-taking, locus of control, social skills, autonomy, innovation and creativity, which have been found to play a significant role in women entrepreneurs' propensity to become entrepreneurs, their financial management, goal achievement and motivation for success.

Education is a significant factor in female entrepreneurship: entrepreneurs are better educated than the general public. Studies show that women entrepreneurs are more likely than their male counterparts to acquire higher education, and they consider it a salient means of preparing for starting a business. Ultimately, education serves mainly for obtaining more knowledge and tools relevant to their businesses, rather than opening traditional avenues such as promotion or rewards.

An early and ongoing influence of family background and parental role models is critical to entrepreneurs in general, women entrepreneurs in particular. There is a strong body of evidence that links entrepreneurs to parents who are themselves entrepreneurs. Social capital and social networking have also been proven to foster entrepreneurship among women; however, studies continually note the impact of male-dominated networks' contribution to the radically accelerated opening of start-ups among women.

SUMMARY

It is widely accepted in academic circles that traditional entrepreneurial models and their consequent practices have a masculine bias. As such, they do not resonate with women entrepreneurs and engender a mismatch between research and practice, as well as between potential and existing female entrepreneurship. Adopting an expanded, but still woman-based approach to the new venture creation process means stepping beyond the masculine bias and conventional gender differences to explore aspects of women-related processes that envelop the new venture creation's dynamics: women's background, experiences, socialization and current social and family roles are assumed to affect their attitudes toward entrepreneurship; such attitudes are conceived as a mental phenomenon, residing inside the individual's head and formed through socialization and that individual's social role. Therefore, topics related to women need to be raised, discussed and disseminated. Adopting a male-based approach in female entrepreneurship, in both research and practice, leads to neglecting the issues at the core of women entrepreneurs' interests.

Several researchers have drawn attention to the male dominance of entrepreneurship, i.e., its concepts are male-gendered and consist of masculine connotations. This chapter uses the female lens to provide a view of female entrepreneurship's uniqueness rather than its comparative differences.

This chapter covers different themes that may reveal how, and explain why, female entrepreneurship is distinctive and unique, by illustrating female-based intricacies in women's world that affect their performance in new venture creation. Drawing on the feminist aspects and linking them to the female entrepreneurial spheres, this chapter offers a broad platform for discussion of female entrepreneurship in the context of the venture creation process, while embracing practices of women from different countries and cultures.

In an attempt to encompass an expanded overview, macro and micro levels of analysis are introduced, and the topics are mostly studied at those levels.

CASE STUDIES AND AT-A-GLANCE CASE[6]

The following two case studies, contributed by Gundolf and Jaouen, illustrate two intriguing processes exhibited by Isabelle, a pastry chef-chocolatier and Céline, a brewer, in their new venture creation journeys.

The authors first link the macro and micro perspectives by introducing several points of interest on female entrepreneurship in France, and then present the individual case studies to describe the challenges and obstacles which the two women entrepreneurs tackled in the pursuit of their new venture creation.

At-a-glance cases are also included in each chapter to illustrate a different avenue to addressing the concepts discussed in the chapters, rather than for analysis.The case studies here are thus followed by the at-a-glance case, "Comparing Paradoxes: the Cases of Norway and Thailand," contributed by Elin M. Oftedal and Lene Foss. It adds new views and subtleties by introducing different ecosystems and illustrating the macro–micro dialogue and its effects on the new venture creation processes of women entrepreneurs.

Female Entrepreneurship in France: Fighting against Socio-cultural Heritage

Katherine Gundolf and Annabelle Jaouen
Groupe Sup de Co Montpellier Business School, Montpellier Research in Management, Montpellier, France

These two case studies will highlight some characteristics of French society. In fact, even if France is considered to be opened to gender equalization, some socio-cultural heritage, hindering female entrepreneurship to develop, persists. The barriers for women persevere mainly in traditionally "men-jobs." Our contribution is offering an insight into some statistical facts on French female entrepreneurship, and also illustrates some difficulties they may encounter.

It is easy to justify the importance of female entrepreneurship, considering their economic and social weight. Indeed, during the last years, several researches have been realized in different countries to underline the role played by female entrepreneurs and to incite governments and economic actors to take this phenomenon into account (Fiducial, 2006).

According to the GEM Global Entrepreneurship Report 2007 (Bosma *et al.*, 2008), France has prevalence rates of entrepreneurial activity (for overall business owners) of 6.66 percent for men and 3.16 percent for women (www.gemconsortium.org), which signifies at least two things: (1) entrepreneurial activity in France is quite low; (2) female entrepreneurial activity is less than half as low as male activity. In fact, according to the GEM data, France has one of the lowest female entrepreneurial activity rates of the examined countries.

Furthermore, the GEM data provide the following interesting information: France is one of the countries where female entrepreneurship is mainly opportunity-driven (as opposed to necessity-driven). This means that entrepreneurship is not considered as an alternative to unemployment (only 2 percent of female entrepreneurs were unemployed beforehand).

Looking now especially at France, we can observe that French data on enterprise creation do not consider the gender of the creators. The only real statistics existing in France on this topic are provided by individual enterprises managed by women: 443,360 in 2006 (INSEE/ Sirene and Dcaspl according to www.apce.com). According to this study, several points can be underlined:

- Women's enterprises are generally smaller than men's (30 percent do not have employees, 18 percent have between 20 and 49 employees, 11 percent between 100 and 249).
- Enterprises are mainly situated in the service sector (38 percent service enterprises are managed by women).
- Fewer women (12 percent) own more than 50 percent of the capital of the enterprises they manage than men (37 percent of men).
- 72 percent of female entrepreneurs are older than 50 years.
- And 73 percent of the enterprises managed by women are older than 20 years.
- Nevertheless, 71 percent of female entrepreneurs think that it is no harder for them to manage an enterprise than it is for men. Even 75 percent of female entrepreneurs declare, if they had to choose again, they would still decide to go for entrepreneurship.

A recent study on female entrepreneurship published for the French government revealed that inequalities still remain important (Bel, 2009). They concern access to full-time jobs (more than 30 percent of women have part-time jobs, as against 5 percent of men), wage (more than 20 percent of difference for managers), position (only 17 percent of women are managers), etc. The study also shows that female entrepreneurs have generally studied longer than men; and that they principally create individual enterprises (no employees), mainly in the social, health, education and real estate sectors. Also, women generally undertake less financial investment than men, and their enterprise is less focused on growth.

Through the two case-studies that follow we will try to understand the obstacles to female entrepreneurship.

Case Study 1 Isabelle, Pâtissier-Chocolatier (Pastry-chocolate Producer)

This is the story of Isabelle, 26 years, former trainee, and now pastry-shop owner.

Isabelle was not supposed to have such "men's work" when three years ago she took over a shop in Montpellier. Today, the young entrepreneur has four employees and many projects.

It was my father's fault. I didn't work enough at school. My father decided to send me for the week-ends doing the dishwashing for a pastry producer, in order to show me how would be the future if I did not work at school. The punishment turned into a revelation. I discovered this job and I fell in love with it. I found it exciting, and I wanted to learn it. I found my way and I decided to prepare a certificate, which I got without any problems, then another one, I also got. I became then a pastry-cook assistant at "Ecole Nationale Supérieure de la Pâtisserie" at Yssingeaux, near Lyon. This school assures a continuing training for pastry-cooks. I had the chance to be in touch with the best of them, I learned a lot. During this time, I also had several work experiences with different pastry and chocolate producers.

Three years ago, when I was with my hairdresser, he told me that the pastry-shop "la Gourmande" in Montpellier was going to be sold. I knew that shop, because I used to admire the great cakes in their window. I always liked this place and I always felt good there. The owner bought the shop ten years ago, but they never felt really integrated in the village. I met them. Then, I really thought a lot about that place, I wasn't even able to sleep at night. Finally, I asked my teacher to evaluate the potentials of this place. He had a look at the pastry-shop and he said: "go for it." I had the opinion of a professional, and this secured me.

The hardest tasks in this project, was to manage the relationship with the banks. It was really hard to get money from them. I was only 23 years old, I was single, and as a woman, I did a man's-job. So the banks were really suspicious. One of the banks even gave me an agreement, but removed it the week before the signature of the selling-contract. I was really too much confident, and very disappointed. Fortunately, my teacher told me before to submit at another bank at the same time. Finally, this bank accepted the loan.

I opened the shop eight days after having it bought. The day before the opening, I was completely overbooked, I called Audrey to help me. Audrey is a pastry-aid I had known before. Now, she works for me. I also employed Cécile, she's in charge of the selling, and I have two trainees, Vincent and Denis, both 18 years old. We are a good team. Without this team, I could have never succeeded. Now, I also invested in new materials, and in a cold room (the former was built in 1924). I was lucky with my clients. First, they came because they were curious, then they were loyal. Since I bought the store, I multiplied my turnover by 300 percent. In four years, I will rebuild my kitchen and open a little tearoom.

Since I manage my enterprise, I have a place in the professional meetings. I'm the only woman among all those men, aged between 50 and 60 years. They are extraordinary and their maturity delights me. Sometimes, they forget that I'm here and they make some remarks. Some of them have difficulties to admit a woman in this profession, they don't understand how we are able to accomplish this job and have a family. It is true, a lot of women, stop working once they get pregnant, stop working. It is hard to start at 4:30 a.m. and to find somebody to take care of a baby. While the boss would only have to organize differently the work . . . I have done this, since Audrey got a child. And the enterprise works still as well.

We should not always blame the men. In my job, some women made a bad impression in the enterprises they were employed. When you really want to succeed, you have mainly to behave professionally, the rest is less important . . . I also observed that in this profession, as elsewhere, women have to prove more. They have to deserve twice as much their place. Especially, when she is an entrepreneur.

Case Study 2 Céline, Brewer (Home-made Lemonade and Beer)

She was 25 years old when she stopped working as an employee in order to create a factory for lemonades and beers. Having learnt the profession of a brewer, she created the home-made brewery in Dinard (Bretagne). A real adventure . . .

After her scientific baccalaureate, she started a two-year diploma at a university institute of technology, and specialized in biology, especially in food-processing industries. There she developed her passion for the brewery process, and decided to work on home-made beer, popular at this time.

I worked as a brewer in Alsace, then in Bretagne, but I always felt like creating my own brewery. To do this, I took a diploma on management. The financial and accounting courses I followed were very helpful to establish my forecasts . . . In April 2003, I decided to quit my job and to concentrate completely on my project. This brewery should produce all types of beers, lemonades and low alcoholic aperitifs. I wanted to sell them to bars, restaurants, home-made product shops; and this from Bretagne all over the region up to Paris.

Céline was helped by the chamber of commerce and succeeded in convincing some stakeholders to follow her.

They are five, three of them are brewers. They did not only provide a capital of 150,000 euros but also helped me by giving me advices.

Their competences are complementary to mine. Concerning the banks, it was not easy. When you are young, you're not considered as serious. But I never gave up.

These two case studies underline some of the most important barriers for female entrepreneurship in France: gender-specific job attribution, difficulties in getting financial support, hostile men, problems in managing job and family, etc.

Bel's study (2009) concludes that the obstacles for female entrepreneurship in France are mostly:

- the socio-cultural heritage;
- the scholar system implementing some gender-specific choices;
- the limited possibilities for women to access continuing education;
- the irresolution of men to ask for flexible working hours in order to take care of the family;
- the sectors chosen by women are more competitive, thus the profitability may be lower and the banks are more cautious.

The results of different studies, as in the cases we examined, stress the disparity between men and women, and the need for further efforts to reduce these inequalities in France.

Questions for Discussion

1   Identify the links between the macro and micro factors in both cases; indicate the similarities and dissimilarities in these links.
2   How did the women manage to succeed in these male-dominated jobs? What is the macro-related atmosphere needed to engage in male-dominated jobs?
3   Will it be easy to change socio-cultural heritage? Discuss this in the context of your country's cultural norms.
4   Select one of the feminist models introduced in this chapter and rewrite the two cases through that theory's lens. Discuss your insights and implications.
5   Select one macro factor and one micro factor from those discussed in this chapter; explain the cases by focusing on these factors. Are your analyses and views regarding Isabelle's and Céline's performance different? Explain your answer.
6   What could the government do to facilitate female entrepreneurship in the two introduced cases? What would the government in your country do? Explain your answer.
7   Why are some entrepreneurial sectors considered to be gender-specific?

Case References

Bel, G. (2009). *L'entrepreneuriat féminin*. Conseil Economique, Social et Environnemental.

Fiducial (2006). *L'observatoire fiducial de l'entrepreneuriat féminin* (www.fiducial.fr).

Bosma, N., Jones, K., Autio, E. & Levie, J. (2008). *Global Entrepreneurship Monitor—Executive Report 2007* (www.gemconsortium.org).

AT A GLANCE[7]

Comparing Paradoxes: The Cases of Norway and Thailand

Elin M. Oftedal and Lene Foss

Tromsø University Business School, Universitetet i Tromsø, Tromsø, Norway

Introduction

Entrepreneurship is considered a crucial activity for overall economic progress. However, it is often claimed to be a "male activity" since the general, cross-cultural pattern shows that men are 50 percent more likely than women to become entrepreneurs (Minniti *et al.*, 2003). Female entrepreneurship is argued to be an under-researched area with tremendous economic potential and one that requires special attention (McClelland *et al.*, 2005). Since a recent theoretical framework suggests that gender achieves its form in the relation in which it is situated and the context in which it is expressed (Bruni, Gherardi & Poggia, 2005; Haraway, 1991), we hold that the context in terms of structure affects female entrepreneurship.

This study focuses therefore on two country cases which demonstrate quite different/opposite governmental policies for female entrepreneurship. The Norwegian governmental sector has performed numerous initiatives and regulations for women's participation in work life in general and for promoting women into more powerful economic positions, but without achieving the intended results (Foss, 2005; Spilling, 2004). On the other hand, the Thai society has no legal intervention to promote female participation, yet the female participation in entrepreneurship is higher than usual, and also as compared to neighboring countries (Hatcher *et al.*, 2007; Minniti *et al.* 2003). How may we understand this obvious paradox? This chapter invites a discussion about how both structural and cultural factors may be intertwined in a more complex way than realized. In line with that, we are inspired by Giddens (1984) who claims structures are both outcomes and resources for actions and can be constraining as well as enabling. As Giddens' framework of dualities of structures sketches a dynamic picture, this chapter will be organized around the entrepreneur as the agent role and a description of the embedded structure in each of the cases.

The Norwegian Paradox

Norway is a rich, highly organized western country with a high degree of equality and emancipation. First, a description of the situation for female entrepreneurs is discussed, followed by a discussion of the unique structural properties of the country.

Agent

Women owners account for approximately 25 percent of business establishments in Norway. This pattern has been stable over the last 10–15 years (Alsos & Kolvereid, 2005; Ljunggren, 1998). Interestingly, this proportion is 10.5 percent lower than for similar European countries. The role of women as entrepreneurs and managers of businesses reflects to a great extent their traditional roles in the labor market (Foss, 2005), and thus the most important sectors for women to start and organize businesses are mostly "soft sectors" like personal services, retail, consultancy services and also in agriculture. There is a tendency for women entrepreneurs to start businesses in sectors which have a lower need for venture capital and are also slightly in the lower performance end of the scale (Spilling, 2004).

Structure

The United Nations documents Norway as a leading nation with regard to providing equal opportunities for men and women. The Gender-related Development Index (GDI), which measures human development in a society, including the distribution of welfare between men and women, ranks Norway as number one in the world (UNDP, 2010).

Norwegian women can be said to be champions of equality in the area of politics as their participation in politics started to rapidly increase in the 1970s, and, in 1981, Norway's first female Prime Minister was elected. She served three terms and pioneered feministic political work. Female political participation has been the norm in the years since.

There is also a high degree of female participation in the labor market[8] and, with an increasing fertility rate,[9] Norwegian women seem to handle both working and family life well. Nevertheless, it is claimed that the statistics "hide" the fact that women work fewer hours than men.[10] Furthermore, an even lower number of Norwegian women have management positions.[11] The largest proportion of female managers is in the public sector, whereas the private sector is lagging behind.[12] Seventy-three percent of the owners of public limited companies and limited companies are men and this role is also looked upon as being "masculine" (Foss, 2005; Statistics Norway, 2010). Further, men spend on average twice as much time on their careers as women do (SSB, 2000). With eight out of ten women working in health or education and far more women than men working part time, Norway stands out as the fifth most gender-segregated labor market by OECD countries, both horizontally and vertically.

Norway's main culture has been more one of egalitarian art, which may contradict the perception of an entrepreneurial culture. The belief that you, in some way, are better than others is considered rare in Norway. A famous Norwegian writer (Sandemose) labeled the phenomenon the "Jantelov." This law may affect women to a stronger degree since the female role is looked upon as nurturing and caring, thus to stand out or rise above their position for career reasons is not considered an egalitarian or even feminine activity. In the Norwegian debate, this cultural norm is often argued as being a barrier for entrepreneurship in general. The above points are illustrated by the following quotes from a study of cultural acceptance of being a female entrepreneur in Norway (Settem, 2009).

> I think it is easier for men than for women. I have been on different arrangements where I am the only woman among at least 17 men. It is a clear difference in the way you are presented and perceived. When I am presented, it's all about how many children I have. None of the other participants are asked about that. Then I think—of course—this is typical. . . .

> To be an entrepreneur is not easier for men than for women, but it is easier to receive resources and be valued as a man. . . .

The social norm of putting each other down (janteloven) is strong.

> In-laws are the worst. Clearly, when we are doing what we are doing: Stick our heads out, it's not just positive. A lot of people are waiting to see us fall "what does she think she is, etc." Both family and other people are among those.

Norway has a "dual breadwinner norm" requiring both men and women to earn a living and support a family. Part-time work has been an adaptation to this norm (Foss, 2005). The majority of Norwegian households consist of "nuclear" families with mother, father and children.[13] For parents with small children, a gendered pattern seems to exist; women spend more time on domestic work than men. Further, every third manager finds that their work affects their family or social life (SSB, 2000). This is illustrated by the following quotes from a study of cultural acceptance of being a female entrepreneur in Norway (Settem, 2009).

> I guess there are no ideas anymore that a woman should stay home with the kids, that was more a reality 10–20 years ago. I don't know any woman who stays at home now. . . . However, I have noticed that people approach my male partner more than me. Further,

people never ask me about what I do for work but they ask my male partner.

. . . my husband can't stay away from work as much as he thought . . . I think there will be some hindrances because of this.

It is hard. I have to go home at four o'clock to make dinner and do homework. However, I can go back to work, but it is the work–life balance [that] you always have to attend to.

Some female entrepreneurs attribute their ability to start and run a company to a supportive environment:

I am very good at taking weekends off. I have a great support at home and I have family on both sides who are very proud of what I am doing and say that "you have always been so clever—and this you can manage well."

The Thai Paradox

Thailand is situated on mainland Southeast Asia. Thailand is a transitional economy country with and unequal distribution of resources, resulting in a high degree of poverty. This section discusses the structure-agent relationship in Thailand. First a description of the situation for female entrepreneurs is discussed, followed by a discussion of the unique structural properties of the country.

Agent

The status of women in Thailand has changed a great deal. The country is now found to provide the highest opportunities for women to hold executive positions in private organizations compared with others in the world, according to the annual business report of Grant Thornton (2011). In this report, 45 percent of the Thai executives are found to be women, which is the highest in the world.[14] Similar results are found within entrepreneurship, where research shows that men had a 33.5 overall entrepreneurial activity prevalence rate and women had a rate of 32.5. Other studies show marginally higher entrepreneurship for women (Minniti, 2003).[15]

Structure

In Thailand, as in most other Asian countries, politics has traditionally been a male preserve and women's interests remain neglected (Atal, 1993; Iwanaga, 2005; Thailand Human Development Report, 2007).[16] The ratio of women both appointed or elected to political offices, as compared to men, was so low that female representation in politics could be deemed insignificant.[17] There is still little analysis on the participation of women in politics at various levels of government in Thailand and research to date is fragmentary (Iwanaga, 2005).

Although playing a minor role in Thai politics, Thai women have held a strong position in the household economy (Atal, 1993). According to the Thailand Human Development Report (2007), the labor force participation rate of Thai females (67.5 percent) is only slightly less than that of males (77.8 percent), although earning significantly less. According to gender roles, both men and women do agricultural work, and although some tasks tend to be assigned mainly to men and others mainly to women, that division of labor is not adhered to rigidly. The women have traditionally been looked upon as an economic force (Atal, 1993). An underlying reason for the distinctive phenomenon of gender relations in Thailand is argued to be the unique characteristic of Thai society (Ractham & Nuttavuthisit, 2011). This is also reflected in the old Thai proverb cited below.

> Marriage is like an elephant with the husband as the front legs that choose the direction and the wife as the back legs that provide support.

There are no legal restrictions on women owning and managing businesses, as the following quote from a Thai entrepreneur indicates:

> Thai women are fortunate. We have enjoyed equality with men, have played roles in the family and society, and there are no social taboos against women working outside the home or having a public role, even after marriage.
>
> (Hatcher *et al.*, 2007)

Although female participation in economic life is strong,[18] gender inequality is manifested in violence against women, societal discrimination against women, and trafficking in women for prostitution. However, looking at history, role modelling and celebrating women as heroines was emphasized by drawing on the traditional and long culture of Thailand. Another important theme among Thai women has been the Buddhist idea of perfecting behavior. This is reflected in the following quote:

> Being successful means being a perfect mother, perfect wife, perfect daughter, perfect sister, perfect boss and perfect social contributor and to be No. 1 in all fields.
>
> (Hatcher *et al.*, 2007)

Further, Thai women are surrounded by extended families and often women take responsibilities for each other's children and elderly. This releases time and monetary resources for the woman (Ractham & Nuttavuthisit, 2011). Further, according to the gender roles, the man is expected to support the family. This division appears clearer as one rises in the social system (Atal, 1993; Iwanaga, 2005). However, this may take pressure off the women to seek employed work.

> Women's work is just seen as a hobby, so there is not so much fear about failure. If it works, it is good and seen as an extra income, if not, it can be quickly forgotten.
>
> (Hatcher *et al.*, 2007)

In Thailand there is also an acceptance of earning money as a way of serving your family: In addition, the Thai female entrepreneur takes on a role where she looks after her workers and their families:

> I look after not only my employees but their families too—their uncles and mother.
>
> (Hatcher *et al.*, 2007)

Thus, in Thai society, there is no fundamental difference between being a caring female figure and a provider. The Thai women may show care by providing monetary benefit, although they have to balance this with other gender expectations. The following quote illustrates this observation:

> I have proven that the work we have done benefit the people and the community—that I am not just a business person looking for profits and you have to get peoples heart to work with you. I look after not just the person but the family too.
>
> (Hatcher *et al.*, 2007)

According to Hatcher *et al.* (2007), responsibility, connection and caring were strongly and repeatedly asserted by the female entrepreneurs. Hatcher (2007) argues that female entrepreneurs are then allowed to fulfill the culturally induced gender expectation even when starting new businesses; they continued the "nurturance" of the company and the society, thus shifting the focus from the individual to the collective.

Notes

1 OECD, at: http://www.oecd.org/document/49/0,3746,en_2649_34417 _17947825_1_1_1_1,00.html; http://www.oecd.org/document/16/0,3746 ,en_2649_34417_44938128_1_1_1_1,00.htmløc
2 Based on the Diana Project, and studies published by renowned researchers in the field of female entrepreneurship, e.g., Brush, Gatewood, Greene, Carter, Hart, Henry, and others. Available at: http://www3.babson.edu/ ESHIP/research-publications/dianaproject.cfm

3 The well-known picture symbolizing "feminism" is taken from "Feminism is not a dirty word," November 3, 2010, at: http://stephanierapp.blogspot.com/2010/11/feminism-is-not-dirty-word.html

4 Available at: http://plato.stanford.edu/entries/feminist-power/

5 Based on integration of data and results from: Allen, Elam, Langowitz, & Dean (2008), Commission of the European Communities (2001), and Franco & Winqvist (2002).

6 The author(s) of the case studies and at-a-glance cases are fully and solely responsible for their content, phrasing consistency and flow, terminology, English proofing and reference lists.

7 At-a-glance cases are included to present different ecosystems and their effects on the concepts discussed in the chapter; they do not include questions for discussion.

8 In Norway, 68.6 percent of the population are employed (SSB, 2011: the labor force), which means that we are in the top rank compared with the EU and EFTA countries. Employed women accounted for 66.6 percent of the female labor force, while men account for 70.7 percent (Statistics Norway, 2011: the labor force).

9 The fertility rate is 1.9 children per woman in 1991, and 1.8 in 2004, making it the highest fertility rate in Europe.

10 Of all employed women in Norway, 43 percent work part time compared with 13 percent for men (Statistics Norway, 2010: Ola & Kari). The part-time women workers are often found in the sales and service occupations and the caring professions. Women's labor is used extensively in the public sector, where they constitute 70 percent of all employees, while those in the private sector accounted for 37 percent. Men represent about 63 percent of employees in the private sector (NOU, 2008: 6 Equal Pay Committee).

11 Six percent of Norwegian women are senior managers, compared with 15.7 percent in the U.S. and 9 percent in the UK (Catalyst Inc., 2002). The proportion of women who are managing directors of a public limited company (ASA) is 6.5 percent, but the proportion of women who are managing directors of limited companies is 14 percent (Samfunnsspeilet, 2010). Today, one in ten Norwegian top managers is a woman. The proportion of women managers declined from 23.8 percent in 1999 to 21.4 percent in 2002 (Colbjørnsen, 2004). Women hold 40 percent of leadership positions in the public sector, but only 20–21 percent of those in the private sector.

12 In 2006 women's representation on the boards became regulated; a quota system was applied to company boards of public limited companies, where 40 percent of board members must be women. This resulted in an increase of 196 percent of the proportion of female board members in public limited companies in the period 2004 to 2010 (from 254 women to 751 women). For ordinary corporations, where no such quotas are introduced, the percentage of female board members is 17 percent, a proportion that has been steadily low since 2004 (Samfunnsspeilet, 2010).

13 Divorce rates have highly increased in the last twenty years, and governmental support (tax reduction) is given to split-up families who have children to care for. Many divorcees' families do share so that the children stay every other week with one of the parents. However, in the case where the child may stay with one parent, this is more often the mother.

14 Following Thailand in the ranking are Georgia with 40 percent, Russia with 36 percent, and Hong Kong and the Philippines with 35 percent.

15 It is also interesting to note that female entrepreneurs in Thailand identified 62 percent of their practice as limited company opportunity, rather

than necessity-driven. This is a high percentage for a country in the middle-income cluster where typically results for necessity-driven entrepreneurship are higher than in the high-income country cluster and suggest that entrepreneurship activities have some cultural support when compared with other Asian countries (Minniti, 2003).

16 Recently Thailand has elected a female prime minister, Yingluck Shinawatra. However, she is the sister of the former prime minister Thaksin who was overthrown and had to leave the country. It is reasonable to believe that Shinawatra acts according to her brother's political claims.

17 Malee Pruekponsalee (1986) pointed out that discriminatory laws against women did exist and could be found in the following areas: Laws pertaining to women's rights to education and training. Laws pertaining to women's economic rights. Laws pertaining to family and citizenship rights of women. Laws pertaining to women's rights over their own bodies. Laws pertainining to women's political and administrative rights.

18 Efforts to improve the status of women have increased, and the 1997 constitution provides women with equal rights and protections, although, some inequalities in the law remain. Domestic abuse affects women in all social classes. Sexual harassment in the workplace was made illegal in 1998, but only in the private sector, and no cases have been prosecuted.

Case References

Alsos, G.A. & Kolvereid, L. (2005). Entrepreneurship among women in Norway. In E.S. Hauge & P.A. Havnes (Eds.), *Women entrepreneurs: Theory, research and policy implications*. Kristiansand: Høyskoleforlaget AS.

Atal, Y. (1993). *Women in politics: Australia,India,Malaysia,Philippines,Thailand*, Guest Editor: Latiku Padgaonkar. Unesco Principal Regional Office for Asia and the Pacific—Bangkok. Krusthap Series on Monographs and Occasional Papers.

Bruni, A., Gherardi, S. & Poggia, B. (2005). *Gender and entrepreneurship: An ethnographical approach*. London: Routledge.

Foss, L. (2005). The Norwegian paradox: World champion in gender equality—loser in female management recruitment. In A.M. Fuglseth & A.I. Kleppe (Eds.), *Anthology for Kjell Grønhaug in his celebration of his 70th birthday* (pp. 237–260). Bergen: Fagbokforlaget,

Giddens, Anthony (1984). *The constitution of society. Outline of the Theory of Structuration*. Cambridge: Polity.

Grant Thornton International Business Report (2011).

Haraway, D.J. (1991). Situated knowledges: The science question in feminism and the privilege of partial perspective. In Haraway, *Simians, cyborgs, and women: the reinvention of nature* (pp. 183–201). New York: Routledge.

Hatcher, C. (2007). Leading women entrepreneurs in Thailand. In M. Radociv (Ed.) *The perspective of women's entrepreneurship in the age of globalization*. University of Florida Press.

Iwanaga, K. (2005). *Women in Politics in Thailand*. Working paper published for the Centre for East and South East Asian Studies, Lund University, Sweden.

Ljunggren, E. & Foss, L. (2004). *Women's entrepreneurship in Norway: The need of and access to new venture capital*. 13th Nordic Conference on Small Business Research, Tromsø.

Ljunggren, E. (1998). *The new business formation process: Why are there so few women entrepreneurs in Norway?* FE-publikationer 1998: 159, Umeå School of Business, Umeå: University of Umeå.

McClelland, E., Swail, J., Bell, J. & Ibbotson, P. (2005). Following the pathway of female entrepreneurs: a six country investigation. *International Journal of Entrepreneurial Behaviour and Research*, 11, 84–107.

Minniti, M. & Arenius, P. (2003). Women in entrepreneurship. Paper prepared for the conference on the entrepreneurial advantage of nations. First Annual Global Entrepreneurship Symposium, United Nations, April 29.

Pruekpongsawalee, M. (1986). Women and law. In Amara Pongsapich (Ed.), *Women's issues: a book of readings*. Bangkok: Institute of Social Research, Chulalongkorn University.

Thailand Human Development Report (2007). United Nations Development Programme (http://hdr.undp.org/en/reports/national/asiathepacific/thailand/THAILAND_2007_en.pdf).

Settem, L. (2008). Kvinnelig entreprenørskap: En kvalitativ studie av kvinnelige gründere med vekstambisjoner.

Spilling, O.R. (2004). *Women entrepreneurship, management and ownership in Norway 2004: A statistical update*. Oslo, NIFU STEP.

SSB (2007). Rolleinnehavere i personlig eide foretak, etter kjønn, næring organisasjonsform og antall ansatte.

SSB (2010). Agnes Aaby Hirsch (red.) Dette er Kari og Ola. Kvinner og men i Norge.

SSB (2010a). Statistikk. Bedrifts og strukturregister. Personlig eide foretak, etter organisasjonsform og rolleinnehavers kjønn. Nyetableringer i 2009.

SSB (2010b). Tabell: 03824: Fullførte utdanninger ved universiteter og høgskoler, etter kjønn, nivå og fagfelt.

SSB (2010c). Tabell: 05215: Rolleinnehavere i personlig eide foretak, etter kjønn, alder og utdanningsnivå (2004–2009).

SSB (2011a). Arbeidsstyrken http://www.ssb.no/aku/tab-2011-05-04-03.html.

SSB (2011b). Statistikkbanken, utdanningsnivå i 2010. Tabell 06983.

Samfunnsspeilet (2010). http://www.ssb.no/samfunnsspeilet/utg/201004/02/

Vathanophas Ractham, V. & Nuttavuthisit, K. (2011). Why More Female Executives Prosper in Thailand: The Counterbalanced Power of Women in Thai Society. Accepted to present at Global Business & International Management Conference (GBIM, 2011), Seattle, Washington, USA. July 7–9, 201

UNDP (2010).

2 Motivations for Becoming Entrepreneurs

A Woman's Perspective

Chapter Objectives

- Understanding the "dynamics" of motivation in the individual–business–environment context;
- Becoming acquainted with women's main motivations for becoming entrepreneurs; discussing the differences from men's motivations;
- Learning the concepts of necessity- and opportunity-driven motivation and their relevance to women entrepreneurs;
- Delineating the female entrepreneurship mindset, and the roles of cultural and social influences;
- Discussing the impact of education, experience and family influences on shaping women's motivations to become entrepreneurs;
- Recognizing the versatility of the concepts of work–life conflict and work–life balance, as well as work-to-family conflict (WFC) and family-to-work conflict (FWC);
- Characterizing the different avenues that entrepreneurship provides for women juggling multiple roles.

Women entrepreneurs' motivations to start a business include: independence, being one's own boss, pursuing one's dreams or interests, and making more money. This chapter discusses the different motivations that attract women to entrepreneurship.

The chapter includes a section on opportunity versus necessity entrepreneurship that deals with a differential classification of the elements that constitute the motivation to become an entrepreneur and that are echoed in business success. Since necessity entrepreneurs are typified as being less successful than opportunity entrepreneurs, the existing literature portrays women as more prone to necessity entrepreneurship. This topic is discussed in light of the different approaches and includes examples of women whose enterprises began as necessity entrepreneurships but, by their use of the relevant strategies and assistance measures, became successful entrepreneurs. In this context, the chapter, and in fact the entire book, highlights the need to fight labels and preconceived ideas and to strive to realize one's dreams.

MOTIVATION TO START A BUSINESS: A FEMALE OUTLOOK

In the entrepreneurship literature, a number of different definitions can be found for the motivations to start a business, deriving from different theoretical frameworks. Entrepreneurial motivations include the urge to fulfill a need for personal development, to achieve financial success, and to gain more autonomy, independence and control of one's time schedule and tasks.

Entrepreneurial motivations do not guarantee entrepreneurial activity: there may be a time lag between the desire to become an entrepreneur and the implementation process, or the two can be completely disconnected. Some individuals report that they would like to start a business yet the business never materializes due to external conditions or lack of capabilities, either tangible, e.g., money, team, etc., or intangible, such as personal characteristics, e.g. risk-taking, hard work, a good idea, etc. (Bay & Daniel, 2003; Krueger, Reilly, & Carsrud, 2000; Locke & Latham, 2002; Shane, Locke, & Collins, 2003).

The research on motivation can be traced to Freud's work on instincts (Freud, 1976) and the research that followed (Maslow, 1946) referring to the instincts (motives) for a particular survival behavior aimed at escaping failure or pain and accomplishing success and self-fulfillment.

Traditionally, motivations have been classified into intrinsic and extrinsic, and in entrepreneurship these have been interpreted as motivation to become an entrepreneur due to: an internal inclination, such as the motivation to accomplish a goal, i.e., intrinsic motivation; pursuit of an external reward such as money, status, i.e., extrinsic motivation (Carsrud & Olm, 1986; Festinger, 1957).

Motivations, however, are not an isolated phenomenon; rather, they are shaped by the individual–business–environment context. Motivations can change with changes in the individual's needs, attitudes, competence, or in his/her educational achievements or job experience, among others; changes in external effects, such as relocating and thus changing the environment, changes in the environment itself, for example, development of a new business area in one's hometown resulting in increased employment opportunities, and finally, changes in the business, for example, advancement in the business stages, acquisition of financial investment, or expansion of products and services. Each of these changes creates a sequence of effects on the content of the individual's motivations to start the business: motivations that are relevant to one condition may seem irrelevant under others. For example, a need to control time and assignments at work may be a leading motivation for young women entrepreneurs who are mothers of young children, but would no longer apply once the children have grown up.

In the entrepreneurial realm, this is often the case. Entrepreneurship is dynamic and rapidly changing, and entrepreneurs may quickly change their motivations to start a venture, as the initial motivations may be rapidly accomplished: "I want to be my own boss" is accomplished immediately at start-up, and is therefore no longer a motivating factor, and the next challenging motivations are then sought.

The New Venture Creation Process—This phenomenon presents an additional set of motivations, derived from the specific conditions typifying it. In the new venture creation phase, most of the activities take place in obscure, unfocused and unpredictable settings, where most factors are still latent and unknown, as shown in Figure 2.1. The motivations, reflecting the accumulation of environmental effects, individual needs and the business's competencies, are affected by each of these factors. Because most of the

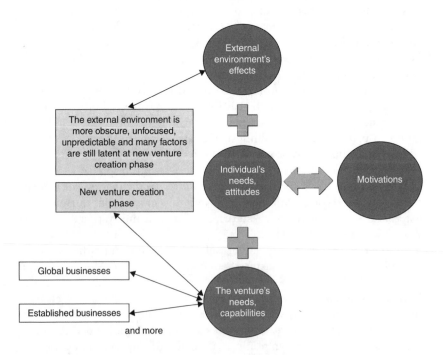

Figure 2.1 Motivations and the New Venture Creation.

determinants of the environment's effects are unknown in the new venture creation phase, the content of the motivations at this phase changes rapidly.

Women Entrepreneurs—While motivations in the new venture creation process are strongly dependent on the link between external environment and the business's competencies, needs and stage of development, motivations among women entrepreneurs are heavily dependent on the link between external environment effects and the individual. Women pursue a typical track in society—the family setting, the labor market—but this track is distinctive in different countries and cultures; hence, differences or changes in the external environment, such as attitudes toward women's employment or independence, national rates of divorce or of unemployment, have a direct and significant impact on women's attitudes and their capability to start a business, and subsequently, on their different motivations to start a new venture. For example, in an affluent economy, women may perceive entrepreneurship as a way of obtaining the best fit between their professional abilities and prospective rewards. In an oppressed economy on the other hand, women may perceive entrepreneurship as a way of escaping unemployment. These individual–environment effects may shape the agenda in women's motivations to create a new venture.

Research reports on different factors as prime motivators among women to start a business, including the desire to implement a new idea, a wish for independence and being one's own boss, the desire to put a skill to work, financial ambition, such as earning more money, choosing how to allocate the budget, avoiding a "glass ceiling" at work, being flexible in terms of schedule (Minniti, Allen, & Langowitz, 2006b; Orhan & Scott, 2001; Orser, Riding, & Manley, 2006). These factors can be better understood in the context of the following four key drivers of entrepreneurial motivations that are imperative in female entrepreneurship:

Self-fulfillment—Independence, autonomy, greater control, managing one's time and assignments, exploiting one's abilities and developing an undertaking that is one's own: these represent a set of significant reported motivational factors for embarking upon entrepreneurship among women.

Monetary motives—Money is an important factor reported by all prospective entrepreneurs, though gender differences exist with regard to this motivating factor: women are driven by money yet, relative to men, they place less emphasis on money and more on the non-monetary components of entrepreneurship (e.g., time flexibility, being one's own boss, etc.)

Work/family-related factors—Different motivations originate from the constant endeavors of women, especially mothers, to craft the best match between work and family and still get paid, fulfill their potential and satisfy their needs, and exploit their capabilities and academic or professional accreditations.

The meaning of work in one's life—This category addresses women's desire to be valued in the labor market and avoid unfortunate experiences, including unemployment, redundancy, underemployment, the "glass ceiling" and a lack of job satisfaction or career prospects due to gender-related issues (e.g., motherhood incurs fewer working hours and more frequent non-attendance at work due to family-related issues). Gender differences are found with respect to this category due to women's historical experiences in the labor market in terms of career path, rewards and contentment.

OPPORTUNITY AND NECESSITY MOTIVATIONS

One predominant categorization of the motivations for creating a new venture is opportunity- vs. necessity-driven orientation.[1] This categorization originates from the individual level, but it is also frequently addressed in research on local or national entrepreneurship. Opportunity and necessity types are most relevant to better understanding women's entrepreneurial motivations, as this categorization helps organize women's recurring responses when asked about their reasons for creating a new venture. The motivations behind new venture creation do not stem from any one single factor; rather, it is the combination of factors that together constitute the "motivation."

Embarking on entrepreneurship always reflects one's desire to improve an existing situation. Yet, while opportunity orientations refer to perceiving entrepreneurship as an appealing alternative chosen from a range of possible options, necessity-driven orientations refer to choosing entrepreneurship in order to escape specific conditions, while the entrepreneur has, or perceives to have limited alternatives in the labor market. These orientations are then echoed in one's aspirations, decisions and potential performance along the venture creation process: opportunity-driven orientations are related to higher motivation and aspirations toward success and growth, and necessity-driven orientations are more rooted in the survival phase of the business.

Opportunity and necessity orientations have been associated in research with the pull–push model. The opportunity side has been associated with "pull" factors originating from environmental factors that prompt the desire to gain more from the entrepreneurial path; they are often seen as a way of achieving upward mobility and of accelerating socioeconomic status by, e.g., making money, being independent, tracking one's work toward one's interests. The necessity orientations have been related to "push" factors that are seen as the invisible barriers facing individuals' career-advancement prospects in the corporate world. The most common opportunity-hindering factors found in the research are unemployment, underemployment, discrimination in the labor market or in a prior job, severe dissatisfaction in a prior/concurrent job with respect to future career opportunities, and unrewarding relationships with co-workers, among others. Thus, push factors force the individual to take some action that involves inherently higher risk, such as starting a business that may eliminate the experienced discrimination or dissatisfaction, and that would not be an alternative under normal circumstances (Allen, Langowitz, & Minniti, 2007; Brush, Carter, Gatewood, Greene, & Hart, 2006b; Holmquist & Sundin, 1990; Riverin & Filion, 2005).

While "pull" factors emphasize the benefits of the "outcome," i.e., the new venture, the "push" factors symbolize the benefits of escaping concurrent situations, as presented in Figure 2.2.

The Gender Perspective—Gender differences have been found in entrepreneurial opportunity and necessity orientations: men more than women are mostly found to be attracted to entrepreneurship by their opportunity orientations while women more than men are influenced by their necessity orientations.

Along their labor market track, women face situations, including underemployment, the "glass ceiling," lower wages relative to men, barriers to entering prestigious positions; these mold their perceptions regarding their future prospects in the corporate market. Consequently, women are attracted to entrepreneurship to avoid such experiences. In addition, women's dual role and their responsibility to their family and households

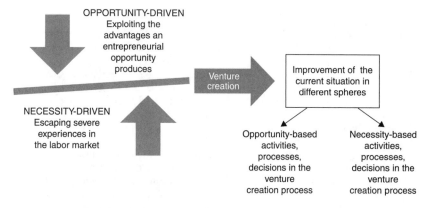

Figure 2.2 The Push–Pull Tradeoff for Women Entrepreneurs.

raise another hurdle that is more easily resolved by the flexibility that entrepreneurship provides. Starting a business to enable managing both roles may also be considered a necessity-driven orientation (Amit & Muller, 1995; Hisrich & Brush, 1984; Kariv, 2010; Orhan & Scott, 2001; Thurik, Carree, van Stel, & Audretsch, 2008; Verheul, van Stel, & Thurik, 2006).

Table 2.1 summarizes the main components representing women's motivations to become entrepreneurs, categorized by opportunity and necessity entrepreneurship and focusing on the micro level, which reflects their personal and family-related issues.

As illustrated in Figure 2.2, these orientations, opportunity or necessity, target the same aim: improving one's work life and the other spheres, i.e. family life, personal life, financial status, etc.

In the case of women, opportunity-driven motivations are perceived as promising improvement in the conditions of women's working lives, including financial status, better fit between work and abilities, pursuit of one's dreams, balancing the stress between working and personal/family lives, among others. In many cases, women who are driven by opportunity-based motivations are already employed in fulfilling jobs, have various alternatives in other labor markets, have sufficient resources to make a successful living, and are satisfied by their existing careers: they could choose any career path or any other job, yet they consider entrepreneurship to be the best alternative.

In the case of necessity-driven motivations, women want or must go out to work, but encounter limited opportunities and thus cannot play a significant role in the labor market due to visible or invisible constraints that

Table 2.1 Opportunity and Necessity Entrepreneurship—Micro Perspective

Opportunity	*Necessity*
Attraction to a business opportunity	Unemployment; sudden lay-off
Pursuing an idea and developing a subsequent niche in the market	Underemployment
Being one's own boss	Discrimination, stereotypes
Independence at work	Limited opportunities for re-employment
A desire for career change	Changes in the family financial situation
Flexibility in working hours, prioritizing work assignments, time management	Changes in the family needs (birth, health-related issues, change of residence; change in family status)
A potentially profitable economic activity	Lacking or inadequate experience in the labor market
Varied experience in the labor market	Lacking or inadequate relevant education in the labor market
Partnership; investment	Undergoing severe experiences in the workplace; e.g., "glass ceiling," sexual harassment, discrimination

push them away from it. Women then create their own labor market, i.e., business, out of necessity, in an attempt to create rules and norms that will support their stay in the labor market. In this case, women may be either unemployed, or employed in jobs that do not allow them to manifest their real potential and capabilities; they may face discrimination in the labor market or gender-based stereotypes in their local markets or in their family's norms; they may have undergone harsh experiences in the work-place, e.g., hitting the "glass ceiling," sexual harassment, or deliberate discrimination in promotion or rewards or while attempting to climb the managerial ladder.

Such conditions are then reflected in women's choices of different entre-preneurial forms. Some necessity-driven women entrepreneurs strive to make "lemonade from lemons" by introducing creativity and innovation, exploiting different opportunities, searching for collaborations with existing companies, looking for potential investments and planning long-run and strategic cooperations. Despite the different starting point, these necessity entrepreneurs and opportunity entrepreneurs perform similarly. Oprah Winfrey[2] is the best example of this form of entrepreneurship. A different resulting form of necessity entrepreneurship may manifest itself in women's selection of a business in their "comfort zone," such as choosing only local, nearby or "female-oriented" opportunities, which tend to have lower rewards and potential at the outset. This form reflects women's insecurity in the labor market and their lower self-esteem, derived from their history. Many of these women establish businesses in segments such as cosmetics, manicures/pedicures, or care-giving for the elderly or young children, and feel incapable of extricating themselves from the conditions that first pushed them into entrepreneurship. By "letting go," these women would be unable to provide themselves with the different world they dreamt of implementing through entrepreneurship. A third form of necessity-driven entrepreneurship reflects poverty and social immobility: a lack of relevant skills, severe family constraints or ongoing discrimination against women in different regions around the world may result in being swept into the lowest ranked segments, or to illegal entrepreneurship, such as merchandising of products on the streets or in the market. As this vicious cycle escalates, ethnic women entrepreneurs and immigrants are frequently pushed into these segments (Hechavarria & Reynolds, 2009; Hessels, van Gelderen, & Thurik, 2008; Kariv, Menzies, Brenner, & Filion, 2009; Shane, Venkataraman, & MacMillan, 1995).

THE FEMALE ENTREPRENEURIAL MINDSET

The entrepreneurial mindset comprises motivations, aspirations, interpre-tations and perceptions of the different concepts relevant to entrepreneur-ship, including: success/failure, self-fulfillment, personal goals, business goals, business's competitive advantage, etc. The entrepreneurial mindset originates and develops from one's history and consequently, it is reflected in one's decisions and behaviors. Entrepreneurs are commonly portrayed as having attitudes and approaches to life, work and career that are unusual, in the sense that these attitudes "urge" them toward proactiveness, risk-taking, passion, constant alertness to potential opportunities, and productivity; they appear to possess a perpetual spark.

Women hold an entrepreneurial mindset that reflects their own experiences and biography combined with the culture and the leading attitudes toward female entrepreneurship that they have tackled in the course of their lives. It is thus plausible to conceive of women and men seeing things differently. In entrepreneurial terms, the genders should hold similar definitions for the *core* of the entrepreneurial mindset, that which involves the entrepreneurial spirit and approaches. A place should be created for a representation of the differences between the genders, those that reflect the genders' different worlds and those that enhance diversity and prompt creativity and innovation in entrepreneurship.

As already noted, the entrepreneurial market is male-dominated, and thus includes male-based perceptions and definitions that are communicated and disseminated in ways that represent the male-oriented mindset, rather than the *core* of the entrepreneurial mindset. Because the genders encounter different life experiences, those defining "success" or "failure" for men may not reflect the female mindset.

Women entrepreneurs tend to regard their entrepreneurial business as an integrated facet of their own identities rather than as a separate economic unit. Their typical approach to failure is associated with an internal locus of control. Men, on the other hand, are more inclined to consider success as their own achievement, i.e., internal locus of control, while attributing failure to "others"—an external locus of control. The meaning of business "success" or "failure" is embedded in women's deepest existential essence; it is rationalized differently by men. These different mindsets have significant effects on the genders' resultant decisions and performance. For example, to avoid existential "collapse" due to a business's failure, women entrepreneurs tend to limit their expectations and aspirations concerning their business's performance at the outset, allowing a potential floor effect to shield their identities. For men, business failure is considered the failure of others, and is managed accordingly (Ajzen & Fishbein, 1977; Krueger, 2000; Krueger & Brazeal, 1994).

Yulia Gal,[3] a 29-year-old female Israeli immigrant from Uzbekistan, perceives "success" as redefining and reinventing the conventional approach to manicures and pedicures. Gal established a business based on the innovative concept of "instant-beauty salon" that promises services taking no more than 25 minutes. Her choices and decisions regarding the business sector, its innovative form and the potential profits may be irrelevant to some male entrepreneurs, but they reflect her world, desires and identified needs. If she had tried to adapt to the male-based mindset, it is doubtful that Gal's business would have been established.

In the context of diffuse, male-dominated entrepreneurial mindsets, women entrepreneurs may easily adapt to the "rules of the game" and adjust their mindsets accordingly; in this case, Yulia Gal would hypothetically have strived for profitability in more rewarding, less female-oriented business sectors. Others might strive to allow their own mindset to take center stage, rather than closing the gap between their own and the male-based entrepreneurial mindset, because they are unwilling or unable to adjust themselves to the "rules of the game."

Entrepreneurship is about realizing goals that are outlined by the wishes and needs of the entrepreneur. It consists of a mindset and subsequent processes that are symbolized as being independent, open and free. Under the obligation to adjust one's mindset to one that is already known, the core and essence of entrepreneurship collapse. Thus women should deem entrepreneurship an autonomous territory that can provide the best match between their capabilities, resources, and their own desires and needs. Women who pursue male-based definitions of entrepreneurial achievement may end up discarding entrepreneurship or their entrepreneurial mindset; they may find themselves in the pursuit of goals that do not match their own "just because these are the common goals." Entrepreneurship means preserving and protecting a free, independent territory, to be fueled by a personal entrepreneurial mindset, even when the mindset is unusual or unpopular. This is the real essence of taking risks, standing up for one's choices and ideas and protecting them. Entrepreneurship means unleashing the entrepreneurial mindset in one's own life and allowing one's own life to break into the entrepreneurial mindset (Carsrud, Brännback, Elfving & Brandt, 2009; Kor, Mahoney, & Michael, 2007; McGrath & MacMillan, 2000).

Cultural and social influences play an important role in crafting women's entrepreneurial mindset. Some cultures associate entrepreneurship with masculine characteristics (e.g., aggressiveness, decisiveness, risk-taking); others associate it with a male-dominated career path (e.g., provides higher income, allows control over others, being the boss), and as such it is considered as capturing men's interest. Yet other cultures transmit a negative message to women who choose entrepreneurship by "excluding" them from the normative course of life, by stereotyping them as possessing "masculine" traits. There are many examples of women who wanted to start their own businesses and were warned that it would lower their odds of getting married and becoming good mothers. In her videotaped speech at TED,[4] Sheryl Sandberg, Chief Operating Officer at Facebook, tells the story of a young woman who shared her concerns of embarking on a demanding job due to domestic and family responsibilities; when asked if she was expecting a child, the young woman disclosed that she was not yet married and did not have a boyfriend. This story echoes the culture in which this young lady was raised, and shows how culture molds entrepreneurial mindsets, explaining why some women are reluctant to choose entrepreneurship.

On the other hand, some other cultures encourage entrepreneurial mindsets. This is manifested in their educational systems' curricula and attitudes toward entrepreneurship, innovation, initiatives and discoveries. It is also manifested in support at the country level for young entrepreneurs and venture creation processes; higher education and the labor market are harnessed to foster entrepreneurship, the media covers successful entrepreneurial stories, and even the day-to-day interactions can indicate a culture's maturity, in embracing entrepreneurship and providing an honorable place for entrepreneurship and the entrepreneurial mindset. I interviewed Sveta Sheransky, the founder and owner of music schools in Ottawa, Canada, on her venture creation process. In describing her entrepreneurial path, it is obvious that Sheransky was self-driven toward entrepreneurship; yet, as an immigrant for the second time (from Ukraine to Israel and then to Ottawa), she faced different immigration-related difficulties in adjusting to her host country, including language barriers. She overcame the hurdles and established her first school in Montreal. She felt that the Canadian atmosphere was very supportive: people admired her for being "courageous" and "proactive"; she obtained positive feedback from her Canadian surroundings on her entrepreneurial undertaking, even before it became profitable.

Education is a significant factor in the construction of the entrepreneurial mindset. Education gives entrepreneurs cutting-edge knowledge and tools in entrepreneurship, and exposure to entrepreneurial success stories. By attending courses in higher education, the relevant networks are intensified and grow.

Research stresses women entrepreneurs' proclivity to acquiring education prior to establishing their own businesses. Unlike men, women consider education not only a salient means but also a crucial mechanism in preparing for entrepreneurship and achieving potential success. Education is perceived as the anchor for entrepreneurial success among many women entrepreneurs. Emerging statistics from different parts of the world show that more women than men sign up for academic programs in entrepreneurship to prepare themselves for this undertaking, as well as in areas pertaining to what their future businesses will focus on. In different virtual weblogs for entrepreneurs, many women can be found sharing their ideas regarding different programs in entrepreneurship. One woman from India, for example, revealed that she had recently resigned from a gas company in India and wished to open a business for hand-made jewelry; she asked the blog participants for advice in directing her to academic programs in entrepreneurship in her area. Other chats on entrepreneurship present posts from women entrepreneurs who are searching for, or advising on education and training programs to prepare for entrepreneurship.

The explanation for this difference between the genders is based on women's reported tendency to take less risky decisions, including the decision to start a business. Research points to women's tendency to prepare more systematically for processes and actions that involve risk or ambiguity, by acquiring more information, knowledge and the formal qualifications offered through education. In higher education programs, women can take on the role of apprentice, which will assist them as future entrepreneurs in developing the relevant strategy for establishing their own ventures. Some programs involve internships in which the interns are exposed to a variety of experiences and opportunities that allow testing the waters with a safety net, and women entrepreneurs perceive these as significant groundwork and preparation for the venture creation.

Relevant experience in a business environment is crucial for starting a business. Typically, this experience is gained from previous jobs and role models, including parents and family. Prior experience as an entrepreneur is the ideal incubator for women entrepreneurs, offering them the opportunity to manage challenges and difficulties by grasping the overall operation of the business and learning as many aspects of the business as possible, experience that would not otherwise be accessible to them (Bowen & Hisrich, 1986; Coviello & Jones, 2004; Powell & Butterfield, 2003; van de Lippe & van Dijk, 2002).

Family influences—Family background and parental role models are associated with women's motivations to become entrepreneurs. There is a strong body of evidence linking entrepreneurs, mainly women entrepreneurs, to parents who are themselves either self-employed or entrepreneurs. The behaviors, ways of thinking, attitudes toward risk-taking, unstable career or independence displayed by these parents provide a positive role model and a source of inspiration for the child. In the case of female entrepreneurship, a mother's entrepreneurial career plays a salient role on the individual level; however, as few of the mothers developed independent careers, it is striking to note that at the macro level, this appears to be an insignificant factor.

The natural implication is that women entrepreneurs should become role models for the next generation of young girls who are exploring their future career paths. In the absence of female role models in the family, young girls should be exposed to role models in the media, literature and films about successful women entrepreneurs, and become familiar with existing successful female entrepreneurs and the success stories of past women entrepreneurs. These should be inherent in schools, academic institutions and daily routines.

Social expectations and socialization craft female motivation toward entrepreneurship by intertwining the roles of a woman's life and work through early childhood, and during the course of the woman's life. Socialization and social expectations illustrate women as mainly responsible for the family's well-being and household basics, even at the expense of their professional aspirations, which they will renounce if they overlap with their family responsibilities. These views are mirrored across different spheres, including children's books, media advertising and coverage of male entrepreneurs' success stories, analyses of male-based case studies in academia, and so on.

Such traditional approaches to entrepreneurship depict it as a process that is detached from family and social life. It is considered to absorb the entrepreneur's time and energy and its outcomes are disembodied and unclear, and thus apparently inapplicable to women. Given these messages, women's motivations to start a business decline and become more necessity-oriented: entrepreneurship can only be considered a preferred employment path when escaping harsh conditions in the corporate labor market (Ahl, 2006; De Bruin, Brush, & Welter, 2007; Powell & Greenhaus, 2010; Renzulli, Aldrich & Moody, 2000; Wilson, Marlino & Kickul, 2004).

WORK–FAMILY TOPICS

Traditionally, "home" has always been the woman's domain. Today, greater emphasis is being placed on the division of work within and outside the home: both men and women find themselves engaged in home-related duties, thus enabling women to assign time, thoughts and energy to work and business. For many years, research treated work–family as a "zero-sum" equation, i.e., spending more time at work means less time with the family, consequently "neglecting" the family and domestic demands, while spending more time with the family means less time at work, resulting in "neglecting" work-related demands and obligations. However, recent years have seen acceptance of the notion of work and home being the two main driving forces for women, who can easily juggle work and family duties with the cooperation of their family members, and particularly their male counterparts.

These concepts originate from role theory and the scarcity perspective (Katz & Kahn, 1978), according to which individuals have a limited amount of time and energy to divide among various roles. The premise that multiple roles inevitably create a strain emphasizes their negative effects on women's well-being and self-fulfillment. In addition, the literature on gender stresses women's identification with social roles associated with their family duties, suggesting that the gender's actual behavior at work and at home (household duties and domestic matters) originates from individuals' self-categorization into groups of members who view themselves as belonging to the same social category. Accordingly, role identities are socially defined and derived primarily from the individual's membership, or perceived membership, in social categories and roles. Individuals may identify with multiple roles (e.g., employee, family member, community member) and thereby exhibit a range of role identities and behaviors. The subjective importance held by women or men for a given role will be reflected in their invoking that role's identity in a variety of situations, and investing more time and energy in performing according to the expectations attributed to that role.

Female entrepreneurship has spread worldwide in recent decades, inducing two significant trends in women's reality that have changed the traditional work–family segmentation:

1 Women entrepreneurs strive for quality time spent with the family rather than just fulfilling domestic tasks and family-related obligations.
2 Women want to maintain their independence and place high importance on their personal well-being, such as having personal time for hobbies, recreation and meeting with friends.

Figure 2.3 illustrates the contradictory demands of work and family.

Work-related demands:
Long hours, time pressures, inflexibiltiy of the work schedule, role overload
Responsibility—employees, clients processes, outcomes
Solving strategic and ad hoc problems

Family-related demands:
Household chores
Childcare—practical aspects
Responsibility for the children's well-being-emotional aspects
Raising children for excellence and competitiveness-educational, academic, social aspects

Figure 2.3 Work–Life Conflict.

These new trends are being molded into women's new realm and are redefining their feminine, maternal and business/profession-related identities. Specifically, while segmentation of work and family refers to keeping work and family separate by maintaining highly impenetrable boundaries around work and family domains, its counterpart is integration of these two domains, referring to the merging of various aspects of work and family by maintaining highly permeable boundaries around the two domains (Table 2.2). These changing trends, as presented above, are enabling women to adapt to either segmentation or integration, as long as these are compatible with their preferred identity and serve to increase their quality time with the family as well as allow them their independence and ability to create their personal territory in a daily context. For example, some working women may refrain from checking their work e-mail account at home because they want to maintain the boundaries between work and family; others, who maintain permeable boundaries between their family and work domains, prefer to accomplish some of their work at home, after spending quality time with the children.

Entrepreneurship as a means of juggling multiple female roles   Entrepreneurship is a successful means of achieving work–family balance; it allows women to shape their work assignments and schedules to their obligations and demands in the domains of the family, household, personal and social lives. Studies show that "quality" rather than "quantity" in the roles may produce positive spillover effects among women entrepreneurs: when women feel self-fulfilled at work, achieving their goals and managing challenging responsibilities, such a meaningful role, even if not suited to the family domain's demands, energizes them and promotes their self-esteem, confidence and sense of being empowered. Multiple roles may be viewed as an opportunity to juggle exciting roles and domains and benefit from increasing one's skills, capabilities, networks, knowledge, and fun. It is a win–win situation, as shown in Table 2.3, which summarizes the main benefits of work–family balance for the individual, for the family and for the business.

Managing both their own business and their family satisfactorily is a continuing challenge for women entrepreneurs: it requires unique self-operation, such as rescheduling and re-prioritizing some work and family matters, re-planning expected goals in both worlds—work and home—and much flexibility and many adjustments, especially in handling urgent, unexpected "emergencies." Every mother has experienced the situation in which her child calls from school saying that he/she is not feeling well while she is still at work with many tasks to complete. Most mothers' main concern in this situation is their children, ignoring the impact of their consequent decisions on their work.

Table 2.2 The Leading Work–Family Perspectives and Their Implications for Entrepreneurship

Theme	Definition and context	Managing the difficulties
Work–family conflict	• A form of inter-role conflict that arises when the pressures stemming from one role are incompatible with those stemming from another. • Work–family conflict is a critical issue in female entrepreneurship as traditionally, obtaining certain rewards associated with their homes and ignoring their family members' well-being. • Identifying with either of these roles means time allocation, energy and strain associated with being committed to multiple domains. • Women experience greater conflicts between their multiple roles than men, resulting in frustration and negative effects on their well-being and self-fulfillment from both work and family spheres. • Many women choose the traditional path and leave work to spend more time at home.	• Managing the demands of both work and family is a continuing challenge for women. • Entrepreneurship is considered the best way to balance work and family demands. • The ability to balance work and family seems to have a positive effect on women's well-being, enabling more time for their responsibilities in their different roles, flexibility and independence, along with enhanced financial opportunities, finding interest and obtaining a better work–family balance.
Work–family balance	• The equilibrium between the roles, i.e., the amount of time, energy and effort devoted to work relative to other aspects of life. • The root of work–family balance is embedded in the changing structures of both the family and work, and the consequently changing roles for women, from taking care of the household in the traditional family structure to a more balanced division of tasks and responsibilities at home between the family members.	• Work–family balance is not guaranteed by, nor is it an inherent condition of entrepreneurship. • Women need to develop a time schedule, task and assignment plans, as well as management strategies that will allow them to balance their business and home responsibilities, and enable them to navigate the borders between work and family domains.

(Continued overleaf)

Table 2.2 Continued

Theme	Definition and context	Managing the difficulties
	• Other changing configurations of the family, manifested in increased rates of divorce, step-families, single mothers, non-traditional families, require a more balanced role for women, allowing them to go out to work.	
Work-to-family conflict (WFC) and family-to-work conflict (FWC)	"Two unidirectional conflicts" that represent the interference of one domain with the other; these conflicts are distinct yet reciprocally related.	

WFC	• The negative interdependencies between work and family roles, in which the work role interferes with the family role.
	• A representation of personal and organizational cultures that favor work and career and influence women to choose spending time at work, even when there is a spillover between their roles at work and at home.
	• This concept is reflected in practice by three components: time, strain and behavior.
	  – Women will experience WFC when *time* pressures at work make it difficult for them to meet the demands of their family role.
	  – Work-related stressors cause frustration, fatigue, irritation and other symptoms of *strain* that negatively affect their performance in their family role.
	  – Choosing behaviors corresponding to work might have a negative impact on women's role in the home; for example, when a board meeting at work and a child's final basketball game are scheduled for the same time and the mother chooses to attend the board meeting, this might produce a WFC.
		• Regaining work-to-family balance and finding a positive spillover between work and family: this might be achieved by embracing the coexistence of feelings of competence, autonomy, and relatedness deriving from being active and indentifying with roles in both domains simultaneously.
		• Work-to-family balance can be achieved by engaging in tasks that have visible functions in both constructs, thus minimizing role- and identity-related conflicts.
		• Some theories stress that occupying multiple roles is more beneficial and more self-fulfilling for individuals than focusing on a single role; it is a chain that connects two different constructs.

FWC

- This condition appears when family demands and obligations interfere with work time and incompatible obligations.
- As the family domain is considered a greater source of conflict for women than for men, this conflict is associated with a number of dysfunctional outcomes for women, including decreased well-being, and dissatisfaction with the job and with life in both the family and work domains.

Family-to-work balance might be achieved by accepting both domains, perceiving both as salient in one's life and as fueling one's energies.
Family support is another important factor that may transform potential conflicts into positive spillover. Assistance in domestic households is helpful to achieving a positive family-to-work balance.

For further reading: Edwards & Rothbard (2000); Frone (2003); Greenhaus & Powell (2006); Netemeyer, Boles, & McMurrian (1996); Welter (2004).

Table 2.3 Benefits of Work–Family Balance

Work–life balance benefits for the individual	Work–life balance benefits for the business	Work–life balance benefits for the family
• Minimizing the feeling of constant rush • Allocating time for hobbies, outside-work interests • Going back to school • Assigning quality social time, meeting with friends • Being involved and active in the community • Having the time to reflect, think, plan for the future • Increased productivity in many aspects of life • Reduced stress • Self-fulfillment, self-actualization • Less health-related issues associated with stress and conflicts	• Better productivity at work • A role model for the team • Improved teamwork • Better communication and atmosphere at work • Being happier, more creative, more stimulated from work • Positive spillover • An opportunity to learn from the other roles rather than "fighting them". • Less negative stress-related organizational symptoms	• Stronger feelings of relatedness, attachment and affection toward the family • Better relationships and communication with family members • More balanced division of household tasks at home • More time to devote to loved ones • Engaging in family activities • Being more involved in family members' lives

The tension between work and family still exists among women entrepreneurs, despite the autonomy, independence and flexibility that typify the entrepreneurial life. Women entrepreneurs are typically pushed by an inherent determination to be "the best," the leader and the role model, in both domains, i.e., to establish the most successful business, raise their children as the most successful and popular students who are highly motivated to achieve the "right" goals, and manage the most organized and cleanest houses. When one of these components does not match their expectations, even temporarily, the work–family tension emerges. Table 2.4 shows three ways for women entrepreneurs to cope with the work–family conflict.

SUMMARY

This chapter presents women's motivations to become entrepreneurs from different angles. First, the typology of necessity and opportunity

Table 2.4 What Women Entrepreneurs Need to do to Cope with the Work–Family Conflict

Asking for assistance	Formal assistance	Different forms of business
• Women entrepreneurs need to "learn" to use assistance; asking for assistance from a neighbor or family member in taking care of the children when duties demand longer hours at work might be pleasant for the children and build a "give-and-take" relationship with the neighbor. • This is an efficient way that encompasses different values, of assistance, friendship, community care. • "Informal" assistance reduces stress and pressures.	• The support systems provided by organizations devoted to women entrepreneurs offer a variety of programs that develop women's relevant skills and capabilities to run successful businesses. • The outcome of these programs is a positive effect on the work–family issue both psychologically—perceived as a challenge rather than a conflict; and in practice—women are better equipped with skills to manage time and assignments, conflict resolution, decision-making processes; etc.	• Home-based businesses: allows flexible working hours and simultaneous presence at work and at home. • E-based business: enables flexibility, working hours are not confined to tasks (meetings with clients; managing employees) • Partnership: sharing decisions, obligations and responsibility by partnership is a practical solution for women entrepreneurs, as it facilitates the business burden, by breaking it down to "responsibilities per partners." • Hiring people to the business: psychologically and practically, division of the labor is effective and reduces stress; sharing the tasks is cost-effective on the long term.

entrepreneurship is presented and discussed in the context of women's more reluctant entrance into entrepreneurship, as the pull–push factors that affect their motivations to embark upon entrepreneurship. Then, the female entrepreneurial mindset is debated, offering a different approach to the continued quest of women's motivations to venture into their own businesses, stressing that in addition to the "typical" entrepreneurial mindset, women entrepreneurs tend to regard their entrepreneurial businesses as integrated facets of their own identities, including their family roles, and as a vital part of their family context. These factors craft a unique structure for their entrepreneurial mindset. The work–family conflict and balance is debated, and the role of entrepreneurship is presented in this context.

Finally, a broad overview of the contexts relevant to female entrepreneurship is presented, including issues such as family support and work–family balance, maintaining that a requisite condition to successful entrepreneurship and higher well-being is achieving a satisfactory work–family balance. This balance will be shaped by each woman's needs, constraints and desires and by avoiding "protocols," such as working more hours from home or keeping a clear separation between home and the business. For some women, such "protocols" will work and will enhance their work–family balance, while others will form their own "protocols" from different components.

CASE STUDIES[5]

The following two case studies, contributed by (a) Clare Brindley, Carley Foster and Dan Wheatley and (b) Janice Byrne and Alain Fayolle, provide a deep and most interesting look into women's motivations, entrepreneurial mindset and necessity-based entrepreneurship through the lens of (a) qualitative research aimed at deepening our understanding of women entrepreneurs in the UK, the reported reasons for starting their own businesses, their levels of success and the realities of running their own businesses, from their own points of view; (b) Olivier Dubout, entrepreneurship professor and researcher in France, who investigates the forces that push/pull women into entrepreneurship; the case takes the reader on an exciting journey into female necessity-based entrepreneurship from a non-traditional perspective, i.e. the consultant's eyes.

These pieces thus offer quantitative and qualitative perspectives on motivations and mindsets in the context of female entrepreneurship from two leading, opportunity-based entrepreneurial countries, the UK and France.

Marketing Women: A Sector Experience

Clare Brindley, Carley Foster and Dan Wheatley
Nottingham Business School, Nottingham Trent University, Nottingham, UK.

The research moves away from a comparison with men by focusing on the experiences of women in marketing to elicit the women's views of their experiences. These are women who have moved their professional competencies across into self-employment.

The case study focuses on a particular functional context, marketing; the implications for policy and the encouragement of women business owners are a wider one.

Marketing is a recently feminized industry yet there is little knowledge about female careers in the profession and the extent to which they reflect the non-linear career paths of many other women

Introduction

The case study explores the experiences of self-employed women who have their own marketing business. Women with marketing qualifications, employed in large organizations, who then move into self-employment provide a rich narrative on the actual challenges starting up a business involves and their experiences challenge the consensus that women owned businesses "under-perform" (Ahl, 2006; Watson, 2002).

The research presented in this case study forms part of a larger, longitudinal study into the careers of women in marketing. The marketing industry is a feminized one because women form the large part of the workforce. The case study begins with data drawn from the UK Labour Force Survey (2008) to contextualize the qualitative study that follows later in the Chapter. Conclusions from the findings are then discussed.

Women in Marketing the Context

The UK Labour Force Survey (LFS) has been collected on a quarterly basis since 1992 and approximately 120,000 individuals form the sample of the fourth quarter LFS in 2008, which we use below. The LFS includes a range of variables that are key to researching occupation and work patterns. International definitions of employment, unemployment and economic inactivity are used, combined with a wide range of related topics such as occupation, training, hours of work and personal characteristics of household members aged 16 or over. Using the LFS we were able to investigate the employment patterns of women working in marketing.

Table 2.5 Breakdown of Marketing Occupations by Gender[a]

Occupation (Marketing only)	Male (%)	n	Female (%)	n
Marketing and Sales Managers	50.7	667	15.5	286
Advertising and Public Relations Managers	3.7	49	2.6	48
Designer (Advertising)	1.0	131	2.8	52
Buyer (Advertising)	5.1	67	2.6	48
Marketing Associate Professionals	6.5	86	7.8	144
Filing and Records Assistants (Marketing)	4.6	60	12.6	233
Market Research Interviewers	1.1	15	1.0	19
General Office Assistants (Marketing)	18.3	240	55.1	1019
Total	100.0	1315	100.0	1849

Source: UK Labour Force Survey 2008.
Note: [a] X^2 tests confirm that the patterns observed in the proportions of men and women by marketing occupation group are statistically significant (p-value 0.000), and as such are representative of the wider population.

The LFS 2008 (fourth quarter) identified a sample of some 1,849 women working in marketing roles compared with 1,315 men. The women work in a number of different roles (see Table 2.5).

If we then look at self-employment in particular, across all occupations, 7.9 percent of women report being self-employed, compared with 18.3 percent of men (LFS, 2008). Comparatively fewer women in marketing (and associated occupations)—approximately 5.5 percent identify themselves as self-employed. Further analysis of the data shows that self-employed women marketers were on average older (46.1 years) than their employed counterparts (39.5 years). The self-employed women were likely to have more dependent children under 16 (younger children) (0.57 for employed but 0.66 for self-employed) and children under 19. Women in marketing reported working 33.0 hours per week when employed but just 26.7 hours per week when self-employed. The figures are indicative of issues of flexibility and greater household responsibilities which are also supported by the fact that most self-employed marketers worked from home. The self-employed marketers were also well qualified—some 38.2 percent of self-employed women in marketing occupations have a degree or equivalent qualification compared with just 23.6 percent of employed women. The LFS (2008) data thus supports extant literature, for example, the glass ceiling (Marshall, 1984), industry experience/qualifications and work–life balance (Krider & Ross, 1997), views on risk toward self-employment (Brindley & Ritchie, 1999) which all influence the careers of women in marketing.

Women in Marketing—Their Voices

Although the LFS (2008) data provides a picture of women's employment in the marketing industry in the UK it does not capture the experiences of self-employed women in the sector. Hence, interviews were undertaken with five UK-based women who had their own marketing business and who had previously worked in marketing in a large organization. The sample of businesses was a convenient one (Easterby-Smith *et al.*, 2008). The interviews were designed to capture both the demographic character-istics of the women and why they became self-employed. The study answered Patterson and Mavin's (2009: 177) call that "[F]ew studies explore women's post hoc experiences to assess how women analyse their original motivations from their current position as an established entrepre-neur." In addition, Beetles and Harris (2005) identified a lack of gendered research focusing on marketing work.

Table 2.6 provides an overview of each case business.

Interview themes were drawn from the literature and included: the purpose and nature of their business, their role in the business, their career history, their personal and business-related aspirations, their experiences of running the business, reasons for starting the business and why they worked in marketing. Personal story-telling was encouraged, to identify the influences on their career choice and the relationships between them (Broadbridge, 2008; Brush *et al.*, 2009). The findings are presented around specific themes. Template analysis was used because, as Patterson and Mavin (2009: 179) argue, template analysis offers "a flexible yet systematic approach for organizing information to provide lucid final accounts." The interview analysis yielded five major themes which are discussed in turn below.

Table 2.6 An Overview of the SMEs

	SME 1	SME 2	SME 3	SME 4	SME 5
Age of business	10 years	6 years	13 years	12 years	1 year
Service provided	Strategic Marketing	Strategic Marketing	Market Research	New Product Development	Online Marketing
Age of owner	47	45	48	50	34
Marital status	Single	Married	Married	Married	Divorced
Children's ages	N/A	7 and 11	11 and 13	14	7 and 11
Highest qualification	BSc	BSc	MA	Diploma	BTec
Hours worked per week	Varied	22 hours	20 hours	50 hours	50 hours
No. of employees	0	0	0	0	0

Source: Beetles and Harris (2005).

1 Trigger events to starting the business   All five women reported that they had become self-employed due to a trigger event. For SME 3 and SME 4 it was redundancy and for SME 4, the redundancy payment had funded her initial start-up phase. For SME 1, the fact that her temporary contract in a large organisation had not been renewed was the prompt. The owner of SME 5 explained how she had been overlooked for a promotion as a result of a company restructure. This combined with a change to her role meant that she began to evaluate working for the organization. For the owner of SME 2, the need to be in control of her working life had been a key reason for starting her own business.

2 Reasons for staying in marketing   All the sample had chosen to remain as marketers when they started their business. SME 2 said ". . . I could have gone and made biscuits but I wanted to use the knowledge and skills I'd built up . . . I'd worked out what I could charge for a day of my time . . . and actually I'd have to sell a hell of a lot of biscuits to make that kind of profit." All five women had marketing qualifications and although these qualifications gave their business credibility they did not feel their qualifications were instrumental in staying as marketers.

3 Definitions of success   Success was defined in a number of different ways but most women were in agreement that financial success was not always a priority. This was reflected in the range of turnover levels generated by each business with the highest turnover level being £60,000 per year, although all five businesses had experienced significant fluctuations in turnover over the life of the business. Flexibility was also considered to be a way of measuring success for the owner of SME 5 who stated that "I work longer hours but I have more time . . . I can do what I want when I want and to me, that's brilliant."

4 Responsibilities outside work   Four of the women had children but family responsibilities were not always referred to when asked about the other responsibilities they had which had a significant impact on managing their work. Instead, all the women commented on their social and business-related activities which included charitable, religious and community activities. Only one of the women engaged with the more formal, traditional business network organizations, as they were seen as not particularly women oriented.

5 Defining their work role   All of the women hesitated when asked to describe their work role. None of the women described themselves as an "entrepreneur" mainly because it was not a term they could relate to, preferring to use "business owner" or "business woman," and in some instances they also referred to their marketing specialism.

Conclusions

The case study has looked at the context of self-employed women marketers in the UK and through qualitative research identified the reasons why these women started their own business, their demographic details, their levels of success and the realities of running their own business, importantly from their own interpretations/recollections. It has therefore attempted to address the gap in knowledge which exists in relation to the challenges entrepreneurial women face (Marlow *et al.*, 2009) even in a feminized industry. All the women deliberately stayed working as professional marketers and although all had gained marketing qualifications, they were not seen as crucially important to their businesses. Their decision to stay as marketers was predicated on their desire to use the experience and skills they had gained whilst employed. This resonates with the observation made by Brindley and Ritchie (1999) that women are risk-averse when seeking self-employment, preferring to stay in the industry where they have the most skills. Risk aversion was also evident in the fact that none of the women considered working for themselves when they started their working career and all the women started their own businesses in their mid–late 30s. Like Patterson and Mavin (2009) found, these women were not initially ambitious to start their own businesses. Instead, "trigger events" whilst working for a large company had prompted their move into self-employment. It would be true to say that there was a package of influences on the decision to become self-employed.

Rather than monetary rewards, flexibility and control were the key drivers for these women. Although, despite the initial view that self-employment gives flexibility, the women still experience role conflicts, with their businesses and domestic responsibilities. These women are still having to juggle. Interestingly, the responsibilities these women had outside of their business were largely related to local organizations with altruistic aims, which may be indicative of different ethics. The women in the study felt most comfortable describing themselves as a business person/woman or by referring directly to their profession. Other terms, such as "entrepreneur" were associated with risk and innovation and not a true reflection of them. Traditional networking activities also did not motivate them and they had mitigated this through their community roles and support from other women sole traders.

It is acknowledged that the generalisability of the findings are limited as the qualitative study draws from a small sample based in one area of the UK. However, by utilizing data from the LFS (2008) and by focusing on one sector it does provide useful insights into the experiences of self-employed women in marketing and the careers they have. Future qualitative research will increase the number of cases and historical analysis of the LFS will be undertaken to identify employment trends.

Questions for Discussion

1 What kind of entrepreneurial mindset can you identify in this case study?
2 (a) Are you familiar with any other feminized industries?
   (b) What self-employment opportunities would be open to women in other feminized industries?
3 What challenges do women face if they move into self-employment that is not related to their professional/industry expertise?
4 Do you think the experiences of the UK women reported here would be similar to those of women in other countries/cultures?
5 How can industry experience help self-employed women with respect to networking?

Case References

Ahl, H. (2006). Why research on women entrepreneurs needs new directions. *Entrepreneurship, Theory and Practice*, September, 595–621.

Beetles, A. & Harris, L. (2005). Marketing, Gender and Feminism: A Synthesis and Research Agenda. *The Marketing Review*, 5, 205–231.

Brindley, C. & Ritchie, B. (1999). *Female Entrepreneurship: Risk Perceptiveness, Opportunities and Challenges*. 22nd ISBA National Small Firms Policy & Research Conference, Leeds, November.

Broadbridge, A. (2008). Senior careers in retailing: An exploration of male and female executives' career facilitators and barriers. *Gender in Management*, 23(1). 11–35.

Brush, C.G., de Bruin, A. & Welter, F. (2009). A gender-aware framework for women's entrepreneurship. *International Journal of Gender and Entrepreneurship* 1(1), 8–24.

Easterby-Smith, M., Thorpe, R. & Jackson, P. (2008). *Management Research* (3rd edn.). London: Sage.

Krider, D. & Ross, P. (1997). The experiences of women in a public relations firm: A phenomenological explication. *Journal of Business Communication*, 34(4), 437–455.

Marlow, S., Henry, C. & Carter, S. (2009). Introduction: Female Entrepreneurship. Special Edition. *International Small Business Journal*, 27(2), 1–9.

Marshall, J. (1984). *Women managers: Travellers in a male world*. Chichester: Wiley.

Patterson, N. & Mavin, S. (2009). Women Entrepreneurs: Jumping the Corporate Ship and Gaining New Wings. *International Small Business Journal*, 27(2), 173–192.

Watson, J. (2002). Comparing the performance of male and female controlled businesses: relating outputs to inputs. *Entrepreneurship, Theory and Practice*, 11(2), 129–143.

Necessity Entrepreneurs in France: Women and Business Support Services

Janice M. Byrne[a] and Alain Fayolle[b]

[a]*Department of Management, Law and Human Resources, EM Lyon Business School, Lyon, France;* [b]*Entrepreneurship Research Centre, EM Lyon Business School, Lyon, France*

This case study looks at the phenomenon of necessity entrepreneurship and entrepreneurship policy. The case focuses on female necessity entrepreneurs in France and their use of a business advisory/coaching service. The chapter raises theoretical issues concerning (1) the interplay between gender and entrepreneurial motivations, (2) the coaching process and (3) the gendered provision of training/business support. We explore "push" and "pull" entrepreneurial motivations and try to better understand the needs of necessity entrepreneurs. This case study demonstrates the precarious and fragile lives which some women entrepreneurs lead in a developed and innovation-based economy. This case prompts students to consider the wider implications of government policy in entrepreneurship.

Introduction

On October 25, 2010, Olivier Dubout, entrepreneurship professor and researcher at a leading French business school, re-read the email from Marie Grandval, an official at the Department of Trade and Enterprise. Marie was compiling a report on *necessity entrepreneurs* in France. She had invited Olivier—a recognized expert on entrepreneurship and entrepreneurship policy in France—to prepare a report on necessity entrepreneurs and the business support services available to them. Over the course of his research, Olivier had discovered that many "necessity entrepreneurs" were in fact women. Olivier didn't consider himself to be a feminist but he had been saddened and shocked by hearing of the extreme and unjust situations in which these women entrepreneurs found themselves. He was determined to paint an accurate and honest picture of the reality that these women "necessity entrepreneurs" faced and to make recommendations as to how best they could be helped.

Setting the Scene: Entrepreneurship Policy in France

As early as the first oil crisis in the 1970s, Raymond Barre, France's Prime Minister at the time, promoted the idea of business creation as a viable alternative for the unemployed. Shortly afterward, in the mid-1970s, the first entrepreneurship incentives and measures began to appear in French economic and social policy. Without being explicitly expressed in these terms, such incentives and political measures have generally targeted two particular types of entrepreneurship: *necessity* and *opportunity entrepreneurship*.[6] *Necessity entrepreneurship* is about having to become an entrepreneur because you have no other choice, while *opportunity entrepreneurship* is an active choice to start a business based on the perception that an unexploited (or underexploited) opportunity exists.[7] Opportunity entrepreneurship arises from positive "pull" factors, such as the desire for greater autonomy, independence, freedom, financial gain, social status, or even recognition.[8] By contrast, necessity entrepreneurship results from "push" factors which are more negative in nature, such as long-term unemployment, being laid off, or the threat of losing one's job.[9]

The particular form of entrepreneurship is an important consideration for government policy makers. Necessity entrepreneurship provides individuals with employment and a revenue source but has been found to have no effect on economic development.[10] Opportunity entrepreneurship, however, has been found to have a positive and significant effect on economic development.[11] Businesses started by entrepreneurs with push motivations are less successful (financially) than those built upon pull factors.[12] Those who are pushed into entrepreneurship are often less dynamic and entrepreneurial.[13] In fact, many recent studies linking firm survival and growth to entrepreneurs' motivations show that firm survival is all the more uncertain when motivations relate to "push" factors.[14] Necessity-based entrepreneurs are more vulnerable then their opportunity-based counterparts and have more precarious businesses.

For over thirty years, the persistence of various schemes and recurring incentives for entrepreneurship in France has legitimized the creation of new ventures out of *necessity*.[15] Such measures have succeeded in making entrepreneurship appear possible and more appealing to a larger number of people. In France today, it has never been easier for job seekers to start their own business. The government has made considerable efforts to lower the administrative, social and fiscal barriers associated with starting a business. A recent study shows an increase in the numbers of individuals engaging in early stage entrepreneurship.[16] Schemes like the "#eu1 firm" or the recently created "auto-entrepreneur" status have been warmly received. The "auto-entrepreneur" legislation came into force on January 1, 2009. Since then, 551,500 individuals have registered, of which 524,000 were considered "active" by the end of July 2010.[17]

The advisability of entrepreneurship as *the* solution to unemployment warrants further debate.[18] Olivier feels that while entrepreneurship may hold economic and social promise, its promotion through political discourse and public infrastructures in France is questionable. Entrepreneurship can be seen as a means for job seekers to bounce back and find employment,[19] or as a response to fate,[20] but not all unemployed people or marginalized individuals *want* to become entrepreneurs. Nor do they always have the *resources* (in the broadest sense) which are necessary to succeed in this field.

Setting up in business is only half the battle. Once the firm is founded, the entrepreneur needs to ensure the long-term viability of their business. Throughout the process of business creation and development, entrepreneurs may draw on a wide range of support structures and resources, both privately and publicly provided. The quality and availability of such support services are key to helping small businesses survive and grow. It is with this in mind that Marie Grandval has asked Olivier to make particular recommendations about support structures for necessity entrepreneurs.

Entrepreneurship Support Structures

Common small business supports include funding, structured training, access to university or third-level expertise, networking, mentoring and coaching.[21] Entrepreneurship training is the building of knowledge and skills in preparation for starting and running a business.[22] Networking is one of the most widely accessed supports by entrepreneurs, followed by funding and mentoring.[23] Olivier has been asked to assess the informal entrepreneurship training support structures available to necessity entrepreneurs in France. Informal training is that which operates outside formal programs, for example, non-credit bearing courses provided by universities, local business organizations or government agencies.[24] Business advisory services may also be included in this category of informal training. The terms "coaching," "counselling," "consulting," "tutoring," "mentoring" and "sponsoring" are often used interchangeably to describe the general business advisory services which may be given to budding entrepreneurs.[25] Such a service generally involves an external coach or "mentor" providing continued assistance to an individual in the process of business creation. Ideally, it is a relationship which permits the entrepreneur to learn and develop while at the same time accessing resources (be they human, financial, skill or knowledge based) which enable him or her to realize their project's potential.[26] Coaching may take numerous forms depending on the entrepreneurs' needs as well as the consultants' approach.[27] (See Appendix 2.A2 for a breakdown of varying coaching approaches.)

Olivier began his review by contacting a local consulting company which specialized in providing business advisory services for small business creation. He established contact with five of their permanent consultants and arranged meetings with each of them. All the consultants held a higher education qualification (degree or masters) from one of the country's established business schools and had considerable experience in the domain of small business creation. The support services which their consulting company provides are delivered in close collaboration with "Pole Emploi"— the French employment assistance agency. As such, many of their clients may be classified as *necessity-based entrepreneurs*. They had been put in contact with this service as a result of their unemployed status and their stated desire to begin their own business. Olivier organized to meet some of these entrepreneurs. In their meetings, the consultants and entrepreneurs were asked to speak freely about their experiences and feelings on their decision to start their own business as well as their experience of coaching/mentoring. All interviews were recorded and Olivier arranged for them to be transcribed for ease of reading and analysis at a later point (see Appendix 2.A3 for an overview of the interviewees).

Support Structures and Gender

Olivier found that most of the consultants' clients that could be classified as "necessity entrepreneurs" were in fact women. Finding data on women entrepreneurs in France is difficult given the nature of how entrepreneurship statistics are recorded in the country but very basic national statistics indicate that around 30 percent of firms in France are owned and managed by women.[28] Olivier found no relevant research which specifically raised the question of *necessity entrepreneurs* and women. He wondered about the link between gender and necessity entrepreneurship. It is more difficult to start a business after a break in activity and there are more women than men who decide to start a business after having been absent from the labor market.[29] This may be because women's unemployment is often higher than men's unemployment, because of maternity leave, or breaks to raise children. In France, 20 percent of women who started a business in 1998 were back on the labor market following a period of inactivity, whereas only 6 percent of men had not been working the year preceding business creation.[30]

Olivier was aware of a long-running policy debate concerning the need for business creation support services just for women.[31] From his reading, he discovers that globally the incidence of gender-based small business assistance (i.e., support services targeted just to women) is increasing.[32] However, researchers dispute the extent to which differences between male and female entrepreneurs exist[33] and hence questions have been raised as to the grounding rationale for gendered training provision.[34] Indeed, in some cases such gendered support has been resisted as some women resent the existence of gendered provision of training.[35] However, a recurring argument appears to be that while men and women business owners' needs are often similar, women-only support services can help address the common problem which women face: the gender-system in society and the expressions of this that they encounter (i.e., discrimination or stereotyping).[36] Some researchers have suggested that women often feel more comfortable discussing their business problems with other women.[37] Olivier learns that mentoring programs are thought to be particularly effective for women. Mentoring/coaching facilities can be used to help women overcome cultural barriers and develop their feelings of competency, personal control, self-efficacy and self-esteem.[38] They provide reassurance and trusting relationships. Olivier wonders if this perhaps accounts for the high number of female necessity entrepreneurs availing of the business assistance services? Or could it be that many necessity entrepreneurs in France are women? He also wondered if these support services for these necessity-based women entrepreneurs should differ from those given to men? Olivier decided to look more closely at the reasons why these women became entrepreneurs.

Examining Motivations

Entrepreneurs are often either "pushed" or "pulled" into entrepreneurship. Some research has suggested that women and men have relatively similar motivations for entrepreneurship.[39] Generally speaking, there are four key drivers of entrepreneurial motivation:[40]

1   A desire for **independence** and related factors such as autonomy and greater control are often considered as "pull" factors for both men and women.[41]
2   **Monetary** conditions are also usually classified as a pull factor. Women who are historically lower wage earners than men are often pushed into entrepreneurship.[42]
3   Motivations related to **work**—such as unemployment, redundancy, and a lack of career or job prospects—are often considered as push factors[43] but according to existing research men and women do not differ so much in this regard.
4   A number of **family** related factors have been found to be important in influencing the decision to be an entrepreneur, i.e., fit with domestic commitments, desire for work–family balance, combining wage and domestic labour, family obligations. These factors are often found to be more prevalent among women.[44]

Olivier reviewed the transcripts of the interviews he had carried out with the consultants and the entrepreneurs (see Appendix 2.A3 for a detailed breakdown of the interviewees). He took out a blank page and pen and made notes on how the women he interviewed ended up as entrepreneurs. What were the forces that pushed or pulled them? Olivier tabulated the responses given by the entrepreneurs in their sample to give an over-view of the factors that motivated them to start their own business (Table 2.7). Neither the consultants nor the entrepreneurs in his sample mentioned control or desire for independence. This affirmed Olivier's belief that he was looking at cases of "pure" necessity entrepreneurship. These women did not feel that they had a choice other than starting their own business.

In order to get a clearer picture of the reality faced by these entrepreneurs, Olivier began to scan the transcripts for some recurring topics in their discussions. He started to piece together some general themes arising

Table 2.7 Motivation Factors

Factors	Cited by the consultants		Cited by the entrepreneurs
Work related	"I have met individuals who had been morally harassed by their companies who did not want to lay them off, but tried to force them to resign." (C1)	"They have experienced extremely tough layoffs . . ." (C2) "These are people who face an immediate difficulty of lack of resources, who can't find employment and who are obliged . . . to start their own business."	"I've seen many necessity entrepreneurs who were forced into starting a business because they had no other option." (C4) ". . . some people tell me they feel they have been cheated by their employers." (C4)
Family, household situation	"We meet women who have to cope with extremely tough situations, because they have kids to look after." (C1)	"We sometimes see people in situations of personal, professional, and family distress." (C1)	"We meet lots of single parents. Women who raise their children alone and want to start their own business because they can't find work." (C1) "What if I give up? What will I do? I'm 55, I'm a single-parent . . ." (E5)
Monetary	"Some of the people we meet have no initial capital at all, they survive on the RMI or RSA." (C2)	"We see more and more people who live in precarious situations and have no personal capital." (C2)	"These are people who have no resources and . . . are obliged, by default, to start their own business . . . in a rush." (C3) "There's two of us, . . . so we make ends meet." (E4)

Source: Byrne and Fayolle.

Note: RMI (Revenu Minimum d'Insertion): minimum subsistence allowance. RSA (Revenu de Solidarité Active) Active solidarity income (designed to replace the RMI from June 1, 2009, compensatory benefit for job seekers to encourage them to get back to full-time employment as well as for people with low-paid jobs).

from the discussions which help paint a picture of these entrepreneurs (see Table 2.8 below for details). He finds that they are described by the consultants as vulnerable people with low self-confidence who struggle to survive in business. They themselves describe the daily struggle that they face. They often feel lonely and without adequate guidance.

Olivier is also conscious that he needs to better understand how the coaching and mentoring process works. In particular he needs to find areas of weakness so that he can make recommendations for providing business

Table 2.8 Profiling the Necessity Entrepreneur

	Consultants' Remarks
Vulnerable, low self-confidence, burdened	"They have experienced extremely tough layoffs that they did not understand."
	"These people need to bounce back and get their confidence back."
	"They have been through a lot, they have been traumatized, they have lost their confidence, their landmarks and they feel betrayed."
	"These layoffs can be distressing . . ."
	"Some entrepreneurs have been through depression and have found it hard to get their heads above water, and with these people, we have to do a lot of social and psychological coaching."
	"These people are extremely vulnerable."
	"A lot (of them), when they arrive, start crying, they get their burden off their chests . . ."
	"People's vulnerability stems from their lack of self-confidence."
	Consultants' Remarks
Conflict and struggle	"The people who succeed are those who, when faced with an obstacle, fight and overcome it."
	"It all depends on the person's state of mind, how strong they are . . . it is not something everybody has in them . . . it requires a lot of energy . . . you must have a lot of drive, and thrive on autonomy."
	"We sometimes meet people who have become extremely aggressive in the face of adversity."
	"When somebody is made redundant, everything can go downhill from there . . . their relationships can suffer, they start to have money problems, people don't feel good in themselves . . ."
	"Since I have started, I don't have any revenue . . . thank god I have my other activity alongside it . . ."
	Entrepreneurs' Remarks
	"Let me tell you, it was hard at the beginning for me, you must be ready for a long fight, you'll need staying power, patience, availability and a sense of sacrifice, especially for the first few years when you don't get any income."

(Continued overleaf)

Table 2.8 Continued

	Consultants' Remarks
Isolated; forgotten and lost	"So many entrepreneurs feel lost, once they find themselves on their own, they try to move forward the best they can . . ."
	"I've met many fragile entrepreneurs who felt pressured into starting their business as they had no other choice . . . for some, being an entrepreneur is just escaping reality."
	Entrepreneurs' Remarks
	"I realize it's an obstacle course, it's extremely difficult . . . you often feel lonely . . . I've often felt very lonely, I'm not even from the area, I don't have a network here."
	"I opened my coffee shop six months ago, and since the opening, I've seen the advisor from the Chamber of Commerce and Industry who dealt with my application stroll past my shop every single day, he's never stopped once."

Source: Byrne and Fayolle

support and assistance to necessity entrepreneurs. He looks again to the transcripts and begins to tabulate some comments (Table 2.9).

Both the consultants' and the entrepreneurs' accounts are fraught with emotion. Olivier knows that he needs to carefully analyse their responses if he wants to pinpoint the crucial problems, and propose appropriate

Table 2.9 Reflections on the Business Support Process

Entrepreneurs' Reflections

"It is really difficult to have access to the relevant information. Fortunately, there's the APCE website, otherwise it's very difficult, even with state support schemes . . . the people you seek help from don't always have the answers . . . I'm not even from the area, I don't have a network here . . ." (E1)

"The thing is, sometimes you only discover afterwards that you were entitled to some help, but you didn't know it . . . I learnt too late that I could have benefited from financial support to start my company, but I didn't know it. . . I discovered it when it was too late, it's such a shame! . . . the same goes for support in general, I didn't know there were infrastructures that would deliver consulting services for free . . . sometimes I felt like it was the jungle out there." (E3)

"I opened my coffee shop six months ago, and since the opening, I've seen the advisor from the Chamber of Commerce and Industry who dealt with my application stroll past my shop every single day, he's never stopped once." (E4)

"What really bothered me (when starting up my business) was the bureaucracy, the slowness of the administrative procedures . . . there are lots of things that don't seem clear and all of that takes up lots of time." (E3)

Consultants' Reflections

"Sometimes their situations affect me personally, and I find it hard then to stick to my consulting role with them . . . Our objective is first and foremost to help them regain their confidence, strength and energy." (C4)

"These people start businesses as they face difficulty and have no other choice . . . these aren't favorable conditions under which to start a business . . . especially not when it's done in this spirit of urgency and in a rush . . . in a rush, nothing works out well." (C3)

"You need good listening skills and other such skills, our job goes beyond just putting together a forecast balance sheet or a feasibility study. . . these people need a place where they can be listened to, and we have come to realize that our job reflects the changes in society, with the emergence of new expectations, new difficulties resulting from isolation and distress, issues that are distinct from the process of starting a business in itself, although the business start-up process is embedded in this context." (C2)

"There is no follow-up . . . I think many entrepreneurs are simply left to their own devices . . . you're busy with your consulting projects, I sometimes have up to eight appointments in a day, you think, well, I should give them a call . . . but it's hard to find the time . . ."

"At the end of the day, I feel drained . . . they need constant reassurance . . . I try to pass on some positive energy." (C1)

"There should be a post-start-up support scheme." (C3)

"I think that today there is a significant increase in the number of unemployed people . . . Pole Emploi are also under pressure . . . before we used to meet with people for an hour, now we meet with them for less than 20 minutes, ten minutes . . . In ten minutes, it's difficult to identify their background. We squeeze, we manage flows (of people), statistics . . ." (C2)

"We follow people over a period of three months . . . you have to be realistic, you don't become an entrepreneur in three months . . . business creation, on average, takes from six months to two years . . . to go from idea to concept, a feasibility study and actually starting up your activity . . . it takes time and maturity and every phase is important." (C3)

Note: APCE (*Agence Pour la Création d'Entreprise*): French business start-up agency

solutions for both the consultants and the entrepreneurs. He wonders is it just coincidental that in this one agency there are a high number of female necessity entrepreneurs availing of the business assistance services or is it a more widespread phenomenon? He also wondered if these *necessity-based* women entrepreneurs need specialized support services. He scratched his head and began to think about formulating his analysis for Marie Grandval from the French Department of Trade and Enterprise.

APPENDIX 2.1 NECESSITY AND OPPORTUNITY
ENTREPRENEURSHIP EXPLAINED

These two types of entrepreneurship depend on the varying aspirations, motivations and external factors that influence human behavior (Acs, 2006; Hessels *et al.*, 2008; Reynolds *et al.*, 2001). People launch businesses for a variety of reasons: they may be led into entrepreneurship out of necessity, i.e., they have no other choice, or their efforts may be driven by the desire to maintain or improve their income, or to increase their independence (Kelly, Bosma & Amoros, 2010). This table helps further distinguish between these two types of entrepreneurship:

Table 2.A1 Necessity and Opportunity Entrepreneurship Explained

	Opportunity-based entrepreneurship	*Necessity-based entrepreneurship*
Push or pull ?	Individual is "pulled" towards entrepreneurship	Individual is "pushed" into entrepreneurship
Objective	Individual seeks greater autonomy, independence, freedom, financial gain, social status, or even recognition (Carter *et al.*, 2003; Kolvereid, 1996; Wilson *et al.*, 2004)	Individual needs a source of income; individual pursues self-employment because there are no better options of work (Kelly, Bosma & Amoros, 2010)
Trigger	Individual recognizes an opportunity that can improve or maintain their income or increase their independence (Kelly, Bosma & Amoros, 2010)	Often result of long-term unemployment or being laid off, or the threat of losing one's job (Thurik *et al.*, 2008)
Economic impact	Concerns projects with growth potential; at a macro level, opportunity entrepreneurship spurs innovation and dynamism in economy (Kelly, Bosma & Amoros, 2010)	Provides employment options and means of revenue generation for otherwise unemployed (Kelly, Bosma & Amoros, 2010). Businesses are less successful (financially) than those built upon pull factors (Amit & Mueller, 1995)
Examples	Innovation based economies such as The Netherlands, Sweden, Denmark and Iceland show especially high proportions of opportunity motives (Kelly, Bosma & Amoros, 2010)	Factor-driven economies such as Ghana, Uganda, Zambia, Pakistan and Bolivia have the highest proportion of necessity-driven motives (Kelly, Bosma & Amoros, 2010)

APPENDIX 2.2 COACHING/MENTORING AND BUSINESS SUPPORT PROVISION

Table 2.A2 Coaching/Mentoring and Business Support Provision

Coaching and business assistance typology			
	Functional coaching	*Interpretative coaching*	*Reflexive and critical coaching*
Individual seeking:	Help, protection, specific assistance in dealing with a particular problem, challenge or objective	Assistance in clarifying business development options; planning for business evolution; help defining personal and professional development options	Assistance in identifying alternatives and making decisions
Methodology employed:	Rely on rules and technical procedures; problem resolution; mobilising means/ resources	Interviews/discussions; active listening; creating conditions which facilitate sense making and in-depth understanding	Confrontation and dialogue; implementing contracts and plans of action
Centred on:	The problem	The relation between the individual and their problematic	The overall situation
Coaching is	Lending the coach's expertise as an active resource	Unlocking and mobilising the individual's resources	Confronting the coach and coached individuals' points of view
	↑↓	↑↓	↑↓

Coaching needs linked to entrepreneurial project			
	Technical	*Psychological*	*Global or methodological*
Centred on:	The project itself, i.e. financial questions, legal issues or sales and marketing related queries	The business founder	Dynamic between founder and project; project/ founder "match" and internal coherence; choice of strategic directions
Role of Coach:	Provides technical expertise	Coaching the project founder	Heightening the founder's awareness of choices and consequences

Source: Adapted from Verzat, Gaujard & Francois, 2010; Paul, 2004; Cuzin & Fayolle, 2004.

APPENDIX 2.3 OVERVIEW OF INTERVIEWS: CONSULTANT AND ENTREPRENEUR PROFILES

Table 2.A3 Overview of Interviews: Consultant and Entrepreneur Profiles

Name	Gender	Age	Role/Activity	Years experience (in this role)	Interview date	Interview location	Duration of interview
Alexandra C1	Female	35	Consulting and coaching/ business mentoring	1.5	02/04/10	Toulouse	75 minutes
Claire C2	Female	42	Consulting and coaching/ business mentoring	5	19/03/10	Toulouse	90 minutes
Françoise C3	Female	51	Consulting and coaching/ business mentoring	10	22/03/10	Toulouse	90 minutes
Laurent C4	Male	45	Consulting and coaching/ business mentoring	6	15/03/10	Toulouse	60 minutes
Vanessa C5	Female	43	Consulting and coaching/ business mentoring	3	23/03/10	Toulouse	60 minutes
Amandine E1	Female	48	Entrepreneur (Cultural activities for young children)	1.5	17/03/10	Toulouse	40 minutes
Natasha E3	Female	53	Entrepreneur (Event communication)	4	05/04/10	Toulouse	30 minutes
Dominique E4	Female	49	Entrepreneur (Tea salon)	1.5	27/11/09	Avignon	65 minutes
Héléna E5	Female	52	Entrepreneur (Interior design, chair upholstery)	3.5	11/01/10	Avignon	85 minutes

Notes

1 In research, this classification is variously termed opportunity/necessity, pull/ push, voluntary/non-voluntary, and evolutionary/deliberate approaches to entrepreneurship.
2 *Oprah Winfrey* official website at: http://www.oprah.com/index.html
3 Career and managing entrepreneurship. Ido Salomon, The Marker, March 8, 2011 at: http://www.themarker.com/tmc/article.jhtml?ElementId =is20110308_58867 (Hebrew).

4 TED talks: Sheryl Sandberg—Why we have too few women leaders; at: http://www.ted.com/talks/sheryl_sandberg_why_we_have_too_few_women_ leaders.html

About this talk-Facebook COO Sheryl Sandberg looks at why a smaller percentage of women than men reach the top of their professions—and offers three powerful pieces of advice to women aiming for the C-suite.

About Sheryl Sandberg—As the COO at the helm of Facebook, Sheryl Sandberg juggles the tasks of monetizing the world's largest social networking site while keeping its users happy and engaged.

Long before Sheryl Sandberg left Google to join Facebook as its COO in 2008, she was a fan. Today she manages Facebook's sales, marketing, business development, human resources, public policy and communications. It is a massive job, but one well suited to Sandberg, who not only built and managed Google's successful online sales and operations program but also served as an economist for the World Bank and Chief of Staff at the US Treasury Department.

Sandberg's experience navigating the complex and socially sensitive world of international economics has proven useful as she and Facebook founder Mark Zuckerberg work to strike a balance between helping Facebook users control privacy while finding ways to monetize its most valuable asset: data.

5 The author(s) of the case studies are fully and solely responsible for their content, phrasing consistency and flow, terminology, English proofing and reference lists.

6 See Appendix 2.A1 for a more in-depth description of these concepts.

7 Acs, 2006.

8 Carter *et al.*, 2003; Kolvereid, 1996; Wilson *et al.*, 2004.

9 Thurik *et al.*, 2008.

10 Acs, 2006.

11 Acs, 2006.

12 Amit & Mueller, 1995. See page one for reminder of what "push" and "pull" factors constitute.

13 Hytti, 2010; Tervo & Niittykangas, 1994.

14 Ashta & Raimbault, 2009; Caliendo & Kritikos, 2009.

15 Fayolle, 2010.

16 Kelly, Bosma & Amoros, 2010.

17 Levratto & Serverin, 2011.

18 Hytti, 2010.

19 Brasseur, 2010.

20 Glée, 2010.

21 De Faoite *et al.*, 2004.

22 Martinez, Levie, Kelley, Sæmundsson & Schott, 2010.

23 De Faoite *et al.*, 2004.

24 Martinez *et al.*, 2010.

25 Paul, 2004.

26 Cuzin & Fayolle, 2004.

27 Verzat & Gaujard, 2009.

28 Orhan & Scott, 2001.

29 Ionescu, 1999.

30 Ionescu, 1999.

31 Byrne & Fayolle, 2010; Carter, 2000; Richardson & Hartshorn, 1993; Welter, 2004.

32 Orser & Riding 2005.

33 De Bruin, Brush & Welter 2007.

34 Byrne & Fayolle, 2010.

35 Carter, 2000; Orhan & Scott, 2001; Nilsson, 1997.
36 Tillmar, 2007; Marlow & Patton, 2005.
37 Orhan & Scott, 2001.
38 Carter 2000.
39 Rosa & Dawson, 2006.
40 Kirkwood, 2009.
41 Wilson *et al.*, 2004.
42 Clain, 2000.
43 Kirkwood, 2009.
44 Kirkwood, 2009.

Questions for Discussion

1 Why do governments need to think carefully about the entrepreneurship incentives and measures they introduce?
2 Do necessity-based entrepreneurs represent a favorable phenomenon?
3 What can the government do to help necessity entrepreneurs? What are the training and support needs of such entrepreneurs?
4 What is the consultant's role as business coach?
5 In your opinion, are necessity entrepreneurs more likely to be women?
6 Should training/business support services exist which are targeted strictly to women? If so, what factors should constitute these business support services?
7 What could be some negative repercussions of such programs?

Case References

Acs, Z.J. (2006). How is entrepreneurship good for economic growth? *Innovations, Winter*, 97–106.
Amit, R. & Mueller E. (1995). "Push" and "pull" entrepreneurship. *Journal of Small Business and Entrepreneurship, 12*, 64–80.
Ashta, A. & Raimbault, S. (2009). Business perceptions of the new French regime on autoentrepreneurship: a risk-taking step back from socialism. *Working Paper Centre Emile Bernheim*, No. 09–058.
Brasseur, M. (2010). *Entrepreneuriat et insertion.* Bruxelles: Bruylant.
Byrne J. & Fayolle A. (2010). A feminist inquiry into entrepreneurship training. In D. Smallbone, J. Leitão, M. Raposo & F. Welter (Eds.), *The Theory and Practice of Entrepreneurship: Frontiers in European Entrepreneurship Research* (pp. 76–100). Cheltenham, UK: Edward Elgar Publishing Limited.
Caliendo, M. & Kritikos, A.S. (2009). *I want to, but I also need to: Start-ups resulting from opportunity and necessity*, IZA DP no. 4661.
Carter, S. (2000). Improving the numbers and performance of women-owned businesses: some implications for training and advisory services. *Education and Training, 4/5*, 326–334.
Carter, N.M., Gartner, W.B., Shaver, K.G., & Gatewood, E.J. (2003). The career reasons of nascent entrepreneurs. *Journal of Business Venturing, 18*(1), 13–39.
Clain, S. (2000). Gender Differences in Full Time Self Employment. *Journal of Economics and Business, 52*(6), pp. 499–513.

Cuzin, R. & Fayolle, A. (2004). Les dimensions structurantes de l'accompagnement en creation d'enterprise. *La Revue des Sciences de Gestion, Direction et Gestion*, *210*, 77–88.

De Bruin, A., Brush, C. G. & Welter, F. (2007). Advancing a Framework for Coherent Research on Female's Entrepreneurship. *Entrepreneurship Theory and Practice*, *31*(3), 323–339.

De Faoite, D., Henry, C., Johnston, K. & Van der Sijde, P. (2004). Entrepreneurs' attitudes to training and support initiatives: evidence from Ireland and The Netherlands. *Journal of Small Business and Enterprise Development*, *11*(4), 440–448.

Fayolle, A. (2010). Nécessité et opportunité: les "attracteurs étranges de l'entrepreneuriat, *Revue Pour*, no. 204, 33–38.

Glée, C. (2010). La création d'entreprise comme réponse au destin. In Martine Brasseur (Ed.), *Entrepreneuriat et insertion* (pp. 179–196). Bruxelles: Bruylant.

Hytti, U. (2010). Contextualizing entrepreneurship in the boundaryless career. *Gender in Management: An International Journal*, *25*(1), 64–81.

Ionescu, D. (1999, October). *Women Entrepreneurship: Exchange Experiences between OECD and Transition Economy Countries*, paper presented at the OECD, LEED Project Conference, Brijuni, Croatia.

Kelly, D., Bosma, N. & Amoros, J. E. (2011). *Global Entrepreneurship Monitor*, 2010 Global Report, Babson College.

Kirkwood, J. (2009). Motivational factors in a push–pull theory of entrepreneurship. *Gender in Management: An International Journal*, *24*(5), 346–364.

Kolvereid, L. (1996). Organizational employment versus self-employment: reasons for career choice intentions. *Entrepreneurship Theory and Practice*, *20*(3), 23–31.

Levratto, N. & Serverin, E. (2011). Become independent! The paradoxical constraints of France's Auto-Entrepreneur regime. *EconomiX working paper*, 2011–6. University of Paris West, Nanterre La Défense, EconomiX.

Marlow, S. & Patton, D. (2005). All credit to men? Entrepreneurship, finance and gender, *Entrepreneurship Theory and Practice*, *29*(6), 699–716.

Martinez, A., Levie, J., Kelley, D., Sæmundsson, R. & Schott, T. (2010). Global entrepreneurship monitor special report: a global perspective on entrepreneurship education and training. *The Global Entrepreneurship Research Association* (GERA).

Nilsson, P. (1997). Business Counseling Services directed towards female entrepreneurs—some legitimacy dilemmas. *Entrepreneurship and Regional Development*, *9*, 239–258.

Orhan, M. & Scott, D. (2001). Why women enter into entrepreneurship: An explanatory model. *Women in Management Review*, *15*(5/6), 232–243.

Orser, B. & Riding, A. (2005). Evaluating a gender-based training program. *Journal of Small Business and Entrepreneurship*, *19*(2), 143–167.

Paul, M. (2004). *L'accompagnement, une posture professionelle spécifique*. Paris: L'Harmattan.

Richardson, C. & Hartshorn, P. (1993). Business start-up training: The gender dimension in business. In S. Allen & C. Truman (Eds.), *Women in Business: Perspectives on Women Entrepreneurs*. London: Routledge.

Tillmar, M. (2007). Gendered small-business assistance: lessons from a Swedish project, *Journal of European Industrial Training*, *31*(2), 84–99.

Thurik, A. R., Carree, M. A., Van Stel, A. J. & Audretsch, D. B. (2008). Does self-employment reduce unemployment? *Journal of Business Venturing, 23*(6), 673–686.

Rosa, P. & Dawson, A. (2006). Gender and the commercialization of university science: academic founders of spinout companies. *Entrepreneurship and Regional Development, 18*(4), 341–366.

Tervo, J. & Niittykangas, H. (1994). Effects of unemployment on new firm formation: Micro-level panel data evidence from Finland. *Small Business Economics, 19*(1), 31–40.

Verzat, C. & Gaujard, C. (2009). Expert, conseiller, mentor, confident ou tout a la fois? *L'Expansion Entrepreneuriat, 2*, 6–12.

Verzat, C., Gaujard, C. & Francois, V. (2010). Accompagner des futurs entrepreneurs en fonction de leurs besoins a chaque âge de vie. *Gestion 2000, 3*, 59–74.

Welter, F. (2004). The environment for female entrepreneurship in Germany. *Journal of Small Business and Enterprise Development, 11*(2), 212–221.

Wilson, F., Marlino, D. & Kickul, J. (2004). Our entrepreneurial future: Examining the diverse attitudes and motivations of teens across gender and ethnic identity. *Journal of Developmental Entrepreneurship, 9*(3), 177–197.

3 Female Venture Creation Process in Emerging Markets

BRIC and MENA

Chapter Objectives

- Characterizing the interdependencies between national economic development, national innovation levels, the prevalence of high-quality educational institutions and the country's ecosystem in shaping female entrepreneurial market and dynamics;
- Delineating the exclusiveness of emerging economies in their reflection to national entrepreneurship;
- Typifying attitudes, perceptions and approaches to female entrepreneurship in BRIC and MENA countries;
- Portraying the changes in transition countries emulated by changes in the attitudes, atmosphere, processes and dynamics of female entrepreneurship;
- Necessity and opportunity entrepreneurship in BRIC and MENA economies and the impact on women's new venture creation processes;
- Illustrating the support systems prevailing for women in emerging economies;
- Increasing the awareness of women's conditions in BRIC and MENA countries, and emphasizing the benefits of female entrepreneurship for the country's well-being, employment rates and general attitudes to women's position in the society.

The BRIC (Brazil, Russia, India and China) and MENA (Middle East and North African region) countries have experienced a transformation in recent years in terms of embracing more global approaches, understanding the benefits of strategic collaborations and opening themselves to different markets. This approach has already been translated into rapidly growing and emerging markets in BRIC countries. Recent events, including the 2011 Arab Spring,[a] have been echoed in the entrepreneurial realm in these countries.

While these economies' dynamics are attracting growing interest among researchers and decision-makers, there is still much to learn about female entrepreneurship there. The transformation in these countries' economic and employment attitudes has penetrated differently with regard to female entrepreneurship, hence their challenges and difficulties are still pertinent and require a deeper understanding. This chapter addresses different themes in female entrepreneurship among these economies.

A country's ecosystem shapes its entrepreneurial market and dynamics. Characterized by interdependencies between economic development and institutions, the ecosystem has a critical impact on different factors associated with new venture creation, such as attitudes toward entrepreneurship as a favorable employment path, access to capital and other resources, and public support systems to educate and train nascent entrepreneurs.

The ecosystem's level of development is reflected, according to Porter (Porter, 1990; Porter, Sachs, & McArthur, 2002), in three stages, with each stage affecting the activities and dynamics of the new venture: (1) factor-driven stage, (2) efficiency-driven stage and (3) innovation-driven stage. These stages occur at the macro level, specifically at the country's economic, social, and cultural levels, but their effects are reflected at the micro level, shaping businesses. The factor-driven stage is typified by low-cost efficiencies in the production of commodities or low value-added products; economies typified by this stage's characteristics tend to create very limited innovative businesses and are deprived of the knowledge creation that can be used for innovation, technologies or breakthroughs. Such conditions obviously affect attitudes toward, and the structure of, entrepreneurship, which more closely resembles self-employment in its traditional form than entrepreneurship, i.e., innovation, proactiveness, thinking "big," having a vision. Female entrepreneurship is portrayed in research as more focused on the service and caretaking sectors and on average, less innovative, regardless of the country's entrepreneurial stage. Under the entrepreneurial conditions of the factor-driven stage, entrepreneurship prevails in its most basic and traditional form; the environmental atmosphere and dynamics do not assist in stimulating women to leap forward by choosing entrepreneurship, or in promoting their business to the next stage.

---

[a] *The New York Times*, at http://www.nytimes.com/2011/09/23/world/middleeast/israeli-palestinian-dispute-upstages-arab-spring-at-united-nations.html?pagewanted=all

The efficiency-driven stage is typified by a country's endeavor to increase its production efficiency by allocating money to educating the workforce to adapt to subsequent global developments. Such conditions are depicted in most emerging economies, including Brazil, Russia, India and China (BRIC countries), while the innovation-driven stage represents economies of the most developed countries.

To move into the innovation-driven stage, environmental conditions conducive to entrepreneurship must be established. This transition to the third stage has been implemented in Korea, Ireland, Israel and Taiwan (Acs & Szerb, 2007). Accordingly, in innovation-driven countries, female entrepreneurship has flourished and reveals itself in its advanced form: more women are enrolled in academic technological programs that may pave their way to technological businesses, start businesses in sectors that are typically male-dominated, and are highly motivated to become global entrepreneurs.

The ecosystem dynamics has a significant impact on entrepreneurship, and the impact on female entrepreneurship is even more pronounced, for the following reasons:

- Women, more than men, engage in necessity entrepreneurship.
- Relative to men, there are higher rates of female unemployment and under-employment.
- Women are at a disadvantage in entrepreneurship, originating from lower levels of relevant education, limited relevant job experience, limited effective networks, and a lower inclination toward risk-taking, among others.
- Topics related to gender discrimination in the labor market.
- Women encounter more difficulties integrating into the corporate labor market, due to the conflict of home responsibilities and no suitable complementary arrangement for the children.
- Women face a slower promotion pace, limited possibilities to reach the highest management levels, and lower salary rates in the corporate market.

Any transitions from one stage to the next, i.e., from factor-driven to efficiency-driven and then to the innovation-driven stage, require the implementation of changes in the existing settings, and therefore courage and a risk-taking attitude. To enable the transition in female entrepreneurship toward its advancement, countries should carefully study the conditions experienced by women in their respective labor markets, understand the atmosphere and attitudes toward female entrepreneurship, then establish reforms and improvements to mitigate the difficulties and promote the benefits associated with female entrepreneurship.

More than a decade ago, the World Bank Development Report (1996) addressed women's quest and their ecosystems, and noted:

Transition affects women much differently in some ways than it does men . . . Women are no longer seen as having a social duty to work, but reform has also brought a dramatic decline in affordable child care facilities and a deterioration in health care systems. In addition, economic hardship and uncertainty during transition make it more difficult to feed and clothe the family—responsibilities that have always fallen predominantly to women in these countries . . . Moreover, women's employment choices may be constrained by increased labor market discrimination, as evidenced by layoffs of women before men and open discrimination in job advertisements.

(World Bank, 1996)[1]

A Macro Level Look into Transitional Economies and Female Entrepreneurship

A basic and leading assumption in female entrepreneurship is that women, like men, create a new venture to pursue an opportunity; they foresee the prospective fruits of engaging in the entrepreneurial world. However, the sources of their motivations and orientations to start a new venture, as described in the previous chapters, may stem from either necessity- or opportunity-driven conditions, depending, at least in part, on the country's stage of development. The environment's impact on necessity and opportunity orientations has been proven at various levels; in transition countries, with the fall of the communist regime, the role of women in society has changed, but these changes can differ according to country. For example, in Hungary, it has become socially acceptable for women to have professional careers, including entrepreneurship, whereas in Croatia and Slovenia, the status of women has decreased, and structural inequalities between men and women have become evident: women are discouraged in their attempts to improve their own status in society through work and career advancement; subsequently, opportunity-based entrepreneurship is not considered an option for women. These barriers to female entrepreneurship originate from the often prevailing attitude that a woman's place is in the home and that her first and foremost priority should be taking full responsibility for that home and her family.

Cross-country studies have provided empirical evidence for narrower gender differences in starting a new venture than in maintaining a business (Figure 3.1). However, a more pronounced gender gap in creating new ventures is revealed in high-income countries, whereas the smallest relative gender difference emerges in low-income countries. The implication is that in low-income and transition countries, everyone, regardless of gender, needs to make money. The economies are fluctuating and vulnerable, employment in the corporate market is limited, and thus people choose entrepreneurship out of necessity to escape unemployment and provide their families with food and shelter (Gatewood, Shaver, & Gartner, 1995;

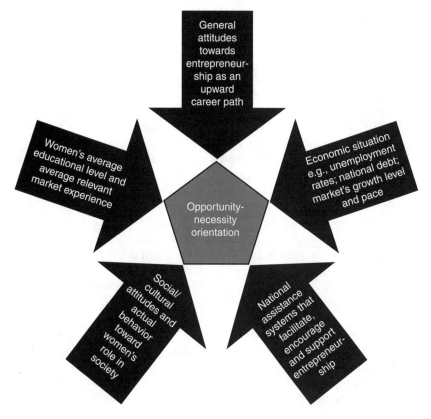

Figure 3.1 Necessity–Opportunity Demonstrations at the Country Level: The Case of Female Entrepreneurship.

Izyumov & Razumnova, 2000; Manolova, Manev, Carter, & Gyoshev, 2006; Reynolds, Bygrave, Autio, Cox, & Hay, 2002a; Shabbir & Gregorio, 1996; Shane, Kolvereid, & Westhead, 1991; Smallbone & Welter, 2001; Taniguchi, 2002).

Changes in transition countries at the macro level are emulated by changes in the attitudes, atmosphere, processes and dynamics of female entrepreneurship. Consequent changes in transition countries and emerging economies can also be presented as follows:[2]

• Limited or discriminatory national laws toward women in the labor market have changed in some countries to more permissive rules, and to the development of laws that consider women's specific needs, targeted to enhance women's participation in the labor market, entrepreneurship and technology.

- Prejudices against women and their ability to run businesses, which produce lower prospects for women-led businesses, are undergoing a transformation in several countries and a new atmosphere is emerging for women entrepreneurs, as reflected by women's presence in the media, academic institutions, government, etc.
- Biases against women's involvement in technical matters, which impede their self-track enrollment in technological programs and lead to discrimination in accepting women into them, are being changed in many transition countries, encouraging women's participation in such academic programs.
- Difficulties in providing women with security and stability in the labor market are being amended by implementation of new rules supporting women in various countries.
- Lack of credit for women entrepreneurs is being transformed into various means of support and sources of financial support for women-led businesses.
- The lack of development and provision of support systems for women entrepreneurs is being largely transformed: many governments are allocating resources to the development of programs to support, educate, train and mentor women entrepreneurs.
- The existence of few contacts in the bureaucracy and little access to policy makers or to representation on policymaking bodies, which have typified women in many countries in transition, is being studied with the aim of changing these conditions.
- Countries in transition have developed an acute awareness of the lack of access to information, which limits women's knowledgeable input into policy.
- Difficulties in, or lack of English-language skills, which are pertinent to both women and men: many countries are devoting time and money to advancing their population's proficiency in English.

(Acharya, 2001; Charumathi, 1998; Gillani, 2004;
Izyumov & Razumnova, 2000; Tominc & Rebernik, 2007;
Welter, Smallbone, Mirzakhalikova, Schakirova, &
Maksudova, 2006; Wennekers, & Thurik, 1999)

THE EMERGING BRIC MARKETS

BRIC—Brazil, Russia, India and China—has become a popular acronym as these countries are identified as emerging markets with growing power and influence in the global economy. A general snapshot of these four countries shows that they contain more than 25 percent of the world's land and more than 40 percent of its population, while accounting for about 15 percent of the world's economy and about 40 percent of global currency reserves; the BRIC countries are positioned, respectively, 8th,

10th, 11th and 2nd in the world in nominal GDP;[3] 5th, 7th, 2nd and 1st in the world in labor force;[4] 18th, 11th, 16th and 1st in the world in exports.[5] Thus, the BRIC countries clearly stand out in terms of both their economic and demographic sizes.

Predictions for the future of the BRIC economies are even better. The well-known Goldman-Sachs report:[6] "Dreaming with BRICs: the Path to 2050" (2003) asserted that over the next 50 years, the BRIC economies will become the largest force in the world economy; together, these four countries will be larger than the G6 in terms of US dollars; China could overtake Germany in the next four years, and India's economy could be larger than all but the US and China in 30 years; Russia will overtake Germany, France, Italy and the UK; the BRIC countries already have a bigger share of world trade than the US.

The BRIC's rapid economic growth in recent years has also been revealed in these economies' higher levels of entrepreneurial activity, especially in Brazil, India and China. These extreme economic and entrepreneurial, and consequently social and cultural, changes have affected the ecosystem in many ways, and academic institutions the world over are paying greater attention to the BRIC's entrepreneurial dynamics. For example, Babson College[7] launched a new Overseas BRIC Program, in which students explore the four biggest rising economies; in addition, the BRIC group has been established in LinkedIn;[8] websites for the trade of goods have been established for BRIC sellers and buyers;[9] more than 23,395 views have been registered on YouTube for "Empire—BRIC: The New World Order" on the BRIC summit;[10] investments are targeted to BRIC companies, among others.[11]

The emerging economies have been attracting entrepreneurial firms in partnerships, and multinational corporations as strategic alliance partners, with no regard as to whether they are owned and led by either men or women. Such transitions reflect a significantly improved understanding of entrepreneurship in the BRIC transition economies, be it those arising from a similar historical path of socialist command (China, former Soviet republics and Eastern European countries) or those originating from similar deprived economic conditions that were echoed in their institutional and social systems (India, Brazil).

Economic reforms and empowering policies have attracted enormous interest in these economies, which have been assessed as comprising "economic value." Such internal and external influences have promoted the release of people's entrepreneurial spirit and actions, which in turn has enabled a boom in private entrepreneurship. Women's role, i.e., as fully responsible for their families and household duties, and the normative restrictions women have tackled over the years, hindering their participation in the labor market, have been shattered. For example, in China, statistics show that since 1995, the number of women involved in private economy has risen by 60 percent; to date, 63 percent of enterprises are run by women entrepreneurs, and women's business ventures create opportunities for other women's employment (Lee & Peterson, 2000; Tan, 2008; Wong, 1988).

Nevertheless, there are voices criticizing the BRIC predictions—asserting that there are many uncertainties concerning the BRIC thesis on living up to their promise, and stressing that the economic emergence of BRICs will have unpredictable consequences for the global environment.[12]

THE EMERGING BRIC MARKETS AND THE FEMALE PERSPECTIVE

In most high-income countries, men are about twice as likely to be entrepreneurially active as women, whereas in the BRIC countries, the gender gap is narrower; overall, the levels of female new venture creation activity in the G7 and BRIC countries appear to have been static since 2002 (Brush, Carter, Gatewood, Greene, & Hart, 2006c; Domeisen, 2003; Levie & Hart, 2009; Minniti, 2009; Minniti, Allen, & Langowitz, 2005, 2006a).

Figure 3.2 illustrates the gender gap in three G7 countries, three BRIC countries and Israel, in the early and established stages of venture creation.

Despite the reforms in BRIC countries, the general attitudes toward female entrepreneurship are still hindering women's attraction to the entrepreneurial world. As compared to some more developed countries, e.g., the US, Canada, Western European countries and Israel, where

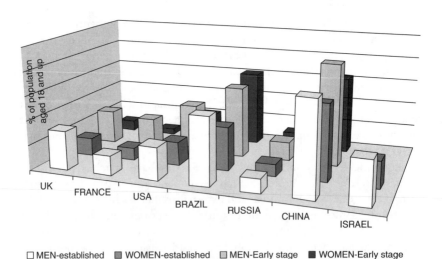

☐ MEN-established   ■ WOMEN-established   ☐ MEN-Early stage   ■ WOMEN-Early stage

Figure 3.2 BRIC vs. G7: Gender Participation in Entrepreneurial Activity.

Source: GEM 2009 APS; Levie & Hart, 2009; the Central Bureau of Statistics, Israel report 12.20

entrepreneurship is linked to more positive attitudes and considered a favorable, rewarding career path, BRIC countries are typified as boosting their economic activity and budding motivations to embrace the private sector, and therefore entrepreneurship, yet face difficulties in renouncing the normative-based and culture-related roles and responsibilities attributed to women in their respective countries. It appears that while policies are being developed specifically to foster female entrepreneurship, the widespread culture and norms in the BRIC countries are hindering these improvements (Aidis, Welter, Smallbone, & Isakova, 2006; Arbaugh, Camp, & Cox, 2005; Bhagat, Kedia, Harveston, & Triandis, 2002; Hofstede *et al.*, 2004).

In their paper in the *Harvard Business Review* (May, 2008),[13] Sylvia Ann Hewlett and Ripa Rashid discuss the talent shortage in emerging markets and the unique difficulties encountered by women in these markets, by tackling the traditional approach to woman's role in society and her consequent marginal role in the labor market. To become a talented labor force suited to global companies and to the fast-growing national businesses, the authors suggest developing the best-educated and best-prepared women managers in those markets. As increasing numbers of highly ambitious, educated women enter the BRIC professional workforce, their potential will become better recognized, thus providing them with the required opportunity to break through a very thick glass ceiling. Not all educated women can accomplish this: many well-educated women from BRIC countries are still embedded in their social traditions and endorse women's domestic-based role while neglecting their potential career path in the labor market. Entrepreneurship in such social environments is thus a comfortable way of maintaining a traditional role while developing a fulfilling career path.

Newsweek (July, 2010) published a column by Jessica Bennett and Jesse Ellison, "Women Will Rule the World,"[14] showing that well-educated women from BRIC countries constitute between 30 percent and 50 percent of BRIC workers as a whole, and in three of the four BRIC nations, female labor-force participation is on the rise from previous years. The authors believe that this trend will accelerate in the coming years, mainly due to women's ambition and aspiration to break into the labor market.

Engaging women from BRIC countries in entrepreneurship lies mainly in mentoring them to accomplish both the emotional aspect—reinforcing their belief in their own abilities to start and develop a business, and the practical aspect—training them simply and clearly, using tailor-made means, to start a business.

Support systems for women entrepreneurs in BRIC countries should focus on:

- Maintaining their traditions while starting a business.
- Mounting women's confidence in their own capabilities and skills.

- Stimulating and inspiring them through examples of successful female role models.
- Learning the basics of new venture creation, e.g., developing a new, yet feasible and relevant concept; planning the next practical steps in a mini business plan; establishing the business model, including answering the question: How will the business make money?, and segmenting potential clients, among others.
- Being less hesitant in asking for assistance at home while creating their new ventures, e.g., in taking care of the children, general household duties, and other domestic tasks.
- Understanding and recognizing the benefits of sharing, emotionally and practically, responsibilities, assignments, duties and reflections related to the business: sharing is time-efficient and more fun; it enables working in a less stressful and more relaxed environment and appreciating the benefits of brainstorming with partners and colleagues.
- Engaging F-F—family and friends—in different aspects of the business, and making their engagement beneficial for them as well. This will enable preserving a sense of family and community and minimizing the painful detachment from tradition and community.
- Successful women entrepreneurs should dedicate some time to mentoring nascent and novice women entrepreneurs from their environment.

THE MENA COUNTRIES

A different group of countries that have attracted attention for their economic development, including budding entrepreneurial activity and its prospective value—consists of the countries of the Middle East (except Israel) and North Africa—termed MENA. This economically diverse region includes both the oil-rich economies in the Gulf and countries with scarce resources relative to population size, such as Egypt, Morocco, and Yemen. MENA mainly addresses the following countries: Algeria, Bahrain, Egypt, Iran, Iraq, Jordan, Kuwait, Lebanon, Libya, Malta, Morocco, Saudi Arabia, Syria, Tunisia, United Arab Emirates, The Palestinian Authority and Yemen.

According to the GEM-MENA (2009)[15] and World Bank[16] reports, both women and men in MENA countries are becoming more and more entrepreneurially active. However, delving into the statistics, the gender gap in the new venture creation phase is more pronounced in Syria and Palestine, less so in Yemen and Algeria. Statistics on the MENA countries show that the general entrepreneurial population is less educated than in the BRIC and developed countries. More educated groups and those in higher-income households are found in early-stage entrepreneurial activity, while involvement at these stages is about equally likely in urban and rural areas. About a quarter of the entrepreneurial activity is necessity-driven, especially in Palestine, Syria, and Yemen, while a prevalence of opportunity-driven entrepreneurship is found in Algeria and Lebanon.

Data show that millions of new ventures have been or are in the process of being established in MENA countries, mainly in the consumer-oriented sector (retail, hospitality, personal and social services). In some MENA countries, a relatively high proportion of businesses are observed in the extractive sectors (farming, fishing, mining); in others, they are found in the transforming sectors (manufacturing, construction, distribution). The vast majority of new ventures led by women or men represent an adaptive rather than innovative form of entrepreneurship in terms of products, services, technology or business concept. Thus, when penetrating their respective markets, they face many competitors. MENA entrepreneurial businesses are mainly micro-enterprises. They are locally restricted, although they are in the process of developing collaborations outside the country. The World Bank projects that as developing countries reach full capacity, growth will slow from 7.3 percent in 2010 to around 6.3 percent annually from 2011 to 2013. High-income countries will see growth slow from 2.7 percent in 2010 to 2.2 percent in 2011, before picking up again to 2.7 percent and 2.6 percent in 2012 and 2013, respectively (GEM-MENA, 2009[17]; Lagoarde-Segot & Lucey, 2005; World Bank report[18]).

WOMEN'S ENTREPRENEURIAL PERSPECTIVE

The MENA region is undergoing a demographic transition characterized by a rising proportion of young people in the population. According to the World Bank (2010) and GEM-MENA (2009) reports, women in the MENA region are more likely than men to attend university, yet face a considerable unemployment challenge.

The gender gap in entrepreneurial activity in MENA countries is one of the highest in all GEM countries: women encounter very limited entrepreneurial opportunities. In fact, MENA countries have a lower participation of women than the low-income countries in Asia, Latin America, and the Caribbean according to GEM and World Bank reports. Research explains this lower female participation in entrepreneurship by cultural and social factors regarding women's role and status in MENA countries, e.g., women's lower participation in the general labor market, the lower levels of education and job experience that impede their ability, self-confidence and resources to create new ventures, and the general attitudes toward women's role in society and family, which again limit women's motivations to create new ventures.

Improved access to entrepreneurial training and finance, particularly for young women and those in rural areas, is imperative: enhancing women's participation in entrepreneurship is of prime interest for improving national welfare, because establishment of businesses not only generates income for women's families, but also creates jobs for men and women alike.

Different perceptions and attitudes toward entrepreneurship prevail in MENA countries. Most women do foresee the benefits of creating new ventures yet are reluctant to implement their desire to become entrepreneurs due to lower self-confidence in their abilities to start a business, including lack of knowledge, skills and experience. In addition, they report a high fear of failure.

MENA women's lower involvement in social networks, as well as their tendency to use limited external assistance for their entrepreneurial undertakings, places them at a disadvantage in entrepreneurship. The recent (2010–2011) protests and revolutions in the Arab world have raised political and social challenges that affect many Arab countries, and have transformed the area into a turbulent economic environment.[19] Such conditions also have a major effect on MENA female entrepreneurship.

Increasing the awareness of women's conditions, while emphasizing the benefits of female entrepreneurship for the country's well-being, is crucial. Changes in the perceptions of women's role in society should be complemented by the development of support systems to facilitate financing of women-led businesses, assist the businesses with developing international collaborations as well as mitigating poverty by encouraging women to create new ventures (IFC-GEM 2005a, 2005b, 2005c, 2005d, 2005e, 2005f, 2005g; IFC-GEM, 2006a, 2006b, 2006c; IFC-GEM,2007a, 2007b, 2007c).[20]

SUMMARY

The economic, social, political and cultural changes affecting countries in transition and emerging markets have set new challenges for these countries' respective economies. The impact of these changes on female entrepreneurship is even more pronounced. Female entrepreneurship is vulnerable due to women's relatively lower participation in early-stage entrepreneurial activities, their limited relevant experience in entrepreneurship, and attitudes toward women's role and status in society. The cultural implementation of the improvements and developments which have occurred during the transitional period is not yet complete, and therefore not yet reflected in women's involvement in the new venture creation process. In different BRIC and MENA countries, women are still at a disadvantage, facing hurdles to engaging in entrepreneurship due to perceptions regarding their main role as responsible for home and family, and their lack of confidence in their ability to become successful entrepreneurs.

This chapter illustrates the reciprocated effects of the ecosystem and the environmental stages of development in molding women's involvement in the new venture creation process. The BRIC countries represent emerging economies which are expected, according to the world's foremost economists, to accelerate and grow; their women are still necessity-driven entrepreneurs, but well-educated women are starting to develop into opportunity-driven entrepreneurs. In MENA countries on the other hand, women are still reluctant to start businesses, but their changing attitudes toward entrepreneurship are promising. The premise of this chapter lies in revealing the successful entrepreneurial experiences of women entrepreneurs in emerging economies and countries in transition, to foster entrepreneurship among other women.

CASE STUDIES[21]

In the following, inspiring journeys of women from BRIC countries are thoughtfully conveyed, sketching their venture creation process in the context of their unique, transitional ecosystems.

Wenxian Zhang and Ilan Alon introduce three case studies of women entrepreneurs from China: the story of Shi Xiaoyang who, upon graduating from nursing school in Beijing, paved her way to the entrepreneurial world; Yu Yu, the co-founder of China's largest online retailer and the world's leading online seller of Chinese language books, movies and music, and Zhang Yin, the chairperson of China's Nine Dragons Paper, the wealthiest self-made woman in the world. The Chinese culture is entwined in these case studies and provides a solid basis for understanding these women's challenges along the roads to their current achievements. Tatiana Iakovleva, Jill Kickul and Lisa Gundry contribute the case study of Marina Kretova from Russia who founded Deonis, which is now registered as a Limited Liability Company. By carefully and captivatingly drawing a picture of the turbulent entrepreneurial environment in Russia, the authors take the readers on Kretova's exciting journey from Bryansk, Russia, educated as a catering engineer but with high motivation and determination, to a most successful entrepreneur. Meenaz Kassam, Bhagyashree Ranade and Femida Handy introduce the readers to the Indian realm with the story of Manisha Gupte, co-founder of MASUM, a successful rural women's NGO that focuses on sustainable development. The special challenges of Indian women entrepreneurs are sensitively introduced, giving the readers a deep acquaintance with the context of MASUM. Finally, from Brazil, Maria Salete Batista Freitag and Cândido Borges contribute the case study of Wanusa, a social entrepreneur who founded an association of recyclable material collectors in the city of Goiania, taking us from opportunity exploitation through the challenges she tackled in the unique Brazilian culture.

CHINA

The Rise of Select Female Entrepreneurs in the Economic Reformation

Wenxian Zhang[a], Ilan Alon[a] and Shirley Ze Yu[b]
[a]*Rollins China Center, Rollins College, Winter Park, Florida, USA;*
[b]*China Central Television*

Shi, Xiaoyang (史晓燕 1962–)

Shi Xiaoyang is the CEO of the Beijing-based Illinois Investment Company Limited, a furniture company targeting on middle-class, white-collar workers. In seven years, Shi has made a huge leap forward in her life: from a nurse in a Beijing hospital to a student studying abroad, from a housewife to a millionaire and the boss of a famous furniture company, and from owning a small shop to running a large auto theme park. With personal assets amounting to US$160 million, she was ranked in 2006 by *Hurun Report* as number 32 among the richest Chinese retailers and 21 of the richest women in China.

After she graduated from a nursing school in Beijing, Shi first worked as a nurse at the Beijing Union Medical College Hospital. However, she not only was frustrated by the tedious and boring nature of her assignment, but also could not bear her low monthly salary of RMB70 yuan while struggling to make a living in the Chinese capital. Being a woman who could not be content with a stable life, Shi job-hopped to a foreign company in 1984, although at that time changing careers was quite unimaginable in China. Working for the new company, she did not even know how to use a typewriter or a computer. But as a smart, capable, and quick-minded individual, she still won the appreciation of her employer. Later Shi reflected upon this experience: "even today I am not really able to use the computer. What I am interested in is dealing with people. That is my principle: I will do what I can and I won't bother to do what I am not skilled at."

After marriage, she was still not satisfied to be a housewife. A trip abroad inspired her to enter into the furniture industry. In 1989, her husband moved to Singapore to work in the headquarters of an IT company. There she realized that personal values are usually embodied in ones' lifestyles, and noticed the delicate design of furniture and other household appliances in developed countries. Therefore she decided to major in interior design at the University of Chicago, while keeping eyes on both the international fashion trends and China's economic development. From 1993 to 1994, she studied high-quality materials, brands and design concepts, which provided a solid foundation for her future career success. "Almost all my lessons in the U.S. were taught in museums, instead of the classrooms with boring theories," Shi noted, "for example, I learnt most of the knowledge about the wooden veneer from a veneer processing manufacturer. So I know about wooden skin products and ways they combine together." Even today, Shi still spends a lot of time visiting museums and art exhibitions to seek inspiration.

Realizing the huge potential of the domestic furniture industry, Shi returned to China in the mid-1990s to begin a new career in the field. After losing US\$3 million and a few other setbacks, she, together with her husband, established a small furniture factory and imitated the design and style of foreign brands as well as importing actual foreign products. Because of the low price and novel style, her Illinois brand was gradually accepted by customers in Beijing. Yet this strategy of copying western designs did not last long, and Shi started to think about setting up her own furniture design shop. Since 2000, after researching the international furniture market, she defined and developed Illinois' unique style—new classic, postmodernism. This soon became a real hit, which attracted not only Chinese customers, but also interest from abroad. Shi often says, "Style keeps changing and I never stop working." Whenever she encounters difficulties, she is able to find a solution. She always brings her camera to every exhibition, and takes pictures of whatever she likes. She continues to travel abroad monthly to keep up with the latest trends, and invites top designers around the world to design in her studio. Her insight into the market and sense of aesthetics enables her company to stay at the cutting edge of furniture design.

Shi never stops expanding her business. In addition to the 10,000 sq m furniture outlet and her own product lines, Illinois is also an agent for many famous brands, including Giorgetti from Italy, Rolf Benz from Germany, and Roche Bobois from France. Apart from running a furniture company, Shi has also established China's first auto theme park located near Beijing Capital International Airport. With an investment of over 50 million yuan, it is the only one of its kind in Northern China, where people can purchase automobiles and participate in auto racing and other related activities. Looking forward, Shi has even more ambitious plans of building shopping malls, hotels and golf courses in the surrounding area.

Case References

Hurun Report (2006) 2006 Richest Women in China List, *Hurun Report*, December, http://www.hurun.net/detailcn57,people36.aspx

Women of China (2007) Shi Xiaoyang: from a Nurse to a Billionaire. *Women of China*, 3 December, http://www.womenofchina.cn/Profiles/Businesswomen/200571.jsp

Lujin Huang
East China University of Science & Technology

Yu, Yu (俞渝 1965–)

Also known as Peggy Yu, Yu Yu is the co-founder and co-president of Dangdang.com along with her husband Li Guoqing. Founded in 1999, Dangdang is China's largest online retailer and the world's leading online seller of Chinese language books, movies and music. As one of the best-known "sea turtles" (*Hai Gui*, students with overseas education who return to China; see China Today, 2004) today, Yu Yu came back to China in 1998 after eleven years in the U.S. to start Dangdang.com, a successful online bookstore dubbed as the Amazon.com of China (New York Times, 2005).

Born in 1965 in Chongqing, China, Yu Yu received her bachelor's degree in English literature from Beijing Foreign Studies University in 1986. She first worked as an interpreter and secretary for a joint venture in Beijing, and then went to the U.S. to pursue graduate studies a year later. As a starry-eyed 22-year-old, Yu first enrolled at the University of Oregon, but found the courses uninteresting, so she went to New York University instead, and received her MBA degree in 1992. From there she began her adventure in Wall Street by working five years for Tripod, a consulting firm specializing in mergers and acquisitions and providing an advisory service to corporate clients.

In the mid-1990s, while engaging financing on Wall Street, Yu was fascinated by the monumental success of online bookstore Amazon.com. At that time she conceptualized the idea of a similar e-commerce web site for China. However, upon returning to China she found the country had only a tiny community of Internet users, and there was no comprehensive, up-to-date database on books in print in China, an essential for establishment for an online bookstore. Yu was not disturbed. As an experienced financial professional, she knew well that there was great potential for an online bookstore in the near future, and she and her partners began to build a large database of books in China, a tedious undertaking that required both money and time. So Yu began to find foreign investment partners. Soon Boston-based International Data Group and Luxembourg Cambridge Holding Group became the main investors, holding the majority of equity stakes in the newly formed Beijing Science and Culture Book Information Corporation. This large database, finished in three years, laid the foundation for Yu's future online bookstore.

While the database construction was under way, the Internet community in China was growing at a dizzying speed and by late 1999 the country had over 8.9 million Internet users. So in that year she and her husband founded their Chinese bookstore Dangdang, which quickly became China's leading online destination for retail shopping and has recorded significant growth in a few years. Yu personally named the store for cultural and business-savvy reasons. "A good company name should combine cultural cohesiveness and auspiciousness," she noted, "Dangdang can be read smoothly in any dialect" (China Today, 2004).

Managing an online bookstore in China was not an easy job. Since Chinese people lack meaningful online experience, Yu had to change not only customer purchasing habits but also the attitude of her employees. Moreover, she has had to struggle with consumers' hesitance about online shopping, inhibiting credit card regulations and an ineffectual delivery system. Despite all those drawbacks, Dangdang's business has grown steadily. Within several years, Dangdang grew into the largest Chinese Internet bookstore in the world. By 2005, the company aggressively transitioned itself from an online bookstore to a mass merchandiser featuring everything from digital products to cosmetics. The success of Dangdang was truly remarkable, as noted by the chief of China's Press and Publication Administration, "it's tremendous help in accelerating the development of China's book industry in the new millennium makes Dangdang the bellwether for China's e-commerce" (China Today, 2004).

Case References

Businesswomen (2007) Peggy Yu: the Clang of Dangdang.com, *Businesswomen*, February 5.
China Daily (2005) A Woman-Created E-Commerce Legend, *China Daily*, May 18.
China Today (2004) The Return of China's "Sea-turtles," *China Today*, May, retrieved from http://www.chinatoday.com.cn/English/e2004/e200405/p24.htm
New York Times (2003) Leaping Forward Online, with Amazon as Her Guide, *New York Times*, October 25.
TMCnet.com (2006) Dangdang Closes US$27 Million Round Led by DCM, *TMCnet.com*, July 6.

Michael Moodian
Chapman University

Zhang, Yin (Cheung, Yan 张茵 1958–)

Chairperson of China's Nine Dragons Paper, Zhang Yin is regarded by many sources as China's wealthiest person, and the wealthiest self-made woman in the world (surpassing Oprah Winfrey of the United States and J.K. Rowling of the United Kingdom). Meanwhile, Nine Dragons is currently on pace to be China's number one producer of packaged paper. Her fortune had grown to $3.4 billion in 2006. The company's current client list includes various multinational companies such as Sony, Coca-Cola, and Nike. She is considered a pioneer among female leaders, breaking gender barriers in communist China and leading a very successful business from the start-up phase to immense growth.

Zhang was born the oldest of eight siblings in the Guangdong Province. Her father was a military officer who was jailed for multiple years for practicing capitalism during China's Cultural Revolution. Upon reaching adulthood, she relocated to Shenzhen in the 1980s, accepted a job as a finance associate with a paper-products company, and developed a keen interest in the industry. Additionally, she realized the enormous potential in market size if she were to embark on her own and enter the recycling sector. Based in Hong Kong with only $4,000 in savings, she started Nine Dragons, a company that buys scrap paper from the United States and reproduces the commodity for use in China. Upon growing Nine Dragons as a major Chinese corporation, her goal was then to grow the company and its brand equity globally. In building the company from the initial start-up phase, Zhang endured numerous financial difficulties, unethical practices from unstable business partners, and intimidating acts by local organized mafia organizations. She would persevere through this by moving to the United States to build her empire and establish herself as a tycoon in the waste paper and paper recycling industry. To date, she has retained nearly 75% of an equity stake in the company that she founded. Her husband, Ming Chung Liu, currently helps run the company as a senior executive.

The success of the company has springboarded Zhang to a number one ranking in the *Hurun Report* of the richest person in China. Before the first announcement of her standing in the *Hurun Report* in 2003, Zhang kept a low profile and surprised many when her net worth was publicized within the Chinese business world. It is reported that Zhang attempted to communicate with the group that releases the report, requesting that her name not be included on the list. The share value of Nine Dragons has nearly tripled since they were initially introduced on the Hong Kong Stock Exchange. When she earned the number one ranking she surpassed Huang Guangyu, the retail mogul of Gome Electrical Supplies. She is one of 35 women in the 500-person *Hurun Report*. What is perhaps most noteworthy is that she has succeeded as an entrepreneur in an economic and political system that is heavily skewed toward male dominance, and features a business system in which several male-dominated networks control the flow of commerce within the country.

Zhang currently resides in Los Angeles, CA, USA, and is a member of a political advisory body in China.

Questions for Discussion

1   Research shows that most BRIC women do not embark on entrepreneurship. The women described in this case study are not just entrepreneurs, they are successful entrepreneurs. Which main factors enabled these women to (a) become entrepreneurs, and (b) succeed as entrepreneurs in their ecosystems? Explain.

2   Address the cultural, traditional and social aspects of the ecosystem. Explain the effects of the ecosystem on the difficulties encountered by the female entrepreneurs described in this case study.
3   Address relevant education and prior experiences of the ecosystem in China. Explain the effects of these parameters on the difficulties encountered by the female entrepreneurs described in the case study.
4   What main advantages in their respective ecosystems do these women benefit from? Do they leverage these advantages? If so, how?
5   Which support systems from those discussed in the chapter fit the difficulties and challenges illustrated in this case study? Explain your choices.
6   Choose one of the described cases and advise the entrepreneur on how to promote her business to a sustainable and successful one. Explain.

Case References

BBC News (2006) Woman Tops China's New Rich List, *BBC News*, online at http://news.bbc.co.uk/2/hi/business/6039296.stm, October 11.
China Daily (2006) Woman Tops List of China's Richest, *China Daily*, online at http://www.chinadaily.com.cn/china/2006-10/11/content_705535.htm, October 11.
Flannery, R. (2006) Dragon Lady, www.forbes.com, November 13.
Hurun Report (2003) www.hurun.net.
Terra Daily (2007) Cheung Yan: Dragon Queen of Waste Paper, *Terra Daily*, online at http://www.terradaily.com/reports/Cheung_Yan_Dragon_queen_of_waste_paper_999.html, September 23 .
Watts, Jonathan (2006) Worth $3.4 billion, Ms. Cheung is Richest in China, online at http://www.guardian.co.uk/world/2006/oct/12/china.jonathanwatts, October 12.

RUSSIA

Marina Kretova and Deonis: Entrepreneurial Growth in the Russian Context

Tatiana Iakovleva[a], Jill R. Kickul[b] and Lisa K. Gundry[c]
[a]*Stavanger University, Stavanger School of Business, Stavanger, Norway;*
[b]*Stewart Satter Program in Social Entrepreneurship, Berkley Center for Entrepreneurship & Innovation, NYU Stern School of Business, New York, USA;*
[c]*Center for Creativity and Innovation, DePaul University, Chicago, Illinois, USA*

Introduction: Entrepreneurship in Russia

At one time, Russia was the largest country in the former Soviet Union. Today, the Russian Federation is still an important player in the world economy, with its rich natural resources and population of 150 million people. The concept of "entrepreneurship" emerged in Russia in 1989 when the law concerning entrepreneurial activities was passed. The "Perestroika" period was associated with a reconstruction of the economy and the collapse of the Soviet Union. During this period, self-employment was often necessary for many people, and thus numerous small, privately-owned businesses were started.

However, Russian entrepreneurial activity is relatively low in comparison to many other countries (Verkhovskaya *et al.*, 2007). As we discuss below, this is partly explained by the challenging operating environment for entrepreneurs and small businesses that is characterized by extensive bureaucracy, corruption, weakly developed financial markets, and lack of state support mechanisms for nascent entrepreneurs (Iakovleva, 2001; Karhunen *et al.*, 2008; Verkhovskaya *et al.*, 2007). Moreover, the Russian entrepreneurial culture is young and entrepreneurial attitudes of many older Russians are still influenced by the Soviet past, where private enterprise activity was considered immoral and even a criminal activity.

Nevertheless, this turbulent environment did create new opportunities for emerging organizations. Women entrepreneurs constitute only one third of all start-ups in Russia, which is similar to the trends observed in other countries (Kickul *et al.*, 2010). At the same time, women typically enter service and trade industries and also prefer to establish their businesses as individual entrepreneurs rather than other types of enterprises, which can be partly explained by the more complicated accounting system for other enterprise forms in Russia. While earlier studies of female Russian entrepreneurs depicted a stark contrast between them and their US counterparts with respect to their major issues of concern (Babaeva, 1998), recent research suggests that the goals and concerns of women entrepreneurs across cultures may be more alike than dissimilar. For example, the Wells *et al.* (2003) study of over 500 Russian women business owners reported that growth and expansion were their most important business goals. Their research indicated they were pursuing innovative strategic practices and import/export initiatives at a rate that exceeded their American counterparts. This is in line with recent findings on female entrepreneurship in other post-Soviet economies (Welter & Smallbone, 2008).

Russian women generally have a high level of education and many possess more than one degree from institutions of higher education. This factor, combined with their responsibility, their patience in running their businesses and their ability to establish relationships, leads to higher levels of employment and income generation in women-owned companies. The present case represents many of these similar characteristics and behaviors of today's Russian woman entrepreneur.

Evolution of the Business Idea

Marina Kretova was born and raised in Bryansk, Russia. She was educated as a catering engineer. When she completed her studies in the College of Commerce, she worked as Head of Production in the canteen. Her perseverance and hard work were noticed and soon she was appointed as a head of the canteen. In 1989, Marina moved to Lyudinovo, her husband's home city. She naturally wanted to get a job in catering. The country soon was in the midst of restructuring. After Perestroika, for the first time entrepreneurial activities were officially allowed. Everywhere there were cooperatives, and private enterprises starting up. The Director of one of these, a café, was pleased to accept Marina's expertise based on her positive recommendation from her previous work. Marina recalls:

> I wanted to get a job as head of the catering department of a public company. They told me, "we would love to give you a job but our enterprise is for sale now, due to the privatization process. Why don't you start a small café?" So I invested my money and we established one here on Fukin Street. We called it "Pelmeni" because we served dumplings (pelmeni) in the café, which is a Russian version of Italian ravioli, filled with meat, in addition to a variety of confectionery products. I had no choice but to start this business, since I needed to work. I had two small children, so I bought the café and began to work. As time went on, I bought the land and began construction on the site.
>
> (Interview, 2011)

Marina's husband joined the business later, after his factory job was lost. With the assistance of Fund Microloans, Kretova's family began opening mini-bistros in different stores. This was a completely new service for the residents of Lyudinovo, and it proved to be very popular. As the concept grew, from focusing on mini-bistros they gradually began opening fully-fledged cafés. By 2002, Kretova's business had expanded to a network of eight cafés.

Emergence and Growth of the Deonis Complex

Before long, Marina was finding it difficult to manage the many cafés. That is when the idea arose to build a restaurant complex. She took the bold step of selling the entire network of cafés in order to get the necessary funding to invest in the new project. Maria and her husband completely renovated an old building and opened a modern restaurant complex, Deonis ("Dionysus"), and opened its doors to customers in 2004. Overseeing the construction of the complex was quite challenging, and Maria believes that it was particularly difficult since she was a woman dealing with primarily male construction owners and employees. As Marina recounts,

Being a woman is generally difficult in business here. During construction, there were so many problems, and the work was typically not exactly what I asked for. I felt they thought I would accept anything. As an example, during inspections I was working with men who were physically much bigger than I am, and it was clear to me that they did not take me seriously. But I'm so persistent, and I'm not sure how many women there are here who are this way. You need perseverance to achieve. You might be pushed away, but then you need to come back again tomorrow, knock again on a closed door until it opens.

I do have women entrepreneur friends, including one in the construction business, as well as others, mostly younger women, in small businesses who are quite successful. I sometimes need to have heart-to-heart talks with them, to complain, and to share.

(Interview, 2011)

Maria is continually looking for business development opportunities. As she describes:

Because I have so much experience in the catering industry, I view myself as an engineer technologist in catering. I looked at my restaurant business, for example, after it was open and starting to grow, and I noticed that it was not enough to stop there, with just the restaurant. I felt that youth have different tastes, and may not like the music we have in the restaurant. They want something else, so I came up with the idea of a discotheque.

If I do not like something I can close it, and open something else in the same place. Perhaps it doesn't meet consumers' taste, or my own. My soul doesn't rest. One example is slot machines. They were eventually forbidden in many places. I didn't like them, and despite the fact that I was offered significant funds to install them, I refused. I didn't have to engage in that type of business that was often perceived as unfair in Russia. I always had an "open" business, a solid business.

(Interview, 2011)

In 2006, when the city of Lyudinovo celebrated its 380th year, Marina opened her new "Yard of Dionysus," which brings together family recreation and entertainment in one complex. Marina made the sketches and layouts herself. The complex is built of timber, provides feelings of safety and warmth, and an aroma of the forest. The complex has a unique style, decorated with Russian wood patterns on the exterior and a modern design inside, with stage and dance hall. The dance hall is used as a playground for children during the daytime, with different attractions inside, such as a laser shooting area, and trampoline. In the evening the dance floor becomes a room for youth activities. This is the first entertainment complex in the city and it entertains both adults and children.

The complex was a large undertaking, both strategically and financially. One of the obstacles for women entrepreneurs can be access to financing. During the economic crisis, Marina had to take on a bank loan. While there is a Women's Microfinance Network in Russia, Marina believes the funding available is small and more suited to minimal needs for business. In most banks, loans are available, but the interest rate is extremely high. As an example, the interest rate for the loan that Marina took on during the financial crisis a year ago is about 24 percent per year. In part, this is why Marina is now selling the first floor of the retail/office center to Magnet, a business in Russia that sells food and household goods. Marina views this as a positive step, since she has so much to do managing the restaurant and entertainment complex.

Deonis has been very successful. It has grown into a family business with both of Maria's daughters joining the business after completing their schooling. They chose to work with their mother rather than accept disadvantageous conditions as legal professionals, including low pay and lack of support. Marina believes this is one reason why entrepreneurship is so attractive in Russia. She cites the example of a specialist in history who earns only $100 (2,000–3,000 rubles) per month. She notes that there is risk for women who do decide on a path of entrepreneurship while they are raising children, as she did when her children were small. There is risk either way, she notes; it is up to the individual woman which path she chooses. With both daughters planning to continue in the business, she plans to pass the business to her daughters in about ten years.

Residents of the city frequent the Deonis restaurant for dinner and for business meetings. Special events such as weddings or anniversaries must be booked four to five months in advance. Quality is very important to Marina, and locating fresh, high-quality ingredients is central to the business. There are primarily women employees in the business, since there are more women than men in the region. Marina notes that men are moving elsewhere for employment opportunities, including Moscow. She explains, "Entrepreneurs are attempting to change the cultural scene and create opportunities for young people so they don't leave the city."

As the business grows, it has become a champion in reducing the level of unemployment in the Kaluga region. Maria provides charitable assistance for many of the groups in the city, including police officers, school children, and others. "I always find a bowl of soup and a kind word for those in need," she says. In winter, she plans to set up a skating rink with music and video effects—an idea she hopes will delight the residents.

In 2006, Marina Kretova was awarded the Russian Prize for Microenterprises, recognizing the best individual entrepreneur among trade enterprises. She was among four winners recognized in the competition. Women represent a minority of Russian entrepreneurial businesses, and, as Marina encourages, "We could have many more women in business. I would advise them not to give up."

Questions for Discussion

1   As a woman entrepreneur, what "entrepreneurial" qualities have made Marina Kretova so successful?
2   What do you believe were some of the unique challenges encountered by Marina as she created and developed her business?
3   Following through on question #2, consider the Russian context and the environment that supports or creates barriers to entrepreneurship.
4   What do you believe motivated Marina to grow and scale her business, the Deonis Complex?
5   Marina says that "Entrepreneurs are attempting to change the cultural scene and create opportunities for young people so they don't leave the city." What incentives should a region offer to promote and support entrepreneurship? What more can be done to stimulate growth for women entrepreneurs?

Sources

Interview with Marina Kretova, conducted and translated by Tatiana Iakovleva, April 2011.
Success stories, issued by Russian Women Microfinancial Network, 2006.
Results of the competitions "Russian Microentrepreneurship Awards with the support of Citigroup Microentrepreneurship" 2006 in *Questions of credit cooperation*, launched on 25.02.2010 from http://www.credit-union. ru/magazine_nc/48.html (in Russian), (2006) No 4 (18).

Case References

Babaeva, L. (1998). Russian and American female entrepreneurs, Rossiskie I Americanskie genshini predprinimatelnici, *Sociological Review* (*Социологические исследования*, Sociologicheskie issledovania), 8, 134–135.
Iakovleva, T. (2001). *Entrepreneurship framework conditions in Russia and in Norway: Implications for the entrepreneurs in the agrarian sector.* Hovedfagsoppgaven, Norway: Bode Graduate School of Business.
Karhunen, P., Kettunen, E. Sivonen, T., & Miettinen, V. (2008). Determinants of knowledge-intensive entrepreneurship in Southeast Finland and Northwest Russia. *Helsinki School of Economics*, Mikkeli Business Campus Publications N-77.
Kickul, J., Griffith, M., Gundry, L., & Iakovleva, T. (2010). Mentoring women entrepreneurs in the Russian emerging market. In Brush, C., Bruin, A., Gatewood, E., & Henry, C. (Eds.), *Women entrepreneurs and the global environment for growth: A research perspective.* Cheltenham, UK, Northampton, MA, USA, Edward Elgar, pp. 303–322.

Verkhovskaya, O.R., Dermanov, V.K. Dorohina, M.V., & Katkalo, V.S. (2007). Globalnyi monitoring predprinimatelstva (Global Entrepreneurship Monitoring), Country Report on Russia 2006, St Petersburg State University, Higher School of Management (in Russian).

Wells, B.L., Pfantz, T.J., & Bryne, J.L. (2003). Russian women business owners: evidence of entrepreneurship in a transition economy. *Journal of Developmental Entrepreneurship*, 8 (1), 59–71.

Welter, F. & Smallbone, D. (2008). Women entrepreneurship from an institutional perspective; the case of Uzbekistan. *International Entrepreneurship and Management Journal*, 4, 505–520.

INDIA

The Profits of Non-Profits: Women Entrepreneurship of NGOs

Meenaz Kassam[a], Bhagyashree Ranade[b] and Femida Handy[c]

[a]*Department of International Studies, American University of Sharjah, American University of Sharjah, Sharjah, United Arab Emirates;* [b]*The Institute for Women Entrepreneurial Development in Pune, India;* [c]*School of Social Policy & Practice, University of Pennsylvania, Philadelphia PA, USA*

The BRIC Thesis posits that emerging economies, namely India, China, Brazil and Russia, have a leading role to play in economic growth in the 21st century. Currently in a transitioning phase, these societies are undertaking domestic and political reforms to sustain economic growth and replace failed interventionist government policies. In India, along with the public and private sectors, nongovernmental organizations (NGOs) have become major partners in the development process. More than a million NGOs, covering all development sectors, are currently operating in India (Manerkar, 2010: 64). Moreover, women are increasingly being involved in non-profit organizations both as volunteers and founders. Participation in the NGOs has given many middle-class and affluent and well-educated women the opportunity to enter social and political spheres in a socially sanctioned manner, develop leadership and organizational skills as well as obtain personal fulfillment while partnering in the development process (Handy *et al.*, 2006). It is important to understand these women entrepreneurs who have impacted the society around them and brought about meaningful change.

Here, we examine the precedent set by non-profit entrepreneurs like Manisha Gupte. Manisha co-founded Mahila Sarvangeen Utkarsh Mandal (MASUM), a successful rural women's NGO that focuses on sustainable development. MASUM's community level involvement is primarily with rural women in the perennially drought-prone areas of Pune, Maharashtra. Streamlining women's access to health, confronting violence against women, developing economic resources, working with youth and children on issues of gender, caste discrimination, equality and peaceful co-existence are some activities undertaken by MASUM. Increasing participation of women in politics, both as elected representatives and as empowered citizens, and strengthening child rights through village-based children's councils are issues rapidly gaining attention. All programs run by MASUM are interconnected to ensure that the impact is optimized.

Manisha Gupte has a post-graduate degree in microbiology and hails from a middle-income family. She has been inspired by her parents, both of them social democrats, freedom fighters and trade unionists, to pursue a career in non-profit entrepreneurship. Like other entrepreneurs, Manisha admits to being a risk taker who enjoys finding innovative ways to manage her enterprise. Working in an emerging economy where many still do not have basic necessities to support a comfortable life, she is motivated to fulfill this need rather than to pursue profit. She is a feminist and an egalitarian who encourages collective management and grass roots participation.

While she was growing up, however, Manisha had not planned her current lifestyle. She took up the natural sciences, a field traditionally taken up by all academically high-achieving students. As she recalls, much of what she had done was "mindless, oblivious of social issues and so typical of middle class children's lives." She would have "stayed on this conveyor belt of existence: going on to doctoral work, taking up a job and treading the usual comfortable path, until the day when one dropped off the belt and could do no more." However, political events intervened and gave Manisha, then a teenager, the opportunity to pause and think. As her short biography puts it, ". . . her involvement with India's budding feminist movement, forced a choice between the laboratory and life outside it." "In the laboratory, the whole world seemed to be under the microscope. But when I got involved in the women's movement, focusing only on the microscope seemed so inadequate. I loved microbiology but I had to choose what my heart told me" (Shetty, 2010: 1,215).

In 1975 when Indira Gandhi was the Prime Minister of India she imposed an Internal Emergency Rule in an undemocratic manner and clamped down on the civil liberties that Manisha's parents had earlier fought to establish. The political events caught Manisha's attention. Manisha was pursuing her undergraduate science degree at the time. She became sensitive toward the injustices and inequalities. Although the seeds of social action existed in the family for two generations—her grandfather and father's siblings also having been freedom fighters—Manisha felt that she was sort of "born again" during the 19-month long Emergency Rule. It was then that she fervently turned toward making right the wrongs in her country. However, she knew she could not do it alone. With her parents' blessing, she joined a progressive youth group that was committed to bringing about social change by promoting grassroots democracy. She remembers vividly the large anti-Emergency rallies that were held amidst police threats. Ramesh, her future husband who was then doing his doctoral work, was a speaker at one of these rallies.

When the Emergency Rule ended in 1977, Manisha and Ramesh remained committed to social change. They began working in the Mumbai slums, fighting against demolitions and setting up local democratic structures for local-level decision-making. After getting married in 1982, they lived in a rather dilapidated one room tenement. They both joined the Foundation for Research in Community Health (FRCH) in Mumbai. They researched and wrote about rural health services and the creation of poverty.

As India progressed economically, Manisha became aware that the for-profit health sector was growing at the cost of the public sector. She believed that the State was abdicating its responsibilities and the poor were left to fend for themselves. At this time, nongovernmental organizations were sprouting up to fill the gap and offer basic services to the very poor. However, very few were involved in making the State fulfill its obligations of making health care a fundamental right in India. Manisha and Ramesh, having chosen to fight for health care, wrote a proposal to the Indian Council of Medical Research for strengthening health education at the grassroots. In 1987, they secured funding of Rs. 12,000 ($300) and moved to a village amongst the hills in Pune district. Here, they began training poorly educated local women and men to become health educators who would in turn create demand for comprehensive health care from government health services.

In his book, *India's emerging economy: performance and prospects in the 1990's and beyond*, Amartya Sen lists the challenges facing rural India—endemic hunger, continuation of massive illiteracy and ill health, enduring inequality of class, ongoing denial of gender inequity, survival of social barriers of caste, lack of development of economic opportunities (Sen, 2004: 37). This accurately describes the scenario that Manisha and her husband faced when they moved into the village. Initially they had to feel their way around local customs while the village folk wondered when they would give up on their efforts and return to their city. Their efforts kept getting stymied by barriers of caste, gender and community—certain castes just could not get involved in certain works, women simply could not do certain things and communities just would not work collectively.

Eventually they won over the trust of the villagers and the word about their efforts spread. As Manisha puts it, "women's groups just began happening" around her. Though the women first came in with their health problems, it was soon apparent that these were intricately linked with other problems such as wife battering, alcohol abuse, sexual violence, drought and poverty as well as problems involving caste, class and gender issues. Manisha dealt with such issues with equanimity. Therefore, women gathered around her from the most subordinated of the castes as well as from religious minorities. Collectively, Manisha and the women addressed issues first by understanding them politically and then by training women to deal with them on a day-to-day basis, both within the home and outside it. Once the women were adept at confronting their own problems, they were encouraged to take leadership roles to form village-based committees on pertinent issues that completely disregarded caste barriers. Thus a new community of empowered people was gradually being created that had broken through the barriers of caste, community and gender and was willing to facilitate other people to deal with similar problems. The myriad of problems led Manisha to think about starting her own organization. However, it was not easy to start MASUM. She had to deal with barriers of caste, class, patriarchy and sexuality that intersected to obstruct every move. The small, empowered community was a signal to take such a course—empower rural women to help themselves by encouraging them to break through their traditional barriers, learn how to deal with their own problems and then form committees for collective action. Meanwhile they focused on the leadership of subordinated castes and communities.

MASUM began without a fixed plan or a blueprint, except that it was to remain committed to progressive social transformation and that Manisha and Ramesh would work with the local community for 25 years. Manisha began the venture adding sections intuitively as the need arose. For instance, she trained village women to become health care workers. When it became apparent that there was a great need for health care, workers who specialized in the needs of maternity to ensure healthy pre-natal care and delivery, a section of birth attendants were trained, to reduce the control of local money lenders, a woman-centered saving and credit program was initiated. It was later felt that a section of paralegal workers was required to help women know their rights and sort through a maze of laws. When these paralegal workers were helping women with the understanding of savings and credit, a new branch of workers were created to focus solely on accounting.

In the early stages of the organization, there was little distinction among the workforce—sometimes the same woman worked as a paralegal and as a counsellor in accounting. Overtime the distinctions became specializations and an organization of quasi professionals began to form. A somewhat formal structure emerged. The founders, Manisha and her husband Ramesh, acted as the co-convenors who set out the programs of the organisation. Along with them were three program coordinators who worked with six team leaders. Each team was led by committees of women trained to do particular tasks and oversee the project at each of the locations.

Now, most rural women who run the organization have basic education and many have completed high school. Women are trained in areas according to their abilities and inclinations. Those who are willing and able to take on more responsibility are accorded more influence and decision-making. The governing board is made up of the two founders as well as a media specialist, a well-known feminist and an activist who specializes in the rights of Muslim women. The salaries are mainly paid by funds received through grants. These were deliberately kept small initially to keep the organization manageable. As the organization grew gradually, Manisha applied for larger grants.

MASUM now has a staff of 60 full-time paid employees from the local villages. There also exists a vast pool of volunteers who work toward solving matters of health, providing shelter to women who face the risk of homicide or suicide, understanding constitutional rights, increasing political participation by women, monitoring government programs and even monitoring MASUM's local activities. In this process, the village activists create networks that act as social capital for the hitherto marginalized people, empowering them with knowledge, leadership skills and the ability to run and rely on their own networks. More importantly, they are now relatively less encumbered by caste and gender barriers, are aware of the dangers of religious bigotry and can now count on each other's support.

Manisha sees MASUM as scaffolding that would support the society in anticipation of the fact that the government fulfills its responsibilities in the many areas that are left untended in the social fabric of an emerging economy. Moreover, it prods the government to fulfill its role and the people to take on more responsibility for their own lives. For instance, MASUM had been training village women to teach at pre-school level in order to advance literacy. When the government offered to hire these women at government schools, MASUM gladly relinquished these women to the government and encouraged them to fulfill their role in education. Now Manisha is in the process of handing the rural work of MASUM over to the village women who have been running the organization. Her husband has been requested to stay on for the next five years as mentor to guide the management team as it attempts to function on its own and also to help impart the art of proposal writing and dealing with local powerful vested interests. Manisha and Ramesh now concentrate more on the National and Asia level interventions of MASUM, mainly as resource persons on issues related to gender, violence against women, economic and social rights and minority rights.

It was thus that MASUM was born to empower women through community participation and to promote women's health and welfare. It has been running for over two decades and is now recognized as a credible training and capacity building institute even at the international level. It continues to be inspired by Gandhian, socialist, feminist and democratic values and operates within a collectivist egalitarian structure. MASUM's salary structure is transparent and modest, but includes strong social security benefits. Its accounts and finances are open to the local public. The continuation and sustainability of the rural interventions has been assured by formally handing over the decision-making to the local staff and by setting up vigilance committees of trained village women. MASUM has striven to accomplish a number of objectives—to create human capital instead of material wealth, to establish a methodology for change instead of following a fixed and given blueprint, to develop a belief in individual and social change through self-reflection and conviction and to present positive role models of leadership for children to observe and emulate. The sustainability of these ideals is Manisha and MASUM's success.

For further information on the organization please visit www.masum-india.org.

Questions for Discussion

1   Why are middle- and upper-class women in India getting involved in NGOs as both volunteers and founders?

2   What were the events that precipitated the changes in Manisha Gupte's life as an ordinary student?

3   List some of the challenges facing rural India. Why were these challenges compounded for Manisha when she tried to help?

4   What does Manisha do to help bring about sustainable development for women?

5   Examine the current organizational structure of MASUM within the framework of a feminist organization.

6   Visit the website for MASUM at http://www.masum-india.org and examine its programs. What do they all have in common?

Case References

Handy, F., Kassam, M., Feeney, S., & Ranade, B. (2006). *Grass-roots NGOs by women for women: The driving force of development in India.* Sage Publications, New Delhi.

Manerkar, Preeti (2010). Corporate Governance is Growing Modestly in India. In Svetlana Borodina & Oleg Shvyrkov (Eds.), *Investing in BRIC Countries: Evaluating Risk and Governance in Brazil, Russia, India & China.* McGraw-Hill, London and New York.

Shetty, Priya (2010). Manisha Gupte—working to empower women in rural India. *The Lancet, 376*(9748), 1,215.

Sen, Amartya (2004). Democracy and secularism in India. In Kausak Basu (Ed.), *India's emerging economy: performance and prospects in the 1990's and beyond.* MIT Press Cambridge, MA.

BRAZIL

Balancing Work, Family and Social Entrepreneurship: A Woman Entrepreneur in Action

Maria Freitag[a] and Cândido Borges[b]
[a]*Faculdade de Administração, Contábeis e Economia, Universidade Federal de Goiás, Brazil;* [b]*Faculdade de Administração, Contábeis e Economia, Universidade Federal de Goiás, Brazil*

In Brazil, as in the world, social entrepreneurship has been shown to be an alternative to the promotion of a more sustainable and socially equitable society.

This case study aims to highlight the role that Wanusa has as a social entrepreneur. She is developing an association of recyclable material collectors in the city of Goiânia, located in Central Brazil.

Knowing the World of Recyclable Materials

Wanusa was born in 1970 in the city of Juazeiro in the State of Bahia. At that time, people in the northeastern region of Brazil lived in unfavorable climatic and economic conditions. A prolonged drought reduced the opportunities for agricultural production and work, often leaving people to live in situations of hunger and poverty, leading many to seek better living conditions in other regions of Brazil.

For Wanusa it was no different. She was rather poor and still very young when she moved with her parents to the city of Uberlandia in Minas Gerais State, in southeastern Brazil. There, Wanusa met Raniere whom she married and they moved to Goiânia city in the center of Brazil, located in the State of Goias and only 200km from the capital, Brasilia. The couple had three children, in addition to one daughter of Raniere's from another relationship.

In Goiania, the couple initially lived in a shantytown. The slums of Brazilian cities are regions where people generally live in precarious conditions. Few or no public services (such as water, sewerage or energy) are offered and the buildings are small and fragile. Due to the difficulties of such a life, Wanusa had interrupted her studies early, having attended school for only four years.

In 2000 Ranieri, Wanusa's husband, began working for a recycling company. Wanusa saw in her husband's work an opportunity to develop an activity that could improve her life and family. "[. . .] At the time I discovered that working as collectors of recyclable materials gave a gain that could help my livelihood and my family [. . .]." She then decided to start working as a stand-alone collector of recyclable materials.

From Self-employment and Precarious Work for a Collective and Dignified Action

Wanusa walked the streets of Goiânia collecting recyclables—cans, paper, cardboard, bottles and other materials—which she placed in a cart and then sold to recycling companies. More than just a way to make money, she saw her job as a contribution to the city, which she also saw as a contribution to the city: "[. . .] my job contributed to make the city a cleaner and healthier place to live [. . .]."

Acting as a collector of recyclable materials in the street and socializing with the co-workers of her husband, she had the opportunity to meet other people who did the same work. Wanusa recognized other collectors' dissatisfaction with their work practice. People were working in poor conditions, such as having to exert excessive physical effort, as they walked several miles of city streets in sun and rain pulling the heavy cart in which the recyclable material was placed; they received little money for the material collected, had no employment contract or formal record of their work and were still ignored by the general population, which marginalized them as scavengers.

Wanusa had the idea of creating an association for the recyclable material collectors to act as a group, united in the collection and sale of recyclables. As freelance scavengers, they collected their own supply of material and sold it to buyers themselves; they had no bargaining power. If they joined forces, however, there would be a system of cooperation and a greater bargaining power with buyers, Wanusa thought.

She began to talk to other collectors about her idea. Some liked the idea and engaged in the project to found an association of collectors. The result was the *Associação de Catadores de Materiais Recicláveis Beija-Flor* (Association of Recyclable Materials Collectors Beija-Flor) founded in 2008.

Leading the Association as a Social Enterprise

Wanusa was elected to be the first president of the Association Beija-Flor. As she reported, "[. . .] the way I act, my responsibility and curiosity to learn and pursue what is good for me and for people was a major reason for me to become leader of the Association [. . .]." The Association led by Wanusa works in a poor neighborhood in the city of Goiania, with 10 members. Each member of the association participates equally in the decision-making of the organization, including decisions about the allocation of the funds raised by the association.

The working process of the Association begins with the arrival of the material that has been collected, not only in the streets, but also from companies, public organizations and residential condominiums. Then the material is sorted according to destination. Next it is pressed and this generates a heavy volume of processed material at the rate of 21 tons per month. Following processing, the association contacts companies interested in buying. All processing stages are overseen by Wanusa and negotiation at the time of sale is made by her due to her skills in that area of operation.

The broad meaning given by Wanusa to her practice was the two factors which originally aroused her to a different motivation for expanding her areas of expertise in this activity. As a recyclable material collector, she saw beyond the possibility of financial gain, another way of collaborating with the environment. She saw, through the concept of the Association, that there was an opportunity to develop the activity of collecting recyclable materials on a more organized basis and mainly play the role of social entrepreneur by taking up the social issues of the Associates.

Most members are migrants from other regions of the state or country, most, are semi-illiterate, young poor people (mean age not over 27 years) and with little or no contact with family. Some are former drug addicts and former prisoners. "[. . .] They are poor people coming from other states, and [have] many problems with alcoholism and drug addiction and also have some problems with the law," says Wanusa on the profile of people seeking to join the Association.

For her, the Association is an "[. . .] opportunity to improve the lives of these people trying to recover them [. . .]." Along with her husband Raniere she created a different way of working with these people. "[. . .] we know these people better and so we divided the responsibilities and activities of the association with them. [. . .] they will be benefited by the results, will become more involved with work and moving away from addictions [. . .]."

The Association is a mechanism for the social inclusion of those people who join it. Besides an opportunity to earn an income, these people develop Wanusa's sense of property and participation; they perceive the Association as an enterprise for collective ownership and management. This search for development of associates is reported by Wanusa: "[. . .] we encourage associates to build their dignity. Being able to make a profit on it, to dress decently and be able to go to a mall [and be] treated as a citizen and not as a thief."

All the care taken by Wanusa with the Associates beforehand has strengthened the ongoing process of achievement so that the Associates are encouraged to feel they are also entrepreneurs, with responsibility in building the Association. Besides the benefits to health and quality of life of members, this process of empowerment initiated by Wanusa has thus resulted in greater involvement which in turn has direct impact on the gains of the Association, increasing overall gains for all its members.

Entrepreneur, Wife and Mother

Wanusa, taking into account the need to reconcile her activities as entrepreneur, wife and mother, along with Raniere and with the approval of other members has organized a residential space for living at the place where they work. This makes it easier for her and other family members to share their daily work at the Association. The workplace has also become the residence of the family. Wanusa and Raniere work together and close to the children, who, as far as possible, are also integrated into the activities of the Association.

As leader of the Association, wife and mother, Wanusa begins to reconcile her time around two main strands interwoven into everyday routine. On the one hand, there is the commitment to actions that mobilize members around the goals of social business developed by the leader. On the other hand, this entrepreneur also mobilizes the members' families with a view to help them establish a relationship with the Association's work, not only as a means to survival, but also as an educational experience.

Wanusa believes that the practices developed through the Association while representing work experiences that will contribute to her livelihood, also have a social function in that she acts as custodian of the environment, keeping the city clean and offering more health and quality of life for society.

Supported by this belief and by the discourse of public policies and social responsibility, regarding environmental conservation and social inclusion, this woman entrepreneur, as a result of her behavior and her attitude, has created a pervasive culture in favor of the Association, which leads the development of the shared activities of a team in a favorable way, focused on both the livelihood of the members' families and environmental preservation.

The Association "Beija-Flor," under Wanusa's leadership, has continued to arouse the interest of other collectors evidenced by the increasing numbers of Associates. Due to her resourcefulness, Wanusa is the person who makes the Association's contacts with enterprises, residential condominiums and public organizations in order to educate them about the process of selecting and gathering the material to be recycled. This new responsibility is a great challenge to Wanusa, as she reports in one of her speeches: "[. . .] I had to face the fear and build courage to talk to these people. But I thought it could help in the work of the Association and then went to take the job [. . .]."

The uncertainty expressed in the fears of Wanusa about daring to create an innovative action, and her courage to take risks arising from this action, characterize her entrepreneurial attitude, which will increasingly reinforce her role in the Association Beija-Flor, making it a stimulating factor in the search for other opportunities. Considering herself as an entrepreneur, Wanusa declares in one of her speeches: "[. . .] the courage I had to go outside the Association to get knowledge from a world [of which] I knew nothing [. . .] acting differently within the Association with its members, knowing how each one can help and also their problems and [. . .] it makes me feel like an entrepreneur."

Questions for Discussion

1   What factors led this woman entrepreneur to have the idea of creating the Association? How did the context influence her idea?
2   To reconcile family chores with professional activities, this woman entrepreneur chooses to stay in the workplace and integrate her family with the activities of the Association. What are the advantages and disadvantages of this approach? Do you think it is proper to join family with work?
3   The Association works through a process of participatory management. Although Wanusa acts as the main leader, all participants have a voice and an equally weighted vote in the decision-making. What are the advantages and disadvantages of this approach?

4   Which of Wanusa's behaviors are similar to those normally assigned to an entrepreneur?

5   Does a social entrepreneur need to exhibit behavior, attitudes and strategies that differ from those of traditional entrepreneurs?

Notes

1 World Bank (1996). *From Plan to Market: World Development Report 1996* (The World Bank, Washington, DC), at http://www-wds.worldbank.org/external/default/WDSContentServer/WDSP/IB/1996/06/27/000009265_396121418 1445/Rendered/PDF/multi0page.pdf

2 Based on the following sources: Commonwealth Secretariat, Commonwealth Business Women: Trade Matters, Best Practices and Success Stories (London), 2002, and United Nations ESCAP publications, at http://www. unescap.org/publications/index.asp; http://www.unescap.org/tid/publication/indpub2401_chap4.pdf

3 Global Economist Paper no. 134, at http://www2.goldmansachs.com/ideas/brics/how-solid-doc.pdf

4 From: The Kauffman Foundation. The State of Entrepreneurship in Europe—An Investor's View. An interview with Sir Ronald Cohen: Cofounder and former Chairman, Apax Partners; Author, The Second Bounce of the Ball: Turning Risk into Opportunity. Available at: http://www. kauffman.org/entrepreneurship/state-of-entrepreneurship-in-europe.aspx

5 Kauffman Foundation.

6 Economic Research from the GS Financial Workbench®. at https://www. gs.com

7 At   http://www3.babson.edu/Centers/Glavin/GPS/Academics/UG/Study-Abroad/BRICs.cfm Podcast interview with Undergraduate Dean Dennis Hanno: http://www.babson.edu/podcast/2009-09-08DHanno.mp3; Photos from BRIC session in Russia: http://www.babsonbric.com/

8 At http://www.linkedin.com/groups?gid=90634&mostPopular=&trk=tyah

9 At http://www.bric.com/php/home.php

10 At http://www.youtube.com/watch?v=OjR1GGP_Vns; AlJazeeraEnglish.

11 For an inclusive overview on the BRIC economies, the Goldman-Sachs reports, at http://www2.goldmansachs.com/ideas/brics/BRICs-and-Beyond.html

12 The Economist column, Another BRIC in the Wall (21 Apr 2008) at http://www.economist.com/node/11075147?story_id=11075147

13 The Globe: The Battle for Female Talent in Emerging Markets, at http://hbr.org/2010/05/the-globe-the-battle-for-female-talent-in-emerging-markets/ar/1

14 At   http://www.newsweek.com/2010/07/06/women-will-rule-the-world.html. For more reading on BRIC: Kowitt, Beth (2009-06-17). For Mr. BRIC, nations meeting a milestone, CNNMoney.com at http://money.cnn. com/2009/06/17/news/economy/goldman_sachs_jim_oneill_interview.fortune/index.htm. Retrieved June 18, 2009; Global Economics Paper No. 99, Dreaming with BRICs and Global Economics Paper 134, How Solid Are the BRICs?; Economist's Another BRIC in the wall (2008). How Solid are the BRICs? (PDF). Global Economics at http://www2.goldmansachs.com/ideas/brics/how-solid-doc.pdf. Retrieved September 21, 2010; Reuters 2011 Investment Outlook Summit, London and New York, December 6–7, 2010. bricnation. com at http://bricnation.com/?p=24. Retrieved October 15, 2010, at http://www.investordaily.com/cps/rde/xchg/id/style/801.htm?rdeCOQ=SID-3F579BCE-819F182C; Brazil, Russia, India and China (BRIC). Investopedia

at http://www.investopedia.com/terms/b/bric.asp. Retrieved May 11, 2008; BRICs helped by Western finance crisis: Goldman. *Reuters*. June 8, 2008. at http://www.reuters.com/article/ousiv/idUSL071126420080608?pageNumber =2&virtualBrandChannel=0; Carl Mortished (May 16, 2008) Russia shows its political clout by hosting Bric summit. The Times (London). At http://business.timesonline.co.uk/tol/business/markets/russia/article3941462.ece. Retrieved April 26, 2010; Halpin, Tony (June 17, 2009) Brazil, Russia, India and China form bloc to challenge US dominance. *The Times*, Retrieved from http://www.timesonline.co.uk/tol/news/world/us_and_americas/article6514737.ece.

15 At   http://www.gemconsortium.org/download/1319958704319/GEM%20 MENA%202009%20-%20ENGLISH.pdf; survey of the following countries: Algeria, Jordan, Lebanon, Morocco, Palestine, Syria, and Yemen.

16 The World Bank report. Vishwanath, Tara (2010) Bridging the gap: improving capabilities and expanding opportunities for women in the Middle East and North Africa region, at http://www-wds.worldbank.org/external/default/ WDSContentServer/WDSP/IB/2010/10/27/000334955_20101027074715/ Rendered/PDF/575180WP0Box353768B01PUBLIC10Gender1pub.pdf

17 Global Entrepreneurship Monitor: GEM-MENA Regional Report 2009 (Middle East and North Africa). International Development Research Centre (IDRC), at: http://www.gemconsortium.org/download/1319958704319/ GEM%20MENA%202009%20-%20ENGLISH.pdf

18 World Bank reports.

19 The New York Times, Egypt News—Revolution and Aftermath, Friday, July 22, 2011 at: http://topics.nytimes.com/top/news/international/countriesandterritories/egypt/index.html

20 All reports appear at: IFC-GEM, Gender Dividend: Growth Through Gender Equality (2005a). Summary of PREM Week symposium. At http://www.ifc. org/ifcext/gempepmena.nsf/AttachmentsByTitle/News_Events_Egypt_ GenderDividend/$FILE/Egypt_Gender_Dividend_April2005.pdf

IFC-GEM, Egypt Gender and Entrepreneurship Market (GEM) Study (2005b). International Finance Corporation.

IFC-GEM, Morocco Gender and Entrepreneurship Market (GEM) Study (2005c). International Finance Corporation. At IFC-GEM, GEM Country Brief-Morocco. (2005d). International Finance Corporation. English at http://www.ifc.org/ifcext/gempepmena.nsf/AttachmentsByTitle/Morocco_ Country_Brief_Oct05. pdf/$FILE/Morocco_Country_Brief_Oct05.pdf

IFC-GEM, GEM Country Brief—Oman (2005e). International Finance Corporation.   At   http://www.ifc.org/ifcext/gempepmena.nsf/AttachmentsBy Title/Oman+Country+Brief/$FILE/OMAN+Country+Brief+v.+29+March+ 2006.pdf

IFC-GEM, Yemen Gender and Entrepreneurship Market (GEM) Analysis Report (2005f). International Finance Corporation. At IFC-GEM, GEM Regional Brief—Middle East and North Africa (2005g). International Finance Corporation. At http://www.ifc.org/ifcext/gempepmena.nsf/AttachmentsByTitle/MENA_GEM_Brief_Oct05.pdf/$FILE/Regional+MENA+GE M+Brief+v.+19July+2006.pdf

IFC-GEM, GEM Country Brief—Yemen (2006a). International Finance Corporation.   At   http://www.ifc.org/ifcext/gempepmena.nsf/Attachments ByTitle/Yemen_GEM_Country_Brief_July+06/$FILE/YEMEN+GEM+Cou ntry+Brief+v.+July+18+2006.pdf

IFC-GEM, PEP-MENA, Middle East and North Africa (MENA) Regional Directory of Businesswomen's Associations (2006b). International Finance Corporation. At http://www.ifc.org/ifcext/gempepmena.nsf/Attachments ByTitle/MENA+Regional+Directory+of+Businesswomen%27s+Association +June++2006/$FILE/~8678358.pdf

IFC-GEM, GEM Country Brief—Egypt (2007a). International Finance Corporation. At http://www.ifc.org/ifcext/gempepmena.nsf/Attachments ByTitle/EpyptGEMCountryBrief2007/$FILE/Egyptfinalgemmarch6.pdf

IFC-GEM, GEM Country Brief—Jordan (2007b). International Finance Corporation. At http://www.ifc.org/ifcext/gempepmena.nsf/Attachments ByTitle/Jordan_GEM_Country_Briefv2/$FILE/JORDAN+GEM+Brief+with +out+Survey+info+for+posting+now.pdf

IFC-GEM, GEM Country Brief—Lebanon (2007c). International Finance Corporation. At http://www.ifc.org/ifcext/gempepmena.nsf/Attachments ByTitle/Lebanon_GEM_Country_Brief/$FILE/Lebanon+GEM+Country+Brief +Feb+2007.pdf

21 The author(s) of the case studies are fully and solely responsible for their content, phrasing consistency and flow, terminology, English proofing and reference lists.

Part 2

The Venture Creation Process

Part 2 focuses on

- The pre-launching stage(s) of the new venture creation from women's perspective;
- The main processes, challenges and difficulties faced by women entrepreneurs during these stages;
- The significance of these initial stages to the robustness and sustainability of the business;
- The individual's required core competencies relevant to these stages;
- Women's skills and capabilities, and their contribution to enhancing creativity, innovation and the competitive advantages of the business from the initial stages;
- This part includes chapters and case studies on the processes typical of the pre-stages of new venture creation and on the personal core competencies needed for such stages to achieve growth and success.

Part 2 addresses the pre-launching stage(s), and presents the main processes, challenges and difficulties faced by women entrepreneurs during these stages. Specifically, because in the pre-launching stage the business has not yet been formalized, structured or made tangible, the founders have the freedom to plan, reflect, act and adjust, under less risky conditions. Nevertheless, it is a most demanding phase, because the pre-venture has not yet been funded, the team has not been assembled, and the feasibility of the venture's concept is still uncertain and erratic.

This part of the book delves into the main processes typifying the pre-launching stages in female entrepreneurship by classifying them into two themes: the pre-business processes and the individual's required core competencies.

Women's experiences at these stages are most interesting and intriguing due to the distinct path they follow in their entrepreneurial course. This section presents the woman's perspective, and the practices, skills, capabilities, and processes required to face the unique challenges and demands placed on the modern woman entrepreneur in these stages.

4 The Pre-venture Stages

Chapter Objectives

- Typifying the pre-venture phase in terms of processes conducted to link the entrepreneurial idea, drive and spirit with the future venture;
- Representing the "quest" stage of the business's life cycle and becoming acquainted with leading models of the new venture's life cycle;
- Listing some core principles required to create a new venture;
- Connecting women's different cultural backgrounds and encountered gender-based expectations with their reluctance to embark on the new venture creation process;
- Uncovering the main opportunities and threats typical of the initial stages of the new venture creation through women's outlook;
- Discussing the main practices used by women to negotiate the passage, typical to these stages, from ideas and theoretical plans to implementation and practical processes;
- Articulating women's decision-making processes in the pre-stages of the new venture creation; linking these processes to leading models, characteristics and techniques;
- Listing the main entrepreneurial strategies used by women in these stages to enhance the value of their future businesses.

It is often stated that "the first success achieved in the prospective new venture is actually in getting it started": turning ideas into a real venture is one of the most difficult challenges in the entrepreneurial realm. This chapter traces practices in the pre-launching stages, and presents the typical processes characterizing these stages, from a woman's perspective. The pre-launching stages are "latent": the business still does not exist in any recognizable form, i.e., it is not registered or licensed and usually does not include any formal procedures (taxing, licensing, investments). Nevertheless, business activities ensue rapidly, perhaps even more intensively, as "timing" is a critical factor for the business's materialization. To illustrate this: when an entrepreneur has an idea for a venture, he or she is encouraged to communicate it, so as to get a feel for its feasibility among its target customers; at the same time, the idea becomes known and widespread among the audience that might be the most suited to appreciating it, and therefore also, purposely or inadvertently, adapting it, imitating it or using it. Therefore, for the entrepreneur, the time elapsed between communicating the idea and implementing it should be short, focused and valuable for the potential customer. This stage is essentially a sprint, during which resources, capabilities, a team and money are sought.

The challenges and difficulties encountered in the pre-launching stages are anchored in women's entrepreneurial experiences, as they take on distinct forms and are unearthed in a variety of contexts that typify women's environments. Accordingly, this chapter discusses the processes, activities, challenges and difficulties characterizing the pre-launching stages in women's entrepreneurial experience, and illustrates how women respond to these challenges under the conditions faced at these stages.

A GENERAL LOOK INTO THE PRE-LAUNCHING STAGES

The stages typifying the pre-venture phase are basically deliberate actions of volition conducted to link the entrepreneurial idea, drive and spirit with the future venture in its specific ecosystem. New venture creation represents "the quest" stage of the business's life cycle, i.e., its stages of development over time. As shown in Table 4.1, which exemplifies some of the leading models developed to represent the business's life cycle, the pre-launching stages revolve around processes such as opportunity, idea, intention, conception, entrepreneurial intent, initiation and gestation. While the pre-launching stages may appear to be distinct, these models essentially describe different approaches to the same ultimate goal: bridging between an idea and a business. New venture creation is a process, and much like any manufacturing process, it is aimed at turning raw materials into finished products, in this case accelerating the translation of ideas into ventures, and building sustainable value.

The pre-launching stages are characterized by intensive work. The proposition suggesting that actions begin when the business starts

Table 4.1 Leading Models of the Business Life Cycle: The New Venture Creation Outlook

Stages of new venture creation					Authors
Opportunity	Technology set-up and organization; creation	Exchange			Bhave (1994)
Idea	Pre start-up	Start-up	Post start-up		Clarysse & Moray (2004)
Intention	Boundary	Resources	Exchanges		Gelderen, Bosma, & Thurik (2001)
Conception	Gestation	Firm birth	Grow or Persist or Quit		Reynolds (2000)
Entrepreneurial intent	Search and discovery	Decision to exploit	Exploitation activity		Shook, Priem, & McGee (2003)
Initiation	Acclimatization	Consolidation	Start-up	Childhood	Tesfaye (1997)
Concept	Planning	Implementation	Proprietary product	Multiproduct	Vesper (1990)
Gestation	Planning	Contract services			Van de Ven, Hudson, & Schroeder (1984)

up is not upheld by empirical evidence or entrepreneurs' narratives: much work is required to prepare for implementation of the new venture and creation of the future business—determining its content, structuring the business model, becoming thoroughly familiar with the business's niche, its ecosystem, and customers' tastes, alternatives and purchasing habits.

The challenge in the process of new venture creation is to qualify the underlying competitive advantage of a still non-existent, future venture through a still theoretical process that will determine whether the venture has a viable product, a growing market and an achievable plan, along with existing resources, knowledge and capital.

The processes required to create a new venture are thus complex, multi-faceted and most challenging at these stages; they comprise some core principles:

- Coming up with an innovative yet feasible idea.
- Exploiting opportunities in creative ways.
- Finding suitable resources (e.g., partners, team members, money, location).
- Collaborating with highly qualified entrepreneurial personnel.
- Possessing/learning skills relevant to initiating a venture (decision-making, creative thinking, negotiation skills).
- Visualizing . . .

The characteristic activities identified for these stages follow the vision. The vision is a key way to create a new venture and cross this phase effectively. It enables dreaming, sketching the future business and seeking out this dream. It helps maintain optimism and dedication to the dream, even when that dream appears to be far off or even unreachable. The vision is the anchor that keeps the entrepreneur from drowning in the choppy waters of venture creation. The role of the vision is best demonstrated by the case of Gete Dessalegn, Dejyitnu Bisetegn and Sinkinesh H/Wold, visually impaired women entrepreneurs in Ethiopia:

> Despite their considerable difficulties the women are optimistic. They are proud of their achievements in a country in which begging is still the main occupation of many visually impaired people. Managing their savings and loans, taking on the role of breadwinner in their later years and guarding their dignity, the women continue to dream of the better life they could have with more opportunity and support.[1]

The vision and its ensuing simple and practical implementation steps enable pinpointing what attracts customers and acquiring knowledge of the missing links, i.e., what is not yet there, and combining these into a vibrant venture.

The vision, its implementation and the actions associated with the pre-launching stages are all embedded in the specific conditions imposed on the entrepreneur. These, in turn, shape the various strategies that will be employed to respond to the external conditions being tackled in the pre-launching venture phase (Bhave, 1994; Churchill & Lewis, 1983; Hanks, Watson, Jansen, & Chandler, 1993; Kazanjian, 1988; Kazanjian & Drazin, 1990; Pensore, 1959; Shane & Venkataraman, 2000; Wennekers, Van Wennekers, Thurik, & Reynolds, 2005).

THE WOMAN'S VIEW

The pre-venture processes and the entrepreneur's ensuing actions are all embedded in their specific ecosystem. Accordingly, women initiate and manage the pre-launching stages of the new venture in ways that echo their distinctive, female-based background and experiences.

Women are exposed to distinct triggering events, having grown up in different cultural backgrounds and encountered different expectations regarding their prospects of becoming successful entrepreneurs, and therefore women develop attitudes in this venture phase that reflect a context in which not much credit and confidence is attributed to their potential success as entrepreneurs. Many women entrepreneurs report being reluctant to formalize their ideas, vision and dreams into a real venture. They prolong the moratorium by going back to school and taking programs in entrepreneurship, before daring to create a new venture. Many women entrepreneurs confirm that they considered their knowledge and experience prior to starting their ventures insufficient or irrelevant in terms of competing in the market; in fact, women are known to be less self-confident regarding their own capability of creating a venture. They assign time at these stages to studying the entrepreneurial realm and the relevant skills, and they opt to ask for assistance; in addition, many women favor partnering with others, women or men, to start a business. Although women may be less confident about their own abilities to start a business, they are quite confident in their ideas for a business. Many women entrepreneurs affirm that they were self-assured about the need for, and validity of their ideas in their particular markets. Susanna Simpson,[2] founder of the London-based Limelight Public Relations and awarded Young PR Professional and successful entrepreneur at the 2003 PR Week, was quoted as saying: "The most powerful advantage that I think women have is a real sense of intuition about people and situations. I believe that this is arguably a more important skill."

A main concern is women's reluctance to implement their ideas into new ventures: shying away from the pre-launching stages means withdrawing from the potential entrepreneurial course. One way to understand these concerns is to look at them through the lens of women's ecosystems.

Women's entrepreneurial ecosystems confront them with different situations in the pre-launching stages that require high self-confidence in their methods and course of action. The strategies used by women at these stages reflect the ways in which they interpret the competition in their ecosystems and treat the attitudes toward women entrepreneurship.

The Kauffman Foundation published a most intriguing interview with Ms. Shaherose Charania, CEO of Women 2.0 and Ms. Sharon Vosmek, CEO of Astia,[3] where it is stated that: "While the numbers of highly educated women who have the potential to start scalable ventures have reached record levels, these women are not pursuing entrepreneurship or being exposed to entrepreneurial possibilities through networking," suggesting that the difficulties perceived by women at these stages are hard to handle.

Typical strategies used by women at these stages include: taking a longer time to prepare the business, going back to school to acquire the needed competencies to start a business prior to actually starting it and, correspondingly, hanging on to work rather than delegating, showing a tendency to partner up with someone, and sharing their options and future profits with more partners than men do. Women are more open to revealing their ideas at the pre-launching stages, to seek assistance from friends, family and professionals, and to follow suggestions and recommendations. Despite these strategies, not enough women who have great ideas are entering the early stages of new venture creation to implement those ideas (Bhidd, 2000; Brockhaus, 1980; Bygrave & Hofer, 1991; Carland, Hoy, Boulton, & Carland, 1988; Chandler & Hanks, 1994; Gartner, Shaver, Gatewood, & Katz, 1994; Katz & Gartner, 1988; Mitton, 1989; Stuart & Abetti, 1987; Westhead & Wright, 1998).

Opportunities and Threats at the Pre-launching Stages

The pre-launching stages of the new venture are typified by higher levels of uncertainty, coupled with a lack of resources and relevant information. The venture at these stages is more vulnerable to external threats. Entrepreneurs at these stages, both women and men, face conditions that need to be responded to properly to enable the potential business to start and eventually succeed.

The categorization of opportunities and threats has two different forms: the objective form refers to any conditions that can promote or damage the business idea, concept, processes or development; for example, when an expert is interested in collaborating with a start-up and finds an entrepreneur's business concept appealing, an opportunity is presented that should be leveraged for the business's future success; on the other hand, when investors who initially expressed their interest in the business renounce their potential collaboration, this can be seen as a threat. The subjective form refers to the entrepreneur's perceptions of these conditions; some entrepreneurs may interpret the investor's withdrawal from potential collaboration as an opportunity to grow and advance in different ways, while others may interpret this as holding back the business concept.

Typical opportunities identified at the pre-launching stages might be either internal, i.e., stemming from the business concept, the team's capabilities or the technology's implementation, or external, i.e., originating from the financial situation in the business's environment, the saturation level for the product, or the "trends" in the region.

The conditions typically unveiled at the pre-launching stages of businesses led by either women or men are fairly similar, but have two relevant distinctions: (a) the subjective form, i.e., women's and men's perceptions of these conditions, differs; (b) the encountered conditions are affected by the attitudes toward women's role in their society and women's entrepreneurship.

The subjective form involves recurring conditions encountered at the pre-launching stages that can be assessed as threats by women, while men may consider them challenges, or vice versa; subsequently, women and men use different actions to best adjust their own capabilities and the business's resources to the conditions interpreted as threats or opportunities. For example, limited knowledge and experience in the mechanics of starting a business can be interpreted by women as a threat, with the potential to impede plans for the pre-launching stages; in response, they will go back to school and learn the relevant know-how, ask for assistance, or partner with more experienced entrepreneurs. On the other hand, if this lack of knowledge does not appear threatening to male entrepreneurs, they are not likely to perform any of the activities executed by women in response to these conditions. Namely, the activities exhibited in the pre-launching stages represent, in many cases, a response to perceived threats or opportunities: when the genders perceive the conditions differently, their subsequent actions will differ as well (Davidsson & Honig, 2003; Delmar & Shane, 2002; Keh, Foo, & Lim, 2002; Reynolds, 2007; Rotefoss & Kolvereid, 2005; Van Gelderen, Thurik, & Patel, 2011; Wennekers, Uhlander, & Thurik, 2002).

The reflection of attitudes and norms associated with women's role in society can be seen in cases such as a bank's refusal to provide loans for women-led businesses, or a potential partner's hesitation to collaborate with a women entrepreneur or to support a system that controls, rather than empowers women entrepreneurs.

The Unexplored Gaps

Moving from the pre-launching stages to the set-up stage requires more than a plan: it represents the passage from theory to practice. The competencies typifying many entrepreneurs, such as proactiveness, entrepreneurial spirit and drive, risk-taking and a firm determination to overcome the difficulties and hurdles that pop up, are critical at such passages. The difficulties tackled by women in the pre-launching stages were discussed in the previous section; the difficulties encountered by women in passing from the theoretical phase to practice are even more pronounced, yet little is known about the preparations, competencies and actions needed to navigate this passage successfully.

Figure 4.1 illustrates the unexploited gap between the theoretical phase and practice, to be fueled with processes that will ease the passage of women entrepreneurs.

To cross this gap successfully, women use:

- Assistance—women ask for functional and practical assistance from professionals, experienced entrepreneurs, support systems, governmental-based programs for women entrepreneurs.
- Partnering—women gain more confidence for crossing this gap by partnering with others, thus sharing the responsibility, decision-making and tasks.
- A team—the presence of a supportive, professional and reliable team in a woman's new venture journey is imperative. Women favor collective work and are empowered by their teams; many tend to share their dilemmas with their teams and adopt the team's suggestions regarding different aspects of their business. A leading, loyal team is most helpful for women to cross the gap from theory to practice.
- Role models—living examples that "it can happen." Successful women entrepreneurs who mentor nascent and novice women entrepreneurs empower those women by providing them with the confidence that they can become real entrepreneurs and materialize their dreams in a real venture.
- Emotional support—it is common knowledge that women appreciate emotional dynamics, and encourage, and make room for emotions in their business's world, and that emotions exhibited in their businesses are well imprinted in the business processes and structure. Because women accept feeling different emotions during the early stages of the new venture creation process, they embrace emotional support, and allow it to lead them to be more self-confident and trust their instincts, feelings and ultimately, their decisions.
- Just start . . . —when the ecosystem signals that any entrepreneurial experience is acceptable, that any entrepreneurial outcome is eventually for the best because it is in essence a platform for a constructive and valuable experience, concerns related to "making mistakes," "failing," and "disrupting the harmony" are eliminated. Many women entrepreneurs admit that visualizing the business is an ideal phase, while starting a business means abandoning the harmony and starting the real work: it is less appealing, they depend on others,

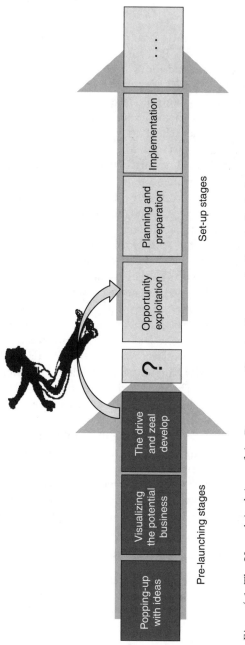

Figure 4.1 The Unexploited Area of the Pre-venture Creation Process: the Female Outlook.

they can make mistakes or even fail. Nevertheless, this huge leap from theory, or vision, to practice must be made in order to create a venture.

The following example illustrates how this complex passage was successfully navigated by Ms. Norma Peerson, an elementary school teacher in Helsinki, Finland. Norma had dreamt of becoming an entrepreneur from early childhood, but she followed her parents' advice and became a teacher. Her zeal for entrepreneurship, however, never faded. As a teacher, she developed a special program in mathematics for children with learning disabilities and then executed it at her school; the results were amazing and she was excited to transform it into a web-based program so that children around the world could use it. Norma admitted that: ". . . it took me about one whole year to make the arrangements to implement my dream. It is not lack of enthusiasm and not fear from failure; it is a different feeling of leaving behind the great ideas, planning, vision, and starting to manage the nitty-gritty. This was so discouraging; it felt like falling from the uppermost spheres to the lowest spheres . . ." Norma regained her enthusiasm by approaching the school principal, Ms. Swann Ring, and asking for assistance; "I did not determine what kind of assistance I needed, I suppose that at this stage I just needed a good listener . . ." says Norma. While at first, Ms. Ring was not excited about Norma's initiative, mainly because it would take up so much of Norma's time, after several meetings, Ms. Ring realized that Norma was determined: she had filtered and focused her idea and Ms. Ring felt that its implementation was feasible. She decided to allocate the school's resources to assist Norma in materializing her vision, and made some formal arrangements. The main assistance consisted of technological support from the school's technological staff. After some time, Norma began to face other difficulties associated with the creation of new ventures and asked Ms. Ring to partner with her in the undertaking; Ms. Ring agreed. Today, Norma and Ms. Ring are the owners of a two-year-old web-based teaching business for children facing mathematics-related difficulties; their team consists of four teaching-program developers, a marketing staff and an administrative staff. The two have already signed collaborative contracts with teaching institutions in Norway, Denmark and New Zealand.

Female-oriented Processes: Insights Obtained

The model in Figure 4.2 presents the processes typifying the pre-launching stages of new ventures and demonstrates the unique content contributed by women to these processes. This uniqueness reflects the women's world. Their entrepreneurial preferences and decisions reveal their needs, motivations and interests.

The model is structured to depict women's uniqueness: while the general model (on the left) lists typical processes in the pre-launching stages in sequential order, the women's model (on the right) spans the "traditional flow" and extends it, by bridging the different processes, to either bypass difficulties or exploit advantages associated with women's tendencies and the conditions women encounter as entrepreneurs.

Accordingly, female-oriented performance in the pre-launching stages proceeds as follows:

- *Coming up with* ideas—the intuition to design new products, services or methods to capture unexploited markets is rooted in the entrepreneur's characteristics, spirit and drive. As women pursue a course in life that embodies the conditions, expectations and challenges unique to their gender, they develop specific interests, and interpret their needs in ways that are relevant to their own experiences and insights. This results in generating ideas in the sectors and niches that are more closely associated with the women's world, in ways and along paths that typify how women think, reflect and create.
- *Filtering the ideas—focusing on one idea?*—a common recommended practice for entrepreneurs is to focus on one, best idea in the pre-launching stages to ensure the successful establishment of a business; the implication is that more than "one, best idea" might damage the business's establishment. Yet, many ideas that eventually materialize into ventures are the consequence of a combination of ideas, rather than of "one, best idea." Women are known to possess lateral thinking and more imaginative, creative thinking styles, implying that they are more apt to successfully blend ideas, which may then stimulate other ideas, resulting in the emergence of a new, combined idea. Therefore, the general recommendation to focus on "one, best idea" may be insufficient or even irrelevant in the context of female entrepreneurship (Carland, Carland, Ensley, & Stewart, 1994; Feingold, 1988; Hyde, 1981; Lippa, 2002).
- *Reflecting (decisions, motivations)*—reflecting on ideas and their outcomes, deciding on the steps to be followed while acknowledging the different scenarios—the best and worst cases. Women exhibit an openness to change, by adjusting and even renouncing parts of their planned ideas and processes. Reflections on their ideas are associated with their motivations, decisions and needs.
- *Visualizing the business*—women can envisage several scenarios for their potential business concurrently; this appears to distract their focus and sidetrack their venture creation-related activities. However, women can more easily plan different scenarios without being distracted, benefiting from a comparative assessment of these simultaneous planning processes, which may produce an improved result.
- *Communicating and collecting feedback*—women use assistance systems with ease, and foresee their benefits for their future businesses. As such, communicating their ideas, tackled challenges, difficulties,

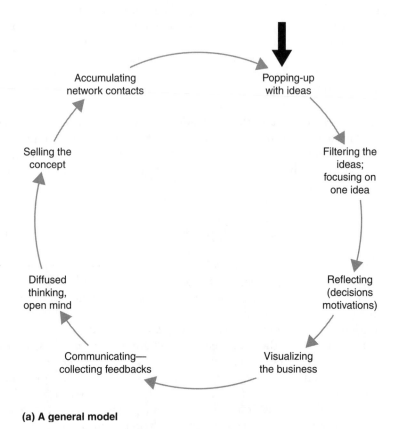

Accumulating
network contacts

Popping-up
with ideas

Selling the
concept

Filtering the
ideas;
focusing on
one idea

Diffused
thinking,
open mind

Reflecting
(decisions
motivations)

Communicating—
collecting feedbacks

Visualizing
the business

(a) A general model

Figure 4.2 The Pre-launch Steps in the New Venture Creation Process.

doubts and even uncertainties or fears, is natural for women. They proactively collect feedback from a wide range of people, rather than just professionals, friends or colleagues; they then identify the most suitable assistance path to approach, in order to exploit the opportunities as well as cope with the threats that emerge from the collected feedback. Women will not hesitate to amend their ideas accordingly; as they visualize different future businesses, such amendments seem much less threatening and much more promising.

- *Diffuse thinking, open mind*—diffuse thinking comes naturally to many women; in the context of entrepreneurship, an open mind and flexibility are central to handling these stages until a satisfactory result is established. The previous stages, i.e., communicating their ideas and visualizing alternative businesses deriving from their ideas, converge with keeping an open mind in the "Sisyphean" process of crafting ideas and solidifying them into a real venture.

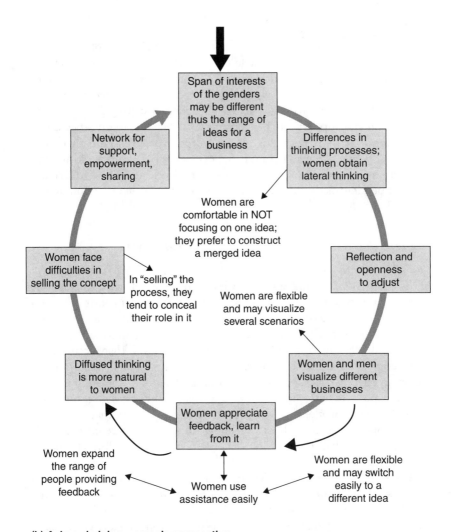

(b) Acknowledging women's perspective

- *Selling the concept*—at the pre-launching stages, entrepreneurs are focused on self-persuasive processes regarding their idea's feasibility, innovation and competitiveness; yet, almost concurrently, they need to sell the concept outside their immediate circle. Such outreach processes are imperative to sensing their idea's saleability and potential. Women often tend to conceal their central, vital role in the entrepreneurial process during the selling of their ideas, focusing instead on the concept's advantages, and even on the advantages of the team. As such, they paint a false picture, one in which the concept may appear too simple or redundant, as it does not appear to require its leader's (the woman entrepreneur's) intensive involvement.

• *Accumulating networks, contacts*—the social capabilities of women are well-documented; the female inclination toward emotional and expressive communication is echoed in women's social patterns and relationships. Yet, women tend to separate between "business and pleasure": they do not utilize their networks to gain more information and support for their businesses. In fact, initially, they do not accumulate their networks for the purpose of leveraging their business. While women maintain emotionally based networking, men maintain functional, practical-based networking. These differences can be identified in the structure and content of their communication and network dynamics.

Pre-launch Decision-making: Is there a Female Style?

Decision-making is a complex, multifaceted process that is the backbone of the business's dynamics and activities at any stage. At the pre-launching stages of the business, the complexity of the decision-making process is even more pronounced, as expectations from entrepreneurs are extremely large, i.e., to create a business under vague and uncertain conditions.

Research in entrepreneurship continually shows that accumulated knowledge and experience in entrepreneurship and management are core factors in effective decision-making. Prior experience is known to improve various aspects of entrepreneurs' performance, including using some decisions that have "worked" in the past and avoiding others that have led to undesirable results, as well as psychological facets by strengthening the entrepreneur's self-confidence in taking decisions, because it has been done in the past.

According to world statistics, many women enter the entrepreneurial realm with limited experience in entrepreneurship, and are thus lacking the "best practices" that are typically based on prior experience. Therefore, the female decision-making process will be based on trial and error, consequently reducing self-confidence and trust in the ability to start a business. This vicious cycle may escalate, as lower self-confidence may lead to decisions that are not carefully analyzed and these, in turn, may result in repeating bad decisions.

Studies in decision-making processes and gender stress that women are more apt to exhibit emotion-oriented styles. They embrace decisions taken at an emotional level. Women also prefer a narrative, a story with faces, interactions and relationships, rather than just relying on numbers and statistics to make their decisions. Women tend to ask people for their opinions in order to craft their own decisions; thus, their decisions may be the outcome of a combined solution developed from the opinions and insights gathered from others, joined to their own initial opinions.

Women are also quick to build relationships to get the task done, and this is also reflected in their decision-making styles in the pre-launching stages; specifically, it is most important for women to commit their founding staff to their idea and the future undertaking. Consequently, their decision-making approach is socially oriented. In addition, women incorporate intuition into their decision-making. These tendencies are reflected in women's decision-making and consequent activities exhibited in the pre-launching stages.

It is difficult to determine whether this style, which is best suited to accomplishing the pre-launch business goals, i.e., planning a long-term, sustainable business, is suited to launching a business. Clearly, a combination of both genders' tendencies in the decision-making process would result in generating more useful results over the long term in new ventures.

To facilitate women's decision-making processes at the pre-launching stages, the models in Table 4.2 are introduced.

COMMUNICATING THE IDEA

The stakeholders need time to approve new concepts and ideas. When ideas are original and innovative, the stakeholders' resistance to them can be higher, and thus the feasibility of these ideas and concepts will be more complex, along with penetration in their respective market.

Statistics are constantly providing empirical evidence of failure of very early entrants. This phenomenon can be partially explained by the introduced ideas and concepts, which develop in unsuitable environments, for example, when:

- the environment is saturated for the idea or concept (for example, if an entrepreneur develops an idea on social networking in an environment saturated with social networks);
- the idea/concept is ahead of its time; the general state of mind is still premature for such ideas/concepts;
- customers and investors do not see the true value created by the newly introduced idea/concept, e.g., strong performance, time-saving, cost-saving;
- there are different players in the entrepreneurial realm for similar ideas/concepts. When the entrepreneurs introduce their ideas/concepts, they signify to the other competitors that they may think of new angles to differentiate between the competing ideas/concepts.

Such situations may impede the business's ideas/concepts, yet the pre-launching stages are ideal for checking the idea's/concept's feasibility, competition, and appeal among the target customers. Communicating the business's idea/concept in the early stages is therefore critical. It also serves

Table 4.2 Models Introduced to Facilitate Women's Decision-making Processes

Models	Characteristics	Techniques	Practical in . . .
Rational decision-making models	Rational models represent systematic, validated and reliable ways of analyzing both internal and external environments to base decision-making on evidence and espouse the decision-making process	Rational models include: SWOT Cash-flow projections Balance sheets/balance score cards Income and financial statements Pareto analysis Grid analysis Force field analysis	Situations that require practical evidence, data, figures, calculation. Situations where financial, fiscal or legislative situations are at stake. Situations in which measures are required by external bodies (e.g., banks, potential investors, partners).
Intuitive decision-making models	Intuitive models refer to creative methods of decision-making, which involve ideation of new and unexplored perspectives and entail visualizing things from original, unconventional or innovative angles.	Intuitive models include:' Methods and techniques for creative problem solving (CPS) such as The Five Whys technique, Mess-finding, the Six-Hats analysis Brainstorming Positive thinking and positive alternatives	Starting a project, when strategic thinking and a wide-ranging perspective are required. Tackling complex problems, and where an outside-the-box solution is needed. Situations in which there is a need for a "wake-up call," when things appear to be flowing smoothly and the drive for new ideas is imperiled.

to prepare and familiarize the stakeholders with the idea and carefully construct their anticipation of its implementation. For example, many entrepreneurs use their business's website or their social networks as "trailers" for their business in the pre-launching stages: surfers come across an "under construction" website that communicates the business's ideas/concepts to acquaint the customers with the business's ideas and to develop expectations.

While research shows that entrepreneurs are generally reluctant to disclose their business idea or concept at these vulnerable stages, women entrepreneurs are more secure in doing so, thus gaining more feedback on those ideas, and enabling them to adjust accordingly (Bower & Christensen, 1995; Carpenter & Nakamoto, 1990; Seth & Ram, 1987; Suarez, 2004).

Women's communicative style assists in understanding the customers' needs, adjusting the business's idea or concept and disseminating its advantages and true value for the stakeholders. Women's communicative styles are documented in research; they are more willing to "spread the news," and thus obtain more information at the less risky stages. The following styles are more often used by women:

- *Questioning style*—women typically ask questions, and consider questioning to be a functional vehicle to connect, show interest, and keep the conversation flowing. For the pre-launching stages, this style assists in obtaining responses that reflect the stakeholders' thoughts on the business idea, and provide more accurate information on how they perceive it in view of their needs, tastes and existing solutions.

- *Lateral thinking*—women are portrayed in research as lateral thinkers: they define topics broadly and shift topics naturally while maintaining their thinking flow and coherence; as such, women's communication may seem unfocused to their male counterparts because their interpretations of situations are broad and less confined to a determined analytical style. Lateral thinking is most functional in communicating the business idea; women can easily follow comments on their business idea coming from different people and representing different angles; they can switch easily between topics; the broader picture in analyzing situations facilitates their consequent decisions on whether to adjust their business ideas according to the comments raised, as different aspects emerge and are seen as relevant to their decisions.

- *Expressive style of communication*—women favor an expressive style of communication in both delivering the message and obtaining feedback and new comments that reflect on what has been said. This style is most functional at the pre-launching stages in attracting people's comments, feedback and insights regarding the entrepreneur's future business.

- *Hesitant in authority-driven statements*—studies reveal that women rely on hedging statements to avoid seeming overly aggressive when communicating; consequently, women hesitate to deliver their message with authority or assertive tactics, or to control the conversation. Such strategies may be a drawback in the pre-launching stages, as potential investors, customer and partners expect confident, declarative and determined statements when pitching a business idea.

The Main "Entrepreneurial" Strategies in the Pre-launching Phase

To enhance the value of their future businesses, the best fit between their firm's future performance and the demands of the external environment should be sought. The strategies used by women entrepreneurs at the pre-launching stages are still unclear and have scarcely been investigated (Barney, 1991, 2001; Pfeffer & Salancik, 1978; Wernerfelt, 1984; Zahra, Sapienza, & Davidson, 2006). Drawing on women's strategies that have already proven successful in their entrepreneurial businesses is important to train women at the pre-launching stages in the most effective strategies for their businesses.

Pre-launching Stages and Entrepreneurial Strategies—A Woman's Perspective

- *Opportunity exploitation*—women are known to be attentive and to see the details of the "big picture"; opportunity exploitation requires careful identification of unresolved niches, a thorough look into the potential customer's needs and demands, and an open mind to the general trends in the local regional and global markets. Being attentive to early warning signs, and then correcting the course of action, learning from prior experience or from outsourced models for the first stages of the business, are all valid strategies for establishing a sustainable new venture.
- *Creativity and innovation*—women are portrayed in research as creative, sometimes perceived as "fantasizers," as they seem to dream and visualize unrealistic goals for their businesses. Such creativity and "big dreams" should be directed to innovation in products, services, and business processes such as marketing, advertising, branding and R&D.
- *Networking*—friends, colleagues, professional websites and blogs are useful for networking, sharing, mutual learning, disseminating, absorbing information, getting a sense of market needs or saturation levels, and finding potential clients, investors and suppliers. Women are typified as possessing proficiency in social interactions, initiating and handling open communication and sharing their insights and thoughts; however, research shows that men more than women use networking for their business needs. Women should embrace

networking as a core process in the pre-launching stages and engage themselves more deeply in a goal-oriented networking dynamic that will promote their business's goals.

- *Marketing strategies*—it is imperative to develop a plan that suits the entrepreneur's temperament and routines; women should sketch their own marketing plan, be it general or detailed, in a feminine or other style, yet this plan should echo women's reflections, desires and needs. Marketing plans embody core marketing strategies to be pursued and practised, such as finding the niche, using the best techniques for branding, advertising, sales and marketing, focusing effort on reaching clients, i.e., outreach. A plan designed to match women's thoughts and reflections will serve as a valid anchor in their business's dynamics.
- *Finance*—many women tend to avoid the financial part of their businesses; studies continually show that women delegate finance-related activities and responsibilities to their male counterparts (partners, team members, outsourcing assistance, family members). Women need to embark upon the financial topics of their businesses; they may still accept assistance while remaining hands-on, taking finance-based decisions and leading the financial processes in their businesses.
- *Managing teams*—women have to learn how to recruit and manage the most outstanding team in order to establish their business and lead it toward success. No compromises should be made on staff professionalism or suitability to their business's character.
- *Knowledge management*—women must update themselves on a daily basis, be informed about their competitors, clients, suppliers and potential clients. Moreover, they must proactively seek material that is relevant to the core products/services of their business (e.g., owners of arts and crafts firms should read and learn about innovations, technologies and the "latest" know-how in art; while owners of counseling firms should keep themselves updated on the latest counseling research, theories and articles published in this area).
- *Self-management*—juggling entrepreneurship, family time and personal time is becoming more challenging for women as they engage more and more in the role of entrepreneur; the burden and demands imposed on women's time, e.g., business, family, personal, social, become congested and may result in a decline in women's quality of life. Self-management means prioritizing, setting personal goals, including activities that fuel both the entrepreneur and their close circle with positive energy. Different entrepreneurial-related programs, such as coaching, mentoring and training sessions, are offered to entrepreneurs in the pre-launching stages; programs assisting in balancing the work–home conflict are especially constructive for women entrepreneurs.

SUMMARY

The pre-launching stages arise in an atmosphere that is still abstract, theoretical, i.e., in the entrepreneur's mind or in written sketches, when these are not yet a tangible business; however, these stages represent a crucial moratorium in the new venture creation, particularly because other, future activities will be executed at a higher cost, e.g., adjusting the business's concept at these stages is cheaper than adjusting it when a business is established. Therefore, this is a relatively less risky phase that needs to be meticulously exploited to ascertain that the required plans have been assessed in advance and that these are the best plans to be implemented for a business.

Managing an abstract, theoretical venture is complex and demands specific capabilities, including coming up with creative ideas, planning, assessing the ideas by communicating them, accumulating a team of people before there is an actual business, making decisions that are relevant for the future business. These activities, among others, require competencies that women possess: in-depth yet flexible thinking and creativity, which assist in making decisions for the future business, being attentive to opportunities, including others' comments on the business idea or concept, gathering together a team, communicating ideas, social and emotional decision-making, embracing the environment's comments and insights, partnering, and asking for assistance.

CASE STUDIES AND AT-A-GLANCE CASE[4]

Two exciting case studies are included in this chapter to illustrate the new venture creation process as a phenomenon that takes on different forms in different contexts: Martha Reeves takes us on a journey with Ms. Rachel Weeks, who received a Fulbright Scholarship to investigate the garment industry in Sri Lanka, lived in Sri Lanka for a time and started an ethnic clothing line that sells through college and university bookstores in the US.

Mason, Dana and Anderson trace the fascinating ways of two Inuit women entrepreneurs, Ms. Tara Tootoo Fotheringham and Ms. Robin Goodfellow-Baikie of Northwest River, and draw their entrepreneurial path in the context of the Inuit community.

An "at a glance" story of Ms. Vongpackdy Sithonh, is also introduced to add an international, yet unknown flavor of entrepreneurship in Laos and Thialnd. Ms. Sithonh's story contributed by Professor Leo-Paul Dana tells the story of a woman that started her business by taking advantage of the new opportunities for trade resulting from the opening of a new land route between Laos and Thailand.

Supply Chain Management in Sri Lanka

Martha E. Reeves
*Markets and Management Studies Program, Duke University,
Durham, North Carolina, USA*

Rachel Weeks earned a Women's Studies degree at Duke University, graduating in 2007. During her years at Duke, she had become interested in women in developing countries working in the garment sector. She had read a great deal about the exploitation of garment workers in Asia and Central America and how they were generally treated poorly and paid wages that could not support themselves or their families.

As part of her undergraduate experience, she participated in an internship in Washington, DC working for Women Thrive Worldwide, a nonprofit organization interested in new approaches to driving innovation that might improve the lives of women in developing countries. The organization specifically looked at how corporations affect supply chains and how corporate social responsibility initiatives could improve women's lives.

With this early interest in women's issues and her experience in the nonprofit organization under her belt, she applied for and won a Fulbright Scholarship in 2007–2008 to investigate the garment industry in Sri Lanka. She had an eye toward possibly starting her own ethical clothing line, but realized that she needed on-the-ground experience to understand the complexity of the garment industry and to develop contacts with manufacturing facilities. Excited for the adventure of learning more, she packed her bags for South Asia.

During her extended stay in Sri Lanka, she became more convinced that she wanted a career in ethical fashion, but had no real idea of how to go about it. She began meeting with organizers from Garments Without Guilt, an association of garment managers. The mission of Garments Without Guilt is to support higher labor standards and women's empowerment. The organization had links to Victoria's Secret's top suppliers.

The Textile Industry in Sri Lanka

In the 1960s and 70s, the Sri Lankan State invested heavily in textile manufacturing facilities in an effort to become more self-sufficient. These State-run facilities, which concentrated on the cotton sector, predominantly employed men. At the same time, there was an increase in the handloom industry, which employed mostly women. The textile industry was split into three main sectors—the State-owned cotton sector, the privately-owned synthetic sector, and hand-looms which were either cooperatives owned by the workers themselves or were owned by the private sector. By 1977, only two mills were State-owned. Today, women constitute 85 percent of textile workers and work in all types of jobs, but dominate weaving and knitting roles. The entire industry has become export-driven, as the demand for clothing is much greater outside of Sri Lanka. By 1986, garments in Sri Lanka accounted for the largest share of its exports.

Cheap labor and the institution of EPZs (Export Processing Zones) by the government encouraged rapid growth of private investment in the textile industry. EPZs are special zones in a country where trade barriers for foreign investors, such as tariffs and quotas, are relaxed or lifted altogether. This lack of regulation, private ownership and the constant pressure to ramp up production leaves employees at risk of mistreatment.

Several human rights issues have arisen due to the lack of oversight of textile factories. Women are often isolated, having come to the EPZ from rural areas of the country. They have left their support system behind and are often powerless to protest unfair treatment. Unrealistic production targets, verbal abuse, sub-human living conditions, long hours, and sexual assault have been reported. Privatization of the National Textile Corporation's mills left employees without employment protections, formerly guaranteed by the State.

The Market Niche and Rachel's Business Concept

The retail clothing business is fairly saturated, with large multinational players such as LL Bean, Abercrombie and Fitch, Zara, and the Gap. It was clear to Rachel that she could not go head-to-head with these juggernauts, but instead needed to find a smaller market where there was far less competition. She also knew that she could not compete on price with these volume manufacturers. While at Duke University she noticed that University branded T-shirts, pants, jackets, hats, and other apparel were one-size-fits-all and rarely catered to young women. Many of her women friends shunned buying branded Duke wear because they found it unappealing.

Before she left for Sri Lanka she had the idea for School House, the proposed name for her ethical clothing line that would be sold through University bookstores. Colleges and universities in the US have on-campus bookstores, where a variety of goods—textbooks, clothing, and sundries—are sold. Rachel also capitalized on the fact that individual colleges and universities had different personalities, different traditions, and different rituals. These differences would come alive in her apparel designs. For example, Duke University has a fun-loving, sports-oriented culture where the mascot and Duke symbol is a Blue Devil. MIT, on the other hand, is known for its science and math-oriented students and the Berkeley School of Music had no identifiable logo at all. Research on the different cultures in these schools yielded original designs. For example, the design of the T-shirts for MIT sported equations while the Berkeley School of Music's clothing was screen printed with musical staffs. The feedback she received on these designs was very positive; people liked the fashion sense of the designs and the individual pride they instilled in their own school.

The Early Challenges of the Business

I had to figure out how to make the numbers work. How was I going to deliver a high quality product at the right price, make a profit, and still offer a livable wage at the factory site? Eventually, I just backed out of the problem, by just putting numbers to it. How much was a living wage? How much would the inputs be, the shipping and delivering? I needed to figure in the cost of licensing and the cost of paying royalties to the universities for each item sold. It all starts with the cost of yarn and ends with the Federal Express Truck at a US port.

Of course, a second challenge was finding someone in Sri Lanka who would help me identify a manufacturing facility that could make the product. I found Upali Weerakoon who became my trusted business advisor. He knew the garment industry upside and down and the technical details of apparel manufacturing. He told me I didn't need a huge business plan—I just needed to show demand. I needed my first order.

It became clear that Rachel would not get an order unless she could show a prospective customer what the product looked and felt like. So the challenge to get the order was preceded by the task of creating samples of the clothing line. Rachel's first major financial investment, $20,000, was used to hire a freelance designer from New York City who would design the product. Colleen McCann produced several sketches that were then used to design the samples. At this stage, Rachel began to trust her own judgment about what the product should look like—at age 22 she was very close in age to her target market. By July 2008 she had 45 samples.

Rachel's first customer was her alma-mater, Duke University. The Duke Stores manager gave her an order of 6,000 units with cash-on-delivery terms. She was elated as she left the meeting with him, but soon realized she had no money to pay the factory for the product until she was paid by her customer. Luckily, she was able to negotiate terms with the factory for payment; they would accept payment after she was paid by Duke Stores.

A third challenge, although not as daunting as the previous two, was raising sufficient funds to ramp up the business. Over the course of the business, she has raised $1.3M from angel investors, family and friends. Investors were able to buy shares in increments of $10,000 up to $250,000.

Ongoing Challenges—Competition and Supply Chain Problems

During the early stages of her business concept, Rachel shared her idea with many people in Sri Lanka. One such individual was the Vice President of a large holding company and a manufacturer for a well-established product line of women's wear. Just as Rachel's product was about to hit the market and she was seeking licences from universities, she discovered that he had taken her idea to his largest client. The women's wear company quickly began rolling out their newest product, a line of university-branded clothing.

Rachel was not deterred; she still felt passionate about her concept of ethical fashion and the market she had chosen for it. She had meetings set up with book store managers at the University of North Carolina, North Carolina State, Wake Forest University, and Eastern Carolina University. In order to keep a factory committed to producing her product, she needed to guarantee them a certain level of business. Fortunately, all of the afore-mentioned schools became customers.

After these early contracts, the factory began hiring more workers to ramp up for the additional orders. Unfortunately, the factory manager used it as an opportunity to hire more workers than were needed. They hired 100 workers when Rachel needed only 20! As a result, Rachel was pressured to accept inventory from them that she didn't really need, because with the extra workers they produced more than was required. In addition to the maverick approach of the factory, management in the factory began selling her product on the black market. This is unfortunately a familiar story in many factories in developing countries. After this blow, Rachel decided she had to look for another factory that would deal more fairly.

At this time, her business began growing exponentially. She made a sales call to Barnes and Noble, the largest bookstore retailer in the US. Barnes and Noble has a college bookstore division where they manage bookstores for approximately 600 colleges and universities. After seeing samples of the School House product, they agreed to conduct a test at their Harvard and Yale stores. It proved to be very successful, and Barnes and Noble agreed to add 48 schools to Rachel's roster of business. By this time, Rachel had located another manufacturing facility in Sri Lanka that would take on her business. Stewarts, the new facility, promised to process her orders in a timely fashion. Unfortunately, this manufacturing facility also took on work for Lands End, and placed their business ahead of hers, causing her orders to be late.

It was time to rethink the entire supply chain. Rachel became increasingly frustrated at the lack of goodwill between her business and the manufacturing facilities she had chosen. She realized that the factories did not see the contracts they had signed as binding agreements, and she did not have the resources or the time to pursue legal action against them. She was not even sure that these contracts would be enforceable in Sri Lanka. Perhaps there was simply too much temptation in Sri Lanka for people to try to earn a little extra money through unethical approaches to business. She knew that she could not continue trying to market the company, visit potential clients, and make trips to oversee activities in the manufacturing facilities.

Hiring Staff and Moving Manufacturing Facilities

Up until this point, Rachel had managed the company with just a designer, an assistant and a few student interns. She decided she really needed to hire a chief operating officer whose job it would be to figure out production. With the advice of the new COO, she moved manufacturing facilities to Wendell, North Carolina near the capital city of Raleigh, and began production there. Everything is made and sourced in the US now, including the cotton. Rachel still believes in the livable wage concept, and is implementing it in North Carolina.

To date, Rachel has grown her business from one customer to ninety-one customers. In 2009, she had revenues of $310,000; in 2010, $690,000; and in 2011 she expects $1.4 million in revenue. Her goal is to grow revenues by 100% each year.

She has a new opportunity with The Follet Education Group, which, like Barnes and Noble, manages college book stores. Follet Group has 800 stores under management. In the fall of 2011, School House will test the product at several of their stores—Stanford, Vanderbilt, and the University of Cincinnati, for example.

Reflecting on the Challenges

Rachel has found starting her own business exciting and energizing. It has, however, been a steep learning curve. She did not anticipate the challenges with the manufacturing facilities and still wonders whether or not they could have been avoided. Being young and female may have made some feel they could take advantage of her. On the other hand, the culture of business practices in Sri Lanka may just be radically different than those in the US.

Although she believes passionately in the living wage concept, she doubts whether this is a key selling point for her clothes.

> Many people have no idea how the clothes are manufactured and many probably don't care, unfortunately. For that reason, I believe so strongly that sustainable, ethical fashion has to be as much about fashion as it is about sustainability and ethics. My hope is that our customers fall in love with the way our clothing looks, and love it that much more when they learn our story.

Questions for Discussion

1 What challenges did Rachel face in the early stages of her business?
2 Cash flow is often a problem for small businesses. What potential problems did Rachel have with cash flow and how did she solve them?

3   Rachel trusted many people. Do you think she was naïve? Could she have taken more precautions or was she just unlucky?
4   Rachel wanted to provide livable wages for employees in Sri Lanka. Using the web, investigate what livable wages are in countries that manufacture textiles (Malaysia, Honduras, Mexico, Sri Lanka, and China, for example).

Case References

Kelegama, S. (2005). Ready-made garment industry in Sri Lanka: Preparing to face the global challenges. *Asia Pacific Trade and Development Review*, *1*(1), 51–67.
Nordds, H.K. (2004). *The global textile and clothing industry post the agreement on textiles and clothing*, Discussion Paper #5, 1–41. World Trade Organization, Geneva.
Personal Interview. Rachel Weeks, April 18, 2011.
Tennekoon, R. (2000). *Labor issues in the textile and clothing industry: A Sri Lankan Perspective*. International Labour Organization. Geneva. Retrieved May 12, 2011 from http://ilo.org/public/english///dialogue/sector/papers

Inuit Women Entrepreneurs Recognizing Opportunities

Aldene Meis Mason[a], Leo-Paul Dana[b] and Robert B. Anderson[c]
[a]*Faculty of Business Administration, University of Regina, Regina, Saskatchewan, Canada;* [b]*Groupe Sup de Co Montpellier Business School, Montpellier, Research in Management, Montpellier, France;* [c]*University of Regina, Regina, Saskatchewan, Canada*

This case study makes a unique contribution by highlighting Inuit entrepreneurs as role models. It illustrates opportunities arising from the Inuit land claims settlements. It introduces Inuit values, principles, and context when recognizing opportunities and developing Inuit enterprises. It honors two female Inuit Elders as role models who began trading and selling their clothing products many years ago and are transferring their skills to younger generations. Students can apply key concepts necessary for opportunity recognition.

Sheila Watt-Cloutier (2003) explained the importance of entrepreneurship to the Inuit,

> The Inuit measure success one person, one family at a time. So a business that may seem insignificant elsewhere, perhaps supporting five families is of considerable importance to us. While our lands lend themselves to mega projects, our sense of sustainability lends itself to smaller entrepreneurial businesses . . . With the growing realization that strong economies are essential for cultural survival, we have come to attach more importance to economic and business development.

She went on to say,

> Inuit have many of the skills that characterize successful entrepreneurs in the global marketplace: creativity, the ability to judge all risks, a positive and forward looking nature, and of course, the ability to adapt and use wisdom to make the best use of novel situations. And, we bring strengths that are a great advantage over many non-indigenous entrepreneurs, the strength of our communities. . . . Our traditional knowledge is a source of our strength and can also be a foundation for a growing Inuit entrepreneurial sector.[5]

The Inuit have recently settled several comprehensive land claims with Canada: the James Bay and Northern Quebec Agreement (JBNQA) in 1975 (the first modern treaty); the Northeastern Quebec Agreement in 1978; the Inuvialuit Final Agreement in 1984; the Nunavut Land Claims Agreement in 1993; and the Labrador Inuit Land Claims Agreement in 2005. The Inuit see the land claim settlements as an opportunity to regain control of traditional lands and activities, to develop economies more in tune with Inuit values and resources, and to improve their socio-economic conditions and quality of lives for individuals, families and communities. As a result of the land claim settlements, Inuit have gained ownership of land and resources. They also gained rights to develop their resources; to form business enterprises; to sell, barter or trade their products and services; and to make decisions for themselves about which products are developed and used. Inuit were guaranteed the right to preserve Inuit culture and to ensure appropriate Inuit education. As Inuit beneficiaries, they also received an infusion of capital which could be used to purchase homes and businesses. Special funds became available for Inuit economic development in the form of loans, grants and equity. With resource development, more people are coming to work in the remote Inuit and northern communities and there is more business travel as these economic developments are explored.

Several Inuit values and principles are important in Inuit entrepreneurship and economic development:[6]

- *Pilimmaksarniq*: Acquire skills & knowledge & build capacity; empowerment to be productive, resourceful, capable & successful.
- *Qanuqtuurungnarniq*: Be resourceful to solve problems, through innovation and creative use of resources; constantly exploring new opportunities; show adaptability, flexibility and persistence to improve Inuit well-being.
- *Piliriqatigiingniq*: Collaborative relationships or working together for common purpose and good (stress group over individual), supportive & builds relationships. Everything is interrelated and must be in

balance and harmony. All things in life (living and non-living) have a purpose and are interconnected. Mental, physical and spiritual dimensions of the individual, the family and the community.

*   *Avatimik Kamattiarniq*: Global stewardship for land and the environment; respect for mutually interdependent relationship with the environment and the world; seek to improve and protect the relationship; a related Inuit value is not to waste.
*   *Pijitsirarniq*: Service to the Family and Community and Leadership. Commitment to serving the common good; each person has a valued contribution to make.
*   *Aajiiqatigiigniq*: Consensus decision-making by thinking and acting collaboratively, consulting & developing shared understanding & goals. Helping each other to become informed. Patiently communicating. Being committed to the process.

Elders Lizzie Ittinuar and Elisipee Inukpuk—Master Inuit Seamstresses and Doll Makers[7]

Inuit women have made and sold traditional clothing and household items in their communities for many years. Elder Lizzie Ittinuar of Rankin Inlet, Nunavut remembered, "When I went to Chesterfield Inlet as a girl, I noticed women selling their sewing and fox furs. The Hudson Bay Trading Post used wooden sticks for money. While I was young, I learned how to scrape, stretch and soften skins. I was taught to make clothing from caribou and seal. My first sewing project was a pair of boots. When my children were young, I started selling clothing made from caribou and seal like *kamiks (boots)*, pants and *amautiks* (parkas) as a way of helping with the family finances . . . Later, I wanted people to know that my work was different so I started decorating my *amautiks* with beads. While watching TV, I saw collector dolls and thought that I could do better than that if I try." Today, Lizzie's dolls with their detailed bead work are in museums and private collections around the world.

Elder Elisipee Inukpuk of Inukjuak, Nunavik, Northern Quebec learned from her mother to sew and make dolls. In the 1950s, a federal government officer encouraged her to make dolls for sale. She made the dolls in her tent and igloo from little pieces of clothing and their faces were made from socks. The community of Inukjuak was known internationally for its soapstone carvings. Elisipee carved expressive soapstone faces for her Inuit dolls. They wore miniature Inuit traditional clothing made from seal or caribou skin, jeans or cloth. Preserving and passing on Inuit culture is very important. Elisipee created families of Inuit dolls (*inuujaq*) and used these to tell stories which "represent our Inuit culture, our way of life."

As many young people had not learned traditional Inuit skills, both Elder Lizzie and Elder Elisipee taught workshops focusing on skin preparation, sewing clothes, and making dolls. While delivering the workshops, they also tell stories and communicate Inuit values and principles.

Tara Tootoo Fotheringham—Tara's Bed and Breakfast[8]

Tara Tootoo Fotheringham lived in Rankin Inlet located on the west edge of the Hudson's Bay about 500 km north of Churchill, Manitoba. With a population of 2,239, Rankin Inlet was the second largest community in Nunavut. Its population was 79 percent Inuit and 21 percent non-Inuit. Rankin Inlet had served as a regional center for the government of the Northwest Territories (NWT). Over the years, many people moved to the community to work for the federal and territorial government and Inuit organizations as those were the major employers. The signing of the Nunavut Land Claims Agreement in 1993 led to the creation of the territory of Nunavut in 1999. As infrastructure was moved and some levels of government were devolved, Rankin Inlet's population expanded. Also, more Inuit were employed by government and businesses.

In 1993, a regional community birthing center was opened in Rankin Inlet to handle low-risk births. Place of birth was very important to Inuit identity. Previously Inuit women who were pregnant were sent to hospitals in Winnipeg and Churchill, Manitoba to await the birth of their child. As Inuit extended families were very close, this was very disruptive and hard on the families. In addition, the births in southern Canada had used modern medical sciences and did not allow for Inuit traditional birthing practices and rituals.[9] In 1996, Tara started working for the Northwest Territorial Government as an Aboriginal Adoption Commissioner arranging adoption for Inuit babies. At that time, the rate of pregnancy in teenagers aged 15–19 in the Northwest Territories was 123.3 pregnancies per 1,000; by far the highest rate in Canada.[10] Pregnant mothers came to Rankin Inlet from surrounding communities for medical care at the regional hospital. Tara also served her community as an elected councilor for the hamlet of Rankin Inlet.

Rankin Inlet had only two hotels. According to the 1994 Northwest Territories Exit Survey, Rankin Inlet had 1,245 travelers—829 business and 416 vacational over the four-month busy season from May to September: local hotel managers commented that 90 percent of their clients were business travelers with the rest being tourists. Hotel annual occupancy rates ranged from 50 percent to 70 percent.[11] Tara noticed a lack of accommodation for pregnant mothers and decided to open Tara's Bed and Breakfast operating out of her home in 1999.

She registered Tara's Bed and Breakfast as an Inuit business and listed it on the Nunavut Tunngavik Inc. (NTI) Inuit Firm Registry. This registry was established in 1994 under Article 24 of the Nunavut Land Claims Agreement. Registration allowed an Inuit-owned enterprise to qualify for preferential government procurement under the Canadian Aboriginal Procurement Program as well as the Nunavut government's preferential procurement policy for Inuit-owned and northern businesses. As an Inuit-owned enterprise, it also qualified for special grants, loans or equity financing.[12] One major obstacle Tara encountered was that government employees could only stay at commercial hotels and not in bed and breakfasts.[13]

In 2005, Tara bought the Sugar Rush Café. She serves the community by having no minimum charge; creating a welcoming, comfortable and inclusive atmosphere for young and old; operating extended hours, and providing foods such as arctic char and caribou chili. She also sells Inuit carvings, jewelry and artwork made locally.

Tara's maternal grandmother was an inspirational role model. She sewed traditional clothing for her 15 children and also sold clothing in surrounding communities. She earned enough money to buy her family their first house. Tara's father, Mike Carruthers, was a heating engineer with the Department of Public Works. He became an entrepreneur in 1999 as owner of the Inuvik Funeral Services.[14]

Robin Goodfellow-Baikie, Inventor and Social Entrepreneur[15]

Robin Goodfellow-Baikie of Northwest River, Labrador had the idea to weave caribou hair in 1981. A university professor had suggested she "felt" the hair. She applied for a research grant under the Canada Council Exploration Program in Domestic Sciences. Robin experimented until she developed a technique to felt the hair and called the product "mouffelt." Product tests indicated that it was twice as warm as wool, with 65 percent of the weight. Robin commented, "At the time I did not have the confidence to take the product further."

After moving to Winnipeg, Manitoba in 1984, Robin worked as an industrial sewer for seven years. Through consulting Innu Elders, she learned how to take hair off hides efficiently. She applied for and received Canadian patent 1,255,997 on June 20, 1989 and US Patent 4,751,117 on June 14, 1988 for "moufflibou," a textile. The patents covered both caribou and deer hair.[16] She registered a logo with the caribou profile and had associated this with the caribou-fur felt product. The caribou fur-felt liners could be used for gloves, hats, vests, and sleeping bags.

Since the mid 1990s, Inuit commercial caribou harvests had occurred annually in several northern Canadian communities. About 3,000 caribou were harvested under each license. The hides were generally discarded and burned. Caribou hair was available as a by-product. Using her patented process, the caribou skins were first soured and the hair was removed by scraping. The hair was carded then spun with a mix of sheep's wool. The wool was then woven and felted to make a fabric. During felting, the caribou hair/wool combination collapsed after exposure to steam and formed caribou-fur felt.

In 1987–1988, Robin carried out a prototype project in Nain, northern Labrador with the Labrador Inuit Development Corporation's commercial caribou harvest and processing plant. They made caribou hair/wool felt batting by hand and created twelve pairs of snowmobile mitts. Local Inuit hunters testing the product said these were the warmest mitts they had ever worn and the mitts remained warm even when wet. Robin tried to generate interest in a project with the Inuit First Nations community of Sheshatshiu for a sustainable cottage industry making caribou fur-felt. After several years, this project did not go ahead.

Robin had the special "GOODFELLOW FELTMAKER" designed and built to her specifications in 1997. The machine, which measured eight feet by eight feet, collapsed to fit through 32-inch wide doorways and was ideal for a home-based or small-scale industry. The equipment also was designed to be very strong yet gentle with the fragile caribou hair.

Because of the downturn in the fishing and forestry industries, North West River was identified as an economically depressed area. The community created the North West River Industrial Association (NWRIA) as a not-for-profit community development corporation in 1999. The NWRIA project received $144,000 for three years under the Canada-Newfoundland Agreement for the Economic Development Component of the Canadian Fisheries Adjustment and Restructuring Initiative. The project's objectives were to assess the technical and market feasibility of using caribou hair as a liner for mitts and other garments. The project would help to look at the type and scale of operations which could be established in Labrador. The NWRIA also received funding and technical assistance from Carleton University's Community Economic Development Technical Assistance Program (CEDTAP) in the form of strategic and operational planning, selection of a corporate structure and training in negotiation skills with investors.[17] The project received $12,683 in funding from the Atlantic Canada Opportunities Agency.[18]

Although they envisioned handling 2,000 caribou hides per year, the cottage industry was based on 370 hides per year. It required one manager and four full-time workers. For two seasons, they purchased caribou skins for $5.00 each from Uncle Sam's Butcher Shop which held the Inuit commercial caribou license in Labrador. They also got hides from local hunters. They proved that the caribou fur-felt could be put into production. The project made 300 pairs of high-quality cold weather mitts with insulated liners. Robin sold the mitts at trade shows for $175 per pair. Scraps from the felt cutting were put into round pillows which people used as seat cushions at hockey rinks. Each hide also had three to four pounds of caribou meat which was removed and could have been used for pet food.

The National Research Council had found waste caribou meat could be added to bark for compost. Goodfellow-Baikie was told funds were unavailable from Atlantic government agencies for further commercialization because the project involved sewing and clothing production. She indicated some communities were interested in purchasing the equipment and the rights to the technology. The Central Labrador Development Board indicated they had supported the NWRIA in its project and were currently working with a local entrepreneur to revitalize it.

Questions for Discussion

1   To what extent do the described Inuit women's enterprises meet the model of pre-launching stages discussed in this chapter? Could you pinpoint the main differences between these two women's enterprises? Explain.

2   What environmental trends, such as political and regulatory changes, technological advances, social, cultural and demographic factors, or economic factors are working in favor of Tara and Robin? What might be working against them?

3   Personal characteristics of the entrepreneur, including prior experiences, cognitive factors such as sensing opportunities, social networks and creativity, are also important in entrepreneurs' recognizing opportunities. How are these being demonstrated by the Inuit women entrepreneurs?

4   Choose one technique from the Rational decision-making models and one technique from the Intuitive decision-making models. Analyze Tara and Robin's decision-making by these two techniques. What are your conclusions? Are these women different due to the context they live in?

5   How might other Inuit women capitalize on Inuit culture, values and principles in creating a venture? What aspects of the Inuit culture, values and principles hinder creating a venture?

Case References

Arnakak, Jaypete (2002). Incorporation of Inuit Qaujimmanituqangit or Inuit traditional knowledge in the government of Nunavut. *Journal of Aboriginal Development*, 3(1), 33–39.

Buckler, Carolee, Krueger, Audra, Poelzer, Greg, & Normand, Laura. (2009). *The Northern entrepreneurship workshop proceedings and report: Fostering entrepreneurship in the North.* University of Saskatchewan International Centre for Governance and Development. Retrieved from http://www.iisd.org/pdf/2009/northern_workshop_2009.pdf.

Canada's Rural Secretariat. (2000). The Canadian Rural Partnership. Newfoundland & Labrador, Northern Sustainable Industry. Pilot Projects 2000–2001

(Round 3). Funding Approved: $12,683. Federal Partners: Atlantic Canada Opportunities Agency. Retrieved from http://rural.gc.ca/programs/projects00_e.phtml.

Community Economic Development Technical Assistance Program. (2000). Approved Initiatives (Archives). North West River Industrial Association, Labrador, Newfoundland. Carleton University. Retrieved from http://www.carleton.ca/cedtap/app_ini/initiatives%20%28archives%29_e.html.

Douglas, Vasiliki K. (2011). The Rankin Inlet Birthing Centre: Community midwifery in the Inuit context. *International Journal of Circumpolar Health,* 70(2), 178–185.

Dryburgh, Heather. (2003). Teenage pregnancy. *Health Reports,* 12 No. 1. Statistics Canada Catalogue 82-003. Retrieved from http://www.statcan.gc,ca/kits-trousses/preg-gross/preg-gross-eng.htm.

Government of Nunavut. (2002). *The First Annual Report of the Inuit Qaujimaja-tuqanginnut (IQ) Task Force.* Retrieved from http://www.inukshukmanage-ment.ca/IQ%20Task%Force%20Report1.pdf

Government of Nunavut. Human Resources Department. (2005). *Inuit Qaujima-jatuqangit (IQ).* Retrieved February 2, 2006 from http://www.gov.nu.ca/hr/site/beliefsystem

May, Katie. (2009). "I'll look after everything." Northern News Services. Published Thursday, July 2, 2009. Retrieved from http://www.nnsl.com/frames/newspaper/2009-07/jul6_09job.html

Meis Mason, A., Dana, L. P., & Anderson, R. B. (2009). A study of enterprise in Rankin Inlet, Nunavut: Where subsistence self-employment meets formal entrepreneurship. *International Journal of Entrepreneurship and Small Business,* 7(1), 1–23. Translated into Inuktitut 2009.

Nunavut Tunngavik Incorporated. (2006a). *Inuit Firm Registry Data Base.* Retrieved from http://inuitfirm.tunngavik.com

Pauktuutit Inuit Women of Canada. (2006). *The Inuit Way: A Guide to Inuit Culture.* Retrieved from http://www.pauktuutit.ca/pdf.publications/pauktuu-tit/InuitWay_e.pdf

Pauktuutit Inuit Women of Canada. (2006b). *Inuit Women in Business Facilitator's Handbook.* Retrieved from http://www.pauktuutit.ca/economic/downloads/IWB%20Faciliator's%20Handbooik%20ENG.pdf

RT Associates. (2005). *Rankin Inlet Restaurant, Hotel and Retail Market Study.* Retrieved from http://www.atuqtuarvik.com/documents/rankin-market-study.pdf

Watt-Cloutier, S. (2003). *The indigenous entrepreneur: Sharing a path to global sustainability.* Keynote presentation to the 2003 World Summit of Indigenous Entrepreneurs. August 18–20, 2003 in Toronto, Ontario, Canada. Retrieved November 15, 2004 from http://www.inuitcircumpolar.com/index.php?ID=77&Lang=En

AT A GLANCE[19]

Madame Vongpackdy Sithonh[20]

Leo-Paul Dana
*Groupe Sup de Co Montpellier Business School, Montpellier,
Research in Management, Montpellier, France*

Situational Summary

A gift from the people of Australia, the Friendship Bridge across the Mekong
River between Laos and Thailand was finally opened in 1994. For Madame
Sithonh and her family, this might lead to unprecedented opportunities.
However, Laos, having been a relatively closed country, lacked experience in
international business. As the hot season was giving way to the rainy season,
important decisions had to be made, but only after opportunities were evaluated. As well as having a 23-year-old son living with her and her husband,
Madame Sithonh had another son and two daughters studying in Vientiane,
less than one kilometer from Thailand. All had agreed to meet together the
coming weekend. Their international opportunities were to be discussed.

The Entrepreneur

Born in a small village in the Vientiane province of Laos, Vongpackdy
Sithonh went to study in Vientiane prefecture. She obtained her *brevet*
diploma from the Lycée Vientiane, in 1966. Mastering French, English
and Thai, in addition to her native Lao tongue, she worked as a typist and
later as a secretary for an American in Laos.

　In 1974, Ms. Sithonh got married. Meanwhile, the war in Indochina had
heated up, and as the United States was preparing to withdraw from
Vietnam, Vongpackdy lost her job when her boss returned to America.
Time would come for Madame Sithonh to create her own job.

Methodology

The research leading to this case study used an holistic-inductive design.
While a hypothetico-deductive methodology imposes the researcher's
values (e.g., predetermining which variables are worth measuring, i.e.,
what to ask on a survey), an holistic-inductive design allows the researcher
to be open to whatever emerges from the data. The holistic-inductive
approach thus requires a flexible design, which is in constant evolution.
Since the researcher does not impose *a priori* categories or hypotheses, but
rather attempts to understand phenomena based on field research, new
questions must constantly be formulated. The researcher is inspired by
observations to seek more answers, which in turn inspire new questions.

This allows the researcher to acquire an understanding of the environment for entrepreneurship, as well as the entrepreneur as an individual.

Laos

The Lao People's Democratic Republic is one of Asia's most undeveloped nations, and among the five poorest in the world. The landlocked country, enclosing 235,000 sq km, is nestled between Cambodia, China, Myanmar (Burma), Thailand and Vietnam. In 1994, there was one television set per 142.9 people in Laos, 111.1 in Cambodia, 25.6 in Vietnam, and 8.9 in Thailand; Laos had 4,380 people per doctor, almost twice the ratio in Vietnam.[21] Large corporations in Thailand each earn more than the value of all the goods and services produced in all of Laos.

Laos is sparsely populated, and among the least urbanized nations in Asia. Its population in 1994 was estimated at 4.5 million people, living in an area about the size of Britain. Yet the population's rate of growth was 2.9 percent per annum, double that in neighboring Thailand. With 120,000 inhabitants, the largest city, and capital of Laos is Vientiane, situated at a bend along the Mekong River, near its very fertile alluvial plains. Recent government figures suggest that 90 percent of the Lao population are farmers. Given that over 60 percent of the GNP comes from agricultural output, the government has introduced reforms providing incentives to farmers. The plan increases agricultural investment, especially in irrigation work. It also raises the prices of agricultural produce, links remuneration with output and employs preferential agricultural tax policies.

Per capita rice output in Laos is 350 kg. Nevertheless, some provinces experience occasional rice shortages. Many farming communities are migrational, deforesting land for a crop, and then moving elsewhere. There is a constant breeze of smoke and ashes over the Mekong River. Opium is an important crop, of which Laos produces about 300 tons annually. Although the State no longer has the monopoly on supply, purchasing and marketing since wage and management reforms have increased the autonomy of firms, manufacturing is very limited.

Traditionally, business activities in Laos have not been associated with high social status. Cultural values, stemming from religious beliefs, emphasized instead the elimination of desire. Commerce, on the other hand, is perceived as a means to satisfy desire. Social forces thus discouraged enterprise, and trade has usually been the role of those with inferior social standing. The communist takeover further discouraged entrepreneurial spirit. The result is a generally non-entrepreneurial society.

Infrastructure

Communication and transportation links are particularly poor in Laos. In 1994, there were 510 people per telephone.[22] That year, telephone numbers in the capital city were changed from having four digits to six digits, but telephone numbers in Savanket still consisted of two digits, as the metropolitan area had fewer than 100 telephones. A telephone number configured for international direct dialing (IDD) is costly; consequently, many entrepreneurs in Laos have been using portable phones linked to the telephone system of Thailand.

Given the generally poor conditions of the roads (often flooded during the rainy season) and the lack of a railway, a quarter of all traffic in Laos uses the Mekong River. People and buffalo stand side by side, on boats or barges, for hours.

Just over two miles from the city center of Vientiane, is the capital city's international airport, known as Wattay. A new airport was supposed to be constructed in 1969; however, the cement allocated to it was instead used to build a monument downtown, the Arc de Triomphe. Interestingly, although many flights arrive at Wattay in the afternoon, the money-exchange facility is closed then.

The national airline of Laos, called Lao Aviation, recently retired its Soviet helicopters in favor of Boeing aircraft. Still, its international routes are limited to Cambodia, China, Thailand and Vietnam.

A positive step toward improving infrastructure in Laos was the opening, on April 8, 1994, of the Friendship Bridge. Funded by the Australian International Development Assistance Bureau, the bridge crosses the Mekong River, downstream from Vientiane, at Nong Khai, thereby linking Laos and Thailand. It is expected to significantly boost regional trade and facilitate entrepreneurial activity. Nevertheless, as shall be explained in a following section, the belief system in Laos is likely to restrain entrepreneurship among Lao men.

Culture

Traditional Beliefs

Some East Asian nations believe in the virtues of hard work, frugality and savings. Laos, today, is still more noticeably influenced by traditional folk tales, superstitions, and the beliefs of the national religion, Theravada Buddhism. An article in the August 28, 1992 issue of *Asiaweek* explains that it is commonly believed that the Mekong River gets "hungry" for human souls, without which the annual rains will not arrive:

> A little girl (was) swept away by the current while picnicking with her family on a sandbank. Her mother and father made no attempt to save her. Two foreigners snatched the child from the swift water after a desperate effort. The parents were fearful because the river had been thwarted in claiming the child.

(p. 63)

Wats

Across Laos, Theravada monasteries, known as wats, dominate every town, and almost every house, shop and office has a private temple. It is even common for boats cruising the Mekong River to dock for the crew to jump ashore, light incense and pray.

The Lao wats are architecturally distinct (e.g., large terraces, and flare symbols on the roofs) from monasteries elsewhere in Asia. Monks are many, as *every* male is expected to serve as a monk at some period of his life; this involves 227 precepts. Women, in contrast, do *not* have such an obligation, nor is high social value attached to being a nun, which involves only eight vows.

Monks

Theravada monks are highly influential in Lao society. They are consulted on virtually all matters, thereby playing a role in a diversity of spheres, ranging from private life to government policy. They have traditionally had a great impact on the educational system; it used to be that the only schools were in wats.

Calendar

The official calendar used in Laos is that of the Lao Buddhist era (not to be confused with the Thai calendar); the Christian year 1995, for example, corresponds to 2633 in the Lao calendar, and 2529 in the Thai calendar.

Values

Central to Theravada values is the ultimate goal to extinguish unsatisfied desires. Its doctrine focuses on aspects of existence, including *dukkha* (suffering from unsatisfied desire), and *anicca* (impermanence). Assuming that unsatisfied desires cause suffering, then suffering can be eliminated if its cause (desire) is eliminated. A respectable person then, according to this ideology, should *not* work toward the satisfaction of materialistic desires, but should, rather, strive to eliminate the desire itself. A monk, for instance, is specifically prohibited by the religion from tilling fields or raising animals.

Lao folk tales reinforce the belief that a religious man should not labor on a farm; yet the same folklore conditions women to accept a heavy burden in exchange for honor, protection and security. Even the Lao currency portrays agricultural work being done exclusively by women.

Numerous Lao families who farm during the wet season become self-employed gold-diggers during the dry season. The prospectors camp along the Mekong River, especially in the region of Luang Prabang. The women do the heaviest work, digging for dirt and panning it in wooden trays. The men weigh the gold, up to one gram per day.

In a 1994 article entitled "Indochina," the *Far Eastern Economic Review* (May 5, 1994) quoted a London newspaper as saying that "Lao rice farmers have a reputation in this dynamic region for lying down, closing their eyes and listening to their crops grow in fertile paddy fields [p. 60]." It is very true that neither entrepreneurial spirit nor work ethic is prevalent in the Lao belief system.

The Small Business Sector

Given the Laotian belief system, the small business sector in Laos consists largely of foreigners. Most restaurants, movie theaters, hotels, repair shops and jewelry shops in urban areas are owned by ethnic Chinese. Some of the Chinese entrepreneurs interviewed claimed to be descendants of entrepreneurial families who established themselves in Laos several generations ago. There are about 2,500 ethnic Chinese in Vientiane, most of whom are involved with small-scale business. Muslim men are also very active in the small business sector of Laos.

As well, Thai and Australian entrepreneurs have recently created numerous new ventures in Laos. Unlike the Chinese and the Muslims who reside in Laos permanently, the Thais and Australians in Laos tend to be sojourners.

Whereas United States involvement in Lao business tends to be in the form of large business, Thai investments tend to be in the medium-size category, as are Australian ventures. More involved in small business is France, with 42 ventures. As of January 1, 1994, there were 421 licensed foreign enterprises in Laos. The Foreign Exchange Decree allows foreign entrepreneurs to lease to repatriate profits as well as negotiables.

In April 1994, Laos and Vietnam signed an agreement on goods in transit, which allowed these commodities to be transported across either Laos or Vietnam, on the way to the other. It was expected that this would benefit local and foreign enterprises.

In May 1994, Laos introduced a new, liberal, foreign investment law which streamlined foreign investment regulations and tax structures. Legislation included tax holidays, a 1 percent import duty on capital goods associated with production, and a flat-rate corporate tax of 20 percent. This was to lead to a major influx of foreign capital to create joint ventures as well as 100 percent of foreign-owned investments in commerce, industry and services. Furthermore, the government committed itself to expedite the business application process. Although the Laotians lack a reputation for industriousness, Japanese and Taiwanese investors expressed considerable interest. The geographic position of Laos could help it become an important assembly and trans-shipment center.

Yet, the traditional belief system in Laos keeps most Lao males away from entrepreneurship. Lao folk music is still very popular, and men are encouraged to pray and play music, rather than work as entrepreneurs. Their self-employment is largely limited to hunting, fishing and making utensils by hand.

Lao women, in contrast, are often self-employed, although these tend to be informal, marginal earners. Some are street vendors and others have shops. Since the 1987 liberalization of economic restrictions, many women have obtained stalls at expanding markets. Some sell rats and spiny anteaters at the Ban Thalat market of Vientiane. At the Ban Thong Khan Kham market of Vientiane, other women sell charcoal-broiled duck eggs along with bear paws and snakes.

Some Lao women also operate food establishments. The national dish involves taking glutenous rice with one's fingers, and dipping it in spices. Fancier restaurants also have forks and spoons, but knives are rare. Food tends to be quite fresh, as it is often purchased after the clients make their order. Service is therefore rather slow.

Lao women are also involved in black market money exchange, trading Lao kip for US dollars. Although these entrepreneurs offer the convenience of being able to change money after banking hours, their exchange rates are slightly lower than official bank rates. (This is quite a contrast with the situation elsewhere.)

Madame Sithonh's Enterprise

Madame Sithonh inherited her father's house in the city of Vientiane; however, rather than live in it, she leased it to cousins. She chose to reside in the outskirts of Bolek, in a house worth one million kip. There, she raised two sons and two daughters.

Bolek is a small town 35 km from the nation's capital. Located in the fertile Mekong River Valley, the area is ideal for growing rice. Most Bolek people derive their livelihood from rice. The poor gather frogs in rice fields, and sell them in town for 300 kip per kilo.

Separating rice seeds from the husks is a very laborious and time-consuming task when done manually. Yet, machines can do the job very efficiently. Surprisingly, until 1991, there was no rice-processing machine in Bolek. This prompted Madame Sithonh to import one from Thailand. A dog called Vilie would guard the machine at night.

Madame Sithonh decided that she would not charge anybody for using her machine. She would simply keep the husks for use as animal feed.

Her rice-processing machine soon became very popular, working some nights as late as 10 p.m. In addition to having her eldest son working with her full-time, Madame Sithonh hired an assistant for 500 kip per eight-hour shift.

As a sideline business, Madame Sithonh raised pigs. She would sell a full-grown hog for 100,000 kip; a young one was worth 20,000 kip.

With rental income from her inheritance, Madame Sithonh acquired a 9 million kip diesel truck to transport rice. Her husband operated the truck, charging 300 kip per 60 kg bag. The capacity of the truck was 150 bags, while the price of diesel fuel in Laos was 215 kip per liter.

Toward the Future

The opening of a new land route between Laos and Thailand presented new opportunities for trade. Madame Sithonh's truck might be used to export her pigs to Thailand; rather than return empty, it might be feasible to bring to Laos Thai-made products. The Lao Soft Drink Co. was bottling Pepsi, 7-Up and Mirinda in Vientiane, but Coca-Cola, Sprite and Fanta had to be imported into Laos, as were Chiclets, toothpaste and numerous other consumer goods. Madame Sithonh had an entrepreneurial spirit, but she was not sure whether to, nor how to, expand internationally.

Notes

1 International Labour Organization, Doing Business in Addis Ababa: Case Studies of Women Entrepreneurs with Disabilities in Ethiopia (2003). GLADNET Collection. Paper 189, p. 4. At http://digitalcommons.ilr. cornell.edu/gladnetcollect/189
2 Case Study: Being a Female Entrepreneur, by Susanna Simpson, at Fresh Business Thinking.com, p. 2 of the web version at http://www.freshbusinessthinking.com/business_advice.php?CID=17&AID=2480&PGID=1
3 The Decade of the Woman Entrepreneur, p. 1 at http://www.kauffman.org/ entrepreneurship/the-decade-of-the-woman-entrepreneur.aspx
4 The author(s) of the case studies and at-a-glance cases are fully and solely responsible for their content, phrasing consistency and flow, terminology, English proofing and reference lists.
5 Watt-Cloutier (2003).
6 Sources of information about Inuit values and principles were:

- Arnakak (2002.
- Government of Nunavut (2002).
- Government of Nunavut, Human Resources Department (2005).
- Pauktuutit Inuit Women of Canada (2006a).
- Pauktuutit Inuit Women of Canada (2006b).

7 Information about Elders Lizzie Ittinuar and Elder Elisipee Inukpuk was based on interviews with Aldene Meis Mason.
8 Information about Tara Tootoo Fotheringham was based on personal communication with Aldene Meis Mason and:

- Aboriginal and Affairs and Northern Development Canada. Biography— Ms. *Tara Tootoo* Fotheringham—News Release. Retrieved from www. ainc-inac.gc.ca > . . . > Media Room > 2008 News Releases.
- Business Development Canada. *Tara Tootoo Fotheringham Adds New Flavour to Hospitality in Rankin Inlet*. Canada News Centre. Retrieved from http://news.gc.ca/web/article-eng.httphttp

- Jennifer Macphee (2009). *The Whiz Kids*. Up Here Business - The Magazine of Canada's North. August 2009. http://www.upherebusiness.ca/node/341.

9 Douglas (2011).

10 Dryburgh (2003).

11 RT Associates (2005).

12 Inuit Firm Registry Data Base. (2006). Nunavut Tunngavik Incorporated. Inuit Firm Data Base. Retrieved from http://inuitfirm.tunngavik.com

13 Buckler *et al.* (2009).

14 May (2009).

15 Information about Robin Goodfellow-Baikie and the Nain and North West River Industrial Association was based on an interview with Aldene Meis Mason.

16 Robin Goodfellow. Canadian Patent 0125597 and US Patent US4751117.

17 The Community Economic Development Technical Assistance Program (2000).

18 Canada's Rural Secretariat (2000).

19 At-a-glance cases are included to present different ecosystems and their effects on the concepts discussed in the chapter; they do not include questions for discussion.

20 This case was researched and written in Laos and in Thailand, by Professor Leo-Paul Dana, with the cooperation of Mrs. Sithonh. Research for the essay was done by the author in French, and subsequently translated.

21 Source: Ministry of External Economic Relations, Vientiane.

22 Source: Office of the Foreign Investment Management Committee.

5 Personal Core Competencies in Starting a New Venture

Chapter Objectives

- Establishing the extensive meaning of personal competencies as the main assets in the first stages of the new venture creation for growth and a sustainable competitive advantage;
- Linking the concepts associated with the relevant core competencies to the resource-based view (RBV) and the dynamic capabilities (DC) approach;
- Categorizing the three groups of competencies identified as relevant to a successful new venture creation process: human capital capabilities, personal traits or characteristics, and know-how in management, marketing, etc.;
- Identifying the competitive advantage brought "to the table" by women entrepreneurs;
- Classifying a gender-based group of relevant traits that can assist women in the new venture creation process;
- Decoding the performance of female entrepreneurs in the new venture creation process, and determining the sources of their respective entrepreneurial actions;
- Recognizing the critical roles of networking and social capital in the female new venture creation process;
- Identifying women's entrepreneurial needs and linking these to the relevance of support and accelerating systems for women entrepreneurs;
- Conceptualizing the ethical zone in female entrepreneurship (e.g., social responsibility, respecting diversity, environmental protection) and women's proclivity to exhibit corresponding ethical performance.

This chapter's main objective is to identify the core characteristics that hold promise for success in the process of female new venture creation. The core competencies are articulated in the framework of the resource-based view and the dynamic capabilities approach, and are aligned with the different feminist theory angles—all postulating that some personal, social and societal capabilities can capture sustainable competitive advantages in the female entrepreneurship realm.

This chapter provides fuel for discussion on the multifaceted role of networks as a means of fostering women's venture creation, and analyzes the function of social capital competencies in the new venture creation phase. In addition, assistance and support systems are introduced which offer a possible path for women entrepreneurs to deliberately and proactively achieve empowerment and elevate their self-confidence in their capabilities to start a business.

Finally, a section is devoted to personal ethics in women's entrepreneurial realm, including a discussion on how the topics associated with ethics in entrepreneurship might apply to female entrepreneurship and how these could leverage their business's competitive advantage at the outset.

CORE COMPETENCIES AND THE QUEST FOR CAPABILITY

Vast research in entrepreneurship has debated the topic of entrepreneurs' core competencies as a platform for generating success and competitive advantage at the outset. The resource-based view (RBV) and the dynamic capabilities (DC) approach discussed in Chapter 1, give extensive meaning to the entrepreneur's core competencies at the first stages of the new venture creation; it is common knowledge that a business's effective creation process depends primarily on those raising the bright idea, i.e., the entrepreneurs, rather than on the idea itself, even if it is the brightest or most innovative idea ever invented.

The RBV provides a congruent theoretical framework for the discussion on core competencies in suggesting that accumulating the most relevant competencies at the very first stages of the new venture creation promotes the venture with a stock of valuable, rare, imperfectly inimitable and nonsubstitutable (VRIN) resources that are the most significant source of the venture's sustainable competitive advantage. The RBV refers to the "salient resources"—e.g., management know-how, leadership, culture, professional expertise, technological expertise, informational systems—

which are critical for entrepreneurial ventures, for developing VRIN-based products and services and for the delivery of those functional competencies necessary to run a business (Barney, 1991; Colombo & Piva, 2008; Helfat *et al.*, 2007b; King & Zeithaml, 2001; Lichtenstein & Brush, 2001; Mosey & Wright, 2007).

The DC approach adds the dimension of modification to the discussion on core competencies, stemming from the challenges imposed by the rapidly changing environment on entrepreneurs in the course of their new venture creation process. Having the relevant competencies in a business is not sufficient for a long-lasting advantage: the DC of such competencies can result in a competitive return in the short term, and superior returns over longer periods.

The entrepreneur has the particular capacity to purposefully modify by creating, extending, and joining competencies with the founding teams' competencies in order to establish a resource base that is not only compatible with the changing environment but also has the inherent ability to change dynamically when needed. The competencies' ability for dynamic modification enables the coexistence of the business's concept/idea, the process of opportunity exploitation and the generation of a sustained competitive advantage (Helfat *et al.*, 2007; Teece, 2007; Teece, Pisano, & Shuen, 1997; Winborg & Landström, 2001; Winter, 2003; Wu, 2007).

The modified competencies may be personal or, more often, co-specialized; thus, core competencies in the new venture creation process will embody the DC of the entrepreneurial team rather than the entrepreneur's competence.

These competencies are tuned to the changing needs of the business during the course of its life cycle, e.g., competencies of sensing the market's needs in the opportunity exploitation stage and sensing the investor's demands in the financing phase.

Core Competencies—Three groups of competencies have been identified as relevant to a successful new venture creation process: human capital capabilities, e.g., education, more firmly ensconced experience in entrepreneurship, management, and starting or owning a business; personal traits or characteristics, e.g., creativity, innovative thinking, proactivity, productivity, psychologically based ability to execute ideas into reality; know-how, e.g., in management, marketing, sales, managing teams. These groups of competencies have been found to be key success factors in entrepreneurship, as demonstrated in Figure 5.1. Such competencies are sought after by entrepreneurs, investors and groups of shareholders, due to the added value for the sustainable competitive advantage of the venture "from day 1." Jill, a 40-year-old female medical entrepreneur from Singapore, launched an auto-injection and monitoring device for cancer patients two years previously. She manages a 40-person business that has contracted with more than 2,000 hospitals and clinics around the world. Yet the

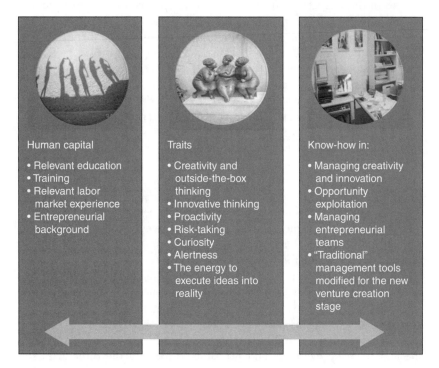

Human capital	Traits	Know-how in:

• Relevant education
• Training
• Relevant labor
  market experience
• Entrepreneurial
  background
	• Creativity and
	  outside-the-box
	  thinking
	• Innovative thinking
	• Proactivity
	• Risk-taking
	• Curiosity
	• Alertness
	• The energy to
	  execute ideas into
	  reality
		• Managing creativity
		  and innovation
		• Opportunity
		  exploitation
		• Managing
		  entrepreneurial
		  teams
		• "Traditional"
		  management tools
		  modified for the new
		  venture creation
		  stage

Figure 5.1 Core Competencies.

start was not easy: she took over a year to assemble the best people for the founding team; she contacted the most renowned academic institutions, laboratories and hospitals to attract their staff for a "part-time entrepreneurial undertaking" and was willing to pay them full-time salaries. From the very start, Jill stabilized a solid professional authorization for her business; she believed in her staff's competencies and considered them assets that should be cultivated.

THE COMPETITIVE ADVANTAGE BROUGHT BY WOMEN ENTREPRENEURS "TO THE TABLE"

The above three groups, human capital, traits and know-how, can be categorized into core competencies that are more frequently used by women and those more frequently used by men to generate a sustainable competitive advantage at the outset of the new venture creation.

Human Capital—Research in entrepreneurship repeatedly shows that men possess higher levels of the relevant education and labor market experience that can be leveraged to establish a successful business, whereas women lag behind in these aspects. However, other research has revealed that women are more likely to ask for assistance in their entrepreneurial pursuit: they use more training, counseling and mentoring facilities than men; they ask, more often than men, for informal assistance from family members, friends and colleagues and, generally, women start a new venture by first acquiring formal knowledge and tools on entrepreneurship know-how and on the core content of their projected business (e.g., education, caring for the elderly, leisure time, social entrepreneurship, internet, etc.). In addition, data based on statistics from different countries show that women that embark on entrepreneurship are on average older than men, suggesting that they participated in the labor market prior to becoming entrepreneurs. Such experiences may not be perceived as directly associated with the relevant experience required for entrepreneurship, yet may be useful and even advantageous for the projected entrepreneurial undertaking. The following example demonstrates this. Ms. Adele Novak, a 33-year-old woman entrepreneur from Budapest, Prague established a store and an accompanying website for candy wedding bouquets. Prior to setting up her business, Adele was employed as a kindergarten teacher's assistant for five years, then as a secretary at a spa in Spain for one year. While her labor market experience seems irrelevant to the competencies needed to create a venture, Adele confirms that her experience eventually turned out to be most beneficial; for example, she reflected on different scenarios in which she had to make decisions and was able to identify the difficulties she encountered in the decision-making process; she also learned from her experience of being abroad; accordingly, she developed entrepreneurial competencies that were relevant to her current undertaking.

Thus, formal education that is not directly related to entrepreneurship or management can also leave its mark: while men are more apt to enroll in technological programs that provide them with the advantage in setting up high-technology start-ups, women can leverage the knowledge they have obtained in their higher education, the different rational ways of analyzing case studies, and the networking that they have established with academic staff, students and alumni.

The well-accepted, absolute "equations" determining that only specific education tracks or specific labor market experiences—mainly those employed by men—can be considered useful for the new venture creation process should be reassessed, then refined into those components in any education or market experience that can form core competencies relevant for the creation of a new venture.

Traits and Personal Competencies—Certain traits have been identified as relevant to successfully setting up a new venture. These include a strong drive to achieve, an orientation toward proactivity and action, a tolerance for ambiguity, risk-taking, dedication to a goal, curiosity, alertness, optimism, creative thinking, independence, tenacity, and internal locus of control.

Table 5.1 Categories of Relevant Female/Male Traits

Female-based	*Male-based*
High achievement drive (mainly in academic matters)	High achievement drive
Tolerance for ambiguity	Proactivity and action orientation
Curiosity	Risk-taking
Alertness	Dedication to a goal
Creative thinking	Curiosity
Optimism	Independence
Internal locus of control	Tenacity

Research probes the most promising competencies for the successful new venture creation through their sources, e.g., gender-based traits, socialization and social roles, self-stratification, environmental effects and triggering events, among others. These are relevant to the quest of female entrepreneurship. Research discusses forces originating from internal or external influences which are relevant to the entrepreneurial process and cultivates entrepreneurs and new venture creation. For example, the rationalization that female and male traits are differently molded and represent congenital needs, interests, desires, etc., that women and men are essentially different, stems from feminist theories such as social, psychoanalytical or radical theories; while socialization as impetus for the gender's differences in their traits can be understood by theories of construction of femininity and masculinity. Accordingly, some entrepreneurial traits are gendered, as they are considered innate or socially espoused by one gender group, i.e., "feminine" or "masculine." While, on the face of it, new venture creation appears to be "masculine," a closer look shows that women possess a critical mass of traits relevant for this process. A categorization of some relevant traits is suggested as follows:

This categorization displays a group of relevant traits possessed by women that can assist them in the new venture creation process, while external effects stemming from the environment can indicate that women and men are essentially similar, as derived from theories such as feminist empiricism and liberal feminist theory.

Know-how—Some skills, strategies and aspects of know-how in the new venture creation process are learned or acquired in prior, relevant employment experiences, such as in corporate management positions, management of a family business, small business ownership, etc. Others are more naturally exhibited by certain individuals, because they possess the relevant traits or have experienced this know-how in different, although not necessarily entrepreneurial, contexts (e.g., university student council, parent committee at school, etc.). While women are at a disadvantage relative to men with respect to formal means of acquiring the "right" know-how (e.g., relevant educational attainment or relevant market experience), such know-how can be obtained through studying, on-the-job training and/or practical performance to gain the relevant experience, and thereby achieve a high level of performance in the concurrent new venture. Informal means to this end are an advantage in the woman's world, as women's natural inclination toward people, teams, delving into details and being aware of risks, among others, enables them to bring skills to the table that are crucial for the new venture creation process. Such know-how might include managing creativity and innovation, managing entrepreneurial teams, or modifying "traditional" tools into modern ones, which are even more pertinent to the new venture creation. This know-how has to be remolded, however, as women have not formally learned which skills are relevant and how they are set into motion. Nevertheless, it is this modification that fuels the performance with more user-friendly and innovative aspects.

Women entrepreneurs bring different advantages "to the table" in the new venture creation process. Yet they are often reserved, or insecure, as regards demonstrating their advantages and prefer to adjust their entrepreneurial-based behavior to that of men, thereby abolishing their own advantages and reproducing a male-dominated, entrepreneurial market.

Decoding the performance of female entrepreneurs in the new venture creation process, and determining why they behave in specific ways and the sources of their respective performance, can lead to a better understanding of the assistance required to facilitate their preparation for creating a business and the subsequent implementation process. Understanding a behavior can also mean accepting, or even encouraging it. In addition, in the course of the new venture creation, a turbulent period, many entrepreneurs, women and men, tend to execute different entrepreneurial-based activities intensively, intuitively, without having thoroughly reflected upon them. Providing women entrepreneurs with the tools to analyze their behavior in the new venture creation process may better prepare them for this process and equip them with strategies to manage the conditions they are encountering, or will encounter (Bhide, 2000; Gupta, Turban, Wasti, & Sikdar, 2009; Hodgetts & Kuratko, 1995; Jennings, 1994; Kuratko & Hodgetts, 1998; Lambing & Kuehl, 1997; Scarborough & Zimmerer, 2000; Stevenson, Grousbeck, Roberts, & Bhide, 1999; Timmons, 1999; Vesper, 1996).

NETWORKING AND SOCIAL CAPITAL

According to Pierre Bourdieu (1986):

> Social capital is an attribute of an individual in a social context. One can acquire social capital through purposeful actions and can transform social capital into conventional economic gains. The ability to do so,

however, depends on the nature of the social obligations, connections, and networks available to you.

(p. 242)

Social capital is essential to the myriad resources and transactions that are critical in the early stages of the new venture process. Entrepreneurs at these stages draw heavily upon their networks in mobilizing resources, gathering ideas and receiving feedback on those ideas, exploiting opportunities, eliciting finance at the start-up phase, getting referrals, and establishing client bases, as well as potential investors, employees, distributors, suppliers and customers, among others. In addition, networks can provide friendship, emotional support and trust.

The resources engendered by the networks can be either tangible or intangible and of different natures, such as functional, professional, referred and emotional, as shown in Figure 5.2 (Anderson & Miller, 2003; Coleman, 1988; Evald, Klyver, & Svendsen, 2006; Granovetter, 1973; Greve & Salaff, 2003; Shane & Cable, 2002; Verheul, Risseeuw, & Bartelse, 2002; Verheul, van Stel, and Thurik, 2006).

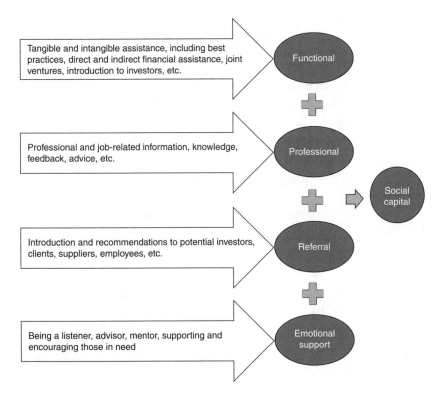

Figure 5.2 Social Capital Avenues.

Individuals who have accumulated social capital possess the following characteristics and abilities: to properly and promptly respond to social circumstances, to foster interpersonal trust, to provide social support, connectedness, sociability, cooperative ability, civic participation, among others (Adler & Kwon, 2002; Burt, Hogarth, & Michaud, 2000; Lee & Jones, 2008; Mosey & Wright, 2007; Paxton, 1999; Portes, 1998). Some of these characteristics and skills, however, seem to counteract the documented entrepreneurial characteristics and skills, such as being individualistic, independent, focused and target-oriented, etc. While entrepreneurial characteristics are considered to fortify success in the course of the new venture creation, they can be seen as impeding the acquisition of social capital. For example, being individualistic (entrepreneurial characteristic) may oppose the ability to be cooperative (social capital characteristic), and being focused and target-oriented on the topics associated with one's own venture (entrepreneurial characteristic) could nullify characteristics associated with social support for others (social capital characteristic), which is clearly an emotion-based, unfocused, time-consuming action. Women entrepreneurs can blend these opposing characteristics and create a more holistic set of core competencies that will be valid for the new venture creation process. A wealth of empirical evidence suggests that there are robust gender differences with respect to social and emotional characteristics and skills relevant to social capital: women have repeatedly been found to possess higher interpersonal, social and emotional abilities than men. In addition, women's communication skills, verbal and nonverbal, are far more advanced than males'; thus, women more easily and effectively encode and decode human messages and pinpoint the subtexts and hidden agendas; women demonstrate greater perceptiveness, empathy, and adaptability than men, as well as greater emotional intelligence. These competencies and others enable women to respond to different situations in more compatible ways, subsequently establishing their social capital (Argyle, 1990; Eagly, 1987; Hall, 1985, 1998; Petrides & Furnham, 2000; Riggio & Friedman, 1986).

Women's social environments have become increasingly demanding, diversified and heterogeneous as a result of their increasing participation in the labor market, their moves through their career tracks—changing positions, jobs or organizations and relocating—and their growing participation in entrepreneurship. There is vast potential for women to accumulate solid and valid networks and pertinent connections in such environments and harvest them to create their new ventures. Concurrently, female environments can also be considered to impede women's access to resources relevant to new venture creation, due to their deliberately segregated access to some networks and therefore valuable contacts. Research shows that compared to their male counterparts, women encounter a network deficit and are kept away from the most privileged contacts, either by being reluctant to approach them, or by not being taken seriously by them. Either way, such inaccessibility creates extremely difficult barriers for women in raising the resources that can accelerate the competitive advantages for their new ventures through their networks (Aldrich, 1989; Bolton & Thompson, 2000; Bourdieu, 1986; Granovetter, 1973; Renzulli & Aldrich, 2005).

While the role of social capital in the new venture creation process is unarguable, there is still no clear model that guarantees the generation of valuable resources through social capital. The relevance, direction, solidity, length and trust of the network are imperative factors upon which the role of social capital in the entrepreneurial course is shaped.

THE "FLIP SIDE" OF SOCIAL CAPITAL IN THE FEMALE REALM

While it is well-established that social capital provides a variety of different advantages to entrepreneurs in the new venture creation process, research drawing on feminist theories suggests that some social institutions, especially economic ones, do not function similarly toward women and men. As such, while women have the ability to blend their entrepreneurial and social capital-related competencies, they may confront institutions that intentionally favor "doing business" with men, and establish processes that do not reinforce female participation.

The following cases illustrate the "flip side" of social capital for women entrepreneurs. Ms. Dalal Tay, a 30-year-old woman entrepreneur from Singapore, has always been entrepreneurial, as well as a leader of different institutions at school, at the university and in her community. She accumulated a diverse and most influential range of contacts from her various entrepreneurial undertakings throughout the years; she was also aware of the significance of maintaining connections and developing unique ways to get in touch with her contacts from time to time. Nevertheless, she tackled rigid barriers when looking for financial sources for her new venture, based on a unique leisure-based concept, kiting, which combines leisure, sports and quality family time. Ms. Joanna Smith, a 29-year-old woman entrepreneur from Illinois, USA, faced similar difficulties from the governmental institutions in her country when approaching the patent registration office for her technological development to quit smoking. Like Dalal, Joanna held the relevant competencies required for mounting solid social capital: she was the initiator and driving force of a most successful professional, virtual network at her university; a representative in her school's student association and the initiator of a most effective campaign against smoking in her community. She had amassed a large network, yet her abilities and achievements were insufficient for getting patent approval for her development. These examples provide further evidence for the research findings in female entrepreneurship on women's difficulties in obtaining full benefit from their social capital. While entrepreneurs in general face difficulties with various institutions, the situation is more acute for women entrepreneurs. The institutions' asymmetrical gender-based conduct is a main hindrance in women entrepreneurs' accrual of the reciprocal advantages that lie in social capital (Adler & Kwon, 2002; Brush, 2008; Brush, Carter, Gatewood, Greene, & Hart, 2006d; Nahapiet & Ghoshal, 1998; Nahapiet, Gratton, & Rocha, 2005; Neergaard, Shaw, & Carter, 2005; Taylor, Jones, & Boles, 2004; Uzzi, 1996).

Women therefore need to forge their own way to escape the institutional barriers and generate the benefits that their social capital can give them.

THE FUNCTION/MALFUNCTION OF SUPPORT SYSTEMS IN THE WOMAN ENTREPRENEUR'S REALM

Support and accelerating systems are significant in facilitating the entrepreneur's path from raising an idea through the process of preparing the set-up of a venture and eventually creating a business that makes a change and a sustainable contribution. Support systems refer to the more traditional concept of assisting with financial and operational resources, as well as with enhancing the individual in question's core competencies which can then increase the business's chance of growth and success. Whereas support systems are aimed at facilitating the entrepreneur's path and enabling her/him to start a business, accelerating systems represent a fairly innovative concept which seeks to push entrepreneurs to a significant change by focusing directly on commercialization and exit strategies. In a certain sense, accelerating systems resemble the university experience—from application, to the move, interactions with experts, time limits and finally, graduation. Accelerating systems stress the critical role of time in the failure/success process and move the entrepreneur forward to reorganize and remobilize her/his resources to find different, creative ways of enhancing the business's growth.

Yet the quest for support and accelerating systems in the entrepreneurial realm raises some interesting questions that should be addressed in research and practice, for example: What is the main goal of these systems and, consequently, how do we ensure that such systems do not "mold" a single type of entrepreneurship, based on the similar best practices that such systems assimilate? Who decides whether the gender groups need different assistance and subsequently what is the message of gendered support and/or accelerating systems? Is the implication that women need more assistance than men, or are they incapable of establishing their own businesses? Furthermore, who protects the barriers between an entrepreneur and the different support system, so that the entrepreneur maintains an independent, free environment for her/his own entrepreneurial activity? Accordingly, is it really best to keep entrepreneurs from experiencing and making mistakes, failing, and restarting the whole process, undergoing the trial-and-error process, by equipping them with the best practices at the outset? Finally, who assesses the outcomes and how are such finds then implemented into ongoing learning from experience?

To address these questions, scholars and practitioners should first determine the entrepreneurs' needs. Women entrepreneurs are considered to encounter some unique circumstances that may cultivate specific needs, which should be addressed. The needs reported in research are summarized and presented in Figure 5.3.

However, it is the conceptual framework that will determine the thematic approach of the support systems: a liberal feminist theory,

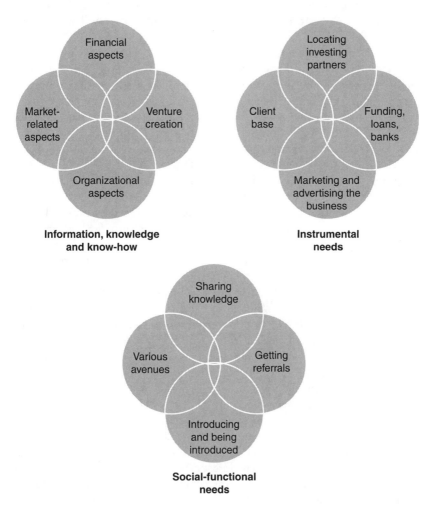

Figure 5.3 Female Entrepreneurial Needs.

stressing the similarities between women and men and considering "gender" a factor like any other, such as "age" or "education," would suggest similar support systems for entrepreneurs despite their gender. A social or radical feminist theory, on the other hand, whose concepts are founded on the principle that women and men are innately different and postulate that their respective interpretations of the same situations differ, would target different programs that suit each gender group's exclusive needs. Along these lines, there is a vast body of research stressing that female entrepreneurs have different training and mentoring needs which should foster the development of different programs or even different support systems; accelerating women's entrepreneurial performance thus seems relevant in providing women with the systems and "space" to plan, operate and manage their new ventures in their own ways, in a framework that aims at chauffeuring their businesses to significant growth and success (Carter, 1989; Hisrich, 1989; Hisrich & Brush, 1983, 1984, 1987; Nelson, 1987; Pellegrino & Reece, 1982).

A different look into entrepreneurs' needs focuses on the process, i.e., input, process, or output. Support systems can assist in developing or strengthening the "right" capabilities and competencies for a new venture creation, such as the most compatible entrepreneurial characteristics (creativity, innovative thinking, tolerance to ambiguity, risk-taking, proactivity, etc.), internal factors such as motivation and self-confidence, social capital, and financial capital, reflecting a focus on input. The programs allied to such an outlook are mainly counseling, training, on-the-job training, and networks, and such programs can then be categorized with respect to the different feminist perspectives to determine whether they will be developed and delivered as one general mix for both genders or segregated by gender. A process-based focus would emphasize assistance in strategies, practices and actions that are most crucial in the pursuit of the new venture creation; e.g., negotiating with collaborators, presenting the idea to investors, differentiating the business from its competitors, establishing the relevant connections, recruiting people that will enhance the business's progress, etc. Support programs with a process focus would offer mentoring, role models, learning from one's own and others' experiences, among others. Both the input and process foci endeavor to empower women by accepting and encouraging their particular ways. These programs show them the ways followed by other women or men entrepreneurs to their entrepreneurial success, facilitate the interpretation of such entrepreneurial experiences and their subsequent implementation in their respective concurrent entrepreneurial undertakings.

The support and accelerating systems focusing on output start from a contextual perspective that acts to adjust external factors, e.g., barriers, difficulties, special needs, in favor of women entrepreneurs, to open up opportunities that would otherwise be unreachable. In this sense, a focus on output means sustaining the core competencies and processes exhibited by women while changing their ecosystems. Taking such an angle is a most compli-cated, lengthy and risky endeavor, as environments persist against changes; in addition, it delivers a message that releases women from responsibility and action. Specifically, adopting programs that stem from an output focus prevents women entrepreneurs' empowerment and their ongoing learning, by not equipping them with the tools to cope with situations in which they will face difficulties. The main support systems under this outlook center around setting policy, attempting to impact local and governmental initia-tives, lobbying, publicity and propaganda. Figure 5.4 illustrates the different support means that steer women to empowerment.

Women's needs should be broken down to develop the relevant thematic scope of support systems: *professional support* emphasizes start-up know-how or the core business (for example, technology, pharmaceuticals, gardening, etc.); *emotional support* refers to reflecting on successful and unsuccessful experi-ences, including encouraging women, strengthening their self-confidence, introducing them to role models, etc.; *functional support* can emphasize ad-hoc, specific inquiry or dilemmas that arise from time to time as the venture develops, or ongoing issues, such as seeking international connections for the business or searching for staff members, that tend to change over time (Ang

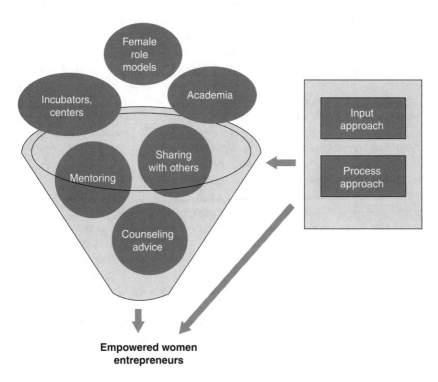

Figure 5.4 Support Means for Women Entrepreneurs.

& Hong, 2000; Autio, Keeley, Klofsten, & Ulfstedt, 1997; Begley, Tan, Larasati, Rab, & Zamora, 1997; Henderson & Robertson, 2000; Lee, Chang, & Lim, 2005; Lüthje & Franke, 2003; Parnell, Crandall, & Menefee, 1995; Turker, Onvural, Kursunluoglu, & Pinar, 2005; Veciana, Aponte, & Urbano, 2005; Wang & Wong, 2004).

MAPPING THE FUZZY ZONE OF ETHICS IN FEMALE ENTREPRENEURSHIP

In the new venture creation phase, entrepreneurs strive to beat the competition and uncover their business's competitive advantage, because they consider failure at these stages a stark reality with a second chance rarely being offered. They are under pressure to make critical choices that will eventually determine survival or death. Entrepreneurs are often faced with situations that defy a simple choice between right and wrong; many of the situations tackled by entrepreneurs that require decisions create tensions between ethics-related issues and possible optimization of their business profits.

Taking a macro perspective, many countries bear, from time to time, a slew of fraudulent business activities that raise ethical dilemmas. Researchers conjecture that the erosion of business ethics echoes a turbulent global economy, which causes scarcity in resources and hence intense competition for them, including competition for clients, investors, employees, social and financial pressures, and pressure from the whole ecosystem: shareholders demand a better stock price, customers want higher quality at lower prices, banks want their loans repaid, suppliers require a timely payment, staff members want to get paid, among others. Such cumbersome situations, intertwined with a lack of well-accepted means to prioritize the right way to respond to ethics-related issues, cause a multiplicity of business responses to ethical dilemmas, as reflected by the plethora of studies whose primary thrust is to elucidate how ethics are incorporated into decision-making and work practices.

The following simple example illustrates a common ethics-related situation: an entrepreneur generates an investment from an external business angel (i.e., an investor) and needs to decide between cheaper production that can cause some degree of environmental pollution or more expensive, non-polluting production. There is no precedent to emulate, and the resolution of such a dilemma demands careful consideration of the angel investor's expectations, as well as those of other stakeholders. When looking at the ethical options of such a simple decision, entrepreneurs must consider not only the immediate solution, but also a solution that is aligned with the ethical code that the entrepreneur aims to apply in the business.

Some empirical evidence, drawing mainly from social feminist and radical feminist perspectives, shows that women and men construe the same ethics-based situations differently (e.g., environmental pollution, full disclosure to shareholders, recruitment of "cheaper" labor). Consequently, the genders might respond to these situations by implementing ethical rules that they consider appropriate for the perceived situation. As there is no unique, specific type with respect to ethical issues, the differences in ethical actions manifested by gender groups can be regarded as "ethical" or "unethical."

Ethics in the entrepreneurial new venture creation process focuses on the free behaviors of entrepreneurs aimed at crafting ethical and socially responsible entities in their businesses. This goes beyond simply meeting local rules and legal requirements, while balancing business interests and the interests of its ecosystem. It inspects the inherent morals of the entrepreneur and not simply her or his adherence to regulations or even values. The culture is shaped by the very first decisions and actions of the entrepreneurs and it involves the societal, ethical nature of the norms that they put forward, their morality, and their awareness of diversity and responsibility to their communities and environments, among others.

Ethics constitutes a fuzzy zone in entrepreneurship. The genders may interpret the same situations differently, due to their distinct traits, core competencies, interests, needs, access to information, and strategies used. Consequently, they may promulgate situations associated with ethical issues in a gender-based way and handle such situations differently, such that each gender group may assess their counterpart's performance as unethical. For example, a situation in which an employee asks to be excused from work for several hours in the middle of the day for family-related reasons, during a critical period at work, and a woman entrepreneur consents to this request, while a man entrepreneur refuses: this does not automatically mean that the woman behaved more ethically because she was more concerned with the employee's well-being; it may point to the different meanings women and men entrepreneurs attribute to such employee requests, and reflect their own view of "ethics at work." Questions that some situations introduce may encompass complex, indefinite scenarios and pressures that are difficult to deal with, e.g., could "rightness" in one situation influence "wrongness" in other situations or in other people's view? If so, how do we make the right decisions? Does a moral decision as the entrepreneur sees it guarantee that it is moral for the people affected by this decision? How can entrepreneurs manage situations in which "significant others" urge them to make decisions that contradict their own ethics?

Ethics is gauged through different measures that reflect one's approach to ethical issues along the new venture creation process, thus reflecting different societal standards of ethics adopted by entrepreneurs in the new venture creation process (Azmat, 2010; Buttner, 2001; Cable & Shane, 1997; Dyer & Whetten, 2006; Ibarra, Kilduff, & Tsai, 2005; Robinson, Davidsson, van der Mescht, & Court, 2007; Waddock, 2009). Some of the basic ethical categories are summarized in Table 5.2.

According to the table, women's core competencies and traits are compatible with dealing with dilemmas effectively through an ethical

Table 5.2 Main Ethical Concepts in Entrepreneurship

Concepts	Application to female entrepreneurship
Social responsibility to customers, suppliers, other shareholders (Kovács, 2008; Longenecker, McKinney, & Moore, 1989; Moak, 1993; Morris, Schindehutte, Walton, & Allen, 2002; Velasquez, 1997; Wilson, 1980)	Women hold a service-oriented approach; they charge a fair price for a quality product/service; women are committed to their suppliers; women respect the customers' freedom to choose
Social responsibility to the community (Azulay, Lerner, & Tishler, 2002; Brown & King, 1982; Chrisman & Fry, 1982; Christenson, 1984; Joyner, Payne, & Raiborn, 2002)	Women value "giving back"; women care about their communities and are willing to allocate time and money to get involved
Corporate responsibility—employees' well-being, culture, shareholders (Bucar & Hisrich, 2001; Hayton, 2005; Longenecker *et al.*, 1989; Welsh & Birch, 1997)	Women value relationships and connectedness with others to a great extent Women care about their employees' well-being: they see their happiness as essential to the long-term viability of the planned business; women groom their staff, and promptly respond to their staff's needs Women respect their shareholders and treat them with fairness, openness and disclosure
Individual values, ethics and justice (Barnett & Karson, 1987; Brenner & Molander, 1977; Carroll & Hoy, 1984; Cavanagh & Fritzsche, 1985; Harris, Sapienza, & Bowie, 2009)	Women believe in providing opportunities, and delivering responsibility; they tend to assign time and money to shape an accepted corporate culture that rests on justice and fairness; women's maternal instincts further their protective, compassionate approach toward people
External accountability—organizational citizenship behavior (Ashmos, Duchon, & McDaniel, 2000; Bolino, 1999; Cabrera & Cabrera, 2002; Courpasson & Dany, 2003; DeLeon, 1996; Ryan, 2001; Wat & Shaffer, 2005)	Volunteering is natural for women; women are strategically driven and see the win–win situation in offering corporate charities or sponsorships; they embrace the business's involvement in the community
Environmental awareness and protection (Dean & McMullen, 2007; De George, 1993; Hoffman, 1991; Lynes & Andrachuk, 2008; Olson & Currie, 1992)	Women are concerned about resource-based survival being increasingly eroded by the demands of industrialization and act to protect the environment and balance the inequality in the distribution of natural resources

approach. Different aspects of ethics are manifested in capabilities that are more natural to women; such an approach can be more easily leveraged by women entrepreneurs to create a solid platform for competitive advantage. Yet the alleged progress in ethical awareness seemingly still bears little resemblance to the reality of the entrepreneurial realm, and these emerging operating principles remain in their infancy because they appear at odds with the tension to generate benefits in the short term and manifest a significant competitive advantage in an already male-dominated realm. The gap between theory and practice is exacerbated by the general mindset toward women's core competencies and capabilities to create a new venture, which actively prevents women from allocating time, money and energy to constructing a valid ethical base.

SUMMARY

The amount and variety of work in the area of core competencies that promise success in the new venture creation process appear to be on the rise. Using the RBV and DC approach to delve into the main and core competencies that are explicitly relevant to the successful new venture creation process undertaken by women entrepreneurs, this chapter offers a thorough look into the traits, human capital, social capital and ethical issues that create competitive advantages at these stages. Based on research in female entrepreneurship, this chapter proposes symbiotic relationships between the entrepreneur and the environment that nurture her/his venture, in postulating the core competencies required for creating a new venture. At the same time, the precept of distinct benefits and added value brought to the table by women entrepreneurs is strengthened. The differences between the genders are discussed by independently looking into the general perceptions, stereotypes and "halo effects"[1] that result in a more favorable view of men in the entrepreneurial realm, including the attribution of gendered perceptions on entrepreneurial traits and core competencies, along with the ways in which women and men interpret situations to be dealt with by ethical, societal or network-based means.

The support systems for women entrepreneurs are introduced and their role in empowering women entrepreneurs in the first stages of the new venture creation is discussed.

Understanding the core competencies that apply to women entrepreneurs in creating their new ventures may be quite important, since this information could be one key to their engagement in entrepreneurship and to their successful new venture development. The differences between the genders should be reassuring for both women and men, as both genders are main beneficiaries of their own munificent ideas, strategies and businesses that flourish through diversity and establish their competitive advantage at the outset.

CASE STUDY AND AT-A-GLANCE CASE[2]

This case study, contributed by Edmilson Lima, Brazil, traces Cristina Marques's steps in the process of creating a unique entrepreneurial NGO that stemmed from her social and ecological awareness, and that embraces organizational concepts such as trust, healthy relations, vigorous team work, and other issues of socio-environmental responsibility. Through Cristina's story, the author encapsulates the Brazilian ecosystem as it applies to entrepreneurship and ethics-related issues.

The case features the model of a dynamic, entrepreneurial woman whose creativity, passion for children's literature and networking ability enable merging the interests and efforts of multiple players (people, companies and governmental organizations) in an unusual way, delivering great outcomes to society with respect to social responsibility, environment and children's literature.

This case study provides a sound example of motivation toward entrepreneurial activity that addresses issues which women seem to be particularly sensitive about: social conditions of children and their families in a developing country. It offers helpful points to those wanting to make a transition from entrepreneurial activities in the traditional sector to the third sector. The case highlights the realization of entrepreneurial and innovative activities in a socio-economic context of high resource deprivation.

The case illustrates how a woman can produce major benefits by carrying out associative initiatives in the third sector while complementing them with traditional sector activities. The trajectory of Cristina Marques and Instituto Evoluir provides us with an example of the way in which a special spin-off situation from the traditional sector of activity to the third one might occur, and the practical and theoretical implications of such a situation. It highlights the importance of leadership and interpersonal abilities in a woman who gathered people and their efforts around activities with major potential for contribution to female entrepreneurship.

Cristina Marques and the *Instituto Evoluir*: Start-up and Innovation in the Third Sector

Edmilson Lima

Master and Doctoral Program in Business Management, Universidade Nove de Julho-Uninove, São Paulo, Brazil

This case follows the trajectory of a creative woman entrepreneur, born in 1963, concentrating on her accomplishments. The regional context is predominantly the city of Blumenau, in southern Brazil, where Cristina

Marques founded her company Estúdio Criação, from which began the Instituto Evoluir, an innovative NGO.

The Origins of PROFOUND MOTIVATIONS

Since a young girl in her native city of São Paulo, Cristina presented great creativity and interest in reading. Her father, a traveling salesman for one of the largest book editors in Brazil, as well as an avid reader, inspired her with a love of literature. There was no shortage of books in their home. One of her favorite pastimes was creating children's stories. The constant spiritual encouragement for humanist values was a pillar in her education, as well as for that of the rest of her family. They lived in a middle-class apartment near the city's main bus station. They were also in the habit of inviting recently-arrived and hungry migrants from the Brazilian Northeast, especially women and children, into their home for a meal; Cristina's mother was always ready to make a large pot of soup.

At nineteen, she began her university studies in literature. For her that initiative seemed obvious, given her passion for reading and her desire to be a teacher, which she considered a noble profession. She also began to work for an editing house creating new book collections. Her attention and work remained concentrated on a children's audience. This was also true of her first trips as a missionary, which started in 1982. Cristina was interested not only in evangelizing but primarily in contributing to the quality of life of children in needy communities. She believed that they could change their future and the trend toward reproducing poverty if they began with the right idea—"just as a large beetle uses its tiny wings to fly," she would say. Thus, she focused her activities on culture and reading as things to be fostered in children. At 23, she graduated, and shortly after she began another university program in theology. She faced many prejudices and a lack of support in this typically masculine educational environment.

Innovating, Finding Confidence, and Becoming an Entrepreneur

Cristina did not complete her studies in theology. In 1988, she moved to Blumenau on the invitation of an editor who admired her work and creativity. There, she faced even more prejudices. She did not share the same European ancestry as most of the population and, at times, was perceived as a dreamer. Over the first few years at her new job, she came to the fundamental conclusions that would set her on the path to entrepreneurship. One of these was that it did not make sense to follow the tradition of translating foreign children's literature heavily based on text. After all, Brazilian children usually want to understand the stories through the illustrations.

She began to innovate, creating collections of children's books which used beautiful illustrations as the central attraction. This resulted in one of her collections achieving a long-standing first position among children's books in sales in the country for 2002 and 2003. Her innovations were also incorporated into the creation of toy-books, the illustration of book packaging for door-to-door sales, and in books with CDs containing audio effects used in films. Cristina left her job in 1999 to open her own company: Estúdio Criação. She wanted to explore other innovations with potential success that were incompatible with the editorial lines of her former employer. One of these was the successful collection *Frutolândia*, which sought to awaken a desire in children to eat fruits and vegetables. Another idea was the 2002 collection of books about the environment with a new style of text and visuals. This publication was an allusion to the Environmental Conference held in Rio de Janeiro in 1992—ten years earlier.

At this time, as a mother with two children around six years of age, her commitments outside of work were heavy, but they also guaranteed her a major accomplishment and an important source of inspiration. "With all sincerity, they have been the first judges of my creations," Cristina relates. Her husband and partner was an important supporter, handling the complementary activities to her creative process. For Cristina, working in this way was a great happiness, for she could unite her two great passions: family and creation.

Major Social Needs, Innovative Ideas

One event had a major impact on Cristina during her activities as a missionary, which now occupied less of her time. During a speech that she was giving, she noticed a little girl who was rushing to read a book before the end of the presentation. It was one of the children's books that Cristina had brought to show the youngsters. She left the hill community with this image in her head as she passed trash and recyclable materials discarded among houses. It became more important than ever to her to provide these poor children with the possibility of having "books as their own personal cultural property," as she usually puts it. But would it be possible to do this without monetary payment? Then she asked herself: "Why not exchange them for recyclables in the communities?"

Very quickly, a few months later, she announced *Troque Lixo por Livro*— TLL (Exchange Recyclables for Books)—her new project. With this, she wanted to help needy children. However, she also believed that her company, through retraction of sales, could be strengthened by new income from author's rights and project execution services.

She developed a partnership with the Municipal Secretary for Education, a retired teacher also aware of the lack of access to literature for needy children. In addition, she received the support of a large company whose directors wanted to finance part of the project as one of their social responsibility initiatives. The TLL program involved the idea of children persuading their parents to collect one kilogram of recyclable waste to exchange for each book in an attractive and colorful new collection. There were 12 high-quality books and a music CD created by Cristina, a singer, and a foreign painter. Under Cristina's coordination, a small team of volunteers began the exchange program in municipal public schools. Through this initiative, the sponsor received a national environmental award in 2005.

The Genesis of Instituto Evoluir

As creator, Cristina obtained growing renown but began to face a serious problem. She could not continue her socio-environmental project in the context of her small business without incurring high costs and paying taxes typical of profitable activities. In addition, her company began the project with a budget lower than necessary, not receiving adequate compensation. The primary cause for this snag was the lack of experience of this type of activity and its complexity—involving multiple partnerships, a differentiated creative team, logistical challenges, and a large execution team.

With the assistance of consultants, she began to analyze possibilities for solving the problem. Cristina's network of contacts was important for identifying and accessing consultants at reduced cost. It confirmed the incompatibility of the socio-environmental project with the conditions of a for-profit organization. There was clearly a need to apply a traditional solution to such a challenge: create an NGO. However, finding the right formula for creating this type of organization was not a simple task. There were many subtleties to consider and important decisions to make concerning the development of the statutes that needed to be made, for example. They also had to choose one of two possible configurations: association or foundation.

Cristina considered the support of the consultants from Instituto Exitus, of Blumenau, specialized in creation and management of third-sector organizations, to be valuable. For her, the assistance of the coordinator of the Sistema de Apoio Institucional—SIAI (Institutional Support System)—a frequent collaborator in Instituto Exitus activities, was also decisive. SIAI is a third-sector organization operating nationally in Brazil with the mission of supporting the development of other third-sector organizations. The assistance of organizations such as Exitus and SIAI is well received by those in the start-up of an NGO. This is not by chance; management of this type of organization and its creation continue to be unfamiliar and are not part of the Brazilian university curriculum.

Cristina and her work team held discussions with the consultants and the coordinator of SIAI about the possibilities of beginning the Instituto Evoluir. The entrepreneurial actors gradually formed a shared vision for the creation of an association of which they would be members. For this purpose, and following the legislation, an association appeared to be a more flexible and less bureaucratic option than a foundation. The numerous articles of the statutes to be adopted were carefully studied and defined initially by the actors, under the guidance of the collaborators and a lawyer. This assured a statutory structure coherent with the legal exigencies so that the future NGO could, in short term, be qualified by the judicial system as an Organização de Sociedade Civil de Interesse Público—OSCIP (civil organization of public interest). This qualification allows NGOs to collect financial resources from numerous public and private sources.

In December 2006, Cristina and her team promoted a general voting assembly to create the Instituto Evoluir. The participants were invited according to strict criteria through the network of the entrepreneurial actors, respecting aspects such as trust, good relations, complementary competencies, and respected public image. The board was composed of six people and supervised by two others from the fiscal council, according to the minimum number of people required by law. Exceeding this number was seen as something that would unnecessarily complicate the start-up. Given that the preliminary statutes had already been read and adjusted by the present founders in the assembly, its approval was fast. Cristina, naturally, received the position of president.

The first work of the Instituto Evoluir was the development and implementation of projects of socio-environmental responsibility for companies involving children's literature—exactly the same work done by the Estúdio Criação for the TLL project. Compensation for this enterprise would be via payment of licensing for content creation in the books to be used.

Creation, Project Implementation, and Recognition

In 2005 and 2006, during the unintentional incubation phase of the Instituto Evoluir, Cristina was co-author and creative coordinator for two book collections and a separate book. This last book, entitled *Fábulas Ecológicas* (Ecological Fables), was used as an attention-getter at launch events for the various editions of the TLL project.

The collection, entitled *Cantos e Encantos* (Chants and Enchantments), was designed for children and composed of 12 short books, each with a children's story illustrated with vibrant colors by an Argentinian painter and with lyrics of a song at the end. The story texts were developed by Cristina. In all, there were 12 songs related to the stories presented that were created and recorded on CD by a Blumenau singer. The lyrics were composed to aid the development of phono-audiological abilities in children, containing tongue-twisters and different word games. During some period of the public school year, TLL established an exchange for each book of one kilogram of recyclables. The CD, of particular interest to the children, would be delivered to all of those that completed the book collection. "To offer a good example," as Cristina says, the teachers, in turn, were invited to exchange recyclables for books on children's literacy.

Financed completely with public resources and investments from partner companies, the project established that the direction of each school should choose a recycler to commercialize the recyclables obtained with the assistance of the students' families, as well as apply the amount obtained with the sales for school improvements. In the two editions of the project in the city of Blumenau, in 2005 and 2006 respectively, many schools increased their resources and improved their libraries and/or acquired necessary audio-visual equipment.

The second collection of books, *Jóias Literárias* (Literary Jewels), was finalized in the beginning of 2007. Its conception arose from the interest of the entrepreneurial actors at the Instituto Evoluir, led by Cristina, to create new editions of the project in Blumenau or other cities, but this time for adolescent students. The new collection was composed again of 12 books, with 11 of these written by different individual authors and the last being a collection of poetry by 10 writers. Each of the books focused on a specific genre: poetry, terror, self-esteem, adventure, chronicles, etc. Their content was based more predominantly on text than illustrations.

The creation of the NGO brought as its primary advantage the possibility of submitting requests for financing from government agencies. If approved, the requests would allow large companies to apply part of their taxes in the realization of projects promoted by Evoluir. Additionally, a practice used previously would continue to be viable: partner companies could sell part of their recyclable residuals to invest in the projects and also make donations to support them.

By the beginning of 2007, TLL had already distributed 132,000 books to around 11,000 students and promoted the collection of approximately 132 tons of recyclables in Blumenau. In the 10 days of the launch of the *Jóias Literárias* collection, held at the city shopping center in July 2007, 670 books were exchanged for around 1.8 tons of recyclables. Such results and the benefits generated for the youngsters, adolescents, schools, recyclers and partner companies were the object of a large-scale spontaneous and free promotion by the press and television in many regions of the country. Cristina received various regional and national awards, among which was the 2006 Woman Entrepreneur Award given by SEBRAE, the largest and principal agency for training and consulting services to support entrepreneurs and micro and small companies in Brazil.

It did not take long for Cristina's pioneering ideas to be imitated in other, more distant, cities. In southern Brazil, the directors of other large companies, influenced by the project's repercussions, sought to increase their socio-environmental projects in partnership with Evoluir. It was the beginning of a new developmental phase for the NGO and of the entrepreneur's activities.

Expanding Projects, Preparing for the Future

The first year of Evoluir was characterized by key events in its development. Initially, for practicality and to maintain reduced costs, the board decided that the NGO headquarters would be in one of the work rooms of the small company Estúdio Criação. This, then, began receiving rent payment for the space. The launch of the second collection of books allowed for increasing actions to include an adolescent public. Subsequently there came the possibility, among others, of offering TLL again in cities such as Blumenau or neighboring Gaspar, where another large company was already financing the project's implementation. Activities at the end of 2007 amply utilized the collection *Jóias Literárias*.

Cristina's many years participating in the Blumenau Câmara da Mulher Empresária (Chamber of Business Women) was an important driver for her contact network and continued to generate important connections for creating attractive opportunities for the NGO and her company. The first significant contribution of this participation for the entrepreneur was the obtaining of the lead user in 2005, a major company partnership that received a national environmental award.

The positive repercussions produced opportunities in different cities across southern Brazil, primarily in the states of Santa Catarina and Paraná. Nevertheless, the impetus for rapid growth was cooled by logistical difficulties and the need to further develop the NGO to make it possible to decentralize with remote teams. The base of operations needed to be Blumenau, and the growth needed to be gradual and secure in and around this city.

Despite the growth trend, the NGO activity level was low in 2008. As it was a municipal election year, the state and federal governments did not approve requests for funding with company fiscal resources. Therefore, there was no book distribution project during this period. However, Cristina worked intensely with her creation team on two new book collections for children, adolescents, and teachers: *Toda Arte* (All Art) and *Outras Fábulas* (Other Fables). These were finalized in 2009 and assured new possibilities for the NGO's growth. The first collection consisted of 10 books on the different arts, such as literature, ballet, photography, music, etc. The second dealt with philosophical themes in a simple and attractive manner.

In 2009, the directors of a large company in neighboring Jaraguá do Sul created a partnership with Evoluir to benefit their city with a project called Livro Livre (Free the Books). It differed from TLL through the considerable volunteer participation of company employees. In September of that year, many teacher training workshops were held. From April to November of 2010, the volunteers used all four Evoluir collections and exchanged 130,000 books for recyclables (180 tons). The objective was to benefit 12,000 children. Forty-five tons of recyclables were collected in the period from April to June of that year, the sale of which was reverted to improvements in public schools participating in the project.

Cristina and her team faced many challenges during the creation and development of the NGO. In this entrepreneurial struggle, she made mistakes but also did much that was right in operations and leading this team to new accomplishments. Her work heading this organization provided her with much recognition, albeit mainly social development and countless smiles. Her plans for the future did not reduce the challenges. One of these ideas is to strengthen the entrepreneurial training of children.

Another focuses on increasing the geographical regions covered, which will be through the growth in understanding and development of a manual of procedures to aid remote teams.

Questions for Discussion

1 What aspects of Cristina's background do you consider to be most important to constructing the way she is? What role did each aspect play in this?
2 Which core competencies are involved in Cristina's business? What competencies were important in the process? Why?
3 Which ethical aspects are encompassed in Cristina's entrepreneurial actions throughout her life? Explain their role in her subsequent business success.
4 How can a woman work and succeed in third-sector entrepreneurial activities, taking into account this sector's specific challenges? How can she be successful in the spin-off process of creating an organization in this sector?
5 Do you think a man performing the same activities as Cristina would behave differently? If so, why? What kinds of differences would emerge? Explain.
6 Considering this case study, do you think family plays a special role in the female entrepreneurship process? If so, why? What are those special roles and their influences on the process? On women entrepreneurs in general? Explain.
7 Would you do the same thing as Cristina if you were in her shoes? Why? What would you do differently if you were her? Why?

AT A GLANCE[3]

Women's Empowerment and Poverty Reduction through Mobile Phone Micro-enterprise: a Follow-up Study of the Village Pay Phone Program of the Grameen Bank in Bangladesh

Linda Hultberg[a] and Mohammad Sahid Ullah[b]
[a]*School of Communication and Education, Jonkoping University, Sweden;*
[b]*Department of Communication and Journalism, Chittagong University, Chittagong Bangladesh*

Introduction

The Village Pay Phone program (VPP), well known as "Palli Phone" in rural Bangladesh, is an information and communication technology (ICT) development program initiated by Grameen Telecom to diffuse the access to and advantages of the mobile phone to rural people who have no other access to telecommunications services. In 1990, only 0.21 percent of the population had a fixed line telephone. The mobile phone soon came to replace the fixed line telephone enabling interconnection to a much greater extent. As a result of several mobile companies entering the market, the number of cellular subscribers increased, from 0.06 percent in 1998 to 31.18 percent in 2009 (United Nations Statistics, 2007; BTRC, 2009). The initiative also aims to enable women to combat their poverty through micro-enterprise by targeting rural women, and it encourages them to start a small enterprise by renting their mobile phone to others. By 2007, more than 297,079 VPPs had been established in 61 of the 64 districts of Bangladesh (Grameen Bank, 2007).

Typically, the hard-working women in rural Bangladesh perform demanding and repetitive reproductive work. However, women's contribution to the family income is not recognized to the same extent as men's, even though the women are involved in many income-generating activities. It should be noted that money made through these activities is seldom considered a woman's own since she is financially dependent on her father, then her husband, and, thereafter, her son for economic security (Hartman & Boyce, 1998). In addition, only one third of Bangladesh women can read or write, largely because of their families' reluctance to pay for their daughters' education (Landguiden, 2008). Along with the State's inability to restrain poverty, ensure security, and combat illiteracy and corruption it has deeply affected the lot of women and their opportunities to become entrepreneurs. In spite of the constitution trials to promote equal rights for women, women still suffer from discrimination and violence (Ministry of Women and Children's Affairs, 2008).

This qualitative follow-up study, based on interviews with women from representative areas of Bangladesh, investigates the experiences of women involved in the Village Pay Phone program. It discusses the way these women have participated in the program as entrepreneurs as well as the way the program has impacted their everyday life and how it may have reduced their poverty.

Telecommunications and the Village Pay Phone Program

Bangladesh—a densely populated, South Asian country—has developed rapidly in the past ten years, but is still among the world's least developed countries (Landguiden, 2008). The VPP program concept was introduced to the Grameen Bank in 1994 by its designer Iqbal Quadir and is widely cited as a successful example of shared access to or shared use of the information and communication technologies (ICTs) provision model (Cohen, 2001). The Grameen Bank, founded by Professor Muhammad Yunus who was awarded the 2006 Nobel Peace Prize for combating poverty through the micro-credit program, is unique in its focus on women (with women comprising 97 percent of its loan recipients) (Grameen Bank, 2008). According to Iqbal Quadir, VPP's sustainable economic development initiative is "of the people by the people and for the people" (Quadir, 2006) designed to maximize gains for villagers in several ways. Researchers (Aminuzzaman *et al.*, 2002; Bayes *et al.*, 1999; Molina, 2006; Richardson *et al.*, 2000) enumerate the reasons for Grameen Telecom's initiation of the VPP program to be: (a) to diffuse the advantages of the mobile phone to rural people who have no access to telecommunications services; (b) to include rural women, in particular, as participants in the VPP program in an effort to combat their poverty; (c) to target women in rural areas to become owners of a mobile phone, thereby enhancing the economic independence of families and societies as a whole; and (d) to empower female owners of the VPP and enable them both to generate their own income and participate in decision-making at the family level.

Women's Access and Use of the VPP and the Mobile Phone

Out of sixteen VPPs owned by women, seven were operated by the owner's husbands or a male relative. In six families the husband or other male relative operated the VPP, receiving help from the owner or sometimes the owner's daughter. Two VPPs were mainly or exclusively operated by the owner. Most of the women were pleased to let their husbands operate the VPP, and the most frequently given reason was seclusion. As women are not allowed to visit public places or invite unknown men to their house, they cannot operate the VPP as a business. One woman, Dipali Shaha from Dinajpur, believes that women in general do not wish to operate the VPP because family members impose seclusion restrictions since they do not want to risk a bad reputation. "If steps are taken against these restrictions, women will be able to start a business," Dipali says. Six of the owners said that they did not want to operate the VPP because their domestic work was too time-consuming. As Rabiya Khatun of Gazipur said:

> I am a very hardworking woman and have many children and grand-children and I am rearing cows and ducks and growing vegetables in the backyard garden. Because of so much work at home, I would not be able to run a business from outside the home. Just give me some work in home, within two hours I will have it completed.
>
> (Rabiya Khatun-Gazipur)

Ms. Rabiya understands that men and women supposedly have equal rights, but she thinks that cultural and social norms preclude sharing responsibility for domestic work with male counterparts. One woman said that she could not operate the VPP since her work at BRAC (Bangladesh Rural Advancement Committee) includes traveling around to various villages to collect loan-repayments. Women with different, though fairly low levels of education, said that their skill levels were too low to participate in the VPP successfully. Rabiya Khatun explained;

> I never thought I would operate the VPP. As I am an illiterate one, and can't even count the money; I think it would be a problem for me to run the business. Rather my son and my nephew can do it.
>
> (Rabiya Khatun-Gazipur)

Three women bought the VPP because a husband, son, or male relative needed employment. Consequently, it was decided beforehand that the husband would operate the VPP. Three of the respondents believed that business is not for women and therefore handed the VPP over to their husbands. Shamima Akter from Brahmanbaria said: "He [her husband] decided that business is not a matter of women, so it is not for me. It is rather for my husband to operate it." Thura Bewa from Rajshahi voiced a similar view as she thinks that it is her husband's duty to run a business since he is the "guardian of the family."

In seven cases, the female owners help their husbands or sons operate the VPP in the evenings when their husband has finished his work at the shop or when he comes home for lunch and rest. Women send their children to deliver the phone to users. Two of the surveyed women take the main responsibility for operating the VPP. Parul Akter from Brahmanbaria decided, together with her husband, to buy the VPP from Grameen Bank. She started a shop and operated the VPP business from there. The shop is actually part of her house, which is located near the center of the village. She decided for herself that she needed a mobile phone to keep in contact with her parent's family when she moved from Dhaka to her husband's house in Brahamenbaria. She also thought that the VPP could generate an additional income. Marzina Begum of Bagerhart operates the VPP herself from 8 am until 2 pm and from 4 pm until dawn, feeling safe working near her relatives and leaving her children safe with relatives at home. During the breaks she does her domestic chores. She joined the VPP business to earn money. She explained:

> I have three sons and a married daughter. In 1999 only one of my sons was old enough to work, and he has a farm to spend some time for. So there was no one else in my home that could operate the VPP but me for meeting our living expense. Also, I feel secure operating the mobile phone as all businesses around my shop are run by my relatives.
>
> (Marzina Begum-Bagerhart)

There is a range of uses and the reasons for operating the VPP, showing that women and men use the mobile phone for different personal purposes. In almost all cases, women used the mobile phone to call relatives in distant places. Men used it to enhance their businesses efficiency in addition to calling relatives and friends. Ms. Dipali is the only woman in the sample who uses a mobile phone in her work. She uses it to keep close contact with office staff at BRAC and her husband while traveling between villages. Five women did not know how to use the mobile phone, but let other family members dial the number, or even speak for them. They were either not interested in using the phone or even learning how to use it, or they were incapable of using it because of illiteracy. Three women had not used the mobile phone.

> My son discourages me to learn the mobile phone as he will always be available to help me when I need the mobile phone.
>
> (Saleha Khatun-Bagerhart)

With some respondents, the subjects of the VPP and the mobile phones as male domains were touched upon, revealing different opinions. Tapoti Paul from Feni believes that the mobile phone is for both men and women, but that renting it is for men only.

> Though I cannot operate the mobile phone because of my illiteracy, my daughter can. It proves that it is for both men and women. [. . .] But operating the VPP in the village is a male task, because women cannot go there.
>
> (Tapoti Paul-Feni)

Some women think that the VPP and the mobile phone are for both men and women. "We are all equal in my family. So it is not a matter of male business only. I can also operate this one," Dipali Shaha says. Marzina, who operates the VPP herself, believes that "it depends on the borrower's mentality" whether or not a woman will become an operator.

VPP Benefits and Restraints among Women

The women have derived a few benefits and restraints from the VPP-enterprise accordingly. To begin with, many of the operators and owners of the VPP experienced an increased income from the VPP. The income was often spent on the family as a whole rather than on individuals, and enabled a woman to support her family herself. In three cases the VPP was bought to provide employment for the husband. Men who operated the VPP from their shops enhanced their businesses. Two of the respondents used the money from the VPP to send their male family members abroad for work, and two respondents used the money to initiate other businesses that still are prosperous. Two families used the money to pay for their daughters' dowries and weddings. None of the women uses the money from the VPP for personal benefits; rather, they see the increased income as beneficial for the family and thus also them. "I never bothered about my personal profits. If my son earns some money it would probably benefit my family too," Rabiya Khatun says. All of the owners and operators experiencing an income from the VPP have also experienced a gradual decline over time. Rabiya Khatun says: "Now the mobile phone is so common that even the rickshaw pullers have one. [. . .] Even the fishermen, who barely have any clothes over their body, have one also." In two cases, the VPP have made the family even poorer. One operator claims that Grameen, not the VPP operators, makes the profit. A few of the respondents insist that the call rate is too high, and they have purchased a mobile phone from another company instead, handing the VPP back.

Only two women of the sample did not mention any social gains from the VPP-enterprise, and one woman said that people did not perceive her differently. Most of the women experienced a positive change in their social standing after receiving the mobile phone even though they did not operate the business. The other women became prestigious and received attention and respect from others, particularly from women. The owners of the VPP are still well known as "Phone lady," among the villagers in the surrounding areas, though this distinction has diminished over time.

> At the beginning, many people gathered in my house. As the mobile phone is available everywhere now they do not come to my house anymore, but if I meet them when I go shopping they soon recognize me. However, I believe that the mobile phone have given me the opportunity to meet more people, which I enjoy very much when I go to the market.
>
> (Jobayeda Khatun-Chittagong)

Some of the women continue to experience increased social standing and prestige. For example, Tapoti Rani Paul, a Hindu woman, said that even the Muslim people came to her house to use the mobile phone, an uncommon inter-belief association in Bangladesh. Still, she has retained a very good relationship with the Muslim families nearby. However, two women lost some friendships because the neighbors could not pay for the phone calls made, and one of the female operators quarreled with parents who had teenagers using the VPP.

The women also experienced some changes in the family atmosphere as six women said that family members respected them more as an owner of an income-generating source. Two of the women felt that their family had become more prestigious, and one woman noted that the VPP-enterprise as an income-generating source had lessened the quarrels among family members, and that her husband had started to treat her better. Most women, however, did not notice any changes in the family resulting from the VPP. Khatija Begum of Gazipur once asked her husband to hand the phone back to Grameen Phone, but he did not agree as he needed it in his shop. She had no decision-making power in that case, although she has that power in other income-generating activities. She says, "I am just the manager of the house. As a woman I have to sacrifice a lot, they never hear my voice." For Saleha Khatun's family the VPP was a reason for many quarrels, because the family lost much money from that business.

> I have to pay the bill, meanwhile my son or husband claims that they will not continue the business, and by that time I have to pay the bill to Grameen Bank.
>
> (Saleha Khatun-Bagerhat)

From her experiences, Ms. Khatun has gotten the courage to argue with her son, who is the operator, and has gained the power to place responsibility for paying the bills in her son's hands. None of the women experienced any individual constraints with the VPP. Instead, all the women were pleased to be able to maintain regular contact with family members and relatives living in distant places through mobile phone. Khatija Begum of Gazipur says that after getting the mobile phone she feels proud of being able to generate some income, and now she also feels that she is an important person in the area. Similar views came from Dipali Shaha, who said:

> Before, I considered myself a weak woman because I had no mobile phone and felt shy in front of other people.
>
> (Dipali Shaha-Dinajpur)

Jobayeda of Chittagong learned, from Grameen Telecom, how to operate the VPP-enterprise and aided her husband to run the business. She maintains that the VPP made her rely on her own capabilities since she managed the VPP operation successfully, and she would like to initiate another business. Nevertheless, since the business is no longer income-generating, her self-esteem has decreased as concerns the business, but is maintained in terms of social relationships.

Discussion

This study reveals that after ten years of the project, the female VPP owners and operators have almost totally ceased operations. The various follow-on studies clearly show that: the characteristics of the technology, social communication and behavioral norms, gender attitudes, everyday work demands, education levels, and male family member employment status have strongly influenced women's access to the VPP-enterprise. Even though women gained priority for the VPP-enterprise their precedence did not last because the mobile phone became accessible to non-members of Grameen Bank.

From the initiation of the program, a VPP generated an excellent extra income source for the family. Still, the VPP-enterprise did not improve women's financial position as no women surveyed mentioned any personal economic benefits from the VPP. The profits, in general, were spent on the family or invested in the husbands' businesses, sons' education or daughters' dowry, which contradicts the result of Bayes' (2001) study that shows women's increased financial independency.

It should be noted, however, that female VPP owners who consider themselves "Phone ladies" claim that they now have more self-confidence, and that they have some voice in decision-making concerning household issues though still not in issues of business. Still, participation in the VPP-enterprise project made some respondents feel more "valued as humans," due to both the contribution to their family income and their gained knowledge. They also experienced a higher level of confidence that allowed them to encounter strangers more confidently than before and even achieve a somewhat wider understanding of the world beyond their village. The surveyed women's experiences of benefits from the VPP is closely linked to their involvement in happenings around them and the increase in respect they receive, rather than an increase in material assets, authority, participation in the enterprise and money.

Reasons for the failure of the VPP-enterprise to include women and make them financially independent from others include: (a) the process of selecting VPP owners propagated inequity by disallowing participation by the most disadvantaged rural women; (b) inadequate monitoring by local Grameen Bank officials encouraged women to hand over their VPP sets and operations to males; and (c) the lack of proper strategic planning by the Grameen Telecom managers caused the previously mentioned problems during the VPP program operation. To take programs for women's entrepreneurship in Bangladesh further, it will be imperative to baseline and monitor gender relations and thus men and women's access and benefits from the enterprise. Longitudinal follow-up studies will also be required to determine the local conditions and contexts under which the program is implemented, developed, and modified in order to provide detailed examinations of access and benefits for men and women to such programs as they evolve over time.

Positive social and economic benefits among users and owners should not be taken for granted, since training and effort is required to assure that the device is used efficiently and in ways that suit the users' cultural rules and conditions and make access possible.

Case References

Aminuzzaman, S., Baldersheim, H. & Jamil, I. (2002). Talking Back! Empowerment and mobile phones in rural Bangladesh: A study of the Village Pay Phone of Grameen Bank. Paper presented at the fifth conference of the meeting, *Transforming Civil Society, Citizenship and governance: The third sector in an era of global (dis)order*, Cape Town, South Africa.

Bayes, Abdul (2001). Infrastructure and rural development: Insights from a Grameen Bank Village Phone initiative in Bangladesh. *Agricultural Economics*, 25: 261–272.

Bayes, A., von Barun, J., & Akhter, R. (1999). Village Pay Phones and Poverty Reduction: Insights from a Grameen Bank Initiative in Bangladesh. Centre for Development Research (ZEF), Universitat Bonn, Discussion Papers on development policy, no. 8, http://www.zef.de/publications.htm (accessed August 27, 2005).

BTRC (Bangladesh Telecommunication Regulatory Commission) (2009). http://btrc.gov.bd/newsandevents/mobile_phone_subscribers/mobile_phone_subscribers_february_2009.php (accessed April 19, 2009).

Cohen, N. (2001). *What works: Grameen Telecom's village phones*. Washington, DC: World Resource Institute.

Grameen Bank (2007). Current status of Village Phones in Bangladesh. <http://www.grameentelecom.net.bd/vp_status.php> 31 July (accessed August 19, 2008).

Grameen Bank (2008). Grameen Bank at a Glance. http://www.grameeninfo.org/bank/atagrlance/GBGlance.htm 20 April (accessed August 19, 2008).

Hartman, Betsy & Boyce, James K. (1998). *A Quiet Violence: View from a Bangladesh Village*, Food First.

Landguiden (2008). Bangladesh. In *Landguiden*, at http://www.landguiden.se.bibl.proxy.hj.se/ 7 May (accessed August 19, 2008).

Ministry of Women and Children's Affairs (2008). International Women's Day 2008. *The Daily Star, Dhaka*, March 8: 14.

Molina, Alfonso (2006). *The village phone constituency in Bangladesh: A case of a sustainable e-inclusion enterprise*, Social Policy Research Unit 40th Anniversary Conference, University of Sussex, the United Kingdom, September 11–13, 2006.

Quadir, Iqbal (2006). Talks Iqbal Quadir: The Power of the Mobile Phone to End Poverty. http://www.ted.com/index.php/talks/view/id/79 October (accessed August 19, 2008).

Richardson, Don Ramirez, Ricardo & Haq Moinul (2000). Grameen Telecom's Village Phone Programme in Rural Bangladesh: a Multi-Media Case Study. *TeleCommons Development Group*.

United Nations Statistics (2007). Cellular subscribers per 100 population. http://mdgs.un.org/unsd/mdg/SeriesDetail.aspx?srid=756 August 16 (accessed August 19, 2008).

Notes

1 The halo effect is a cognitive bias that influences people to attribute traits to other people based on the latter's different traits; this might push people to

attribute different traits relevant to entrepreneurial productivity to the different genders (a trait), such that men are perceived to be more productive than women in the new venture creation process.

2 The author(s) of the case studies and at-a-glance cases are fully and solely responsible for their content, phrasing consistency and flow, terminology, English proofing and reference lists.

3 At-a-glance cases are included to present different ecosystems and their effects on the concepts discussed in the chapter; they do not include questions for discussion.

Part 3

Women's Ride across the River[1]

From Creativity, Innovation and Vision to Implementation

Part 3 focuses on

- The main characteristics and energizers of entrepreneurship—creativity, innovation and the vision;
- The bridge between the pre-launching stages and start-up;
- The challenges and risks tackled by women entrepreneurs in the "bridging" stages, traversing from theory into practice;
- Tracing the ways in which creativity, innovation and vision are exhibited among women entrepreneurs along the new venture creation through to implementation;
- This part consists of chapters and case studies addressing themes of creativity, innovation and the vision.

The drive to create a venture, energized by creativity, innovation and a vision, enables entrepreneurs to move from an idea to a business by allowing them to envisage and prepare for that business before it exists. This part of the book describes another stepping stone in this adventurous journey of new venture creation process, a stepping stone that bridges between the pre-launching stages (discussed in Part 2) and the start-up stage. The "ride across the river" symbolizes the challenges and risks characterizing this stage: like the river's waters, the environment may be turbulent; akin to the ride, entrepreneurs may have to tackle unexpected conditions and should

---

1 The title is adapted from the Dire Straits song: "Ride across the River."

be self-dependent as there will be no help from anyone else when such conditions arise; like sailors, entrepreneurs should be able to see beyond the obvious and clear scene, foresee the broader picture and reflect upon their current decisions and activities. However, unlike sailors, rides and rivers, entrepreneurs must actively raise the full force of their creativity and innovation, and combine them with their knowledge, experience and instincts to create a vision that will take them to the next level of implementation.

One of the main processes distinguishing entrepreneurs from visionaries is implementation; yet, the vast majority of business plans developed by women are never launched or, if they are, they never completely fulfill the potential that their plans appeared to encompass. This part of the book traces the ways in which creativity, innovation and vision are exhibited among women, and looks into the different strategies used by women to implement their creativity and innovation in the entrepreneurial course, and how these are infused in that implementation.

6 Celebrating Creativity in the Female Entrepreneurial Realm

Chapter Objectives

- Defining the role of creativity in the new venture creation;
- Tracing the advantages brought by women to the new venture process with their unique creative thinking;
- Understanding creativity in the context of the processes typifying the pre-launching stages, e.g., planning, familiarization with the market, disseminating the idea, etc.;
- Encouraging creativity in the business's spirit, team, and implemented practices;
- Sketching the behavioral patterns of creativity that differ for women and men;
- Discovering more about the different practices, means and tools to manage creativity in female-led new ventures;
- Understanding the process of cultivating new, creative ideas.

Creativity is a mental process that encompasses the generation of new ideas to creating or problem-solving, using different methods, techniques and knowledge. Entrepreneurship has sparked renewed interest in the area of creativity in this context, and there have been some significant attempts to decode the role of creativity in new venture creation. In all of those studies, the concept has been linked to originality, different thinking and openness to new experiences.

This chapter traces the role of creativity in the female entrepreneurial world by stressing women's distinct styles and methods of developing and managing businesses, and how these are compatible with creating a venture that is original, different and open to new means of development. Creativity is the backbone of entrepreneurship, and as such it is embraced in all aspects of the new venture creation. Women's propensity to develop teams, for example, can be leveraged to develop teams that exhibit creative thinking and originality. This chapter draws special attention to the role of creativity in raising the business idea, and in putting creativity and its deliverables into practice, while it introduces the exclusive ecosystem encountered by women entrepreneurs through the new venture creation process.

CREATIVITY AMONG WOMEN ENTREPRENEURS

"To create" means to produce something new and ingenious; the word creation entails creativity; creation and creativity derive from processes involving discovery, invention, originality, imagination and curiosity.

Creativity is defined in research as the process through which entrepreneurs produce ideas that are valuable to them and to their wider communities of practice. Unlike innovation, which is the transformation of creativity into profit and a finished article, creativity is the internal process that stimulates innovation, originality and creation, and that provides a solid platform for the entrepreneurial ride.

In new, dynamic markets there are few, if any, previous entrepreneurial experiences, accumulated and proven knowledge or established organizational routines to guide the entrepreneur on how to cope with uncertainties, risks and obstacles involved in the venture creation process. Such uncertainties require entrepreneurs to "create new realities," improvise, think differently, that is, be creative, as these are the essence of creativity (Amabile, 1983; Barron & Harrington, 1981; Covin & Slevin, 1991; Csikszentmihalyi, 1996; Davis, 1989; Kao, 1991; Woodman & Schoenfeldt, 1989).

The seminal works of influential researchers in entrepreneurship such as Schumpeter (Schumpeter & Clemence, 2004), Mintzberg (1987) and Drucker (2002), as well as of practitioners such as Peters (1997), established the notion that creativity, like innovation, is a requisite backbone for new entrepreneurial businesses, and that entrepreneurs in the new venture creation process need to adopt strategies involving creativity and innovation as stimuli for defining and creating their businesses. The leading and most established theories in entrepreneurship—the resource-based view (RBV) and the dynamic capabilities (DC) theory, discussed in Chapter 1—have confirmed that creativity is a key asset in creating and sustaining the business's competitive value (Lawson & Samson, 2001; Loscocco, Robinson, Hall, & Allen, 1991; Petty & Guthrie, 2000; Rosa, Carter, & Hamilton, 1996; Smith, Collins, & Clark, 2005; Ward, 2004).

One main factor that differentiates entrepreneurs from business owners or self-employed individuals is creativity: it is an informal prerequisite to starting a business and a necessary capability to be implemented throughout all stages of the venture creation, due to the high levels of uncertainty and risk introduced in almost every aspect of the venture creation process, e.g., decision-making, problem-solving, planning, process assessments and resource management. By applying creative ideas, solutions and decisions, entrepreneurs use different approaches to tackle the uncertainty and suggest different lenses through which to understand, plan and perform within the business (Amabile, 1988; Amabile, Conti, Coon, Lazenby, & Herron, 1996; Baas, De Dreu, & Nijstad, 2008; Baron & Tang, 2009, 2011; McClelland, 1987; McMullen & Shepherd, 2006; OECD[1]; the World Bank[2]).

Creativity, however, is not a stand-alone construct that can boost the new venture creation process by automatically turning ideas into practice: it involves creative thinking, prior knowledge and motivation, as shown in Figure 6.1.

Creativity embedded in the new venture creation is entwined in the processes typifying the pre-launching stages, e.g., planning, familiarization with the market, disseminating the idea, adjusting the business concept (see Part 2 in this book), which produce the basis for an internal business's capacity that is difficult to imitate or compete against (Albrecht

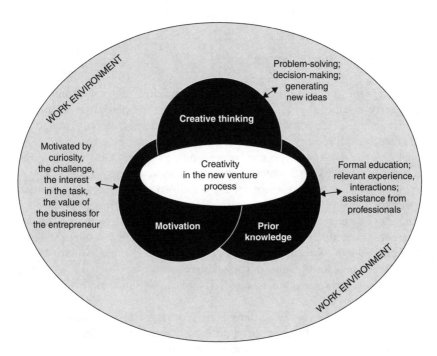

Figure 6.1 The Factors Involved in Creativity.

& Albrecht, 1987; Amabile, 1983; Kaufman, Baer, Agars, & Loomis, 2010; Rickards & Moger, 2006; Sternberg & Lubart, 1993).

While creativity is the driving force for the new venture creation process, it should be intertwined with the different practices in the new venture's course; e.g., it is a necessary asset for modifications of original ideas or the original business concept, for importing or developing new ideas, for differentiating the business from its competitors, and for adjusting the business model to the potential customers' needs, trends, or demands. In equal measure, creativity adds new flavor to the business atmosphere: it makes things "fun," without neglecting professionalism. Creativity stimulates teams, encourages "outside-the-box" thinking, and is most inspirational.

Encouragement of creativity among entrepreneurs and their teams keeps the body of knowledge updated and vibrant; it is introduced into the processes shown in the list below.

- *The determinants*—R&D, product development, and technology; development of the technology; entrepreneurial capabilities of the team; entrepreneurial culture, spirit and drive.
- *The entrepreneurial performance*—Processes conducted throughout the course of venture creation: decision-making, problem-solving, assembling the teams, structuring the planned business.
- *The outcomes*—The product's innovation and/or originality; the business concept; the business model; the pricing structure.

CREATIVITY AND GENDER

The impetus for gaining a better understanding of how women use creativity during the venture creation process derives from empirical evidence in the research showing gender differences in creativity, including in creative thinking, learning styles, processing creative cognition, openness to new experiences and impressions. In general females, i.e., girls, female adolescents and women, emerge as more active in seeking new experiences and more tolerant of the unknown. In their youth, creative girls are more calm, balanced and carefree, even in stressful situations, and are outgoing; they describe themselves as more self-confident, active, energetic, cheerful and optimistic (Boling & Boling, 1993; Dudek, Strobel, & Runco, 1993; Kogan, 1974; Lau & Li, 1996; Tegano & Moran, 1989; Zhao & Seibert, 2006). Some of these differences are manifested in women's new venture processes, where creativity plays a significant role in their routines.

Creativity encompasses different behavioral patterns that differ for women and men, and that are used differently during the course of the new venture creation. There are two prevailing lines of research on creativity and gender:

1   The sociocultural approach—Social expectations define the way in which creativity is manifested by the genders. These expectations originate primarily from sociocultural attitudes toward girls and boys from early childhood. In many cultures, girls are traditionally expected to be "followers" rather than leaders, and they are encouraged to see their main social role as wives and mothers rather than establishing an independent career. For example, a popular song by the American pop singer Britney Spears was released in 1999, entitled "I Was Born to Make you Happy"; in such an atmosphere, females have developed qualities, such as conformity and reactivity, which are directly opposed to the factors yielded by creativity. These social gender-based expectations and attitudes have a major impact on the ways in which women implement creativity in their lives and at work. Creativity requires a freed mind: when women are restricted by social expectations, this has a direct negative effect on their use of creativity.

2   The psychological approach—Creativity is differently represented by the genders from childhood, meaning that there are different creativity-associated traits characterizing men and women from a very early stage. In both of these lines of research, creative thinking and performance are manifested in several representations, e.g., in higher levels of independence, rebellion, sensitivity, non-conformity, curiosity, tolerance to ambiguity, persistence, openness to new experiences, willingness to take risks, courage to defend one's own convictions, self-confidence, and autonomy. As such, creativity may reveal itself differently among men and women and still be essential, albeit in different ways, to their venture creation process.

Females and males have been found to differ with respect to the core issues around which they build their creativity in real life, including its use for solving complex problems, or in the complexity of the solving methods. Empirical findings show interrelations between gender, age and creativity; for example, young boys were found to be more creative than girls, while as teenagers, girls significantly excelled over boys in several measures of creativity—figural fluency, flexibility, uniqueness, verbal flexibility and unusualness. Thereafter, the gender differences narrowed again.

For more reading on this topic, see: Baer & Kaufman (2008), Birley (1989), Kaufman (2006), Kaufman, Niu, Sexton, & Cole (2010), Malach-Pines & Schwartz (2008), Negrey & Rausch (2009), Sarri & Trihopoulou (2005).

Social Messages

Books and films deal with society's expectations for women by showing extreme situations, that is, stories of ambitious women who attempt to fight back against traditional expectations, and strive to change the attitudes toward them that prevent them from achieving their dreams, oppress their ambitions and their inclination to create, change or lead in their environments. Some of these films have won Academy Awards. For example, Barbra Streisand played a Jewish orthodox girl in Poland who decides to live like a Jewish man so that she can receive an education in Talmudic Law after her father's death, in *Yentl* (1983)[3]; in *G.I. Jane* (1997),[4] a female senator succeeds in enrolling a woman into Navy SEALs training where everyone expects her to fail, while in *Erin Brockovich* (2000),[5] based on a true story, Erin Brockovich's legal battle against the US west coast energy corporation Pacific Gas and Electric Company is depicted; *Norma Rae* (1979)[6] presents the story of a factory worker from a small town in Alabama who becomes involved in labor union activities at the textile factory where she works to help unionize her mill, despite the problems and dangers involved.

Music, movies and other media still illustrate women in a different social position, which quite naturally has a significant impact on shaping the manifestation of their creativity in the venture creation process.

Boys, on the other hand, are expected to be creative from childhood. Other competencies, such as proactivity, dominance, risk-taking, independence and responsibility for "serious" matters, are also perceived as male spheres. The implication of such social expectations is that boys create and use creativity to manage "serious" matters, such as work, money and personal status. Books and films that address topics such as men crossing into the woman's world are mainly comedies, reflecting society's attitude toward such "situations." *Tootsie* (1982)[7] tells the story of an unemployed actor with a reputation for being difficult, who disguises himself as a woman to get a role in a soap opera. *Mrs. Doubtfire* (1993)[8] is about a male actor who, after a bitter divorce, disguises himself as a female housekeeper to spend time in secret with his children who are in his ex-wife's custody.

MANAGING CREATIVITY IN WOMEN-LED BUSINESSES

Studies stress that fostering creativity to manage people, new knowledge and business processes and resources provides the business with substantial benefits in the different stages of the venture creation: at start-up, by introducing creative ideas and obtaining a competitive advantage; at the next stages of the business by providing creative solutions when tackling difficulties; at the advanced stages by introducing creative methods and processes for sustaining the business. Studies in entrepreneurship and management, however, have proven that there are gender-related differences in managing creativity in the business (Carland, Carland, & Stewart, 1996; Drucker, 2002; Hamel, 1998; Henderson & Clark, 1990; Kanter, 1989; Kariv, 2008, 2010a; Littunen, 2000; Schumpeter & Clemence, 2004).

Management creativity is a distinct field of research (for a review, see Burns & Stalker, 1994; Howell & Higgins, 1990) defined as a managerial process that targets development in the business, particularly by encouraging the people involved, e.g., employees, freelance workers, partners, etc., to be creative in all or most business aspects. Strategies include encouraging workers to include creativity in their work processes, creating supportive environments that foster creative solutions to problems tackled in the business, serving as a role model for employees on how to foster creativity in the business. Two different approaches, macro and micro, have been introduced in the area of managing creativity in entrepreneurial businesses.

The macro approach is result-oriented, and is introduced in research by decoding how management strategies cultivate creativity in the business (Olin & Wickenberg, 2001; Van Beveren, 2002). Case studies on these topics have provided empirical evidence that successful businesses use creative capabilities coupled with effective management of these internal capabilities (Kristensson, Magnusson, & Matthing, 2002; Kylén & Shani, 2002; Napier & Nilsson, 2006).

At the micro level, the individual influences his/her subordinates toward applying creativity in their daily work by being a role model, that is, by infusing creativity in every capability: cognitive, i.e., adopting flexible, outside-the-box thinking, letting imagination take part in planning, finding solutions, decision-making; affective: being enthusiastic about work, being enthusiastic about others' creativity regardless of the outcome, following the business's vision; behavioral: taking some risks, supporting creative initiatives taken by others in the business, applying strategies that involve creativity on a daily basis, circulating success stories among the business staff involving creativity (Chen, 2007; He & Wong, 2004; Sandberg, 2007; Wang & Casimir, 2007).

Obtaining a competitive advantage requires assembling creative teams and creative projects. Creative teams are developed by creative managers who, in a top-down strategy, hire the most creative people, assemble the most creative teams, and manage those teams through strategies in which creativity is inherent, including brainstorming sessions, encouragement of creative ideas, tolerance of creativity even when it exposes the business to potential risks by taking the project or process in different, unplanned or unconventional directions. Creative teams will survive in a business when they feel secure and can manifest their creativity at those junctions at which decisions are to be taken and the traditional, less risky method seems preferable. Encouraging the team's creativity in such situations crafts a long-term creative environment that will maintain and cultivate those creative teams. This, however, can be obtained when a shared vision exists, which delineates the aim and general ways in which this aim can be achieved. A vision is not a specified plan, and this sometimes allows, even encourages, deviation from the planned path, while the target remains

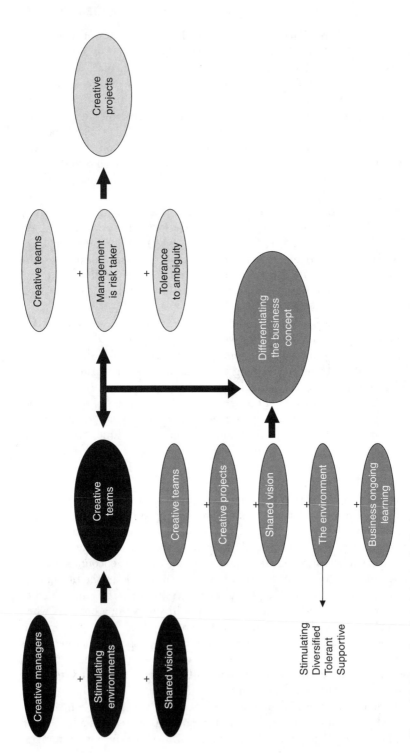

Figure 6.2 Managing Creativity in the Business.

clear and accepted. Women entrepreneurs are naturally oriented toward and proficient at developing and managing teams; they are tolerant of ambiguity and supportive of creativity and consequently, creative teams are nurtured in women-led businesses. Women entrepreneurs create an environment that stimulates creativity; they share their vision and business concept with their teams to commit them to the business.

Enhancing creativity in their chosen projects, women find it natural to engage in creativity-driven projects and activities. It is critical to choose, operate and disseminate the business's creative projects at the initial stages of the new venture to demonstrate to the shareholders that creativity is forged in the genes of the business and its team. However, women are considered less likely to engage in risk-taking behavior, despite the fact that any new venture needs to take some risks to rise up and succeed. Women need to be more aware of their reluctance to take risks and to consider the benefits of embarking on more risky projects, e.g., acquiring experience in new projects, expanding their networks, playing with the "big boys."

To differentiate the business from others and eventually achieve a competitive edge, the business should produce creative projects and creative teams—the business's resources. Creative teams produce creative processes and projects that can be more effective, more rapidly completed and less costly, while creative projects, embedded in a stimulating environment, can stimulate teams.

Inclusion of creative projects requires that the entrepreneur and founding team take risks, as creativity typically has no previous experience to rely on and adapt to; rather, it is original and unique. Hence, differentiating a business means embracing the ongoing learning approach, in which creativity and innovation are sought. Any "slip" into the comfort zone should be confronted by the entrepreneur; the development and production of creative solutions and ideas are possible when the entrepreneur and the team learn from their own and others' experiences and foster their creativity accordingly.

Ms. Monique Murielle, a French entrepreneur, owns a winery in Provence that has been in her family for 80 years. Monique's family owned a large grape-growing field in the region which cultivated the well-known winery; however, with time, more wineries developed and competition in the region grew. Monique's winery started to lose money. Monique tried different finance-based methods to cope with the profit losses: these provided temporary, but no long-term solutions. Then, Monique decided to try a different approach, by adding more products to the winery. She started to produce and sell different products from grapes, especially for health and cosmetic purposes. She also assigned some acres in the fields that were originally intended for grape cultivation to grow therapeutic plants. Sales seemed promising, but opposition to her creative "project" came from the stakeholders of the winery and her family. They wanted the winery to be represented by its fine wines and were against any other type of production. They were also against her decision to grow other plants in the fields. The opposition worsened, until Monique was sued by the stakeholders and her family; at the same time, she was going through a difficult divorce and finally, by court decision, had to withdraw from her creative "project": she could no longer sell any products other than wine in the winery. Shortly thereafter, Monique decided to start a new business in therapeutic products and she ended up running both businesses with the help of her then grown-up children.

It should be noted that Monique's experience is not typical of women entrepreneurs, who generally take fewers risks than men, and are more apt to withdraw from risky situations. Nevertheless, it is a stimulating illustration of what creativity can promote in the female venture creation process, as shown in Figure 6.3.

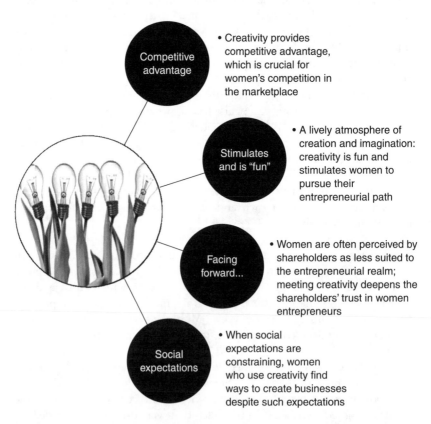

Figure 6.3 Creativity and its Functions in the Female Venture Creation Process.

THE "IDEA"

The idea for a new business is not a trivial matter. Despite entrepreneurs' characteristic creativity, coming up with the best idea is most difficult, as most ideas do not materialize into businesses.

There are general "guidelines" for successful ideas that turn into real ventures, yet every successful entrepreneur admits that it takes more than following such guidelines to be able to give those ideas a stage. Entrepreneurial ideas embody creativity, novelty, originality, innovation, breakthrough, lateral thinking, and outside-the-box thinking (Gartner, 1985; Gatewood, Shaver & Gartner, 1995); but they must also be attractive, sellable, provide a solution for a need, facilitate access to or use of existing products or services, shorten and simplify existing processes or provide them at lower cost. These factors, among others, require creative thinking to sell the idea's originality.

There is extensive debate in the research and in practice among practitioners, entrepreneurs and venture capitalists who assist companies in their early stages on the nature of ideas, specifically, when an idea should appear: is it a prerequisite to establishing a business? Does it evolve, change or adjust in the first stages of the business creation? How an idea evolves: is it a spontaneous construction, the result of a structured need-assessment survey, or a natural evolution of processes already existing in the business? Who is mainly responsible for emerging ideas: is it the entrepreneur, the management team, other people involved in the venture creation process, or anyone in the business? Where the ideas pop up: is it during the planned, structured R&D sessions, at the brainstorming meetings, in the workplace, anywhere?

Ideas are not confined in time, by the stages of business development or by the position or role of the idea's generator. In some cases, entrepreneurs organize their business around a clear idea, whereas in others, they start with a vague idea but in an environment that cultivates ideas, and their idea then evolves later on; yet others tackle ideas that have been transformed from their original form, or merge or add new ideas to the original ones. The only conclusion that can be drawn is that ideas simultaneously derive from creativity and shape the business's creativity.

Ideas in the Female Entrepreneurial Realm

The business idea, the one that is expected to evolve and transform into a real business, starts and develops in the entrepreneur's mind; it reflects the entrepreneur's ecosystem, and therefore ideas arising among women entrepreneurs will differ from men's ideas.

The effects of the association between business idea and business ecosystem in the female realm are manifested as follows:

- The individual level—female entrepreneurs possess distinct traits and capabilities, and have needs and interests that differ from men's.

Ideas evolving among women will mirror these individual requirements; for example, more entrepreneurial undertakings in the areas of
cosmetics, baby supplies, or women's wear are initiated by women.

• The process—ideas develop in different ways: some individuals tend to
focus their ideas, while others elaborate on them; some tend to connect
their ideas with other ideas, while others strive to differentiate their ideas
from day one; yet others tend to develop ideas from scratch, while some
favor building an idea from already existing ones. Women's management styles—typified by homing in on details, flexibility, taking into
consideration others' thoughts and suggestions, thoroughly investigating before deciding on important matters—are then also manifested
in the way they manage the process of preparing their ideas for maturity.

• The organization—women find it fascinating to share their ideas
with their staff. They tend to include their staff's suggestions into
amended forms of their own ideas. They foresee how their ideas can
be structured with the assistance of their staff and take their staff's
needs and interests into consideration when developing their ideas. In
the case of women entrepreneurs, the idea is embedded in the organization, it is cultivated in the organization and takes on, at least in
part, the organizational form.

• The environment—economic, social, cultural, environmental, and
political factors have a significant impact on the development of any
idea for a new venture. Women entrepreneurs' alertness to their environment's effects is considered even more pronounced, due to
women's emotional propensity and the importance they attribute to
the factors around them.

Ms. Frédérique Clavel,[9] founder of the first women's incubator, Paris
Pionnières, dedicated to innovation in France, which opened its doors in
March 2005, has been quoted in different interviews addressing the relationship between women and their ecosystems. Ms. Clavel stresses that
women's anticipated entrepreneurial success in their ecosystems is poorer
than men's. She works hand in hand with women who have innovative ideas
for their future businesses; produces a platform for meetings between women
to share ideas and learn from each others' experiences; works with women to
materialize their ideas into real ventures, and initiates workshops in different
areas to empower women and provide them with the right skills, tools and
knowledge to create new ventures from their innovative ideas.

Cultivating Creative Ideas

Creative ideas should be cultivated in an environment that allows their
evolution. To take practical action, women and men entrepreneurs should
be more aware of the distinctiveness of the idea's cultivation process in the
woman's realm, as displayed in Figure 6.4. Accordingly, the pre-idea

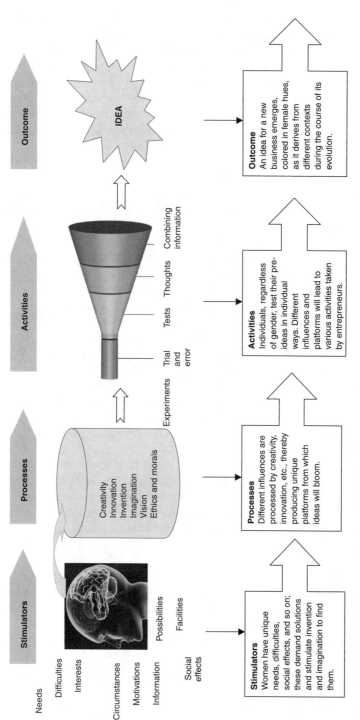

The following labels appear within the figure:

Stimulators
- Needs
- Difficulties
- Interests
- Circumstances
- Motivations
- Information
- Social effects
- Possibilities
- Facilities

Processes
- Creativity
- Innovation
- Invention
- Imagination
- Vision
- Ethics and morals

Activities
- Experiments
- Trial and error
- Tests
- Thoughts
- Combining information

Outcome
- IDEA

Stimulators
Women have unique needs, difficulties, social effects, and so on; these demand solutions and stimulate invention and imagination to find them.

Processes
Different influences are processed by creativity, innovation, etc., thereby producing unique platforms from which ideas will bloom.

Activities
Individuals, regardless of gender, test their pre-ideas in individual ways. Different influences and platforms will lead to various activities taken by entrepreneurs.

Outcome
An idea for a new business emerges, colored in female hues, as it derives from different contexts during the course of its evolution.

Figure 6.4 The Idea in Venture Creation: Its Distinctiveness in the Woman's Realm.

stages: stimulation, processes and activities shape the outcome, that is, the idea. For example, when the "need" (stimulator) is associated with feminine or motherhood issues, such as women's health, babies' facilities, topics associated with sexual harassment or barriers to top positions in their jobs, it affects women differently than men (processes) and energizes women's creativity, imagination, ethics and morals in a way that pushes them to find solutions. The following course of action (activities) will be affected by these processes and the produced idea (outcome) will be unique to women since it derives from women's difficulties, needs and motivations.

Creative ideas that originate from women's needs mainly lean toward traditional businesses (e.g., low-tech and mid-tech, non-innovative, limited R&D), and toward female-dominated sectors, either because these are frequently developed in women-led businesses or because they relate to products/services that are only relevant to half of the population, i.e., women. Whatever the reason, this should not be the case, as a variety of women-related products have been developed in an entrepreneurial, innovative way and have been most successful, for example: Epilady, a hair-removal device that provides a solution for women's esthetics and is aimed at female customers, was developed and patented at Kibbutz[10] Hagoshrim in Israel, employing cutting-edge R&D and innovative technologies; medications to relieve women's PMS[11] symptoms have been developed under high-quality pharmaceutical-grade standards and put through a barrage of testing; even the development of substitutions for breast milk, which concerns mothers more than fathers, emerged from American, Swiss and Japanese food technologists, working together with pediatricians and chemists, who matched, through a complex technology, the essential nutrients of mother's milk in a formula, demonstrating development under the most creative of means, using the best ideas to materialize an idea. These examples, among many others, show that ideas invented and developed by—or for—women should be encouraged as possible businesses and be treated without bias, that is, they should be seen as warranting the pursuit of advanced, creative and innovative implementation methods.

TAKING PRACTICAL ACTION

Creativity serves as a basis for the new venture creation process, and entrepreneurs should strive to make use of it in order to differentiate their ideas, business concepts, methods of marketing or distribution, to build a competitive advantage over companies that already exist. However, most importantly, new venture creation is a practical process, and creativity should be led to facilitate creativity and turn it into a real venture. Taking practical action means using creativity to develop feasible, sellable, profitable and sustainable products and/or services. There are various examples of creative ideas that did not mature into a business, failing because they were not feasible, sellable or attractive. The leap between creativity and practice is a crucial factor in the new venture creation process that should be addressed and attempted; in the world of women, this leap takes on a distinct form.

There is universal, gendered agreement that women are less pragmatically and practically oriented than men in entrepreneurship, mainly because women are considered constrained by domestic-related circumstances. Such agreement strengthens the image of female entrepreneurship as encapsulated in a stereotyped domain to which men are more suited than women. However, studies show that women apply distinct methods to turn ideas into practice (Agars, 2004; Malach-Pines & Schwartz, 2008; Wilson, Kickul, & Marlino, 2007; Wilson, Marlino, & Kickul, 2004; Zhao & Seibert, 2006).

Findings have been presented on strategies, management styles and tendencies that are more frequently found among women entrepreneurs, and which might explain the misleading consensus on women's relatively limited practical approach. As a case in point, women have been found to allocate more time to testing their business idea's feasibility; they spend more time than men in networking to advance their business ideas and concepts; they are more engaged in conducting market research and strategic planning; they are more focused on their teams' development, on empowering them and encouraging their achievements (Bruni, Gherardi, & Poggio, 2004; Brush & Hisrich, 2000; Fischer & Reuber, 2011; Greve & Salaff, 2003; Gundry, Ben-Yoseph, & Posig, 2002; Gundry & Kickul, 1994; Lerner & Almor, 2002; Morris, Miyasaki, Watters, & Coombes, 2006). The ways used by women to test their idea, commit their teams to the idea and manage the start-up phase are time-consuming, and may appear impractical.

A more practical approach can be achieved by enhancing creativity in different elements of the new venture creation: enhancing creativity among the founding teams, developing a business model which is innovative and thus creative in its essence, wrapping the business's concept differently, approaching investors using a creative approach, being a role model for creative thinking, solving problems through unique attitudes, disseminating the business's ideas in original ways.

SUMMARY

This chapter illustrates the underlying essence of creativity in female entrepreneurship and portrays its significant role in different aspects of the new venture creation. The value of creativity in starting a business in the viable, demanding realm of female entrepreneurship is described, including creativity as the impetus for raising the business's idea, and as the driving force in constructing the business's concept, wrapping the business model to differentiate it from its competitors, stimulating the founding teams to think creatively, and choosing projects for the new venture that differ from those on the market, at the outset. Each of these elements requires creativity as a prerequisite for business success; the form of creativity exhibited in female-led new venture processes is distinct and echoes women's entrepreneurial and management styles.

CASE STUDY AND AT-A-GLANCE CASE[12]

The case of Bushra Ahmed, contributed by Dr. Spinder Dhaliwal, illustrates the predicament of Muslim Asian female immigrants in the UK. Bushra had drive, vision and business acumen but faced cultural and social barriers. Bushra, originally from Karachi, immigrated to Lancashire, England in her early childhood, and paved her way from Rose Hill Junior School to dropping out of school and being involved full-time in the family business, to becoming the leader of the company. However, like many Asian women, she is crucial to the success of the business, yet remains in the background. Dr. Dhaliwal takes the readers on an amazing tour of the silent realm of Asian immigrants sensitively yet unwaveringly, without prettifying the situation; with her remarkable story-telling ability, the readers delve, with Dr. Dhaliwal's guidance, into the depths of Bushra's creative journey to entrepreneurial success.

Bushra Ahmed: The Legendary Joe Bloggs

Spinder Dhaliwal
Surrey Business School, University of Surrey, Guildford, UK

Background

Bushra Ahmed is the eldest of five children of Nizan and Saeeda Ahmed. Her brother Shami is the managing director of The Legendary Joe Bloggs Company and she is the Marketing Director in this family-owned business. Bushra was born in Karachi and came to England at the age of one and a half years where she grew up in Burnley, Lancashire. Her parents ran a couple of retail shops and from as far back as she can remember she was helping with the business. At the tender age of six years old she recalls packing tights in boxes so her father could sell them.

Bushra, like all the other Ahmed children, was given a lot of responsibility at an early age, which has been the basis of her personal development and has led to her confidence and strength today. Despite her parents' beliefs in her abilities she still had to prove her credibility to others. As early as 15 years of age she was doing all the buying for the retail shops and had to counteract her three main disadvantages—she was a woman, she was Asian and she was young. She had to overcome the patronizing attitudes of men who wanted to deal with her father. Today respect is automatic due to the phenomenal success of Joe Bloggs. Bushra is now the leading lady of the company and is poised, self-assured and in control.

Bushra is the PR and Marketing Director of the Legendary Joe Bloggs Company. Here she enunciates the challenges and hardships sustained both personally and professionally in the rise to the top. Not content to be just a fashion mogul Bushra has entered the music industry with a vengeance as manager of the rising star, Sabina.

The Ahmed family settled in the North of England, in Burnley. In 1966, Bushra's father set up a market stall selling socks and ladies' stockings. Nizan and Saeeda juggled the responsibilities of raising a young family with working long hours in a strenuous business; all the children were encouraged to help out. Bushra had to shoulder responsibility from an early age. Bushra Ahmed is the eldest daughter and as far back as she can remember she was helping with the business.

The first generation of Asian immigrants in the UK tried to create a secure home environment where their traditions and values could be retained. There was great emphasis on the importance of the family unit and the wider community network. Children were bought up to respect their elders and the elders in turn would do anything to better the situation of the young. Duty, obligation and trust were key words in any Asian household. They were prepared to work long hours and make many sacrifices for a better future. The unusual feature in the Ahmed family is that they do not value formal education preferring the "hands-on" approach instead. Whilst most Asian parents stress the need to study further, and make many sacrifices for their children to gain academic qualifications, the Ahmeds are firm believers of practical experience. The business always came first, education was not important and this was the case for the boys as well as the girls. The lack of academic training has not held them back in any way and this family illustrates the Asian success story where the first-generation parents initiated the business and the second generation made the move from small-time enterprise to the multimillion pound empire. The children were keen to move the business forward and the parents were willing to take the risks to do this. This story illustrates that the success and effort of the first-generation immigrants can be taken forward to the next level.

The comfortable lifestyle that Bushra is now so accustomed to was not in sight in her early years when she attended Rose Hill Junior School and then Walsall High School for girls. These were both State schools and her contempt for academia is plainly revealed by her remark, "I was crap at school and I don't care who knows it." Like her brother Shami, she preferred practical experience to classroom learning. Since she was clearly not academically inclined she left school at the first available opportunity and joined the business full-time, an easy transition for someone who had been involved in it practically from the day she could walk.

This was a strategically important event for the family as it enabled her father to be free to launch a new venture. He was considering venturing into the wholesale business in Manchester, and could concentrate on this now that Bushra was involved full-time. The move from retail into whole-sale was instigated by the younger Ahmeds, Bushra and Shami, who were the real driving force behind this move. The Ahmeds never shy away from the risk and challenge of new ventures and succeeded in setting up Pennywise cash and carry, which is still thriving today.

Bushra credits her formative years of "training," where she was given a lot of responsibility, as the basis of her success today. Those early days strengthened her and made her more streetwise as she had to prove her mettle. Despite her parents' beliefs in her abilities she still had to prove her credibility to others. Being Asian, female and Muslim was interesting and, in addition, she was still only 15 years old when she was given the job of making purchases for the retail shops. Trying to negotiate and haggle, she had to overcome the patronizing attitudes of men who wanted to deal with her father. Today respect is automatic due to the phenomenal success of their businesses. Bushra is now the leading lady of the company and thrives on the fast pace of the industry and loves making decisions, wheeling and dealing and being involved in every aspect of the fashion business. She is strong-minded, sharp and impulsive. For example, she went into a shop to buy a T-shirt and emerged with a Harley Davidson bike! Her philosophy is to see your goals and then go for them, do what it takes to achieve them.

Nizan Ahmed has now passed away and his death was particularly devas-tating to Bushra, who felt acutely the devastation of the loss of a man who had been a tower of strength and source of advice all her life. The shock of the loss left the whole family so shattered they feared they were incapable of carrying on without him. Nizan, however, had left a legacy of strength and unity which paid dividends. The Ahmeds are ultimately survivors and managed to endure the desolation of the following months to rebuild a stronger and more powerful empire. Bushra describes her father as the most honest man she has known, "He was very strong willed but fair," she reminisces. He gave his children much liberty and in return gained their utmost respect. Saeeda, the silent contributor, is credited with originating the business and despite her modest profile is a shrewd businesswoman. Like many Asian women, she is pivotal to the success of the business, yet remains in the background. According to Bushra, "My mother is generous, sensitive to plight, charitable, honest and direct," clearly directness is a characteristic that has been inherited by her children.

Shami was frustrated with producing goods for other designers. He longed for his own name to be recognized. However, he wanted to remain as part of a family business. In 1986 the 24-year-old Shami created the "The Legendary Joe Bloggs" label and it was exhilarating. He could not have known at the time that he had hit on a formula for a global brand. It was his first taste of real success; he was marketing his own brand label instead of other designers'. He was ahead of the game, with his insider knowledge of the trade. Shami had identified a gap in the British market between expensive designer labels and cheaper, mass-produced jeans any old Joe Bloggs could wear.

His timing was perfect, the label was launched on the crest of the Manchester rave scene and even today the marketing team at Bloggs continues to watch movements on the street and in the music industry for inspiration. In the 1980s the designer jeans industry was geared for the elite. Shami felt that everyone should have the right to wear designer jeans. He saw a gap in the market for designer jeans at low prices. This enabled anyone and everyone to enjoy the glamour of designer jeans. He wanted to provide exciting garments with style, choice and, most of all, at a reasonable price.

Marketing strategy was innovative and daring, and in the early stages he worked on gut instinct, never engaging consultants or undertaking market research. He had good instincts and acted on these. His own background made him well aware of class snobbery and the frustrations and dreams of escaping from the working class. Most designer labels were elitist and far removed from the masses he wanted to sell to. He felt it was unwise to compete at that level. There was a niche in the market for the everyday jeans wearer, any old Joe Bloggs. Shami was desperately ambitious and so seized this opening that the million-pound designer jeans companies had left and made his own fortune. He had the ability to gauge the needs of the people in the street and give them what they wanted.

He has since departed from his classless concept and diversified into other ranges such as Katherine Hamnett and Slazenger. He also boasts an elite clientele of pop stars, sports personalities and other notables. The marketing team design and coordinate promotions to specifically meet the needs of individual stockists. They keep their high profile due to their links with pop groups like Take That, Bad Boys Inc, New Order, Apache Indian and Happy Mondays. They were commissioned to produce the most expensive pair of jeans in the world for pop star Prince, valued at more than a £100,000. They are also linked with some high-profile sports personalities such as Brian Lara who holds the record for the highest ever score by a batsman in first-class cricket. But it was their marketing campaign in 1993 entitled, "Everyone Snogs in Joe Bloggs" that catapulted them to success and resulted in 86 percent brand awareness of their jeans; they were now a household name, albeit a classy one. More recently, spoon bender Uri Geller has joined forces with Joe Bloggs to launch a range of clothing with the potential to allow the wearer to fulfill their dreams. In addition, every product will be touched by Uri Geller before it hits the shop floor.

In recent years, the fashion end of the business has been solidified and internationalized; the company now employs more than 2,000 people across the world. The next step is to take the brands online and to grow that way. Joe Bloggs Stores are due to open in Dubai, South Africa, India and across the Middle East.

These openings were through business links and not through family or community connections. The Joe Bloggs brand was sold in Debenhams, Debenhams moved to Dubai and the Middle East and they were approached by people out there. They now sell online too.

The management values in the organization to date have been largely Asian values of family unity and even after the death of the founder, Nizam, his wife has resided over the empire commanding the same respect. The second generation has brought in a lot of the Western business practices and ideologies but has remained faithful to their roots. Shami is currently based in London and the success of the company is now in the hands of his brother Kashif, who is the Managing Director, and his sisters Bushra, Tabasum and Tesneem.

Music

Bushra's secondary career in the music industry started off as a hobby but has now developed into an all-consuming passion and is a field she is determined to conquer. Bushra is the manager of singer Sabina, a talent she discovered eight years ago when Sabina was a close friend of her sister's. Bushra is set on making Sabina a mainstream artist and has consequently invested a lot of time and money in the process whilst fully admitting it is a distraction from the main fashion business. It is an insight to Bushra's character where she has to achieve her goals even if it means clawing her way to the top whatever the odds.

The music industry has proved to be a greater challenge than the fashion industry because here she has no family members to consult. Despite some of her marketing skills being transferable she is constantly treading new ground with this venture and there is definite frustration in the slow pace of ascent. Bushra has come a long way in the last eight years and now she is confident about setting up meetings with executives from the main-stream music industry.

Bushra Ahmed remains the Marketing Director of the Juice Corporation which includes a premium portfolio of designer brands such as Joe Bloggs, Elizabeth Emanuel, Katherine Hamnett, and Slazenger amongst others. The global success that the family-owned and -run company now enjoys is attributed to the foundations laid by Bushra's parents, the late Nizan Ahmed and his wife Saeeda. For Bushra, growing up in an entrepreneurial environment helped as it gave her the experience and responsibility from a young age.

Bushra's aspiration for the future is to work like a maniac for the next ten years and then retire. It seems difficult to see this human dynamo retiring but to have the option to do so is a far more worthwhile goal. Her philosophy is to see your goals and then go for them, do what it takes to achieve them.

Questions for Discussion

1 Discuss the differing importance of men, women and ethnic minorities in entrepreneurship. The discussion should touch on the different gender roles and the support of family and community.
2 Discuss Bushra's creativity as she paves her way in her ecosystem.
3 What are the specific challenges Bushra faced as a female entrepreneur? The discussion should be centered around Bushra's traits and characteristics and you can compare these to other female entrepreneurs.
4 How did Bushra's early involvement in the family business benefit her? Refer to the influence of the environment.
5 What personal characteristics does Bushra highlight?
6 In terms of creativity, what did creativity "do" for Bushra? Where was creativity revealed in her entrepreneurial life and how did she leverage it?
7 How would you recommend Bushra proceed?

AT A GLANCE[13]

Alice Goh: A Female Entrepreneur in Singapore

Rosalind Chew
Division of Economics, School of Humanities and Social Sciences, Nanyang Technological University, Singapore

Alice Goh succeeded her father in running a family business in marble and granite called Goh Teck Wah Company. To be precise, her elder brother succeeded their father and Alice took over from her brother in 1980 when he decided to pursue other interests such as investment in properties instead of running the family business.

Today, Alice is an established entrepreneur. Over the years, under Alice's leadership, Goh Teck Wah has developed a strong local market, with 80 percent of its business being conducted locally in Singapore. The rest of the business covers overseas markets, including Indonesia, Sarawak, Brunei and Malaysia.

The clientele of Goh Teck Wah mainly consists of a few channels provided by established contractors and architects, and by supplying wholesale to other distributors/dealers and stockists of tiles as well as recommendations and referrals from previous clients. Hence, networking with other businessmen in the construction sector is very important for Goh Teck Wah. Alice was once the Second Honorary Secretary of the Singapore Building Materials Suppliers' Association.

With Alice at the helm, Goh Teck Wah has proven itself to be flexible and versatile, able to respond to market needs and trends and to maintain its existing position all these years as one of the more established dealers in building materials in Singapore.

Business Acumen

Alice said that her father and her elder brother were her best teachers. They were willing to teach her everything about the business. Initially, she used to follow her father to his office and business meetings. Subsequently, she learnt from her elder brother. She used to follow her brother to China on numerous business trips during which she learnt to determine the quality of marble and granite, and negotiating with suppliers, among other useful business knowledge. Her brother was smart, very hard-working and generous in imparting knowledge to her. This greatly molded her business ethics. Alice said there is no short cut to success. No one owes you a living. One should be honest and sincere in business dealings but one should not be gullible. Equally important is that one should be kind to people, especially to fellow workers.

When she first took over the construction materials business, Alice had to handle practically everything, from accounting to finance, from inventory to marketing, and from transport to client relationships. There was no such thing as delegation of responsibility and duties. Running a construction materials company means that she has to keep tabs on the latest building trends. The world is her classroom. When she travels overseas, she will study the tiles and marbles used in buildings with a view to learn and formulate business strategies.

Fortunately for her, subsequently her younger sister joined her in the family business and has taken over the role of marketing. This has provided Alice the time to focus on business dealings with suppliers, contractors, architects, as well as with final clients.

Sibling Influence

Alice emphasized that she benefited tremendously from her elder brother in terms of business culture and her sister in helping her to run the family. She also says that there must be harmony at home before you can venture outside to build your business and therefore your career.

Business Strategies

To make her business a success, as an entrepreneur, Alice has to plan the work processes of her business, minimizing inventory cycles and minimizing fixed costs if possible, such as leveraging on the rental of vehicles instead of purchase of lorries, for instance.

Exchange Rate Risk

Alice has to import tiles and marbles. Her costs are nominated in USD and Euros, while her revenue is largely in SGD. The year 2010 was a good year for Alice because the SGD appreciated against the USD and Euro. It is possible that one can make more money in foreign exchange fluctuations than in the normal business dealings but the reverse is also true.

Difficulty in Business as an Entrepreneur

One of the difficulties Alice faced as an entrepreneur is that of setting credit limit terms in business negotiations. If her clients did not know that she is the boss, she would tell the clients that "my boss has set a limit on the terms for business negotiations." But when they knew that she is the boss, Alice could not claim that the boss would not agree to give more discounts.

Expansion of Business and Community Work

Alice said that she does not want to expand her business and has resisted the temptation to pursue a listing on the local stock exchange. This is because being an entrepreneur is only part of her dream. Her other dream is to devote time to charity work. If the business was too big, she would not have time to do work for the community.

Hence, the name of Alice Goh in Singapore is synonymous with various community activities at the grassroots level. She is well known for her contribution of time as well as money. For her participation in grassroots activities over the decades, she was awarded the Public Service Medal by the Singapore government in 1993.

Alice also always encourages other people to do community work. She said: "It is our responsibility to serve the society. When you are in this service, you soon realize that it offers you opportunities to interact with different levels of people."

Long Working Hours

Each day, Alice will be at her office at 7.30 am, and she leaves her office around 6 pm. After that, she will be involved in the organization of and participation in grassroots activities. Much of these activities is to help low-income Singaporeans cope with the fast pace of life in a global city such as Singapore. Nightly, she spends about an hour reviewing her daily activities and making a self-study and critical assessment on how she could improve both her business strategies and her community involvement.

Difference between Self-employed and Entrepreneur

Alice said that the business volume of a self-employed person is small although the business volume of some entrepreneurs may not be big either. Women who are self-employed enjoy certain benefits as it enables them to have the flexibility to look after the family while providing them with a livelihood.

Marital Status

It is tough for a married woman to be an entrepreneur in Singapore as she is expected to play many roles, as a mother, wife and breadwinner. Alice said that she can be an entrepreneur and at the same time still find time to contribute to various activities at the grassroots level because she is single.

Age of Female Entrepreneur

Being young has certain advantages in terms of drive, energy and fewer opportunity costs but the advantage of engaging in entrepreneurship at an older age is that one has more business experience and professional expertise. On balance, being older is an asset.

Education Level of Female Entrepreneur

Alice said that education is a key to business success. A more educated person will be a better entrepreneur as she is more analytical and able to learn fast.

How the Government Can Promote Entrepreneurship

Speaking as a businesswoman, Alice says that the government should lower the corporate tax rate and create the infrastructure to lower the cost of doing business in Singapore.

The government can promote entrepreneurship by encouraging public institutions to conduct more evening classes for the community, as not only employees but also entrepreneurs need to engage in lifelong learning in order to improve themselves and develop their enterprises. The range of subjects can include business law, accounting, personal finance, e-business, business strategies as well as human resource management.

How the Government Promotes Female Entrepreneurship

Law and order is the key to protecting women's rights. With low crime in Singapore, opportunities for women to succeed either as a salaried employee or as an entrepreneur is enormous. Women in Singapore can come home late without worrying about safety. She said that if there is no law and order in Singapore, she will have difficulty getting a job, let alone becoming an entrepreneur. With law and order, a low crime rate, and absence of female discrimination at all levels, from the family to the educational system and the workplace and in business, female entrepreneurship will thrive.

Notes

1 At http://ec.europa.eu/education/lifelong-learning-policy/doc/creativity/report/oecd.pdf; http://www.entrepreneurship-indicators.net/
2 At http://www.doingbusiness.org/research/starting-a-business
3 *Yentl*: directed, co-written, co-produced by and starring Barbra Streisand; based on the play of the same name by Leah Napolin and Isaac Bashevis Singer.
4 *G.I. Jane*: directed by Ridley Scott and starring Demi Moore.
5 *Erin Brockovich*: directed by Steven Soderbergh and starring Julia Roberts.
6 *Norma Rae*: directed by Martin Ritt and starring Sally Field.
7 *Tootsie*: directed by Sydney Pollack and starring Dustin Hoffman.
8 *Mrs. Doubtfire*: directed by Chris Columbus and starring Robin Williams.
9 Ms. Clavel is also founder and Chair of the new Federation Pionnieres since 2008 which coordinates and develops the network of Pionnieres incubators; she is also founder of the company Fincoach since 2001, at http://www.apce.com/cid83569/a-rencontre-paris-pionnieres-incubateur-dedie-aux-femmes.html ; http://www.easybourse.com/bourse/international/interview/276/frederique-clavel-paris-pionnieres.html; http://www.tivipro.tv/chaine.php?id=3483
10 A kibbutz is a collective community in Israel.
11 Premenstrual syndrome (PMS) is a group of symptoms linked to the menstrual cycle.
12 The author(s) of the case studies and at-a-glance cases are fully and solely responsible for their content, phrasing consistency and flow, terminology, English proofing and reference lists.
13 At-a-glance cases are included to present different ecosystems and their effects on the concepts discussed in the chapter; they do not include questions for discussion.

7 Innovation in the Context of Female Entrepreneurship

Chapter Objectives

- Outlining innovation process flow in the female entrepreneurial realm;
- Emphasizing women's contribution to innovation at the business level and that of women-led, innovative businesses at the macro level;
- Discussing women entrepreneurs' involvement in fields involving high levels of innovation, growth and professional standards;
- Understanding innovation's role in the new venture creation through the resource-based view (RBV), the knowledge-based view (KBV), and the dynamic capabilities (DC) approach;
- Establishing the concepts of innovation and adaptation in the female entrepreneurship framework;
- Becoming familiar with women's breakthroughs and inventions in academia and research;
- Acknowledging the barriers set up against women entrepreneurs in implementing innovation in their new ventures.

Women are innovators. They have bright ideas and are adept at pioneering and breaking new ground in a variety of different realms; e.g., Jo Rowling emerged with an imaginative idea for a book that became one of the most profitable bestsellers worldwide; Professor Ada Yonath was the 2010 winner of the prestigious Nobel Prize for her cutting-edge, highly innovative achievements in chemistry; Dr. Grace Murray Hopper invented the computer language COBOL, to name only a few. To turn innovation into entrepreneurship however, innovative ideas have to be feasible, practical and saleable. Innovation is the backbone of entrepreneurship but can also be its biggest threat, since innovation introduces products and services that are original: customers cannot assess their quality from experience, and may thus be reluctant to accept them.

This chapter deals with the roles of innovation, invention, breakthroughs and risk-taking in the female new venture creation process, and imparts the message that innovation is an important element in establishing a venture, as long as it serves the demands and needs of its shareholders and is well aligned with the entrepreneur's passion, dedication and interests.

THE ROLE OF INNOVATION IN THE FEMALE VENTURE CREATION PROCESS

Innovation is the use of new ideas, technologies, methods or processes in places where people have never seen them before. Innovation includes the interaction between the innovator and the process: the players turn an idea into innovative output through a process that enables the transformation of ideas into a tangible business.

Innovation is the heart of entrepreneurship. At the same time, according to Joseph Alois Schumpeter (1950, 1954) and many other scholars in the field, it creates new capabilities, i.e., technological, social and scientific. The development of new products, services, processes or technologies is thus the outcome of the generation of such new capabilities, intertwined with new value added to existing businesses. As such, innovation is not a stand-alone phenomenon in entrepreneurship: it is associated with feasibility, value for the shareholders and production.

Macro Level—The process that typifies innovation in the entrepreneurial market begins in entrepreneurial businesses, mainly small and medium-size ones (SMEs), that introduce innovative products, services or technologies. It is risky, and therefore most of the innovative businesses that attempt to penetrate the market are perceived as valueless and they vanish. Those few that are perceived as having value are sustained in the market and establish the temporal dominance of the innovation, by bringing in newly developed products, services, technologies, etc. As the leading, established companies' tendency is to sustain their own dominance in the market, they operate to exclude the innovative SMEs and regain their dominance. However, at a certain point, the customers who have already experienced the innovation presented by the SMEs will not accept its elimination. In fact, they demand the innovative products and services. The established companies are left with the option of taking over the SMEs to control the innovative products and services. SMEs assess this takeover as a sign of approval: their innovation is deemed worthwhile, and it means that the established companies will invest time, talent and money in building value through the SME's innovation. SMEs profit from such processes by being bought out, merged with or acquired, as shown in Figure 7.1 (Loring, 1991; Mirowski, 1994; Schumpeter, 1950, 1954; Shane, 1992, 1993; Solow, 2007;[1] Utsch & Rauch, 2000).

The track pursued by women entrepreneurs in the new venture creation process is demonstrated in Figure 7.1. Women are typically more risk-averse than men, and this includes introducing innovative deliverables that are exceptionally original. Women therefore break into the market with products, services or technologies that are less innovative relative to men; they develop their innovation in their businesses more prudently and at a slower pace and, as a result, the innovation introduced by women entrepreneurs to the market is less intense than men's. At a stage at which established companies are endeavoring to dominate the SME, women will choose an even slower pace of development of their innovation. This appears to be due to women's more natural tendency to conform to and accept social expectations. Established companies negotiate takeovers more easily with women entrepreneurs than with their male counterparts, buying the former's businesses at lower prices. This outcome is therefore a matter of negotiation and adjustment to the market's dynamics, rather than being a consequence of the development of less innovative products, services or technologies by women entrepreneurs (Figure 7.2).

The frequency of innovation among the genders for the EU-27 in 2009 was broken down as follows: on average, women represented 37 percent of all researchers in the higher education sector, 39 percent in the government sector, and a mere 19 percent in the business enterprise sector (European Commission, 2009). In the US, women accounted for around one third of all scientists and engineers in business or industry. Overall, entrepreneurial businesses headed by women are more likely to be found in personal services and retail trade and less likely to be found in manufacturing and high technology (Anna, Chandler, Jansen, & Mero, 2000; Brush, Carter, Gatewood, Greene, & Hart, 2006). In addition, studies stress that the social change brought about by the elimination of overt gender discrimination has effected a disappointing change in the areas of innovation in business, science and academia, which continue to shun gender parity. Instead, more sophisticated barriers have emerged which continue to limit women's advancement in the spheres of innovation. Both women and their supporting spouses were totally unprepared for this social change, which has proven much more difficult to combat because it often precludes collective action— the only source of power for members of disempowered groups.

Micro Level—Although the contributions of women to innovation at the business level are outstanding, they remain unnoticed: in their 2010 article "Athena in the World of Techne: The Gender Dimension of Technology, Innovation and Entrepreneurship," Marina Ranga and Henry Etzkowitz

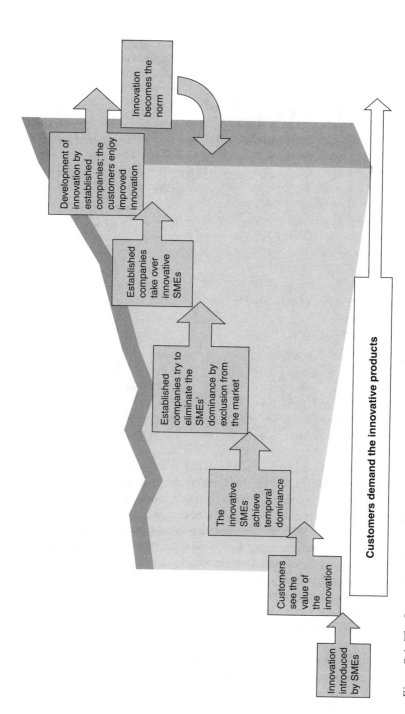

Figure 7.1 The Innovation Process: A Macro Perspective.

Innovation introduced by SMEs

Customers see the value of the innovation

The innovative SMEs achieve temporal dominance

Established companies try to eliminate the SMEs' dominance by exclusion from the market

Established companies take over innovative SMEs

Development of innovation by established companies; the customers enjoy improved innovation

Innovation becomes the norm

Customers demand the innovative products

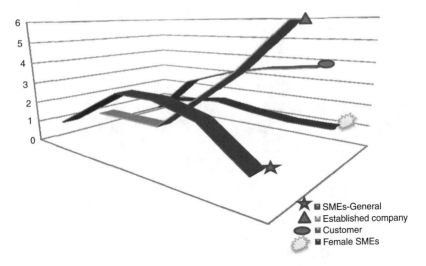

Figure 7.2. Innovation Flow: A Woman-led Perspective.

ask: "Why so Few? Why so Slow? Why so Low?" The relatively lower numbers of women in academia, business, science, technology, high-tech sectors and other fields associated with innovation, their lower positions in the hierarchy, their lower enrollment in technologically oriented education, and their slower pace in developing inventions and scientific breakthroughs, sum up to limited participation and involvement of women in innovation.

Yet women who create new ventures in the high-tech sector, medicine or the sciences, those in academia or those creating initiatives in collaboration with academics are intensively involved in innovation. These fields are rapidly changing and require matching innovative thinking and performance. At the same time, the number of women involved in these areas is limited and most of the new ventures developed by women are in other sectors. The fields involving high levels of innovation embody high professional standards, high demands and an intensive workload involving, among other things, long and unconventional working hours and numerous trips abroad. Women, especially mothers, who could easily meet these high professional standards find it difficult to "choose" between their family-related and work-related roles, and thus avoid, or abandon, their involvement in areas of innovation. Women who hold relevant academic degrees or work experience in areas associated with innovation choose different jobs, such as in the education services sector, to be able to juggle their two roles and reduce their potential work–family conflict. In addition, the market competition in areas of innovation is evident and somewhat aggressive: thus many women avoid it at the outset.

While there has been a rise in women's participation in sectors associated with innovation in the last two decades, social stereotypes that relegate women to domestic activities or that denigrate their biological or psychological inclinations or their suitability for endeavors associated with innovations, breakthroughs and inventions exist, and still have a crucial impact on women's engagement in businesses associated with innovation. However, studies of innovation usually focus on the team rather than on the individual—the innovator, and therefore research on the gender dimension in innovation, especially in the entrepreneurial context, is still lacking. Consequently, the exclusion of women from areas of innovation or the barriers they encounter when attempting to enter these areas have been treated as peripheral matters that are not worthy of research. Thus women's role in innovation and their contribution to their businesses by being innovative are often invisible, even when they hold key positions in the process (Birley, 1989; Bonnett & Furnham, 1991; Bowen & Hisrich, 1986; Boyd & Vozikis, 1994; Kariv, 2010a, 2010b; Strohmeyer & Tonoyan, 2005; Utsch & Rauch, 2000).

THE RESOURCE-BASED VIEW ON THE QUEST FOR INNOVATION

The resource-based view (RBV) pinpoints the prominence of innovation as a stimulus for entrepreneurship. The RBV asserts that a business's innovation depends on its assets and competencies: coordinating the deployment of those assets and competencies, be they tangible or intangible, endows the business with a competitive advantage that is more difficult to imitate. Because businesses rarely present innovations to the market, their scarcity promotes curiosity, which provides a competitive advantage, similarly resources that are more valuable, rare, imperfectly imitable and non-substitutable produce higher competitive advantages to a business.

Research on the RBV of innovation is based on the fundamental premise that the business's resources and capabilities trigger its capacity for innovation. In other words, the business's tangible and intangible resources are assumed to provide the input which is then combined with the business's capabilities to produce innovation (Barney, 1991, 2001; Baysinger & Hoskisson, 1989; Harris & Trainor, 1995; Helfat, 1997; Lee, Lee, & Pennings, 2001; Teece & Pisano, 1994; Wernerfelt, 1984; Zahra, Sapienza, & Davidsson, 2006). In the new venture creation process, even prior to establishing a venture, innovation can be manifested in a way that will place the business in a competitive position in the market. For example, when two entrepreneurs are planning their ventures in the social media arena, and one of them is doing "more of the same" while the other is introducing an original concept in activating the service, the latter is starting on the new venture's path with an evident advantage.

The knowledge-based view (KBV), an extension of the RBV, focuses on the business's stock of knowledge (tacit or explicit) as a strategic resource for the business's competitive success (Decarolis & Deeds, 1999; Kogut & Zander, 1996; Nonaka, 1994). Entrepreneurial businesses create internal knowledge while also exposing themselves to a bombardment of new ideas from their external environment, in order to prevent rigidity, encourage innovative thinking and performance, and assess their developments against those of their competitors. These knowledge-based deliverables trigger the business's capacity to innovate (Helfat & Raubitscek, 2000; Hoopes & Postrel, 1999; Joyce & Stivers, 1999; Leonard-Barton, 1992, 1995; Tiger & Calantone, 1998).

In this vein, while innovation is the critical backbone in the new venture creation process as it places the business at a competitive advantage at the outset, it is not sufficient for success: a sustainable competitive advantage must be sought. Innovation is a key capability in this pursuit as well.

The dynamic capabilities (DC) approach is built around the premise that the business's sustainable competitive advantage lies in combinations of the business's competencies and the resources that can be developed, deployed, and protected to address the changing environment, e.g., technological skills, R&D, product and process development, technology transfer, intellectual property and human resources, among others (Conner & Prahalad, 1996; Nelson & Winter, 1982; Prahalad & Hamel, 1990).

The rudimentary assertion of the DC approach is that innovation is one of the most important keys for a sustainable competitive advantage. Accordingly, successful businesses are those that can exhibit rapid and flexible product innovation, coupled with management capability that can effectively coordinate and redeploy internal and external competencies. Innovation enables the business to demonstrate continual responsiveness and adjustment to the environment's changing demands and thus to the shareholders' changing needs and interests. The DC approach to the new venture creation process can be manifested in the entrepreneur's ability to build competencies that will enable rapidly addressing the changing environment while the venture is still only an idea; that is, to visualize how the planned business's practices will generate different forms of competitive advantage on a continual basis in the face of increasingly demanding environments (Katila & Shane, 2005; Teece, Pisano, & Shuen, 1997).

These concepts stress the importance of innovation in women's new venture creation process: by establishing a competitive advantage via the introduction of innovation to the market, women-led businesses can experience a market dominance that will then encourage and stimulate other women entrepreneurs to develop and present their businesses' innovations to the market. Most importantly, innovation can be manifested in different dimensions of the business, not just in R&D or technology; innovation is based on various combinations of marketing concept, idea, advertising model, niche, internal knowledge developed in the business, among others.

Every business has its actual and potential strengths and weaknesses. Women are more likely to determine those strengths and weaknesses openly, and identify the resources and capabilities that their business can muster.

In addition, female-based traits aimed at people's development and empowerment make the women's impetus and ability to develop their teams feasible.

INNOVATION/ADAPTATION

Innovation/adaptation refers to the manner in which people think, behave, solve problems and perform in their entrepreneurial businesses, by either following the agreed-upon and well-known structures or by inventing new ones.

Adaptors prefer to improve things within the existing framework and well-known structures. They are typified by:

- a focus on restoring balance, i.e., solving problems rather than trying to identify potential pitfalls and problems in advance;
- rarely challenging rules;
- an interest in understanding the problems they encounter and learn from them;
- providing a safe base for the innovator's riskier operations;
- seeing the benefits of implementing solutions which have been developed and approved by others;
- preferring a structure that is consensually agreed upon when problem-solving;
- risk aversion.

Innovators prefer to do things differently; they are less concerned with acting in accordance with existing structures. They have a tendency to overhaul the entire work process. Innovators are typified by:

- being seemingly undisciplined, approaching tasks from unexpected angles;
- providing the dynamics to produce revolutionary changes;
- treating accepted means with little regard to the pursuit of goals;
- challenging the known;
- being less concerned about restoring balance, but rather advancing thoughts and experiences, and engaging in a trial-and-error style;
- taking risks.

(Drucker, 1985; Foxall & Hackett, 1994; Hutchinson & Skinner, 2007; Kaufman, 2004; Kirton, 1976; Kwang *et al.*, 2005; Meneely & Portillo, 2005; Quinn, 2000; Schilling, 2005; Skinner & Drake, 2003)

Table 7.1 Innovation/Adaptation: Leading Research

Entrepreneur's problem-solving styles	Styles of managerial creativity	Personality, cognitive style	Performance and leadership
Buffington, Jablokow, & Martin (2002); Buttner & Gryskiewicz (1993); Summers, Sweeny, & Wolk (2000)	Foxall & Hackett (1994); Shiomi, & Loo (1999); Woodman, Sawyer, & Griffin (1993)	George & Zhou, (2001); Kaufman (2004); Meneely & Portillo (2005); Tierney & Farmer (2002)	Kirton (2003); Skinner & Drake (2003); Shin & Zhou (2003)

Table 7.1 presents some of the leading empirical research in the context of innovation/adaptation.

While innovation in the entrepreneurial context is praised, it is not the only way to manage an entrepreneurial business and it is not categorically better than adaptation. However, in the first phases of the new venture creation process, it regenerates the drive and provides the first and deepest impression that customers and other shareholders will get of the business.

Are Women Innovators or Adaptors?

Entrepreneurs raise various ideas and implement them in their ventures; they export ideas from different domains, merge ideas, adjust already known ideas to the environment's dynamic changes and create original ideas, among others. Creativity, imagination and vision, coupled with the drive to act, change and succeed engender new, original ideas; by appending originality, innovativeness and invention, these ideas are transformed from "just" ideas to innovative ones.

Women entrepreneurs dare, provoke and challenge the known and the obvious; they introduce innovation into female-oriented and traditional sectors of activity, foster innovation among their teams and serve as a role model for innovation among their staff. However, women downplay the innovative parts of their business concepts or performance: their relatively lower confidence in their ability to leverage their innovation and sustain it results in their withdrawing those innovational aspects that might be perceived as controversial by their customers. For example, women may craft an original way of financing their business, but they will return to the more conventional way of tackling this issue if they perceive, or are told, that their way of financing is too innovative. Women prefer to rely on previous experiences than to break through on a path that has never been traveled. As such, women are regarded as adaptors more than innovators— not because the level or pace of their innovations are lower, but because of personal or social-related factors such as self-efficacy, lack of self-confidence and a desire to "follow" rather than "lead."

Yet this is not always the case among women: some of them are more courageous and rebel against tradition by proudly introducing their innovations. Ms. Adina Bar Shalom,[2] the founder of higher education for the ultra-Orthodox in Israel, provides an example of breaking through by introducing innovation in a traditional sector. Bar Shalom initiated, founded and manages an innovative concept, aimed primarily for Jewish ultra-Orthodox women but secondarily for men as well, that offers them academization, better employment opportunities, and career options. Bar Shalom, an ultra-Orthodox Jewish woman, followed a risky innovation path: the female ultra-Orthodox segment has been marginalized and neglected for decades, yet these women are the core workforce in their families, as their spouses are studying at the Yeshiva[3] and cannot provide for their families. Any type of academic education was considered impermissible in this community, yet Bar Shalom catered to the special needs of her target customers with academic quality and attracted clients. She took the huge risk of being criticized by her own community, or of being unable to attract ultra-Orthodox women to higher education due to the extreme innovation of her concept. But she exhibited determination, and a deep belief and confidence in both the concept and her ability to activate it properly. This enabled her to start and manage her business successfully. Her most successful entrepreneurial undertaking has produced unequivocally successful results among ultra-Orthodox women and men.

Women entrepreneurs are proficient in managing teams toward innovating, thinking outside the box and creating; this is essential to achieving innovation in the business. Women possess a natural ability to empower teams by unleashing and managing them through a "hands-off" approach when required. Women are instinctively more attentive to their teams, provide them with the needed flexibility and can easily pinpoint the staff members who tend to think more originally, and empower them. Such practices are of prime relevance in enabling the people involved in the new venture to spawn innovation across all of the business's processes, activities and plans.

Another feature of innovation concerns women's breakthroughs in academia and research: women initiate and advance sophisticated experiments, make extraordinary discoveries and exhibit risk-taking, outside-the-box thinking and performance by challenging the known and using complex models to prevail over the "obvious" with their discoveries and innovation. Despite their emergence in academia and research, however, women innovators are still at a disadvantage, and their innovation remains hidden. Thus, again, women are regarded as adaptors more than innovators. Breakthroughs and discoveries in research are mainly communicated and published by research or laboratory teams, and awards for those discoveries are also mainly given to teams rather than just one contributor. As women rarely occupy the formal position of team leader, their contribution as innovators is barely recognized.

Women are also corporate innovators. They are loyal to their workplace and challenge real life in the business by promoting its practices and competencies through the introduction of innovation and originality. An interesting example of this appeared in an episode of the ABC television series "Grey's Anatomy,"[4] when the chief challenged the hospital's residents by setting up a competition between the hospital's departments with an over one million dollar prize; the doctors were asked to come up with the best and most innovative ideas for improving their departments and making them more competitive. This episode revealed the significance attributed to corporate innovation. Female residents in this episode addressed innovation as the primary challenge, while the men were more concerned with efficiency, finance and the quality of their departments. Reflecting on this episode, such competition is the best way to encourage corporate innovation as well as to reveal the daily needs of the business.

Research shows that corporate innovations are mainly ignored, as they expose the company to costs, uncertainty, and unknown outcomes. Thus, women's role in developing such innovation and inventions is accordingly ignored; again, women may be considered adaptors rather than innovators as their innovation is rarely recognized by corporations.

To emphasize their ability, desires and achievements as innovators, women should fight for their innovation, encourage other women to reveal their innovations and empower themselves and their female counterparts, staff members or colleagues in order to inspire more women to innovate. Women's contribution as innovators is demonstrated in Figure 7.3.

Barriers in the Way of Innovation

There are different dimensions of hindrances to women entrepreneurs' leadership in innovation: some of these stem from women's personal barriers, while others are associated with women's status in society and the labor market.

Figure 7.4 illustrates the dimensions associated with barriers to women on their path to innovation. As shown in the figure, labor market inequality (the broadest circle) is manifested, in the context of innovation and gender, in different forms, including a reluctance to provide bank loans to women vs. men for their innovations, praising and spreading the word about innovations initiated by men vs. women, and regarding innovations developed by men as the standard and those developed by women as the suspicious exception that needs to be thoroughly reviewed, among others. These are then echoed in each of the progressively smaller circles presented in Figure 7.3. Starting from the first dimension, self-direction to the conventional and avoidance of the innovative (inner circle), many women avoid careers as entrepreneurs, researchers, managers of

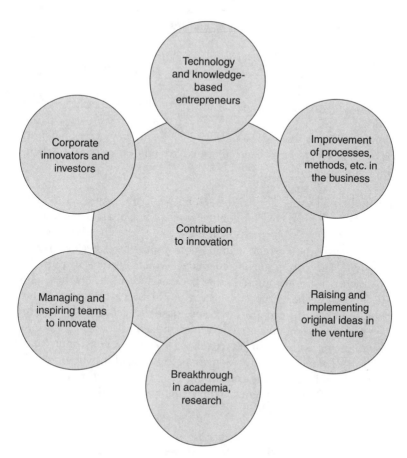

Figure 7.3 Women as Innovators.

technologically innovative companies and start-ups, or taking the top
technological responsibilities, such as CTO,[5] regardless of their talents,
capabilities and desires. Self-direction is related to the general inequality in
the labor market and is manifested as follows:

- lack of self-confidence with regard to one's potential and capacity for
  innovation as well as for managing innovation;
- lack of leadership experience; too much experience as a follower;
- lack of belief in being taken seriously as an innovator and in having
  one's innovation be considered as feasible;
- lack of self-assurance in sharing one's ideas with others, due to loosely
  developed relevant networks and a general fear of imitation;
- concerns about failure, humiliation, being embarrassed by one's
  innovation;

- perceiving innovation as "too much to handle," as not having obtained sufficient competencies and resources to effectively set it up in one's business;
- regarding one's own innovative ideas as futile;
- adopting the victim's point of view: " 'they' will think there is nothing in my ideas . . .";
- considering that innovation is not worth the risk, because it "never works . . .";
- concerns about being responsible for the money, time, and other resources which have been allocated to innovation, rather than to more tangible goals.

Family and social expectations, the second circle in Figure 7.4, represent the impact of this close environment on women: it is often "recommended" that women follow the conventional, non-risky path. The effect of people who are close to the entrepreneur is more pronounced because they are familiar with the entrepreneur and know "which buttons to push." For example, when a mother suggests that her daughter withdraw her innovative ideas because her time and energy could be better spent at home with the children, this proposition is specifically targeted to the daughter-entrepreneur situation, and as such is most influential.

The following salient barrier is related to family constraints and to work–family balance/conflict. Women perceive working in innovation-based sectors as hugely time-consuming, due to the long hours spent at work to manage and implement their innovation, and meetings at all

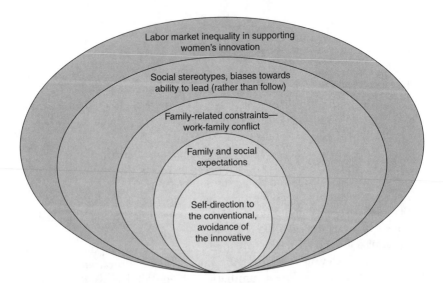

Figure 7.4 Barriers to Innovation: The Female View.

different hours of the day—including after-school hours which therefore cannot be spent with the children. In many cases, innovation is linked to global businesses and demands frequent travel, as well as working at non-conventional hours (when there are time differences between countries). Innovation is demanding and spills over into family time, setting up dilemmas regarding time allocation and quality of life while being engaged in innovative projects. Some women can manage the work–life conflict and achieve a balance by implementing innovation in their family routines, for example, "re-starting" their work day after the children have gone to sleep, or involving the children in their businesses (this is even possible with young children in some areas of the business).

A broader barrier, almost entirely affected by labor market inequality, is gender-related stereotypes and biases, which have an impact on women's decisions to enlist in innovation-oriented undertakings. In fact, this barrier is mirrored in a variety of institutions, such as schools, higher education, employment, social and cultural institutions: for example, girls tend to choose a more traditional path at school, and their numbers in science and technology courses are consequently relatively low. This barrier demands a choice between following the social identity of women in the respective country or confronting and fighting these social perceptions. Many women choose to avoid such a fight. The result has many manifestations: any endeavor of women entrepreneurs to take part in hard-core innovation and R&D raises doubts in their social environment via rumors on their family status, sexual preferences or feminine characteristics, consequently counteracting women's participation in a position involving innovation.

Understanding the barriers faced by women is an important factor in facilitating their involvement and leadership in areas associated with innovation. However, this is only one part of the equation; the other is expanding our understanding of the unique paths taken by women who have attempted to break through the barriers and penetrate "male-dominated" sectors.

Due to the fluidity and instability of innovation in the new venture creation process and the difficulty in actually pinpointing it in this process, little has been investigated or is known about women's working practices to overcome the aforementioned barriers. This creates a void in our knowledge of their unique processes and achievements, and such a void cultivates stereotypes, biases and discriminatory approaches (Cockburn & Ormrod, 1993; Pelkonen, 2003; Rosser, 2004, 2006; Sonnert & Holton, 2006; Xie & Shauman, 2003).

According to Kofi Annan, "no tool for development is more effective than the empowerment of women";[6] pursuant to this proclamation, women can overcome the barriers by:

- studying the subject matter of their business deeply and rigorously, so that their innovation can be based on solid ground;

- training themselves prior to starting an innovative undertaking to possess the relevant skills to deploy innovative competencies, processes and outcomes;
- surrounding themselves with experts, counselors, and people with experience;
- sharing their ideas with people they trust;
- taking a flexible rather than rigid approach to their innovation, thereby allowing easier adjustment of their innovation when the environment's demands change;
- using innovation in different spheres of their lives, including children, spouses, domestic household, friends, etc.;
- fighting for their ideas;
- maintaining support networks;
- developing and/or maintaining relevant networks to support their innovations.

INVENTIONS AND BREAKTHROUGHS AMONG WOMEN ENTREPRENEURS

The essence of entrepreneurship lies in being a revolutionary, embodying an innovative nature and outside-the-box thinking, capitalizing on the unexpected, unrecognized and unique, and being the rebellious spirit that captures innovation.

Research on topics related to women's inventions, breakthroughs and discoveries is limited, as these areas are traditionally characterized by either gender blindness or male dominance. The few studies that have addressed gender in the context of inventions and breakthroughs explain women's avoidance of careers involving originality and novelty by their nature and culture. Even when women have made substantial accomplishments in innovation and breakthroughs, they are presented in ways that reduce their net accomplishments in these fields, by showing their talents in the areas of sociability and family, i.e., the traditional female sphere.

Yet there are many examples of women innovators: Professor Ada Yonath was the first female recipient of the Nobel Prize in her field since Dorothy Hodgkin received the Nobel Prize for chemistry in 1964, and Professor Maria Goeppert Mayer shared the Nobel Prize in Physics in 1963 (e.g., Abir-Am, 2010; Bray, 1997, 2007; Etzkowitz, Kemelgor, & Uzzi, 2000; Haraway, 1989, 1997; Wajcman, 2007).

Nobel prize laureates and patent recipients are mainly associated with men, despite the fact that amazing breakthroughs have been initiated, managed or facilitated by women: Catherine Greene is said to have presented both the problem and the basic idea to Eli Whitney, who received a patent for the cotton gin and was a pioneer in the mass production of cotton; Stephanie Kwolek, one of Dupont's leading chemists, discovered the "miracle fiber," Kevlar, which has five times the strength of steel by weight, and is used for ropes and cables on oil-drilling rigs, canoe hulls, boat sails, automobile bodies and tires, and military and motorcycle helmets. Kwolek was inducted into the National Inventors Hall of Fame in 1995. Gertrude B. Elion, 1988 Nobel laureate in Medicine, is credited with the synthesis of two of the first successful drugs for leukemia and a breakthrough treatment for AIDS, among others; Elion was the first woman inductee into the National Inventors Hall of Fame in 1991. While Margaret Knight, considered "the female Edison," received some 26 patents for such diverse items as a window frame and sash, machinery for cutting shoe soles, and improvements to internal combustion engines, workmen reportedly refused her advice when first installing the equipment because, "after all, what does a woman know about machines?"

The role of female home economists who helped develop specific functions of the microwave oven was not acknowledged as part of the innovation process. Cain Miller (2010) tells the story of a female high-tech entrepreneur in Silicon Valley who waited a long time—until she gained experience in several start-ups—before undertaking her own, being well aware, based on their track record, that male-dominated venture capital firms were less likely to fund women's ventures. These are but a few examples showing the little attention and biased treatment women have received in the context of innovation and entrepreneurship, breakthroughs and inventions.

Little is known about the innovative patterns of women inventors. Hence there is a need to proactively locate such stories, as well as encourage innovators to communicate and disseminate their own stories: it is only through inspiration from other women's experiences that women will follow their desires and use their skills and abilities to promote their potential breakthrough to the world.

RISK-TAKING: THE ENIGMA OF INNOVATION—A FEMALE VIEW

Innovation means taking risks, be they radical or moderate. These risks are related to the ambiguous, vague and unpredictable process and outcomes of innovation and its side effects. At the same time, most studies in entrepreneurship have concluded that gender differences clearly exist in entrepreneurs' strategic behavior; e.g., women are more cautious, less confident, less aggressive, easier to persuade, and take fewer risks than men. However, more recent studies have revealed more similarities than differences in the genders' risk-taking performances (Chaganti & Parasuraman, 1996; Hudgens & Fatkin, 1985; Johnson & Powell, 1994; Powell, 1990; Powell & Ansic, 1997). While research into gender performance in risk-taking has given mixed results, it has revealed that women have a lower preference for risk-taking and are hesitant in their ability to make decisions in risky situations, and will therefore avoid situations that can lead to risk, such as innovation (Levin, Snyder, & Chapman, 1988; Masters, 1989; Schubert, Brown, Gysler, & Brachinger, 1999; Sexton & Bowman-Upton, 1990; Stinerock, Stern, & Solomon, 1991; Zinkhan & Karande, 1991).

Risk-taking is a major component of entrepreneurial activity and success. Showing reticence toward bearing substantial risk means being at a disadvantage when entering into cutting-edge entrepreneurial activities to achieve business success. Thus, a vicious circle is formed: women are prone to risk aversion and refrain from choosing areas that carry risk, such as innovation, science, breakthroughs. Consequently, they are underrepresented in the entrepreneurial undertakings that promise the best potential profits, and women's success rates in entrepreneurship remain mediocre.

Nevertheless, studies investigating gender differences in risk-taking propensity continue to provide mixed results; for example, no significant differences have been found in different studies regarding risk level of decisions in venture innovation or strategies chosen by business owners, or regarding entrepreneurial values given to innovation, risk-taking and courage to "dive into the water." This indicates that men and women entrepreneurs are more similar than different in their risk-taking behavior and that being an entrepreneur, regardless of gender, determines a higher propensity for taking risks. However, other studies have found that in the case of active entrepreneurs, women minimize risks in different aspects of the business; e.g., in finance-related issues, they make less risky financial choices than men, are more prudent in using funds and stakeholders' money, are less risk-seeking, are more conservative when making decisions under uncertainty, and engage in less risky projects in their business to reduce the probability of failure. Findings on potential entrepreneurs, however, are scarce, and therefore this second view does not indicate whether, among potential entrepreneurs, it is women's risk aversion or some other determinant that explains the difference in men and women's likelihood to start a business in areas that are prone to higher risk (Arch, 1993; Baker, Aldag, & Blair, 2003; Byrnes, Miller, & Schafer, 1999; Fagenson, 1993; Jianakoplos & Bernasek, 1998; Powell & Ansic, 1997; Sonfield, Lussier, Corman, & McKinney, 2001; Thomas & Mueller, 2001).

Reflecting upon the accumulated research results on risk-taking and innovation, the implication is that women entrepreneurs' risk aversion is significant in their initial motivation, willingness and attraction to opportunities involving risk, and that the trade-off foreseen by women entrepreneurs between risks and business outcomes differ from that foreseen by men. Simply put, women see the potential failure, while men see the potential success that might result from taking risks in the business. Both views may be valid, depending upon personal, organizational and environment-related variables that may affect whether risk is leveraged to achieve success, or is underestimated or misused, resulting in failure

(Brockhaus, 1980; Masters & Meier, 1988; McGrath, MacMillan, & Scheinberg, 1992; Mueller & Thomas, 2001).

Gender differences in the propensity to take risks in entrepreneurial undertakings involving innovation and R&D might be attributed to the following:

1 Social norms and entrepreneurial history present women's role in society in a way that reduces their confidence in their ability to handle innovative undertakings; they therefore favor traditional and known areas in entrepreneurship, mainly typified by female-oriented businesses.

2 Social norms regarding women's role and status have a significant impact on the way others see women entrepreneurs, especially those involved in male-dominated areas such as innovation; women are taken less seriously as business people, and find it difficult to gain support for their entrepreneurial activities from potential shareholders and stakeholders.

3 Family, friends and colleagues "protect" women by advising them to pursue a less risky course of action, including refraining from entrepreneurship, innovation and inventions.

4 The shortage of female role models in the areas of innovation, cutting-edge science and breakthroughs is discouraging to women; they interpret this lack as reflecting failed experiences that do not merit exploration.

5 Due to greater household burdens and childcare responsibilities, women have more trouble balancing the formation of a business and family responsibilities. In such cases, any additional risks or demanding challenges in the business are perceived as exceeding their abilities.

6 Women have more difficulty obtaining adequate mentorship for their venture creation efforts, which discourages them and leads to more traditional endeavors in female-oriented areas.

SUMMARY

The concept of innovation as the backbone of entrepreneurship has been shaped by Schumpeter (1939, 1943), followed by leading scholars and practitioners and it continues to be advocated today in both research and practice. It is described in this chapter in the framework of the RBV and DC approach to emphasize its role in providing a more valuable, rare, imperfectly imitable and non-substitutable, higher competitive advantage to the business.

Innovation stems from different dimensions of the business and its environment and weaves the processes and practices executed in the new venture creation, from the development of the idea to its implementation. In this framework, the quest of women entrepreneurs for innovation and the ways in which they integrate it into their new ventures are outlined.

Women's achievements in innovation, inventions and breakthroughs are presented, along with the hindrances women encounter in accessing and leading innovation-driven projects. Their remarkable achievements in science and research are contrasted with the limited dissemination of those achievements.

This chapter conveys the message that women entrepreneurs can and should embark on innovation. The relevant circles surrounding them should congregate to facilitate their way in the realm of innovation, starting with a change in their own attitudes regarding their ability to develop and deploy innovation and ending in a change in social ordering, perceptions and biases pertaining to women as innovators.

CASE STUDIES[7]

The following two case studies, contributed by Professor Sundin and Professor Holmquist, describe the intertwining of entrepreneurship and innovation in a non-innovative sector, i.e., the real-estate maintenance sector, and an innovative sector, i.e., a high-tech business. They carefully trace the different dimensions in which innovation is manifested by the two women entrepreneurs. Drawing on the realm of Swedish women, the authors guide the reader from opportunity identification to successful implementation of innovative ideas into real ventures, though the course is sometimes twisted and the success potential blurred.

In both cases, the significance of engaging in a strategy of innovation is emphasized and the message that innovation is the backbone of any entrepreneurial undertaking is clear, regardless of the sector of industry.

SWEDEN

Women's Entrepreneurship in a Scandinavian Welfare State

Elisabeth Sundin[a] and Carin Holmquist[b]
[a]*Business Administration at the Department of Economic and Industrial Development (IE) and Helix Vinn Excellence Centre, Linköping University, Sweden;* [b]*Family Stefan Persson Chair of Entrepreneurship and Business Creation, Stockholm School of Economics, Sweden*

In international comparisons Sweden scores high on the position of women. An important dimension for this position is that women to a large extent are on the labor market. In some municipalities women have even higher labor-market participation than men. Other dimensions are the social security and support system. Care for the elderly and care for children, considered to be the responsibility of women all over the world, are to a comparatively large extent financed and even handled by the public sector. That is the main reason why Sweden is classified as a Scandinavian welfare state by Esping-Andersen (1996) and others after him.

Esping-Andersen has been criticized by some feminist researchers for a gender-biased view of the world. Another puzzling fact is that Swedish women score low in international comparisons of the extent to which women are owner-managers. Twenty-five to thirty percent of all owner-managers are women. Although their share of new-starters is higher overall, their share seems constantly to stay at the same low level. The reasons for this situation are discussed among both researchers and politicians. An often-discussed question is whether the welfare state is a hindrance for women to establish themselves as owner-managers and self-employed—or whether it has been genuinely positive as it has given Swedish women a women-friendly labor market. Other types of explanations concern the gender-segregation of the labor market and the gender-labels on occupations and positions including self-employment and entrepreneurship.

Women as Owner-managers in Sweden Today

The entrepreneurial strategies of Swedish women can be described both as very similar to the strategies of men and as very different from the strategies of men. Both trends are illustrated through data presented by Statistics Sweden, an agency which collects adequate figures every year. The similarities concern such important attitudes as willingness, or rather unwillingness, to grow and hindrance from being a successful entrepreneur. The differences concern family-obligations and sector-specific realities. Both of these are variants of the gender system and the gender-regime. From the gender system and gender-regime it follows that the innovations of women often are not acknowledged as innovations.

Women as owner-managers are very different. All they have in common is that they are women and that they are owner-managers. Also, if we restrict ourselves to owner-managers of innovative enterprises the differences are striking. We will illustrate this by presenting two examples of Swedish women who started innovative enterprises at a young age—and still are very different. We will start with Malin Bodén who started a cleaning company as we think that the prejudice toward cleaning, labeled as something everyone (at least every woman) can do, blocks our recognition of the innovativeness of her actions.

Case A: The Innovative Entrepreneur in a Non-innovative Sector

The Swedish entrepreneur presented as a case here is in the real-estate-cleaning sector. To understand the innovativeness of her thoughts and actions some information on the sector has to be given. Real-estate was long considered as a local market-industry protected from national and international competition by the fact that the services provided have to be done in a specific place. Now this has changed as multinational companies also are active in every small village. An absolute majority of all companies are small, very small. Some of them delivering their services from the "black side" of the market. The serious small local companies are consequently caught between the big internationals and the self-employed. A majority of the individuals working as cleaners are women. They have the lowest salaries on the labor market. Many of the employees are working part time, some of them just a few hours a week, and uncomfortable working hours that are very early mornings or very late nights. Health problems are a well-known phenomenon among cleaners.

When Malin Bodén left school at the beginning of the 1990s she found her first job with a real-estate-cleaning company. After only a few years the company left the market and she became unemployed. She was just 20 years old. Her work had given her experiences which she wanted to use and she had seen practices she wanted to change. So she took the opportunity to follow a start-your-own-company course given to young unemployed individuals by the Employment Services. Subsequently, after a few years she decided to diversify her services among real-estate-cleaning, real-estate-services and graffiti removal and for this purpose she allowed two men to join her as partners. They get 20 percent each of the shares and she keeps 60 percent herself. She is married to one of these men and she has one son.

It is the cleaning part of her services that is closest to Malin's heart. "Cleaning is important! And it is the employees who do the job. They are the company. If you do not take care for the employees you have nothing. They are the professionals. They are the ones that really know the customers."

Bodén's conviction is demanding for other actors and actors' groups. First, her employees must have the same feeling of conviction about her business. They must think of the cleaning provided as an important service and not just one that anyone could do. They have to be committed to and really want to work full time—not look upon their work solely as a way to get some extra money. To get that feeling Bodén thinks she has to show that she really means it by paying more than the mini-wages that characterize the sector. However, that gives her higher costs for an hour of cleaning than her competitors. To handle the situation Bodén has different strategies.

Bodén's strategy may also be demanding for her customers. She tries to show them that they get a high-quality service by hiring her cleaners. For the customer the cost per item is more relevant than the cost per hour for the cleaners. Her employees are less frequently on sick-leave than other cleaners so she seldom has to "summon reserves" as many other cleaning-companies often have to do.

Her strategy also extends to restricting her clientele to just those customers that share her values. Many pay lip-service to her ideas but when it comes to practice price is still of great importance. To convince the customers of her "high-quality-strategy" she discusses the service provided with them. "Often I do the budget together with them because then I can influence them and help them. Because I am the expert. I can present them an offer and a price and if they take it they get no unpleasant surprises. Others may promise them a very low hourly rate but then present them with many hours for services they may not foresee. I will not do that."

Bodén is also demanding for the other companies working on the local market because she wants them to share her values on the importance of cleaning. She initiates networks and meetings for the big providers and the big customers although she herself is a rather "small player" on the local market. She presented the idea of establishing a company owned by the local cleaning companies to provide all cleaners with full-time employment. The owners, the cleaning companies, in that way would not have to handle the full-time positions themselves. That idea, however, was never realized because not enough businesses supported her by being willing to join. Bodén illustrates their argument by reproducing a conversation: "we cannot share staff" they said "they may tell you about our customers." Then I asked straight on: "I suppose you do not hire idiots! Isn't it talented employees we want? If I need someone for twenty hours a week and you need the same what's the problem? If we cannot provide a full-time position then we will lose this person in cleaning. She will leave us and go somewhere else."

In summary, we state that there are many reasons for calling Malin Bodén an innovative entrepreneur and owner. As shown above, she is seeking solutions in new ways of organizing and defining the services provided. These solutions have to be transformed into a strategy for employees as the companies in the sector are the employees and the employees are the companies in the sector. To change the sector Bodén has to change the working conditions for the employees as well as their identity and ambitions. This also may make her a social entrepreneur and the sector-changing ambitions may also make her a societal entrepreneur. Without going into these discussions further, the conclusion can be made that entrepreneurship which from the outside looks conventional and straightforward at a closer look appears both innovative, complex and multifunctional.

Case B: The Owner-manager in the High-tech Sector

Mai-Li Hammargren has always been entrepreneurial. She comes from a family where her mother is very strong and active and Mai-Li has actively chosen not to follow stereotypical gender roles. Her appearance, though, is very conventionally feminine. She is a student of the Stockholm School of Economics and started her present company, Mutewatch, at the age of 21—parallel to her studies. She is the CEO of the company, which she founded in 2008 together with an engineering student, Oscar Ritzén Praglowski. Mai-Li was the one who had the original idea—a vibrating wristwatch. She and her boyfriend had very different working hours so she pondered on a way to set the alarm without waking him up. The idea she elaborated won a prize in a business idea competition—and after that Mai-Li was hooked on the idea.

Her idea of how to run a venture is to engage her networks and today the team of Mutewatch consists of nearly a dozen people, not including the wider networks of mentors, supporters and friends. Since Mai-Li is not an engineer she has recruited team members who are, while she herself takes on the roles of securing capital, managing the company, marketing the product and setting up networks. The idea has evolved and prototypes have been developed. Today Mai-Li describes her product as a time management tool with a strong fashion character. Her mission is even wider than this— in an interview she stated that she truly believes her product can help people attain mindfulness in an easier way.

All of Mai-Li's time is dedicated to her company; she has no leisure time. There have been, and are, a lot of issues to deal with—setting up the company was one thing, engaging friends to join the team another (most people have worked on a non-profit basis since Mai-Li has convinced them of the potential of the product).

Mai-Li has no problems with gender roles, in fact she believes that entrepreneurship is very good and suitable for women—as she says in the interview on Mini Max USA, Spring 2010:

> Running your own business is a good arena for showing what you are capable of, taking a lot of responsibility and at the same time retaining power. It is not that unusual to be given a high degree of responsibility as an employee early on in your career, but to also have a decision-making role is very uncommon. And I can tell you, it is extremely satisfying to experience that your decision sticks and to see it implemented in practice!

The company development has not run smoothly. Mai-Li has had to struggle in many arenas.

The main problems have been product development and capital acquisition. She has managed to get lots of attention for her idea but in order to be able to sell Mutewatch products she has to get capital for production in advance. And in order to get capital she needs to show that she has a market, which is not easy to prove for a totally new product.

After years of constant work, the product—a silent alarm in the shape of a vibrating wristband—was presented in August 2010 and pre-orders were taken. Investors started to sign up and Mai-Li became confident that her networking entrepreneurial style would succeed.

Questions for Discussion

1   Do you think that the two women in these case studies are innovative? Why/why not?
2   What are the differences between the women in terms of innovativeness? Why do you think they are different?
3   Is there anything in the case studies that you think has to do with the gender of the entrepreneurs? Or could the two examples just as well have been men? Why/why not?
4   Do you think that there is anything specifically Swedish about these examples? Why/why not? Could these two examples have come from your country?
5   The case presents rather young entrepreneurs. Do you think that the age of women entrepreneurs affects their entrepreneurship? Why?

Notes

1   Solow (2007).
2   At http://israel.ashoka.org/en/adina-bar-shalom
3   At http://theyeshivaworld.com/
4   At http://abc.go.com/shows/greys-anatomy
5   CTO—chief technology officer.
6   From remarks by Secretary-General Kofi Annan at the opening of the 49th session of the Commission on the Status of Women (Beijing+10), New York, February 28, 2005.
7   The author(s) of the case studies are fully and solely responsible for their content, phrasing consistency and flow, terminology, English proofing and reference lists.

8 The Vision

The Foundation of Entrepreneurship

Chapter Objectives

- Recognizing the vision's role in the new venture creation phase and its significance to the growth and success of the business;
- Linking the vision's characteristics to women entrepreneurs' core competencies;
- Embedding the concept of vision in feminist theories;
- Analyzing women entrepreneurs as visionaries;
- Understanding the vision in the framework of mental models;
- Understanding the power of vision from women entrepreneurs' success stories.

The vision is the imagined business, the wish, the drive. It is seeded long before the venture has been created, and accompanies the entrepreneur along the creation process. It flourishes in the entrepreneur's mind and functions as the business's North Star as the venture creation process evolves. The vision is not dependent on the entrepreneurs' environment, though the entrepreneurs' visualization is embedded in their culture, as well as in their knowledge and experience.

Unlike other processes, the vision is rarely adjusted, blended with other ideas or modified along the new venture creation; rather, it remains the solid ground of the future business, and molds the business's structure and content.

This chapter introduces the role of vision in the new venture creation process from the female entrepreneur's perspective, and discusses how the vision's deliverables shape her new venture creation process.

The uniqueness of this chapter lies in introducing the vision through the biographies of well-known women entrepreneurs that had visions which were realized and turned into successful ventures, e.g., Estée Lauder: "I have never worked a day in my life without selling. If I believe in something, I sell it, and I sell it hard," and Debbi Fields: "Good enough never is."

VISION IN THE VENTURE CREATION PROCESS

... it is this perception of the invisible linkages between knowledge and experience, fueled by creative insight, which allows an individual to develop a vision of a venture which does not yet exist. It is much more than simply recognizing an opportunity, although the vision may involve exactly that. It may be a vision of an approach which is tried and true, or a complete copy of another's concept or idea. Alternatively, there may be no opportunity existent at all. The vision may be of a process which can create an opportunity which does not yet exist.

(Carland & Carland, 2000, p. 38)

The vision is the dream, the wish, the imagination, a visualization of the business that the entrepreneur envisages, regardless of whether the vision emerges as a venture that the entrepreneur is actually willing to launch. The quest for the vision in the new venture creation process has been awakened with some emerging approaches (e.g., Filion, 2005; Filion & Ananou, 2010) that treat the entrepreneurial process holistically, and through the lens of the entrepreneur's intuition, reflection and synchronization. These approaches emphasize the significance of the vision in pursuing the entrepreneurial course of action: the entrepreneur "sees" what is still not there. The vision is the insight that identifies the fitting market and the intuition that designs the business's products and services to capture these markets.

Thus, by mentally molding business structure and content, and how the business will appear and function in the future, the entrepreneur can start the business with a clear advantage: the desired business is already constructed, mentally, and this is a huge step toward starting a business. The vision is the core component in the venture creation process at the phase of idea formation and harmonization, followed by the start-up phases. As it is the anchor of the business as well as the stimulator of the other components needed for the new venture, e.g., opportunity identification, risk-taking, proactivity, exploration of the environment, etc., the vision subsequently produces the required equipment to start a business— capabilities, motivations, tools and resources. Moreover, infusion of the vision enables the entrepreneur and founding teams to move through the daily and problematic situations tackled in the new venture creation process.

Visions can be vague or precise; they can be visualized as the "outcome" or as the process directed at reaching the "outcome"; they can fuel the entrepreneur with passion and enthusiasm or create feelings of caution and concern; they can originate from the experience of an existing business or reflect "wishful thinking." Visions are independent, limitless, unconstrained mental and emotional entities that take on multiple configurations. Visions echo personal dimensions such as the entrepreneur's emotions, wishes, aspirations, dreams and aims, as well as environmental dimensions such as society, culture, economics, politics and the world (Baum, Locke, & Kirkpatrick, 1998; Carland & Carland, 1992, 2000; Carland, Hoy, Boulton, & Carland, 1984).

The vision is not intended to provide a practical roadmap for the new venture. Instead, it is meant to motivate the entrepreneur, stimulate the founding teams and elevate the confidence of all involved in the business toward its successful implementation. In fact, according to Filion (1989, 1990, 1991, 2004), we can distinguish three main categories of visions: emerging visions, central visions and complementary visions, representing an interdependent flow. The central vision develops from emerging visions, and its realization and evolution depend on complementary visions. Emerging visions are represented by different ideas for products and services that pop up while still immature, yet they stimulate the entrepreneur and create a vigorous and dynamic atmosphere. The central vision refers to the chosen vision that is the core of the business's subsequent activities. Complementary visions usually take the form of managerial activities, such as marketing, finance, operations management, information systems, human resources and so on, or they may be related to any other sector within the organization. The interrelationships between the vision and the venture creation's action are mediated by innovation, intuition and creativity, i.e., the key components in establishing a business. The ultimate outcome of this process, stimulated by entrepreneurial drive, tempered by knowledge and experience, filtered by intuition and evaluated on an ongoing basis, is the main entrepreneurial vision. It can be adjusted, amended or abandoned for other visions, but it always exists in an entrepreneurial action. The absence of a vision in the process means that the action taken is not entrepreneurial.

Figure 8.1 illustrates the three entities entwined with the vision.

Separating Idealistic and Realistic Aspects

The vision's main advantage is also its greatest shortcoming: it addresses an imaginary, non-existent and therefore idealistic entity that can encompass elements which are utterly impossible to implement, detached from the market's demands, or unfeasible for the markets to which the vision is destined. Hence, a dynamic, continual assessment of the vision is needed, to be able to separate its imaginary and practical aspects. The entrepreneur

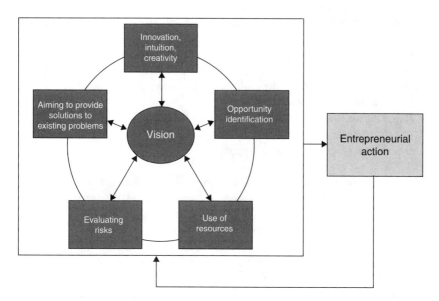

Figure 8.1 The Vision: A Core Component in the Venture Creation Process.

should be able to ask and answer questions such as: Can the vision rally around the entrepreneur and founding teams? Is the business concept, based on the vision, obtainable and feasible? Is the vision a driving force for implementing the business or does it impede the entrepreneur and the teams, who are trapped in its imaginary aspects?

The vision has a crucial impact on the opportunity-exploitation process, which is most notable during the new venture creation process. The vision sharpens the entrepreneur's alertness to opportunities, and thrusts the entrepreneur toward exploitation of those opportunities that will eventually promote the vision and turn it into a real venture. Concurrently, opportunities demarcate the vision and enable an ongoing assessment that enables separating the vision's idealistic aspects from its realistic ones.

The business's resources, e.g., financial state, human capital and knowledge, are main factors in the ongoing assessment of the vision. These resources mirror the business's concurrent situation clearly and soundly, thus clarifying whether there is enough capital, knowledge, networks, etc., to implement the vision. Having insufficient resources does not, however, mean retracting the vision; instead, it may push the entrepreneur to take the plunge by extracting the resources and enabling implementation of the vision. It can also push the entrepreneur to use more creativity and outside-the-box thinking, and to adopt originality in order to nurture the vision out of the concurrent resources.

The vision is of significant relevance to the business when it faces difficulties and challenges. In such times of real or perceived chaos and ambiguity, the vision can delineate the way and hearten the entrepreneur to cope with these difficulties. For example, when a developed product prototype does not sell and customers are disappointed with it, keeping the vision enables thinking of different ways to "make it work" and adjusting the prototype to the customers' tastes.

The Cherie Blair Foundation[1] works globally to provide women entrepreneurs with access to business development support, networks, finance and technology. In Ms. Blair's words:

> Our vision is of a world where women have equal access to the tools and support needed to establish and grow successful businesses. By supporting women entrepreneurs, we are building a brighter future for them, and their families, for communities and economies.

The operationalization of the vision is then delineated as follows:

> Women who are financially independent have greater control over their own and their children's lives. Economic security gives women a more influential voice in tackling injustice and discrimination in their own communities and in wider society. By supporting women entrepreneurs, we build a brighter future not just for the women themselves, but for their families and communities too.

VISION AND GENDER

Do women and men hold different visions? Do they visualize their businesses differently? Are their aspirations for business success different?

The differences in women and men's motivations to start a business, their exclusive ways of managing their businesses and their different definitions of sustainable, successful businesses suggest that the genders emphasize different factors as critical for crafting a vision—the business of their dreams—which are basically embedded in their respective environments. The reciprocal effects of gender-based expectations and environmental conditions demarcate the vision that each gender group is more apt to create. For example, social expectations of women in MENA[2] countries, as compared to social expectations of women in the USA, combined with the respective economic, financial, political, policy and cultural conditions, result in different visions for women entrepreneurs. Mrs. Hela Chadi from Tunisia, owner of SOCADECO handicrafts noted: "The idea started when I got married and wanted to build my own house, furnish it and design its own elements myself,"[3] reflecting the context of the social expectations rooted in her vision for change, advancement and progress; on the other hand, Ms. Marissa Evans,[4] founder of GO TRY IT ON, a social retailing start-up based in New York City, conceptualized the idea as a student at Harvard Business School, and recently raised $3 million. Evans said she hopes her website will be more about helping a person with thoughtful reviews or product suggestions on how to get dressed. Evans is eager to see her vision be made public: "We're excited to get the product out there and see how people want to use it," Evans said. In both examples, the business focuses on services for leisure activities and items that are "nice-to-have," rather than on necessities. The vision of a woman entrepreneur from Tunisia appears to stem from her family, her house and her social role, while the vision of a young woman entrepreneur based in New York City appears to be much freer of gender-based constraints, originating from a more personal point of view.

Drawing on feminist theories in the entrepreneurial realm, the vision can be depicted as an entity embedded in the different feminist theoretical views. Thus, a "gender zest" can be recognized in different types of visions. Figure 8.2 shows possible associations between the vision and the contexts from which it originated; e.g., a vision expressed in "academic-leadership colors" may stem from a liberal feminist view, in which the postulated context for women is discrimination or lack of opportunities in accessing prestigious companies or higher education. Differences found in the literature in the genders' participation in academic, scientific, entrepreneurial undertakings, for example, have been attributed to, among other things, a paucity of opportunities for women scientists to work with companies, less access to important networks and more difficulties than their male colleagues in obtaining external funding and being published (Benschop & Brouns, 2003; Brush, Carter, Gatewood, Greene, & Hart, 2001; Ding, Murray, & Stuart, 2010; Hsu, Roberts, & Eesley, 2007; Jacobs & Winslow, 2004; Jain, George, & Maltarich, 2009; Xie & Shauman, 2003). Such difficulties may push women to form a vision that will eventually illuminate the scarcity in resources and the discrimination they were subjected to.

On the other hand, "being the next Google" is a vision that can be derived from a social feminist view, a context in which women encounter differences in the distribution of power between the genders along with deliberate socialization. Visualizing the business as the next "most successful business" is a representation of overcoming male dominance in the area and celebrating the fair distribution of power among the genders: where Mr. Marc Zuckerberg is the male CEO of *the* most successful company today, Mrs. X will be the female CEO of *the* most successful business tomorrow. Radical feminist theory stresses that men and women are seen to be essentially different: cultures differentiate between the genders, and feminine traits should be perceived as benefits rather than drawbacks and as resources to be used constructively. As such, social entrepreneurship may be a vision that is derived from environments in which culture reflects a male-dominated world and the environment/community is "tinted" in

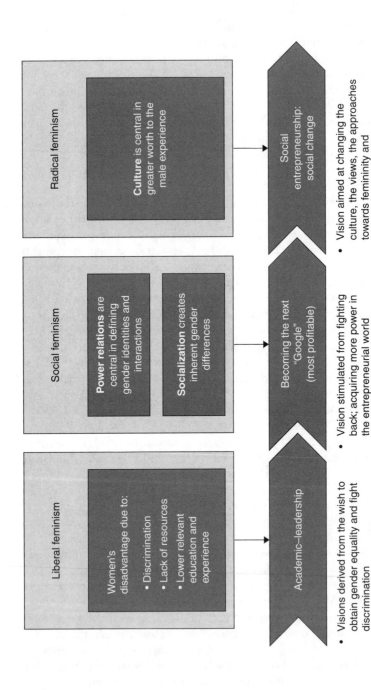

Liberal feminism

Women's disadvantage due to:

- Discrimination
- Lack of resources
- Lower relevant education and experience

Academic–leadership

- Visions derived from the wish to obtain gender equality and fight discrimination
- Vision embedded in education, skills, training, experience

Social feminism

Power relations are central in defining gender identities and interactions

Socialization creates inherent gender differences

Becoming the next "Google" (most profitable)

- Vision stimulated from fighting back; acquiring more power in the entrepreneurial world
- Starting education towards gender equality from an early age

Radical feminism

Culture is central in greater worth to the male experience

Social entrepreneurship: social change

- Vision aimed at changing the culture, the views, the approaches towards femininity and masculinity

Figure 8.2 A Look into the Vision as Embedded in Feminist Theories.

mannish colors. Such a vision can be a woman's manifestation of her feminine traits employed in the entrepreneurial realm, such as ecological consciousness or community awareness.

THE FEMININE VISION AND WOMEN VISIONARIES

Social and cultural influences play an important role in how women experience entrepreneurship and shape their entrepreneurial interests, and they determine how women define concepts such as success or failure in their businesses. These, among other experiences of women entrepreneurs, are restructured into a collective feminine vision.

The feminine vision reflects the environment and spheres in which women work. It represents their motivations, dreams and desires, and it fits their needs. The feminine vision is the safe place where women are comfortable and do not need to justify their dreams; for example, some women entrepreneurs' visions involve being the most significant player in the area of cosmetics, a famous brand in social media, or "just" establishing a business in their area of expertise. There is no pressure to compete with men's visions and their consequent business successes, or to defend their choices in the sector, area of expertise or level of expected success for their businesses.

In point of fact, the feminine vision creates businesses that meet women's needs, address their world and reflect their values. This may play prominently in the significant increase in female-owned entrepreneurial ventures. It is strongly affected by the gender approach to entrepreneurship, and assists in mitigating the typical masculine context that rewards and supports businesses headed by men over those headed by women. Understanding and accepting the differences in the attributes that create different visions for women and men will help in recognizing and rewarding women who are able and motivated to grow businesses in their own way and according to their needs and interests, rather than attempting to adjust their vision to meet society's expectations of women (Bird, 1989; Bird & Brush, 2002; Birley, 1989; Calas, Smircich, & Bourne, 2009; Gatewood, Shaver, & Gartner, 1995; Orhan & Scott, 2001; Scott, 1986; Segal, Borgia, & Schoenfeld, 2005).

Are Women More Visionary than Men?

Visionary entrepreneurs usually possess a detailed picture of the future "outcome" they yearn for. Recurrently, their vision is already found in their childhood or adolescence; for example, Leanna Archer,[5] the founder of Hair Inc., was listed in Inc.com Magazine's Youngest 30 Entrepreneurs under 30 (at 8 years of age). Using a family formula for hair repair, she began her career by selling her product to her peers. Leanna is developing new products, and has even been offered a scholarship to Harvard; Cameron Johnson[6] started his first business at the age of 9 and was recognized as one of the most successful young entrepreneurs in the world. As a teenager, he started a dozen profitable businesses and at 15, he became the youngest American appointed to the board of a Tokyo-based company. Last year, Cameron was a finalist on Oprah Winfrey's first prime time series, *The Big Give*, which aired on ABC. Most recently, he hosted Season 4 of *Beat the Boss* which airs on the BBC in the UK.

Visionary entrepreneurs are tied up in each of their visualized business aspects, although they are not "hands-on" when the vision materializes into a new venture. Visionary entrepreneurs are theoreticians; they are the architects of their future businesses. They can lose interest when the vision becomes a tangible business, yet they do not cease visualizing when the vision has been implemented; they never tire of the visionary process. On the contrary, it fuels them with positive and stimulating energy. When they implement their vision into a real venture either they improve their original vision and promote their business accordingly, or they move on to crafting the "next," different vision.

Entrepreneurs anticipate different possibilities for their future businesses by following the needs and trends that exist all around them and exploring unexploited opportunities. Visionary entrepreneurs differ in daring to "change" the existing trends to materialize their vision, thus creating opportunities and giving their vision some space to take root.

Women are often accused of being unfocused, and sometimes unrealistic dreamers in that they consider the marginal factors rather than the primary ones in the new venture's creation. For example, rather than searching for financial resources at the outset, women focus on "how the product will be designed" or "who will use the service."

Consideration of these "marginal" factors, however, might also imply that women are visionaries. They see things beyond the "here" and "now," and let their mental models combine with their emotions to craft an ideal type of future business, i.e., the vision.

Visionaries may be regarded as unrealistic or unfocused, as are women; but this simply means that the ways of thinking and developing a vision are differently experienced by the genders. Visionaries think in details, as do women; again, they are often considered to neglect the essence because they emphasize the details.

The vision enables entrepreneurs to craft a change in their "little paradise" and visualize the business they always longed for, and as such is imperative in a woman's world. The vision and its consequent practices are internalized as individuals construct personal gender identities and apply them in the actions taken to create their ventures. Women manage different gender identities that can intersect and conflict with each other in certain situations, making crafting a vision complex. It is most important that women should have the opportunity to embrace their gender identities and preferences and strategize their vision in a desired direction, rather than maneuver their vision relative to the degree to which it meets the social expectations imposed on them.

VISION AND MENTAL MODELS

The outside world is filtered through mental models which give the situations being tackled a meaning, some rationale, whether we are aware of it or not, and enabling us to act on what we see. Mental models are central in crafting a vision: they reflect the way individuals interpret a situation, a need, a difficulty encountered; there are no "right" or "wrong" mental models or interpretations of situations or needs, as they reflect who we are and where we live.

The power of mental models is multifaceted as they translate the world, intervene between the objective and subjective and subsequently generate thoughts, plans and actual action. Peter Senge's book: *The Fifth Discipline: The Art and Practice of the Learning Organization* (Senge, 1990) delivers a message of the essence and centrality of mental models in our working realm; accordingly, mental models are deeply embedded assumptions, generalizations, pictures and representations that influence our understanding of the world and, subsequently, how we take action to handle the world and our surroundings. Mental models comprise a set of expectations that people develop for others. Filion and Ananou (2010) add two main components to this definition: reflection and knowing the environment; according to Ananou, visions are representations of mental models that originate from the information in the environments around us: a thorough knowledge and deep understanding of these environments, followed by comprehensive reflection on the emerging needs of society in specific environments, serve to construct mental models that can then be transformed into visions.

For example, the entrepreneurial vision of Gerber[7] stemmed from a personal view, but Daniel Gerber's thorough familiarity with the needs in his surroundings turned the vision into a worldwide, most successful baby food industry. However, it began with a woman's vision, and the mental model held by this woman played a large part in stimulating this entrepreneurial business. The story begins with a pediatrician's suggestion to put Sally, Daniel's daughter, on a diet of strained fruits and vegetables. Gerber's wife, Dorothy Gerber, started making homemade strained baby food from fruits and vegetables to feed to Sally. Dorothy suggested turning ordinary peas into strained baby food and canning it for production. Gerber understood the needs of his environment and times—baby food was uncommon and relatively expensive—and suggested that his father produce the baby food through his company, Freemont Canning Company (Bentley, 2002; Ingham, 1983). Gerber's success story represents the synchronization of environment and reflection into a vision.

COMMUNICATING THE VISION

The vision is not a confined entity that addresses only the business. Many women entrepreneurs hold visions addressing their communities, environments or even the whole world. They expect to achieve their vision's delivery via their business's influence and outcomes. For example, Ms. Ishita Gupta, the founder of *Fear.less Magazine* and *Touchpoint Speaker*, describes her drive to create her venture as follows: "What inspired me was the fact that I learned through specific people's stories—not general advice . . . and the fact that I was in a fearful moment and needed to hear what others were doing to combat their fear." *Fear.less* is a digital magazine that empowers people through stories of overcoming fear.[8] Ms. Krystal O'Mara is the founder of ReMain Eco Design and Consulting. O'Mara began transforming bikes into living room décor in February 2010. O'Mara articulates her aim—to educate people about environmental stewardship—as follows: "I feel like I'm doing something that is going to benefit the earth," she says, "but it's also benefiting our economy."[9] Ms. Linda Rottenberg is the founder of a nonprofit endeavor exporting American entrepreneurship and networking to countries in Latin America and beyond, with the aim of boosting their employment and GDP. She aspires to building profitable small businesses on a global scale.[10]

These examples illustrate visions that addressed a general, rather than personal need, and were cultivated into a business. The visions presented in these examples could appear too big or too general and therefore unfocused or unfeasible. Yet, these, among many others initiated and managed by women, are functioning ventures, in which the founder had higher aspirations to reach high levels of performance and power, and have an impact on their surroundings.

Impact can also be achieved throughout the course of the business's action, by sharing the vision and communicating it. The shared vision is a collective experience and a commitment to common goals; it is a most important asset that should turn into a communication-based process during the course of venture creation, as shown in Figure 8.3. Women entrepreneurs are typically seen as more proficient than men in communication skills, yet research finds that they obtain less external funding and shareholder support than men. Communicating their business vision in a "WOW" style may turn this reality upside-down, provided the vision is well and clearly communicated and that women use the feminine traits and capabilities known to be to their advantage.

According to Peter Senge (1990), the following strategies are required to craft a solid vision that will have a significant impact on its environment:

- the ability to create or elicit the initial vision;
- the ability to translate that vision into the tangible activities required to achieve it;

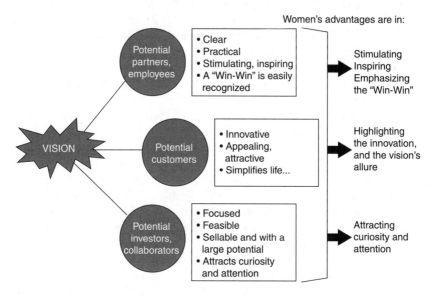

Figure 8.3 Vision: A Communication-based View.

- the ability to articulate and sell this vision to others as either the right or best way to reach a goal;
- the ability to hold true to the essence of the vision when reality changes plans.

VISION AS THE DRIVING FORCE

Insight from Estée Lauder's and Debbie Fields' Success Stories

Estée Lauder—Estée Lauder's amazing success story clearly demonstrates the significance of the vision as a core component and driving force in the subsequent success of a company.

The Estée Lauder company was founded in 1946 by Estée Lauder and her husband Joseph, and grew to be one of the world's leading producers and marketers of upscale cosmetics, fragrances, and hair-care products, with a market share of about 46 percent, products sold in over 100 countries, a listing as a Fortune 500 company, and a large line, including skin treatment, makeup, and fragrances (e.g., Aramis, Clinique, MAC, Tommy Hilfiger fragrances, grooming products, cosmetics, and more).

Estée Lauder was born as Josephine Esther Mentzer in Queens, New York, in 1908, the ninth child of Rose and Max Mentzer, immigrants from Hungary. Lauder was attracted to cosmetics and beauty care from childhood and was looking for opportunities to enter this area. The opportunity revealed itself at her uncle's laboratories in Brooklyn, where she began selling her uncle's cosmetic products in New York City and then in Miami Beach as well.

Lauder has been characterized as highly determined, motivated and entrepreneurial, following her vision of leading the cosmetics sector. In 1944, Lauder began working in various New York salons and smaller department stores, selling her own product line from behind a counter, while exploiting opportunities to materialize her vision. Lauder's next goal was to get her products into Saks Fifth Avenue. After a successful lecture and demonstration at the Waldorf Astoria, Saks' managers realized that there was a demand for her products as customers were lining up outside for more product information. The Saks connection helped Lauder achieve a reputation that allowed her to sell her products nationally.

In pursuit of her vision, Estée Lauder traveled the country, making personal appearances in specialty and department stores and training staff in proper sales techniques. She made impressions on influential people early on. Against the advice of their lawyer, Lauder and her husband entered full scale into an industry known for extreme market swings and short-lived endeavors. Joseph Lauder worked every day in the small space they had rented, while their oldest son, Leonard, made deliveries to Saks and other stores on his bicycle.

Lauder has been quoted as saying: "I loved to make everyone up . . . I was always interested in people being beautiful . . . [people] who look like they have a cared-for face." This was the driving force; she visualized her dream and strove to advance it.

Lauder was innovative, as proven in every aspect of her company. She was also practical and directed her innovation into real action. She was the pioneer of the gift-with-purchase offer, a technique which gained her a loyal following and helped establish her business. She continually introduced new developments in her products; in the early 1960s, Estée Lauder joined Rubenstein, Arden, Revlon, and Cosmetiques in the race to develop a skin-care cream with the ability to revitalize skin and eliminate wrinkles. Lauder was determined to prompt innovation even in the advertising aspect: Estée Lauder Inc. developed its own unique image—since the company could not afford color ads, they used black-and-white photos instead—and a model portraying the elegance that Estée Lauder wanted to present was hired for the advertising campaign. In addition, Lauder's innovation manifested itself in her penetration of different niches, such as men's cosmetics by introducing the male fragrance.

Estée Lauder founded her company's action and innovation on a strong vision: "Bringing the best to everyone we touch. By 'The best', we mean the best products, the best people and the best ideas. These three pillars have been the hallmarks of our Company since it was founded by Mrs. Estée Lauder in 1946. They remain the foundation upon which we continue to build our success today"[11] (Lauder, 1985; Severo, 2004).

Debbi Fields—The founder of Mrs. Fields' Cookies, one of the largest retailers of "freshly baked on the premises" specialty cookies and brownies in the United States, holds a vision that turned her passion for making cookies into a million dollar business. She is also famous as the author of *The New York Times* bestseller: *Mrs. Fields' Cookie Book: 100 Recipes from the Kitchen of Debbi Fields*, which has sold more than 1.8 million copies and was the first cookbook to top *The New York Times* bestseller list. Fields was quoted as saying: "I've never felt like I was in the cookie business. I've always been in a feel good feeling business. My job is to sell joy. My job is to sell happiness. My job is to sell an experience."

Fields was born in Oakland, California in 1957. At the age of 20, as a young housewife with no business experience, Fields had a dream and a passion for baking and selling her chocolate chip cookies. She could not afford realizing her dream without financial support and turned to a bank to finance her business concept, a concept which had never before been proven. When Fields received the support, she opened Mrs. Fields' Chocolate Chippery in Palo Alto, California, in August 1977. Debbi Fields believes in excellence; accordingly, her motto is: "Good Enough Never Is." Excellence is mirrored in every aspect of her company, which has earned a reputation for providing the best in product quality and superior customer service.

In pursuing her vision, Debbi Fields could be classified as an opportunity exploiter. Her alertness to the "next move" directed her to take advantage of advances in computers: in 1989, she introduced state-of-the-art computer systems to streamline the business operations; her company was among the first to embark on the use of computer technology for such programs. This helped her franchise the business concept to interested franchises. Today, her program is used as a model for business efficiency at Harvard Business School. More than 30 years later, Debbi Fields' company had expanded from one shop to supervising operations, brand name management, public relations and product development of her company's 600+ company-owned and franchised stores in the United States and 10 foreign countries. In 1993, Fields sold the company to private investors.

Mrs. Fields' vision of excellence and her greatest priority—customer satisfaction, were echoed throughout the venture creation process, from the day her store first opened: when by noon there was still not a single sale, Fields decided to reach out to her potential customers by handing out free cookies to the people walking by. They liked her cookies and came back as customers to buy more.

These exemplars of visions that pushed women to successful entrepreneurial undertakings are summarized in the following insights:

- Being committed to the dream.
- Some dreams, passions and visions are transparent in childhood; each dream deserves serious attention and cultivation.
- A strong vision can be persuasive and influential for potential stakeholders; e.g., investors, suppliers, collaborators, customers. (Estée Lauder's uncle, who collaborated with her in her first steps in the cosmetic world; Debbi Fields' bank, which supported her in opening her first store; Fields convincing passers-by to become loyal customers.)
- Innovation and vision constitute a winning combination for successful businesses.
- A vision is a solid, trustworthy anchor in times of comfort and affluence as well as when tackling paucity and fruitless experiences.
- There are multiple ways to realize a vision; the selected ways should be those having the best fit to the environment's trends.
- The vision should be clear, simple and easy to identify with, so that people can unify around it.
- A strong vision provides confidence, even in cases where the exact process delineating how to implement the vision is still vague and unconfirmed.

(Bunker & Smith-Doerr, 2005; Ding, Murray, & Stuart, 2006; Frietsch, Haller, Funken-Vrohlings, & Grupp, 2009; Thursby & Thursby, 2005; Wyer, 2001; Xie & Shauman, 1998)

SUMMARY

This chapter focuses on a broad perspective of the vision, including its definition, meaning and power in the context of the venture creation process, particularly in female entrepreneurship. The vision is rooted in the entrepreneur's mental models, affected by, but nevertheless independent of environmental influences. It offers a framework for reflection and actions and serves as the "North Star" for the entrepreneurial path, no matter how convoluted and blurred.

The vision is discussed through the lens of feminist theories and mirrors their different dimensions. The common ground, however, is the framework the vision creates, fueled by the entrepreneur's mental models.

Different configurations of the vision are illustrated through the stories of two successful and visionary women entrepreneurs, highlighting the vision's limitless nature, along with its "elasticity" and ability to suit any type of business.

This chapter transmits the message that constructing a vision means bridging the gap between women and the businesses they have always longed for. Yet, the chapter also discusses vision as a complex entity that is still difficult to crack, due to a lack of research on visions in female entrepreneurship.

The significance of communicating the vision is articulated as a promising means of encouraging more women to pursue their dreams and embark on entrepreneurship to implement them.

CASE STUDY[12]

This case study, contributed by Geneviève Guindon and Louis Jacques Filion, illustrates the significant role of vision in the new venture creation process and entrepreneurial way of Ms. Chantale Robinson, a 34-year-old veterinary technician, writer, counselor and artist from Montreal, Canada. Driven by a deep-seated passion for animals, entwined with her vision to raise awareness and action toward animal welfare, her entrepreneurial action, e.g., her books, courses and counseling, were all designed to improve the lives of pets based on her approach of a human–animal relationship tailored to the nature of the animal.

The authors build the story of Chantale's entrepreneurial path around her vision and passion by revealing a convoluted journey, fraught with difficulties, different jobs, passages and separation from her loved ones, but also by addressing her influential role models, in order to understand how she became who she is and what she does.

Professor Filion is one of the pioneers in the research area of the visionary process; he has published hundreds of papers and books on this topic as well as on other areas in entrepreneurship.

Chantale Robinson and Kilookas: Barking up the Right Tree!

Geneviève Guindon[a] and Louis Jacques Filion[b]
[a]Professional; [b]Chair of Entrepreneurship, HEC, Montreal, Quebec, Canada

A Passion for Animals

Take the pulse again. Give two rescue breaths.
Don't forget that someone's life may depend on you!

It's a Saturday morning in March 2002. Chantale Robinson, 34 years old, a biologist and animal health technician, is taking a cardiopulmonary resuscitation course offered by the St. John's Ambulance organization. She's a veterinary technician at the Holistic Veterinary Clinic and her boss has sent her to do the course, as recommended by Québec's Workplace Health and Safety Commission. Chantale already knows what to do in an emergency—for pet animals at least, if not for humans! But the exercise sparks her imagination and she has an idea: why not offer first aid training to animal health workers and pet owners? And just like that, another business opportunity joins Chantale's long list of activities in the dog world.

In 2002, Chantale had already worked for several years at an emergency veterinary clinic and had witnessed the death of some four-legged patients that could have been saved if only their owners had known how to administer first aid. And so Montréal's female Dr. Doolittle[13] began to write her first book, in French, on the subject of first aid for dogs and cats. It was published in the fall of 2002.

Below is an excerpt from the book:[14]

> The first step in assessing your pet's health is to identify what is normal and what is not, so that you can give the necessary care or consult a veterinarian . . . Breathing rhythm is another way of assessing the physical condition of an animal. Breathing that is too fast or too slow may signal discomfort at best, or a serious pathological state at worst.

The book launch coincided with the creation of Chantale's new company, Kilookas. The name is a combination of the names of her two cats, Kiloo and Lookas. She began by marketing two first aid kits for animals, and went on to write a second book on animal nutrition, as well as offering a number of training courses (Appendix 8.2). She was able to obtain assistance from several government programs and signed a number of professional collaborative agreements.

> I applied to every available support program![15]

Chantale's reputation is now well established. Her second book, on the subject of animal nutrition, is now used as a reference by animal health students in college technical programs. Chantale herself has been a member of Québec's Union of Artists since March 2006. She writes regularly for the French-language pet animal magazine *Poils et Compagnie*, and has also become a sought-after resource in the dog world, giving speeches across Canada and in Europe. She has her own monthly radio program (Appendix 8.1).

Chantale is driven not only by her success, but by a deep-seated passion for the animal world. Her primary goal is animal welfare. Her books are designed to raise awareness and recommend actions that will improve the lives of pet animals and their relationships with their owners. In her books, her first aid courses, her massage workshops and her speeches on animal nutrition and health, Chantale proposes approaches based on a human–animal relationship tailored to the nature of the animal.

A Passion Dating Back to Childhood

Chantale Robinson spent most of her childhood in Longueuil, on the south shore of Montréal. She was the second in a family of three children, with an older sister and a younger brother, and admits to being fascinated by animals from a very young age. Her mother, Yolande Durand, had a breeding pair of Siamese cats. Chantale loved them and developed an almost human connection with them. Her maternal grandmother, Denise Lambert, had worked for some years in a travelling circus. She would often tell Chantale tales from her childhood and talk about the circus animals— the tigers in their cages and the elephants with their trunks. It was a whole new world for Chantale, and it is not hard to understand how her two great passions in life—animals and show business—were born.

Five-year-old Chantale had already decided she would be a veterinarian one day.

> I was always telling my mother I wanted a pet, so she gave me a kitten for my fifth birthday. I didn't have it for long—it ran away. I asked my mother if there were any jobs that involved working with animals, and she answered "a vet"! So that's what I decided to become!

Unfortunately her dream never became a reality because her application to Montréal University's oversubscribed Veterinary Medicine Faculty was turned down. Although she was accepted for a veterinary medicine program at the University of the West Indies in Trinidad, she was unable to gather the necessary funds. Instead, she enrolled in the Vanier College animal health program to become an animal nurse. Here is what she has to say about this turn of events:

> When I was turned down for vet school, it was as though my whole life had failed. Over time I learned to accept things, though, and I realized there was more than one way of helping animals. By giving massage and first aid courses and educating people on how to feed their pets, I'm helping to improve the quality of life of pet animals. My contribution is preventive, and complements what vets do. The fact of not being able to become a vet forced me to develop other types of activities and go into business in the animal world.

Inspiring Models

Chantale recalls her childhood and describes herself as having a strong personality and good social skills. Her teacher did not like the straightforward, confident attitude of seven-year-old Chantale, misreading it as insolence. She tried to destroy the child's assurance, but Chantale will never forget how her mother came to her defence:

The teacher didn't like me and had started to be really unpleasant towards me. She told my mother I was mentally retarded and should see a psychologist. My mother was furious and confronted the teacher, before taking me to see a psychologist or some kind of therapist for an evaluation. The psychologist told her, look, your daughter is entirely normal, brilliant in fact, there's absolutely no problem. So my mother went back to see my teacher, who apologized and started being kind to me. But my mother went to see the school principal about the whole situation, and the teacher eventually lost her job. Imagine if my mother hadn't had the courage of her convictions! She'd have said, oh no, there's something wrong with my child, and she'd have sent me to another school. She'd have let the other kids bully me. What kind of woman would I have become?

Chantale admires her mother tremendously. Although no longer alive, she remains a model of determination and courage for her daughter, and Chantale speaks of her with a great deal of emotion:

My mother gave me a lot of courage. She was my inspiration in life, especially when I was a kid. She barely finished her elementary education as a kid, but went back to school when she was thirty or so and completed her secondary, college and university studies. She was a good example for me as a young teenager. She taught me that anything was possible.

Her mother qualified as a criminologist in her late thirties. The other family models that helped forge Chantale's entrepreneurial nature were her maternal grandmother and adoptive father. In her youth, her grandmother had worked for a circus and sung in night clubs, while her adoptive father was manager and musician at the popular Montréal jazz club Rocket Paradise. The club no longer exists, but when one of the authors of this case study was younger, it was a veritable institution, hosting jazz stars from as far away as New Orleans. On Fridays and Saturdays, shows went on through the night, and the club was often open until five o'clock in the morning.

A Childhood Marked by Discipline and Stability

At high school, Chantale was involved in a number of extra-curricular activities. Among other things, she helped produce the school's television show.

We produced our own show in a real studio. It was broadcast weekly on the community television channel. My job was to present and describe the school's activities. It was a great experience!

Chantale was also inspired by Nadia Comaneci, a 16-year-old Romanian gymnast who was the star of the 1976 Montréal Olympic Games, and practised gymnastics between the ages of 5 and 21, training three or four times a week. Gymnastics took up much of her spare time. She competed until she was 16, and then began to teach.

> When I was eighteen, I decided to teach a course that I had designed myself . . . I was quite the entrepreneur, doing the whole thing from A to Z. And I worked for the City of Longueuil after school and on weekends, teaching community courses, mainly to little girls around four years of age. I like children and loved teaching them.

Chantale started work early in life. By the time she was 12, she was baby-sitting her neighbors' children and already had her own network of customers! At age 14 she met her first boyfriend, through her babysitting activities, and they went out together for eight years, living together for four of them. However, she did not feel ready to set aside her personal and professional ambitions in favor of marriage and children, and chose freedom instead. Freedom is precisely the element of self-employment that she prefers and enjoys the most.

A Career Path Rich in Experience

Fast-forward to the spring of 1990, and Chantale Robinson is now looking for a job in her chosen field. A qualified animal health technician, she already has some work experience at the Montréal Zoo and the Hochelaga Veterinary Clinic, as well as three workplace training placements.

> The summer after my first year in the animal health program, I got my first summer job in the field, at the Hochelaga Veterinary Clinic, working with Dr. Lise Laliberté. I still hadn't finished the program, of course, and asked a lot of questions. Dr. Laliberté was impressed by my enthusiasm. Here's someone who wants to do something in life, she thought! Just before I left, she took me out for a meal to congratulate me. The other employees told me I must be something really special, because she didn't usually take people out for dinner. I'm still in touch with her. She was a tremendous inspiration for me. I was really lucky.

Great minds think alike! Dr. Laliberté began to practise homeopathy a few years after Chantale's summer placement.

Chantale's job search soon led her to the Lachine Veterinary Clinic, where she worked as a veterinary technician for the next year and a half, learning to care for exotic animals in the process. She then moved on to the Westminster Veterinary Clinic and the Metropolitan Veterinary Clinic, where she learned first aid for animals, did laboratory tests and assisted the veterinarian during surgery.

In 1994 she decided she wanted to live by the sea and left Québec for Jamaica. One of her jobs there had a particular impact; it was a management position at the Phoenix Veterinary Clinic in Kingston. Although the job was interesting, she came up against some cultural problems:

> There I was, the white girl who became the boss. The employees were unhappy about this, and wouldn't do what I asked. They just didn't listen. It was their way of saying they didn't want me around. It was very hard for me to function in that kind of environment. You can be as nice as you like to people, but if they're not open to it . . . I was completely alone. That's not what delegating is all about! I'd never worked anywhere with as many outside dog runs. I had to take care of between 30 and 50 dogs every day, with more inside. By the time I went home at night, I was exhausted.

After a year in this difficult environment, Chantale returned to Montréal and decided to continue with the university course she had begun before leaving for Jamaica. She completed her bachelor's degree in marine biology at Concordia University in 2000, after several years of part-time study.

> It wasn't easy to finish my studies, and the fact that I succeeded gave me a lot of confidence. The degree helped solidify my reputation and credibility.

In the meantime she took a job as an animal health technician at the Holistic Veterinary Clinic, where she remained for the next eight years, until 2002. This is what the Clinic director, Dr. Paul Guindon, has to say about her:

> I enjoyed working with Chantale. She's dynamic, always smiling, and her experience helped us to improve our services. Our customers always liked her. When she left, several people asked why she wasn't there any more. They were disappointed. There were even some customers who would call the clinic and ask to speak to Chantale instead of me![16]

In her early 30s, Chantale Robinson had more than fifteen years of experience in the animal care field, including twelve as an animal health technician. She had also taught at the ICARI cartoon school for two years, in addition to her gymnastic courses. By 2002, she had seven years of experience as a teacher.

Dr. Paul Guindon: Teacher, Guide and Mentor

Chantal Robinson maintained a close relationship with Dr. Guindon as she progressed through the animal welfare world. At long last, she had found a mentor who shared her view of the human–animal connection. Dr. Guindon was generous with his knowledge and taught her his expertise. This is how Chantal describes the multifaceted teacher–student, employer–employee and mentor–entrepreneur relationship:

> From our very first meeting I felt we were truly on the same wavelength. He had tremendous confidence in me. We worked as a team. I never felt any kind of hierarchy between us. There was a lot of mutual respect. He helped me develop many different aspects of my work, and we learned from one another. He opened my eyes even further to the natural approach, holistic medicine and homeopathy. There was always something else to learn. We communicated so well that I didn't want to leave . . . I still go to see him if I don't know what to do, if I need advice or if I have a problem I can't solve.

In fact, Chantale Robinson and Dr. Guindon still work together; Dr. Guindon has converted his former surgery into a classroom, and says the courses given by his young colleague create a dynamic atmosphere in his veterinary clinic. In addition, many of Chantale's customers are animal care professionals, and therefore potential customers for his veterinary business. He is proud of practising natural preventive medicine. Chantale's services complement his own. In short, their relationship has been transformed from one of mentor–student to an equal partnership where both benefit from the other's input. This is what Dr. Guindon says about it:

> When I began to practise homeopathy in 1990, it was in some ways a reaction to a pharmaceutical market that was becoming increasingly mercantile, more focused on its shareholders than on its patients. I wanted to offer my customers a more natural alternative and improve the health of their animals. In 1995, when I hired Chantale, it was important for me to have an employee who was open to alternative medicine and natural products—someone who thought like me. Chantale was the ideal candidate. She was passionate about animals, already had considerable experience, and was interested in natural medicine. Now that she has her own business, she's continued in the same vein and she does it very well. Chantale is a generous person who needs to help animals. She enjoys teaching, and I'd go so far as to say that she needs an audience. She's a natural leader and uses her leadership skills well.

Self-Employment Assistance to Launch Her Business

In October 2002, Chantale published her first book, on the subject of first aid for dogs and cats. Dr. Guindon, her employer at the Holistic Veterinary Clinic, had decided to close down his surgical practice and devote all his time to homeopathy. As a result, he needed only a receptionist, not an assistant. Chantale viewed this change of circumstance as an ideal opportunity to go into business for herself. Because she was now unemployed, she was eligible for Emploi-Québec's Self-Employment Assistance (SEA) Program, which helps unemployed people to go into business while still receiving their employment insurance benefits.

Chantale Robinson was born in 1968. In 2002, she was 34 years of age and at a major crossroads in her life. She decided to enrol for the SEA Program offered by the Metropolitan Montréal SAJE, a para-governmental non-profit agency created to support 18–35-year-old entrepreneurs. Chantale really appreciated the help it was able to give as she launched her business. She took courses in administration and also received assistance with her business plan. The process of drawing up her plan allowed her to think about what she wanted to do and target her actions accordingly. She also became better organized.

Once completed, her business plan served as a point of reference for many of her subsequent decisions concerning her business project and activities. The fact of preparing the plan also qualified her for several government subsidies. Not only were her living expenses paid by the SEA Program for a full year, but Chantale also received a $6,000 working capital grant from the Government's "Young Promoter" Program as well as $1,000 to pay for training courses.

In addition, because her business plan was so good, she also won first place in the regional component of the Québec Entrepreneurship Competition, which came with a $1,000 award. Then, having already signed a contract with Les Éditions de l'Homme, a publishing house whose books are distributed throughout the French-speaking world, she was invited to France, Switzerland and Belgium to promote her book. The Franco-Québécois Youth Office paid her air fair and one night's accommodation. And in 2003, the Québec Youth Fund paid one full year's salary for a young animal health technician, whom Chantale employed as her assistant.

Kilookas

It's now the winter of 2002–2003. Even before she launched her business, Chantale had tested her market. Wanting to sell first aid kits and courses was all very well, but she needed to know there was a market for them! Her business plan showed that women and people living alone tend to take better care of their animals, and the older and younger age groups are most attracted to natural medicine.

In 2000, Canadians spent a total of $3 billion on their pets. Clearly, the products offered by Kilookas were aimed at clients who took good care of their companion animals. The market existed in theory, but in practice the question was: were they prepared to spend $125 on a first aid course?

> I had teaching experience but I wanted to test the market first. I talked about my plans and ran classified adverts. There was a real interest. Dr. Guindon let me use the room under his clinic. I started out slowly, giving a few first aid courses and animal massage workshops on weekends.

Fast-forward to the spring of 2003. Chantale's business plan is now complete and her company is in the start-up phase. Business is growing, and there's no shortage of things for Chantale to do. She has to promote her products, teach her courses and put together her first aid kits . . . Who said start-up was easy? Then she heard about the Québec Youth Fund and immediately filled out the forms. She got the grant and hired Geneviève Limoges.

> The technician I hired with the money from the Québec Youth Fund was extremely helpful to me. She spread the word to pet stores throughout Québec. Her promotion really helped publicize my company.

In the spring of 2004, Chantale contacted Eagle Pack, a pet animal food manufacturer. She liked its products; some were organic and all were made from meat fit for human consumption, without preservatives. She entered into a partnership with Eagle Pack, and since then has worked from time to time with Brian Drake, the company's Canadian representative. Brian promoted Chantale's book (translated into English for the purpose) among Eagle Pack's customers, and the company bought approximately 4,000 copies, which it distributed in Canada and the United States. It intends to do the same thing with her second book, on animal nutrition.

> I work in partnership with Eagle Pack, a holistic food company. It provides me with a tremendous amount of visibility. It hires me to give conferences on nutrition and first aid, and organizes promotions. Last year, anyone who bought a large bag of its food got my book free—a gift worth the same as the product.

In the fall of 2004, Chantale developed and offered a series of new courses. The authors of this case study interviewed some of her students. The following comment, made by Nadia Nadski, a groomer who has taken virtually all Chantale's courses, is typical:

Chantale is passionate about animals. You just know her work is also her pleasure, and she has a real desire to teach what she knows. When she organizes her courses, she tries to form small groups, usually no more than eight people. Many of the courses require people to practise techniques, and she needs to be able to see what we're doing and correct us when necessary. Chantale is a wonderful leader and her courses are very informative. She should advertise more.[17]

During the same period, in late 2004, Chantale published her second book, on the subject of animal nutrition. The second book created shock waves among animal lovers. The following excerpt (translated from the original French) calls into question many of the diets traditionally offered by the pet food market:[18]

Animal by-products can hardly be described as quality protein. And yet, they meet the minimum standards of the Association of American Feed Control Officials (AAFCO) . . . By-products are made from the unused parts of animal carcasses and flesh considered unfit for human consumption . . . They also contain out-of-date or tainted foodstuffs from restaurants and food markets, along with their plastic and Styrofoam packaging, not to mention dead or euthanized animals from veterinary clinics. All this finds its way into your pet's bowl!

In the winter of 2004–2005, following the launch of her book on animal nutrition, Chantale began to offer her services as a consultant. The animal nutrition market is an interesting one. In 2000, according to Statistics Canada, pet owners spent an average of $304 per year on dog and cat food. Nearly six million Canadians have a pet, so the calculation is simple; the pet food market is worth $1,824 million per year. Chantale's book reveals that many different grades of food are available, and it can be difficult for people to choose. Here is what Dr. Guindon has to say on the subject:

There's a new popular awareness of all things natural. People want to eat well and be healthy. So the trend is really there. Logically, these same people will want to feed their pets well too. So there's a growing demand for top quality pet food.

Chantale's expertise in the area of natural diets for pets is a rare commodity. Her customers fall into two categories—tradespeople wanting to market new pet food, and individuals wanting to give their pets customized meals. The second group often includes people whose pets are sick with cancer, diabetes and other similar diseases. For them, diet is a form of treatment.

In early 2005, Chantale's mother, whose discipline and lifelong learning had made her a model for Chantale, died suddenly. The period that followed was extremely difficult. Chantale recovered slowly from the shock, and for several months her heart just was not in her work. However, by the spring of 2006 she was back on her feet. Like many entrepreneurs, the first few years are both difficult and crucial from a financial standpoint. As Chantale's company entered its fourth year, it finally began to make a profit. At long last she was able to pay herself a living wage.

> I'm now fairly well-known in the pet community. People recognize my name. I'm really starting to be respected. My products are original, well put-together, credible, and have a good reputation. I don't need to solicit new customers quite as much as before. They come to me now, because they've heard of me.
> The Veterinary Academy and the Association of Technicians both hire me. Animal health technicians take professional development courses to earn points, rather like vets. Their Association credits my courses. I'm really pleased about that. I give the participants a certificate or attestation that they can frame and display.

Some of the Obstacles Encountered by Chantale

When asked about the problems encountered during start-up, here is what Chantale has to say:

> Marketing my products and providing follow-up. Not that I'm no good at it, but I just don't like being a sales representative. I don't like knocking on pet shop doors. I did it in the early years, to get myself known. It's easier to teach courses because they're already prepared. I love teaching. It's like being on stage. The hardest aspect is finding customers.

Chantale offers a number of services and products. Her teaching is very successful, but she does not enjoy selling her first aid kits, which contain bandages, scissors and other medical items, all of high quality. The first aid kit therefore seems to have potential. Chantale's lack of interest in the selling aspect may well be part of the reason why most sales are made at her first aid courses, when the bulk of her turnover should come from pet shops and veterinary clinics. When someone goes into business, they often have to wear a lot of different hats in the early days—manufacturer, accountant, sales representative, personnel manager and so on. Very few people can claim to perform well in every area. To overcome their weaknesses, they need access to skilled resources. But things are not always that simple!

In 2003, Chantale hired a young animal health graduate with the aim of delegating the job she disliked the most—sales. But when the 12-month wage subsidy ended, she could no longer afford to pay her. How can she achieve her sales targets without having to sell the product herself? This is what Carl Bélanger, Chantale's advisor at the Metropolitan Montréal SAJE, has to say:

> Chantale is very resourceful and has worked hard on her business project. She and I have worked mainly on reducing the cost of her first aid kits. Personally, I believe the kit has good market potential. We met with the Costco buyers to see if we could get Costco to carry a new composite product composed of Chantale's first aid book and kit. The concept was good and we were just in time for Costco's Christmas stock. In the end, though, it didn't work out. You have to have a solid base to sell at Costco; you need a product with good sales potential and a competitive price. I'm currently working with several start-up entrepreneurs, and it often takes several years to bring down a product's cost price. You have to look at alternative materials, join forces with someone else to buy them, and sometimes even develop a new process. You really need to be creative! I believe Chantale prefers to develop her courses, and that's fine too, because she's good at teaching. However, I still think that if she can reduce the cost price of her kits, she might be able to pay an intermediary to distribute them, because distribution is the key development factor for that particular product.[19]

Carl Bélanger's recommendation is to reduce the kit's cost price in order to release a margin for the distributor. Chantale, however, feels she has invested enough in the kits. Reducing the cost price would involve a lot of research and further expense, with no guarantee of success. At best, if she makes enough profit, she is considering redoing the kit's graphics. In reality, if she could start over, she would have invested a lot less in the development of the kits. But as she herself admits, the product helped publicize her name throughout Québec, thanks to the efforts of her sales representative. So who is right?

Animal Care Courses and Show Business: Two Visceral Needs for Chantale

Despite these various problems, Chantale is perfectly happy in her role as a self-employed entrepreneur. She says it doesn't seem like work! She went into business because she likes to create, direct, make decisions and show leadership in an area she loves, and in which she believes. In her opinion, entrepreneurship is the best job in the world. What she loves most is being able to decide how to use her time. No more nine-to-five for her! She organizes her schedule so as to be able to take acting classes. She dreams of having her own television show, and is working hard to turn her dream into reality. She already has a business plan for the show, as well as an agent, and her efforts are beginning to pay off. She has won a contract for an advertisement and has recently been to several auditions. She also joined the Artists' Union, an initiative that has opened a number of doors for her. It seems that her success is limited only by her ambition.

> I don't want to have to choose between Kilookas and acting. Whatever happens in my life, I want to keep helping animals and be involved in show-business. I need them both to be happy and balanced. Depending on how successful I am, there will probably come a time when one of the two will take up more time, that's all!

Chantale Robinson has decided to concentrate on her courses and entertainment industry activities, and is wondering what to do with the kits, about which she is less enthusiastic. She is looking for ways of targeting and recruiting customers for her courses, and ways of breaking into the entertainment industry that will allow her to share and convey her love of animals while developing a profitable and perhaps even lucrative career. She has hired you as a consultant, and has asked you for suggestions. Based on her strengths and weaknesses, what would you advise her to do?

APPENDIX 8.1

Chantale loves sport and trains at least twice a week. Her favorite activities are kick boxing and dance, but she also enjoys skateboarding and weight-lifting, as well as skiing in winter. Her spiritual life is also important to her; she is a practising Buddhist. (Website: www.kilookas.com)

Table 8.A1 A Typical Working Week for Chantale

Monday	Writing, updating the Website
Tuesday	Consultation with an animal feed manufacturer
Wednesday	Acting course, radio program and gym
Thursday	Course given in Montréal or in the regions
Friday	Course given in Montréal or in the regions
Saturday	Eagle Pack Open Day
Sunday	Gym

APPENDIX 8.2

Main Elements of Chantale's Résumé

Education

BSc, Bachelor's Degree in Marine Biology, Animal Biology and Environmental Science, Concordia University, Montréal, 2000.
Technical Diploma in Animal Health Techniques and College Diploma in Health Science, Vanier College, Montréal, 1987–1990.
Canine Massage Certificate, Optissae, Ohio, USA, 1998.

Professional experience

Animal Health Technician, Holistic Veterinary Clinic, Montréal, 1995–2002.
Teacher–Animal Biology, ICARI, Montréal, 1998–1999.
Teacher and Clinic Manager, Phoenix Veterinary Clinic, Jamaica. 1994.
Animal Health Technician–Head Nurse, Metropolitan Veterinary Clinic, Montréal, 1992–1994.
Animal Health Technician, Westminster Veterinary Clinic, Montréal, 1993.
Animal Health Technician, Lachine Veterinary Clinic, 1990–1992.
Animator, Montréal Zoological Garden, and consultant researcher for the development of the Montréal Biodome, Montréal, 1989 and 1990 summer seasons.
Trainee Animal Health Technician, Westmount Animal Hospital, Montréal, January–February 1990.
Trainee Animal Health Technician, Montréal Institute of Cardiology, Montréal, 1990.
Veterinary Technician, Hochelaga Veterinary Clinic, Summer 1988.

Questions for Discussion

1   How did Chantale's vision guide her entrepreneurial path?
2   Reviewing Chantale's role models' influences on her, in your opinion, how did they impact her central vision? Explain for each role model separately.
3   Chantale encountered difficulties on her entrepreneurial path. What roles did they play? Were these roles consistent with her vision? If so, explain how.
4   Appendix 8.1 reveals Chantale's typical work week and includes a description of her leisure time. What are your observations on Chantale's schedule? Do you think a diverse schedule can impede the entrepreneurial course of action? If so, what are the factors that can tie up the entrepreneurial action?
5   Chantale's job experience (Appendix 8.2) illustrates many passages and moves. How did these moves affect her vision? How does any move affect one's vision in your opinion?

6 Chantale said, "I don't want to have to choose between Kilookas and acting . . . " How are her vision and passion intertwined in her decision to combine helping animals and an involvement in show business?

Notes

1 At http://www.cherieblairfoundation.org/
2 At http://www.ifc.org/ifcext/enviro.nsf/AttachmentsByTitle/rep_GEM_MenaWomenEntrepreneurs/$FILE/MENA_Women_Entrepreneurs_Jun07.pdf
3 At http://www.ifc.org/ifcext/enviro.nsf/AttachmentsByTitle/rep_GEM_MenaWomenEntrepreneurs/$FILE/MENA_Women_Entrepreneurs_Jun07.pdf, page 26.
4 At http://wearenytech.com/72-marissa-evans-ceo-go-try-it-on ; http://www.foxnews.com/scitech/2010/03/13/need-stylist-new-web-site-offers-free-wardrobe-advice#ixzz1UzCkvsRT
5 At http://www.cosmoloan.com/investments/10-inspirational-child-entrepreneurs.html
6 At http://www.cameronjohnson.com/his_companies.htm; http://7million7years.com/2009/05/31/speaking-of-child-entrepreneurs/
7 At http://www.gerber.com
8 At http://startupprincess.com/meet-ishita-gupta-founder-of-fear-less-magazine-touchpoint-speaker/
9 At http://www.entrepreneur.com/article/220021
10 At http://womenentrepreneursgrowglobal.org/category/social-entrepreneurship/
11 From: Estée Lauder company, at http://www.elcompanies.com/; The Estée Lauder Companies Inc. at http://www.fundinguniverse.com/company-histories/The-Estée-Lauder-Companies-Inc-Company-History.html; Estée Lauder Biography, at BIO: http://www.thebiographychannel.co.uk/biographies/estee-lauder.html; case study: Estée Lauder in Strategic Management, at http://mmu-strategic-management.blogspot.com/2010/02/case-study-1-estee-lauder-external.html; *The New York Times*, at http://www.nytimes.com/2004/04/26/nyregion/estee-lauder-pursuer-of-beauty-and-cosmetics-titan-dies-at-97 html
12 The author(s) of the case studies are fully and solely responsible for their content, phrasing consistency and flow, terminology, English proofing and reference lists.
13 The name given to her in an article entitled: "Elle a trouvé sa niche," published in *Affaires plus*, March 2004, p. 48.
14 *Premiers soins pour chiens et chats*, Les Éditions de l'Homme, Montréal, 2002, pp. 11 and 13, free translation from the original French.
15 The quotations are taken from an interview carried out by the authors of the case study on February 23, 2006, in Chantale's Montréal office, and a follow-up interview on April 6, 2006, in a classroom at the Holistic Veterinary Clinic at 1895 de Salaberry in Montréal.
16 Dr. Paul Guindon's comments are taken from an interview held on April 4, 2006, in the offices of the Holistic Veterinary Clinic at 1895 de Salaberry, Montréal.
17 Nadia Nadski was interviewed on May 19, 2006.
18 *Mon animal mange-t-il bien?* Les Éditions de l'Homme, Montréal, 2004, 223 pages.
19 Carl Bélanger was interviewed on March 15, 2006, in the SAJE offices at 505, boul. René-Lévesque Ouest, Suite 510, in Montréal.

Part 4

The First Steps in Venture Creation

Part 4 focuses on

- The processes typifying the first steps of a start-up;
- The challenges and difficulties faced by women entrepreneurs in the new venture's first stages;
- Women's "interpretations" of external effects on their new ventures and their corresponding reactions;
- The resources needed to accelerate the business and enable its growth and success, including financing and networking;
- This part includes chapters and case studies on women's opportunity identification, the ways in which women acquire capital for their new venture and to finance their businesses and their entrepreneurial paths.

The entrepreneur encounters a variety of different challenges and difficulties along the business's life cycle: when the business has just been set up and takes its first steps in the real world, i.e., moves from theory, plans and sketches into practice, such challenges and difficulties are very distinct from those encountered at the previous stages, when the business was only an idea.

One of the predominant, multifaceted processes that a business undergoes in its first stage is the translation of its theoretical plans into practical action, while maintaining its original concept and business model.

The ways in which women tackle this multifaceted process echo their ecosystems, specifically, the external effects—challenges and difficulties—that women encounter at this stage, their "interpretations" of such external effects and the "translation" of these interpretations into action. Hence, the strategies taken by women at this business stage, addressing the external effects, e.g., coping with the difficulties and sustaining, or leveraging the challenges into keys to success, represent a unique, female-oriented activity.

Part 4 introduces the process typifying the first steps of a start-up. Drawing on the resource-based view and models of business life cycles, the chapters forming this part of the book focus on the resources needed to accelerate the business and enable its growth and success.

In the opening chapter, the process of opportunity exploitation, planning, the main hurdles typical of the start-up stage and subsequent strategies used at this stage are examined. The second chapter introduces financing the business at the early stage, by discussing the different financing methods used by women, and those that they avoid. Another chapter discusses networking and social capital as a valid and most promising way of starting and stabilizing a business. Part 4 concludes with a chapter on the entrepreneurial avenues women choose as part of their career course.

9   "In the Midst of Difficulty Lies Opportunity"[1]

A Woman's View

Chapter Objectives

- Recognizing the core elements of opportunity exploitation in the start-up phase from the female perspective;
- Distinguishing between the different forms of opportunity exploitation and understanding what each entails;
- Discussing the impact of gender background on the ways in which women exploit entrepreneurial opportunities;
- Detecting the significance of opportunity in the business's life cycle through the framework of leading theoretical models;
- Positing networking as a fundamental practice in female new venture creation, and social capital as an essential asset in female entrepreneurship;
- Understanding the planning process in the context of opportunity exploitation;
- Portraying women-related strategies for exploiting opportunities that will grow into successful ventures.

Opportunity exploitation is introduced in this chapter from the female perspective, by presenting the pursuit of opportunities as the accelerator of any entrepreneurial action and proposing the different ways in which women exploit them: looking for unexploited opportunities, creating new ones, reshaping existing ones and grabbing opportunities, among others.

This chapter propounds the view that the pursuit of opportunities can be managed and accomplished in different ways, which involve different characteristics: creativity, attentiveness, proactivity, flexibility, among others, that are matched to the major processes at each phase in the first steps of the new venture.

The chapter portrays the difficulties, barriers and mental blocks encountered by women during their pursuit of opportunity and discusses ways to manage these, by shaping their own female-based approach, rather than ignoring it and adopting a male-based one.

THE PROCESS OF OPPORTUNITY EXPLOITATION

Opportunity exploitation reflects the entrepreneur's ability to identify opportunities more accurately and rapidly than others and leverage them into a competitive and sustainable business advantage. Opportunity exploitation involves sensing the market's needs where resources are still under-employed, or not at all; identifying the gaps, or needs, in the existing market and creating an adjusted or elaborated "fit" between the market's needs and the outcomes that will be based on the respective business's resources.

Opportunity exploitation draws on the business's internal capabilities to obtain a sustainable competitive advantage. Alternatively, when the entrepreneur founds the business's prospective success on external forces, such as affluence in the economy, an emerging technological boost in cellular appliances or a significant development in China's economy, while disregarding her or his business's capabilities, the business concept becomes more risky as it can only be marginally amended while resting on the impact of external forces. Relying on internal capabilities, in line with the resource-based view (RBV) and dynamic capabilities (DC) approach, enables the business to employ various tangible and intangible resources to develop an opportunity into a valuable asset for the business (Barney, 1986b, 1991; Eisenhardt & Martin, 2000; Helfat, 1997; Helfat & Peteraf, 2003; Makadok, 2001; Teece, Pisano, & Shuen, 1997; Winter, 2003).

The case of Jean-Christophe, a 27-year-old student from France who launched a promising entrepreneurial project, illustrates this point. Jean-Christophe failed after a very short time and then reestablished the project as a successful business by adjusting its concept, demonstrating the essential need to explore internal capabilities in the opportunity-exploitation process in order to survive and grow. As part of his study assignments, Jean-Christophe identified an unexploited need: visitors at the beach or at outdoor swimming pools often neglect to bring sunscreen, yet are aware of the damage caused by the sun's rays and want to protect their skin. Jean-Christophe exploited this opportunity and developed the simple but most promising concept of establishing automatic machines as selling points for tubes of sunscreen; he installed the first automatic machine at a friend's family-owned swimming pool and it immediately attracted a lot of interest among the visitors—sales were very high. However, despite much effort, he could not find any other location in which to install his machines. The undertaking shut down, to Jean-Christophe's great disappointment. A second attempt to succeed in this same undertaking was made the following year with the collaboration of his roommate, Miriam, who reconceptualized the business model. The founders recruited people with experience and expertise in marketing, business development and sales. The model was then based on a win–win situation, i.e., the founders located owners of swimming pools in the area and suggested sharing the sales profits in return for a space in the swimming pool area free of charge to place the automatic machines. Just as the opportunity-exploitation process had been successful, the restructuring of the business model with a view of the business's internal resources enabled its success; the venture is growing and has managed to collaborate with more than 200 swimming pools.

There is still no accepted definition of what, exactly, constitutes an opportunity or what the best process or best circumstances are to exploit them. Yet there is wide agreement regarding their key role in entrepreneurship, in distinguishing between entrepreneurs and business owners, and in paving the way for sustainable competitive advantage and growth: entrepreneurs who are more proficient at exploiting opportunities and promptly transforming them into a practical process that meets the identified needs or gaps are more apt to generate competitive advantages (Alvarez & Busenitz, 2001; Ardichvili, Cardozo, & Ray, 2003; Shane & Venkataraman, 2000).

The prevalent approaches in opportunity and entrepreneurship research today are:

- opportunity identification, referring to opportunities that are formed by discovering a need and are exogenous to the entrepreneur (Alvarez & Barney, 2007; Eckhardt & Ciuchta, 2008);
- opportunity creation, referring to opportunities that are formed endogenously by the entrepreneurs themselves through an enactment process (Aldrich & Ruef, 2006; Venkataraman, 2003).

Accordingly, opportunity exploitation—via identification or creation—is exhibited in different forms, e.g., identification, creation, development, recognition and imitation. Each of these forms centers around some core elements, while at the same time highlighting unique elements that differentiate it from others (Table 9.1).

The core elements are based on the following:

- Entrepreneurial alertness
- Information acquisition
- Prior knowledge
- Social capital and networks

- Human capital acquisition
- Styles of exploiting opportunities (e.g., creation, identification, development, imitation, assessment)
- Personality traits (e.g., optimism, self-efficacy, creativity)
- The type of opportunity itself.

Table 9.1 reveals the characteristics of the different forms of opportunity exploitation.

Table 9.1 The Opportunity Exploitation Process in the New Venture Creation

Form of opportunity exploitation	What does it entail?	What differentiates it?
Identification	Identification of opportunities that already exist but are still un- or under-exploited	Being alert; generating ideas from any circumstance, experience or interaction; cracking the codes of successful businesses and following their steps; deciphering the best practices to follow.
Creation	Creating a need for a product, a service or a technology; e.g., it is easier to use, cheaper, more reliable, higher quality	Convincing potential customers and shareholders to accept a new idea, concept or need, although this need has not yet evolved. For example, environmental awareness and its various entrepreneurial deliverables were created long before anyone anticipated the need for them.
Development	Development of an existing opportunity by adjusting, adding or excluding elements associated with it to expand the scope of its customers to non-traditional ones	Requires a deep familiarity with the existing customers and identification of their core need for a product/service, to leverage the need to different groups of customers. For example, developing the concept of travel packages into theme-based travel packages, e.g., trips for the elderly; a journey through a movie (the *DaVinci Code*); gastronomic travel, etc.
Imitation	Using an existing product, service or process for either its traditional or new customers	This process draws on the concept that there is room for everyone in the market; thus a product that is successful in Europe could, or should, be exposed in Asia as well.

| "Grabbing" | Capturing opportunities by disregarding rational analyses on their profitability prospects; basing the decision on intuition; taking risks yet being the first to exploit the opportunities | This process is riskier yet entails a faster track. Individuals can take credit for being the first to exploit the opportunities. It suits individuals who are naturally more opportunistic, risk-takers and driven by enthusiasm and passion. |
| Reshaping existing opportunities | Opportunities that are well-known, well-accepted and treated as routine, are reshaped, e.g., updated, technologically advanced, etc., for the same traditional customers | The idea is to retain the customers yet provide them with higher value for the same products/services/processes; for example, integrating automatic bank services through mobile phones; selling sugar-free bread in addition to traditional bread, etc. |

IS THERE A GENDERED STYLE IN OPPORTUNITY EXPLOITATION?

Research in entrepreneurship reveals that women and men interpret "opportunities" differently: they consider the attractiveness of unexploited niches through gender-based lenses, hence the desirability and feasibility of a potential business are differently perceived by the genders. Such differences are explained by:

- *the unique gender socialization background*—women and men undergo different experiences during the course of their lives and are raised under different social messages. These effects shape their consequent perceptions, including those associated with opportunities, which reflect their background;
- *human capital acquisition*—women and men have distinct job experiences, entrepreneurial experiences, and educational attainment. As prior knowledge and experience are crucial factors in the opportunity-exploitation process, the genders' exploitation processes differ;
- *the gender-based inclination toward specific sectors/industries/interests (e.g., women being more attracted to cosmetics, fashion, nurturing, etc., less attracted to mechanics, technology)*—whether it is an innate inclination or an outcome of the socialization process, women and men are fascinated by different rudimentary opportunities; these, in turn, correspond to their general tendencies; e.g., women more than men create ventures

in sectors that involve care-giving, an artistic bent, esthetics and creative interests.

As such, an unexploited market for motor vehicle carburetors may seem more appealing to men than to women. Alternatively, each gender might address this same unexploited opportunity differently, resulting in different exploitation performance, i.e., creation, invention, imitation or improvement of the existing performance of these carburetors.

The *search* process for business opportunities also differs between the genders and reflects their distinct ways of applying the search actions. For example, women more than men tend to use more formal means while men use more informal means. The pace of the search action is gender-oriented as well: women intertwine the search with different activities while men focus on the search activity, thus appearing to pursue it more intensively. Women and men differ in their employment of different human and social capital to search for opportunities. However, both genders employ innovation, uniqueness and feasibility in the search for opportunities; in these aspects, women and men are more similar than different (Davidsson & Honig, 2003; Shepherd & DeTienne, 2005; Singh, 2001; Ucbasaran, Wright, & Westhead, 2003).

Drawing on the feminist approaches, the elements with a major impact on opportunity exploitation among the gender groups are illustrated in Figure 9.1.

The following examples demonstrate the opportunity-exploitation process followed by two young women entrepreneurs using the virtual

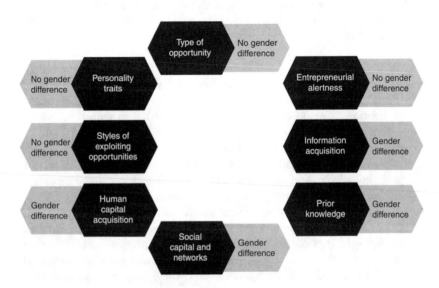

Figure 9.1 Opportunity Exploitation and Gender.

social media and networks. They provide a glimpse into opportunity exploitation and the young and promising Generation Y women entrepreneurs—Facebook, Twitter and YouTube.

Ms. Natasha Nelson, founder of a self-serve frozen yogurt company, Yogurtini, California, is a persistent advocate for good ingredients and good causes. She was always entrepreneurial; but Yogurtini started because she was not satisfied with the flavor of the yogurt products she tasted in her home town. Opportunity exploitation according to Ms. Nelson is the next online marketing tool. She says that those who aren't using Facebook and Twitter are way behind. Her tip is "Study, study, study"; she explains the internet as follows: "It's fast and immediate; I can create my own brand and impression I am in control of."	Melani Gordon, founder of Gwave consulting, internet marketing, focuses on generating publicity through social media. In her YouTube interview Ms. Gordon strongly advises entrepreneurs to be strong networkers; and if they are not, she urges them to learn it and take networking classes. She encourages women to "just start" a business; those too analytical will never start the business. A major focus for women entrepreneurs is "have fun . . . to keep us fun and motivated," and concludes by "have fun and do new things."
Read more at: http://www.retireat21.com/interview/natasha-nelson#	Read more at: http://www.youtube.com/watch?v=IjxgWjbdmEo

OPPORTUNITIES AND THE BUSINESS LIFE CYCLE

The focus of entrepreneurial businesses is to generate a sustained competitive advantage from their unique set of internal resources; starting from the very first days, start-ups target the production of such competitive advantages to facilitate their penetration into the market.

Most research on sources of sustained competitive advantage focuses on models that isolate the business's opportunities and threats, describe its strengths and weaknesses (Ansoff, 1965; Porter, 1985), analyze how these are matched to the strategies taken by the entrepreneur at the different stages of the business, and focus on the internal power of the business, to create a combined outcome that will be attractive to the business's stakeholders. Most of these models have been introduced by scholars of the RBV (Barney, 1986b, 1991; Peteraf, 1993; Wernerfelt, 1984).

The RBV and the business life cycle model, as relevant to the female new venture creation process, converge in an understanding of the sources of the challenges and difficulties identified by women in the start-up phase and the consequent strategies they use to face them.

Table 9.2 introduces leading models of the new venture creation life cycle in its different characteristic stages; the second section of the table

Table 9.2 The New Venture's Life Cycle, Resources Needed and the Female View

Stages of new venture creation

1st stage	2nd stage	3rd stage	4th stage	5th stage	Leading models
Opportunity	Technology set-up and organization; creation	Exchanges			Bhave (1994)
Idea	Pre start-up	Start-up	Post start-up		Clarysse & Moray (2004)
Intention	Boundary	Resources	Exchanges		Gelderen, Bosma, & Thurik (2001)
					Reynolds (2000)
Concept	Gestation	Birth of the firm	Grow or Persist or Quit		Shook, Priem, & McGee (2003)
Entrepreneurial intent	Opportunity search and discovery	Decision to exploit	Opportunity-exploitation activity		
Initiation	Acclimatization	Consolidation	Startup	Infancy	Tesfaye (1997)
Concept	Planning	Implementation			Vesper (1990)
Gestation	Planning	Contract services	Proprietary product	Multiproduct	Van de Ven, Hudson, & Schroeder (1984)

Resources and capabilities needed: a female view

1st stage	2nd stage	3rd stage	4th stage	5th stage
Networking skills, social capital	Planning	Proactivity	Exploiting opportunities	Implementation
Opportunity identification	Mobilizing resources	Determination	Strategic view	Learning from experience
	Consulting with professionals	Managing the best staff	Deciding on ways to pursue	Production
		Empowering the personnel		Managing people, projects

1st stage	2nd stage	3rd stage	4th stage	5th stage
Creativity Sharing the idea and concept Flexibility Adjusting the concept according to accumulated feedback	Management skills combined with creativity and innovation Allocating the most suitable people	Exchange of services, ideas Identifying the best internal resources and capabilities and exposing them	Practical view Implementation of ideas Risk-taking Decision-making	Decision-making

Resources and the new venture's life cycle: a feminist-based view. Women are typified in research as:

1st stage	2nd stage	3rd stage	4th stage	5th stage
Creative, innovative and using flexible thinking Proficient in networking and possessing the relevant skills to amass the needed social capital Insufficient materialization of creativity and innovation into products or projects	Skilful in planning; looking into details and planning accordingly Embracing, consulting feedback from external and internal people, brainstorming with experts Favoring management processes focused on people rather than exclusively on tasks	Adept in managing the best staff Tend to empower their staff Identify the strengths/weaknesses of their business easily and daringly Tend to be less proactive than men Considered less determined in fighting for their business, and are more easily affected by external effects	Creative in exploiting opportunities Having a sophisticated strategic view More theoretical; less practical Risk-averse Unfocused: appreciate different scenarios rather than one decisive scenario for their venture	Fine learners; learn from their own and others' experiences Skilful in managing people; people-oriented Using flexible and evidence-based decision-making Less productive Less good at implementing Less good at managing projects

(Continued overleaf)

Table 9.2 Continued

Resources and the new venture's life cycle: a feminist-based view. Women are typified in research as:

1st stage	2nd stage	3rd stage	4th stage	5th stage
Insufficient endorsement of networks for the business's growth	Employing intuition in recruiting staff	Tend to handle unbalanced exchange of services, ideas: tend to demand less and give more than their male counterparts	Less efficient in exploiting opportunities, due to their characteristic blend of detailed and lateral thinking	
Hindrances such as the "men's gang" impede women from grabbing the benefits of their social capital	Combining organizational orientation with creativity and innovation			
	Mobilization of resources			
	Task-oriented management			
	Sometimes multiple feedback and comments make it difficult for women to choose their way			

presents the converging crossroads of the business life cycle models and the RBV by listing the resources and capabilities—tangible and intangible—that are needed for each stage of the new venture creation process. The last section of the table offers an outlook on women's world by summarizing the main capabilities and actions taken by women entrepreneurs in the respective stages and those capabilities and actions that women avoid.

Some of the action-avoidance by women stems from female-based preferences, demands or needs, while some is embedded in women's ecosystems, including the socialization process that "teaches" them to follow rather than lead, the dominance of men in different areas, and their exclusion from different niches because "this is not a job for women," "women should focus on their own niches" or just because men strive to maintain their exclusiveness in different niches.

NETWORKING AND SOCIAL CAPITAL

Networking is fundamental for making the most of the opportunity-exploitation process. It produces the most relevant connections and contacts with people who might invest, collaborate or introduce the entrepreneur to others. It assists in retrieving critical information. In fact, it consists of collecting prior knowledge of customer problems before the competitors, thus understanding the context in which the future business may or may not be developed. Obviously, different types of networking, e.g., sources of information, styles of approaching these contacts, the "use" of contacts for business versus social needs etc., reveal different types of opportunities.

Women and men have access to different sources of information about opportunities and their styles of exploiting opportunities differ. Men have more access than women to investors, people in local and national politics and bankers; women have access to the social-based interface, e.g., friends and family. Men approach their networks in a more straightforward and direct fashion; they develop networks that will simplify their venture creation process and its expansion, and they focus on attracting investors, co-founders and collaborators, sometimes even prior to finalizing the structuring of their idea. Women, on the other hand, are more thorough and systematic: they first tend to finalize structuring their idea, and only then will they try to attract investors. But even then, women would prefer being introduced to investors, rather than approaching them directly. The following examples illustrate the differences. Ted, a 35-year-old male entrepreneur from London, UK, created a start-up in the field of semi-conductors; he needed money to start the business and he approached one of his schoolmates, the son of a well-known investor in the UK, to get an introduction to his father. "When I raised the idea for my business

I knew I could not lose time because somebody else could raise similar ideas, be ahead of me with its production, leaving my idea behind and no longer relevant, so I started approaching investors very quickly," Ted disclosed. However, Ted was refused by his schoolmate's father and went on to receive further refusals since his idea was still not completely configured and not fully clear; but he was persistent and improved his idea while approaching investors. It took him more than 60 meetings with investors to find an angel investor from Spain to partner with. Annabelle, a 29-year-old female entrepreneur from Rotterdam, the Netherlands, was a school graduate who developed an internet-based technique for dating (providing a better match between people who are looking for a life partner). She did not approach any investors for one year, but during this year she intensively developed her invention; it was only when she completed the prototype that she felt more confident in presenting it to investors. "I felt that it is rude to spend an investor's time to present a half-finished device, it could also jeopardize my chances to attract investments for my business . . . I had no idea how I would locate the first investor; I did not have any familiarity with investors, no networks or contacts and did not find a proper list in the internet of investors for my invention." She approached a few investors using a trial-and-error technique, did not find anyone willing to invest and decided to take a loan from the bank.

These typical examples illustrate the differences between the genders' approaches to opportunity exploitation, including acquisition of information, approaching investors, and developing the concept through the opportunity's exploitation, as shown in the Table 9.3.

Table 9.3 Networks; Locating Investors; Financial Approach

Women	Men
• Hesitant approach	• Use of networks, connections, both direct and indirect
• Trial and error	• More methodical
• Sporadically	• Intensively
• Focused on developing the business concept first	• Focused on finding financial sources from the start
• Approaching a few investors and then looking for other financial sources	• Approaching many investors
• Information gained from alertness	• Information gained from connections
• Fragility in the face of investors: refusals discourage women	• Persistence
• Approaching investors when the prototype is ready	• Approaching investors from "day 1"

Social Capital

Social capital is the backbone of a sustainable network, although the members of a particular network can change with time. In today's Facebook, LinkedIn and Twitter applications, engaging in "groups," "blogs," "forums" and "interest groups" on the popular virtual networks gives entrepreneurs the needed exposure by being connected through the most relevant groups and people.

Women and men differ in developing and maintaining their social networks. In their renowned book *Start-up Nation: The Story of Israel's Economic Miracle,* Senor and Singer (2009) affirm that the Israeli army serves as a platform for engaging and being involved in the most relevant networks and forming the most valuable social capital . . . for men! Such army-based networks shorten the opportunity-exploitation process and promise higher entrepreneurial success; however, since this valuable network is male-dominated, it either sets up barriers against women entering or sets up hurdles for women who seek to maintain their participation and involvement in such networks. In fact, women entrepreneurs who confront the hurdles typical to the start-up phase disapprove of such male-dominated networks that impede their entry for the "wrong"reasons, that is, just because they are women, yet they address this difficulty by pursuing the same, alleged "wrong" way, developing their own, woman-dominated networks. Research reveals that both gender groups favor networking with people of the same gender. However, strong ties in the same gender group are less beneficial in that the information from homogeneous interactions lacks diversity and tends to be redundant: women will benefit more from interactions with men and vice versa. This is a setback that both genders need to address (Barrett, 1995; Dillman, 2000; Gatewood, Shaver, & Gartner, 1995; Renzulli, Aldrich, & Moody, 2000).

Virtual social networks: Facebook, LinkedIn, Twitter—Ever since 2000, there has been an increase in entrepreneurial businesses introducing virtual, social utilities such as Facebook, LinkedIn and Twitter, among others, which have changed the social interactions and connective pathways between people.

The main innovation in the most popular virtual services is their power to connect people from different countries, sectors of industry, cultures, etc., and to enable instant messaging, introduction to people sharing one's interests and/or taking part in virtual interest groups, etc. Such virtual networks consist of direct connections, and potential expansion of the network via connections of each of those connections, thus allowing introductions to different people and crossing the "barriers" that are more transparent than in face-to-face interactions. People of different ages, professions, academic degrees or interests use these virtual networks to find business opportunities. As these virtual networks are based on trust, i.e., people are connected to each other through mutual acquaintances, they facilitate the opportunity-exploitation process.

LEARNING AND INNOVATING IN SHAPING NEW OPPORTUNITIES

The above discussion depicts opportunity as a possibility that emerges in situations where competitive imperfections surface, e.g., customers' unfulfilled needs, existence of under- or undeveloped products or services, insufficient market competition for a product, service or niche, etc. To take advantage of these imperfections, entrepreneurs fuel the existing opportunities with innovative solutions and ideas. This means that rather than "just" identifying opportunities, entrepreneurs develop, create, shape and reshape opportunities, and reap the advantages of being the first to acquire the information on an opportunity and promptly exploit it. Processes of opportunity-exploitation that incorporate innovation in the method, practices or essence of the opportunities are highly sought after by entrepreneurs. In line with RBV concepts, such processes energize the start-ups and foster their potential competitive advantage by being more complex to imitate, and therefore more rare and perceived as more valuable.

An interesting categorization of the opportunity-exploitation processes was developed by Chandler, Lyon, and DeTienne (2005): (1) Learn/Replicate—represented by corporate workers who identify an unmet market demand at work and replicate the corporate product/service by satisfying this unexploited market; (2) Learn/Innovate—representing corporate employees who identify an unmet customer need and develop a product/service that does not exist and that will satisfy that unmet need; (3) Learn/Acquire—representing individuals who identify a promising business concept and take advantage of existing income streams by acquiring the business (e.g., spin-offs, buyouts, licensing agreements); (4) Innovate/Educate—representing individuals who innovate by developing a product/service and then educate potential customers to use it by "selling" its benefits relative to other competing products.

In the context of the genders, women exhibit innovative and creative thinking during the opportunity-exploitation process; they learn from their own experiences and are attentive to others' experiences; they learn from and reflect upon their successful practices. Yet they favor the identification of opportunities rather than shaping or creating new ones, a tendency that might be associated with being less confident about their abilities to create a business and their inclination to be risk-averse. Men, on the other hand, are profiled in research as motivated by achieving the "bottom line," i.e., success and profits; they use innovation to achieve their goal, yet assign less time than women to learning from others' experiences.

Thus, the innovation used by the different genders originates from different motivations and approaches and is subsequently differently manifested in the genders' opportunity-exploitation (Kariv, 2010a).

Innovators and Adaptors in the Opportunity-Exploitation Process

Recent studies in the area of opportunity-exploitation and gender have proposed that in exploiting opportunities, men perform more as innovators, women as adaptors, i.e., women use modifications of existing products rather than product innovation.

Innovators are defined as generators of "outside-the-box" ideas, creating the unexpected, novel solutions; they are attracted to the less structured problems and are more likely to change the context of the situation in generating solutions. Adaptors, on the other hand, are eminently capable of initiating changes that improve the current system, but are less likely to think outside the box and for the most part do not change anything that is outside the accepted pattern; they are portrayed as more conservative, and tend to solve problems that are more clear and defined, rather than vague, in a more efficient, conformist way.

While women are profiled as adaptors more than innovators, they employ unique methods to develop and reshape existing opportunities. For example, in the case of Ms. Gina Schaefer,[2] owner of a few cool hardware stores, there was always a small kernel in the back of her mind about someday owning her own business and becoming an entrepreneur. She enrolled in an entrepreneurial training program, but was still unsure about the kind of business she wanted to start, so she poked around a couple of possibilities. She realized that 95 percent of independent hardware stores belonged to one of three co-ops or a couple of manufacturer buying groups. She sent out inquiries to all of them and was immediately contacted by Ace Hardware. In March 2003, Gina opened Logan Hardware, now with 130 employees in 7 stores. Gina Schaefer's story illustrates how opportunities are developed, even when they are already there.

The research associates women's opportunity-exploitation process, be it innovation- or adaptation-oriented, to their background, experiences and ecosystem:

- *Limited entrepreneurial experience*—women tend to be watchful and hesitant regarding information, informal agreements or friendly promises concerning opportunity-exploitation; they undergo more learning-by-doing and trial-and-error experiences along their opportunity-exploitation process.
- *Higher tolerance for external assistance*—women leverage their opportunities by approaching mentors, consultants and experienced friends and family members for assistance.

- *Creativity*—women use creativity, flexibility and their ability to develop skills over time, respond to the challenges they meet in different contexts and eventually survive; as such they are more apt to structure and change situations or circumstances that can then be developed into business opportunities. Training and mentoring can improve both the number of ideas generated and the innovativeness of those ideas.
- *Coping with the difficulties*—it is common knowledge that being off-balance enhances innovation, while being in one's "comfort zone" reduces the urge to exploit different opportunities. Women face different types of difficulties in the new venture creation process associated with being women and being entrepreneurs; these, in turn, stimulate their yearning to innovate in order to respond to the difficulties in ways that have not yet been implemented.

Inno-daptation is a newly introduced construct representing the combination of pure innovation and adaptation, producing outcomes that originate from existing, yet independent and not normally compatible products/services/technologies, combined into new products or services. For example, satellites, high-technology and transportation were combined to produce the GPS device; combining love and technology has resulted in multiple dating websites; Facebook facilities combined with social or political movements have resulted in mass protests in different countries.

Grabbing Opportunities!

The extensive conflicting expectations encountered by female entrepreneurs—that they should differ from, yet resemble their male counterparts, i.e., preserve their gender-based, traditional parenting and domestic responsibilities, while performing as successful entrepreneurs in similar ways to men, all the while dealing with additional barriers to women's equality in opportunity exploitation, have pushed women toward two different actions: (a) avoiding entrepreneurship and (b) grabbing opportunities.

(a) *Avoiding entrepreneurial opportunities*—a decision taken by women to disregard or not develop the opportunities they encounter. This can be accompanied by deciding to work in the corporate market or remaining unemployed, to avoid any possibility of being attracted to entrepreneurial opportunities, especially when the entrepreneurial zeal is still there. Avoidance is associated with multiple stressful forces imposed on women entrepreneurs; e.g., stresses stemming from either the home or work sphere that arise on top of the demanding, sometimes frustrating pressures of the other sphere.

Many women that are entrepreneurial take a decision to focus on their traditional responsibilities or traditional social expectations and step away from entrepreneurship. These women suppress their internal tendency to create, invent and innovate, in exchange for a calmer atmosphere and social desirability.

(b) *Grabbing entrepreneurial opportunities*—refers to seeing an opportunity and "taking it," regardless of diagnostic analyses of its profitability prospects; grabbing opportunities is based primarily on intuition, on an internal feeling regarding the opportunity's potential. It is thus a riskier technique of opportunity-exploitation, yet it places individuals on the fast track to the new venture creation process, as it enables the "first dibs" advantage, i.e., those that exploit an opportunity first can take credit for being the first, while individuals that avoid an opportunity cannot claim rights over its exploitation. However, the opportunity can be, at least theoretically, worthless.

Women are generally less involved in the opportunity-exploitation process: they face more difficulties in using networks and social capital, and therefore grabbing opportunities could correspond with their needs. In addition, it is common knowledge that women effectively use intuition and internal feelings about their surroundings.

Women need to respond to opportunities in a brisk, active manner in a brief time to manage the male dominance in opportunity exploitation. Women who ignore or dawdle in grabbing an opportunity endanger the "momentum," which may take a long time to return. Yet, being more risk-averse than their male counterparts, grabbing opportunities may not be the natural choice for women entrepreneurs.

Many successful women entrepreneurs, especially younger ones, are less and less reluctant to grab opportunities. They embark on opportunities without thinking too much about their effects and consequences. One high-tech woman entrepreneur from Israel, Ms. Gali Ross, co-founder of Razoss,[3] was quoted as saying: "try, grab any opportunity; you might be surprised, it may work, or not work, but you should try it. Some people have great business plans but they are so hesitant in exploiting opportunities that they miss them. They then stay at home, frustrated by 'missing the boat'; there is not much to lose from just grabbing opportunities, it is worth trying . . ."

Opportunities do not manifest themselves in a vacuum. Sometimes opportunities are latent and require a thorough search to detect them; sometimes the exposed opportunities are in a raw condition and need to be cultivated prior to their exploitation. Women must be alert to opportunities, while being concurrently ready to act in order to exploit them in any of the aforementioned ways that suit the context and conditions. Women should attempt to exploit those opportunities that seem more feasible, desirable and within the scope of their interests, in order to nurture them into the business they have been dreaming about.

HURDLES TYPICAL TO VENTURE CREATION OF WOMEN-LED BUSINESSES

Women's actions in the start-up phase are often debated in comparative terms, deliberately implying that men are the ultimate model in entrepreneurship. Any entrepreneurial action is thus regarded through the lenses of men's actions, e.g., women are portrayed as *less* prone to take risks at this stage compared to men; women interpret business success in a *different* way than men; women entrepreneurs are *too* concerned with their dual roles in their business and family, etc.

The commonly held approach to women entrepreneurs regards their supposedly insufficient capabilities to create a venture, e.g., lower motivation to start a business, mediocre aspirations of financial success, and lack of critical entrepreneurial characteristics. This approach has permeated different countries and, as a result, women are deemed "unsuitable" for entrepreneurship not only by men, but also by women—even women entrepreneurs. Given the pattern of girls out-performing boys in academic achievements in school and higher education, their high motivation in school, their creativity and their ability to think outside the box, such perceptions are puzzling.

Table 9.4 categorizes the main reported hurdles reported by women entrepreneurs.

One main explanation for these perceptions lies in the presence of gender-specific hurdles to the start-up phase in the new venture creation. These hurdles have been documented and analyzed in feminist research and are categorized as follows:

Hurdles Originating from Women's Choices

- Hurdles derived from women's self-stratification and their own choice of directing themselves toward traditional, women-dominated sectors that have lower prestige and are less rewarding relative to men-dominated sectors.
- Women's relatively lower aspirations to start a business.
- Women's interpretation of business "success" is confined to "just" starting a business rather than aspiring to businesses with high growth.

Table 9.4 Main Hurdles Reported by Women Entrepreneurs

Business unit	Strategies	Management styles	Motivation	Sectors of activity	Requisite skills
Fewer resources at start-up	Limited strategies developed to access to resources	"Relational strategy" when working with clients, partners	Different socialization experiences—home and children are the first priority	Women's choice of smaller, traditional businesses in retail, service and caring	Limited business skills
Focusing on industry specific experience	Limited strategic and tactical decisions	Focus on development of teams, employees, empowering, perseverance	To cope with the work-family conflict by working independently	Women's avoidance of high tech manufacturing or non-traditional and "too" innovative sectors	Limited managerial experience
Smaller businesses comparatively to men's	Development of strategies emphasizing product quality; neglecting strategies addressing to cost efficiency	"Feminine" management style, i.e., informally structured	Turning their hobbies into businesses	Choices of educational and professional tracks that are less rewarding in the labor market	Limited entrepreneurial experience
More work from home thus less exposure of the business' products or services.	Women entrepreneurs are more risk averse		"... just to make a living"; "I do not necessarily have to be profitable"; "It is not catastrophic just to be balanced ...."		Limited employment of negotiation skills
Discrimination—lenders discriminate women entrepreneurs as well as prefer to lend to larger and more established firms; which are usually male-dominated.					Limited employment of financial management skills

- Women's lower commitment to their businesses when there is spill-over with their family-related responsibilities.
- Less relevant experience.
- Poorer leadership capabilities relevant to entrepreneurship, e.g., proactivity, decisiveness, risk-taking, persistence even when feedback is discouraging.

Hurdles Originating from the Environment

- General perception of women's inadequacies for creating a venture; this is even more pronounced in the high-tech sector.
- Unbalanced public opinion about women entrepreneurs who are mothers of young children—compared to men under the same conditions—and their likelihood to start a business and advance it toward success.
- Less access for women to equity markets.
- Relatively restricted financial sources that are actually open to women (formally all sources are open to any individual).
- Less access to relevant networks such as those including people who make decisions on financial investments, influential people in business sectors, etc.

Symbiotic Hurdles that Combine Women's Self-stratification and the Public's Approach to Women

- Women's lower enrollment in MBA programs is reflected in a lower probability of achieving the same level of executive authority or being able to tap into groups of decision-makers.
- Women's lower enrolment in technological programs deprives them of the possibility of engaging in high-tech start-ups.

Yet the blame for the fact that women are still tackling these realities lies with lingering cultural perceptions that form a gendered outcome which reverberates through the social-cultural barriers that females face in school, in the family, in higher education and in the labor market.

The main hurdles depicted in the research on female entrepreneurship (Buttner, 2001; Chaganti & Parasuraman, 1996; Robb & Coleman, 2009; Scherr, Sugrue, & Ward, 1993) are collected and summarized in Figure 9.2.

Women's entrepreneurial course of action should be understood through the lens of women; the best practices that are delivered to entrepreneurs should apply to women; most importantly, the action eventually taken by women in their entrepreneurial realm should be accepted, rather than compared to men's, and encouraged by their environment.

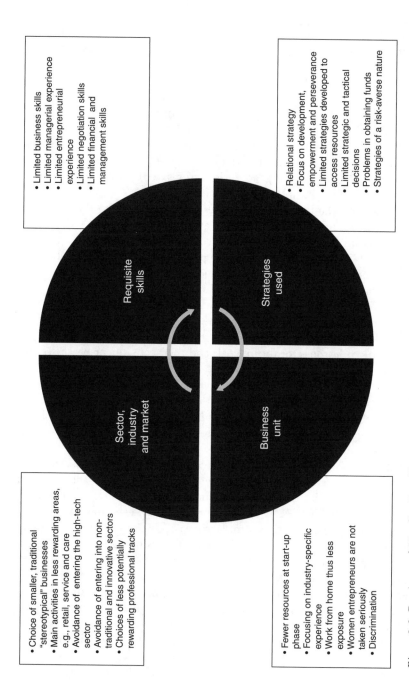

Figure 9.2 Barriers and Hurdles Faced by Women Entrepreneurs: The Main Research Findings.

PLANNING THROUGH A FEMALE PERSPECTIVE

Planning is essential in the new venture creation process, mainly to organize one's mission, goals and vision. Planning encompasses different aspects such as:

- declaring the goal, objectives, mission and vision;
- knowing the market, competitors, main supplier;
- understanding the ecosystem, trends, needs, etc.;
- listing the activities and actions that have been taken to accomplish the business's goals and objectives;
- listing the forthcoming activities/actions to be taken in order to accomplish the business's goal and objectives;
- calculating the fixed costs, expenses and earnings from the activities, machinery, technology, personnel, etc.;
- calculating the prospective fixed costs, expenses and earnings from the activities, machinery, technology and personnel that will be used to accomplish the business's goal and objectives;
- reflecting on the team's qualifications relevant to the business's goal and objectives;
- reflecting on the venture's strengths and weaknesses in terms of its market, competitors, environment, mission and vision;
- setting milestones for future goals and their consequent processes and actions.

Women plan. Women reflect upon processes that have been conducted in their ventures, and plan the ones that will be undertaken to accomplish the business's goals and objectives; they are hands-on regarding their teams, processes, contracts and technologies used.

Statistics show that in many countries, women entrepreneurs, especially opportunity entrepreneurs, are highly educated, and use the methods learned in academia, hence, women allocate more time and thought to planning their businesses. While the entrepreneur in the start-up phase is driven by passion and enthusiasm, at times the planning process is overlooked; women are less impulsive in starting a business and tend to "think it over," plan their upcoming activities, base their plans on the deep learning process they have undergone, and consult with colleagues, their staff or experts on potential scenarios of their prospective business activities from different angles. Women enroll in courses on business-plan writing; they pay a great deal of attention to the preliminary process of their start-up's planning and consider it a building block in the whole process.

Women's proclivity to take fewer risks, think creatively, widely and strategically, consult on their plans, share their thoughts and delve into details, among others, are reflected in their planning process.

Consequently, the planning process executed by women entrepreneurs is relatively long and is applied in a step-by-step fashion along the new venture's life cycle.

The planning process is typified by the inclusion of multiple potential risks and analyses of different scenarios in order to craft, in advance, ways to overcome or even avoid potential risks. The dynamic of the planning process conducted by women is characterized by teamwork, the sharing of thoughts, concerns and insights, and the raising of inquiries to be addressed later on. Women exhibit a meticulous planning process that offers some significant advantages for nascent and novice entrepreneurs but also presents some disadvantages: while it enables organizing the resources, allocating the relevant capabilities, setting priorities and avoiding wasteful consumption of time and energy, it takes longer, and raises more unsolved concerns and questions that may seem too difficult to implement.

A planning process that inspects the business's market and environment, and provides a thorough outlook of the business-to-be, yet includes "open spaces" for uncertainties and unplanned scenarios that will be exposed but not yet answered, may set the required balance between the two approaches to planning.

BREAKING DOWN THE RISK BARRIERS

Many women entrepreneurs fight the barriers they encounter in the entrepreneurial realm using a variety of different strategies. Women that want to become entrepreneurs enroll in academic programs, e.g., MBA programs or technological programs, training themselves for the creation of high-growth business. Women entrepreneurs ask for assistance from experts, colleagues and their staff members, they use formal and informal sources, they network to support each other with ideas, brainstorming, referrals or service provision.

Many younger women entrepreneurs are more persistent in entrepreneurship, and treat failure as a learning experience: they put their next entrepreneurial endeavor on the market more rapidly the second time around. In their subsequent entrepreneurial undertakings, these women are more confident and much more experienced; they are more familiar with the keys of success and know how to avoid the pitfalls they encountered in their previous experiences. They have already acquired the techniques that suit their goals and needs, and they know how to address difficulties and overcome obstacles.

In addition, these women break down barriers by empowering themselves, believing in their own capabilities to create a venture, and elevating their confidence in accomplishing their goals and achieving success. The presentation of the self is then persuasive and enables women to convey their business's needs in a clearer, simpler and more convincing way. The message that women deliver to potential investors, banks, angel investors, potential collaborators and the shareholders has a substantial impact.

Ms. Hilla Ovil-Brenner, co-founder of White Smoke,[4] has been quoted as saying:

> We understand that expertise and knowledge are transferred and shared; we do not have all the knowledge. We may think so at first, but over the years we realize how important it is to brainstorm, to analyze what we went through, to proactively ask for comments and actively strive for knowledge transfer. Personally, I would go to every conference, workshop or talk, to share with others my experiences and be the model of a woman who does not let obstacles interfere in her entrepreneurial course of action . . .

Figure 9.3 summarizes the best practices collected from interviews with hundreds of successful women entrepreneurs addressing the general question: "What is your single best advice to a young entrepreneur on how to overcome female-related obstacles on her way to establishing a business?"

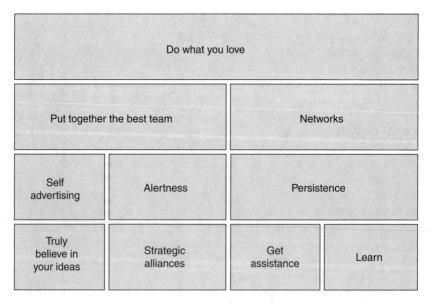

Figure 9.3 Overcoming Women-related Barriers: Best Practices Offered by Successful Women Entrepreneurs.

Accordingly, the practices used by successful women entrepreneurs to confront the barriers they have faced in their entrepreneurial course of action are:

- *Team*—Put the best team together; be confident that all complementary capabilities are represented, e.g., risk-takers, innovators, people-oriented individuals; this is the best, probably only way to gain a competitive advantage in a highly motivated organizational environment.

- *Access to the right network*—Be a member of Facebook, Twitter, LinkedIn. Be active, "invite" friends; write posts and be part of central blogs. Offer your friends comments on their business's websites; start a virtual conversation, so that you can get a "feel" for the trends and expose your business's benefits to others.

- *Advertise yourself*—on virtual networks and the most popular internet marketing sites, such as GoogleAd; hiding oneself and being reclusive damages the business's image and reputation. Women entrepreneurs sometimes tend to stay backstage; they may feel insecure about being noticed, appreciated and a model for others; it takes time and many successful experiences for women to admit that they are successful. Yet, women should be more self-confident, show off their businesses' benefits and advantages, and accept the appreciation and compliments they deserve.

- *Make strategic alliances*—with companies/associations/organizations that can benefit from your products and/or services, or simply from the connection with the new venture. For example, a successful woman entrepreneur from Sweden, who invented an illuminated outdoor billboard and failed to convince investors to partner with her business, "switched" to a different strategy: she turned to a big advertising company in Sweden for a strategic alliance. "I offered free advertising for one year, all around my country, and asked for two technological developers to be dedicated to designing the illuminated billboards. They agreed!"

- *Be alert to market competition*—and grab the opportunity it offers to expose your company and its competitive advantages. People compete for the same opportunities; the quicker ones will grab them first, the most innovative ones will gain a competitive advantage, the ones with better networks will have better access to these opportunities. Women must be attentive, exploit opportunities, look proactively for opportunities and when these opportunities match their needs, they should compete for them.

- *Get assistance!*—Women have a more liberal approach to asking for assistance from others with the different aspects of their business; they do not perceive assistance as an indication of their own inabilities.

Some may think that assistance is time- and resource-consuming and is best skipped; yet in most cases the relevant assistance is worthwhile and it facilitates and shortens the subsequent course of action.

- *Persistence*—People have imperfect knowledge of their own abilities in many of the tasks they face. They search for external clues to understand their abilities more accurately. Rewarding feedback provides the incentive to perform, while negative feedback is treated as a hindrance to the performance of specific tasks. Starting a business presents entrepreneurs, especially women, with difficulties and barriers, but they should not treat these difficulties as a sign of their inability to start or develop a business. Women should know that it takes time. If they are sure about their product or service, they must be persistent and overcome these difficulties.
- *Learn*—It is never too late to acquire the most relevant human capital, e.g., strong management and financial skills, fostering creativity, stimulating the team to innovation and intra-preneurship.
- *Do what you love to do*—To develop and sustain an inspirational, vibrant, stimulating spirit, women should focus on what they love to do; this is the only way to successful entrepreneurship.

WOMAN-RELATED STRATEGIES

Research in entrepreneurship provides conflicting views on the nature of the strategies used by women entrepreneurs in the start-up phase: while some studies have identified distinct feminine strategies, including a "feminine" style or performance in decision-making processes, problem-solving and leadership, among others, other studies argue that women and men entrepreneurs perform more similarly than differently along the new venture creation, specifically since emerging businesses place similar challenges and difficulties upon entrepreneurs, regardless of their gender, and such conditions require a set of universally accepted responses that have been found promising and facilitate the business's set-up.

(a) "Feminine" strategies originate from social and institutional barriers encountered by women in corporate managerial careers, which result in negative experiences for women as managers; such experiences are considered to plague women in different fields, including entrepreneurship. Accordingly, women dawdle in acquiring strategies that are most valuable to creating a venture that will exhibit a competitive advantage at the outset. Some women will refrain from starting their own businesses as a result of their negative experiences, while others react to the corporate-based, negative experiences by embarking on entrepreneurship to establish a company that suits their needs and goals. Due to the inappropriate managerial experience they have acquired as corporate managers, these women develop strategies ad hoc and employ them through trial-and-error; such strategies reflect their "feminine" style.

Specific woman-based strategies echo women's greater emphasis on their teams, and on non-financial goals: women are more likely than men to see quality as their competitive edge; women rely less on systematic practices, they use intuition and respect "feelings" and "common sense" in decision-making processes; women avoid major risks in their strategic decision-making. In terms of behavior, research has revealed that women entrepreneurs use a less aggressive strategic management style than men; they are easier to persuade in negotiation processes, they are less confident; their leadership strategies are reported in research as "inferior" to men's, addressing mainly their problem-solving abilities when making decisions under risk.

Recent studies have also drawn attention to evidence of the budding female entrepreneurship's contribution to the global economy, by providing more and more employment opportunities and generating trillions of dollars in sales annually. These studies suggest that the differences in the strategies used, if they exist, may not be as disadvantageous to women as they appear. The "feminine" strategies seem to match certain types of entrepreneurial businesses, and the conception that women entrepreneurs are under-equipped with the relevant strategic tools, or make unsuitable strategic decisions, may be misleading. Women confront their perceived weaknesses in strategies used by collaborating with people that complement their knowledge or capabilities, creating an inclusive set of capabilities in their business. By being open to identifying the areas in which they lack the relevant strategies, and embracing the idea of joining forces to accomplish their business's goals by either recruiting people or asking for assistance and consulting with people who may complement their immature capabilities, women allow their businesses to be set up more successfully.

(b) A different body of research claims no significant differences between the genders in strategies used, suggesting that environmental effects and common difficulties that are typical to the start-up phase are blind to gender. Individuals tackling such difficulties respond to them with some characteristic strategies, such as focusing on the marketing, developing the product, identifying the competitors, negotiating with suppliers, recruiting people, getting assistance from experts, etc. Any differences are caused by the entrepreneur's personal traits rather than gender-based characteristics.

At first glance, this might be the ultimate perspective, as it represents an unbiased view that does not stereotype women entrepreneurs. However, its major pitfall is in crystallizing a unidimensional perspective for "best practices" and most promising strategies, by erasing any uniqueness that stems from gender-oriented thinking and behavior. Accepting a unidimensional view imperils diversity and the reciprocal learning that is imperative in the entrepreneurial realm. These strategies are then reflected in women-led businesses' lower performance, including their size, growth rate and profitability (Kalleberg & Leicht, 1991; Loscocco, Robinson, Hall, & Allen, 1991; Powell & Ansic, 1997; Priem & Butler, 2001; Sexton & Bowman-Upton, 1990).

SUMMARY

In this chapter we discussed the process of opportunity-exploitation among women entrepreneurs by delving into the different approaches to opportunities and the different types of exploitation that are pertinent in different phases of the new venture creation.

The factors that enhance opportunity-exploitation are presented and debated in light of the difficulties and hurdles faced by women entrepreneurs while setting up their ventures. Women's self-stratification to the less rewarding entrepreneurial sectors, the social expectations imposed on them that hinder their full dedication to their entrepreneurial undertaking, and male dominance in some entrepreneurial spheres coerce women to adopt a flexible and open approach to opportunity exploitation, i.e., use the various types of opportunity-exploitation and subsequent strategies, with each type matching the specific conditions imposed on the business and the entrepreneur. It is only by using such an approach that women entrepreneurs can generate a competitive advantage at the outset.

The typical hurdles encountered by women entrepreneurs in the start-up phase are illustrated and best practices collected from successful women entrepreneurs around the world are offered and discussed, to encourage women entrepreneurs and pinpoint the ways in which such barriers can be avoided or crossed.

The "feminine" styles of opportunity exploitation are discussed in this chapter by addressing the advantages and disadvantages of emphasizing the gender distinction: while a gendered view may produce a bias, implying the predominance of men's styles, an alternative view that erases the gender differences eliminates diversity in the entrepreneurial context, and thus gender sharing and mutual learning.

This chapter concludes with the message that there is no one single way to exploit opportunities. Accepting women's, as well as men's, approaches to exploiting opportunities, which correspond to their thoughts, needs and intuition, means embracing diversity, encouraging mutual learning, and engendering benefits for both genders.

CASE STUDIES[5]

The following two case studies, contributed by Benoît Leleux and Anouk Lavoie Orlick, IMD, Switzerland, and by Kerstin Ettl, University of Siegen, Germany and Friederike Welter, Jönköping International Business School, Sweden, take us into two exciting worlds, consisting of very different entrepreneurial escapades of women who paved their entrepreneurial way by pursuing different paths of opportunity exploitation.

Marta from Bolivia transformed the family pasta business, based in the fertile plains of Cochabamba, from a local wheat pasta producer to a global exporter of specialized gluten-free pastas. Ines from East Germany worked in the commercial cleaning sector. Through her attentiveness to the environment's needs, and to prevent the skin irritation she was experiencing due to exposure to the chemicals in commercial cleaning powders, she created a natural cleaning powder and obtained a German patent for its composition and manufacturing method.

In these two case studies, alertness to opportunities is intertwined with planning and start-up-based management strategies in two very distinct ecosystems with different challenges and difficulties, but with some common barriers typical to female entrepreneurship.

The authors sensitively sketch the exciting and most inspiring voyages of these women while stressing the role of opportunity-exploitation in subsequent business success.

Coronilla of Bolivia: Leading Change in the Family Business

Benoît Leleux[a] and Anouk Lavoie Orlick[b]
[a]*Stephan Schmidheiny Professor of Entrepreneurship and Finance, IMD, Lausanne, Switzerland;* [b]*IMD, Lausanne, Switzerland*

The case documents first the development and then the strategic repositioning of the Coronilla business in Bolivia. After the patriarch retired from active duty, his daughter Marta, then in her forties, took over running the family pasta business. She quickly discovered that not all was well in the Andes Valley, and the business was soon heading for the wall. Margins had been squeezed for years by cutthroat competition, vertical integration failed to deliver its bounties and regular government mismanagement made bankruptcy a real possibility. After three years of haggling with various family members, Marta had to do something to save the company. And what she embarked upon was one of the most amazing corporate transformations in Bolivia. During the next ten years (to 2009) she transformed the family pasta business based in the fertile plains of Cochabamba (Bolivia) from a local wheat pasta producer to a global exporter of specialized gluten-free pastas and snacks made from ancient Andean grains targeting gluten-intolerant people around the world. Teetering on the edge of bankruptcy in 1999, Coronilla pulled itself out of a desperate market situation with the help of risk capital from a Bolivian investment fund.

During the worst of the crisis, CEO Marta Wille also had a sudden revelation: Devoting your life to a company, especially during turbulent times, can only be justified if the company has a social purpose. When she accepted the leadership of the company in 1997, she set a non-negotiable condition on the shareholders: They would let her run the business as she felt best. She took the reins at a difficult juncture and immediately started to make far-reaching changes. She set up a positive discrimination policy to favor the hiring of women and disabled people in the workforce, and she established Fairtrade relations directly with Andean farming communities to procure raw materials. For her, corporate social responsibility (CSR) was a reason to exist and persist, not a public relations tool.

"We entered a period of intense change. Not only a change in the company but also in myself. I saw that it was feasible to operate a radical strategic shift, that others could be convinced of the benefits brought by change. I felt it very deeply . . . but didn't know how to bring it forward."

(Marta Wille, CEO, Coronilla)

In the colonial-style house built by the Wille family on the edge of the factory lands, Marta Wille sat facing her fellow shareholders in the family business. It was a warm Sunday afternoon in December 2000, and the pasta plant was silent. After an hour of intense and, at times, acrimonious deliberations, which had been preceded by months of informal discussions, they could still not agree on the future of Fideos Coronilla S.A.

Three generations of the German-origin Wille family had built the company in Bolivia's Andes Valley, with Marta the current CEO and two of her grown-up children also involved. Coronilla was Wille, and the Wille family lived for Coronilla; the pride was easy to feel, and so was the family's sense of responsibility toward their employees. But the 4 percent gross profit margin on their pasta sales was no longer even covering operating costs. The Willes were confronted with three alternatives. They could continue operating at a loss and hope that the disastrous conditions in the pasta market would improve rapidly. Cochabamba had been an important center for pasta production, with over twenty companies operating plants but, after a string of bankruptcies, only a handful remained. They could decide to close the company, liquidate its assets and lay off the workers. The third path was to seek external capital to modernize and find a new direction for the company, since pasta was going nowhere fast. Marta had an ambitious turnaround plan, but she would need to combine passion and strategic acumen to convince her father and the other family shareholders . . .

Coronilla and the Wille family

There were two important elements in our education: The German-style energy and drive from our father and the emotional side from our Latin mother. The combination of these two lines produced children with high energy and initiative, which is conducive to an entrepreneurial spirit. All six children were entrepreneurs in their own fields.

(Marta Wille)

Guillermo Wille, a Bolivian of German descent, founded Fideos Coronilla S.A. in 1972, his second start-up after he successfully developed a brewing company in Potosí with his father and brothers. The extended Wille family had since established itself in Bolivia's food and beverage industry. However, a serious heart condition forced Guillermo to move to a lower altitude. Marta's son, Diego Pelaez, explained:

In 1971, when my grandfather was the general manager of the brewery company, he suffered his fifth heart attack in as many years, and it nearly killed him. The problem was that Potosí stood over 4,000 meters above sea level, so he had to leave in the blink of an eye.

Guillermo sold his shares in the brewery and brought his family to Cochabamba.[6] There, he assembled his wife and children, with the exception of those too young to give counsel, to decide what could be done. The city of Cochabamba lies in the fertile Andes valley, between the poor and remote western highlands and the more prosperous and populated eastern lowlands that are rich in natural resources. This important decision was to be taken by the family as a whole. Because Guillermo lacked a university education, most salaried jobs within his reach would not pay well enough to support a wife and six children. But he was a natural entrepreneur, and Cochabamba was the nation's granary. His dream became building an industry around staple foods. His experience of running a brewery had been a success, but his long-term goal was to produce healthy foodstuffs. So he bought land in the valley and endeavored to build a pasta plant.

Building the Pasta Business

In 1972, Cochabamba had seen little urban development outside the city core. The Willes dug a well to have clean water for their plant and paid to have a sewer system installed. From the start, the pasta plant was a family endeavor. The children helped in the well-drilling project and Marta accompanied her father to Argentina to buy their first pasta-making equipment. A year later, the plant started producing entry-grade wheat noodles. Coronilla's main market was lower-income families who bought pasta in bulk. The business took off and Coronilla soon achieved a 20 percent national market share. Quite early, Marta showed a strong interest in the pasta business:

> I was not the eldest child; I had an older sister. But I had always been closely associated with Dad and I took after him in my work methods. I shared his drive and his love of the business.

Catalina, the eldest of the Wille siblings, decided to study nursing. Marta, the second eldest, obtained a degree in accounting and business administration. For his two eldest sons (the third and fourth siblings), Guillermo decided they should pursue their university education in Germany. Guillermo held the German education system in high regard, and it was a link with the family's past. Among his six brothers and sisters, two had married German nationals, with in-laws and later generations scattered today in Bolivia, Germany and even Boston! With all three siblings studying either overseas or at home, only Marta remained closely involved with the business:

> I felt a certain amount of responsibility. My father was 56 at the time. It was no small undertaking for a man approaching his sixties to build and run a plant.

Guillermo was nevertheless a very strong leader for Coronilla. According to Diego Pelaez:

> It's not difficult to guess how the management was when my grandfather was in charge of the company. He was god inside the factory. Everything was made according to his wishes. If he needed to buy something, he just bought it and if he needed to change something, he just changed it.

In 1984, the second Wille son, Gerardo, returned from Germany with a degree in mechanical engineering. He immediately entered the company as managing director with strong support from his father. Guillermo, who stayed on as president and technical advisor to the production manager, saw this as the logical course of action. Gerardo managed the technical aspect of the business and Marta handled the administrative side. About her brother, Marta recalled:

> He was very competent, hard-working and had a very strong drive. It was not easy working with him, but I managed it. We worked side by side for more than ten years.

As with many family businesses, spouses also had an important influence on Coronilla, either through their direct involvement or from the sides. Marta reminisced:

> I decided to marry. I was very much in love. And I remember Dad asking, "Are you absolutely sure you want to get married?" I said, "I love him very much." He said to me, "Maybe that's not enough." As the years went by, I realized he was right. I married Gonzalo Pelaez. He never involved himself in the business. He was very independent. I would venture to say that he always thought I didn't earn enough in the family business, that I worked too hard for the returns. He had a fairly critical stance on my involvement with the firm.

By 1987, Coronilla had tripled its production capacity to 2,000 quintals (100,000 kg) per month. All of a sudden, the company reached a plateau; growth pretty much stopped. On top of that, there had been steady erosion of the gross margins on pasta products since the mid-1980s. The company had to find ways to reduce the cost of production and squeeze savings from the cost of raw materials. In 1989, Gerardo Wille initiated the vertical integration of Coronilla with the purchase of a flour mill. Marta recollected:

> When Gerardo suggested that we buy a mill, for my father it was like knocking on Heaven's door; it brought us one step closer to having a bakery, which was the dream he had cherished from the beginning. He thought that producing bread would be the next logical step, so he gave strong support to Gerardo's project.

The vertical integration accomplished its purpose; it rebuilt Coronilla's profit margins on pasta sales by procuring cheaper flour. This in turn boosted turnover, which resulted in a second phase of growth. However, the renewed prosperity was short-lived. The Bolivian economy entered a period of severe crisis. As a result, the government instituted drastic changes in economic policies. Inflation was skyrocketing, so the government imposed rigid price controls on food production. The administrative burden in the industry became mind-boggling. To source raw materials, food companies had to produce dozens of administrative authorizations and follow Kafkaesque bureaucratic procedures. Once the raw materials were obtained and processed, the plant's output was still strictly monitored and the final products could only be sold to designated buyers at predetermined prices.

Reduced employment in Bolivia's coca sector following a coca plantation eradication program also indirectly deprived Coronilla of an important part of its sales, since many families lost their primary source of income and switched from noodles to less expensive local staple food. Conditions for the pasta industry deteriorated further when the government introduced a value added tax of 13 percent on the food industry.[7] Because of widespread tax-evasion, many of Coronilla's competitors enjoyed an unfair competitive advantage.

To make matters worse, the government introduced an ill-fated preferential scheme to incentivize investments in the food industry. Many investors rushed to take advantage of the incentives, launching industrial bakeries and pasta plants on every street corner. The result was a massive glut of production capacity, which ended up vastly underutilized. Functioning at full capacity, the plants could have met the consumption needs of Bolivia six times over. To top it off, the quality of pasta produced did not meet export standards. As a result of all this, most pasta producers could no longer cover their fixed costs. For some, this was not a real issue anyway because the pasta and milling businesses were only fronts for illicit activities.[8]

For Coronilla, the financial problems were exacerbated by the heavy debt incurred for the purchase of the flour mill. The shaky financial situation brought on a family crisis as well. In November of 1997, Gerardo Wille decided to leave the company. With little time for transition, Marta took the reins. While running the company, Marta searched for a way to reverse Coronilla's fortunes.

Marta Takes Over and Prepares for Strategic Change

Under Marta's leadership, Coronilla set up a small research and development initiative to renew the company's product offering. Marta believed that pasta had no future; it was time to look for other lines of business, more creative and different. Marta's younger sister, Cristina, was the only sibling still living in Cochabamba. Both sisters sat down to discuss Coronilla's predicament and the options before them. Cristina suggested Marta attend a three-month intensive course on strategy and change management offered in Spain. She also offered to oversee the business and take care of Marta's children during her absence, should Marta be accepted. After 18 years of marriage, Marta and her husband had decided to seek a divorce and Gonzalo Pelaez had since moved to Canada. Marta received a positive response from the school, as well as a scholarship to attend the program. Leaving everything behind for an extended period was a great struggle, but Marta remembers it as an incredible experience:

> I read enormous amounts, studied like mad and returned with renewed passion. It was like a shot of adrenaline.

Her main take-away from the program was the feasibility study of her strategic revival plan for Coronilla. Upon her return to Bolivia, she began exploring the new possibilities. She had to find a unique differentiator for Coronilla's future line of pasta. The most promising avenue seemed to be in starting to use local grains instead of the traditional and costly wheat. Coronilla started conducting tests with native Bolivian root vegetables, cereals and fruit. To substitute for wheat pasta production, it produced sample batches of yucca, plantain and even banana flour noodles. Initially, both taste and consistency remained unsatisfactory; in fact, in many instances the resulting pasta was barely edible.

After much digging, and very much by accident, they discovered a gem—quinoa.[9] Marta's nephew was (erroneously) diagnosed with celiac disease. This intestinal disorder, also known as gluten intolerance, is the most common genetic disease in Europe. Those affected must adhere to a 100 percent gluten-free diet, eliminating all food containing wheat, rye or barley. Marta remembered that quinoa, a high-protein grain grown in the Andes as far back as the Inca Empire, did not contain gluten. She decided to use quinoa in the next tests to make pasta for her nephew. The results were excellent, better than any of the previous experiments.

With the help of her two eldest children, Marta started to seek information on quinoa. Diego and Ximena Pelaez, who were attending university at the time, assisted their mother in researching the market. What they found confirmed the existence of a very promising niche market for gluten-free products. Quinoa was a perfect alternative to wheat, and in fact, it had superior nutritional value. Gerardo Wille, though he had resigned from the company, supported the new initiative. A skillful technician, he lent his expertise to adapting the flour mill, the pasta machinery and the processes to quinoa and other non-gluten grains.

Resistance from All Sides

However, the adoption of a new product line met with stiff resistance from Coronilla's staff. The plant workers were accustomed to producing at 100 percent capacity. They disliked stopping the machines to make small test batches of new pastas. After 20 years they were set in their ways and could not fathom the need for change. Coronilla's shareholders were also feeling increasingly impatient with the product tests. The pasta trials had been underway for two years and the company finances looked worse than ever. After a string of unprofitable years, cash reserves had melted away. On top of the severe financial crisis that had affected Bolivia's food producers in the previous years, there was now the issue of falling commodity prices. The price of pasta on the Bolivian market had dropped substantially since 1993 because of contraband pasta imports from neighboring Chile and Argentina. These foreign pasta producers, by avoiding corporate taxes, could undercut the local competition. They had modern equipment (unlike Coronilla, whose machines were 25 years old) and produced in large batches, hence capturing substantial economies of scale. Coronilla's sales were still 100 percent local.

Coronilla was bleeding cash. The machines were still turning out wheat pasta, but keeping the plant in operation became more about "moving money" than "making money." Coronilla needed to keep paying its suppliers and its employees. But the situation was totally untenable. Marta confided:

> My only regret was that I was not quick enough. I allowed the company to wear me down. I wasted time before achieving what I sought because of lack of money, on one hand, and lack of confidence in the people surrounding me on the other. Some of the shareholders withheld their vote of confidence. They argued, "Why are you changing things? Don't change anything. If Dad could run the business successfully, follow his lead and it will continue being a success." They couldn't understand that the business was no longer successful because of changes in the business environment, and that the conditions would not improve.

For staff, a series of drastic job cuts were the first sign of how serious the crisis was. Coronilla's difficulties also had a direct impact on the Wille family. In 1997, Marta's eldest son Diego had started a degree program in music at a German university. He was 18 years old and planning a career as a pianist. Diego received a phone call from his mother, saying she could no longer support his studies abroad. To keep Coronilla afloat and continue the R&D initiative, Marta had invested her own savings. Diego flew home to Bolivia and enrolled in a local university, leaving aside his musical aspirations for more pragmatic studies in management. During the company's deepest crisis, both Diego and his sister Ximena worked informally for Coronilla. Diego explained:

> During those crisis years we were often not able to pay salaries for months at a time. Not only to plant workers but also to ourselves. We did not pay management, the president or the general manager. We used to cook all together with the workers in the garden of the factory and they were able to invite their families to eat lunch and dinner in the factory because we had no money but we had pasta. So we found

creative ways to keep on going, and with those small details, they started to become more committed. They started to understand that we were not just talking about change; we had already changed.

Marta's Turnaround Plan

Coronilla's 1997 annual shareholder meeting always took place right before Christmas, since that was when the Wille family converged in the city for the holidays. It was an informal gathering of the nine shareholders: Guillermo Wille Sr., his children, and a Wille cousin who was regarded almost as a seventh sibling. Though Guillermo, as founder and president, had a decisive influence on the future of the company, the Wille family had always favored open discussion of business issues.

Marta needed their support for the turnaround plan, which would clearly require external financing. Marta was convinced that Coronilla's best chance for survival was to switch from bulk wheat pasta for Bolivian consumption to niche-market pasta and snack exports. Instead of competing solely on price, as the company had done in the first 25 years of its history, Coronilla would be competing on quality, product differentiation and brand value. They would also develop export channels since the new products would likely be too expensive for local markets. Sales of gluten-free products were expanding in Europe and North America to meet the needs of celiac patients and natural foods enthusiasts. This would also somewhat insulate the firm from the chaotic changes in local economic policies.

But seeking external financing meant ceding equity to outsiders. The Wille family would probably have to give up close to half its stake in the company—which was what Marta needed to complete Coronilla's transformation into a gluten-free, organic pasta and snack exporter—to launch a venture they judged risky.

Marta argued that continuing to sell exclusively to the local market was a dead end. It was a particularly complicated time for the Bolivian economy and it was difficult to compete because of the situation with formal and informal markets. Despite the far-reaching program of macroeconomic stabilization and structural reforms undertaken by the government six years earlier, Bolivia's economy was still weak, with GDP growth plunging from 5 percent to 0.4 percent the previous year.[10]

The shareholders mulled over the options. Coronilla employed 134 people. Its debt represented twice its yearly sales. It owned the land and the machinery. On pasta sales, Coronilla made a gross margin of only 3 percent but enjoyed 22 percent to 24 percent market share.

Could Marta get them to support the radical move? Was there a way to maintain the family values in the firm, even with large external shareholders? Would this impact what they saw as the strong social responsibility of the company? The company was family.

Questions for Discussion

1   How would you characterize the existing competitive situation in the pasta business in Bolivia? What would you do to compete effectively and get away from this situation?
2   List the hurdles encountered by Marta in the context of Coronilla's strengths, weaknesses, opportunities and threats in 1997.
3   What kinds of opportunities are open for Marta? Explain.
4   What do you think about the Wille family succession process? What is in place already? What is lacking?
5   How would you rate Marta's interventions? What impresses you most in the story of the strategic repositioning of Coronilla?
6   What are the opportunities associated with raising outside financing for a family firm? How do they correspond to different ecosystems?
7   What do you think of the strategic plan? Can it be implemented? What are the major challenges?

Ines in Germany: From Cleaning Lady toward Holding a World Patent

Kerstin Ettl[a] and Friederike Welter[b]
[a]University of Siegen, Germany; [b]Jönköping International Business School, Sweden

Ines is 54 years old and was born in East Germany, the former GDR.[11] After finishing school, she trained as a retail saleswoman and worked as a general manager of a supermarket. During the collapse of Communism and the fall of the Berlin Wall (the German "Wende") she was on a three-year maternity leave with her second son. The reunification led to high unemployment in East Germany and after her maternity leave Ines was made redundant in her former job. She had to realign herself and started further education, in particular to learn about market economies and business management. After her degree, she worked in the commercial cleaning branch. She was responsible for organizing the cleaning of a big supermarket chain in her region; and this constituted her first contact with the commercial cleaning branch—retrospectively an important time for her to gain sector knowledge and experiences for her own business, although Ines never considered having her own business at that time.

After four years, she again lost her job, this time because of internal restructuring in the company. At the same time, her marriage broke up; and Ines faced a totally different and novel situation both in her private and occupational life. "That was the moment I thought about becoming self-employed for the first time. I thought I can do on my own what I've done before on my job." Even though this thought never crossed her mind before, her then situation, having no job, triggered her to start considering self-employment as an alternative, as in no case did she want to take up a new job, only to become unemployed again within a few years. Like Ines, many women entrepreneurs in East Germany have been pushed into self-employment and entrepreneurship, because they faced the (threat) of unemployment, especially after the "Wende" with its impact on German labour markets (Welter, 2006). Women were often the first to be laid off when the transition started and despite their relatively high level of qualification had a hard time finding new employment. However, as qualified female employment was highly valued and participation in the labor market was a "must" in the former GDR, their propensity to become self-employed might have been facilitated. Thus, from 1991 until 2006, women's entrepreneurship in East Germany increased considerably from 99,000 to 232,000 self-employed women, while in West Germany in 2006, 1,032,000 women were entrepreneurs (Statistisches Bundesamt, 2008). The share of female entrepreneurs has been continually higher in East Germany, amounting to 28.4 percent in 1991 and 32.9 percent today, compared to 25.6 percent and 30.1 percent in West Germany respectively.

So, shortly after her second spell of unemployment, in 1995, Ines started out as self-employed in commercial cleaning. At that time, commercial cleaning was classified as a "crafts" business, which implied that starting a business in this sector was regulated according to the "Handwerksordnung" and business owners had to have a "Meister." Therefore, Ines had to take up the "Meister" training course, and that in parallel to her own work as cleaning lady and caring for her children. Retrospectively, Ines states: "It was simply a horrible time. I was a single mother, self-employed and additionally, I had to go to the 'Meister' school every Friday and Saturday and stay there overnight. My children didn't see much of me; I didn't have enough time for them . . . I was lucky that everything with them went relatively well during this period . . . although sometimes I felt really stressed out." The double burden as entrepreneurs and mothers, to organize both household and family and the business, is often picked out as a central theme in the everyday life of women entrepreneurs in Germany. While the former GDR propagated gender equality in the labor market and fostered worker-mothers through establishing widespread public childcare (West) German society (and politics) are built around the image of women as housewives and mothers (Gottfried & O'Reilly, 2002); and widespread childcare is still a major problem. All this favors a traditional labour distribution where men are the main breadwinners and women are mainly responsible for household and childcare still dominating across Germany (Welter, 2002). Moreover, with reunification, the East German society picked up the dominant discourse. Thus, for women entrepreneurs, entrepreneurial strategies and strategies to handle one's own personal life have to be closely linked to each other.

Shortly after Ines obtained her "Meister" certificate in commercial cleaning, the regulations for her sector changed. Immediately, Ines faced an enormous increase in competition, but she was already well established on the market by then. The supermarket chain in her region she had worked for as an employee continued to be her main client. Looking back at her business development, Ines progressed from taking on much menial labour herself during the first years to concentrating on management tasks in later stages. Word-of-mouth recommendation led to more and more jobs, resulting in Ines hiring more and more employees. Reflecting on business development, Ines muses that firm growth just happened, without her applying a specific strategy for growth or this being one of her business goals: "Somehow, business growth happened bit by bit, all on its own, without me doing much—and of course, I always had a bit of luck!"

Over the years, Ines started noticing that her skin was irritated because of her constant contact with aggressive chemicals: "I started facing severe health problems, and then I began to realize that I cannot carry on like this." Additionally, in 2001, Ines again experienced personal problems because of legal proceedings in relation to her house renovations. In order to divert herself from her personal troubles, she focused on solving her health problems, resulting from the chemical substances in the cleaning products: "I think that this is important for all people who want to be entrepreneurs: If you have problems don't be down in the mouth. You have to do something [. . .]. To divert myself from my private problems, I started to engage with totally different issues and solved my business-related ones." Ines began to experiment with various natural substances, and over the next years, she developed a natural cleaning powder based on beetroot as a renewable raw material. In 2003, she obtained the German patent for her manufacturing method and for the composition of the cleaning powder, the European patent in 2005.

And her success story continues, now also involving one of her children: Ines' eldest son, Christian, studied industrial engineering and management for supply and cleaning engineering, graduating from university in 2005. During his studies, he worked on optimizing the composition of the cleaning powder in collaboration with his university. The cleaning powder is fully based on natural ingredients, and thus an eminent important innovation in the field of biologically based cleaning products. In 2007, Christian received the license to produce and sell the beetroot cleaning powder, which resulted in him setting up a spin-off. Today, Ines buys the powder from her son. Nowadays, the beetroot cleaning powder is available over-the-counter and the media shows great interest. Ines, who developed the powder initially to facilitate her own day-to-day work, never thought that the powder would attract such great attention: "Much of what happened was luck and chance . . . I never would have thought that something could come out of it, that this development could happen. I didn't know that so many people would be interested in my product!"

Ines' goal for her (business) future is focused on remaining in the market. Moreover, although she still wants to offer ecological cleaning, she has an open mind toward new trends in the market: "You just have to be bold and come up with ideas. Ideas will come eventually, and then you also can create new jobs, I am pretty sure of this!" Whenever she had faced problems, she set out to do something totally different, and thus was able to find new solutions in due time.

When asked what motivated her to set up a business, exploit her innovation and consequently grow her business, Ines muses: "I guess it's partly my nature. Once I have started working on something, I am interested in this, I need to know everything and I will simply continue working on this and see it through—especially if these are very practical issues." She characterizes herself as a very practically oriented person, who is better at learning through trial and error than through formal education. "I love to experiment . . . Also, I didn't want to stop where I was at that time, I always have worked on something or the other. So I think I motivated myself a lot." She also pointed to the role of social relations, networks and customers in relation to her business development:

> One learns a lot from others, one hears something and never forgets that issue. Also, much is learning by doing. And of course, many clients come with specific cleaning problems. When they ask how to solve that, I listen to them. It is important to listen to client problems, and to progress from there—this helps to develop the business also.

Ines' own recipe for her success is that business and private life need to be integrated. Only if she herself is satisfied, both with her private and business life, will she consider herself open-minded for new ideas and problems of her clients. Naturally, Ines experienced stressful and bad times during the first years of her entrepreneurial activity during which she did not enjoy her business activities. During that time, she looked for satisfaction in her private life. She also realized early on that, in order to successfully balance business and private life, she needs enough time and space to live her personal life. "I never work through weekends. During the week, agreed, I work a lot, but during weekends I need my personal time."

Moreover, as a divorced mother, she had to solve many problems, bearing responsibility for both family and enterprise on her own. Interestingly, she is of the opinion that this actually was advantageous for her: "My divorce wasn't that bad; I am in fact glad that I got rid of my husband, because otherwise I wouldn't have been able to develop myself as I did. I don't want to be held down by anyone, and he would have slowed me down. . . . As a single mother, I can do as I want—although I'd certainly like a partner who would back me all the way and support my ideas." Today, Ines owns a company with 20 full- and part-time employees. Her business has an annual sales turnover of €300,000–400,000 and earns €60,000–70,000 profit per year. This enables Ines to live comfortably from her business income.

Interestingly, Ines' success story is contradicting the discourse dominating German newspapers, which builds on a rather old-fashioned image of women's entrepreneurship, implicitly fostering traditional role models (Welter *et al.*, 2006) and thereby possibly preventing more women from entering entrepreneurship. Moreover, Ines also contradicts a commonly held assumption in entrepreneurship research, namely that necessity-driven entrepreneurs will not contribute to economic development and growth in the long run. Instead, her story illustrates and demonstrates her ability to learn, take up and exploit opportunities and to grow her business from humble beginnings toward one of the more innovative companies in her sector.

Questions for Discussion

1   Does Ines's experience strengthen or contradict the commonly held assumption about women's self-stratification in entrepreneurship? How?

2   List the opportunities that surround Ines; explain how these opportunities are manifested.

3   Which types of opportunity exploitation were exhibited by Ines? Could you explain her decision to choose these particular types?

4   List the direct and indirect hurdles Ines faced; explain in what sense they are hurdles.

5   How did Ines cope with the hurdles she faced along her course of action? Explain her approach.

6   You are hired to assist Ines in developing her business. Ines characterizes herself as a practical person, using trial and error and favoring action over formal learning. What types of strategies would you recommend that she implement?

Notes

1   Adapted from A. Einstein (1988). *Ideas and Opinions*. New York, NY: Bonanza Books, Crown Publishing Co., reprint 1988.

2   At Examiner.com, http://www.examiner.com/small-business-in-arlington/a-woman-entrepreneur-s-success-story

3   At http://www.razoss.com/

4   At http://www.whitesmoke.com/

5   The author(s) of the case studies are fully and solely responsible for their content, phrasing consistency and flow, terminology, English proofing and reference lists.

6   Cochabamba has a relatively low altitude of about 2,500 meters, compared to Potosí's altitude of more than 4,000 meters.

7   Previously, products related to flour, noodles and staple foods had been exempt from tax.

8   Bolivia was the third-largest grower of coca in the world and businesses were used as cover for money laundering. (Source: Crime and Narcotics Center. Central Intelligence Agency, USA.)

9 Quinoa (from Quechua *kinwa*), is a species of goosefoot (*Chenopodium*), a grain-like crop grown primarily for its edible seeds. Quinoa is not *stricto sensu* a true cereal, or grain, but a chenopod, a close relative of beets, spinach and tumbleweeds. Its leaves are also eaten as a leaf vegetable, much like amaranth.

10 Bolivia's Real GDP in 1999 was US$ 8.19 billion compared with $8.16 billion in 1998. Datamonitor, July 2007. Reference code: DMER043.

11 The GDR (German Democratic Republic) was the communist state established in 1949 in the soviet zone of Germany. With German reunification in October 1990 all of East Germany was integrated into the Federal Republic of Germany.

Case References

Gottfried, H. and O'Reilly, J. (2002). Der Geschlechtervertrag in Deutschland und Japan: Die Schwäche eines starken Ernährermodells. In K. Gottschall & B. Pfau-Effinger (Eds.), *Zukunft der Arbeit und Geschlecht: Diskurse, Entwicklungspfade und Reformoptionen im internationalen Vergleich* (pp. 29–57). Opladen, Leske & Budrich.

Statistisches Bundesamt (2008). Gendermonitor Existenzgründung 2006 [Gender monitor Nascent Entrepreneurship 2006]. Wiesbaden.

Welter, F. (2002). The environment for female entrepreneurship in Germany. *Journal of Small Business and Enterprise Development, 11*(2), 212–221.

Welter, F. (2006). Women's entrepreneurship in Germany: Progress in a still Traditional Environment. In C.G. Brush, N. Carter, E.J. Gatewood, P.G. Greene, & M. Hart (Eds.), *Growth oriented women entrepreneurs and their businesses: A global research perspective* (pp. 128–153). Cheltenham, UK: Edward Elgar.

Welter, F., Kolb, S., Ettl, K., & Achtenhagen, L. (2006). *Süßes Leben mit bitteren Noten: Unternehmerinnen und Gründerinnen in der deutschen Presse—eine diskursanalytische Betrachtung.* Düsseldorf.

10 Financing the New Venture

The Untapped Perspective in Female Entrepreneurship

Chapter Objectives

- Outlining the multifaceted process of financing the new venture in the female realm;
- Drawing upon the origins and impact of capital acquisition;
- Understanding the large scope of the process of raising capital, including goal setting, the business structure and the entrepreneur's growth aspirations, among others;
- Identifying the sources of the venture's capital acquisition, and women entrepreneurs' proclivity for specific funding sources;
- Depicting women's financial strategies in raising capital at the new venture creation stages; discussing the gender differences in capital acquisition for their ventures;
- Emphasizing the role of networking in women's capital acquisition;
- Delving into best practices of successful female entrepreneurs' funding strategies;
- Advancing the debate on women's multifaceted interactions with investors to center stage.

Funding of the new venture constitutes one of the major difficulties tackled by entrepreneurs, and these difficulties are even more pronounced among women entrepreneurs who encounter additional barriers, including stereotyping of women's ability to raise capital for their business, a history of loan and investment refusals for women-led businesses, and a lack of relevant education and experience in this area.

This chapter focuses on the process of raising capital for the new venture. We examine several aspects of female capital acquisition and provide insights into women entrepreneurs' strategies to raise initial capital, including a categorization of the different sources for financing a new venture, and women entrepreneurs' preferences among these sources.

The hurdles encountered by women as entrepreneurs and as investors are presented and discussed, e.g., lack of relevant networking, difficulties in accessing the "boys' clubs," discriminatory conditions offered for loans or investments to women-led ventures, limited access to growth and recurring financing. Women's "role" in reproducing their disadvantaged state in generating capital for their new ventures is discussed.

The chapter concludes with best practices used by successful women entrepreneurs to fund their businesses. Case studies and an at-a-glance case illustrate the discussed topics by exposing the different aspects through different entrepreneurial experiences.

Most entrepreneurial ventures start from scratch and need to raise capital to survive and develop. The new venture creation phase sets various challenges and difficulties for entrepreneurs, a main, and apparently most daunting one, being the process of acquiring business capital. This process usually starts in the very early stages, when the venture has still not proven recurrent achievements or vigorous business processes which can sometimes guarantee its future success, or even promise that the venture will accomplish its goals. In many cases, a formal, registered business still does not exist; rather, money is sought for an idea in the seed phase, when it is still risky and uncertain. This is one of the reasons that raising capital in the early stages is considered an *art* which can be significantly improved by learning from one's own experiences, professionals' or experienced people's advice and mentorship, among others.

WHAT DOES THE FINANCIAL PROCESS ENTAIL?

Raising capital is a multifaceted process that encompasses much more than the financial aspects of the business. It originates from financial need, drawn from the business's goals and available resources, the entrepreneur's growth aspirations, external expectations, etc. Subsequently, this process affects different aspects inside the venture, such as its structure, existing and potential processes, relationships inside and outside the venture and growth rate, while the impact of the external environment on this process as well as the consequent effects of this process are also prevalent. For example, an Australian entrepreneurial business in the seed stage, for the production of diet meals, raised a large amount of capital and penetrated the local market; the capital acquisition not only affected the business's marketing concept, product pricing and personal behaviors and dynamics, but also raised community awareness of healthy food and well-being; one manager from a nearby sports club reported that she started renovations in the club because people in the region had become more aware of their health and diet and were interested in different means of becoming healthy, thin and good-looking. Figure 10.1 demonstrates this dynamic.

Furthermore, the process of raising capital requires abilities beyond financial knowledge or expertise, e.g., strategic management, business planning, negotiation expertise, presentation and communication proficiency, as well as the ability and sensitivity to understand people. Similarly, management of the financial aspects is also not financial per se: it includes identifying the relevant financial sources, choosing a source that fits the new venture's capital needs, acknowledging the advantages and disadvantages of the chosen sources for the business's short and long term, securing the business's and lenders' money, managing the relationships with the lenders and financial partners (e.g. uncovering mutual expectations, becoming familiar with the people behind the financial bodies to craft a route to personalized, long-term, relationships, truthful communication), leveraging the capital to implement the business's goals, prioritizing the functions and tasks to be developed with the money obtained, identifying cutting-edge practices that should be incorporated into the business when the capital has been obtained, among others.

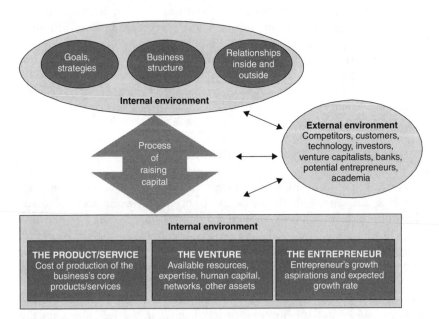

Figure 10.1 The Origins and Impact of Capital Acquisition.

The management of such varied processes, the use of different abilities and preparing for potential effects on different aspects inside and outside the venture, all demonstrate that raising capital is much more than managing the financial aspect of the business. History shows entrepreneurs who started businesses with a sufficient amount of capital and failed, as well as those who started from scratch and succeeded; this implies that while capital is essential for entrepreneurial businesses in the early stages, it does not function in a void; rather, it is embedded in the business's ability to adjust to the environment's demands and is maneuvered by the main interests of the business, the entrepreneur, the financial partners and the shareholders.

SEEKING CAPITAL: IS THERE A WOMAN'S WAY?

The need to identify the abilities and practices associated with raising capital is even more pronounced in the female entrepreneurial realm. Women often start their new ventures at a disadvantage compared to men, e.g., with less capital, less access to debt financing, being broadly regarded as possessing less financial savvy to manage high-growth ventures, limited experience in entrepreneurship or financing businesses, and less knowledge in financial aspects. Therefore, the need to use abilities and practices "that work" is crucial for women entrepreneurs in the new venture creation process.

Generally, the new venture creation is characterized as a financial "rat race" period: entrepreneurs encounter a basically impossible situation in which they must search for financial resources that will enable developing and operating their business, and concurrently they must substantiate their business's development to prove its continual progress to potential financial partners. Hence, they must work intensively to develop the business's products and services, accumulate a client base, claim market space, and establish technology, among others. Their business's development depends on acquisition of capital, which is time-consuming (e.g., outlining the financial sources, analyzing their relevance to the respective business goals, locating potential investors, studying these investors' interests, preparing for presentations, etc.), while in turn, acquisition of capital depends on continual development and palpable progress in the business processes as well as proven achievements, which again, are time-consuming (e.g., research and development, trial and error, testing the concepts and adjusting). The process is like a "zero-sum" situation involving time, priorities and capital. In women's realm, because they start their ventures with lower capital, managing this zero-sum-type process seems out of reach, thus entailing prompt acquisition of capital to enable them to operate their ventures. Yet, women are more reluctant to search for external capital. The zero-sum cycle escalates, but at the same time women use strategies that enable them to endure this phase.

Raising money involves several unwritten "rules," which are followed by a great many entrepreneurs: e.g., preparing a comprehensive and detailed business plan, outlining and analyzing the advantages and disadvantages of different financial resources, presenting the business's concept to potential lenders/investors simply and clearly. Yet research shows that while women entrepreneurs follow these "rules," they raise significantly less capital than their male counterparts, are hindered in receiving equity investments, receive less favorable credit terms, are approved for loans under poorer conditions than men; basically, when lenders consider the ideal type of successful entrepreneur, they conjure up a male profile, and therefore prefer collaborating with male, not female entrepreneurs. Interestingly, investors' reported satisfaction with their collaborations with female entrepreneurs, when they exist, is high due to women's stronger ability to secure the lenders'/investors' money and their calculated, risk-averse approach with the obtained money.

Potential sources of capital are:

- personal savings
- banks and merchant banks
- venture capital (VC) funds
- government funding programs
- selling existing products and services (even if only partially developed)
- business angels
- capital markets
- factoring
- leasing
- existing shareholder and director funds
- family and friends.

Debt Loans and Equity

Entrepreneurs manage the capital-acquisition process by balancing equity and debt to ensure that the funding sources fit the venture's short- and long-term goals and available resources. For example, banks demand interest payments and capital repayments based on entrepreneurs' assets (i.e., the business's assets, the shareholders' assets, etc.); in the case of failure, the bank has the power to declare bankruptcy and the entrepreneur is responsible for repaying the borrowed money. The bank is usually less interested in managing the new venture and gives the entrepreneur space to plan and implement his/her goals and practices, yet, it does not take on the risks of failure, or compensate the new venture for poor performance; in such cases, the new venture has to cover its losses and repay the bank loan.

On the other hand, equity investors take on the risk of the new venture's failing, such that the new venture is not required to pay back any money to investors in cases of failure or poor performance, but investors are "hands-on" and active in piloting the new venture according to their interests and the strategies they consider most suitable. The risk for entrepreneurs is that this can result in transformation of the business's original goals, because the investors decided to nurture different ones. Similarly, the entrepreneur incurs other risks, such as replacement of the team members, even replacement of their own position as founder/entrepreneur by professionals; dramatic changes in marketing strategy and finance management; changes in product development, raw materials used, relationship with the community, etc. In general terms, investors' entrance into a new venture may turn it upside down in the long run. In addition, these investment organizations are the main beneficiary of the new venture's success from their equity stake; frequently, the entrepreneur is left with limited equity or share options when the business succeeds.

For example, a new web-based company for trading vintage clothes using a new concept, founded by two women from Italy in their thirties, needed a massive investment to develop its services. A venture capital (VC) company from the US was impressed by the new venture concept: they funded it with cash money and provided management expertise; at the same time, the VC company took some degree of governance authority over the web-based venture as part of their investment contract by claiming seats on the board of directors. In 2008, during the economic crisis, the web-based venture needed more cash money, which was immediately provided by the VC company in exchange for more control, more participation on the board of directors, and higher equity shares. In finalizing the contract agreement, a dispute emerged between the founders and the VC representatives on the matter of expansion to other products such as antiques and vintage furniture. As a result, the VC company recommended dismissing one of the founders, who was the CEO of the venture, and moving the other founder, the vice CEO, to a consulting position. After a few weeks, the web-based venture had considerably changed its concept and business model, and both founders found themselves out of their own business.

The aim of VC and other investment companies is to gain a large and immediate profit based on the growth and success of the funded new venture. Thus the initial investment criteria are used to select which new venture to fund—draw on its growth potential, its available assets, and the profile of its entrepreneur(s) and management team, including their growth aspirations, entrepreneurial spirit, professional approach, educational and employment background. The degree to which the VC company is engaged in the new venture depends on the new venture's performance in meeting the investors' expectations.

The entrepreneur should strive for balance between the sources of capital obtained, to avoid exposing the new venture to excessively high borrowing, but also to avoid unnecessarily diluting the share capital, as this reduces the entrepreneur's power, control, and decision-making authority.

Due to women's lack of, or lesser experience in financing new ventures and their history of refusals and disappointments from funding companies, women entrepreneurs should be more attentive to carefully choosing the financial sources that promise to implement both short- and long-term goals. Women entrepreneurs should carefully inspect each source, the conditions offered, its advantages and disadvantages for their new ventures. They might ask entrepreneurs who have been using such funding sources for their insights, and brainstorm with professionals on the potential benefits and risks that each funding source entails. For example, women may attract equity capital and be self-assured in their ability to implement their business's short-term goals by using the cash money to advance their business, e.g., by hiring experts, purchasing equipment, obtaining professional counseling. However, they should be aware of the conditions they have agreed upon with the investment companies to secure their long-term goals, e.g., fairness in distribution of the business's equity shares, transparency in the "trade-off" between funds and seats on the board of directors, etc.

Determining a funding source is a long-term engagement which goes beyond the financial aspect: it involves relationships, interests, ongoing negotiations, strategies and practices. Mainly, such engagement involves a constant creative and open-minded approach, in which any potential dispute or disagreement will be solved creatively and positively. Studies reveal that women entrepreneurs are more likely to agree with their investors'/lenders' changing demands and will generally act more as followers than leaders in their relationships with their business's investors/lenders, relative to their male counterparts. Studies show that women entrepreneurs tend to respond to their investors'/lenders' expectations by conforming to their changing demands. This, however, can result in being liked but not respected; as in entrepreneurship, a conformist approach may be interpreted as an inability to make tough decisions. Women should adopt a more self-promoting and self-confident approach and be determined in piloting the venture toward its goals.

In short, women entrepreneurs should trust their instincts and manage their relationships with their business's investors/lenders in line with their vision and goals (Alsos & Kolvereid, 1998; Brush, Carter, Gatewood, Greene, & Hart, 2001, 2002b; Greene, Brush, Hart, & Saparito, 2001; Haines, Orser, & Riding, 1999; Leitch & Hill, 2006; Wallsten, 2000).

WOMEN AND CAPITAL ACQUISITION

Obtaining financial support is a universal requirement for both female and male entrepreneurs to convert ideas into products and services. Studies in female entrepreneurship reveal that women favor types of capital support that differ from those men tend to use. For example, women entrepreneurs tend to use their personal savings first to create a new venture, rather than approach external sources of financing. They favor generating money from internal sources, such as by selling their business's products and/or services, outsourcing their business's services, bartering services for services. Women also approach informal rather than formal sources, such as family members and friends.

Studies confirm that women require smaller amounts of capital to create their new ventures, compared to men. They base their capital-acquisition decisions on informal and restricted sources of information, loosely coupled with the financial market's limitless information. Women entrepreneurs are less likely to apply for loans, credit or debt capital to finance their businesses in its early stages. Furthermore, women are more likely to put off their decisions on the best capital sources to the last minute, and such financial management may affect the suitability of their chosen financial sources. For example, if time is a main constraint, then female entrepreneurs will choose the most available source rather than the most suitable one.

Looking from the market functioning side, there is a significant inequality between the proportion of women-led businesses and the proportion of those that have obtained equity capital. The share of equity invested in women-led businesses is low; there is gender inequality in the credit decision-making process, such that loan officers evaluate female and male applicants not just on relevant criteria, but also on the basis of their own gender-based perceptions which have been imbued with gender socialization processes. As such, women are considered unqualified to manage growth-oriented businesses, or are suspected of being liable to neglect the business for family issues, and they are therefore less commonly approved for loans, credit and capital support from formal sources relative to men.

Research in entrepreneurship has offered different insights into why there are still relatively few venture-funded companies led by women, such as: investing and lending bodies' higher rates of refusals of women entrepreneurs' capital requests at the early stages of the new venture; women's disappointing experiences in such matters, termed "discouraged borrowers" in the research, i.e., trustworthy borrowers who avoid applying for loans because they feel that they will be rejected; the less favorable conditions offered to women in terms for loans and investments, along with women's lower self-confidence in their ability to effectively manage the capital-acquisition process, resulting in lower capital investments and poorer loan conditions and/or equity share distribution (Alsos, Isaksen, & Ljungren, 2006; Carter, Shaw, Lam, & Wilson, 2007; Cavalluzzo, Cavalluzzo, & Wolken, 2002; O'Gorman & Terjesen, 2006; Orser, Riding, & Manley, 2006).

Concurrently, there is a growing body of research in female entrepreneurship that has introduced different aspects in female capital acquisition, proving minimal gender differences in this area by attempting to dispel some prevailing gender-based perceptions of women entrepreneurs' lower ability to acquire funds for their new ventures. Based on a number of studies, women and men entrepreneurs have been found to be alike in raising capital, confirming that more similarities than dissimilarities exist between the genders, including in the genders' perceptions of the difficulty in obtaining financing, business growth aspirations, or management of networks (Cavalluzzo & Cavalluzzo, 1998; Kon & Storey, 2003; Menzies, Diochon, & Gasse, 2004).

Of the influential publications in this new area, the Diana project published *Women Business Owners and Equity Capital: The Myths Dispelled*[1] (Brush, Carter, Gatewood, Green, & Hart, 2002b), which offers insightful empirically based explanations that systematically dispel myths rooted in women's financial strategies, including women's lower aspirations to own high-growth businesses, lack of relevant educational background and experience to manage their business's finances efficiently, lack of relevant networks to access external financial sources, lack of financial ability, know-how and knowledge, as well as business planning and choices of industry sectors that are unattractive to venture capitalists, among others (Gatewood, Brush, Carter, Greene, & Hart, 2009; Gatewood, Shaver, & Gartner, 1995). In line with these studies, it is probable that the differences between the genders are manifested in structure rather than content, specifically: while they may perceive similar sources of financing as the best fit for their new venture's needs, they might use them at different business stages, for different purposes (e.g., marketing, technological developments, recruitment of experts), prioritize the sources' feasibility differently, etc.

Figure 10.2 illustrates the main sources of financing a business from the female perspective.

Women tend to delay the use of external finances to the more advanced business stages, when they are more confident of the robustness, feasibility and potential of their business concept and its implementation. Women are less likely to engage in sources involving other people's money (OPM), unless they have already proven that their business is able to repay the loan or generate a profit for its financial partners.

However, while the entrepreneurial market is vibrant and dynamic, depending only on their personal savings might endanger the business's penetration into the market, its reputation and continual development. Male-led entrepreneurial businesses tend to attract external capital, and men entrepreneurs use varied and more sophisticated money-raising strategies, as well as higher amounts of money to develop their new ventures. As a result, they can grow their businesses from an earlier stage. Women-led businesses use more conservative funding strategies, applying funding at

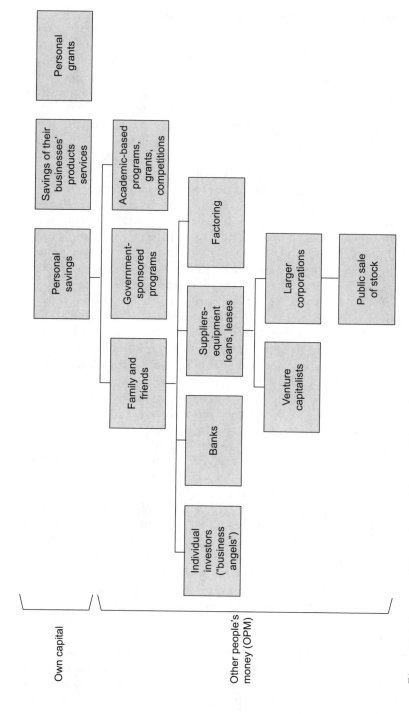

Figure 10.2 Sources of Financing the Venture: Women's Outlook.

more advanced stages in relatively limited amounts, and their business's development therefore lags behind.

While the dynamics of entrepreneurial businesses can fluctuate, those processes set up in the early stages of the new venture are fixed in the shareholders' minds, and therefore crucial to the business's long-term development. In the early stages, entrepreneurs can more easily sculpt the business's processes, activities and strategies, including product price or form; however, attempting to develop such processes in the more developed business stages means attempting to change the shareholders' image of the business. Thus the challenge becomes not only selling the business's products/services but selling a different concept. For example, it took Amazon.com a long time to profit from offering their customers furniture or beauty products; customers were used to purchasing only books, because this was Amazon's initial business model. Moreover, introducing novelty or changing the existing processes at the advanced stages is costly; therefore, the capital acquired in the early stages of the new venture process is critical to boosting the development and penetration of the new venture; delaying business development results in lagging behind at these stages, and this will be further echoed in the more advanced stages, as well as in the difficulty in generating a competitive advantage relative to other companies in the market (Carter & Rosa, 1998; Coleman, 2000, 2002a; Coleman & Carsky, 1996; Constantinidis, Cornet, & Asandei, 2006; Degryse & van Cayseele, 2000; Fabowale, Orser, & Riding, 1995).

Sylvie Hutchison, a 37-year-old woman from Missouri, USA, wanted to start an after-school program for young children aimed at preparing kindergarten children for school. As a teacher in the public school system for more than ten years, she had some personal savings which she assigned for her new venture. She rented a location, purchased some equipment and educational tools and was about to search for teachers, when she ran out of money for her new venture. People advised her to "start big," as an after-school chain, in order to generate a competitive advantage over the multiple existing public and private undertakings providing similar services. However, this required raising a large amount of capital from external sources, as well as taking loans from banks, applying to venture capitalists, submitting proposals for grants and competing in local competitions for SMEs. Hutchison was very reluctant to approach external financing sources, so she decided to start her business with the available resources, i.e., modestly, as a home-based business, by selling her educational services, and saving the money to develop the after-school chain in a year. She had to renounce the place she had rented and with the few educational tools she purchased, she started the home-based educational service for young children. She anticipated that this first phase, the home-based entrepreneurial business, would assist her in establishing a reputation and would facilitate her future business's penetration into the market. However, a year later, when she was out of alternatives and she approached banks and investment companies to raise money for the after-school chain, she was refused for loans, and investment bodies did not take her calls. One officer at the bank told her: "You are great in providing home services but you did not prove your ability to manage a national chain, we cannot take the risk of lending you money from our bank . . ." Hutchison ended up partnering with her sister in a beauty-products franchise; but she is still dreaming of her after-school chain.

Hutchison's experience raises different questions about the decisions to be taken when searching for financial sources, e.g., were there any guarantees that by raising capital from her own abilities at the early stages she could have developed the after-school chain in the future? Was her reputation as a successful home teacher an impediment to her future plans? Should any business start "big," so as not to risk its future success? Above all, do the existing early-stage financial sources suit women entrepreneurs' approach to the new venture creation, or is there a need to develop different alternatives?

Figure 10.3 introduces different classifications of capital acquisition for new ventures which may assist in identifying the preferred financial sources; for example, using money from individuals rather than from bodies; preferring to have resources, such as equipment or expertise, rather than "real" money. As such, women have different alternatives from which to choose their financial source, rather than restricting their use to a few sources.

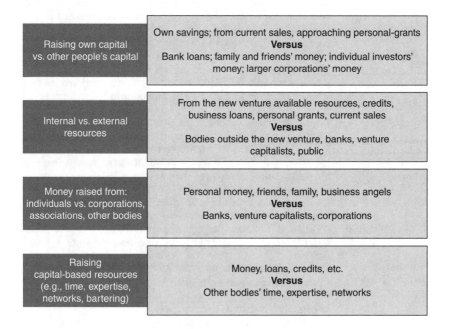

Figure 10.3 Different Classifications for Financing the New Venture.

THE REASONS THAT WOMEN AND MEN USE DIFFERENT STRATEGIES TO RAISE INITIAL CAPITAL

The financing "issue" is, or is perceived as, particularly difficult for women entrepreneurs: most studies and statistics consistently show that the hurdles and barriers faced by women entrepreneurs in financing their new ventures are more pronounced than among their male counterparts, e.g., in raising external financing, being approved for bank loans, taking part in the relevant financial-based networks, in the conditions obtained in equity shares, stock offers, supplier credit facilities, among others (Brush, Carter, Gatewood, Greene, & Hart, 2001; Carter, 2000; Carter & Rosa, 1998; Carter *et al.*, 2007; Hisrich & Özturk, 1999; Marlow & Patton, 2005).

Different explanations have been proposed for the gender differences in raising capital in the new venture creation stages, presented in four main groups in the Table 10.1.

Table 10.1 Gender Differences in Raising Capital in the New Venture Creation Stages

Structural factors	• *The business's potential*—women usually operate businesses in lower-potential-growth sectors of industry such as retail, educational services and industries, and caretaking; these sectors are thought to include less sophisticated practices, to use limited levels of high technology for the process of operating the business or its products, and in general, to offer limited potential for profit and growth, because the markets for these sectors are mostly saturated.
	Women-led entrepreneurial businesses are generally perceived as being of modest growth relatively to men's, and thus less attractive to banks, potential creditors and investors who are motivated by having their loans returned on time or by profiting significantly from financing these ventures.
	• *Women entrepreneurs' aspirations to grow*—some studies stress that relative to men, women's aspirations for their business's growth are moderate; accordingly, their motivations to innovate, enter new markets, venture into new areas, expand into global markets, enlarge their customer base, product or service lines are low. They therefore ask for significantly less initial capital for their new ventures.
	• *Networking*—while women's communication proficiency is considered high, their capital-oriented networking processes lag behind. Use of their networks for concrete financial purposes is generally less common or intense among women entrepreneurs. Women tend to allocate less time to initiating and developing networking strategies that will enable easier access to financial sources, either formally or informally, for example with officers and representatives directly affiliated to banks, investment firms, venture capitalists, governmental funding bodies (direct

access), or to contacts who are well networked and willing to introduce women to these financial sources, as well as facilitate their access to acquiring capital, by supporting them, connecting them with top decision-making figures, etc.

Women are significantly less involved and less present in networking-related events, e.g., attending conferences, fairs, meetings, participating on boards of directors, initiating finance-related events related to financial people from the community, etc.

Women's limited participation in networks relevant to financing the new venture has a domino effect on potential women entrepreneurs, women entrepreneurs who are considering approaching external funding sources, etc., because they can be discouraged from the quality of their network with other women entrepreneurs. Undertakings such as the successful Springboard Enterprises,[1] women in technology Meetup groups,[2] among many others, are most valuable for women entrepreneurs (Boden & Nucci, 2000; Carter & Allen, 1997; Kallenberg & Leicht, 1991).

Demand for funding

- *Sources of capital*—women more often use financial sources that are more limited in providing growth and development; for example, women prefer raising money from individuals than from organizations; they are more likely to use informal rather than formal services; they use their own savings rather than OPM and prefer exchange services such as bartering, or use factoring and leasing rather than raising real money. Such financial sources are mainly unsophisticated financing practices, and provide a limited amount of capital; this is subsequently echoed in the business's growth potential.
- *Management of their business's financial sources*—women are considered risk-averse in managing the business and its financial aspects; they use substantially less capital in the early stages of the new venture than do men; they select more conservative financial alternatives, avoid investments, and are more likely to avoid bank loans, whereas once they use a loan, they tend to reduce it and then are worried about paying it back, and they therefore hardly leverage this money for growth-oriented practices.
- *Terms of capital raising*—women tend to obtain loans and credit under poorer terms than men; they are required to put up more security capital than men; they are offered credit at higher interest rates, investors ask for higher equity shares and stock options in women-led businesses than in men-led businesses; this could be due to either structural factors of their businesses, e.g., their smaller size, sector of industry, or a lack of history in relationships with financial institutions which lowers their self-confidence to negotiate or even refuse the offers that do not meet their expectations.

Due to their basic risk reluctance, women avoid seeking external financing (Arenius & Autio, 2006; Bennet & Dann, 2000; Coleman & Robb, 2009; Watson, 2000).

(Continued overleaf)

Table 10.1 Continued

Feminine style in financing	• *Negotiation style*—the genders employ different communication styles which are echoed in their negotiations with officials and representatives of formal financing sources, who are mainly men; women's style, in contrast to men's, is characterized as indirect, less focused on a specific topic and encompassing various ideas simultaneously. Therefore, negotiating with men would appear to exemplify the concept of "Men are from Mars, Women are from Venus".[3.] Moreover, due to the obvious differences in hierarchy in the negotiation situation (i.e., women are asking for money and men are selecting the applicants), women entrepreneurs tend to accept offers and avoid longer negotiations; some may fear that the latter will reduce their odds of being approved for capital and compromise in order to receive the funding.
	• *History of refusals*—capital-acquisition dynamics are also affected by prior experiences and women's perceived chances of breaking through prior hurdles. Within the prevalent male-dominated investor communities where women have endured refusals from representatives of formal financing sources, their reaction to raising capital from external sources is either avoidance, or in deep contrast, acceptance of any offer received by these sources, probably because women feel fortunate to be heard by banks and investing companies' representatives, regardless of the offer they get. Research on gender reveals that women's history of raising funds effects gender differences in negotiations, e.g., differences in negotiation style, propensity to negotiate, negotiation for oneself (women negotiate well for others but not for themselves), and the content of the negotiation, for example, women tend to avoid negotiations on topics related to money, improving their condition or their stock shares, etc. (Babcock & Laschever, 2003; Kolb & Williams, 2003; Putnam & Kolb, 2000).
	• *Self-confidence and financing*—women have lower self-confidence in managing an effective, profitable capital acquisition for their businesses relative to men; they assess their knowledge in this area as limited, as well as their experience, access to information and general ability to manage this multifaceted process.
	• *Delegating financial matters*—women tend to delegate the management of their venture's financial needs to others, mainly men, who are trusted family members, friends, or professionals. Similarly, women tend to delegate the negotiations on capital acquisition for their new ventures to their male lawyers, partners and even spouses or other family members.
	• *Financing by selling*—another style typical to women entrepreneurs is using internal resources; women favor financing their businesses from internal and their own means; as such, they are more motivated to build a viable client base to sell their products/services, even if these are only partially developed, and to get the business to a break-even financial status, and even to positive profitability.

Experience,
education,
networks and
mentoring

- *The art of financing the new venture*—locating the most suitable financial source is multifaceted; it requires a thorough understanding of the business's potential, its added value, competitive advantage and the market's current and future trends. Concurrently, it requires knowing the advantages and disadvantages of the source of capital, in both the short and long term, with respect to the meaning of the partnership, of sharing management and control with the investors, of losing parts of their shares, among others. This is a learned or acquired art that must be experienced, taught or advised, in order to get the most out of it. The situation in financing entrepreneurial businesses is uncertain, potentially unstable and may fluctuate, and entrepreneurs should pilot and maneuver this situation strategically, carefully yet creatively in ways that will induce profits and success.

  Women entrepreneurs are less experienced in founding and managing the financial aspects of the entrepreneurial business; women's education is also irrelevant to financing their businesses; their choices of training and mentoring are less relevant to financing their ventures and in general, they are at a disadvantage in operating the art of financing.

Stereotyping
and
discrimination

- *Country context*—country context can be manifested in several aspects: some explanations for women's financing preferences and styles emanate from their national cultures, gendered expectations and social norms with respect to their involvement in male-dominated matters, such as finance, banks, negotiations with investors, etc.

  Other explanations refer to the effects of the country context on push/pull entrepreneurship among women at the country level and its subsequent impact on perceptions of women as successful entrepreneurs; specifically, women that were pushed to entrepreneurship and start businesses with lower potential growth capabilities, face stereotyping by banks and potential loaners, regardless of the business's performance or women's growth aspirations.

- *Gendered discrimination*—different studies show that women entrepreneurs are discriminated against by banks and investment institutions. These studies explain this phenomenon by the male dominance in the investment and banking community, and men's struggle to reproduce their dominance by impeding women's access to external sources of capital. In some national cultures, stereotyping of women entrepreneurs still prevails; some others may perceive successful women as a social and domestic threat that should be controlled by not financing women-led ventures and "returning" women to their main social role, i.e. taking care of the family and household duties (Haynes & Haynes, 1999).

Notes:

[1] At http://www.springboardenterprises.org/

[2] At http://witi.meetup.com/

[3] Adapted from the title of the book: Gray, J. *Men Are from Mars, Women Are from Venus.* Harper Collins 1992.

NETWORKS GENIUS: THE ROLE OF NETWORKING IN CAPITAL ACQUISITION

Networking is a natural social process: people interrelate, chat, recommend each other—these are the basic and most common social interactions among people. The concept of networking draws on the premise that people who are attracted to each other and network possess similar characteristics, share mutual beliefs and attitudes, and have stronger ties and mutual trust.

While networking seems to be a natural social process, its practical roles, including facilitating capital acquisition for new ventures, have attracted the interest of scholars and practitioners in entrepreneurship for the last few decades. One fundamental proposition in social capital theory and networking is that a network provides access to resources, assets and sources of information, capital, social capital, etc. It is therefore considered a valuable business asset which can increase competitive advantages and is significant in the development of different business aspects, e.g., growth rate, innovation rate, recruitment of experts; largely, the process of networking strongly promotes the new venture.

Today, social networks are prosperous. Entrepreneurs are connected through Facebook, LinkedIn and Twitter, as well as through more substantial networks where they meet their contacts regularly (e.g., their staff members, people meeting on a regular basis for events, conferences, associations, boards of directors of other companies), or through abstract, non-web-based networks (e.g., members from their previous workplaces, alumni, friends from their childhood), which may seem loosely tied, yet are most advantageous in times of need. Contacts through networks can be obtained via the individual's personal connections, her/his contacts' connections, or randomly: the larger the network, the broader the opportunities it can provide. For example, it is already common to find requests for assistance in finding business partners or investors, recruiting employees, among others, through networks. Apparently, people trust their contacts, and even their contacts' contacts, more than the formal system (agencies for connecting businesses with investors, partners, employees) to refer the "right" people for their business's needs.

Networks are therefore not only a matter of quantity (number of contacts) or quality (1st, 2nd, 3rd circle of familiarity; frequency of chats), but also of the individual's perceptions regarding the firmness of the network, and consequently, the use the individual makes of the network to facilitate the process of capital acquisition.

These networking practices and perceptions differ between the genders. Moreover, the specific use of their networks for capital acquisition is differently interpreted and managed by women and men entrepreneurs.

Women are active in developing and maintaining vigorous networks; women entrepreneurs are considered most involved and dynamic in different networks. The quantity and quality of their networks' contacts and interactions are similar to those reported by their male counterparts. Yet, women entrepreneurs still lag behind in using their networks as a significant circle of tight and trusted contacts that can facilitate access to external financial sources, and acquisition of the best conditions from such sources. It is common knowledge that the effectiveness of meeting with investors for capital acquisition hinges on referrals, e.g., the meeting has been set up by a mutual friend's recommendation, by a personal contact, or even by recommendations of people that hardly know the person they are recommending, but are familiar with that person's contacts (Adler & Kwon, 2002; Burt, 2001; Cohen & Prusak, 2001; Coleman, 2002b).

Women use such contacts for the purposes of capital acquisition less often than men, and maintain more social than practical interactions, while the reverse holds true for men. Furthermore, men's domination in circles that are closely related to financial organizations provides a sort of gatekeeper system which pushes women away from these circles, while strengthening men's ties with the organizations within them. As such, women's networks become less relevant to accessing the financial community and raising capital for a new venture; in a vicious cycle, the marginal numbers of women in finance-related networks affect their access to external financial sources, their odds of attracting high investments or debt capital, and negatively affect their subsequent desire to approach these sources of finance.

Networking is known to be a vital means of connecting entrepreneurs to potential investors, partners or lenders, as the sides use their networks to receive information, advice and recommendations. However, the role of networks exceeds the financial aspect: entrepreneurs and investors/lenders use their contacts as a window to "observe and be observed"; people provide details in their Facebook or LinkedIn profiles to let other people view different aspects of their experiences, expertise or other activities which they are, or have been, involved in; in fact it is an "open secret" that entrepreneurs and funding representatives meet only after "Googling" each other, and gathering information from their networks. This phenomenon even goes beyond these searches to more proactive operation of networking; for instance, a woman investor from Dublin disclosed in an interview that when she gets interested in a new entrepreneurial venture, prior to recommending funding, she uses her contacts, mainly the entrepreneurs that have already been funded by her company, to recommend her company to the potential clients; more specifically, she connects her existing clients with the potential ones, to enable the latter to "inspect" her company through her contacts' eyes; she believes that this strategy is most valuable for the negotiation process.

Women rarely network with investors, investment or lending firms, thereby often missing the valuable assets associated with these external sources for financing their ventures. Specifically, women restrict their search for capital acquisition to internal and personal sources, while men search for external sources. The interactions with representatives of external sources are beneficial, regardless of the funding outcome: interactions between entrepreneurs and investors/lenders enable the new venture's exposure, dissemination, and furthering of networks and contacts. When entrepreneurs discuss capital acquisition with their potential investors, partners or lenders, they can benefit from the information, knowledge and expertise of these people, who could, and should, be their next contacts. Many investors, business angels and potential partners are seasoned entrepreneurs in their own right, so that in addition to capital, they can also provide functional and financial expertise, information about suppliers, customers, etc., which can greatly contribute to the new venture's development and growth. Therefore, the benefit of meeting and networking with these people does not end in being "approved or disapproved" for the capital; more importantly, it adds these people to the circle of networks that can more easily be approached. Women's preference for internal sources of finance means renouncing the extra benefits associated with networking.

Figure 10.4 illustrates the effects of female entrepreneurs' marginal role in finance-related networks.

Accordingly, while from a bird's-eye view it appears that women entrepreneurs lack the ability to raise money for their businesses, and that their ability to raise capital for growth-oriented businesses is even poorer, a broader perspective can be applied to understanding women's capital acquisition. As shown in Figure 10.4, gendered social expectations, women's educational and employment background and past experiences, manifested in their relatively moderate growth aspirations, have a considerable effect on women's underrepresentation in financial bodies, organizations and networks which are closely associated with financing entrepreneurial businesses. As a consequence, women are practically excluded from the most significant decision-making layer, where formal and informal information flows and contacts emanate and extensively facilitate the process of raising capital for the new venture. The exclusion is latent and therefore difficult to detect; the decision-making layers include mainly men who share interests, hobbies and a specific style of communication, dress code, and lifestyle preferences. Joining meetings or events that are theoretically open to anyone means "playing on the same field"; women, however, typically do not chat with other men about new car models or their partners' intimate behavior, and therefore find themselves to be outsiders at such events.

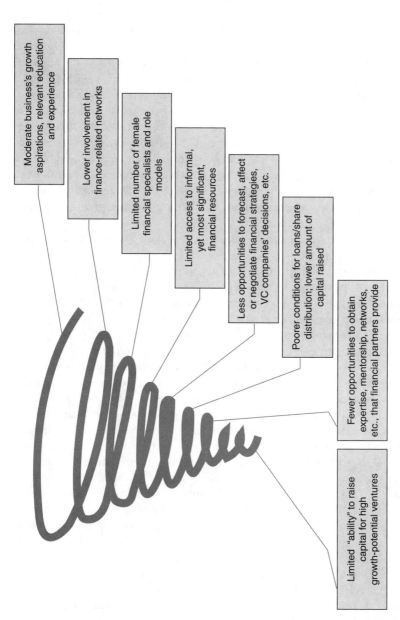

Figure 10.4 The Spiral Dynamics of Female Capital Raising and (lack of) Networking.

Moderate business's growth aspirations, relevant education and experience

Lower involvement in finance-related networks

Limited number of female financial specialists and role models

Limited access to informal, yet most significant, financial resources

Less opportunities to forecast, affect or negotiate financial strategies, VC companies' decisions, etc.

Poorer conditions for loans/share distribution; lower amount of capital raised

Fewer opportunities to obtain expertise, mentorship, networks, etc., that financial partners provide

Limited "ability" to raise capital for high growth-potential ventures

Missing such events or meetings can then escalate to being underrepresented in top management positions where the decision-making processes occur on topics related to business growth and success. There are no advocates to support women's enrollment in such top positions; as a result, there is also a massive underrepresentation of women as role models in the financial arena, which affects women entrepreneurs' proclivity to approach external financial sources. For example, in one case a woman entrepreneur from Montreal reported that during the process of raising capital she met with potential investors and representatives of private associations dedicated to nurturing early-stage entrepreneurial businesses; she had the feeling that ". . . there were some unspoken codes between these men that I could not follow; they seemed all very similar to me, they said the same things, asked the same questions, even the nasty ones, were even dressed the same. I could feel the latent 'fence' they set up between us, to put very clear boundaries between us and emphasize that I am not one of them." This woman finally obtained capital from a VC company that was dedicated to supporting women entrepreneurs.

Women entrepreneurs may identify or feel more comfortable with other women. In fact, models in social capital and networking base their premise on people's attraction to those who are similar, including in gender. The number of woman financial experts who are considered professional authorities in this area and can serve as role models is limited, affecting women entrepreneurs' access to financial resources, and especially their access to information, advice, relevant contacts, and the "hidden agenda" that is most critical in capital acquisition, e.g., referrals to potential investors in women-led businesses, formal and informal endorsements of a woman-led business, and even active involvement in financing a woman-led business. Women entrepreneurs choose internal sources of finance, and therefore reproduce the gendered status quo, rather than changing the existing conditions to more balanced ones. They fail to obtain different contributing deliverables associated with acquisition of capital from external sources, such as mentoring and consulting from financial partners' experts, or an introduction to their networks, which is known to be most valuable. The consequence of this dynamic is manifested in women's alleged inability to raise capital for their entrepreneurial businesses.

The rising number of successful women-led businesses proves that those women's financial strategies can work, but should be more carefully studied, understood and most importantly, accepted as the standard, rather than deeming them exceptions who "surprisingly, achieved success . . ." (Donckels & Lambrecht, 1995; Granovetter, 1983; Johannisson, Ramírez-Pasillas, & Karlsson, 2002; Koka & Prescott, 2002; Kostova & Roth, 2003; Krishnan, Martin, & Noorderhaven, 2006). The points in the Table 10.2 summarize the best practices obtained from women entrepreneurs[2] on how to raise capital for entrepreneurial ventures.

Table 10.2 Best Practices Obtained from Women Entrepreneurs[1] on How to Raise Capital for Entrepreneurial Ventures

Demographics	Quotes	Implications and insights
A 37-year-old, high-tech woman entrepreneur, Tel-Aviv, Israel; co-founder (with her husband) and CEO of a 7-year-old business	"I faced many difficulties in raising money for my startup; although I was, and still am, expert in the relevant technology; venture capitalists and investors were skeptical about my ability to start a business. I decided to make an internal 'switch', and implement the concept of the well-known song '. . . anything you can do, I can do better.' When I met with investors, I always put on my 'self-confident face'; I was very attentive to my body language; I did not show any signs of tension. Instead, I spoke most professionally and gave my potential partners the faith that I can lead my business to the highest achievements."	Self-confidence Professionalism Body language
A 50-year-old immigrant from Taiwan to Germany, managing a 5-year-old, highly successful Taiwanese restaurant; it is a family business	"I started a business with no money; my family and I cooked our traditional food in the restaurant kitchen; it was very tiny, not fancy but people loved it. My family did not speak German so when we decided to expand the restaurant, I was the one searching for financing. I tried to use the 'regular' financial sources, but was refused. Then I approached people from my community in Germany, during one of our traditional Taiwanese celebrations . . . then, it became surprisingly easy to receive their engagement; some Taiwanese people introduced me to their connections, some became my business partners. . ."	Approaching the community Finding the organizations/people most interested in your business Leveraging "demographics"; people support their peers, the ones who identify with their norms, heritage, shared barriers, e.g., ethnicity, race, gender, disabilities
A 32-year-old serial entrepreneur from Utah, USA; currently founder and director of a non-profit association for nascent entrepreneurs	". . . The most important thing is to show the shareholders that you are a hard worker, and guarantee that if you do not get their money, you will find other partners. Financial bodies look for the entrepreneur behind the new venture; they invest in the person, or in their perception of the person. I showed them that I am a person that any financial partner would wish for. I worked so hard and proved that my startup is needed and valuable; then, the bank approved a loan with excellent conditions; then a business person partnered with me. . ."	Emphasizing the value of the person behind the venture; her entrepreneurial characteristics Fighting the stereotypical perceptions about women as entrepreneurs Hard work pays; even when there is still no capital and work is unpaid, or might never be paid

(Continued overleaf)

Table 10.2 Continued

Demographics	Quotes	Implications and insights
A 27-year-old scientist from Singapore started a global business in technological innovations in neurobiology; currently CTO and co-founder of a startup laboratory	"I encountered many difficulties in attempting to finance my laboratory; I presented empirical proof of my innovation's relevance and feasibility, but kept receiving comments on my inability to manage a global laboratory due to my lack of experience in this area. I was determined and knew I would manage the laboratory successfully; so I decided to find other solutions: 'if you can't beat them, join them', I thought. I decided to partner with a man who managed the strategic and managerial aspects of the laboratory and investors were more willing to partner with us. It is discouraging to tackle such gender stereotypes, but there are always organizational solutions to manipulate them."	Organizational solutions: partnering, deciding on the team's composition, choosing the timing, showing proofs of product feasibility Determination; do not let discouragement destroy your dream
A 33-year-old entrepreneur of a web-based cosmetic brand from Slovenia; franchiser	"When I approached the 'call' for franchising, I was most welcomed, but then I figured out that the owners were looking for a woman because the brand is in cosmetics. I took the franchise, but showed the owners that I was a real leader, in fact, that I not only served a marketing function, but was the strategic leader. I suggested creative ideas on the business's concept to the owners, attracting new customers, maintaining existing customers; I signed a contract with a web-based chain in Croatia and launched a spin-off in Serbia. The owners understood that I was their most valuable asset. They provided my business with more money."	Being proactive, daring, making a change Leading, suggesting creative ways to profit, advancing the business Taking risks
A 45-year-old woman from Quebec, Canada, owner of a hobby-based startup that turned into a North American bakery chain	"I manage a 10-year-old 'boulangerie' chain that started as a home bakery and has only recently been financed by a well-known corporation. I had great dreams for my home bakery; after 2 years, I wanted to move it out of my home kitchen, but banks did not approve my loans; investors were uninterested. I had my family savings, which we were keeping for our retirement, and my mother's pension money; it was only when the profits of my bakery reached 1M Canadian Dollars that I had the courage to ask for a loan from the bank; I wanted to start a chain all over Canada, but was again refused. I lived for more than eight years very modestly; people did not believe that I did not travel, did not take vacations, owned an old car and lived with my family in an old, crowded apartment. I wanted to start a chain and believed it would work; again, I used my savings and borrowed money from my sister and friends. I used factoring, partnered with an advertising company for service provision. One day I received a surprising phone call from a well-known company that wanted to partner with us; this time it was on MY terms . . ."	A long way to success should not be discouraging Belief in the business's success, sooner or later Using capital from close circles Finding ways to obtain paying services in creative ways (e.g., factoring, service exchange, borrowing equipment) Do not be blinded by "fantastic proposals," be attentive and pursue your own needs and terms

Description	Quote	Best practices
An accountant from Nigeria, in her forties, opened an import–export business two years ago; currently the general manager of the UK office	"I started my business in Nigeria, when I was dismissed from my job after the birth of my child. I needed money to rent a place and start my work but faced many difficulties with the bank and governmental associations and grants. My husband worked at the university and was invited for a three-month visiting position in the UK. When the family was set up in the UK I looked intensively for ideas on how to advance my business. I worked online but business was slow; so I decided to study and more thoroughly understand how to finance my business. I studied through books, internet and associations for entrepreneurs. I became an expert in financing! When we returned home, I met with venture capitalists; I was expert in financing and suggested great ideas."	Leveraging any situation to own benefits (from dismissal to success) Taking risks and being optimistic Incorporating education as an essential preparation for entrepreneurship Do not fear, be courageous, be determined and articulate the venture's financial needs
A women entrepreneur in internet businesses; in her sixties; has already preformed an "exit" and is currently CEO of her original business and partner in 15 entrepreneurial internet-based businesses	"I was lucky! Not because my business was purchased for such a great amount of money, but because my family and friends were behind me all the way to the purchase. I realized that my success stemmed from the power and energy that I received from my family and friends. I decided to enable women entrepreneurs to succeed by supporting them. With the money I received from the 'exit' transaction, I invested in women-led entrepreneurial businesses. Then I decided to crash the 'boys' club' and I attended any kind of investor event for entrepreneurs; I also initiated events with venture capitalists and business people; I wrote commentaries in the daily newspaper. I did not give anyone the opportunity to ignore me as a valuable power in the finance of entrepreneurial businesses. My advice is, when you have some money, start investing it in other businesses, you immediately turn from 'transparent' to 'apparent', and you have a significant impact in the financing decision-making processes."	Networks, maintenance of relevant networks Developing social capital Taking active part in the most influential networks Investing in entrepreneurial businesses Initiating events, participating in events Proactively becoming apparent

1 The procedure conducted by Dr. Kariv to obtain women entrepreneurs' best practices was built on Skype-based semi-structured interviews lasting around 30 minutes each (some were performed over two or three different sessions) with women entrepreneurs; half of the interviewees were members of the BNI organization; the other half was located by snowball procedure.

BNI is the largest business networking organization in the world. We offer members the opportunity to share ideas, contacts and most importantly, business referrals, at http://www.bni.com/

WOMEN AND THE INVESTORS' COMMUNITY

Women are absent from the investment community. While women's access to business finance has been the subject of extensive research in recent years, the debate over women as investors is scarce, though imperative. Figures show that less than 10 percent of women are investors and venture capitalists; this statistic is most discouraging, not only because it reflects the prevailing gender stereotypes regarding women's abilities in the areas of investment and finance, but also because investment dynamics appear to be based on men's thought, approaches and practices, thus missing the most valuable complementary aspect that women investors can "bring to the table."

Investments are more than probability calculations and financial estimates. An investment decision requires creative thought, an open mind, and outside-the-box thinking; it requires a deep assessment of the people managing the businesses to be funded, and entails strategic predictions on future trends in marketing, product development, and customers' tastes, among others. Such a strategic prediction made by Peter Thiel, co-founder of PayPal, enabled Mark Zuckerberg to receive an investment of US$500,000 for Facebook in June 2004. This investment was based on predictions of customer behavior rather than on pure calculations.

Such personal, social and strategic abilities are women's forte; hence, disregarding women's perspectives in investment decisions can be detrimental to the new venture community as a whole.

Yet, many women tackle difficulties in enrolling as investors or venture capitalists; many investment and financial companies, comprising mainly men, manage a dual life: the formal work life conducted during working hours and a latent life, managed as a "closed club" and conducted informally outside of working hours. Women's access to both formal and informal organizations is limited.

The main explanations found in the research for the underrepresentation of women investors are summarized as follows:

- Women lack experience and relevant education in the areas of finance, investments, and business funding.
- Underrepresentation of females in these areas is rooted in their absence from programs in finance in schools, higher education.
- Lack of governmental and policy-related programs and initiatives to encourage women to choose the areas of finance; this affects their self-confidence in becoming investors, venture capitalists, etc.
- Stereotypical approach to the nature of the investor's role, e.g., powerful, aggressive, hostile, and association is more to masculine than feminine characteristics.
- Gatekeepers and barriers are imposed on women wishing to access the formal and informal organizations of investors and venture capitalists.

- "Boys' clubs," managed according to men's codes, prevail in VC circles; these clubs provide—mainly men—with a prosperous platform for informal interactions where deals are made, decisions are taken and new, highly valuable connections evolve.
- There is a scarcity of women in companies' boards of directors, in senior management positions in investment companies, as well as in non-finance-related companies where they could acquire significant financial experience.
- Women tend to develop limited networks and connections with investment companies.
- Women tend to be risk-averse, and therefore avoid investments which are of a risky nature.
- Women are less likely than men to study know-how in financing and investments: they have less interest in these areas.

Research shows that more women involved in investment companies will be echoed in more women-led businesses obtaining funding. Ms. Amy Millman, president of Springboard Enterprises which links female entrepreneurs with venture capitalists, has been quoted as saying, "You invest in people who are familiar to you. It only makes sense [that] if you're not familiar with women-run businesses, you don't invest in them."[3]

Encouraging women to hold top financial and investment positions will foster entrepreneurship; this should be done through education, mentorship, and a broader openness of existing investment companies to involve women in top positions (Brush, Carter, Gatewood, Greene, & Hart, 2004; Carter, Brush, Greene, Gatewood, & Hart, 2003; Greene *et al.*, 2001).

SUMMARY

This chapter brings to light the complex realm of capital acquisition, by introducing and discussing the ways in which women entrepreneurs manage their ventures' funding practices, the origins of their exclusive financial-acquisition strategies, the challenges and difficulties they tackle in the new ventures and the outcomes of their chosen financial practices. The main message of this chapter draws on accepting diversity, rather than concluding that women should be trained and taught how to raise more capital the "man's way," or how to gain better conditions in equity or debt finance decisions. Being less judgmental while accepting, even sometimes adopting, the "woman's way" may produce more benefits for women-led businesses and for the entrepreneurial realm as a whole. This chapter cites studies showing that raising funds requires more than financial know-how; e.g., it also involves planning strategically, networking, negotiating, inspecting the nature of the people involved in the process more thoroughly, as well as employing creativity and outside-the-box thinking.

While women are found to avoid finance-based programs and thus are considered unqualified to take decisions about their business's finances, they are certainly qualified in other abilities associated with effective capital acquisition, some of which are considered more naturally acquired by women, e.g., networking, people orientation, while others are fields of knowledge that women are attracted to, e.g., planning, negotiations and communications.

This chapter's leading idea is to embrace women's styles and strategies in raising capital, by providing more access for women into formal and informal circles, including circles of venture capitalists and investors, funding new ventures based on relevant criteria rather than their founders' gender and, most of all, changing the rooted stereotyping of women's inability to decide upon their best financial sources. By implementing a broader view in which women and men's strategies are crystallized and harmonized, entrepreneurs, regardless of their gender, can have multiple alternatives, perspectives and opportunities to raise capital for their new ventures.

CASE STUDIES AND AT-A-GLANCE[4]

"When people realize that I am a black female, they are taken aback. Then they try to find out if there is a white Mr. Smith or a white Mr. Whiley . . ." says Gwen, the founder of Smith Whiley & Company. This straightforward example sharply delineates the difficulties and challenges encountered by women entrepreneurs through the process of raising capital to launch their new ventures and manage them to growth and success. The two case studies included in this chapter, the first contributed by Susan Coleman and Alicia Robb and the second, by Benoît Leleux, demonstrate different aspects of the financing process in female entrepreneurship. They trace these women entrepreneurs' steps in raising financial capital in the field of investment management, as illustrated through the intriguing case of Gwen Iloani and Smith Whiley & Company, a woman- and minority-owned investment firm located in Hartford, Connecticut, USA, and by the fascinating story of the "WIP Four," a private equity investment fund empowering South African women in their country's mainstream economic development.

The case studies focus on various angles representing the challenges and difficulties faced by women in raising money and financing their new ventures in the different ecosystems in which their start-ups are operated. The role of education, experience and networks is emphasized throughout these cases, as providing a vehicle for women to finance their new ventures.

The at-a-glance case provides an additional avenue to explore women's challenges in financing their businesses, from India, as illustrated by Ramachandran Kavil and Erin Rogalski who tell the story of Lata, and Bliss Foods tofu products.

Smith Whiley & Company

Susan Coleman[a] and Alicia Robb[b]

[a]Professor of Finance, Barney School of Business, University of Hartford, Connecticut, USA; [b]Senior Research Fellow, Research and Policy, Ewing Marion Kauffman Foundation, Kansas City, Missouri, USA

The Role of Resource-based Theory in Women's Entrepreneurship

Edith Penrose (Penrose, 1959), an entrepreneur in the field of economics if ever there was one, was one of the first economic theorists to address the link between resources, profitable growth, and competitive advantage. Penrose asserted that the entrepreneur's effective management of firm resources allows her to take advantage of productive opportunities in the marketplace in order to achieve profitable growth. Further, Penrose noted that it is necessary for the entrepreneur to continually maintain and develop the firm's resources in order to maintain a competitive advantage. In the case of small and entrepreneurial firms, Penrose observed that opportunities often emerge in segments of the market ignored or abandoned by larger, well-established firms. Finally, Penrose theorized that there is an optimal growth rate for achieving profitable growth. In other words, growth for growth's sake alone is not necessarily the entrepreneur's objective. We will return to this theme repeatedly as we share the stories of successful women entrepreneurs throughout this book. Penrose's early work is important, not only in and of itself, but also because she established the foundation for a Resource-based Theory of the firm which links the fields of economics, entrepreneurship, and strategic management (Kor & Mahoney, 2000; Rugman & Verbeke, 2002).

The Resource-based Theory tells us that the firm is a collection of resources (Bergmann, Lichtenstein, & Brush, 2001; Brush *et al.*, 2001; Hanlon & Saunders, 2007). The task of the entrepreneur is to assemble, develop, and transform needed resources in order to generate unique capabilities that will give her a competitive advantage (Amit & Schoemaker, 1993; Wernerfelt, 1984). Resource-Based Theory goes on to contend that those firms that muster and apply their resources most effectively will also be those that enjoy superior performance (Brush *et al.*, 2001; Sirmon & Hitt, 2003). What types of resources are we talking about? The most obvious resources fall into the major categories of financial capital (debt and equity), human capital (education and experience), and social capital (networks and contacts). The following case, which focuses on entrepreneur Gwen Iloani and Smith Whiley & Company, provides an example of an entrepreneur who effectively leveraged her resources in the areas of human, social, and financial capital to launch a highly successful growth-oriented firm in the field of investment management.

Gwendolyn Smith Iloani and Smith Whiley & Company

Women entrepreneurs in the United States have been growing in both number and economic importance in recent years. The 2007 Survey of Business Owners conducted by the U.S. Census Bureau reveals that there were 7.8 million women-owned firms in the United States generating $1.2 trillion in revenues. This number of women-owned firms represented an increase of 20 percent from 2002 to 2007 compared to an increase of 18 percent for all firms, indicating that the number of women-owned firms grew faster than the number of firms overall for that time period. During the same timeframe, however, the growth rate in revenues for women-owned firms grew by 27 percent compared to a growth rate of 33 percent for all firms. Thus, although the number of women-owned firms grew more rapidly, their growth rate in revenues lagged those of firms overall for the five-year period. This same pattern held true for the 10-year period spanning 1997 to 2007. During that span of time, the number of women-owned firms increased by 44 percent compared to an increase of 30 percent for firms overall. Although women-owned firms also increased their revenues by 46 percent during this timeframe, firms overall saw an increase of 68 percent, suggesting that the firms launched by women tended to be smaller than those started by men. Prior research addressing the topic of firm growth confirms this finding (Coleman, 2002; Fairlie & Robb, 2009; Robb & Wolken, 2002).

Increasingly, however, a growing number of women are pursuing the path of high-growth entrepreneurship. Growth-oriented firms typically consume large amounts of capital, so the entrepreneur needs to raise funds from both internal and external sources. One of the major differences between growth-oriented firms and smaller, life style firms is their reliance on external equity. Entrepreneurs generally finance life style firms with personal and internally generated sources of equity. In contrast, growth-oriented entrepreneurs require substantial amounts of external equity financing from angel investors or venture capitalists. This strategy often entails sharing ownership and control, however. As an alternative, some enterprising women-owned firms use very creative strategies for launching and financing their firms. One such firm is Smith Whiley & Company, a woman- and minority-owned investment firm located in Hartford, Connecticut.

Gwendolyn Smith Iloani started thinking about launching her own investment firm in the mid-90s after rising through the ranks of investment professionals at the Aetna, a large insurance company located in Hartford, Connecticut. Gwen had both undergraduate and graduate degrees, and she had a strong track record of investment performance, having managed over $9 billion in assets. Her goal was to become a CEO. Nevertheless, as she looked around her own firm, she realized that no one at the top "looked like me."

> I started to think about starting my own business as a result of the glass ceiling. When I looked at the CEO office, I wasn't sure where I would fit in, or how long it would take me to get there. I decided to start my own business, because I wanted the freedom to realize my ambitions and to control my destiny.

Smith Whiley & Company was established in 1994 to provide mezzanine and private equity funding to firms at the low end of the middle market. Based on her experience as an investment professional, Gwen felt that this was an underserved segment of the market.

> I identified a niche in the marketplace that I could serve successfully. The opportunities were exceptional, and I could make a nice profit along the way.

One of Gwen's challenges was to raise enough financial capital to start. The sales cycle for the types of investments her firm dealt with was relatively long, and she anticipated that she would need enough capital to stay in business for about three years until she successfully sold her investment funds to institutional investors. To secure this capital, she negotiated a strategic partnership with her former employer, the Aetna, which put in $2.5 million in a combination of start-up financing and support services in return for one-third of the firm. In turn, Gwen supplied "sweat equity" and an investment of approximately $10,000 of her own money. Gwen's strong track record and her relationships with investment professionals and key decision-makers at the Aetna were critical factors in making the strategic partnership happen. Thanks to this source of financing, Gwen did not have to turn to other providers of external capital.

> It was like a marriage of two people who knew each other, as opposed to an arranged marriage of two people who don't know each other. Aetna knew the quality of my work, and they trusted me. I had a history with them.

Gwen also secured financing from the Connecticut Development Authority (CDA), a quasi public–private entity that invests in new firms as a way to promote economic development for the state. CDA invested $1 million in Smith Whiley in return for a 10 percent ownership position in the firm.

Gwen has established Smith Whiley as a series of funds. Investors include pension fund and endowment fund managers who hire Smith Whiley to execute their strategy for investing in firms within the niche that Smith Whiley has targeted. To date, the firm has launched three funds, each in excess of $100 million. Strong earnings allowed Gwen to buy out the minority positions held by the Aetna and the Connecticut Development Authority in the late 90s. Today, Smith Whiley is 100 percent owned by Gwen and by other insiders.

Currently Gwen finances Smith Whiley with earnings from the firm and with a bank loan.

With respect to bank financing, we operate in a complicated business, and banks have difficulty understanding the business and the economics. I always do my homework on the potential lender, and I go out of my way to make the analysis easy for them by giving them all of the supporting documents they will need; this is before they ask for it. I am also very patient with them.

As a woman entrepreneur in the field of finance, Gwen has faced challenges, and she has developed strategies for overcoming them.

The financial field is one of the last male bastions, and is still not fully integrated. When people realize that I am a black female, they are taken aback. Then they try to find out if there is a white Mr. Smith or a white Mr. Whiley. Gender is definitely an issue in the world of finance. As a female, I always have to work harder and be better to get the respect that I deserve. Men tend to gravitate and make eye contact with other men versus women. The challenge is to get them to acknowledge you, particularly when you are making an investment presentation and you are asking them to invest millions of dollars into your business as a client. I had to learn to be versatile in my style and approach, and I learned to use my femininity as a strength along with my size, height, and distinctive clothing.

In spite of the tough investment climate in the current economy, the firm is currently preparing to launch its fourth fund, the largest to date. Gwen continues to see investment opportunities in the marketplace as well as both financial and personal rewards for her and her team.

A major advantage of operating a business is that I used my investment track record to identify an opportunity in the marketplace to sell a high margin product. In a sense I created my own opportunity, and at the same time I took control of my destiny. I like the risk taking that I do daily. The rewards for taking risk are apparent immediately. I also enjoy doing a great job for my investors, the recognition the firm receives in the form of awards and reputation, and the benefits that we reap as a result of these things.

Gwen Smith's story of success illustrates the important role played by both human capital in the form of education and relevant experience and social capital in the form of access to key contacts and networks. Both of these essential resource inputs helped Gwen to secure the financial capital needed to launch and grow her firm. Gwen is also a great example of an "opportunity-driven" entrepreneur. She saw an opportunity in the marketplace and put her human, social, and financial capital to work in order to take advantage of it.

Questions for Discussion

1 What types of human and social capital had Gwen accumulated at the time she launched her firm?
2 How were these human and social capital "resources" instrumental in helping her acquire financing?
3 What other sources of capital might Gwen have used to start her firm? Discuss the pros and cons of these alternative sources.
4 What types of financing does Gwen use for her firm today? Discuss the advantages and disadvantage of these sources.
5 Discuss the extent to which Gwen's financial strategies matched (or did not match) her goals for the firm.
6 In this case we discussed resources in the form of human, social, and financial capital. What other types of "resources" would be needed to launch a firm of this type?

Case References

Amit, R. & Schoemaker, P. (1993). Strategic assets and organizational rent. *Strategic Management Journal*, 14(1), 33–46.

Bergmann Lichtenstein, B.M. & Brush, C.G. (2001). How do "resource bundles" develop and change in new ventures? A dynamic model and longitudinal exploration. *Entrepreneurship Theory and Practice*, 37–58.

Brush, C.G., Greene, P.G., & Hart, M.M. (2001). From initial idea to unique advantage: The entrepreneurial challenge of constructing a resource base. *Academy of Management Executive*, 15(1), 64–78.

Coleman, S. (2002). Characteristics and borrowing behavior of small, women-owned firms: Evidence from the 1998 survey of small business finances. *Journal of Business and Entrepreneurship*, 14(2), 151–166.

Fairlie, R. & Robb, A. (2009). Gender differences in business performance: Evidence from the characteristics of business owners survey. *Small Business Economics*, 33, 375–395.

Hanlon, D. & Saunders, C. (2007). Marshaling resources to form small new ventures: Toward a more holistic understanding of entrepreneurial support. *Entrepreneurship Theory and Practice*, 619–641.

Kor, Y.Y. & Mahoney, J.T. (2000). Penrose's resource-based approach: The process and product of research creativity. *Journal of Management Studies*, 37(1), 109–139.

Penrose, E.T. (1959). *The theory of the growth of the firm*. New York: John Wiley.

Robb, A. & Wolken, J. (2002). *Firm, owner, and financing characteristics: Differences between female- and male-owned small businesses*. Federal Reserve Working Paper Series: 2002–18. Available at SSRN:http://ssrn.com/abstract=306800 or http://dx.doi.org/10.2139/ssrn.306800

Rugman, A.M. & Verbeke, A. (2002). Edith Penrose's contribution to the resource-based view of strategic management. *Strategic Management Journal*, 23(8), 769–780.

Sirmon, D.G. & Hitt, M.A. (2003, Summer). Managing resources: Linking unique resources, management, and wealth creation in family firms. *Entrepreneurship Theory and Practice*, 339–358.

Wernerfelt, B. (1984). A resource-based view of the firm. *Strategic Management Journal*, 5, 171–180.

Women Investment Portfolio Holding (WIPHOLD) of South Africa: Empowerment through Private Equity

Benoît Leleux
Stephan Schmidheiny Professor of Entrepreneurship and Finance, IMD, Lausanne, Switzerland

When women come together simply for the benefit of mankind, we shall see a power such as the world has never known.

Matthew Arnold, English poet, essayist, and social critic (1822–1888)

It was Monday, August 4, 1997 and four women stood in a ground floor office at 53 Main Street in Johannesburg's central business district (CBD). The tension in the room was palpable. Wendy Luhabe's customary outer serenity masked an inner trepidation shared by her three co-founders. Even the normally ebullient Gloria Serobe was silent. Both women stood looking at the traffic going past the window. The remaining two founders of Women Investment Portfolio Holdings (WIPHOLD), Louisa Mojela and Nomhle Canca (formerly) Gcabashe, sat at a table in the center of the room—each woman trying to avoid looking at the telephone on the table, and failing miserably.

Today would be the culmination of an exhilarating three-year journey. They would soon find out if their vision had come to life: to empower post-apartheid South African women through active participation in emerging economic opportunities. The founders waited for a call from Southern Life, the book runner for their initial public offering (IPO) launched six weeks earlier. For three years, they had worked the nine provinces hard to encourage hundreds of South African women from all walks of life to switch from a savings and consumption mindset to one of investment. But WIPHOLD was not a charity or philanthropy, offering cheap micro-loans to rural women. Its vision was more ambitious—it would *take* money from women, invest it in the mainstream economy and make it grow. Grueling roadshows in obscure townships, hours of patient explanation (sometimes in local dialects) and many a setback now lay behind them: But had it paid off? Would those women give them the 40 million rand (US$8.6m) needed to launch their novel investment vehicle?

Pioneering Women's Empowerment

Despite the ANC's women-friendly stance since 1994 (there was a strong female presence in the government and its manifesto was big on female empowerment), most early Black Economic Empowerment (BEE) deals were men-centric and lacked all female empowerment focus. The four founders of WIP (often referred to as the "WIP Four") decided to take on that challenge and engage, mobilize and empower South African women in the mainstream economic development of the country—but not through charity. WIP was not going to be a micro-finance empowerment vehicle dispensing cheap loans or grants to rural women, but rather a private equity investment fund. Through WIP, women could gain some level of financial independence by buying shares in South Africa's largest companies, thus benefiting from the growing phenomenon of black share ownership spurred by BEE.

In South Africa, where there were still deep-seated prejudices about what women could achieve, adopting a gender- rather than a race-centered philosophy was groundbreaking—particularly in a country that was still largely preoccupied with racial issues. It brought the WIP Four one of their first male allies, Geoff Snelgar, then deputy chairman of Hollard, South Africa's largest privately owned insurance group with assets of approximately R1 billion ($217.2m) in 1997. He later became one of the company's closest mentors, recalling:

> At the time they were getting their act together, there was really nobody else taking that women's investment approach. And I've always had a view that women have a different view on life to men, and that adds a richness that you don't get from a purely man's grouping.

At their Tuesday meetings, Gcabashe, Luhabe, Mojela and Serobe hatched their core investment strategy. In South Africa, women—in particular working mothers—constituted the most significant consumer segment. Working women tended to do the grocery shopping, and in high-income households, the housemaid would buy the everyday needs. Women there-fore took most of the buying decisions for household goods and services. Mojela commented:

Women provided labor and consumed goods and services, but they were nevertheless excluded from participating in the economic mainstream. They needed to move beyond this.

WIP's investment strategy would therefore focus on leveraging the female consumer base, targeting the fast-moving consumer goods (FMCG) sector. WIP would add value to its investments by building brand loyalty among its future shareholders for the goods and services produced by its investee companies.

From the beginning, the founders felt a genuine commitment to helping underprivileged women. Articulating their motivation, Serobe said:

> We believed that women were abused because they did not have options. They were too dependent on a man's revenue. However, we believed a lot in family values—getting married and building a family. We were very traditional when it came to family values. But we wanted co-existence with men in equal partnership.

Raising Capital and Finding the First Deals

As the founders tried to raise the seed capital for their venture, they met with disappointment and rejection. Laughing, Mojela later recalled:

> It helped that we did not know that people would not help us!

The eager funding that seemed available to their male BEE counterparts was obviously not for them. Corporate South Africa was overwhelmingly male and lacked confidence in the women's ability to achieve their goals. Indeed, Motlana of Nail approached them to join forces and come under his "protection." To them, this represented the "paternalistic" lack of confidence they were fighting to overcome and they refused. But even among organizations to whom they were already known, they met with little support. As Mojela recounted:

> My own bank manager actually declined my application!

The WIP Four struck several deals, in both listed and unlisted companies. Some deals also went south, costing them dearly. The women attributed some of the early mistakes to insufficient consultation among the founders. With so much going on, the team had to split to address the different issues and opportunities that came along. Although very different in personality, they complemented each other well. Luhabe was a visionary, and she assumed a strategic role, articulating the long-term vision and goals for WIP, together with Mojela and Gcabashe. The latter two also took on operational and hands-on roles, managing the day-to-day business of the company. Serobe provided the intellectual firepower behind the structuring and financing of the deals. All four women were engaged in sourcing deals. On several occasions, the company found itself committed to things before all founders had been informed.

Selling the Dream: Preparing for the IPO

With a vision to bring *all* women into the mainstream of the South African economy, the founders were determined to involve women from all strata of society—no woman would be left out. As one of the company's future directors—Wendy Appelbaum, Liberty Life heiress—noted:

> It wasn't only black women who needed to be empowered. It was all women. Mary Slack [another future WIPHOLD director] and I would have had places on the Anglo American and Liberty Life boards if we hadn't had breasts.

Although it was relatively easy to present their idea to their professional counterparts in Johannesburg, it was a different challenge to present it to the great mass of women in the provinces. These women were among the poorest in the land and those most in need of empowerment to break out of the vicious cycle of labor and consumption. They knew practically nothing about investing, the potential gains and the corresponding possibility of loss. Some of them had already lost money in fraudulent pyramid schemes common in those quarters of society. The WIP women would have to gain their trust. Mojela explained:

> We knew the response from individuals would be: "Who's Wendy? Who's Louisa? They're just girls from Johannesburg who want to make money out of us." We targeted community leaders, church groups, NGOs. This encouraged respect and helped legitimize our concept.

Luhabe added:

> We made a conscious decision to consult with the elders . . . because, historically in South Africa, most of the organizations responding to women's issues have been started or run by women, and these women tended to be in their seventies. So we invited these women to share our thinking and to get their counsel and guidance. But we also hoped that they would become a bridge for us to access their community members.
>
> It was clear to us that we would have to go and sell the idea to the women. But that also meant educating them about how the economy functions. So that became the appetizer in our presentations to them.

First, this is how the economy works. Second, this is the role we play as women. These are the opportunities that we see. Third, this is what we have to propose to you to capture those opportunities. And this is why we are here inviting you to participate and support us.

As soon as they had some deals in place, the WIP Four hit the road. For six weeks they did not spend a weekend at home as they traveled through the nine provinces with their message and vision. They held workshops in the large towns, with women being bussed in from smaller towns. Between 100 and 200 women attended each workshop—and some of them then became "ambassadors" for the WIP concept, carrying the message to their own hometowns and villages for the women who had been unable to attend. At the end of each presentation, the founders would then introduce the concept of WIPHOLD and the coming IPO. They realized it would be difficult to take the women's money when they really did not have anything yet to show as a company. Mojela explained:

> We had to start the other way round by securing investments. But we were able to say, "Continue with your stockvels and your savings clubs, but make sure you set aside money to participate in the public offer from WIP."

As part of the educational process, they explained to the women that this was not like putting their money into a bank. It was to be viewed in the long term, and that they could lose the money as easily as it could grow. This educational process, and the frankness of the founders, also helped to build trust with the women's communities.

The women faced a delicate situation in launching a "women only" IPO. The transaction could potentially be viewed as discriminatory in a newly egalitarian South Africa. Previous attempts at "blacks only" offers had raised public outcries. The women were able to secure permission to launch an IPO targeting women only, a first by any standards. This was partly because they flew "under the radar screen." Most of the business community did not view the new company as a potentially significant player and therefore it was not considered such a big deal. Second, they were able to argue for an exemption on the basis that women were a particularly disadvantaged group in South Africa, and therefore in need of exceptional support.

On June 25, 1997, WIPHOLD launched its women-only IPO to raise money to fund past debt-financed investments, take advantage of future investment opportunities, and to fund working capital requirements. Southern underwrote the minimum subscription of R20 million ($4.4m). Under the terms of the offer, women were invited to subscribe to a maximum of 20 million B shares at 200 cents (or R2) ($0.44) per share. The minimum individual subscription of 300 shares, for individual women, and 1,000 shares, for women's organizations, was deliberately set low so that rural women could participate.

The Results of the IPO

By the time the invitation to buy shares in WIPHOLD closed in August 1997, the company had received applications for 11.3 million shares, exceeding the minimum subscription level of 10 million shares. The company raised a total of R23 million. Equally gratifying, WIPHOLD could count itself as a truly "broad-based" empowerment company; the IPO attracted 18,000 women who had invested either individually or through community groups and credit associations.

The money enabled WIPHOLD to eliminate its short-term debt, fund new investments and set up the WIPHOLD Trust. Six months after the public offer, WIPHOLD established an over-the-counter (OTC) trading facility, administered by Standard Corporate and Merchant Bank (SCMB), to enable women to buy and sell their shares, thus enhancing the liquidity of the shares.

And corporate South Africa's response to the new company? Wendy Luhabe, one of the founders, commented:

> Generally positive. But it was not entirely supported by people bringing us investment opportunities. They were superficially supportive, but they certainly didn't think it was going to work and that we would be successful. If they had, then I think we would have attracted a much stronger pool of investment opportunities. I think it was a reflection of the prejudice they had about what women could achieve. I don't think they were worried about what could go wrong: They just didn't think we would succeed.

The women continued to grow their investment portfolio by buying shares in companies such as African Media, Beige, Software Connection, Specialized Outsourcing, SA Empowerment and Capital Alliance. In less than a year, the company had increased its net asset value (NAV) from 220 cents per share (cps) ($0.48 per share) at the IPO to 630 cps ($1.25 per share) by April. The good performance of its listed portfolio companies was further enhanced as WIPHOLD had acquired most of them at significant discounts to trading prices.

WIPHOLD scored a coup in April 1998 when it acquired a 5 percent stake in Alexander Forbes, one of South Africa's biggest financial services firms. Sourced by Mojela, it was by far the largest deal ever for WIPHOLD. Another controversial deal was the tie-up with Sun International to bid for casino licenses. Although the moral debates nearly split the board, WIPHOLD eventually partnered with Sun to form Afrisun Leisure, which won one of the four Gauteng licenses—among the most lucrative licenses being issued. WIPHOLD attracted criticism for dealing with Sol Kerzner, a controversial figure who was then the subject of allegations that he had bribed one of the homeland leaders during the "bad old days" of apartheid.

Institutionalizing (1998 to 2002)

In April 1998, the board of WIPHOLD was assembled to hear the latest idea from Louisa Mojela, executive chairwoman, and Nomhle Canca, executive director. Nine months earlier, they had raised R23 million (US$5.2m) from 18,000 women and women's groups in support of their original vision. Now, keen to capitalize on that success and to capture a larger slice of the growing empowerment cake, the women wanted to raise more money to fund an ambitious program of growth through acquisition. They were asking the board to approve a preferential rights offer to raise R500 million ($112m) from their original investors and various institutions.

Mojela continued talking, standing up as she spoke, and began counting off each point on the slide on the screen before them. The arguments were persuasive: (i) black-owned companies had now successfully raised money directly from the capital markets and were currently outperforming the market; (ii) it was now clear that the existing special purpose vehicle (SPV) agreements used in their first deals hampered management's room to maneuver; (iii) this and a shortage of funds, more than a lack of deals, limited WIPHOLD's opportunities for growth; and (iv) there was already a lot of interest in the potential issue and the women were confident that the offer would succeed. But, as one of the directors pointed out, WIPHOLD was exchanging one set of constraints for another. The institutional money came with strings attached—a mandatory public listing within six months of the rights offer. Could they be confident that this would be the right thing for the company then?

The first half of 1998 was a great time for South Africa's "black chips," most of which outperformed the Johannesburg Stock Exchange (JSE). It was against this background that WIPHOLD, in May 1998, approached institutional investors and its original group of women investors, and successfully raised R500 million ($98.4m) in a rights offer at 700 cents per share (cps) ($1.39 per share). The offer resulted in a dilution of the women's shareholding to 26.5 percent. However, there was a quid pro quo, as Mojela noted:

> We went back to our women and raised R76 million [$15.1m], triple the amount they had originally invested. The balance we placed privately with institutions in a book-building exercise that was oversubscribed. But much as we were excited, the downside with the institutions was that they gave us a deadline as to when we should list. We had six months to do so, and the clock was ticking.

The tide turned against the black chips in the second half of 1998 as the South African stock market was hit hard by the global turmoil in emerging markets. In August 1999 WIPHOLD announced that as part of a strategic refocus, it would form a niche merchant bank and focus more tightly on financial services. For WIPHOLD, it was clear that it could not remain a passive investment holding company and that it would have to go operational in order to build a sustainable business. The company believed it would be able to leverage WIPHOLD's five-year empowerment track record to unlock deal flow. Speaking at the time, Mojela said:

> We have been disappointed at the discount at which our shares have traded since listing. We decided to reposition WIPHOLD in an attempt to eliminate the discount and we see it as our responsibility to create value for our shareholders and this is a clear way to do so.

But those shareholders were surprisingly ungrateful. Luhabe explained:

> There were two reasons for this. Firstly because we took away skills. We bought people with unique niche skills from institutions that were investors in the company. And we were moving into a sector where they had held a monopoly . . . They also felt betrayed . . . that was not the deal they had envisioned. They had invested in an investment holding company; it was now turning into a financial services firm. But that decision wasn't up to them: It was up to us. We said we didn't think that the previous strategy was sustainable; we had to do something else with the business.

Taking Stock (2003)

February 2003 saw the end of the fiscal year—and a great point for the founders to take stock of the company's position. The IPO had taken place six years earlier, and WIPHOLD had seen many ups and downs since then. However, FY2003 results were looking good and the company expected to report a profit of R25 million ($3.8m) for the year.

In terms of returns, WIPHOLD had done very well for the women who first invested at the IPO in 1997. A woman investing R2,000 ($300) for a holding of 1,000 B shares at that time would have seen her investment grow by 85.9 percent, representing a compound annual growth rate (CAGR) of 11 percent. By contrast, the women and institutional investors who came in during the May 1998 private placement at 700 cps ($1.39 per share) had seen the value of their investment fall by about 50 percent, equivalent to a CAGR of about −12 percent.

While WIPHOLD could easily lay claim to having enabled South African women's economic empowerment, were things significantly better for women now? Not really, said Mojela:

Deals are clearly sourced through networks and we are still very marginalized. Maybe because of the culture of the country itself. We are still very much a patriarchal society. Whenever there was an opportunity, the first thing that comes to mind for the deal owner is the old boys' network. "Let's talk to this man and forget about the girls."

I do not think it has improved much. If anything, it is maybe worse than it was before, because what they were trying to do then was a different form of marginalization. When there is a deal of say R100 million [$11.7m], the man does the transaction and 95 million goes for his own account. Five million [$600,000] is then given to the so-called "women, youth and disabled." We are all lumped together! We are all special! Those special, chronic cases—women, youth and disabled—come together. Here is your 5 percent! So it is in fact worse than before. It makes Gloria so mad to hear that "women, youth and disabled" story. I laugh as she says: "I wonder if they think we are all hunchbacks or something? We are just as normal as they are!" But that is the name of the game.

It is sad that we cannot be seen in our own right as women, able to participate and contribute. Because there is clearly nothing they can do that we cannot do. So this is where we sit back as WIPHOLD and say to ourselves, in spite of being marginalized by these institutions and the men we are still there. And [what about] we "women, youth and disabled"? We are moving forward. Those chosen men? Some of them have fallen flat on their face.

WIPHOLD De-lists

It no longer made sense to remain listed with such a small capitalization of about R165 million [US$20.1m]. The listing was not driven by us; we had to do it to secure institutional funding.

(Louisa Mojela, CEO, WIPHOLD)

With these words, the Women's Investment Portfolio Holdings (WIPHOLD) suspended the listing of its B shares on the Johannesburg Securities Exchange (JSE). It was Monday, March 24, 2003, almost exactly four years to the day the shares first traded on the JSE. A week later, on April 1, 2003, the company terminated the listing of its B shares on the JSE. WIPHOLD's foray into public ownership was over: The company was private once again. In a move overwhelmingly supported by all its shareholders, WIPHOLD used R220 million ($26.8m) of its own money to buy out institutional shareholders and return to its roots as a company controlled by women. Said the parties:

WIPHOLD . . . is set for a total makeover . . . that will see the company restructuring and expanding its role as a full-fledged financial services group. The 1999 listing reduced our women-oriented and black empowerment profile. The de-listing has bolstered them, with women again holding 60 percent of the unlisted WIPHOLD. We will now be able to significantly improve the company's black and women's economic empowerment ownership at shareholder and employee level based on direct economic empowerment participation.

Case Contributions to the Women Entrepreneurship Agenda

The case documents the incredible journey of one of the most original Economic Empowerment vehicles in post-apartheid South Africa, the Women Investment Portfolio Holdings (WIPHOLD), a private equity investment fund which raised its money from disenfranchised (mostly) black women in the townships to invest in mainstream economic activities. From boutique investment fund, it quickly established itself as one of the key drivers of Economic Empowerment and one of the movers and shakers in the South African financial services industry, developing over the years a large range of sophisticated products and services targeting, as a strategy, previously underserved groups.

In 1994, four professional black women took it on themselves to engage South African women and offer them an opportunity to gain access to the mainstream economic opportunities created by the various empowerment initiatives. Women Investment Portfolio Holdings (WIPHOLD) was a private equity investment vehicle determined to make a difference; empowerment would come through *engagement* and *education*, not charity. Eschewing the typical model offering cheap micro-loans to rural women, Wiphold *took* money from women, invested it and made it grow. It succeeded in switching them from a consumption and savings mindset, to one of investment.

Questions for Discussion

1   What are the objectives and means of the Black Economic Empowerment movement? Was it an efficient vehicle to fill the gap left by years of apartheid? How else would you get disenfranchised groups back into mainstream economic activities?

2   To kick-start participation, special purpose vehicles (SPV) were introduced—was this the right solution in this context? What were the major issues with it?

3   What do you think of Wiphold as a business concept, and of its business model? What do you see as the major pros and cons of the envisioned system?

4   How do you evaluate the founders and their vision? Idealists or pragmatists? Opportunists or visionaries? Were they looking for niche

opportunities to invest in or were they true pioneers of empowerment?

5   A women-only IPO? Is positive discrimination sustainable?

6   How would you rate the chances of such an IPO being successful? What would the biggest challenges be post-IPO?

AT A GLANCE[5]

Bliss Soy Cheese

Ramachandran Kavil[a] and Erin Rogalski[b]

[a]*Thomas Schmidheiny Chair Professor of Family Business and Wealth Management, Family Business and Wealth Management, Indian School of Business, Hyderabad, India;* [b]*Freelancer*

Looking down at the week's sales reports, Lata questioned how much longer she could maintain her business at the same growth trajectory. Business had been steadily increasing, but recent capacity constraints created an imposing ceiling. Lata already had 40 percent more orders than she was able to fill running the production facility 15 hours a day. Though current demand was strong, Lata was uncertain about how much longer the Indian market could continue to rapidly expand and whether or not she was positioned to capture incremental growth. Lata had been manufacturing soy food products in Hyderabad for five years and it was still difficult to judge how much market awareness soy was really gaining in India.

Lata was certain that she wanted to pass her business, Bliss Foods, on to her son and daughter in the future but she was unsure about how to grow it in the present. Each day seemed to bring with it a new host of challenges and opportunities. She had many balls in the air in terms of potential customers, new geographies, undependable labor, and capacity constraints. There were so many moving pieces; it was difficult to come to a decision on any one issue. The business had achieved some level of scale and secured many important customers but additional growth was required in order to generate sufficient income and to keep newly interested competitors out of her geographical market. Lata was convinced that the market for soy had significant potential in India but how much effort would be required to unlock it? Lata, a serial entrepreneur, had spent over 30 years in business for herself and as she checked through the customer orders for the next day, she could not help but wonder how much more of herself she could give to her business.

Product Overview

Bliss Foods' primary product is tofu (or bean curd) blocks, which are sold in the format of "soy paneer." The soy paneer product looks quite similar to milk paneer, which is an unaged, acid-set, non-melting cheese made by curdling heated milk with lemon juice or some other food acid. Paneer is one of only a few cheeses indigenous to India and is widely used in Northern Indian cuisine. Though soy paneer and milk paneer are virtually indistinguishable in appearance, the consistency and taste of tofu is quite different than that of the milk paneer. Soy paneer generally sells on a par with milk paneer at approximately ₹ 40 ($0.91 USD) for 200 grams. Lata has set pricing for her soy paneer at small discount at ₹ 35 ($0.79 USD). Bliss has positioned the soy paneer product to retailers as a high protein non-dairy alternative to milk paneer, though none of this is explicitly stated on the product packaging.

Operations and Distribution

All Bliss products are produced in a small facility behind Lata's home using a production crew of seven. In addition to the tofu blocks, the current equipment can also produce a wide range of soy products including milk and flour. A large amount of work is done by hand as compared to larger operations. Batch size for the soy paneer is small and automation is nonexistent. One batch is processed at a time and each batch can produce approximately 15 units. After a twenty-four hour soaking period for the soybeans, batch processing time is under an hour from start to finish. This is also subject to variability due to the lack of automation. Employee turnover is high given the labor requirements of the job, which occasionally disrupts supply. Workers receive market wages but are quick to abandon their post if something less strenuous (and kinder to the senses) becomes available. The production facility runs 12 to 15 hours per day and a night shift is not an option given the facility's residential location. There is space in the current facility for additional equipment, though the location is not central to major distribution points. The finished product is packed in ice and transported to customers via automobile.

Some level of investment is required for Lata to increase capacity in order to meet demand. The next tier of processing equipment costs approximately ₹ 7.5 million (approximately $170,000 USD) and is best suited for high-volume producers. Just recently the same Delhi manufacturer of Lata's small-scale equipment introduced a machine for the middle market, selling at approximately ₹ 0.6 million. There is only one such machine that has been sold, and the durability and efficiency of the equipment are largely unknown and untested. The costs to upgrade in a significant way greatly increases the financial risk associated with scaling up, especially for small manufacturers like Lata who are unsure about the market. Incremental upgrades to fill immediate demand are also available through the purchase of small-batch low automation equipment, which is similar to what Bliss is using now. Additionally, there is a market for second-hand or refurbished equipment but it is unpredictable in both selection and quality.

Cash flow for Lata's business is still relatively tight as the bulk of the family's wealth is tied up in real estate. Recent political uncertainties in Andhra Pradesh, where a bulk of the family's real estate investment has taken place, have significantly impacted the market and as a result many of the family's investments are currently underwater. Working capital for the business is also quite tight given long customer payment cycles. Lata will have no choice but to rely on acquiring bank financing to fund growth-related capital expenditures.

Customer Relationships

Given the scale of Lata's operations, she first targeted several small retailers for initial entry into the marketplace but quickly realized that the effort the sales process required was not worth the returns. There is significant lack of market awareness regarding soy products and their benefits and high levels of resistance to experiment with new products. Additionally, it was difficult to achieve economies of scale as each store owner had to be approached and introduced to the product separately. Lata aggressively began pursuing mid-size retail chains in Hyderabad and was successful in capturing several key market players. Though many of these new customers have eased Lata's burden via central distribution networks, she is unable to keep up with demand and is at risk of losing the business that she worked so hard to attain.

One mid-size retail chain has recently approached Lata to start supplying to Bangalore locations as well, which are over 500 km from Lata's Hyderabad base. Uptake for soy products in urban centers has far exceeded that in rural areas and represents significant opportunity. Urban-based hypermarkets and large grocery chains represent rapid growth avenues for Bliss; however, Lata does not have the bar coding on her packaging required in order to sell to these large customers. Lata was recently approached by the largest hypermarket in Hyderabad to explore a relationship but she was unable to even entertain such a request at that time given her capacity constraints alone. Lata has successfully made a name for herself in Hyderabad but Bliss Foods' dominance of the soy paneer market is currently being challenged. A Chennai-based competitor has entered the Hyderabad market and is aggressively filling orders where Bliss is falling short and representing a credible threat to Bliss's current customer base.

Lata has also explored various opportunities in the hospitality segment and enjoyed some initial success. A five-star Hyderabad hotel purchased the soy paneer from Lata to use as a substitute for milk paneer for many of the hotel restaurant's dishes. Given the difference in taste profile, the soy paneer is not always directly substitutable and requires different prepara-tions. Customers found the milk paneer to be better tasting in the tradi-tional Indian recipes and the hotel discontinued ordering. Lack of education regarding the multitude of uses for soy paneer and the corresponding failure on the part of the hotel to utilize the ingredient in a way that enhances its flavor resulted in the termination of the relationship.

Soy in the Indian Context

India has been identified as a high-potential market for soy food products given the sheer magnitude of vegetarians. Surveys from sources such as the Food and Agriculture Organization of the United Nations estimate that 42 percent[6] of the Indian population is vegetarian. Additionally, meat consumption among non-vegetarians was noted as infrequent, with less than 30 percent of the population consuming meat regularly.[7] Conversely, given the historical reliance on vegetables and legumes as primary components of the diet, Indian cuisine already contains high levels of protein. Indians have traditionally satisfied protein requirements through pulses and a high utilization of legumes as well as through whole wheat flours and cheeses.

Though tofu is positioned in the Indian market as an alternative source of protein there are many other health benefits which are unknown to the majority Indian consumers. Soy is low in fat and calories and has been proven to reduce LDL cholesterol levels. Many other health benefits are derived from the isoflavine content of soybeans including protection against breast cancer, prostate cancer, menopausal symptoms, heart disease and osteoporosis. Though tofu's bland flavor can be seen as a drawback, it is also what lends such versatility to the ingredient. Tofu absorbs the flavors from other ingredients and can be prepared in a number of ways, including grilling, baking, frying and boiling. Soy products and tofu in particular are relatively new to the Indian market. Consumer education on the unique health benefits of soy and uses and preparation of tofu products is virtually nonexistent.

Replacement or substitute foods in India are gaining significant momentum and "sugar free," "fat free" and "all natural" products are slowly transitioning into the mainstream. Innovative soy products are appearing on shelves in the form of meatless meats, bread made with soy flour, soy milk and soy nuggets. Additionally, convenience foods which are virtually ready-made and quick and easy to prepare are gaining popularity among urban professionals that do not have the time to cook. Significant opportunity for healthy convenience products in the Indian market opens up a lot of potential opportunity for soy but also involves a lot of effort to build consumer awareness and provide education.

Conclusion

Lata has many decisions to make, with the first being how much more of her financial and personal resources she can invest in the growth of her business. She could make small adjustments to increase customers or add variations to the main product but her growth would ultimately be constrained by capacity. She could expand her product line in numerous ways and leverage the inroads she had already made in the market but this would require significant capital investment. The possibilities for growth are numerous, but the uncertainty of the market provided no guarantee that the investment would be returned very soon. At the same time, Lata understands that there is a pressing need to increase capacity in order to keep her new competition out of her market. In addition to thinking about growth and capacity, Lata must also consider how to get a more consistent labor force and whether or not to integrate her family into the business.

Notes

1 At http://www.dianaproject.org/Data/publications/publicationsfordow/themyths dispelled/myths_dispelled.pdf ; the sample is based on women participants of the Springboard 2000 forums, at www.springboard2000.org

2 The procedure conducted by Dr. Kariv to obtain women entrepreneurs' best practices was built on Skype-based semi-structured interviews lasting around 30 minutes each (some were performed over two or three different sessions) with women entrepreneurs; half of the interviewees were members of the BNI organization; the other half was located by snowball procedure. BNI is the largest business networking organization in the world, offering members the opportunity to share ideas, contacts and most importantly, business referrals, at http://www.bni.com/

3 Forbes, January 25, 2007, at http://www.forbes.com/2007/01/25/07midas-powerful-women-tech-cz_ccm_0125women.html

4 The author(s) of the case studies and at-a-glance cases are fully and solely responsible for their content, phrasing consistency and flow, terminology, English proofing and reference lists.

5 At-a-glance cases are included to present different ecosystems and their effects on the concepts discussed in the chapter; they do not include questions for discussion.

6 2.3 Growth and Concentration in India, FAO Document Repository.

7 Passage to India, USDA.

11   Entrepreneurial Paths of Women Entrepreneurs

Chapter Objectives

- Distinguishing between career types and their characteristics, e.g., boundaryless careers, protean careers, kaleidoscope careers;
- Outlining the new career paths of women relative to current developments (educational level, entrance to managerial positions) and vis-à-vis the barriers still imposed on women's advancement in the corporation;
- Viewing entrepreneurship as an opportunity and necessity path of employment;
- Typifying different entrepreneurial paths and linking them to solutions that apply to women's needs, hurdles and difficulties;
- Discussing the model of multiplicity of career paths;
- Giving women a glimpse of social entrepreneurship;
- Analyzing women's entrepreneurial intentions and their career transactions;
- Revealing the generational quests in female entrepreneurship.

This chapter introduces new career paths that enable women to embark on entrepreneurship and develop fulfilling careers that match their professional and job-related capabilities and achievements, along with their family and household responsibilities. Female entrepreneurship can be cultivated in a nourishing and vigorous way, as a normative career path—similar to men—when the environment accepts and encourages this form of entrepreneurship.

Consequently, this chapter traces the new avenues that can apply to Generation X and Y women entrepreneurs, including combinations of multiple avenues, quitting a job when "it is not fun" and striving to find the best match between their capabilities, needs and motivations, and the supply of their ecosystems. New career patterns are introduced and discussed to depict women entrepreneurs' different states of mind and approaches, and to analyze how these attitudes can be best incorporated into their entrepreneurial career path.

NEW CAREER PATTERNS AND FEMALE ENTREPRENEURSHIP

The surge of women into the workforce, the exponentially growing ranks of women in organizations, and recent transformations in the nature, meaning and dynamics of the career, e.g., boundaryless (Arthur & Rousseau, 1996), protean (Hall, 1996, 2004), kaleidoscope (Mainiero & Sullivan, 2005), intertwined with the continual barriers imposed on women entrepreneurs, have resulted in fundamentally different career development for women, which embraces entrepreneurship and its deliverables, i.e., entrepreneurial paths. Women define their career differently than do men and interpret different situations as successful or unsuccessful. Subsequently, women's definitions of work-related success focus on factors that differ from those that are central for men.

Women's career development is thus considerably more multifaceted than ever. Barriers imposed on women's careers through gendered social contexts are pertinent but have become more elusive—hidden, but still most conservative; e.g., collective norms still expect women to shoulder the brunt of household responsibilities, in addition to developing a career. Such expectations persist under inconsiderate corporate conditions that include a lack of concern for women's needs. Consequently, women are still at a specific disadvantage when attempting to conform to the traditional career models, and they tend to opt out of their professional development. Yet, contrary to their work–family choices in the past, today many women aspire to fulfilling careers that incorporate their qualifications, credentials, desires and goals. Thus, indifference has turned to frustration, and exclusion from the career to which they aspire has been transformed to a push into other career alternatives. Entrepreneurship represents one such career alternative that enables women to rebuild their undesired, sluggish careers, by taking proactive management of their work life and career path and controlling their time and assignments (Fagenson-Eland & Baugh, 2000; Hewlett & Luce, 2005; Ragins, Townsend, & Mattis, 1998).

The following models are significant in the female entrepreneurial context in that they lead to a revision of some of the conventional thinking about female careers, and stress how careers, such as entrepreneurship, apply to women's needs and wishes by being unlikely to be linear, unidirectional and upwardly hierarchical in character.

Boundaryless careers—a succinct definition of the boundaryless career is a sequence of occupational paths that are not bounded within specific organizations but grow through project-based competency development across firms in an industry network. Such career paths are built upon job mobility across multiple employers, personal responsibility for directing one's own career development, and the development of social networks to shape and sustain that career. Boundaryless career paths require new sets of competencies including referral skills, partnering, and relationship management; e.g., "knowing what," "knowing where," "knowing whom" and "knowing how" (Arthur & Rousseau, 1996; DeFillippi & Arthur, 1994; Jones & DeFillippi, 1996). Lifelong learning is essential in such career paths and accrues along the developmental stages of the new venture creation, dovetailing with the leading concepts in both entrepreneurship and career development.

Protean careers—the protean[1] career concept invokes the notion that individuals can reshape their careers in response to changing life circumstances, through self-directedness and congruence with personal values, rather than relying on the organization to take responsibility for their careers (Hall, 1996).

Protean careers are most relevant to female entrepreneurship as women become self-agents and mold their career course, structure and content, tailor-made to their own constraints and needs. Creation of their own new venture allows women to implement their own definitions of accomplishments and success; they value concepts of psychological success, personal accomplishment and family well-being, even when they are not based on empirical evidence of traditional measures of success, but rather on emotions.

The protean career emphasizes the value of continuous learning and mastery, and it engages individuals in a lifelong series of developmental experiences. Such elements are accepted and highly likely among women entrepreneurs, who appreciate continual learning, challenging work, and incremental career strategies, especially under more favorable conditions where they are less restricted to male-dominated fields.

Kaleidoscope careers—the Kaleidoscope Career Model (KCM) traces the shifts in career patterns over time as individuals' needs and interests change, based on three main career-decision backbones: authenticity, balance, and challenge (Mainiero & Sullivan, 2005; Sullivan & Arthur, 2006). Accordingly, women entrepreneurs decide on their career path by being true to themselves and can shape their entrepreneurial path in the most compatible way with their values, i.e., authenticity; they can more easily integrate their work and non-work lives, i.e., balance; and they can incorporate their own challenges into their course of action, such as their own interests, stretching their work to different spheres, and thus empowering themselves.

These career models refer to the ways in which social practices have become "stretched" over traditional spans of place, conventional career tracks and specific organizations; entrepreneurial careers are then developed, molded through women's needs and cultivated along their life span, congruent with their interests and needs.

Research in entrepreneurial motivation has drawn increasing attention to the advent of women who create their own businesses instead of maintaining corporate careers. The most cited reasons for women leaving their corporate careers and establishing their own businesses are:

- a desire for more flexibility;
- avoidance of the corporate glass ceiling;
- dissatisfaction with the organizational work environment;
- a lack of challenging opportunities in corporate positions;
- prescriptive access to certain projects or activities, including those that could perfectly match women's abilities, expertise or interests;
- escape from a male-dominated ecosystem that gives only limited space to women's discourse.

Female entrepreneurial paths respond to these conditions by providing:

- flexibility, arrangements that fit women's demands and needs without opting them out of their professional expertise;
- career through self-directedness; personal choices; acceptance of transitions within their career track;
- approval of women's personal value congruence;
- requirement for continual learning;
- making room for different activities and for different angles in the same activity;
- opening opportunities;
- shaping "tailor-made" ecosystems that are compatible with women's motivations and aspirations.

Mompreneurship

Mompreneurship is an emerging phenomenon rooted in the everyday experience of mothers, and referring to women struggling to balance motherhood and run their businesses.

The term has been coined to describe mothers running businesses in the entrepreneurial spirit; hence, it links concepts in the new venture creation, motherhood, and society's dual expectations of women that they take on the main responsibility for household-related activities, while contributing to the household's income by going out to work.

The main elements that characterize mother-entrepreneurs, as revealed from the research, are:

- developing and maintaining a balance between women's needs and interests in their careers and their motherhood-related responsibilities;
- the desire for a work environment unencumbered with an immediate supervisor who is impervious to and unconcerned about the needs of one's family;
- the wish to network with savvy mompreneurs who are facing similar challenges and difficulties;
- sharing insights, advice and ideas with significant others, specialists, mentors who can assist in maintaining a balance between career and motherhood;
- the desire to transfer the fulfillment of motherhood to work and vice versa; many women report that spending hours at work/with the children is exhausting and leaves them with limited energy for quality time with the children/at work;
- joining forces with family members toward the challenge of raising healthy children in a working, entrepreneurial environment;
- partnering with others in a business; being inspired by others who share similar challenges and difficulties;
- managing home-based businesses; virtual careers.

Technology and changing attitudes toward career, entrepreneurship and motherhood have made it easier to create new ventures and establish the time frame for their various tasks. In addition, by acknowledging the existence of mompreneurship, the mompreneurship market expands: mothers become the customers of mompreneurs; the dissemination of the concept and its rationale make it easier for mompreneurs to hire people, partner with people, and establish trustful relationships with suppliers and investors (Bechthold, 2006; Bird & Brush, 2002; Bower, 2005; Lichtenstein & Brush, 2001; White, 1995; Winsor & Ensher, 2002). Different life circumstances push mothers to entrepreneurship unintentionally, sometimes even as a twist from a well-structured corporate career path; for example, Jennie, a 39-year-old entrepreneur from the UK, founded an internet magazine when she "discovered" that she was carrying three babies; Accalia, from Canada, a 33-year-old entrepreneur, moved her architecture business to home when her daughter was diagnosed with severe attention deficit hyperactivity disorder (ADHD), and her business received a boost when she transferred it to a home business; Hadar, a 25-year-old Israeli entrepreneur who faced separation from her spouse and had to raise her two 2-year-olds as a single mother, discovered an active, virtual network for mothers by chance while browsing the internet and partnered with one of the network's members to manage a shared blog for mothers; the blog became most successful worldwide, attracted some investments and was then sold to a big, global company for baby products; for Hadar, mompreneurship was a matter of survival, providing for her family, but then it evolved into a satisfying entrepreneurial career. These examples illustrate the significance of mompreneurship and the reasons it should be uncovered and accepted as an independent and valid career path, which should attract people who are juggling work and home, and are struggling to create a balance between the two by taking the plunge through entrepreneurship.

HOME-BASED ENTREPRENEURSHIP

A home-based business is a form of entrepreneurship that is frequently attributed to female entrepreneurship, even though it appears that the number of people, women and men, managing home-based entrepreneurial businesses is on the rise. Home-based entrepreneurship has been precipitated and accelerated by the internet, virtual networks such as Facebook and LinkedIn, and other current and emerging new technologies that facilitate working from home, getting in touch with customers, suppliers and employees at different hours, sharing documents through "interactive white boards," virtually contacting each other face to face or online chatting, among others.

Home-based work is an entrepreneurial form favored by women because it provides an effective way of balancing the demands of paid employment and family responsibilities; the new venture creation process is less risky due to lower overhead and capital outlay for other premises, and is thus compatible with women's risk-aversiveness; it is typically a micro-business, with up to five employees, well-suited to women's lower growth aspirations and their definitions of success and self-accomplishment (Cliff, 1998; Felstead & Jewson, 2000; Moore & Buttner, 1997; Still & Guerin, 1991; Walker, 2003).

With the advent of home-based business opportunities, women can develop a career that suits them, maintain financial independence, e.g. balancing the family budget, save on commuting and other expenses associated with leaving the home to go to work, spend quality time with their children and pursue home-based opportunities at the same time. In addition to solving their work–family conflict, home-based work allows women to save time, and then spend it on other activities, such as leisure time, hobbies, volunteering or donating time to charitable causes, and study, among others.

A home-based path, however, has typical pitfalls that make it unsuitable for some women entrepreneurs; for example, operating a business from home may reduce the business owner's privacy: home is no longer a separate sphere from work. The traditional "roles" within the work and family domains can fluctuate, e.g., the mother is also the CEO of her business. Furthermore, some women, especially those operating internet-based businesses, may find work too easily reached and attractive, and may therefore spend longer hours at their home-based business than in a corporate job; finally, as home-based businesses are usually micro, women may experience some loneliness.

VIRTUAL ENTREPRENEURSHIP

Virtual businesses exist in a virtual rather than physical world, and their presence relies heavily on telecommunications and networks such as the internet. In such a configuration, geographically dispersed individuals can collaborate on the basis of their core strengths from wherever they are and whenever they are able to do so.

Many virtual businesses are established ad hoc to pursue a particular business opportunity. They are typically extremely focused and goal-driven, and managed on the basis of little investment requirements, low start-up and overhead costs, and fast response time. Thus, these are flexible, lively, and fluid businesses that correspond to the entrepreneurial spirit. Often virtual, they disband when their purpose is fulfilled or the opportunity passes.

According to Schon (1987), virtual businesses permit ". . . different paces in doing different things, different ways of doing the same thing, and, above all, reflection in action" (p. 102). Subsequently, virtual entrepreneurship can create virtual alliances with other businesses for the purpose of achieving a specific task, working with international teams, attracting customers worldwide, maintaining trade relations for buying and selling with no geographical limitations.

Women entrepreneurs may find virtual entrepreneurship to be the optimal entrepreneurial configuration, matching their needs which stem from both their family and work worlds. First, virtual ventures enable time flexibility, task prioritization, and reduced time consumed by, e.g., commuting, parking, the so-called "marginal" time spent waiting for meetings, or even the time spent dressing up and applying makeup for face-to-face meetings, among others. Correspondingly, women, mainly mothers who are "juggling" time allocated to their children and their businesses, may benefit from working "behind the computer screen" or the telephone. Second, virtual entrepreneurial ventures require little investment; many web applications can be obtained via an "open source" through the internet, open to anyone, while dissemination of the virtual venture is rapid and with minimal costs. Women are reluctant to address the investment issue and tend to avoid it, delay it or pass it on to their male partners; yet, a virtual setting enables more independence in this matter, thus corresponding to their interests. Third, virtual entrepreneurial ventures are fluid and need to rapidly provide clear benefits to their shareholders so that they will decide to viably maintain and support them in the long run. Women entrepreneurs are cautious and watchful in spending their venture's money; investors favor partnering with women entrepreneurs who provide clear evidence of their financial proficiency in starting and managing a business, though women's self-confidence in their financial proficiency is relatively small. By accumulating more successful experiences in proving benefits, women entrepreneurs may establish their self-confidence in financing their business in the long run. Fourth, many virtual entrepreneurial ventures are temporary: they rise and fall on an ad hoc basis or according to the accomplishment of the original goal. Such a life cycle might be compatible with women entrepreneurs who favor "episodic" entrepreneurial experiences, for example, between pregnancies, when combining studies with work, etc. Fifth, virtual businesses enable prompt interactions, accompanied by lower levels of the "mental blocks" typical to business interactions (e.g., regarding which dress code is suitable for a meeting; language barriers, including accents; fluency in speech; the structure of Power-Point presentations, or even codes related to being punctual, etc.). Women easily and more openly interact, impart their ideas, share their concerns about their tenable plans and expectations and more naturally disclose their achievements as well as difficulties with others; thus, virtual entrepreneurship provides women with the benefit of following this natural inclination. The final point regards the key to achieving success in the virtual entrepreneurship, i.e., lifelong learning. Learning is a must to crystallize the best relationships between their personal/family life and their business's management while promoting their businesses in line with cutting-edge advances, which are even more pronounced in the virtual entrepreneurship realm due to the internet; this learning allows effectively advancing the business, extracting maximum engagement from the virtual teams and using "virtuality" to maximally attract customers. Women are dedicated learners; they are more conformist practitioners and are more willing to put their learning experiences into action. Relative to their male counterparts, women more easily admit that they need assistance and more naturally use learning to improve their business's and their own performance and achievements, allowing for the incremental improvement of their virtual businesses.

MULTIPLICITY IN ENTREPRENEURIAL AVENUES

Different entrepreneurial avenues are open for women: some already exist and are applied by women, e.g., home-based entrepreneurship, self-employment; others comprise a combination of entrepreneurial avenues and employment opportunities, e.g., part-time salaried employee and mompreneur; yet others may be newly introduced or invented avenues that adhere to women's needs. Because the entrepreneurial realm is fueled by flexibility and a broadminded spirit, any newly introduced avenue can apply.

Some avenues that are compatible with women's traits, interests and needs are summarized as follows:

- *Franchising*—women are at a disadvantage in acquiring capital to finance their ventures and are reluctant to take risks. Franchising could be the solution as it provides expedient access to capital, market knowledge, training and ongoing support. Franchising is a well-known business model that has often been touted as a means of providing opportunities to minorities, women and other groups experiencing disadvantages in the marketplace. Franchising is a legally binding business arrangement in which a business owner gives a person/business the rights to manage their business in a prescribed manner within a specified geographical region during an agreed upon period of time and in return for fee payments and royalty contributions. Often, the franchisor's business or trademark is already known, facilitating penetration into different markets and niches as well as shortening the administrative steps to be followed in the case of a brand new business. Although franchising is often promoted as a relatively easier method of starting a business, only a limited percentage of women own franchises (Castrogiovanni, Combs, & Justis, 2006; Justis & Judd, 2004; Kaufmann, 1999). Franchising provides ample entrepreneurial possibilities, e.g., it enables fostering different markets, niches, business-development approaches.

- *Self-employment*—working women who are classified as self-employed are making up an increasing segment in most countries worldwide. This phenomenon refers to women who have won a business, not necessarily by starting it or managing it through the entrepreneurial path, i.e. inventing a business idea, looking for external financing, disseminating the business's innovation and uniqueness, taking risks, etc., but by managing an existing business, running a family business, co-partnering with a business owner, among others.

Research shows that women, particularly mothers of young children, seeking self-employment avail themselves of flexible working hours in order to accommodate family-related obligations. They enjoy widespread policies to encourage business ownership among women, and they experience more job satisfaction. Although they have more of a work–family conflict than their counterparts employed in organizations, many benefit from "being their own boss" and being liberated from a male-dominated environment and the glass ceiling they encountered at their corporate jobs. In most countries, self-employed women have attained higher educational levels and many gain higher salaries. Despite the steady increase in the number of self-employed women over the past three decades and the attraction of self-employment as a practical avenue for women, especially mothers, women's self-employment rates still remain significantly lower than those of men. Reasons for this, revealed in research, refer to, among others, the genders' different motivations to become self-employed, i.e., women seek flexibility, and the planned duration of self-employment; accordingly, women plan to be self-employed for a shorter time, "until the kids grow up," and do not see it as a career path (Fairlie, 2004; Langowitz & Minniti, 2007; Parasuraman & Simmers, 2001).

- *Activists*—this avenue is more political than economic; it refers to women who are active in political ventures that strongly promote female issues. Their motivation is to advocate for the long-term development of women's interests rather than profit-making. The entrepreneurial opportunities are immense, as this avenue focuses on advancing ideas, and thus "the sky is the limit." Ms. Dafni Leef,[2] a 25-year-old Israeli woman who worked at various jobs to graduate with a degree in film from the university, provoked the most significant social protest ever conducted in Israel by initiating an innovative idea: she started a Facebook "event" and invited people to protest against high housing prices; rather than just complaining, she used entrepreneurial characteristics and strategies, e.g., proactiveness, creativity, risk-taking and determination, and erected a tent in a central area of Tel Aviv. Following her act, hundreds erected tents in different cities around Israel. The protest then expanded to the idea of promoting the social well-being of the middle social stratum groups, rather than only the lower social groups.
- *Partnerships*—joining forces to start a business can be most beneficial for women in the new venture creation phase, as it provides them with the opportunity to share ideas, distribute functional responsibilities, expose their expertise (when they function alone they must be involved in different areas, including those in which they are less proficient) and reduce risks. In addition, partnerships expand networks, and intensify the brainstorming process and learning from others' experiences. Establishing a partnership is congruent to many of the business strategies used by women, e.g., sharing ideas and experiences, reflecting on encountered situations, being risk-reluctant. An enriching partnership can be a fulfilling entrepreneurial avenue for women, as it enables them to employ their capabilities, implement their dreams and be their own boss, while availing themselves of the flexibility, controlling their tasks and time and directing their career path to desired destinations.
- *Combinations*—combining corporate and non-corporate work is another career avenue for women; it enables women to maintain their secure working conditions in a corporate job, while planning, preparing and starting a new venture. For women encountering a glass ceiling at their corporate workplace, limited access to projects they aspire to be involved in, or to internal jobs they wish to be a part of, such a combination provides great interest, satisfaction and hope. In addition, different experiences at their corporate job, interactions and networks may be of assistance to their planned ventures; for example, experiences of handling difficult situations with

customers, suppliers or employees could be useful in determining the best practices and methods that worked, to use them in their future businesses. Obviously, such combinations suffer from some shortcomings: because their time is divided into work at the organization and their preparations for the new venture, women may find limited time for their families and leisure; their new ventures will take a long time to become established as they are not allocating full attention to their preparation; finally, some women may find it difficult to keep their "avatar life" a secret.

- *Transforming hobbies into ventures*—entrepreneurship encompasses the principal of implementing one's dream or vision; thus, it is logical to assume that hobbies can be turned into entrepreneurial businesses. In fact, women are more apt than men to turn their hobbies into entrepreneurial ventures; for example, Gili, a 29-year-old American woman who completed her studies as a medical doctor, combined her demanding job at a public hospital with her cooking hobby. At a certain point she decided to concentrate on cooking. She took courses with the best chefs and started a unique catering business; Alicia, a 45-year-old woman from Madrid, Spain, was employed as a nurse at a public clinic for many years, and "used" a simple conflict with her supervisor at the clinic as an excuse to release herself from her job and open a unique place for story-telling for young children; she adored reading and dreamt of turning this into a real venture; while Emiliana from Naples, Italy, a 32-year-old mother of three young children, who pursued her family's tradition and did not go out to work, decided after ten years to turn her pottery hobby into a business and started to sell her merchandise locally. This endeavor met with immediate success, especially among tourists; then she added a "heritage flavor" to her business by pottering Naples-based material, and selling authentic merchandise that attracted even more tourists; her shop was mentioned in tourist guides and people came from distant places to visit her shop; after a few years, she franchised her business. Women's open-mindedness and non-judgmental attitude toward combining work and home/private life facilitate their implementation of such an avenue. This approach, however, does not lessen their dedication to the business and their determination to establish the most vigorous business concept; as women are more open to the spillover between work and family life, they regard it as more natural to combine different spheres into their businesses, be it in the business's concept, structure, physical workplace, etc.
- *Non-profit undertakings*—The main purpose of non-profit organizations is to serve public interest. Women who are passionate about a cause and are thrilled to take action may start non-profit businesses that are dedicated to a cause; e.g., women's rights, environmental awareness, animal protection, protest again child labor. They can use

volunteers, donations and grants, and strive to make a real difference in their cause. Such an avenue is most entrepreneurial as it requires innovation, a focused concept, thorough research to plan the concept and the structure of the business, among others. The documented non-profit orientation is congruent with the perceived female characteristics such as sensitivity, consideration, empathy, and responsiveness; given the clear links between such characteristics and the overall objective of non-profit organizations, a non-profit undertaking can be a valuable avenue for women entrepreneurs. Non-profit businesses require solid plans, fundraising, a business concept, outlining the non-profit's mission statement, marketing efforts, among others, and can be most rewarding. It enables women to gain flexibility as well interlink their ideas, interests and zeal for proactive action with an entrepreneurial undertaking (Dees, Emerson, & Economy, 2001; Di Domenico, Haugh, & Tracey, 2010; Zahra, Gedajlovic, Neubaum, & Shulman, 2009).

- *Breakthrough-ers*—some women face conditions that set severe hurdles in pursuing a desired entrepreneurial way, e.g., financial difficulties, family pressures, etc., yet they do not renounce entrepreneurship; they let their mind "function entrepreneurially" by inventing ideas, improving the things that they encounter daily, including services, facilities, procedures, machinery, etc. These women fuel their world by being committed to their entrepreneurial avenue, which is unusual and mostly unrevealed, but most stimulating for them and their proximate environment. Malina, from Cambodia, had been kept by her family in the traditional woman's role for years and was forbidden to study or work outside her home; yet, as an entrepreneurial spirit, Malina had developed different discoveries in various areas. One such invention actually "released" her from her traditional role, which she considered most frustrating. She was in her thirties, a mother, when she noted that teachers spoke for eight hours a day while the children sat passively, expected to absorb all of the knowledge. Malina thought that children should learn by doing things, practising, taking responsibility for their studies. She stated her criticism as well as her new plan for the school's teaching routines to the school's parents' committee; her plan was accepted with great enthusiasm—the community entitled it "Malina's breakthrough"; it was very rapidly implemented. Today, this school is a pioneer in its unique, breakthrough learning approach, winning an award as the leading school in students' achievements in the area. *The Guardian*, UK, published an article in March 2011 on *100 years of scientific breakthroughs—by women*[3] divulging the great contributions of women in inventions and breakthroughs. The advantage of this avenue is that it can be managed concurrently with other activities, it is not risky and has continued potential of evolving into a venture when the ground is ripe for it.

- *Philanthropy*—entrepreneurial philanthropy involves taking substantial risks to initiate an organization/entity, and having an economic impact. In fact, it is no different from the original concept of entrepreneurship; however, it is said that philanthropy is modeled on the family unit—from helping a family member without expecting anything in return. Consequently, entrepreneurial philanthropy focuses on a specific scope, i.e., creating organizations for the express purpose of making a positive and constructive difference in societal members (Nowell, 1996; Reis, 1999).

Traditionally, entrepreneurship has been associated with financial profits, though this might seem to contradict the philanthropic approach. Yet recent studies have begun to explore the concept of philanthropy and social entrepreneurship, articulating that any historically significant contribution is founded on the creation of wealth (wealth) and the distribution of wealth (philanthropy); in Acs and Dana's words (2001, p. 66): "[P]hilanthropy provides a positive feedback mechanism for future economic growth, and a cumulative causation leading to higher levels of economic development." Shaw and Taylor (1995, p. 88) summed up six categories representing women's given motivations to engage in philanthropic entrepreneurial businesses:

- Change
- Create
- Connect
- Commit
- Collaborate
- Celebrate their philanthropic accomplishments.

THE PREFERRED ENTREPRENEURIAL AVENUE

Entrepreneurship provides ample avenues for implementation, additional to those discussed earlier in this chapter. Other avenues, which are compatible for everyone and do not necessarily address women's needs, can serve as a vehicle to entrepreneurship, e.g., technopreneurship, serial entrepreneurship, portfolio entrepreneurship, corporate entrepreneurship. Women who have the entrepreneurial zeal should not repress it, even when conditions seem complicated. Rather, they may choose a suitable avenue which will allow them to incorporate entrepreneurship into the existing framework of their lives.

Due to its permissive, accommodating and tolerant spirit, entrepreneurship is all-encompassing, especially at the new venture creation phase, and it possesses the fortitude to absorb any type of employment, in any structure or framework. Any idea can captivate vivacious entrepreneurs at the new venture creation phase. Consequently, women may enter any avenue and manage their entrepreneurial path at any pace and intensity which makes them comfortable. The entrepreneurial concept, however, is intolerant toward persisting in the comfort zone; renouncing proactivity eventually results in renouncing entrepreneurship.

In addition to the different avenues introduced, a different angle might be to focus on one or more elements of the new venture to leverage them into a successful business. Figure 11.1 demonstrates some elements that can be leveraged.

Women may chose to focus on product development, technology development, the service, a gimmick, payment arrangement or exploiting a new niche. They should not consider their engagement in the whole entrepreneurial path as a requisite demand at the venture creation phase; focusing on one element can lead to the others and drive women to entrepreneurship with no coercion.

Angelina, a 55-year-old woman entrepreneur from Buenos Aires, Argentina, exemplifies this point; Angelina worked as a librarian for more than ten years, when she felt she wanted to make a career change; she did not consider entrepreneurship at first, but coming across a friend from school that she had not met for years, and who has transformed her life as an international entrepreneur, Angelina decided to explore entrepreneurship. She took a course at the local center for entrepreneurs and felt "it was meant to be . . ."; she used her final assignment in the course, a detailed business plan, to establish a publishing house for children's books (her mentor gave her an A+), and started to prepare for entrepreneurship; but

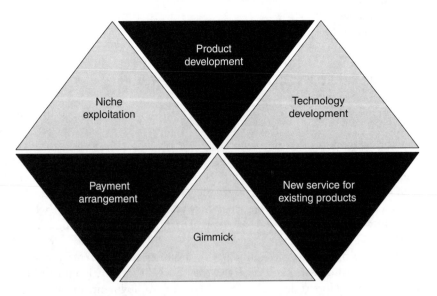

Figure 11.1 Focusing and Leveraging.

she was very quickly overwhelmed and decided to go back to work at the library. During that period, she was frustrated and edgy; she was terrified of entrepreneurship but also most attracted to it, and she dreamt of implementing the publishing house. She consulted her course mentor, Ruth, and Ruth worked with Angelina on the step-by-step technique described in Figure 11.2. The main contribution of Ruth's mentoring was in proving that an entrepreneurial journey can start through different stimulators; while Angelina was thrilled by the product development aspects, its different derivatives were sought; e.g., Angelina was interested in decoding the motivations to write children's books as well as to actually write them; she was attempting to crack the success keys of the most renowned publishing houses in general and analyzed the specific success keys of focal publishing houses, then she turned to those focused on children's books. In contrast to her first endeavor to step into entrepreneurship, the step-by-step technique fueled Angelina with curiosity and drove her to pursue this path. The second step was also quite unusual: Ruth recommended following her "guts" rather than a structured business plan, and Angelina chose the gimmick. Again, she went through an invigorating search, resulting in a marketing-based gimmick called: "dinner with an author"; the author(s) of each selected manuscript were awarded a free dinner with their favorite authors, in or outside Argentina. Angelina felt at this point that she was ready to start the "real" preparations for the

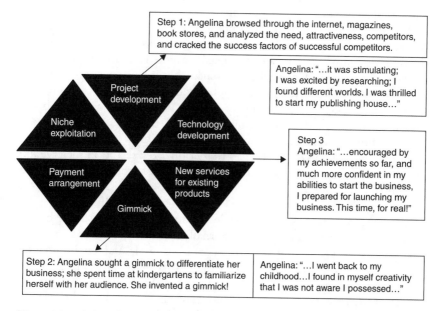

Figure 11.2 A Step-by-step Technique: Example of Angelina's Case of Starting a Publishing House for Children's Books in Buenos Aires, Argentina.

start-up. Delving into one or two elements of the new venture creation, those that are most exciting, attractive, emotionally driven, can be most stimulating and reassuring.

SOCIAL ENTREPRENEURSHIP

Social entrepreneurship integrates social and economic value creation by combining innovation, opportunity and resourcefulness to promote social systems and practices in a wide variety of fields, including ethnicity, immigration, environment, health, employment and education, among others.

It is an emerging and most promising concept, which many countries have aimed to promote in the last decade. Social entrepreneurial ventures are mainly hybrid organizations, i.e., they function according to the well-known entrepreneurial "rules," either aimed for profit or not-for-profit, with the primary goal of promoting social, ecological, or environmental topics. While profit may seem to be the driving engine for entrepreneurship, it does not preclude other motives, thus social entrepreneurship can be profit-based.

Yet, entrepreneurship as a concept to foster social progress has attracted only relatively limited research, though it is embedded in entrepreneurship and in social purpose; the development of social entrepreneurship as a research area closely resembles the development of the "general" area of entrepreneurship. Today, however, social entrepreneurship remains anecdotal and founded on case studies.

Social entrepreneurs share common traits with the "general" entrepreneur in striving to create an innovative business that will prove, and sustain, its competitive advantage; social entrepreneurs are innovative.

The central driver for social entrepreneurship in both not-for-profit and for-profit social ventures is the application of innovative and creative approaches, risk-taking, the ability to seize opportunities and mobilize ideas, capacities, and scarce resources toward their cause, the mission; hence aiming to resolve government or market failures, grasping opportunities, providing goods and services to marginalized sectors of society, and exhibiting a higher sense of accountability for the community served and the outcomes created.

The social entrepreneur is motivated by a cause, a mission; she/he has to achieve a state of alignment both externally and internally among the key components, e.g. the opportunity, people, capital, and environmental context. Due to its sensitive nature, i.e., sensitivity to changes in the ecosystem, and in order to reduce perturbations in the operating systems, social entrepreneurs must be cognizant of any changes in the various elements of their ecosystems, e.g., legal, social, technological, etc., and attuned to the effects of such contextual changes on the original "mission."

Consequently, proposing the social value for realignment is a critical skill for the social entrepreneur. For example, a social entrepreneur that founded the business on a mission of providing pro-bono services for illegal immigrants has to readjust the business's mission when new national regulations facilitating illegal immigrants' status are applied.

The societal demand for social-value creation is enormous; a plethora of opportunities for social entrepreneurs are simultaneously "out there" and tempting to address, yet the social entrepreneur's task is to determine at any given moment the appropriate scope of the opportunity that can be pursued successfully, dependent on ensuring that the scope is aligned internally with the available people and resources.

A social entrepreneur has to determine how best to identify the resource requirements and mobilize them; by building partnerships, alliances, attracting donations and large community interest that will advance the business's mission, for example, Goodwill Industries,[4] the largest private sector employer of people with disabilities that aims to train them and place them in the economic mainstream, established a partnership with the Methodist Church, and used the church's infrastructure and support. This collaboration allowed Goodwill Industries to generate more social value for its clients (Brinckerhoff, 2000; Haugh, 2005; Nicholls, 2006).

Women in the social entrepreneurship realm—like any business, social entrepreneurship can create value by being nurtured and supported by a viable resource-based strategy; the two must mesh together cleanly, so that the entire business model is plausible and the ongoing resource-mobilization process fortifies the new venture creation process. The most fundamental resource is the individual who starts and manages the social enterprise. Women social entrepreneurs are naturally more likely to tackle the human aspect of their ventures and see it as the backbone of their business, e.g., internal partners, management team, other founding members, employees (if there are any at this stage), and their ecosystem, e.g., customers, suppliers, community, investors, among others. While addressing the resource-based view, women entrepreneurs tend to address the human factor, whereas women social entrepreneurs may have a higher awareness of, and responsiveness to the human factor; many have started their social-based undertaking for a human-related cause; many are led by human-related factors while creating their ventures and managing them. Social entrepreneurship has several similarities to female entrepreneurship, as shown in Figure 11.3.

Some similarities can be found in the drivers behind female entrepreneurship and social entrepreneurship, although these are not exclusively drivers of only these two types of entrepreneurship:

- *Opportunities*—the environment provides ample opportunities, e.g., gaps, asymmetries, needs, unfulfilled niches, which are compatible with specific groups as well as generically. Opportunities in this sense do not necessarily refer only to the drivers to start a business, but also to the drivers for women to embark upon entrepreneurship, as such opportunities have the power to establish a context for the new venture as well as attract specific groups of entrepreneurs to create a venture.

- *Human capital*—some personal characteristics have the impact of pushing people into the process of new venture creation; in addition, some personal characteristics predict the attraction of a person to specific topics in entrepreneurship. For example, women are attracted to social-related enterprises; more highly educated people are more motivated to defend their cause, and are thus more attracted to social entrepreneurship; people who have acquired market experience, or even older people, are more likely to become social entrepreneurs.
- *Motivations*—entering the entrepreneurial world through a cause or a mission typifies many women entrepreneurs as well as social entrepreneurs; for both groups, making money is not the main cause, but a secondary one; both women and social entrepreneurs are very devoted to the mission and are willing to defend it by all means.

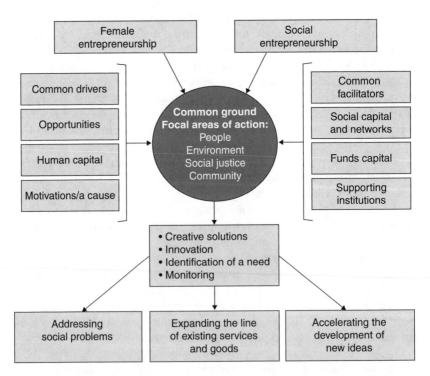

Figure 11.3 The Common Ground of Female and Social Entrepreneurship.

The facilitators that can be found in both female and social entrepreneurship are:

- *Social capital*—for groups that face more difficulties in the entrepreneurial market, social capital and solid networks are valuable assets that can facilitate their new venture creation process. The difficulties can be attributed to tackling unique barriers, such as in the case of women, or in convincing others of their concept's soundness, such as in the case of social entrepreneurs; when women embark on social entrepreneurship, aggregated difficulties may emerge. Social capital and networks, which are properly used for the purpose of the new venture creation, significantly ease these groups' penetration into the entrepreneurial market, alleviate the implementation process by providing the opportunity to share, ask for advice, assistance or even emotional support from their links whenever difficulties emerge, and raise their self-confidence by using their social capital capabilities.
- *Funds*—funding the business permits advancing it to the entrepreneur's original target levels, when it was a vision. Many ideas evolve prior to being financially supported, because entrepreneurs can visualize them and will not cease their activities until they see their ideas being implemented; nevertheless, there is a level at which further significant development cannot be achieved without external resources. At that point, the entrepreneur has to acquire things that cost money and that are imperative for the new venture creation from outside resources, such as human capital, knowledge, expertise, material, databases, among others. Women tend to delay, sometimes even avoid, the fund-raising process, due to, for example, lower self-confidence in their ability to start and manage a business, or uneasiness about raising financial issues; at the same time, the impetus that motivates and energizes social entrepreneurs seemingly contradicts tangible, profit-based matters, such as money, hence, they also tend to avoid the funding process. Women entrepreneurs and social entrepreneurs should consider funds as a significant means and practical resource which will enable implementing their original ideas and causes and harness their driving force into a real business.
- *Supporting institutions*—entrepreneurial spirit and the passion to act for a cause may give evidence of a person's innovative and creative attitudes, of being inspired by a cause, and highly motivated to act, even by taking risks. However, these characteristics do not guarantee any expertise in turning ideas into a business; such a process requires different skills (e.g., planning, researching, analyzing, managing people and projects), and some even run counter to the entrepreneurial nature. Different professional bodies assist female entrepreneurs and social entrepreneurs, among others, in the provision of complementary abilities and skills that entrepreneurs do not possess

but are sought to effectively create the new venture. It is important to get assistance from institutions that understand the entrepreneur's needs; female needs are exclusive due to women's dual role in the family and at work, or their encountering specific barriers; social entrepreneurs are motivated by unique, seemingly not-for-profit, and therefore less attractive causes; supporting institutions that provide the most relevant advice, solutions and assistance can provide short-cuts which will enable these groups of entrepreneurs to compete as equals in the entrepreneurial pursuit.

ENTREPRENEURIAL CAREER CHANGES

Entrepreneurship has been frequently conceptualized as conscious, planned, and intentional behavior (Katz & Gartner, 1988); accordingly, individuals develop intentions to perform in the prospective new venture creation process, based on their attitudes regarding the perceived levels of desirability, feasibility and credibility of this process and its outcomes, and consistent with their needs, interests, human capital, personal and social characteristics, etc. (Ajzen & Fishbein, 1980; Brazeal, Schenkel, & Azriel, 2008; Forbes, Borchert, Zellmer-Bruhn, & Sapienza, 2006). As such, a highly educated woman who intends to be "her own boss," finds this desirable and feasible and has obtained the relevant academic knowledge is more apt to start a business than a highly educated woman who does not see the new venture creation as a desired dream. However, to embark on an entrepreneurial career, these intentions are not sufficient; it is imperative to develop the belief in one's capability for success along the whole process of the new venture creation; cracks in one's self-belief can damage success and one's odds of actually starting a business. The self-efficacy theory addresses the self-belief in one's capability to succeed and postulates that cognitive estimates of the capability to garner resources, being trustful about one's choice of goals, investment of time in carefully selected activities, and perseverance in the face of obstacles, shape one's set of attitudes toward entrepreneurship (Bandura, 2000; Hewlett, 2002; Wood & Bandura, 1989).

According to the entrepreneurial intentions model and the self-efficacy theory, along with models of human capital, women can shape their entrepreneurial career path in a fluid and flexible track. In contrast to corporate careers which are for the most part more planned, except for a few career models,[5] entrepreneurship provides the freedom to more naturally make any choice at any stage; the social environment is much more tolerant and accepting of transitions in the entrepreneurial path compared to transitions in a corporate career. The business's life cycle is typified by targeting a vision, e.g., being the leader in a respective sector, achieving sales of a specific amount, becoming international, etc., and directing toward that

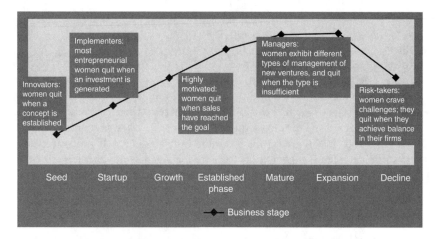

Figure 11.4 Career Transition and the New Venture's Life Cycle.

vision; concurrently, it sets sub-goals pertinent to each stage of the business's development, e.g., obtaining investments, finalizing the development of a prototype, selling the product/service in a specific location such as China or Europe. Women can weave their career path according to goals attributed to each stage; for example, women who are innovators are thrilled by the seed stage, but upon accomplishing its main goals, such as deciding upon the business concept, these women may "quit" and advance to a different undertaking. Figure 11.4 depicts some leading characteristics of the entrepreneur at the different stages, and the "turning point" representing the level at which the entrepreneur feels saturated and is less enthusiastic about pursuing the business's life cycle.

GENERATIONS AND FEMALE ENTREPRENEURSHIP

The concept of generation is mainly identified in research as including members that share common views, values and attitudes as they have experienced similar economic, demographic, political and technological environments. Differences between generations are compounded by changes due to ageing, education, accumulation of work experience, life and career stages; in addition, as each generation was introduced to the work world at different points in time, their work values and behaviors differ (Karp, Fuller, & Sirias, 2002; Lancaster & Stillman, 2002; Martin & Tulgan, 2002; Tulgan, 2000, 2006; Zaslow, 2006; Zemke, Raines, & Filipczak, 2000).

The differences in the generations are identified in their work attitudes, their approach to leisure time, to spending time with the family, to their career path and to entrepreneurship. For example, Baby-Boomers (born in 1946–1959) are typified by a willingness to sacrifice personal or family time for a career, valuing reputation, promotions and positions, and favoring influence and leadership at work; they favor jobs that provide personal growth and gratification, and rewards that include money, titles, and recognition. Technology is the primary driver of growth and change for this generation, who developed and used new technologies to be able to create goods and services that had the ability to change in the face of the market's erratic fluctuations. This also sculpted their work values. Generation X-ers (born in 1960–1980) are typified as more independent, self-motivated and self-sufficient. They expect more balance between work and leisure time which takes into account their life outside the workplace. They do not attribute significance to job security, favor rapid promotion and perceive career as coming from the transferability of one's skills to other jobs. They thrive in a workplace that is flexible, informal and offers freedom with respect to rules, including work hours; they ultimately expect work to be fun. Generation Y-ers (born after 1981) are typified as committed and loyal when dedicated to an idea, cause or product. They expect to be held in esteem, to be listened to, and they believe that respect must be earned.

The generations' different attitudes toward work are reflected in their work-related behavior: Baby-Boomers' socialization has been in the "traditional" corporation and is thus echoed in their strong work ethic and commitment to their business. They tend to associate the number of working hours with higher performance, endeavor to perfectly accomplish their work-related obligations according to professional requirements, tolerate organizational rules and policies, and take a workaholic approach.

Generation X-ers possess more innovative, technologically oriented thinking, and they are more tech-savvy than their generational predecessors. They do not tend to thoroughly study the organization or a task in order to exploit it; most entrepreneurs of this generation are inclined to drop into work in which they find a meaning. They are vivacious, embrace change, lack company loyalty and are willing to change the rules to satisfy their needs. They are individualistic and outcome-focused with regard to getting things done more quickly, even if it means bending the rules a little.

Generation Y is the product of a different value system than the preceding generations. They have witnessed the introduction of quick and endless information by using laptop computers, the internet, cell phones, etc., and have been raised in an era of information and technology explosion. As a consequence, they expect instant results and returns, instant gratification and, ultimately, the virtue of patience vanishes. These experiences are echoed in their impulsive, quick decisions, including in creating a new venture and the risks they are willing to take on.

Women entrepreneurs' attitudes and performance along the new venture creation are influenced by both their gender-related culture and their generation's culture. The new generations have a more flexible culture than their predecessors, thus harmonizing with the entrepreneurial spirit. While Generation Y women entrepreneurs are typified as more flexible, yet suffering from the "instant" syndrome and having a great deal of difficulty postponing their immediate gratifications, they want a business to be created and successful "here" and "now." Yet they meet a more open-minded environment that accepts their difficulties, sometimes sharing some of them. As such, the development of a generation gap has unintentionally paved the way to a potential reduction in the gender gap. In addition, the new generations respect their personal time, family time and the balance between work and family; as such, the family starts to be a shared mission rather than the woman's domain, and this trend can also act as a vehicle to attracting more women to entrepreneurship.

SUMMARY

This chapter draws on the different entrepreneurial paths that women can choose for the purpose of self-realization and fulfillment. As women entrepreneurs meet more pronounced barriers and difficulties than men, it is imperative to identify the avenues in entrepreneurship that can be crafted in ways that will facilitate women's attraction to entrepreneurship.

The main message of this chapter is that entrepreneurship is fluid and open-minded; therefore, any type, dynamic or structure of their chosen entrepreneurial path can be accepted, supported and encouraged. The different examples illustrated in this chapter serve to demonstrate that women coming from different cultures, origins and background constraints, yet sharing an entrepreneurial spirit, can find avenues that will fulfill their entrepreneurial zeal. When the goals of entrepreneurship are reexamined and reconstructed, so that profit is not the ultimate goal or a physical business with tangible infrastructure is not a necessity, then the opportunities to adopt different types, combinations or arrangements of entrepreneurship are enormous. Women should take a proactive stand and create a tailor-made entrepreneurial avenue that they feel comfortable with and will be enthusiastic about. The new generations' changing approaches to career, family and personal life, along with the change to more socially oriented ecosystems can afford the best platform to raise women's attraction to entrepreneurship and push them into successful experiences.

CASE STUDIES[6]

The following case study, contributed by Patrick Valéau from the pastoral, underexploited Réunion Island situated near Mauritius and

Madagascar, tells the story of Corinne's social entrepreneurship undertaking. Corinne's journey is an excellent exemplar of a woman who shaped the entrepreneurial avenue to match her ecosystem's needs combined with her own needs and capabilities. The author describes with great talent Corinne's steps into the new venture creation process from being an active volunteer, and then thoughtfully directs the readers to the reasons that ultimately led her to start her own cooperative, while wrapping the whole journey in Réunion Island's atmosphere.

The second case study, contributed by Ann-Mari Sätre, traces the entrepreneurial avenues from the point of view of an economy in transition, by telling the stories of three women entrepreneurs after the mass privatization in Russia in the early 1990s. Ludmilla, Daria and Anastasia run different entrepreneurial businesses, exploited different entrepreneurial avenues and were originally motivated and oppressed by different factors; they came from three different communities in a Russian region, yet overcame the obstacles and managed to create successful new ventures. Sincerely and tactfully, the author describes the rules, regulations and atmosphere that still exist in Russia to illustrate the entrepreneurial paths these women took to set up their new ventures.

Corinne: A Social Entrepreneur from Réunion Island

Patrick Valéau
Institut d'Administration des Entreprises, CEMOI, University of la Reunion, Saint-Denis, France

Corinne is a 40-year-old mother of three children from Réunion Island, a French overseas department situated near Mauritius and Madagascar. After working for more than fifteen years as a community worker training unemployed adults, three years ago she created Dynamic Services, a "business and employment cooperative." Corinne is the manager. With the assistance of two secretaries, she helps 20 people to develop activities in the sector of "home care services" such as homework support for children, cleaning or gardening. These people, who have often been unemployed for a long time, can thus start their venture as paid workers. Accountancy and administration services are provided for them so that they can focus on developing their activity. The co-op receives 12 percent of the revenues of its so called "paid entrepreneurs," but also benefits from multiple fiscal advantages and subsidies from the French government.

The French government is trying to encourage the development of business and employment co-operatives, but still needs entrepreneurs like Corinne to create them. It is important to understand who these modest but devoted citizens are. This case study first introduces how Dynamic Services functions and then focuses on Corinne's career and personal pathway. Step by step, it details how and why this woman moved from paid work to social entrepreneurship. Like a lot of social entrepreneurs, Corinne is neither a "push" or "pull" entrepreneur; she became a leader, almost through a sense of duty, in order to do something useful for her community.

1.   *A case of social entrepreneurship.* Corinne's co-operative venture falls into the category of what is now called social entrepreneurship: a venture created and developed for social purposes, often combining for-profit and nonprofit activities (Dees, 1988).[7] This "hybridization" gives access to new opportunities, yet, often results in contradictions between economic and social performance, between short-term and long-term goals or between the development of the organization and the interests of its beneficiaries. For instance, the co-op would benefit financially in the short term from taking a higher percentage of its paid entrepreneurs' revenues, but this would reduce the salaries these typically poor entrepreneurs would get at the end of the month. Social entrepreneurship is based on arbitration different values and goals, rather than the optimization of revenue (Valéau, 2010).[8]

2.   *The case of a woman entrepreneur.* Corinne's story is also that of a woman whose entrepreneurial motives are deeply rooted in her occupational vocation. Since the beginning of her carrier as a community worker, her main preoccupation has been to help the long-term unemployed. Disappointed by the results obtained through traditional job search or business creation workshops, she says the co-op was a better "*solution*" to their problems. Although Corinne's profile and approach may not exactly match the image of famous social entrepreneurs such as Baden Powell, Mother Teresa or Bernard Kouchner who developed international nonprofit organizations, it is exactly what territories such as Reunion Island need in order to sustain their development: ordinary citizens accepting to become entrepreneurs, i.e., to create new ventures, to innovate and to take risks in order to serve their community.

THE STORY OF AN OPPORTUNITY

A cooperative is an association of persons united to meet their common economic and social aspirations through a jointly-owned and democratically-controlled enterprise (International Co-operative Alliance, 2011). Business and Employment Co-operatives such as Dynamic Services offer prospective entrepreneurs the opportunity to begin their venture as paid workers (Equal, 2007). Their salaries and associated taxes are paid from their revenue, with 12 percent being given to finance the co-op. The latter will in return provide them with full services including offices, insurance, administration, accountancy and training.

The so-called "paid entrepreneurs" participating in Dynamic Services co-op develop their activities within the sector of "home care services," i.e., services that can be performed at the customer's home such as shopping or gardening. The French government has targeted this sector as one of the most promising for the coming decade in terms of employment opportunities. Some of these activities, like gardening, have always existed within the informal economy, but others, like home beauty treatment, are more innovative. One of the French government's objectives is to make this sector as attractive as possible. For example, wealthy customers are able to deduct half of the money spent on these services from their tax bill. As a result they can afford to pay a high enough price for entrepreneurs to be able to cover their taxes and costs and still make enough money to live on. A second measure is to let these entrepreneurs keep their unemployment benefit in addition to their revenues for the first year until their business is on its feet. A third measure involves distributing vouchers to poor families so that they can afford these services.

This kind of social entrepreneurship is particularly needed in Réunion Island. Situated in the south-west of the Indian Ocean, near Mauritius and Madagascar, it became a French overseas department in 1946. Réunion Island today counts 750,000 inhabitants, the result of African, Malagasy, Chinese, Indian and European immigration, and is often considered as a model of harmonious multiracial society. In 2020, its population will reach 927,000 with a 30 percent increase in the number of people under the age of 20. This is why, despite a 6 percent annual rate of economic growth, the unemployment rate remains around 30 percent. The development of this territory requires more business. The mission of business and employment co-operatives is to accompany the long term unemployed in the creation of small businesses or in becoming self-employed. Réunion Island has been targeted by the French government as a priority area for setting up this kind of structure.

Dynamic Services is the first structure of its type in Réunion Island to actually get off the ground. It started up in 2008 with a capital of 150,000 euros. It welcomed its first "paid entrepreneurs" in 2009. Their revenues reached 30,000 euros in the first year and went up to 60,000 euros in the second. Dynamic Services will probably always need public subsidies in order to finance 150,000 euros of operating costs, but these subsidies should decrease as revenues increase. The survival of a business can never be taken for granted but Dynamic Services seems to be a success. What can we learn from this socioeconomic experience? First of all, there is a real opportunity in France to create business and employment co-operatives in the sector of home care services: financial incentives from the government and assistance and advice provided by the national network of co-operatives obviously help. Yet, this opportunity does not actually exist until someone seizes it. The success of Dynamic Services cannot be fully analyzed without understanding Corinne, the person who created it.

THE STORY OF AN ENTREPRENEUR

Corinne is married to a builder and the mother of three children. She was born in 1970 in Saint Paul. Her mother worked in a hospital and her father was a self-employed taxi driver. She has got a general baccalaureat (equivalent of a high school diploma), a professional diploma in accountancy and a degree in education. Her first work experience was as a trainer in a nonprofit organization where she taught French and Maths for two years to so-called "difficult" teenagers preparing diplomas in horticulture. She then took a year off to get married and have her first child. After this break, she went back to work for another nonprofit organization, but this time to help the long-term unemployed. In order to improve her skills in this area, she took courses in dealing with illiteracy and training adults. After six years, she became involved in the conception of the training courses and began a masters degree in project management. According to Corinne, working with the long-term unemployed, she at last had the feeling that she had found her vocation.

However, after 12 years of working in adult training, Corinne decided to resign.

> After 12 years, I felt disillusioned with these kinds of training schemes. I found their objectives too far removed from those of the beneficiaries. I think it was me who had evolved. My vision was not the same anymore. What put me off was the fact that during the 12 years I worked in this area, I often saw the same people coming back. This, in particular, made me doubt the efficacy of what I was doing and left me with the feeling that I was wasting my time, that I was not bringing anything to these people. I also think that I needed a break, I needed to reconnect with my family. The children had grown up. I had given a lot to work. I needed to stop and think. (. . .) It is true that after school, I had begun my career straight away, I gave 200 percent. This break was an opportunity for me to reflect and see what I really wanted to do and how I wanted to do it. I did not want to carry on seizing any professional opportunity I could for the sake of it.

So Corinne actually took a career break and looked after her family. However, she continued with her masters degree and also had a third child. After a two-year break, Corinne started to think about what she could do next.

This is when Corinne became involved, as a volunteer, in the creation of a new co-operative in the transport and building sectors. An entrepreneur she knew wanted to share some of his costs with fellow entrepreneurs and make his paid workers co-owners. She helped the entrepreneur through the whole administrative and financial process, using her new competencies in finance and accountancy from her masters degree. This gave her the opportunity to go to Paris to meet a national co-operative network.

> I had no experience of this kind of organization. I found it interesting because the co-op retained the commitment and humanistic aspects of nonprofit organizations, but combined with these the economic aspects of business. (. . .) It is true to say that this experience made me more confident in my management skills.

This experience gave Corinne new ideas and motivations, but also new skills.

It also ultimately led her to start her own co-operative when she discovered the existence of a plan especially designed to help the long-term unemployed. Because she had taken part in the creation of the first co-operative, she was contacted by the French administration for an interview to share her experiences as part of a study about the feasibility of creating a business and employment co-operative. This was when the penny dropped.

> This was the connection with my former experience. I knew some people who had training and competences but did not know what to do with them, and they were not psychologically ready, or did not have the management skills, to create a business. What I like about the co-op is that I can take them somewhere.

So Corinne contacted the national network first of all to get information and, later on, to present her project. "I had no hesitation, I did not really take the risks into account. The tool matched the needs so I got started." Conforming to the national network conditions, she started Dynamic Services in association with another co-op within a large nonprofit organization: the Chamber of Social Economy, and was ready to go it alone a year after, in 2008.

Progressively, Dynamic Services has grown to include 20 businesses. Corinne is proud of what she has already achieved and thinks of herself as an entrepreneur. However, being in a leadership role was not what attracted her to the project, and today, she would like to run the co-op on a more collective basis. Entrepreneurs can become co-owners after two years. If they leave to carry on in business on their own, that's fine, but Corinne would like some of them to stay. First, this would increase the level of revenue and the percentage transferred which would allow her to depend less on subsidies. Secondly, this would also create a dynamic motivating newcomers. Finally, even if her management is already very participative, this co-ownership would be the basis of a more formal democracy. Corinne would also like to create partnerships and joint ventures to expand her activity to include a network of like-minded people looking for fair and sustainable development of their island.

Questions for Discussion

1   Is Corinne a typical example of a woman entrepreneur? A woman social entrepreneur? Explain.
2   What entrepreneurial paths did Corinne follow?
3   Do you think that the career breaks Corinne followed are in line with an entrepreneurial mindset?
4   What drivers pushed Corinne to start her entrepreneurial undertaking?
5   Which types of facilitators would you suggest she use to manage her business to sustainability and growth? Explain your suggestions.
6   Do you think Corinne would have started her own co-op without the incentives from the French government?

Women Entrepreneurs in Russia[9]

Ann-Mari Sätre
Centre for Russian and Eurasian Studies, Uppsala University, Uppsala, Sweden

As a consequence of the priority structure, mass privatization in Russia in the early 1990s was far from equitable in many respects, resulting in both "winners" and "losers" of the transition. Amongst the clear winners were the directors of high-priority oil and gas industries, in most cases men.[10] Those in former priority sectors, e.g., within heavy industry, were on average less fortunate as the performance of these branches generally deteriorated and led to closings or bankruptcy, which also meant that owners lost their wealth. Both women and men were among those who lost their wealth. On the other hand, many women benefited from the privatization of the low-priority consumer industry. In the course of mass privatization in 1994–1995, some of these were able to transform their enterprises into private firms. Despite an obsolete structure and need of investment resources, it has been possible also with small resources to build up small-scale production within this sector. Some women who were bosses in other low priority sectors, such as trade, culture, health and education, also benefited in the privatization process.

To set up a private business is a new thing that was not possible during the Soviet period. Women have used the new opportunity to set up businesses in traditionally female sectors which had low-priority status and underdeveloped economic activity during the Soviet era. In the early 1990s, female entrepreneurship was primarily oriented toward science, consulting, retail trade and services. Women also started small-scale businesses in the fields of child care, health care, education, sewing clothes, knitting, handicraft and fruit and/or vegetable production. According to official statistics, 90 percent of production in the female-dominated consumer goods sector takes place in small firms. This sector is growing and it is fairly competitive. Women might also have benefitted from a positive attitude toward female entrepreneurship; women are believed to take responsibility and to be trustworthy in their business relations, driven by the need to support their families and running businesses with social aims.

Meanwhile, women had few resources to succeed in building up sustainable entrepreneurship with a possibility for expansion beyond survival level. According to the national labour force survey in Russia, the share of women among individual entrepreneurs in 2007 was 41 percent. The highest increase in the number of self-employed occurred between 1996 and 1998; it actually doubled during the same period when unemployment reached its peak level. There also seems to be a positive correlation between female entrepreneurship and male unemployment.

The interviews from three communities in a Russian region illustrate that there are many new possibilities for potential entrepreneurs, while there are so many possible and sometimes unpredictable obstacles to overcome.[11] Women have set up firms in trade, but firms have also been set up to process timber, berries and mushrooms and agricultural products, and within the textile branch and tourism. All the interviews provide the same picture. The arbitrariness when it comes to enforcement of rules and treatment by authorities forces the female entrepreneurs to rely on several sources of income. Politicians and community officers are "in the hands of the oligarchs"; consequently, the large male-managed firms do not have to worry about rules that apply to smaller ones. But there are also examples of how mayors have helped small female entrepreneurs, with various facilities, letting locales for rent, or even lending money to them.

The interviews support the impression that it is more difficult to start small businesses in recent times than it used to be just after the privatization reforms in the 1990s. One reason could be that it was easier to get hold of equipment needed to get started as you could take over equipment, or buy it cheaply, from old state firms. Another reason could be stricter rules for obtaining licences. Despite many problems individuals still try to start their own businesses. Possible explanations could be high general levels of tolerance toward risk-taking, too little knowledge of possible difficulties, personal networks, that this is the only way of supporting oneself, or simply that this is something they really want to do. The insufficient legal system is not of major importance as people still try, even if they have difficulties with the registration and licensing of their activities. Several explicitly said they did not want companions from outside the family. The perceived unstable situation has implied that people are hired on an informal basis, especially at businesses run without licences.

The Stories of Three Female Entrepreneurs[12]

The stories of the business development processes of three female entrepreneurs will illustrate what the situation is like.

Ludmila lives with her husband and two children in a community centre with some 10,000 inhabitants, situated 600 km from the residential town in the Archangelsk region. Already as a teenager Ludmila was dreaming that she wanted to start her own business. Anxious to realize her ideas, as soon as she had the possibility in 1992, at the age of 19, Ludmila took over a sewing machine from the textile firm where she was working. It appeared she took a loan to buy all the equipment she wanted from the state-owned firm at a very low price, as this firm was about to close down, and she also took over the ten employees. In this way she was one of those who benefited from privatization reforms in the early 1990s. She registered her firm in 1993, producing traditional clothes as well as working costumes.

Ludmila developed her textile enterprise slowly, and did not invest in new technically advanced machines until there was enough capital within her own. She collaborates with her husband, and she told how he invested money that he earned from timber-cutting in her textile firm, while she helped him with book-keeping. Only after twelve years did she start to make some money. Both explicitly said they did not want companions from outside the family. She also told how her husband stayed at home with the newborn baby when she returned to run her enterprise a couple of days after giving birth.

Ludmila runs the sewing activities connected to her shop in the village. She had employed some young women with small children, they were able to work from home, although this implied a problem as they could not utilize the modern equipment while working from home. She was sewing on orders only, due to the limited buying capacity in the local sphere. These orders included ladies clothes, costumes and work clothes to firms and cloths to restaurants. She said her expansion in the local community was limited by a lack of skilled staff. Her solution was to educate her staff herself (interview, October 9, 2006). In 2008 she had opened a new shop in a town 400 km away. The number of employees had increased to 18. She had been considering moving to the town as she felt it was not possible to expand in the local community where most people are poor apart from those who were already her customers. But she had decided to stay in the village and to keep on with the sewing there, where the rents are low and where she had her sole, while also sewing on orders to the town. Ludmila had also expanded her activity to the sewing of curtains and design of interiors. She learned by attending special courses in the town.

Daria lives with her husband and three children across the river from a village of 5,000 inhabitants, 10 km from the community center and

600 km from the residential town. For five years she tried to get a licence for her tourism business without success and she was one of those who ran her business without being registered and the community knew it. In her case this was due to problems of getting land registered. Daria felt unsafe as they had built houses without being registered as legal owners of them. Finally, at the end of 2006 her firm for "individual living" was registered. Her strategy to obtain financial capital has been to engage in trade through the running of shops and timber-cutting. Together with her husband she started a sports school, free for children. Their salaries for this activity were paid by the State. This couple had also run a shop in the village together with some relatives. Although they earned very little from this shop after the payment of salaries, taxes and repayment of loans that they had taken in order to start the shop, some money was left to put into the development of a business in tourism. As they let the shop for rent, they got money to build a house of their own to live in as well as other houses (the timber you need for building your own house to live in is free).

The tourism business has been built up gradually, step by step. In 2008 five houses were let for rent to tourists, the first of which was built in 2003. From the money earned over the years they have also been able to build a sauna, a café and a building for administration. Gradually the ski and tourism center is being developed partly by State money and partly and increasingly with money from the private sector. Daria expresses a fear of becoming absorbed by one of the local larger entrepreneurs. "As long as the firm is small it is your own, but if you start to grow somebody will buy you up." Nevertheless she is proud to be an example of how to "start with two empty hands" and develop your businesses little by little, using timber and trade as capital for starting up. Daria tells about how she handles all the "begging" she is exposed to, being perceived as a successful local entrepreneur. She has to choose what she wants to support, as she can not contribute in all spheres. She has chosen ski-related activities for children. This means that she would voluntarily contribute in a way that facilitates the good performance of her work in her public employment as a ski teacher/trainer.

The running of food shops in the community center continues to be important as a source of money for the development of the tourism business. But Daria believes that new rules concerning the selling of alcohol will cause problems for smaller food shops and hence lower the possibility of getting financial capital from trade that can be used to develop their business. Daria expresses the opinion that, while it has been possible to earn a lot of money in the food trading business, it has gradually become harder, due to new tax rules and various restrictions. Nevertheless, it had been quite easy to get permits for the running of shops, cafés, restaurants, recreation and sports facilities, while it had not yet been possible to get a licence for running a hotel. The development of the tourism business with the gradual expansion in the number of employees has facilitated life for the private household, which benefits from cooking, cleaning, building repairs, maintenance of vehicles, and even, on some occasions, child care.

Anastasia lives with her husband in a beautiful village with 1,000 inhabitants some 100 km away from the community centre and close to 700 km from the residential town.[13] She was the director of a local child-care unit for 25 years who, in the early years of *perestroika* in the early 1990s, became a local politician; she was in charge at the sub-local level for a couple of years. After not being re-elected, she decided that she wanted to realize her ideas about developing her own business. Consequently, she was eager to apply to take part in the SIDA-financed project, a possibility she became aware of through her engagement in the development of the community. After this course she tried to get started by means of borrowed money, she was running her business for processing berries and mushrooms for almost five years without a licence.

She describes how her proposal was accepted by five officials within the community, while a sixth person said no. She hired an electrician who made the electric installation that she required to get started, but as the inspector found out that the electrician did not have the required permit, she was fined.[14] Then she had to get hold of the only electrician in the region, borrow more money from her son-in-law to pay him, and make the electrician come to her village and redo the necessary installation.

According to Anastasia, community officials have the same mentality as those under the Soviet regime, as they restrain people who have their own ideas.[15] She felt that the possibility to set up a business depended very much on how administrators deal with the different licences that are needed, and she said she noticed right away if it was worthwhile to talk to a particular bureaucrat or not. She felt that administrators and officials behave differently, and as there are many hierarchies to go through, it seems easy to believe that obstacles will appear on at least one of the levels. Anastasia's own experience provides an illustration. She was anxious as the setting up of her business and getting started had become much more costly than she expected. She had borrowed money from relatives, the community administration and three entrepreneurs. She had already invested in modern equipment, but needed to borrow more in order to get the necessary documents to get started.

As long as you are one of the "pioneers" in your field, there appear to be obstacles that the person who is in the process of starting a business is simply unaware of. Anastasia described how she was simply unaware of all the permits she needed to get started. For instance, she needed permission from the health authorities, the fire authorities, the energy authorities, and she did not know in advance how much she had to pay for each permit. Neither was she aware of quality control procedures, how much she had to pay for each product or how often, that she had to give controlling authorities three kilos of dried mushrooms each time, and that she had to go to the center for standardization and certification 300 km away each time. In addition, she says that she did not know that the same procedure was required for each product.

Anastasia described how she and her husband survived thanks to their small pensions, the selling of meat from their own cattle, her little shop and the selling of products from her non-registered business. Her firm was finally registered in mid-2007, but in her daughter's name, within the framework of a family business in the same village.

Questions for Discussion

1   What were the main differences in Ludmila, Daria and Anastasia's entrepreneurial paths? Explain why these differences emerged.
2   How did the situation in Russia affect these women's new venture creation process? Explain.
3   What were the main obstacles these women faced? How do you explain the emergence of such obstacles?
4   Which entrepreneurial traits can you identify in these three women? Accordingly, what would be the most suitable entrepreneurial avenue for each of them? Explain.
5   As an external consultant, what would you recommend to these women in order to maintain an entrepreneurial career path?

Notes

1   The origin of the term comes from the mythological Greek god Proteus who was able to change his form at will.
2   Daphni Leef: How a woman in a tent became Israel's top story. At http://www.thejc.com/lifestyle/lifestyle-features/52718/daphni-leef-how-a-woman-a-tent-became-israels-top-story
3   Athttp://www.guardian.co.uk/society/gallery/2011/mar/09/scientific-breakthroughs-by-women
4   At http://www.wvgoodwill.org/history.htm
5   For example, the protean career, discussed earlier in the chapter.
6   The author(s) of the case studies are fully and solely responsible for their content, phrasing consistency and flow, terminology, English proofing and reference lists.
7   J. G. Dees (1998). *The* Meaning *of* Social *Entrepreneurship*. Kansas City: Kauffman Foundation.
8   P. Valéau (2010). Social Entrepreneurs in Non Profit Organisations: Innovation and Dilemmas. In A. Fayolle & H. Matlay, *Handbook of research on social entrepreneurship*. Cheltenham: Elgar.
9   This is based on A.-M. Sätre, "Women's Work in Transitional Russia: Women's Strategies for Entrepreneurship and Survival in Russian Regions." In M. Kangaspuro, J. Nikula, & I. Stodolsky (Eds.), *Perestroika: Process and Consequences* (330–350). Helsinki: Finnish Literary Society 2010.
10   Putin, however, managed to collect a considerable portion of the income flows that previously went directly into the private pockets of "oligarchs," so that parts of the profits are diverted to the State budget.

11 In 2003, 2005, 2006 and 2008, I conducted 50 interviews connected to the follow-up of a project financed by the Swedish International Development agency (SIDA), which began in 1999. Fifteen persons took part in this project aimed at helping individual entrepreneurs to start their own businesses. I have interviewed 11 women and 3 men (basic information about the situation for a woman who was not interviewed was collected through interviews with others). The project involved education in business development, including the help to develop their own business plans in 2001, law, and a study visit to Sweden, where they visited single entrepreneurs within the same business area. In 2008, one of the three who was running a business, a woman, had run her textile firm since 1993. Another woman had finally in 2006 been able to have her firm for "individual living" registered. A third woman had after a long struggle succeeded in having her processing firm for berries and mushrooms registered in 2007, although in her daughter's name. One of the men had been able to set up a Swedish-Russian timber-cutting firm in 2003, with a Swedish companion, but was out of business in 2008. Some of the others who had tried were running their businesses without being registered. One of the men had died and one of the women had moved to St Petersburg. Apart from the participants in the project, interviews in three communities have been carried out with other individuals who have succeeded or failed to start their own firms as well as with politicians and community officials. At the regional level I have talked to a vice-governor, a vice-chairman and a member of the regional Duma.

12 I have interviewed these three women (we can call them Ludmila, Daria and Anastasia) several times in each of the years 2003, 2005, 2006 and 2008, and also, on a few occasions, some of their family members.

13 She has three adult children. One daughter, one son and three grandchildren live in the same village.

14 According to her, this happened because the inspector had learnt about safer installations in Sweden (Interview, November 23, 2003).

15 She had bribed three persons, but said she would have to bribe another one to get her licence (interview, December 10, 2005).

Part 5

The Future of Female Entrepreneurship

Part 5 focuses on

- The different aspects of promoting female entrepreneurship in research, teaching and practice;
- Learning by role models: entering the world of some of the most successful female entrepreneurs in history;
- Leadership and entrepreneurship: the intertwined concepts in the female realm;
- Breaking the chains of stereotype and crafting a more equal reality;
- This part includes chapters and case studies on themes associated with leadership and breaking the barriers encountered by women entrepreneurs.

This part of the book has a proactive slant, reflecting upon past achievements in female entrepreneurship and on how the subject can be developed in research, teaching and practice in the future. Different aspects of promoting female entrepreneurship are developed by tracing the steps of such well-known successful entrepreneurs as Coco Chanel (haute couture), Marion O'Brien Donovan (disposable diapers), Bette Nesmith Graham (correction fluid), Maria Montessori (children's education) and many others. Also presented are reflections on the future environments that should be crafted and sustained to enable and encourage equality, ethics and integrity for women entrepreneurs.

Two themes are covered: leadership and breaking barriers, by discussing different aspects of the future women entrepreneur who is and will be "shaped" by the perceptions of women entrepreneurs embedded in their ecosystem, images and stereotypes. The message in this part of the book is that by adopting a progressive outlook and liberating women entrepreneurs from the chains of stereotypes and prejudice, a win–win situation will be established, by women, men and the different factors in their ecosystems participating in this context. Such processes should be acknowledged and immediately applied to enable absorption of these concepts for the next generation.

12 Leadership in Female Entrepreneurship

Chapter Objectives

- Linking leadership and leadership styles to entrepreneurship, and identifying the factors that have a significant impact on the successful entrepreneurial course of action;
- Drawing on the main characteristics of leadership and their application in female entrepreneurship;
- The role of the vision as a link between leadership and entrepreneurship;
- Learning more about female leaders and investors in their fields;
- Outlining the leaders' key roles in fostering the staff's entrepreneurial spirit, action and further development;
- Becoming familiar with the key features of female leaders-founding entrepreneurs;
- Recognizing the role of leaders' emotional competencies and their application to female entrepreneurship in the new venture creation phase;
- Learning from the Diva's strengths and applying the "Diva phenomenon," typified by inner passion, enthusiasm for work, composing one's own career path, etc., to female entrepreneurship.

Leadership in the context of female entrepreneurship is presented in this chapter by introducing some well-known models and theories in leadership, and intertwining them with the founders' and entrepreneurs' world, incorporated in the female ecosystem. The reciprocal relationships between entrepreneurship and leadership, leadership in entrepreneurship, and entrepreneurship itself as a vehicle toward leadership—in the community, the business arena, the economy and the international sphere—are presented and discussed. In addition, a glimpse of the Diva phenomenon is afforded, as it is an emerging phenomenon that is most relevant in the face of paparazzi, reality shows and today's culture. Understanding Divas as determined leader-entrepreneurs who started from a rough sketch and established the status of role model should lead to their being praised, and to their feminine competencies in paving their way being studied.

This chapter is aimed at guiding its readers to acknowledge that women have emotional and social abilities that give them a significant advantage in leading their staff members and subsequently, their businesses, to competitive advantage. The traditional models of effective leadership based on male-dominant competencies should be overturned and room should be given to the new models of charismatic, emotional and "tailor-made" leadership which are most relevant to the venture creation process, while at the same time involve characteristics that are embedded in female-based competencies.

ENTREPRENEURS ARE LEADERS

In research, leaders are regarded as individuals who are proficient in the art of inspiring, motivating and stimulating others to follow them toward a common goal. Leaders are typified as possessing relevant internal resources that stem from a combination of personality traits and skills, and that have a cumulative impact on others, i.e., by inspiring confidence and generating followers' enthusiasm and commitment. As a result, others may modify their thoughts, views, feelings or desires, consequently changing their behavior and actions toward following the leader's trail.

A review of the leadership literature reveals an array of definitions concerning its nature, essence, translation in different organizations and different effects on the environment. Leadership is understood as the confluence of positive organizational behavior, ethical behavior, empowering ability and acting as a role model, and as such is detached from negative connotations found in research, such as threatening the staff with punishment for poor achievements, commanding, setting rules that must be followed even if the staff does not accept or identify with them, or just being indifferent to the staff. Rather, leadership is "the reciprocal process of mobilizing by persons with certain motives and values, various economic, political, and other resources in a context of competition and conflict, in order to realize goals independently or mutually held by both leaders and followers" (Burns, 1978: 425); i.e., leadership is a developed and mature type of influence, directing and mainly inspiring, empowering and enabling others to reveal their own strengths for the joint task, based on the main concepts derived from the full range of leadership development models (Avolio, 2003, 2005; Avolio & Luthans, 2006; Schulman, 2002).

Research has identified some traits and skills possessed by leaders, such as being empowering, confident, optimistic, resilient, transparent, ethical, and strategic planners. Above all, leaders affirm that the critical factors in generating a sustainable competitive advantage are likely to come from the human side of organizations. By fostering positive self-development, striving to provide the platform and conditions that can cultivate their staff, leaders encourage their staff to use this platform and experience, try, even when risky, and also fail, but most importantly learn from their actions, decisions and performance outcomes. Leaders motivate their staff to shape their independent identity rather than "follow rules"; they appreciate their staff's independence. Solid and trustworthy leadership is thus considered the backbone of a business that develops the necessary conditions for effective outcomes, improved performance and sustainable competitive advantage by benefiting from its human component's strengths. Leadership respects the process; it emphasizes a trusting environment, builds people's capabilities and relevant skills, broadens their thinking, and equips them with the skills, means and networks that will be valid for their different work and life circumstances.

Leadership and entrepreneurship are intertwined. In these changing, erratic and most challenging of times, comprising market instability and uncertainty, people are seeking a stable place in their organizations and look to their leaders for direction, guidance and self-assurance. In new ventures, the entrepreneur is the figure people are looking at: she/he is the leader. As leaders, entrepreneurs have to direct their staff by establishing sets of rules that are then translated by the staff members as valuable, sound and practical, as well as compatible with their own sets of values, morals and ethics. Therefore, entrepreneurs who display such leadership may be better equipped to withstand the challenges typically faced along the new venture creation process (Argyris, 1993; Avolio, Gardner, Walumbwa, Luthans, & May, 2004; Hitt & Ireland, 2002; Luthans, 2002; Luthans & Avolio, 2003).

LEADERSHIP STYLES AND GENDER IN A NUTSHELL

Different approaches to leadership and gender are pertinent in research. One popular model addresses task-oriented versus people-oriented styles.[1] The first is concerned with accomplishing assigned tasks by being focused on the goal and mobilizing the task-relevant resources accordingly; this style includes encouraging staff members to follow rules, maintaining high standards of performance, and making the leader and subordinate roles explicit. The second refers to interpersonal relationships and a concern for people's well-being; it addresses behaviors such as managing people as individuals with needs, rather than "robots" that follow rules; looking out for their well-being, explaining the procedures, and discussing mutual expectations. These styles have, of course, been stereotypically attributed to the genders: women are considered more apt to adopt a people-orientated style and men a task-oriented style. Another popular model in research is the extent to which leaders behave democratically, i.e., exhibit a participative style, represented by allowing staff members to participate in the decision-making process, versus an autocratic style, i.e., directive leadership which discourages staff participation in the decision-making and encourages following rules. The first has been stereotyped to women and the second, to men (Bass & Bass, 2008; Lewin & Lippitt, 1938; Vroom & Yetton, 1973). A different typology of leadership styles which has been attributed to gender differences is the transformational versus transactional styles: transformational leaders set especially high standards for behavior and establish themselves as role models by gaining the trust and confidence of their staff; they are strategic thinkers and plan for the future; they innovate, mentor, empower and encourage their staff to develop to their full potential. Transformational leadership has more communal aspects, and is thus considered more aligned with the female than male gender roles and with feminine personality attributes. Transactional leaders focus on an exchange of relationships with their staff; as such, goals or tasks that have been achieved are then rewarded by the leaders, while those members who fail to achieve their goals or tasks, or have performed poorly on those tasks, are "punished," corrected, or their rewards withheld. This style clarifies, in a simple way, the responsibilities of the staff members, constantly monitors their work to enable putting the reward system into action, and focuses on correcting mistakes. These styles have been also been connected to the genders, in relation to their social roles and gender-based traits; i.e., transformational leadership typifies women's style while transactional leadership typifies men's style (Cann & Siegfried, 1990; Hackman, Furniss, Hills, & Paterson, 1992; Ross & Offermann, 1997).

In summary, women leaders have been found in research to be more transformational than most men, as well as more participative and democratic (Eagley, Johannesen-Schmidt & van Engen, 2003; Grant, 1988; Helgeson, 1990; Rosener, 1990), by using their interpersonal skills, establishing shared cultures, being transparent, sharing power and information building, striving for deliberated consensus, and fostering empowerment (Brenner, Tomkiewicz, & Schein, 1989; Calas & Smircich, 1992).

WOMEN ENTREPRENEURS AND LEADERS

Ms. Meg Whitman[2] is the President and CEO of eBay, and is considered one of the leading and most influential CEOs not only in the USA, but also around the world. Her particular leadership style is considered one of the main factors directing eBay to its incredible success while so many other internet start-ups have been trying to imitate its concept and structure. Ms. Whitman is typified as a charismatic leader who uses influence rather than force, inspires, and paves her leadership with faith in her staff and in her own abilities to lead eBay to higher levels of success. Her vision is well articulated, yet open to reflection: if required, eBay's goals and actions will be reconsidered in the face of harsh competition in the field. Whitman's vision for eBay has revolved around her intuitive understanding that the key to eBay lies in its people, the users, rather than in any sort of managerial structure or even in the technology per se. While Whitman's experience does not represent the ultimate entrepreneurial pursuit, as CEO of an innovative company, her inspirational experience is the best proof of a successful and most influential female entrepreneurial leader.

Along these lines, *Businessweek Online* published an article in November 2000 entitled As Leaders, Women Rule—new studies find that female managers outshine their male counterparts in almost every measure,[3] stressing that "At the highest levels, bosses are still evaluating people in the most stereotypical ways." Delving into the literature in this area, some leadership styles and behaviors are in fact labeled by gender; subsequently, some leadership characteristics are attributed more strongly to women than men, while some others are more compatible with men than women. Leadership involves people, dedication and commitment, and in different studies in the fields of leadership and entrepreneurship, women have been found to be more accepting of others' directions, supporting and comforting their staff in stressful situations, contributing in situations involving relational and interpersonal problems, willing to sacrifice their own needs in order to enhance a communal environment, less self-centered and willing to "leave the stage" to others when they can identify the prospective benefits. Their style relies on a people-orientation, and emotional and social styles. Men leaders are typified in research as influencing by controlling, initiating activity directed to assigned tasks, and making problem-focused suggestions. According to research in this area, these attributes stem from the genders' roles and their alleged trait characteristics; in particular, such behavior can more naturally be exhibited by men because of the following characteristics which are attributed to men: aggressiveness, ambition, dominance, forcefulness, independence, daring, higher self-confidence, competitiveness (Carli & Eagly, 1999; Eagly & Johnson, 1990; Eagly, Karau, & Makhijani, 1995; Sharpe, 2000).

According to a year-long study conducted in 2005 by Caliper,[4] a Princeton, New Jersey-based management consulting firm, there are several characteristics that typify the female leadership style: women leaders are more assertive, persuasive, and willing to take risks than male leaders; at the same time, they are more empathetic and flexible, possess stronger interpersonal skills than their male counterparts and are able to bring others around to their point of view. They are more alert to changes and read situations more accurately, probably due to their genuine understanding, acceptance and caring of their people, and as a result, their people feel more empowered, valued and motivated. By definition, a woman's style includes limited levels of the genuine male-based characteristics, because women do not feel comfortable using them. The perceived incongruity between the female gender role and such typical leader roles tends to create prejudice toward female leaders, assuming that leadership ability is more a male than female ability. Consequently, women suffer from less favorable general acceptance of their actual leadership behavior, and this is echoed in a lower impetus at institutions such as schools, public corporations and private businesses to pinpoint females who exhibit leadership performance, to allow them a simpler, barrier-free way of reaching leadership and/or entrepreneurial positions.

Table 12.1 summarizes the main characteristics and factors typical of leadership and entrepreneurship and associates them with female entrepreneurship.

Accordingly, many characteristics and factors that have a significant and positive impact on staff members in the new venture creation derive from leadership and entrepreneurial capabilities. Nevertheless, their magnitude in the new venture creation process differs: e.g., popping up with creative ideas is crucial in the entrepreneurial realm and, although recommended,

Table 12.1 Leadership and Entrepreneurship in the Female Context

Styles and characteristics	Leadership	Entrepreneurship	Female-based
Directing and guiding people, resulting in people following the leader	Very high level	Very high level	Directing by emphasizing the "person"; explicating people's unique value to the business outcome
Trusting, emphasizing transparency, ethics, setting the vision	Very high level	High level	Emphasizing trust, vision and ethics; explaining decisions, expecting feedback
Proactive, oriented to action, intolerant of passive, non-reactive, indifferent behavior	High level	Very high level	Proactive, though more tolerant than men to their staff's indecisive behavior; respecting the Q&A process
Enthusiastic about the work, cause, action	High level	Very high level	Enthusiastic, excited and most dedicated to the cause, highly motivated

Confident, sets a direction, follows that direction, stable	Very high level	High level	Confident in explaining their decisions and actions rather than setting rules and direction
Target-oriented, focused on the main goal	High level	High level	The way to the goal is broader, deeper, longer and delves into more detail, compared to men
Demanding, demanding high standards from themselves and others	Very high level	High level	Demanding yet people-oriented, the "person" is important; ready to sacrifice standards for human reasons
People-oriented, empowering, cultivating people	Very high level	Medium-high level	Empowering, encouraging, interested in people; seeing people as the main asset
Idea producer, creative, outside-the-box thinking	Medium level	Very high level	Creative, fostering creativity by encouraging it; rewarding creativity

is less fundamental for leaders. Empowering people, on the other hand, is the core of leadership: it builds the essence of leaders as people who create a nurturing platform upon which others can grow (contrary to managers); yet, in the new venture creation phase of the entrepreneurial realm, the privilege of allocating time to deliberate empowerment systems does not exist, because there are various different goals that must be accomplished in a timely fashion. Entrepreneurs must trust their staff to accomplish these goals, sometimes blindly, and monitor their performance and results regularly.

In the new venture creation phase, women entrepreneurs benefit from some factors typifying their female-based entrepreneurial and leadership style, i.e., their people-orientation and emphasis on empowering the "person." Women value the human capital in their business and see it as the main VRIO[5] asset; they endeavor to extract the most from this precious asset by promoting the business and its people. Empowerment comes more naturally to women entrepreneurs and leaders. They use leadership styles that are well matched to the new venture creation phase, and develop a strong, empowered staff that treats the business as their own, and strives to move it forward toward the full accomplishment of its goals.

VISION—THE LINKING CHAIN

The reciprocal relationship between entrepreneurship and leadership is widely viewed as a combined process, dependent upon the leader and/or entrepreneur and the followers and/or staff members, the former aiming to attract people to rally around their vision and transform it into reality. The consistent influence on people exhibited by both leaders and entrepreneurs depends greatly on a solid, accepted and valuable vision. Accordingly, the main pillars linking leaders and entrepreneurs are:

Envisioning

- developing a vision that is simple to understand, ethical, and easy to empathize with so that it can then be translated accurately into practice by the staff;
- shaping the vision in a premeditated "amoeba-like structure" to enable flexibility and changes in its translation, pace and method of implementation, etc.;
- accepting others' visions and trying to merge them with the main vision;
- wrapping the vision and the envisioning process in updated, advanced and fresh concepts, to rally the staff around it.

Women's perspective—women easily develop visions and are very willing to incorporate their staff's ideas, suggestions and visions into the main vision; their flexibility and openness shape their leadership style as entrepreneurs around a shared vision that is constructed by their staff's input as well. Women are attentive and alert to changes and environmental dynamics, and can therefore adjust the vision's deliverables in line with new jargon, updated concepts and additional parameters that are "in." For example, a vision that emphasizes marketing may include concepts such as "Facebook" and "Twitter," bringing together different generations of staff members and adjusting the vision to today's world.

Role Models

- Entrepreneurs/leaders shape an independent entity, originated from their set of values and deep beliefs, rather than from a desire to be "cool" or charismatic.
- They behave ethically in both routine and unusual or unpredictable circumstances.
- They establish a stable, lasting image of a leader that is not influenced by external pressures (including threats to the business's survival).
- They have dedication, commitment, and respect for people.

- They embrace diversity.
- They are remembered as "the one I wish to become."

Women's perspective—a history of leaders shows that women lag behind in becoming renowned, influential and lifelong role models for leadership in the entrepreneurial realm. Except for a relative few, women are regarded as trading their stable, lasting image as leaders for flexibility. Their openness to and embracing of diversity push women entrepreneurs to change, adapt, adjust, include, or remove concepts, ideas, and suggestions to their image, their vision, the business practices. They do not feel threatened by such adjustments and maintain their confidence in the robustness of their vision and in their image as role model; they can see the benefits of such adjustments and ignore their subsequent effects on their image as leaders. As such, women entrepreneurs increase the fluidity and freshness that typify female entrepreneurial businesses, while endangering a lasting, influential role-model image. However, women's dedication and commitment to the cause, the people and the business, as an entity, along with their proclivity to accept diversity and encourage it, enable them to craft a valid role model as entrepreneur during the new venture creation process, even if this image does not last past this stage.

Expanding the Value of the Business

- establishing pride in being part of the business; expanding this pride as the business develops; "preserving" people's pride, even in times of crisis;
- developing an intrinsic motivation for belonging to the venture; developing the motivation to become more involved in the new venture's strategy and practices;
- evidence-based: showing results that can then be translated by the staff as adding value to the business; e.g., achieving the product development goal in a respectable time; showing survey results supporting the assertion that this new venture is promising; communicating successful experiences, even "small successes" such as exceeding the planned monthly sales, or achieving first place at a local competition for entrepreneurs; giving interviews in the various media.

Women's perspective—women who choose the path of new venture creation are proud and satisfied, by definition; they praise their accomplishments, feel fortunate and rewarded by what they have already achieved and are usually inspired by the dynamic process they are undergoing. They attribute the business's achievements not only to their own capabilities and hard work but also to their staff's capabilities and commitment to the process; consequently, they share their pride with their staff members, glorify them and spread the business's achievements around.

This process introduces positive energy into the business and enhances its value.

Women emphasize the significance of evidence-based results, rather than basing their business's results on intuition or a "feeling"; evidence is persuasive and reliable. In addition, by instinctively going into details, women entrepreneurs detect the "small successes" and celebrate them. These are significant leadership approaches and practices that can expand the value of the business to its staff members.

Entwining the Value of the Business with the Staff's Set of Values, Ethics and Business Ideologies

- being attentive to the staff members' set of values; identifying the leading, key factors that direct the staff;
- being ready to "split" the vision's value into different angles to enable different groups to identify with it; for example, eBay states that it believes in:[6] creating opportunities for people; caring, because people depend on them, and making a change in the world, among others. such a visionary declaration addresses different angles; these angles can be translated by the employees in different ways. More congruence, which is intentionally developed between the vision and the staff's values, can facilitate entwining the value of the business with the staff's values, ethics and business ideology;
- gathering the staff around the business's vision by crafting a value that is important to them, rather than only to the business; respecting diversity.

Women's perspective—women are willing to assign time to linking the business's vision and ethical codes with the staff members' guiding codes, as well as with the staff's different groups; women are sensitive, responsive and can easily identify the staff's set of values and ethical codes. For example, Janice is a 30-year-old activist entrepreneur from Texas who recently started a not-for-profit blog to raise awareness of abuse of women around the globe; Janice figured out that some of her bloggers and users belonged to the homosexual community and decided to expand her vision by adding a mission statement in favor of this community (Dirks & Ferrin, 2002; Eggers & Smilor, 1996; Rhoades, Eisenberger, & Armeli, 2001).

LEADERS AND INVESTORS IN THEIR FIELDS

Coco Chanel—a founder, leader, entrepreneur and visionary—Gabrielle "Coco" Chanel[7] is known as one of the premier fashion designers in Paris, France; she was an inventive, non-conformist, risk-taking designer who created simple suits and dresses, women's trousers, costume jewelry, perfumes and textiles. She was born in Saumur; her mother died when she was only six, one of five children whose father promptly abandoned them to the care of relatives. She adopted the name "Coco" during a brief career as a cafe and concert singer; she used the money she saved to set up a millinery shop in Paris and then in other places in France. She exploited some connections she had established to find customers among society women, and her simple hats became popular. Then, encouraged by her success, she expanded to couture, working in jerseys, a first in the French fashion world. Her business grew, her products were popular. Her fashion was in sharp contrast to the fashions which had been popular in previous decades; her message was much more than fashion, it was a rebellion, through the adoption of liberating and much more comfortable fashions.

Coco Chanel was known for her Chanel No. 5 perfume, which rapidly became very popular and most profitable; she partnered with others to effectively manage this successful undertaking. She designed stage costumes; she introduced the cardigan jacket, the "little black dress," the pea coat and bell bottom pants for women. She was innovative, highly creative and a most successful entrepreneur. She faced difficult times when a romantic affair with a Nazi officer during World War II dampened her popularity and found her exiled to Switzerland. Yet, she overcame these difficulties and made a post-war comeback. During the 1980s, Chanel opened more than 40 boutiques worldwide; Chanel was considered a global leader in the fragrance industry and a top innovator in fragrance advertising and marketing.

Inventor of domestic solutions—Marion O'Brien Donovan and the disposable diaper—Marion O'Brien Donovan[8] designed solutions to everyday problems; as an inventor and entrepreneur, Donovan created products that addressed problems in personal health, beauty, and household needs. She was born into a family of inventors in Indiana; her mother died when she was seven, and she spent most of her time at her father's factory, where he and her uncle developed an industrial lathe for manufacturing gun barrels, founding the South Bend Lathe Works in 1906. After graduation, she married James and became a Connecticut housewife and mother of two; at age 41, she got her Master's degree in architecture from Yale University.

As a mother of babies, Donovan was troubled by the lack of available options to keep her babies dry. She experimented with different solutions and three years later, she introduced the "Boater." Donovan's attempts to sell her idea to leading manufacturers failed, but her product became an instant sensation and commercial success when she began selling the Boater at Saks Fifth Avenue. Eventually, she sold her company, Donovan Enterprises, and her diaper patents to a children's clothing manufacturer for one million dollars. She went on to invent different products such as "The Ledger Check," a combined check and record-keeping booklet; "The Big Hang-Up," a garment hanger and closet organizer; "The Zippity-Do," an elasticized zipper pull; and she launched her largest promotional campaign, marketing DentaLoop directly to hundreds of dental professionals and pharmacists. She was a visionary but also a practical person who was involved in every aspect of product development, designing the product and the machinery. Most of all, she constantly envisioned improvements in every aspect of domestic life.

Bette Nesmith Graham—from secretary to inventor of correction fluid—Bette Nesmith Graham,[9] the inventor of correction fluid or liquid paper, had dreamed of becoming an artist. Yet, as a divorced single mother, the real world "forced" her to work as a secretary in a Dallas, Texas bank. However, creativity and her enthusiasm to create, inherent characteristics of artists, were revealed in her secretarial position; she was fascinated by finding ways to improve the work, and she quickly invented white-out as a way of quickly covering typing errors. She used her limited experience with art— she knew that artists rarely erased their mistakes while painting. Instead, they hid them by painting over them—and decided to use the same approach for correcting typos. She used her home blender to mix colors that matched the stationery she was using. Her invention became very popular with the other secretaries, so she started a home-based business in which she produced and sold her new invention; then she started a company, patented the product, renamed it "Liquid Paper," and obtained a trademark. At that time, she was fired from her job, but her company grew, producing over 25 million bottles a year. In 1979, she sold her company to the Gillette Corporation for $47.5 million. She passed away a year later at the age of 56.

These brief stories of women inventors, entrepreneurs and leaders in their fields prove that some competencies and core characteristics are shared by leaders in different sectors or development stages of the business; e.g., enthusiasm, an inner drive, establishing partnerships and collaborations, dedication to the goal, and overcoming difficulties and barriers.

THE KEY ROLES OF THE LEADER-FOUNDER

In today's competitive entrepreneurial realm, an empowered, highly motivated staff is an indispensable prerequisite for any entrepreneurial undertaking to start, survive and grow; yet, in the new venture creation phase, the conditions required to nurture such a motivated staff may seem unattainable. At these stages, the business suffers from limited resources, barely any finances, and difficulties associated with working with people for the first time with nobody of experience to compare with or lean on; in addition, entrepreneurial settings provide a venue in which the founder's impact is likely to be most pronounced, where the venture is still unstructured, or alternatively is very simply structured, and the leader's/founder's approach, behavior and modeling are crucial assets for the business, or future business. Leader-founders create the right conditions to foster the staff's entrepreneurial independence and filter its strengths for further development; these act as an accelerator which, in turn, increases the leader-founder's ability to stimulate the staff and motivate them to contribute to the startup. The leader-founder should adapt a leadership-oriented, more than a management-oriented approach, and as such give the staff more freedom in order to empower them (i.e., leadership), rather than organizing the staff's tasks and responsibilities in formal frameworks (i.e., management). While it might seem risky and time-consuming in the short run, the leadership approach allows identifying the fundamental strengths of the staff and improving them, which is most promising in the long run as it will eventually enable the staff to complement the leader-founder's abilities. Such dynamics are critical for creating sustainable competitive advantages at the new venture creation stages.

This premise is consistent with those introduced by the transformational leadership and full-range leadership models, proving that when the staff is treated in a fair, caring and respectful manner, and is thus cultivated by the leader, the result is higher job satisfaction, positive attitudes, organizational commitment, and happiness with work, among other factors.

Creating such conditions at the new venture creation phase, however, can be risky: by nurturing the staff, the leader-founder equips it with skills and capabilities, generic or business-specific, that can then be mobilized to other businesses. In fact, there are many examples of empowered and highly motivated employees who turned their backs on the founder by acquiring their networks, managerial skills, specific expertise and market knowledge, among others, then moved on equipped with these valuable assets. These assets are even more valuable at the new venture stage as they provide a solid basis for developing projects/products/services under limited conditions; moreover, changing, adjusting or withdrawing the project/product/service, "because the chief person in the business has left and uses the same social capital acquired at the business," is not an option.

Many founders confront such possible risks by signing structured contracts that hold concealed, threatening implications (the "if . . . then" . . . conditions, among others); yet, the robustness of such methods is limited and short-lived.

A different approach is needed to operate an effective leadership specifically associated with the challenges inherent in the new venture creation process by addressing both the potential benefits but also the potential risks at these stages. Women's leadership style may be most useful at these stages. Table 12.2 delineates key factors in leading during the new venture creation stage and relates these with women's leadership styles.

Table 12.2 The Leader-Founder and Female New Venture Creation

Key factors for leaders-founders	Key factors in female leadership
Taking an holistic view, looking several steps ahead, understanding the complete situation, yet being attentive to the details	Women are strategic thinkers; they plan, calculate and allocate time to learning the "big picture" and understanding it broadly. They are naturally prone to looking into the details. Such combined long- and short-term views along with their continual learning tendency are most relevant to leadership at these stages
Creating a strength-based organizational culture, based on shared values, accepted norms and rules, in which the staff is part of their creation and can easily identify with, as well as transfer this culture further on	Women assign time, thought, reflection and resources to creating a solid organizational culture; they tend to build it jointly with the staff. They truly see the strength of connecting to the staff and of the organizational culture
Establishing positive psychological capital by demonstrating high levels of confidence, trust and fairness, as well as resiliency (e.g., avoiding "ego-related" issues that result in irrelevant inflexibility)	Women lead by emphasizing the psychological aspects; their understanding of, and attentiveness to the positive impact of psychology on the business's culture and consequent outcomes are high; women are much more "ego-free" than their male counterparts and can more easily adopt a resilient approach, despite the consequences of any implication of being wrong
Integrating the staff's interests with those of the business, by explaining, reflecting, assigning time and genuine attention to sharing, discussing and implementing the staff's suggestions whenever possible	Women share, discuss and reflect; they see the importance of such practices and use them more frequently than men
Engaging the staff in positive work attitudes, including happiness, hope, optimism; making such attitudes instructive by cracking the codes of successful experiences, to enable duplicating them and multiplying the positive experiences and attitudes	Many entrepreneurs are positive and optimistic; gender seems to be irrelevant here. However, women are great learners and are willing to allocate time to reflecting upon the situations that engender happiness and self-fulfillment, in order to reproduce them
Encouraging creativity, innovation and outside-the-box thinking; being supportive and tolerant of any idea, allowing the staff to seriously analyze their ideas in order to crystallize them for implementation	Women manage creativity, innovation and originality in most effective ways, by enabling their staff to experience these and by facilitating their implementation, whenever possible. Women assist in crystallizing new ideas into a practical project, when they spot their competitive advantage

Creating a "cultural stickiness," whereby the staff wishes to stay with the business and promote it to success	Women's interpersonal skills, along with their desire to create a shared culture, and appreciation of loyalty and dedication, lay the foundation for staff adherence
Communicating the business, its achievements, praising the staff, disseminating their strengths; being available for the staff	Women are proud of their staff's achievements and will gladly communicate them; they appreciate communal work in the business and do not relate the business's achievements solely to themselves

(For more reading, see: Chandler & Hanks, 1994; Cogliser & Brigham, 2004; Hamel, 2000; Luthans & Youssef, 2004; Luthans, Youssef, & Avolio, 2007; O'Reilly & Pfeffer, 2000.)

EMOTIONAL SKILLS AND LEADERSHIP—THE FEMALE ENTREPRENEURSHIP CONTEXT

The models originating from the transformational leadership perspective stress that social and emotional competencies contribute to effective leadership behavior; these include competencies such as self-awareness, self-monitoring, social control, emotional and social intelligence and charismatic leadership. In terms of the behavioral aspect, leaders emphasizing and using more emotional skills demonstrate a personalized, tailor-made leadership style, in which they know every member of their staff personally, in both their work-related and life-related spheres, recognize and appreciate their work-related accomplishments and praise them. These leaders may display eccentric behavior by taking personal risks to maintain staff unity and high motivation. Emotional skills used for leadership practice act as a source for others' empathy and identification. The staff tends to consider the leader a role model who can be faithfully followed and who inspires them to contribute to the business.

The leadership research typifies women as possessing significantly higher levels of emotional, social and interpersonal abilities than men. These are manifested in their more frequent, open and dynamic communication skills, their more frequent use of informal communication and their "open door" approach to facilitating communication with their staff, and enjoying more personal, open, but confidential interactions with their staff members. Women, to a greater extent than men, have been found in research to be socially sensitive, and genuinely interested in their staff's feelings, thoughts and feedback. Similarly, women demonstrate greater perceptiveness, empathy, and adaptability than men to matters concerning their staff, both as a group and as individuals. Women demonstrate a greater ability to communicate through both verbal and nonverbal channels. Verbally, they tend to explain the tasks so that their staff members will understand the context of their task environment, they correct their staff's mistakes in constructive ways, by clarifying the mistakes and elucidating, mainly jointly with the staff member(s), how such mistakes can be reduced, and they tend to ask questions to verify that their verbal message has been transmitted correctly. Women use nonverbal messages more frequently to encourage, support but also to indicate dissatisfaction or frustration. Specifically, they display a greater frequency of smiling and eye contact, which contribute to a positive atmosphere and openness; they use facial expressions reflecting emotions to transmit their messages. Concurrently, they can easily decode nonverbal and visual cues, and thus are able to react immediately to situations, prior to their verbalization. Overall, women demonstrate superior ability to men in several measures of emotional competency and intelligence (Ashkanasy & Tse, 2000; Conger & Kanungo, 1998; George, 2000; Sosik, 2001). Such benefits could promote their leadership in the new venture creation process.

Women favor "being with" others, and apply this in their leadership style. Such a tendency is relevant to the new venture creation process when the business is unstructured and relationships are more amorphous and not yet associated with a chain of command. Women find participating and sharing, as core segments of their leadership practice, to be fulfilling and self-enhancing. Studies on gender and leadership have shown that creativity and innovation occur more often in situations shared and discussed by women, who feel confident that they are not alone; they experience synergistic growth to a higher extent than men. The implication is that women possess leadership measures that are most relevant to the new venture creation process, in emphasizing the most important asset of their business, the people.

The more frequent use of emotional skills in leadership along the new venture creation process contributes to different business outcomes, while also positively affecting the business's processes, both tangibly—positive effect on the net profit margin, stock value, and intangibly—management team cohesion, staff's positive attitudes toward the business and positive perceptions of the leadership's effectiveness (Lowe, Kroeck, & Sivasubramaniam, 1996; Waldman, Ramirez, House, & Puranam, 2001).

THE DIVA PHENOMENON

The Merriam-Webster Dictionary defines "Diva" as "a usually glamorous and successful female performer or personality." The word originates from the Italian derivation meaning "Goddess." A Diva is labeled as a leader in her field, a metaphor to signify the power of the feminine.

Naomi Campbell, supermodel and actress, was born in the working-class district of South London, the daughter of Jamaican-born dancer Valerie Morris; her father deserted her mother when she was pregnant and Morris forbade her daughter Naomi from meeting him; even her last name is from her mother's second marriage. During her early years, Campbell lived in different places around the world, including living apart from her mother, with her grandmother; her mother was a ballet dancer and traveled frequently. Under such unstable conditions, Campbell became a Diva, as one of the world's top supermodels. At the age of five, Campbell was enrolled at the Barbara Speake Stage School, and at the age of ten, she was accepted into the Italia Conti Academy of Theatre Arts, where she studied ballet. She was seven at her first public appearance, where she was featured in a Bob Marley music video; then she played Snow White in a television series; at the age of 12, she tap-danced in a music video for the Culture Club. While the exquisitely exotic and leggy supermodel began her career on the catwalk, she quickly segued into high-profile advertising campaigns for such fashion icons as Ralph Lauren. She was the first black female model to appear on the covers of French *Vogue*, British *Vogue*, and *Time* Magazine. Campbell has appeared in music videos and films; she is the co-author of the novel *Swan* and she has published a self-titled photography book; she is an ambitious business-woman: with Elle Macpherson and Claudia Schiffer, Naomi Campbell opened the "Fashion Cafe" in New York; she has created two spin-off companies, NC Connect and a perfume line, among others.

Naomi Campbell's story attests to some of the abilities that can be found among leaders and entrepreneurs, which were apparently promoted in paving her way to Diva status; e.g., the ability to exploit opportunities, to leverage her resources, such as her education at that time as a platform to pave her way to becoming a Diva, her proactivity, her determination, her ambition and her growing aspirations: the more she accomplished the more peaks she could envision reaching.

Cher, née Cherylin Sarkisian LaPiere,[10] has led a spectacular life on the road to Diva status, being most successful in music, movies, on television, and on the stage. Cher, born in California in 1946, grew up as a poor, fatherless child whose mother went on to marry eight times. She delighted in watching her mother on stage and living a peaceful life in her family apartment. At 16, she left school and home to take acting lessons in Los Angeles. At 17, unemployed and desperate for work, Cher met and then married Sonny, who had already made many television appearances. They succeeded as a couple and hit gold with their single "I've got you babe," furthering their worldwide success with a variety of hits; yet, her family life was hectic, violent and unstable. At the age of 33, Cher was an unemployed, single mother, with a damaged

TV image and deep-seated emotions: no one in Hollywood wanted her. But this did not discourage her. She was cast in the movie *Silkwood*, acting with Meryl Streep; Cher recounts: "I will never forget the time *Silkwood* premiered in New York and as soon as my name was mentioned, the audience just laughed. I felt so bad . . ." But her performance put her back on the map: she was once again in demand, acting in such movies as *The Witches of Eastwick*, *Suspect* and *Moonstruck*. She used her unique voice to produce an album, but was criticized in Hollywood; she hit back with a slick new disco album. Cher's unstable career and family life did not stop her: today, she is a chart-topping singer, television star, Academy award winner, disco Diva, rock "n" roller and fashion icon.

(Coplon, 1999)

Cher's amazing story demonstrates abilities prevailing among leaders and entrepreneurs, particularly her determination to move forward after unfortunate experiences. Cher's calm appearance, which did not disclose the distress in her family life, the audience feedback or the difficulties faced from Hollywood's critics, assisted in molding her Diva image.

These stories, among others, tracing Divas' journeys, encapsulate these women's capabilities and characteristics: they started from a rough draft and with determination, in some cases even heroism, built their careers, using their leadership skills and characteristics such as proactivity, creativity, opportunity exploitation, risk-taking. These stories shed light on the emerging phenomenon of "Diva" which has only recently become associated with positive connotations of leaders, role models, and determined women who did not consider quitting their dream an option, and thus plowed through under difficult conditions. The Diva is a gendered construct, context-based and represented by different genres: outstanding singers (e.g., Maria Callas, Aretha Franklin, Diana Ross, Björk, Christina Aguilera, Barbra Streisand, Cher, Tina Turner, Whitney Houston, Celine Dion, Mariah Carey); iconic actresses (e.g., Audrey Hepburn, Ava Gardner, Bette Davis, Elizabeth Taylor, Grace Kelly, Greta Garbo, Judy Garland, Julia Roberts, Julie Andrews, Katharine Hepburn); supermodels (e.g., Twiggy, Heidi Klum, Gisele Bündchen, Claudia Schiffer, Cindy Crawford, Naomi Campbell, Kate Moss), as well as other figures that are mostly associated with the arts, show business and putting themselves center-stage.

The notion of Diva was first founded on the concepts of aesthetic and beauty; Diva status was based around the combination of these women's skills, talents, capabilities and beauty; talent alone could not create a Diva. At that stage, being a Diva was associated with negative connotations, such as arrogance, difficult to work with, manipulative, though admired and well-known. The story behind the Diva was only relevant to further public relations and promotion, yet unimportant to understanding their origins, influences and talent.

In the last two decades, the concept of Diva has been transformed. Divas are seen as leaders and entrepreneurs. Divas are perceived as women possessing charismatic abilities; they can communicate their personal achievements to diverse audiences; they can get noticed under a variety of conditions; they overcome obstacles, and are perceived as most determined and powerful. They are typified by inner passion and enthusiasm for work and life, women that compose their own careers, manage to be leaders in their fields and benefit from social status, money and work-related prestige.

In an era which has seen the growing popularity of paparazzi, reality shows, online blogs, gossip websites and ratings, Divas are role models mainly, but not exclusively, for teenagers. They influence other people, many of whom look up to them, admire them, wish to resemble them and trace their steps (Bates, Thompson, & Vaile, 2003; Bomani, 2007; Brooks & Valentine, 2006; Burns & Lafrance, 2001; Hammond, 2007; Smith, 2009).

In summary, the "Diva archetype" is an important addition to the complex concepts of leadership-entrepreneurship in the female arena that underlie the behavior of women who have struggled to establish their status as Divas by implementing abilities and competencies of entrepreneurs and leaders. As leadership scholars continue to investigate such competencies, the importance of uncovering the powerful effects of Divas in different areas: art, science, literature, is becoming clear, as these, among others, are gaining exposure and publicity today. The acknowledgment of these women's exceptional leadership and entrepreneurial-related competencies has important implications for the advancement of Divas as well as of women in leadership roles in the entrepreneurial realm.

SUMMARY

This chapter's aim was to delineate the connections between leadership and entrepreneurship embedded in the female ecosystem, by showing the uniqueness demonstrated by women in their social, emotional and environmental sensitivities, such as identifying their staff members' needs, feelings, abilities, skills, and limitations, and leveraging this to influence their staff by developing mutual affection and respect, specifically by explaining, providing evidence-based proof and reflecting upon the experiences in order to learn more and grow.

Women's "feminine" leadership is manifested and celebrated to release the outdated perceptions of male-dominant skills necessary for effective leadership, such as confidence, task orientation, competitiveness, and assertiveness; and introduce leadership models and concepts, including the Diva concept, which contain skills and competencies traditionally viewed as feminine, yet most successful in obtaining fantastic outcomes from the most precious asset, the staff.

CASE STUDIES[11]

The following fascinating case study contributed by Veronika Kisfalvi and Francine Richer tells, in rich yet sensitive detail, the story of the well-known Maria Montessori and her schools. This case study contributes to our understanding of female entrepreneurship by showing that pioneering women entrepreneurs such as Maria Montessori are not only shaped by their times and their background, but also by powerful personal psychological forces; their vision and action can be said to be "over-determined" by the convergence of a number of influences.

Arnis Sauka and Friederike Welter take the reader on the exciting journey of Ms. Lotte Tisenkopfa-Iltnere, initiator and CEO of the unique Latvian MADARA cosmetics business. Delicately weaving the pieces of her story, the authors show how the high growth ambitions of MADARA Cosmetics' female owners and the choice of production sector contradicted at least some of the characteristics perceived to be typical for female-owned companies, i.e., commonly characterized as less risk-averse, focused on industries with relatively low entry, such as services or retail, small in size and survival-oriented.

These case studies celebrate leadership in female entrepreneurship.

Personal History, Passion and the Entrepreneurial Project: Maria Montessori and Her Schools

Veronika Kisfalvi and Francine Richer
HEC, Montreal, Quebec, Canada

Introduction

A visit to any nursery school or day care, with its child-size tables and chairs, low shelves, and coat hooks and blackboard adapted to the little beings who come there to play and learn, often evokes a spontaneous smile. When the teachers want the attention of their little charges, they invite them to sit with them on the floor, in a circle, and ask them to raise their hands to speak. After play period, they will encourage each child to put away the puzzles, the blocks and the dolls and dishes used in make-believe play. In the yard, there is a slide, a rope to climb, a sandbox, swings . . . But these elements did not always belong to the world of childhood. We owe the creation of such environments, adapted to the needs of children, to the work of doctors, anthropologists, psychologists and pedagogues of the nineteenth century. One of them, Maria Montessori, played a major role in these developments and established an international reputation—and enterprise—in the process.

Few are aware that Maria Montessori-anthropologist, experimental psychologist, pedagogue, feminist, unmarried mother, entrepreneur-was also the first woman to obtain a medical degree in Italy. She was the first to introduce the idea of child-centered education, and saw the teacher's role as that of an observer who creates an environment favorable to the spontaneous activities of the child. Montessori schools can be found worldwide today, and their philosophy enjoys continued popularity. Maria Montessori's concern was to preserve the integrity of her approach, and to promote the appropriate use of the teaching supports she had developed; these supports clearly distinguished themselves from the category of simple educational toys. It is her innovative approach to learning that allowed her to create a movement and to treat the education that she dispensed, the certification that she granted and the material that she developed as a product. The Montessori schools are in fact franchises. The International Montessori Association (IMA) holds all the rights to her work and to the material used in the schools.

To protect a deeply-held philosophy of education, and to support herself financially, Montessori became an entrepreneur. Private groups and individuals-made up mainly of women philanthropists and teachers-were her main financial supporters, although she also received help from various governments. Italy at the end of the nineteenth century, with its poor and largely illiterate population and unstable government, was the setting for much of her life and career. From her birth in 1870 to her death in Holland in 1952, Maria's life trajectory crosses revolutions, the rise of fascism, two world wars, and takes her to the Americas, India and the Far East. Her entrepreneurship cannot be separated from her deep passions and convictions. Very early in her career, she expanded the boundaries of education, because for her, it held the seeds of humanity's regeneration; it was ultimately a work of peace. But her trajectory was also deeply marked by her background and personal experience.

Maria Montessori's Family, Early Childhood and Education

Maria Montessori was the only child of Renilde Stoppani and Allessandro Montessori. Her father had been a decorated career soldier before becoming a civil servant. He had studied rhetoric and arithmetic, wrote well and spoke only Italian, in a country where dialects abounded. He met Renilde Stoppani, eight years his junior, in 1865, when he was posted to Chiaravalle as an accountant. Renilde was part of the lesser nobility, and came from a family of landowners in the region. She was well educated, rare for a girl of her generation, and still rarer was her passion for books and learning. The

Montessoris settled in Rome, where they fitted into the middle class. Rome had a university, libraries and museums, theatres, an opera, and cafés, and Maria benefitted from this intellectual and artistic environment. For her father, intelligence and a quick wit had their place in a girl, as long as these qualities were expressed within the framework of the traditional family. Renilde Stoppani, on the other hand, encouraged her daughter to free herself from traditions and stereotypes. She listened to Maria talk about her dreams and drew pleasure from her daughter's independent spirit. Maria was brought up with the values of self-discipline and helping those less fortunate.

In school, Maria was at first an unremarkable student. Easily bored, she dreamt of becoming an actress. Mathematics finally sparked her interest, and it brought her somewhat closer to her father. At age 12, she enrolled in a technical training school, choosing the most difficult courses. She began to enjoy competition . . . and success! Confident, willful, sometimes arrogant and non-conformist, Maria was encouraged by her mother to read, to question, to develop her interests. Sick at home one day, she said to her anxious mother, "Don't worry, mama, I cannot die. I have much too much to do!"

Maria excelled in math and wished to become an engineer, but on the eve of her graduation abruptly changed her mind and chose medicine, a subject which no woman had ever before pursued in Italy. Although her father refused to back her, she arranged to meat the Dean of the faculty, who also tried to discourage her. Undaunted, as she shook his hand to leave, she said, "I know I'll be a doctor." In the fall of 1890, Maria was admitted to the University, where she excelled, but when she opted for medicine . . . "Unthinkable!" said the officials. But supported only by her mother and, rumour has it, by Pope Leon XIII, Maria was admitted to medical school.

As a woman, Maria was treated harshly. She could only enter the classroom after her male colleagues were seated . . . if there was space for her. They were allowed to make vulgar noises and to whistle at her in derision. But she just said: "The louder you whistle, the further I'll go." Her colleagues, seeing her great determination, gradually accepted her, and eventually, she even obtained prizes and bursaries. Added to the income from a few hours of private tutoring, these allowed her to pay her expenses. Faced with such autonomy, her father could no longer disapprove of his daughter's choice. He would always stay somewhat emotionally distant, but he regularly accompanied her on the way to classes, it being improper for girls to walk in the streets alone. Her mother, on the other hand, provided all the help she could, for example by separating the chapters of the larger books so that her daughter could carry only the pages needed for the day. The last two years of Maria's training were devoted to pediatrics, and at the age of only 25, she was recognized as an expert in childhood diseases. Among the patients that she saw were children unable to function in school and in the family. Asylums were their only refuge. They were abandoned there among criminals and catatonics. Maria saw that the children's environment was devoid of stimulation, both for body and mind, and became preoccupied with their fate.

In her last year, Maria was required to give a talk in front of her classmates. The audience was attentive and obviously impressed by both the content and the style. Allessandro Montessori, informed of the event by a friend, was persuaded to attend. He witnessed the ovation his daughter received . . . and accepted the congratulations due to the father of such a brilliant student. But it was not until her thirtieth birthday that he openly showed his appreciation, presenting her with a leather-bound volume containing newspaper clippings attesting to her many accomplishments. In the spring of 1896, Maria submitted her thesis on paranoia. In elegant evening dress, as was the custom, she defended her work with exceptional success before the eleven men of the jury, who then admitted the first *signora dottoressa* to their brotherhood. A few hours later, as colleagues and friends gathered at the Montessori home, Maria played the perfect hostess and well-brought up daughter . . .

Maria Montessori, Physician and Educator

In the years after her graduation, Montessori pursued her medical career and obtained positions in a number of hospitals in Rome, developing a research program and a private practice consisting mainly of poor women and children. She not only treated these patients' ills, but sometimes also cooked them a meal, made their bed, took care of their children . . . Her mother carefully kept a file of each letter of thanks these patients sent. At this time, Maria began to nurture a network of well-to-do women who supported her efforts with the poor, and later, her other projects.

Her research into mental illness and juvenile delinquency and her experiences as a private physician shaped her ideas about education; in an 1898 paper, she proposed a revolution in the way the "mentally deficient" were treated and taught, revealing her growing interest in education. In it, she articulated the mainstay of her teaching method: "First, care of the body, then training of the mind . . . First, educating the senses, then educating the intellect." Her ongoing efforts in this direction (research, conferences, talks, newspaper articles) led to the creation of the Medico-Pedagogic Institute, whose mission was to educate the mentally deficient. She became its Director in 1900, working closely with a former colleague and co-author, Dr Giuseppe Montesano. In the first year, 22 students were admitted, and Maria began to apply the educational methods she had been developing over the years. One exercise prepared students for the next, more complex one. To teach the alphabet, she used letters made of wood. By handling and examining the letters, the children learned the gestures of writing. The results obtained were extraordinary. Children considered uneducable succeeded and were integrated into regular classes. If this method succeeded so well with "idiots," what would happen with normal children, she wondered.

Maria had occasion to answer this question with the creation, in 1907, of the first *Casa dei bambini*, or nursery school, in the tenements of Rome; the purpose was to channel the resident children's destructive energy into something positive, in order to prevent it from exploding into vandalism later. Having no budget, Maria called upon her network of women philanthropists to help furnish the space. The children were taught basic hygiene, and were stimulated to engage in creative play using Montessori's material. They preferred making things by themselves, with no reward other than mastery of the task. For Maria, the environment must favor children's spontaneous activity and support their autonomy because "no-one can be free unless he is autonomous." It is here that the environment was first tailored to the child; the parents were also involved. Soon, a second *Casa* was opened, then others both in Italy and abroad, with great success. She wrote her first book, *The Montessorri Method*, in 1909, which catapulted her into the spotlight. At about the same time, a dispute arose between Montessori and the owner of the tenements in which the nurseries were housed, and she was ultimately banished from the buildings. From then on, she put all her efforts into promoting her method, which would become her sole source of income, since she had moved far from the world of medicine and the university. This became of utmost importance for a hitherto unsuspected reason.

In 1898, Maria had had a child, Mario, out of wedlock. The father, Dr. Montesano, of the Medico-Pedagogic Institute, had promised to marry her but his family opposed the match. The marriage was called off, and the child's existence kept secret. Arrangements were made to have Mario brought up by a family claiming him as their son; but Maria regularly visited him, bringing him toys and never wearying of watching him play. When Maria lost her mother in 1912, she grieved deeply, but was finally free to contact Mario more openly. He told her that he had always known she was his mother. He took the name of Montessori (and not Montesano) and became the most important man in her life. The father suffered no embarrassment and Maria never admitted to having had an affair with him. Mario became her travelling companion and eventually her agent and faithful collaborator, but was always referred to as her nephew or adopted son. The first time Mario publicly presented Maria as his mother was in 1950.

Maria Montessori, Entrepreneur

With the advent of her added financial responsibilities as a single parent, Marie keenly felt the necessity to protect her sole source of income; she needed to "market" her method and her schools. Knowing that parents and educators were very interested in her schools, books and pedagogic tools, she began to expand internationally, and visited the United States twice in the mid 1910s. But when she saw that her ideas were being co-opted in the U.S., and that her method and her revenues were both in danger, she took rapid action by carefully establishing the copyright to her books and her materials. She eventually disassociated herself from the Montessori schools in the United States, concentrating her efforts in Europe. She had always been very protective of her work, but became even more so, maintaining absolute control over the development of her material, and consistently refusing to teach her method in a university. Her schools were franchises, and only Maria was authorized to train the teachers. Her attitude, seen as a betrayal of her Universalist ideals, eventually led to reproaches from the teaching community both for turning her pedagogy into a sellable product and for her refusal to deviate from her original methods, which some now considered dated. In 1926, she embarked on a disastrous alliance with Mussolini, blind to his intentions which were so contradictory to her espoused pacifist allegiances, in order to gain a greater foothold for her method in Italy. But in 1934, she refused the Mussolini government's offer of the title of Children's Ambassador, maintaining that she had always acted as a representative of IMA and not the Italian government. This act was perceived as open defiance of Mussolini, and all her schools in Italy were shut down the next day. This event marked the end of the Montessori movement in the country which had seen its birth, as well as its general decline, as educators and the public turned to newer pedagogic theories and approaches. Maria moved to Holland in 1937, where her life became more peaceful.

At the age of 69, still determined to spread her method even after these setbacks, Maria took a trip to India, where her approach was still very popular. Intending to stay for a few months, she remained for seven years. Except for a brief period during the war when her son was imprisoned, she seemed very happy, enjoying success and adulation once more. In India, she wrote her last book, *The Absorbent Mind*. In 1945, at age 75, she wrote: "I am well, but my energy and my confidence are gradually decreasing. Perhaps this is because all is well . . . I miss the stimulus of a good fight." Maria returned to Holland after the war, and discovered that she had not been forgotten in Europe. In December 1949, she was awarded the Legion of Honor, and nominated for the Nobel Peace Prize in 1949, 1950 and 1951. In June 1950, when she was a delegate to UNESCO in Florence, the director-general of the organization pointed her out as "the symbol of our great hopes in education and peace." She received a standing ovation.

At the age of 81, she still worked from 7:30 in the morning until late at night. On May 6, 1952, sitting in her garden, she abruptly asked her son: "Am I still of any use?" One hour later, she was felled by a massive stroke. Mario Montessori inherited his mother's belongings, along with all the rights to her work. He succeeded her as president of IMA, and held this office until his death in 1982, when he was succeeded by his own daughter. It is through his efforts that the American associations and the Montessori international movement were reconciled. In her will, Maria Montessori wrote the following about Mario: ". . . may his children bring him consolation and may the world recognize him for his merits, which I know are great and sublime . . . and may the followers of my work and all those who have benefitted from it realize to what extent they are in his debt!"

Questions for Discussion

1   In what ways did the dynamics in Maria Montessori's family contribute to her evolution as a pioneer and female entrepreneur?

2   What were the forces driving Maria Montessori's vision? How do you explain her strong need for control?

3   How would you describe Maria Montessori as an entrepreneur? Do you consider her to be a successful one?

4   What relationships can be seen between Maria Montessori's talents as a doctor, researcher and pedagogue, and her entrepreneurial activities?

5   What ethical issues does this case raise for you?

Case References

Kramer, R. (1988). *Maria Montessori—A Biography*. Cambridge: Perseus Publishing, Radcliffe Biography Series, 410 pages. Preface by Anna Freud.

Montessori, M. (1912). *The Montessori Method*. New York: F. A. Stokes, 377 pp.

Montessori, M. (*c.* 1958). *Pédagogie scientifique : la découverte de l'enfant* / Introduction by Mario M. Montessori. French text by Georgette J.J. Bernard. 27 photos by Jean-Marie Marcel. 3rd éd., Bruges: Desclée de Brouwer, 263 pages. Italian title: *Il metodo della pedagogia scientifica applicato all'educazione infantile.*

Montessori, M. (*c.* 1958). *La messe vécue pour les enfants*, 3rd edition. Paris: Desclée de Brouwer, 122 pages.

Montessori, M. (1995). *The Absorbent Mind*. New York: Henry Holt and Company, 302 pp. Page 165.

Montessori, M. 1965 (*c.* 1917). *The Montessori Elementary Material*. Cambridge, Mass.: R. Bentley, xviii, 464 pp, with engravincp.

Montessori, M. (1975). *L'enfant*. Paris: Denoël/Gonthier, c1936, 184 pages.

Montessori, M. (1932). *La paix et l'éducation*. Genève: Bureau international d'éducation, 23 pp.

Montessori, M. (1932). *Les étapes de l'éducation*. Bruges: Desclée de Brouwer, 40 pp.

Standing, E.M. (1962). *Maria Montessori: Her life and work*. New York and Scarborough: New American Library, 6th ed., 382 pp.

Related Internet Sites

http://www.montessorienfrance.com/index.html
http://www.montessori-ami.org
http://mapage.noos.fr/horizonmontessori/index.htm
http://www.montessori-namta.org/NAMTA/administrators/startsch1.html

Born Green and Global: The Case of MADARA Cosmetics

Arnis Sauka[a] and Friederike Welter[b]
[a]Stockholm School of Economics in Riga, Latvia; [b]Jönköping International Business School, Jönköping, Sweden

MADARA Cosmetics is an example of a business founded in a highly competitive market, but successfully establishing itself in one of its niches (green/ecopreneurship). Here, the ability to spot opportunity in a timely fashion, i.e., realize the high growth potential for eco-products in the world market, played a significant role. This case study demonstrates the innovativeness of the company and its rapid growth through internationalization.

It also demonstrates the successful implementation of the "acting local—thinking global strategy," in particular the opening for business owners to take advantage of the transition environment in Latvia (which is often perceived as less favorable for business expansion), as reflected in, for example, lower wages, to ensure rapid growth of a firm in the global arena.

"The way we came to MADARA Cosmetics was closely linked to our education, experience and lifestyle"—Lotte Tisenkopfa-Iltnere, owner and CEO, begins the story. "I have studied business management and Japanese, lived in Japan and worked for a company in Osaka dealing with logistics and manufacturing processes, and I have gained similar working experience since returning to Latvia. With this I learned to love factories: the bigger and the more complicated, the better!" She is also a vegetarian and a person who really cares about a healthy lifestyle, which happened to have a direct influence on the business start-up. As Lotte remembers, "Before I had an allergic reaction to an eye cream, I had no idea that cosmetics can contain so many unhealthy ingredients, including substances which are used for antifreeze or door lubrication! When I realized this, I simply threw all my stocks away." Since no eco cosmetics that could satisfy Lotte's needs were available on the Latvian market at that time, searching for possible recipes on the internet and exchanging ideas via blogging, she started to make cosmetics for herself at home.

Zane Rugina, who previously worked for the marketing agency McCann-Erickson, was also looking for healthy cosmetics. "We met in a female blogging space and Zane came to me to buy a piece of self-produced soap," remembers Lotte. Both women soon found a common language and, exploring the market needs, realized that they were far from being the only ones interested in eco cosmetics. Indeed, at that time, according to information provided by marketing agencies, the eco cosmetics market was growing by about 20 percent annually, and was the fastest growing segment within the cosmetics market. "This was the rational side of our decision making, but all in all we decided to establish a company because we wanted to produce something which we would use ourselves," says Lotte. "This in turn set a very high quality standard, as happens if you do something for yourself. Being women and the target audience for our own product, we felt in our hearts what the design, product structure, smell, and associations from using MADARA Cosmetics products should be. This was especially crucial at the very early stage of the business start-up as initially most product- and branding-related decisions had to be taken by drawing on our own experience, perceptions, and intuition." Lotte also remembers that "only later could we afford specialists and create surveys and focus groups, compiling thick files with procedures to be followed for each step in the product design." MADARA Cosmetics was established in July 2006 with Liene Darzniece and Lotte's sister, Paula later also joining the team. "Apart from my sister, who was only around 18 years old at that time, we all had management education and work experience," Lotte remembers further. "Even though the Latvian market turned out to be of significant importance in the later stages, we always aimed to stand out among exclusive cosmetics brands in the world market," continues Lotte. "This ambitious aim was another reason for the company to make sure that the quality and appearance of its products is good enough to be able to compete in the global arena." Such an explanation contradicts mainstream female entrepreneurship literature, which characterizes the growth ambitions of female entrepreneurs as being somewhat lower compared to male-owned businesses (Baygan, 2000). Overall MADARA Cosmetics displays characteristics similar to those observed in other studies on women start-ups. For instance, previous studies highlighted that more and more women are now involved in less traditional sectors (e.g., Baygan, 2000), women business owners are relatively young (Carter et al., 2001) and often orientated toward a female target audience (Brush et al., 2006). Furthermore, the high level of education of entrepreneurs is a typical feature of businesses in transition environments (Smallbone & Welter, 2001).

Altogether it took around two years to establish MADARA Cosmetics. Lotte and her colleagues spent most of this time understanding that they could actually dare to establish a company. "When confidence was gained and the idea was clear, we moved along very quickly," remembers Lotte. "Only half a year was needed to introduce the first products onto the market." MADARA Cosmetics received 5,000 euros as well as a network of advisors, which helped to develop the initial idea, from an EU social funds program supporting female entrepreneurship. The owners also approached several banks in Latvia for a loan, but were rejected in each case. "From today's standpoint it is very good that we did not receive a bank loan," says Lotte. "Initially we wanted to enter the market with 20 products, but with our limited resources we could afford only 4. Because of this, we avoided making too many mistakes and also decreased the level of risk, which was already too high."

Apart from the 5,000 euros financial support, their start-up capital consisted of their own savings and loans from parents and relatives. "We risked that money which all of us had saved and our parents were quite nervous about that," remembers Lotte Tisenkopfa-Iltnere, thus not only demonstrating the most common way in which start-up capital is acquired, especially in transition environments where support systems for new entrepreneurs are not yet in place (e.g., Smallbone & Welter, 2001), but also a willingness to accept high risk. Starting one's own production company with limited resources is indeed very risky, because manufacturing companies usually have high fixed costs: "We were well aware that outsourcing the production would be a cheaper and less risky option. But then we would have limited control over the quality of our products, which could potentially destroy the credibility of the brand name," explains Lotte.

MADARA Cosmetics also demonstrates the importance of receiving additional help from families and relatives during the early start-up stage: a characteristic that some research has shown to be of particular importance for women business owners, especially in a transition context (Smallbone & Welter, 2001). As Lotte remembers, "Today we are big enough to be able to pay for professional advice but this was, of course, not the case during the very first year of our operation. Our mothers and fathers supported us emotionally, helped with the printing, worked in the labs and alike; furthermore my husband, a finance expert, offered invaluable support in this area."

Regarding problems young companies might face in the very first years of their operation, Lotte emphasizes that MADARA Cosmetics never really experienced any concerns related to the external environment. In fact, according to Lotte, the external environment in Latvia had a positive impact on the further development of MADARA Cosmetics: "We would never have been able to afford the infrastructure the company has today if MADARA Cosmetics had been established in, for example, Switzerland. Employing a qualified citizen of Switzerland costs 15 times more than having an employee from Latvia." "The only negative issue coming from the external environment I can think of is a stereotype that women can be successful both in their professional career and have family and children," says Lotte. According to her observations, this stereotype in Latvia has been generated by women themselves: "Several successful female entrepreneurs have demonstrated that they can easily combine both, thus putting many women under pressure, as in reality this is very difficult, if not impossible." She adds that "fewer difficulties in this regard arise with respect to work life." The problem starts with expectations regarding what a woman still has to do after she comes home from her job and this can cause difficulties in her personal life.

> The real problem which we faced in the early stage of the company start-up was a lack of current assets: typical for almost any new and small company. For a year and a half we lived with this problem, trying to be as efficient as possible. For instance, there were some 15 employees in the company who simply did everything which had to be done, often outside their competence or working hours. We also had quite a tough situation with suppliers and other cooperation partners, as we were constantly trying to negotiate the best terms.

She adds that despite having big aims, in reality the company had to fight for survival every single day at that time. In order to overcome this problem, the company chose to attract an investor. "This was in 2007, when MADARA Cosmetics was already a success story in Latvia; thus, we could choose the investor we liked," says Lotte. MADARA accepted a local investor, a family company with investment experience in a diverse range of businesses, against minority shares and this allowed them to access the funding necessary for developing the firm. "With an investor participating, we can not claim to be an entirely women-owned business anymore. In fact, it should be emphasized that MADARA Cosmetics was an entirely female-run business only in its first years of operation, and also our first employee happened to be male." Also, today there is only a slight majority of women employed by MADARA Cosmetics. "Later on, apart from an investor, my husband also joined the team of owners, so there are 6 owners now, only 4 of whom are women," Lotte adds.

"Looking from today's perspective," she continues, "we are in the same market niche, with very similar values, as when we started the company. In 95 percent of the cases, our products, including eco cosmetics for kids we introduced relatively recently, are bought by females, our main target audience." The difference between 2007 and today is that MADARA Cosmetics has a much wider product range made possible through their decision to take in an investor. Furthermore, equipped with current assets and an international eco certificate, which is crucial for exporting eco products, starting from 2008 MADARA Cosmetics very quickly moved into the global arena, starting with England and Lithuania. "Today we are working in some 30 markets, the top of them being Switzerland and Denmark." The main focus of the company is Europe as, according to Lotte, "this market is mature enough to accept eco products," but the company is also working in other markets such as Japan and Malaysia.

"Being a high-quality ecological skin care brand in a high price segment, it is very important to enter each new market in the right way," says Lotte, explaining that this can only be done together with a local partner. "In our case, these are distributors who take responsibility for the distribution of the MADARA brand in a specific country or region," she continues, emphasizing that MADARA Cosmetics is very careful in choosing with whom they work. "It is crucial for us that distributors have appropriate logistics, customers and product portfolios, understanding what it means to work with cosmetics, and also that they have a brand manager, PR and marketing people as well as properly trained sales staff: our experience says that only with such a distributor can we achieve success."

The growth indicators of MADARA Cosmetics are quite impressive: having reached a turnover of 170,000 euros in 2007 and 550,000 euros in 2008, the company reached 2.1 million euros in 2010 and is expecting an increase of around 60 percent in 2011. "Do I think that MADARA Cosmetics is a successful business?" asks Lotte rhetorically. "I am sure that people like stable, long-term companies with values, a mission and clear aims; thus, in my opinion, a successful business is a long-term business and MADARA definitely has this orientation." In a way, this contradicts arguments about different success criteria for male and female entrepreneurs (e.g., Buttner & Moore, 1997; Cliff, 1998). "Long term also means safety," says Lotte, "and this has been another crucial value for MADARA Cosmetics: all of us who work for the company know that we are doing something that will be relevant even after many years."

As we talk further about the success formula of MADARA Cosmetics, apart from the focus on quality and orientation toward the global market, Lotte emphasizes the importance of the human factor: "Initially we were four young women, now we are talking about 40 people plus our network of co-operation partners. The professionalism of all these people and the way they are managed is a key determinant of our success story." Other core values of MADARA Cosmetics, clearly reflecting the lifestyle of the company founders, are naturalism and Latvian identity. "In fact, MADARA has always emphasized Latvian identity as a unique selling point: all our products are made in Latvia and come from one of the greenest environments with an ideal climate for growing vulnerary plants," explains Lotte. "By emphasizing Latvian identity, MADARA Cosmetics simply cannot offer a poor-quality product, as the reputation of the country could then suffer as well." In this way, she clearly demonstrates the importance of societal embeddedness as well as of the society for the company's success (Welter, 2011).

The balance between creativity and rationalism is yet another factor contributing to the success of MADARA Cosmetics: "The product development process, packaging, design and creating a visual image are all very creative processes, adding value to the product. Rationalism in turn is important when it comes to the product finding its way to the customers," explains Lotte, adding with a smile: "Interestingly enough, creative people used to say that MADARA Cosmetics is a rational company, but rational people argue that we are a very creative company. The truth, as is usually the case, is somewhere in between." She continues that "all in all, MADARA Cosmetics has now reached a level of stability. We also see how the company has to be managed in the future in order to achieve our aim: to become one of the top 3 brands in Europe in 20 years in the field of eco cosmetics." She concludes by saying: "We know that we can achieve our ambitions if we continue working according to our established values."

Questions for Discussion

1   In the case of MADARA Cosmetics, was the business opportunity created by the entrepreneurs or was it simply "out there," waiting to be discovered?

2   What are the main success factors for MADARA Cosmetics? Do you think any of these are specific to women-owned businesses? Base your answer on the case study, as well as on the discussion in the entrepreneurship literature regarding the success of women-owned businesses.

3   Would MADARA Cosmetics have been as successful if they had not changed their ownership and financial structure? Please explain your answer.

4   As a business consultant you have been asked to assess MADARA Cosmetics' strategy for growth. Please pay particular attention to factors which may foster or hinder further business growth. In addition, prepare recommendations on what the management should do next, in order to sustain its growth path.

5   Would you suggest that MADARA Cosmetics expand its product range, for instance, offering eco-cosmetic products for men? Please explain your answer.

Notes

1   This distinction was introduced by Bales (1950) and further developed in the Ohio State studies on leadership (e.g., Fleishman, 1973; Hemphill & Coons, 1957).

2   Meg Whitman and eBay-Leadership Case Study; at http://www.casestudyinc.com/meg-whitman-ebay-leadership

3   At http://www.businessweek.com/2000/00_47/b3708145.htm

4   At http://www.caliper.com.cn/en/news_women_leaders.asp

5   VRIO is an acronym introduced by Barney (Barney & Hesterly, 2005) to determine the competitive potential of an asset; it refers to the following four characteristics: Value, Rarity, Inimitability, and Readiness of the Organization.

6   At http://www.ebayinc.com/values

7   Harry Berkowitz, Not Everyone Shared Caged Fantasy: Does New Chanel Ad Evoke Freedom or the Same Old Constraining Attitudes?, *Newsday*, August

30, 1992, sec. 1, p. 72; Phyllis Berman and Zina Sawaya, The Billionaires Behind Chanel, *Forbes*, April 3, 1989, p. 104; Catherine E. Hunter, Scientist, Inventor, Futurist, *Drug & Cosmetic Industry*, May 1993, p. 20; Kara Swisher, Chanel Bucks the Trend Toward Tysons Corner, *Washington Post*, May 7, 1990, p. E31.

8 At http://www.women-inventors.com/Marion-Donovan.asp; http://american history.si.edu/archives/d8721.htm

9 At http://web.mit.edu/invent/iow/nesmith.html; "Bette Nesmith Graham". Famous Women Inventors. Retrieved 2010-03-18; Vare and Ptacek (2002).

10 At http://www.sing365.com/music/lyric.nsf/cher-biography/36d174caa94ac6 43482568730010a2de

11 The author(s) of the case studies are fully and solely responsible for their content, phrasing consistency and flow, terminology, English proofing and reference lists.

Case References

Baygan, G. (2000), "Improving knowledge about women's entrepreneurship", paper presented at the OECD Second Conference on Women Entrepreneurs in SMEs: "Realising the Benefits of Globalisation and the Knowledge-Based Economy," 29–30 November, www.oecd.org/dsti/sti/industry/indcomp.

Brush, C., Carter, N.M., Gatewood, E.J., Greene, P.G. & Hart, M.M. (Eds.) (2006). *Growth-oriented women entrepreneurs and their businesses: A global research perspective*, Cheltenham, UK and Northampton, MA, USA: Edward Elgar.

Buttner, E.H. & Moore, D.P. (1997). Women's organizational exodus to entrepreneurship: Self-reported motivations and correlates with success, *Journal of Small Business Management*, 35(1), 34–46.

Carter, S., Anderson, S. & Shaw, E. (2001). Women's business ownership: A review of the academic, popular and internet literature. Report to the Small Business Service, Glasgow.

Cliff, J. (1998). Does one size fit all? Exploring the relationship between attitudes towards growth, gender, and business size, *Journal of Business Venturing*, 13(6), 523–542.

Smallbone, D. & Welter, F. (2001). The distinctiveness of entrepreneurship in transition economies, *Small Business Economics*, 16(4), 249–262.

Welter, F. (2011). Contextualizing entrepreneurship – conceptual challenges and ways forward, *Entrepreneurship Theory and Practice*, 35(1), 165–184.

13 Breaking through the Barriers

Chapter Objectives

- Acknowledging the different aspects of the new venture's growth and their implications in female-led businesses; recognizing the gender differences in this respect;
- Typifying the growth strategies that prevail among women entrepreneurs in the business's early stages;
- Understanding what is required for the pursuit of growth strategies in female-led new ventures;
- Depicting the factors that influence women-led businesses' growth across the different stages of the business life cycle;
- The "growth dilemma" in the female entrepreneurial realm;
- Understanding the origins of women's reluctance toward entrepreneurial growth; listing the different types of hurdles associated with women-led businesses' slower growth rate;
- Demonstrating practical strategies to enhance growth in women-led businesses from the early stages;
- Becoming acquainted with women entrepreneurs' performance and achievements in the high-tech sector;
- Identifying the factors of women who go global;
- Characterizing the practices used by women to break the barriers they encounter in the early stages of the new venture creation.

This chapter delves into the quest for business growth, participation in the high-tech sector, going global, and other practices that can empower women entrepreneurs and enable them to break through the barriers encountered in the entrepreneurial realm. The statistics on women's disadvantaged status in entrepreneurship relative to men should not be discouraging, but rather should stimulate women to take action and eliminate the gender gap.

Gathering together the different concepts introduced in this book, this chapter offers an optimistic, proactive finale for female entrepreneurship, by proposing different avenues for women to break down the barriers, succeed, grow and fulfill their own wishes and desires, according to their own definitions of success.

UNDERSTANDING THE MEANING OF BUSINESS GROWTH

Business growth is a multifarious and complex, but highly desired phenomenon; growing and budding entrepreneurial businesses promise wealth, vibrant market dynamics, incorporation of innovation in the marketplace, and more job offers.

Business growth is thus an evolving area in entrepreneurship literature, mainly understood synonymously with business outcome, e.g., achieving the business's goals, improving the business's value to its stakeholders, developing the number of employees/staff members, sales, profits, etc.

In the literature, several factors related to business growth emerge: the entrepreneur/founder's characteristics—personal (e.g., educational and employment background; intentions and attitudes toward growth), social (e.g., family status, educational attainment) and cultural (e.g., social expectations, attitudes toward successful women entrepreneurs); the business measures (e.g., sector of industry, financial state, location), the market's state (e.g., developed/underdeveloped; affluent/deprived; competition for the product/service; saturation for the product/service), and the general social attitudes toward growth, particularly women-led businesses' growth.

While these factors have been identified, a clear conceptualization of entrepreneurial business growth is still lacking, and the questions of "how" or "why" some female-led businesses grow while others remain stagnant are still open. Most research on business growth addresses the "outcomes," while neglecting the meaning and implications of growth along the business "process"; furthermore, research attributes growth to the more mature stages of the business, rather than to the whole course of the business creation. This appears to be because the new venture creation processes are deemed to consist of resources and capabilities contributing to its survival; once the business is more stable, it can dedicate time, money, human resources and strategies to growth. Yet, only a few entrepreneurial ventures grow extensively. Most of them, especially women-led entrepreneurial businesses, remain small- and medium-sized.

PROMOTING FEMALE ENTREPRENEURSHIP—GROWTH STRATEGIES

The concept of growth strategies is used to identify the set of actions, procedures and processes taken at the business level to spur productive dynamics inside and outside the business in order to develop the business. These include finding resources, assets and financing means, investments, fostering innovation, recruiting skilled workers, among others—all targeted to developing the business in the prevailing market.

Depending on the situation, growth strategies function to either remove the most egregious hindrances encountered, by unleashing a flurry of new ideas, investments, production, and innovation, or develop existing or new processes that will strengthen the competitive advantage of the business in relation to its competitors, promising sustainable success, or both.

According to the 2011 World Economic Forum (WEF) report on *Global Entrepreneurship and the Successful Growth Strategies of Early-Stage Companies*,[1] eight different growth strategies prevail for new or early-stage businesses:

1   wave—a stand-alone product/service, or part of a budding wave that is changing the business landscape (e.g., creating, building or riding new-wave ventures);

2   new product in a new category—potential customers do not have a comparable product to purchase; entrepreneurs should "sell the concept" rather than "sell the product" (new solutions, easier function, longer lasting);

3   new product in an existing category—the key features of the product are well known and are already being experienced by existing customers; the entrepreneurs should strive to raise the competitive advantage(s) of the product and emphasize its benefits for the customers relative to existing and similar products (e.g., innovation, business model, price, new distribution channels);

4   redesign of business value chain—growing sophistication of the business value chain in the emergence of new ventures attempting to either build a position in the existing value chain or play a role in restructuring the existing value chain (e.g., faster, cheaper, better; redesign of value-chain delivery);

5   research or discovery of knowledge—science, research, laboratory work, exploration and practical research that can be implemented in products, services, technologies, processes (e.g., discovery of the genome, new drugs, new treatments, new ways to pay for products through the internet);

6   roll-up (aggregation) of existing players—acquisitions, mergers and joint ventures are an important factor in growth strategies, and a

subset of new ventures make acquisitions the core and major engine of their growth strategy;

7 governmental, regulatory or political change—different incentives fostering growth-privatization efforts by many governments world-wide often lead to the formation of new businesses mobilizing the assets being transitioned from public-sector to private-sector management resulting in wealth creation or wealth transfer;

8 idea transfer or transplant—generation of ideas and implementation of those ideas in different areas around the globe to solve the same needs being tackled.

Research has stepped forward by offering several conceptual frameworks to understand the nature and characteristics of growth strategies in the new venture creation process, including models such as "mice versus gazelles" (Birch, Haggerty, & Parsons, 1993); "flyers versus trundlers" (Storey, 1994); business differentiation emphasizing elements such as quality, innovation, customization of product features, and customer service (McDougall & Robinson, 1990; Porter, 1980); managing growth strategy (Arbaugh & Camp, 2000; Churchill & Lewis, 1991; Weinzimmer, 2000); market penetration, new product development, and new market development (Carter, Anderson, & Shaw, 2001; Hoy, McDougall, & Dsouza, 1992; Ostgaard & Birley, 1995), among others.

Many scholars with an interest in growth strategies in the new venture creation process have focused on the different actions initiated and managed by the entrepreneur that are primarily and deliberately associated with growth, including positioning of the products or services, transferring knowledge or introducing innovation from the entrepreneurial business to the marketplace, in order to engender a *sustainable* advantage and raise the business's competitive advantage at the outset. Specifically, such actions are expected to raise the competitive advantages of a premature, sometimes still non-existent business, to allow the business to cope concurrently with the dynamic competition that new businesses encounter as well as engrave its competitive advantage at the outset. Thus, this specific business will be associated with the potential growth embedded in its growth-related concept, for example: Google is associated with creativity, Mercedes with quality and luxury, Walmart with mass production, among others. However, growth strategies that are planned and applied in the new venture creation phase do not necessarily create actual business growth. One intermediate factor that may foster the actual business's growth is the uncompromised dedication of the entrepreneur to the business's growth orientation, i.e., commitment to continual expansion in the different aspects of the business. As such, the entrepreneur does not aspire to stability but to leadership in the business sector of the industry in question.

Pursuing growth strategies requires developing or locating resources, and bringing in the appropriate organizational capabilities which will make it easier to spot what qualifications differentiate the business from its competitors, such as quality, price, a personalized service orientation. These require a two-faceted strategy: improvement of efficiency, i.e., stringently controlling costs of production, labor, distribution, etc., while concurrently encouraging ongoing developments and conducive productivity improvements, which are costly and thus endanger the business's potential growth (at least financially and in the short term). There is still a dearth of research on female-based growth strategies in the early stages of the new venture creation; therefore, there is still a lack of cumulative knowledge to conceptualize an established framework for the growth processes exhibited by women, as most of the knowledge is based on men's growth strategies or on studies that disregard the gender issue. As such, growth-related hurdles associated with female entrepreneurship are ignored (Du Reitz & Henrekson, 2000; Watson, 2002; Westhead, 2003).

Business Growth and the Business Life Cycle

The life cycle approaches to entrepreneurial businesses introduced by different scholars posit that businesses, like human beings, undergo a development cycle, for example: beginning with entrepreneurial intent, followed by opportunity exploitation, then the decision to exploit toward the firm's birth, resulting in growth, persistence or quitting.[2] These approaches associate the business's growth mainly to its chronological age. The simplicity of these theories and models steers researchers in this field to recognize the importance of the availability of some other factors that are assumed to influence the business's growth in its different development stages; e.g., financial resources, human and social resources, social capital, technical expertise, management skills, ability to adjust to a changing environment, the business's planned opportunity exploitation (as opposed to "good luck" or the emergence of an unplanned opportunity). These approaches refer to the business's growth as a reflection of the relevant capabilities and resources used in each of its stages, for example, use of opportunity exploitation in the birth stages, the ability to negotiate with investors in the maturing stages, and marketing expertise at maturity.

The research in entrepreneurship has identified several factors that influence entrepreneurial businesses' growth in their different life cycles:

1   Entrepreneurial-based characteristics: attitudes, capabilities, and relevant education, training or previous management/entrepreneurial experience (Brush, Carter, Gatewood, Greene, & Hart, 2004; Henry, Hill, & Leitch, 2005; Orser & Riding, 2003).
2   Management competencies: strategic management skills, wide-ranging managerial thinking, the ability to take risks in uncertain

environments that might require minimal costs and result in maximal benefits (Brindley, 2005).

3   Decision-making ability: the ability to apply different types of decision-making processes and their combinations, and look at a challenging situation from different angles and provide alternative solutions (Burns, 2001; Gibb & Davies, 1990).

4   The business's characteristics: referring to factors such as the business's size, sector, age, developmental stage, among others, that echo the business's experiences, networks, and financial acquisition; these have a direct impact on business growth (Johnson & Scholes, 2002; Smallbone & Wyer, 2000). All of these elements and their unpredictable nature apply great force on the direction and pace of the business's growth.

Together, these factors have a significant influence on growth, as shown in Figure 13.1. Developing these factors from the first stages of the new venture in women-led businesses may foster business growth in the more mature phases. Moreover, enhancing the appropriate working environment to enable these growth strategies to function effectively and successfully is a critical element in the business's growth; a supportive environmental effect is even more pronounced in the case of female entrepreneurs striving to grow while they are still in the new venture creation phase.

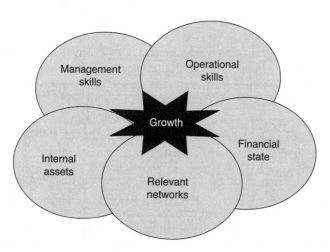

Figure 13.1 Predominant Frameworks for Growth in the New Venture Creation Stages.

THE DILEMMA OF GROWTH IN THE FEMALE REALM

Research-culled gender differences reveal that women entrepreneurs are "slower" than men in several factors associated with their businesses' growth, and that their slower pace prevails from the very first stages of the new venture creation. Only a limited number of women entrepreneurs exhibit strategies aimed at going global to open additional markets for their products/services; few of them participate in the rewarding, high-tech sector; marginal numbers of women entrepreneurs hold leading representative positions on companies' boards of directors, few are involved in mergers and acquisitions. Thus, they avoid strategies that enhance growth. On the other hand, women entrepreneurs introduce innovation for both existing and new products/services, readjust business concepts and models to facilitate and reduce cost and time spent, are attentive to regulations that foster growth, and are active in brainstorming and sharing ideas for implementation. The question is therefore why these strategies have only a limited effect on women-led businesses' growth.

One explanation might stem from the emotional aspect of female entrepreneurship. Research reveals that overall, women are less confident in their ability to grow their businesses, especially in the early phase of their venture creation. This could be the result of their socialization, social expectations regarding women's roles in society at home and at work, or other stereotypes of successful women entrepreneurs implying their inability to maintain a harmonious balance between work and family. In some cultures, successful women entrepreneurs encounter major difficulties in establishing friendships or romantic relationships, because they are conceived as being "bitches," etc. Many women entrepreneurs start the new venture creation with a predefined idea regarding the "cutoff point" for their business's growth and develop the venture accordingly, that is, using a speed and approach suited to this perceived threshold. When asked, many women would respond that they do not aspire to a large business and will not activate any strategy that could potentially grow their business. They do not perceive a non-growing business as an unsuccessful business, quite the opposite: a stable business is sometimes perceived to be the ideal, successful business to which they aspire. For example, when Ms. Viet Chia Ding Li, from Singapore, the founder of an internet fashion-show start-up, received an offer of support from an investor in India, she refused, explaining: ". . it took me more than ten years to find my soul mate, my husband. I want to spend my time with him. In fact, I started a business so that we could spend more time together." Viet justified her refusal with her husband's new job in a governmental company in Singapore and their plans to expand the family; she said that she was not ready to commit to the prospective demanding work life that the growing start-up would require, and therefore she preferred to maintain the start-up at its current size.

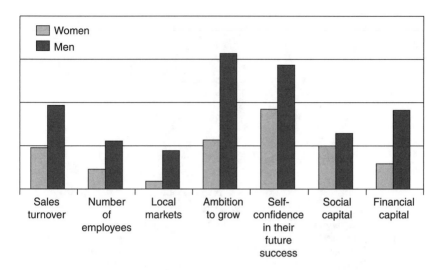

Figure 13.2 Gender Comparisons in some Parameters of Business Growth.

Women entrepreneurs also tend to be more reluctant to take risks, and hence more careful and conservative than men entrepreneurs in implementing growth strategies. Women deliberately choose a slower pace and avoid expanding their businesses. Figure 13.2 provides an illustration of the gender differences in business growth, as discussed in the research (Carter & Allen, 1997; Cliff, 1998; Elam, 2008; Rosa, Carter, & Hamilton, 1996).

GROW OR DIE? THE CONSTRAINING FACTORS IN WOMEN'S BUSINESS GROWTH PROCESSES

The rates at which entrepreneurs, women and men, develop their businesses to growth and sustainable success vary, depending on the joint effects of different factors: the entrepreneur, the business and the contextual factors, as illustrated in Figure 13.3, suggesting that women and men grow their businesses differently at the outset, as they act in different contexts and under different challenges and constraints. Research consistently shows that compared to men, women manage businesses that are significantly smaller and grow at a significantly slower pace. They more frequently encounter factors that constrain, to a higher extent, their business's growth. In addition, as discussed earlier, their growth aspirations are much more moderate than those of their male counterparts and they often maintain a "cutoff point" for their business's growth (Brush, de Bruin, Gatewood, & Henry, 2010; De Bruin, Brush, & Welter, 2006; Delmar & Wiklund, 2008; Morris, Miyasaki, Watters, & Coombes, 2006).

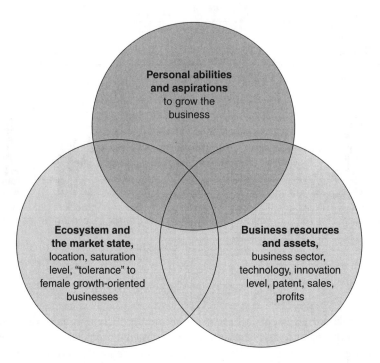

Figure 13.3 Key Factors in Female-led Business Growth.

The following groups of hindrances have been culled from the leading factors found in the female entrepreneurship literature. These factors refer to female-led businesses' growth, and most of them can be classified into more than one group, with multiple spillover effects between these factors and groups. These factors demonstrate the constraints facing women entrepreneurs who are starting a growth-oriented business.

A The Entrepreneur

A.1 Socialization and Background

- While women entrepreneurs are highly educated relative to their male counterparts, their educational attainment and degrees are not in fields that will foster their business's growth (e.g., business, management, technological areas).
- While women's participation in the labor market is expanding, they still tend to have little or no managerial or other experience relevant to starting a growth-oriented business.

- Dissatisfaction with previous employment, where there was no recognition of talent, a lack of autonomy, and stressful working conditions.
- Lower self-confidence in the ability to succeed because women have experienced the glass-ceiling effect, i.e., they have witnessed other people being promoted while they are ignored, red tape, internal politics.
- Psychological influence of their self-confidence on customers, investors and future employees' trust in the business performance and consequently, in their business's growth.

A.2 Relevant Skills: Financing, Management

- women start their businesses with lower levels of overall capital;
- women are much less likely to use private equity or venture capital;
- lack of personal assets to show as collateral and of credit track record;
- disadvantages rooted in lack of experience in management and entrepreneurship;
- difficulties in penetrating informal financial networks;
- lack of proper marketing and effective selling skills.

A.3 Selected Strategies

- women's choice of strategies, which are focused on local markets and traditional technologies;
- compared to men, women are less willing to incur greater opportunity costs for the superior performance of their businesses;
- risk-aversion.

A.4 Home/work

- home/work conflicts—fitting work around family commitments;
- difficulties in dealing with unexpected family circumstances (illness, special needs, etc.).

B The Business

B.1 Business Characteristics and Resources

- business sector (mainly less rewarding), level of innovation, level of advanced technological use;
- business's concurrent financial and human-resource state;
- concurrent sales state;
- lower levels of access to finance/capital for expansion;
- shortage of skilled, dedicated workers at a reasonable, competitive salary;

- high turnover of skilled staff;
- higher costs for training staff.

B.2 Support

- dearth of relevant business support and advice from inside and outside the business;
- internal conflicts (some employees, partners, etc. find it difficult to collaborate with a female leader).

B.3 Opportunities and Strategies

- lack of ability to convert the plethora of network opportunities into potential business opportunities;
- market saturation;
- the business's vision, strategies or leading processes (in product development, marketing, services) are too progressive or new and the market is still ready to accept them.

C The Ecosystem

C.1 Financial Arena

- women are ignored with respect to access to capital for growth when needed due to both internal (management styles, prior experience) and external (intensity of competition, gender stereotyping) circumstances;
- negative attitudes from lending agencies.

C.2 Information, Training and Support

- lack of information on business development;
- lack of access to advisory services;
- very few support programs and services for women entrepreneurs at the new venture creation stages.

C.3 Family-related Issues

- lack of family support to grow their ventures;
- discouragement from family and friends with respect to growth, development, success and risk-taking.

C.4 Socialization and Culture

- socialization in most countries is responsible for women's lower motivation and aspirations to start high-growth businesses;

- definition of "growth," "success" and "growth-orientation" differ in different ecosystems between the genders.

C.5 The Market

- intense competition in a small market;
- use of lower technology, thus higher difficulty differentiating the business;
- stereotypes and discrimination: failure to have their contributions recognized; not taken seriously; feelings of isolation.

(Boden & Nucci, 2000; Brush, de Bruin, & Welter, 2009;
Carter & Rosa, 1998; Gundry & Welsch, 2001;
Lechner & Dowling, 2003; Park & Bae, 2004)

FACTORS CONTRIBUTING TO ACHIEVING GROWTH

Most entrepreneurial businesses remain small during their first years; many of them grow to medium-size businesses later on, but only a few achieve extensive growth. Researchers in entrepreneurship believe that a prerequisite for growth-oriented businesses is to secure growth on the basis of joint strategic building blocks, and accordingly developing growth aspirations and crafting strategies and procedures for growth from the first stages of the new venture creation: capturing growth at the mature phase of the business may be "too late" for extensive growth and sustainable success. In line with the resource-based view (RBV) and dynamic capabilities (DC) approach, new ventures should construct, develop or search for capabilities and resources that promise growth. As such, the platform for a potential business's growth should be set up along with the other necessary processes associated with the new venture creation. Planning growth as a regular process in the new venture creation phase reduces, or even eliminates future costs, as well as the frustration accompanying attempts to grow the business at more mature stages.

Thus, entrepreneurs in the new venture creation phase should secure resource inflow into the business and develop (or recruit) capabilities that will effectively make use of and manage these resources while accomplishing the business's goals. Concurrently, the entrepreneur should develop an internal structure that can organize these resources within and outside the business, in order to expand them in the future. In short, business growth can be captured by planning a growth-oriented platform and embedding it in the business's fundamental tangible and intangible resources.

The phenomenon of business growth does not stand alone in the female context; it can be valuable for women entrepreneurs only when it promotes their work and family lives. Women entrepreneurs should determine the meaning of growth for their businesses and its subsequent implications for their family lives: if growth means sinking into a life without friends because successful women are practically excluded from regular society, this might be too costly for some. However, if the children are already grown-up and embarking on a demanding, growth-oriented path themselves, growth might represent an exciting and challenging journey. Therefore, women should thoroughly clarify the perceived benefits and costs of growth in their specific culture and environment, rather than adopt the traditional growth strategies, or those that apply to men. Growth should be shaped by women's wishes, needs and contextual capabilities.

Business growth should be reconceptualized in the context of female entrepreneurship, to best suit their ecosystem, culture, needs and desires. "Growth" should be understood in a more open, broader context, as it is more personalized and encompasses various definitions, such as growth as a process in progress (rather than an outcome), growth in achieving certain goals (rather than all goals), growth in obtaining sustainable success, among others (Leitch, Hill, & Neergaard, 2010; McClelland, Swail, Bell, & Ibbotson, 2005; McKelvie & Wiklund, 2010).

While aspirations toward growth are relatively limited among women entrepreneurs, they have an established idea of the main drivers most contributing to the growth of their businesses. The main findings in research into female entrepreneurship on the factors that contribute most to their businesses' growth are listed as follows:

- easy accessibility to finance, capital for expansion;
- high quality of products and/or services;
- concentration on value addition for the stakeholders;
- accessing and efficiently utilizing financial resources;
- establishing networks and developing sustainable network contacts to obtain relevant information and emotional assistance and seek out role models;
- dedicated workforce, access to human resources, skilled, professional employees;
- penetrating marketing strategies;
- innovation, development of new products and/or services;
- access to business training.

TOWARD OVERCOMING FEMALE-RELATED HURDLES

Obviously, there is no one inclusive solution that applies to all women entrepreneurs and that can solve the difficulties, barriers and hurdles tackled by women in the new venture creation phase to their business's growth—nor should there be, as women face different hurdles, have different needs, and encounter different experiences, different solutions are needed to enable them to overcome these hurdles.

Figure 13.4 demonstrates two approaches to overcoming female-related hurdles: each encompasses different solutions and techniques which can be combined to create many more solutions, and can serve to invent new solutions or be adapted to solving other difficulties, etc.

The first approach, the "stepwise approach," involves handling each hurdle separately; accordingly, alternative solutions are constructed to overcome the hurdle. The second approach, the "general approach" is of a more inclusive nature, aimed mainly at generally empowering women entrepreneurs and facilitating their new venture creation process, rather than resolving each hurdle separately.

The stepwise approach corresponds to approaches stemming from social or radical feminist theories, i.e., founded on the basic concept that women and men are innately different; accordingly, the "stepwise approach" address the hurdles encountered by women entrepreneurs as more pronounced than those encountered by men. This approach relies on the presumption that responding to a specific hurdle step by step will enable pinpointing the precise, tailor-made solution; obviously, an "exact" solution will be more relevant in dealing with both the specific needs of the woman entrepreneur (e.g., financial needs, partnering, negotiations, marketing needs, psychological support), and in flawlessly responding to the specific hurdle (e.g., addressing its nature, frequency, magnitude, being temporal/permanent, common/rare, latent/apparent, etc.). For example, Ms. Kin Akizawa, a 52-year-old woman entrepreneur from Tokyo in the area of internet services, was distressed by "not being taken seriously" as an entrepreneur; to handle this difficulty she adopted a stepwise approach which enabled her to reflect upon the nature and potential damage of this specific hurdle, analyze its origin and more thoroughly understand its different manifestations (e.g., investors do not answer her calls, however, customers still order her services). Ms. Akizawa decided to handle this by locating a mentor with whom she could develop a trusting relationship and share her distress through discussion, in order to cope with it. In her words: "Most of my women colleagues would probably ignore this hurdle, or alternatively engage in a course for people starting a business; such a course might deliver constructive techniques for entrepreneurs, yet its non-personal nature would not allow me talk about my own difficulty, which would probably persist. Being attentive to my difficulties and addressing each of them independently enabled me to overcome them in the best way."

While the stepwise approach appears promising in handling hurdles, in the new venture creation stages, women strive to overcome as many hurdles as possible in the shortest time, using minimal resources. They may therefore find a stepwise approach non-resourceful. Since women exhibit lateral thinking more easily than men, they can utilize their

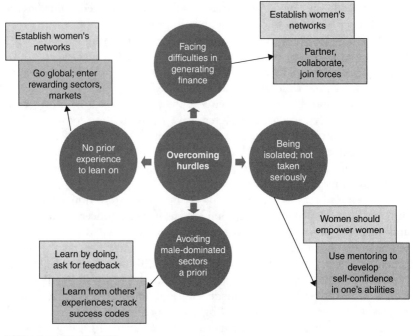

(a) The stepwise approach

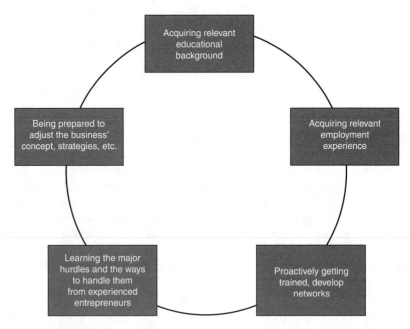

(b) The general approach

Figure 13.4 Two Approaches to Overcoming Hurdles.

capabilities to facilitate executing different tasks simultaneously, yet efficiently. As such, women in these business stages might consider the general approach more appropriate to overcoming their encountered hurdles: they thus obtain an "all-purpose" solution rather than a tailor-made one. They may fail to address their personal hurdles, difficulties or needs, or engage in solutions with which they are unfamiliar or even uncomfortable, yet the general approach is prompt, efficient and resourceful.

The general approach draws on the premise that entrepreneurs, women and men, tackle hurdles. This approach echoes liberal feminist theory, which emphasizes the similarities between the genders and regards any disadvantage felt by women entrepreneurs relative to men as random and easily curtailed. Accordingly, overcoming the female-related hurdles through a "general approach" means developing a modern, highly developed, entrepreneurial entity, e.g., a business, an idea, a project, that will be self-sufficient, autonomous, independent in financial terms and in its choices of strategy and route; an entity that can easily locate capabilities to exploit opportunities and grow. The "general approach" encourages women entrepreneurs (as well as men) to predominate in rewarding and cutting-edge sectors, e.g., finance, manufacturing, construction or high-technology; and to exhibit capabilities whereby success and growth can be achieved from the outset. As such, the general approach goes beyond the "here and now" and recommends that women plan their careers according to their future entrepreneurial prospects by, for example, strengthening their employment background: women should strive to be promoted at their corporate employment, attain managerial positions that will give them the opportunity to acquire and develop relevant managerial skills and experience, face organizational challenges while holding positions of high responsibility, as these can be pertinent in their future entrepreneurial undertakings, such as for financing, marketing, negotiations, managing teams, etc. In a related vein, women should choose major tracks at school and in higher education that correspond to their talents and desires rather than respond to social expectations. As such, women should feel free to study fields such as mechanics, accounting, biotechnology or aviation if this is what attracts them, and to be unconcerned with questions about being accepted or taken seriously when they start a business in these areas. Women should develop their enduring employability, to avoid engagement in a new venture due to absence of employment alternatives.

The "general approach" focuses on the new venture creation process more than on gender; as such, it encourages continual learning, training, and adjustments whenever needed. While such an approach may be effective in promoting entrepreneurs, it may be suspected of improving men's conditions more than women's, as it deliberately disregards any gender-based hurdles (Buttner & Moore, 1997; Mitra, 2002; Zapalska, 1997).

WOMEN IN THE HIGH-TECH SECTOR

The high-tech sector is documented as one of the fastest growing sectors worldwide. While it suffers from episodic fluctuations and is viewed as high risk, it is perceived as the most promising sector, and therefore attracts investments and venture capital, which cyclically promotes knowledge-based and cutting-edge technology, while intensifying job offers and desirable employment conditions. Participation in the high-tech sector is considered most promising and most rewarding for any entrepreneurial business.

Women, however, continue to be vastly under-represented in this sector. Only a small percentage of women are involved in high-tech start-ups and high-growth businesses, as founders, investors, CEOs and workers.

The high-tech sector was founded by men, mainly young White males. It is characterized as a competitive, reckless and most aggressive arena, with traits traditionally attributed to men, e.g., competitiveness, and tasks that come before personal need which are deemed to contribute to growth. Accordingly, growth in the high-tech sector means survival, and subsequently, aggressive competition for financing and venture capitalists' attention; marketing is frantic and hasty. Entrepreneurs who are ready to endure such dynamics are cut out for the rough-and-tumble world of entrepreneurship, which requires extremely hard work and adaptation of typical characteristics to plow through and succeed. Such a context may be deemed opposite to the ascribed female management style.

According to the 2006 GEM report (Allen, Langowitz, & Minniti, 2007), there are limited numbers of women entrepreneurs across countries in the high-tech sector. Women lag behind men in starting and managing typical high-tech businesses, e.g., offering novelty and the most innovative products, services, technologies, discoveries, etc. The GEM also reveals that in the early stages of the new venture creation, there is a significant difference between countries with respect to women entrepreneurs' use of innovative technology: women entrepreneurs in the low/middle-income countries report using the latest or newer technologies more often than their counterparts in high-income countries. The explanation for this, according to the GEM report, is that technologies hyped as high-tech in low/middle-income countries are already in common use in high-income countries. This finding stresses the notion that female entrepreneurship in the high-tech sector enhances potential growth in low/middle-income countries, and complements other findings on the growth prospects of women entrepreneurs in the high-tech sector, regardless of contextual conditions. The high-tech sector has a significant role in female entrepreneurship growth and removal of barriers (Gundry & Welsch, 2001; Lee & Peterson, 2000; Minniti & Bygrave, 2003).

While women avoid high-tech sectors, statistics repeatedly show that in a variety of different countries, women-led high-tech start-ups generate higher revenues per invested capital and have lower failure rates than those led by men. These findings have been strengthened in interviews conducted with investors who confirm that women's cautiousness in decision-making, along with their forethoughtfulness and risk reluctance, are the perfect mix for profitable investments. Such interviews, along with company surveys which can be easily found on the internet, show that venture-backed high-tech businesses founded by women do as well as those led by men, despite often being capital-constrained.

Researchers and practitioners agree that women's underrepresentation in the high-tech sector is strongly associated with their under-participation in executive boards and their preclusion from corporate management and strategic-based company and association boards, where related policies are established and decisions on major business and marketing issues are made, including dividend policies, option policies, executive compensation, recruitment or dismissal of executives, among others. Such encounters, brainstorming sessions and intensive decision-making processes deepen relationships, induce more significant contacts, enable the sharing of knowledge, information and networks, all most valuable assets for entrepreneurs. The absence from such positions can be destructive to women entrepreneurs in the high-tech sector, especially because they remain outsiders in the high-tech community.

This follows from women's difficulty in cracking the "boys" networks that prevail in the high-tech sector. Such networks are knitted around the men's alleged interests (e.g., stock market, cars, technological devices), and women are blatantly prohibited from joining them. Yet, many strategic decisions, relations and contracts are crafted by such networks. The establishment of technological networks for women entrepreneurs is intended to replace the "boy's" networks, as they are designed for the growth of women-led businesses.

Moreover, women are more vulnerable to unexpected or fierce competition with established high-tech companies. They have limited access to financial resources, a smaller amount of available equity capital, limited access to relevant sources of debt financing and to formal and informal networks (e.g., banks, investors, venture capitalists, private financial institutions), and they are more absent from the strategic boards and forums in the high-tech sector. In addition, the differences in the genders' styles of managing their new ventures in the context of the few female-led businesses in the high-tech sector result in the female-based style being less prevalent, and sometimes less adequate for the high-tech ecosystem (Hughes & Storey, 1994; Johnson & Storey, 1993; Maysami & Goby, 1999; Riding & Swift, 1990; Verheul & Thurik, 2001).

Although too few and too rare, there *are* women entrepreneurs who have broken the barriers, penetrated the male-dominated, high-tech sector, and managed successful businesses. These women should be role models for breaking the barriers in female entrepreneurship. Some examples include the following.[3]

Gina Bianchini—Ning, *cofounder and CEO*
A platform for creating social websites http://www.ning.com
Caterina Fake—Flickr, *cofounder*
A platform for sharing photographs http://www.flickr.com/
Eileen Gittins—Blurb, *CEO*
A platform that allows anyone to create customized books http://www.blurb.com/
Sandy Jen and Elaine Wherry—Meebo, *cofounders*
A social platform connecting users with their friends across the web http://www.meebo.com/
Mary Lou Jepsen—Pixel Qi, *founder and CEO*
A business that designs innovative new screens which solve problems not addressed by conventional screens http://www.pixelqi.com/
Tina Sharkey—BabyCenter, *president*
A parenting website providing information on conception, pregnancy, birth, and early childhood for parents and parents-to-be http://www.babycenter.com/
Rashmi Sinha—SlideShare, *cofounder and CEO*
A business that offers users the ability to upload and share PowerPoint presentations, Word documents and Adobe PDF portfolios publicly or privately http://www.slideshare.net/
Mena Trott—Six Apart, *cofounder and president*

A blogging and conversational media company, empowering publishers and marketers around the world to produce influential online content http://www.sixapart.com/

These examples, among others, prove that women can, and do break barriers. These women are enthusiastically and straightforwardly deluging the high-tech sector, determined to develop high quality, perform competitively and offer cutting-edge novelty in technology use, R&D, production, etc.

In 2010, the TechCrunch[4] posted research conducted by Mr. Vivek Wadhwa and the National Council of Women in Technology (NCWIT) on entrepreneurial businesses in Silicon Valley, showing that while there is an imbalance between the genders in entering high-tech fields, in growing their businesses over time, and in the percentage of women CEOs or CTOs of high-tech start-ups, there is almost no difference between women and men high-tech founders in terms of their attitudes and aspirations to grow their businesses. Women, like men, expressed a strong desire to build wealth and capitalize on business ideas. They were attracted by the culture of start-ups, and wished to own a sustainable, successful business.

GOING GLOBAL

Going global is another vehicle for breaking barriers associated with female entrepreneurship. By going global, women can expand the scope of their businesses geographically, culturally and business-wise. Their businesses are more exposed worldwide; consequently, potential customers, investors, partners, suppliers and employees can familiarize themselves with the products and services offered and pool together resources to collaborate on different spheres. Going global enables businesses to conduct benchmarks with other businesses around the world, learn the different tastes and demands for the products/services provided, and adopt best practices that work in different places around the globe. Furthermore, going global means success. In today's dynamic, competitive era, entrepreneurs consider the globe the ultimate marketplace, providing unlimited options, opportunities and customers. Expanding globally is thus promising and longed for by many entrepreneurs.

However, expanding globally also presents a different set of difficulties: it requires taking risks, tolerance of diversity and flexibility, a thorough understanding of the needs in other regions, as well as of language and cultural barriers (e.g., Jewish orthodox men do not meet face-to-face, in private, with women; in some MENA countries, women are not allowed to negotiate in their businesses without a male family member, etc.).

However, delving into the essentials of going global reveals that female-attributed skills and approaches to entrepreneurship can be a great advantage to global success.

The table below summarizes the main factors associated with businesses that go global, while enumerating the female skills that can be advantageous in this endeavor.

Table 13.1 The Main Factors Associated with Businesses that Go Global

Factors related to going global	*Women's advantages for a business going global*
Thinking globally The prism of the business gone global is worldwide, limitless; therefore planning, preparing and activating the business should be more strategic, broader, flexible, and alert to the dynamic changes in the marketplace for managing both short- and long-term processes	Women are strategic thinkers; they emphasize details, but also see the "big picture"; they analyze, reflect and are risk-averse. These tendencies are beneficial for a "going global" journey, as women reflect on the nitty-gritty as well as on the big picture; they do not automatically exploit opportunities; rather, they tend to check and recheck them to avoid unnecessary risks and potential losses. Women analyze the market with a "here and now" perspective as well as a prospective view. *(Continued overleaf)*

Table 13.1 Continued

Factors related to going global	Women's advantages for a business going global
Establish a global brand Marketing, advertizing and business development and growth should be reconceptualized: rather than addressing a certain niche in a bounded region, responding to a particular need, etc., entrepreneurs must capture "the whole world," responding to every person's tastes and needs. They must pinpoint the common and the core in the diversified world arena; the challenge is to understand different local tastes and needs and link them together to craft new, yet relevant, core tastes and needs	Women share, partner, proactively search for advice and implement it. Women are thrilled by understanding people, delving into their tastes, listening to their needs. Such an approach is most useful in "researching" global tastes and needs. As such, women tend to collaborate with local partners who can acquaint them with the local culture, consult with professionals who can enlighten them with knowledge on different niches, and share concerns and brainstorm with other entrepreneurs, as well as obtain their colleagues' best practices, among others. Women are much less concerned than men with "ego"-related issues, and more easily share success with others. This works to their advantage in a going global situation.
Outsourcing To be competitive in the global marketplace, businesses must reduce costs. This can be achieved by outsourcing information technology (IT), accounting or marketing, i.e. non-core business functions	Women are willing to share success with others, and therefore more easily accept assistance from other people to achieve their business goals. However, women appreciate dedication and commitment, while outsourcing emphasizes temporary, short-term relationships. Women may avoid outsourcing and favor corporate workers, yet will consider the former to reduce costs and be more "hands-on" with regard to becoming familiar with different needs and tastes.
Connecting through the web Technology enables worldwide connections in a much easier, faster and cheaper way, and participation in the world economy from everywhere to find cross-border customers, employees, partners and investors	Women are traditionally seen as less technologically oriented than men, and generally technologically reluctant, probably due to their relatively limited participation in the high-tech sector or in acquiring technological degrees. The recent web-based trends prove, however, that women have no mental blocks or inabilities to use the technology. Women are web-shoppers, web-searchers and use the web to blog, share ideas and network. While the web should not be a hindrance to women's "going global" journey, their broader connection should be improved to capture maximum exposure and subsequently, maximize their business.

Cultural differences

Entrepreneurs should sensitively address cultural differences, e.g. gaps in language proficiency (mainly English) or accents, engage tolerance for the "new" and "unknown" including foods, dress codes and religious-based behaviors, and be flexible in terms of amending and adjusting themselves to the local codes of behavior. Some cultural differences are unspoken or concealed, yet when encountered, should be treated with respect; e.g., gender-related manners such as shaking hands, staying alone in a room; eating styles such as Kosher, vegetarian; religious rules, such as wearing hats, dressing modestly, etc.

Women's sensitivity to human nature, their orientation toward people and people-driven situations and their enthusiasm to know more about people, cultures and behaviors are most practical for a global business.

Women are known to be tactful and considerate, and along with their emotional orientation, they can treat cultural differences in a most effective way, which promises a better understanding and acceptance of others.

Awareness of laws, rules, regulations and bureaucracy

There are differences in these issues in both target markets and the global market, including import, export, any cross-country trade, services and relations with the country of origin. In addition, some laws are obscure and can be understood differently, especially by people from different countries; entrepreneurs should be attentive to such interpretations. Moreover, there are differences in definitions and interpretations of terms such as "it is evident," "it was promised," "we agreed upon," and entrepreneurs should be alert to the various meanings of such terms as well.

Women's tendency to delve into details, explore the fundamentals, origins and implications of a project or a proposal's terms, to be "hands-on" and engage in a practical approach to the basics of a project, can be advantageous for the going-global practice. Going into details guarantees being attentive to laws, regulations, and other bureaucratic matters, as well as to any contradictions therein. Along with females' endorsed emotional qualifications, women entrepreneurs can benefit from being attentive to differences in interpretations of laws and rules and in pondering the definitions of terms that are associated with these laws and rules.

SUMMARY

The discussed evidence clearly indicates that women can be successful entrepreneurs; in fact, they already are. They can adopt growth strategies, break through the female-related hindrances and barriers and fulfill their goals and desires. The question is, how much do they want it? This chapter delves into the skills, attitudes, aspirations and strategies of women entrepreneurs in the new venture creation stage, in an endeavor to understand if and how women overcome their disadvantaged state relative to men in the new venture creation, and how they develop their growth-oriented businesses.

This chapter draws upon the main hindrances encountered by women on their road to growth, while portraying the multifaceted ecosystem in which they live, including women's backgrounds, their aspirations to grow, the expectations imposed upon successful women entrepreneurs, their business's state and contextual factors.

The chapter further delves into women's definitions of growth while carefully addressing their array of ecosystems. Women, like men, constitute a heterogeneous group, and the scope of their experiences and life settings is extremely broad. As such, some traditional, male-based strategies for growth do not apply to them. It is therefore essential to clarify, through a more personalized view, what growth entails, and craft strategies that will best suit women's desires and needs.

Two leading strategies for growth are introduced: participation in the high-tech sector and going global, and their advantages and disadvantages are discussed.

Finally, this chapter's main conclusion is that women are equipped with the relevant skills to pursue a growth-oriented strategy, although some of these skills differ from men's. This should be the platform for considering the roles of women and men in entrepreneurship as complementary and harmonious.

CASE STUDIES[5]

A glimpse into the exciting world of women in the high-tech sector is provided through two riveting case studies, contributed by Gilat Kaplan and Ayala Malaach-Pines from Israel, and Barbara Orser from Canada, who tackle women's growth in this male-dominated sector by providing insights into their strategies for jumping the typical hurdles encountered. The vibrant and dynamic paths and approaches in these case studies provide an exemplar of the intensive and demanding environment encountered by women entrepreneurs in the high-tech sector.

By cracking these women's success codes and subsequently learning from the best practices introduced in these cases, these role models can encourage other women with a zeal for technology to embark upon the path to new venture creation.

An Israeli High-tech Woman Entrepreneur: "I Would Have Done the Same Things Again"

Gilat Kaplan and Ayala Malach-Pines
Faculty of Management, Ben-Gurion University, Israel

Sharon is 47, the co-founder of two highly successful Israeli high-tech companies. She is divorced and the mother of three children. When asked about her life as an entrepreneur, she mentions three elements: entrepreneurial personality, the right circumstances and luck:

> This subject called entrepreneurship . . . the big question is where to start. Where does entrepreneurship start? Entrepreneurship can start under two conditions, I think that there has to be a combination of three components: a certain basic personality, about which I am sure we will talk later, but there are two more things that have to be there: circumstances-certain environmental conditions that will lead you to a certain point, and luck. These are two different things.

Before we turn to my personality and who I am and why I turned to entrepreneurship, I want to start by saying that if I had not been married to the man I was married to, who always gave me the feeling that he believed in me, that he saw in me something special, it is possible that I would not have evolved into the person I am today, because after all I started my career as an entrepreneur when I was nearly 35 years old.

> Today there are kids, aged 23 or 24, that all the things we are talking about don't apply to them. They are different type of entrepreneurs. They are entrepreneurs that following the opportunity and success of others said: "OK. Let's try because it's very easy." We are different. My generation is not entrepreneurs of opportunity . . . We all sacrificed a lot to do what we did. That's why the generation we are talking about is not a generation that saw quick success. I didn't take a salary for four years, and so forth. That is why it's not the same personality when you are interviewing old entrepreneurs as compared to 20 year old entrepreneurs. I believe you will discover a very different personality profile. I will give you an example. If we rate the entrepreneurial personality from 0 to 1, then in my generation we had to be the top 10 percent . . . Among the young today, it grew to 25–30 percent and some of them will no doubt succeed, possibly those who earlier were afraid to try.
>
> And then there has to be the circumstance. My circumstance was that I lived with a man that always respected tremendously the fact that I am a career woman. This, even before I was an entrepreneur, when I worked as employee from 5:00 in the morning till 12:00 at night. Even during that period, when it was only a salary, may be

high, but without the potential inherent in entrepreneurship. There was the absolute respect that this is what I do, and this is my career and it was given all the backing. When I did my MA right after my BA, and he didn't do an M.A., if I had a minute of hesitation, he said: "run forward, as much as you can." I didn't do a doctorate, because that was my choice. If it were for him, I would have been a doctor a long time ago, but I chose the business world.

When asked to elaborate on the circumstances of her entrepreneurial career Sharon emphasized her proactive role in shaping the circumstances that enabled her success:

> If you don't have certain environmental conditions . . . I think that very few people would not be influenced by an environment that blocks them and will continue anyway. Another thing, for example, in my case, I had a mother who took care of the children and allowed me to go to work knowing that everything at home is taken care of. It is true that at times I had three women working at home-two nannies and a housekeeper, because it's important to be smart and not take a nanny who is also a housekeeper . . . I took very highly qualified nannies for the kids. I took amazing women that gave a lot to the kids . . . This is a chicken and egg question: was it a coincidence or did I create it? So I will answer: I created it as well. My mother lives in Rehovot. I could have chosen anywhere in Israel to live in. I made sure I lived a walking distance from my mother so she could come and take care of the kids. Which is to say, there are no circumstances that are random, if I will not seize the opportunities, if I will not create them, they will not happen. This gets back to entrepreneurship. This husband of mine, if I did not discover during our courtship that he is this type of a person, I probably would not have married him. So what am I trying to say? That while it may seem very simple, which is to say, that if you don't have certain circumstances to grow in, the platform, the soil on which the flower can grow, that flower will wilt. So I am saying that to a large extent we are responsible for the soil, for making it the best it can be. I am the one who has to consider all the parameters . . . But there is coincidence, a certain circumstance that leads you to an idea, to the thing, and it's always there. With every entrepreneur you will discover that something happened that brought him close to the idea or the topic that he nurtured. And here I definitely include the role of coincidence, because a year earlier or a year later that person would have had another coincidence.

Sharon did not imagine becoming a successful entrepreneur, but she knew from a very young age that she is going to be an engineer and compete with men in a man's world. Even more important, however, was the fact that everyone around her told her she is gifted and expected her to be a great success. As a parent she tried to give similar messages to her children.

> At age 28 I didn't believe I would come so far, and not because I was lazy. At that time it wasn't like it is today that everyone knows this is possible, we didn't see things this way. I'll tell you a story. In 1988, when we founded the first company, we had two ideas: one for a product line, and another for an additional idea for which we needed about $200,000, no more. It didn't occur to us to get funding. If we didn't have it from internal resources, we don't have it and we don't do it. Even though, in fact we were rather close. Today the young guys starting off know that the sky is the limit. In Israel of the 1980s, there were no situations like that. And here comes in the woman element . . . I grew up in a working family, with parents for whom work is the foundation. We weren't capitalists. Even today I don't consider myself a capitalist, no matter how much money . . . The interesting thing is that at the 8th grade I decided to be an engineer. You understand, in 8th grade, in a socialist town, I knew I was going to be an engineer. Believe me that I didn't know what an engineer was . . . . But I decided that if I had a masculine occupation, I was not going to compete in a feminine market place. It was clear to me that I was going to compete in a masculine world . . .
>
> From birth I was told that I was talented. The kindergarten teacher, the first grade teacher, they all told me how smart and how gifted I am. And this went with me. The expectation of me was always to get "very good." It was clear that I have to come back with a very good report card. I was always expected to succeed. And I want to tell you that in my opinion this is the greatest impetus of childhood, the knowledge that you have to succeed and you can succeed. I later transferred this to my children. I told them how gifted they are and how good and how successful. And when someone told me, "you are going to make her a show-off, my daughter," I said: "if it's true, and she has something to show for it, it is an acknowledgement of value." In my opinion being "modest" means you are either dishonest or stupid . . . Acknowledging your virtue and arrogance are very different . . . I need to educate us-myself, the family, the children to acknowledge our value, to believe in yourself, to succeed, to run forward, not to be arrogant. Sometimes you make mistakes, sometimes you fail, but this is the mission.

Sharon is very proud of her children, to whom she tried to give the same encouragement:

> I chose to have three children and I raised them this way, and the results today show that these things are correct. They all have self-confidence; they know they can cope with everything in our world. It

evolved from personal example, from belief and encouragement that went along with them all these years. I did it with awareness. I knew what I was doing. I don't know whether my parents knew what they were doing, but I have no doubt that I received the same appreciation from both my parents and my surroundings. I remember the meeting with my first grade teacher. She told me that I was like her and that I was going to be the best pupil. So if she thought this, I had to prove it. I have no doubt that my whole childhood was this kind of chicken and the egg . . . I had to prove I was the best . . .

Sharon was willing to work hard and continue despite great hardships. She is convinced that the ability to continue after failing is one of the most import characteristics of successful entrepreneurs.

I studied science, because I thought I had to, and I didn't want to compromise. I love literature, but it didn't occur to me to go and do what I love. You go and do what has to be done because in order to succeed you need to work hard. I have never seen and have never believed in success that comes easy. It's not in my nature and not in the nature of the people in my close circle. There are no easy successes. This is typical to my generation, this type of entrepreneurs, of people that didn't feel entitled, that knew that they have to work hard in order to succeed, work very hard. And we were willing to do it. But something else is essential. We learned that if you try hard, you will succeed. Because at times it happens that you try hard and you don't succeed. You will not find an entrepreneur that hasn't. I can tell you many stories of how he tried, before the first time, tried, and I'm not talking about business, tried, it doesn't matter what, tried and failed, tried and failed, tried and failed, tried and failed, tried and failed. Very few people will continue the fourth or fifth time. So at some point we get to a certain age, possibly in this business entrepreneurship, and at a certain point we carry the load of experience, each in his own way, that in most cases, when he tried hard, he succeeded. To say in a metaphor: to try, but not till death, only till bleeding. At a certain point one has to understand that if I drew blood and didn't get it, it's time to withdraw. But you don't withdraw till you draw blood. That's the Motto in this house.

Being a woman and competing in men's arena meant having to be better than men.

Because I chose a masculine field—engineering—I started studying as early as possible in order to have a relative advantage when I graduate. I also understood that as a woman you need a grade of 14 in order to compete with a man whose grade was 9. I had this math, these instincts.

While I did not have the 30 year hindsight, I understood that it's going to be hard and I need to create a relative advantage. I think that through these stories we talk about strength, about the willing to fight and struggle, about all these things that actually are the basic characteristics of an entrepreneur, the basis for risk taking. There were many engineers around me and I had to get a relative advantage, I don't think I would have thought about these things if I hadn't been a woman. My competition is explained by the feminine motives and the need for a relative advantage. Competition also creates envy and this is something I am not willing to accept. I can respect someone who doesn't have the ability who envies someone who has it, but I'm not willing for someone to envy the outcome of hard work. If you want it — then work hard to get it.

Combining a demanding career and a family was not easy or simple:

I had little kids, but I knew that staying home with the children or work from seven till two is Nirvana. You feel like you are retired. I understood that I needed a change. That's when I started my second enterprise . . . My husband was very supportive. I could be abroad for three months installing a system and no one here said a word or thought that it was strange, that I had young children. The systems at home were very supportive and very understanding, which is to say, they let me be the most I could be. They didn't limit me at all and this is crucial. On the other hand, when I got home at nine or ten in the evening, then at ten, they expected me to prepare and serve dinner. It is not like a man who comes home after his wife fed the children and washed them, and he can take the paper and sit next to the TV. I didn't have that. When I came home, I knew that preparing dinner awaits me, because he wouldn't do it. Which is to say, he gave me the freedom to get out, but he didn't take on the responsibility. He was a father who did a lot, but was not willing to be a "house-husband." He was not going to do the wash and hang up the wash, and he was not willing to clean or cook dinner and all these things. But I didn't need it, because part of it I bought with the help of the women I hired to help me around the house. Besides, housework didn't bother me, for me it even felt like vocational therapy. It really didn't bother me. But the story I wanted to tell here is of the support I had, the emotional support, support in the knowledge, support that what I am doing is OK, is important, encouragement. And all these things went with me along the whole way. Today, my kids are my biggest asset. They are leaders, and they are willing to work, they don't expect success that comes easy. They will do it, in their own way and they will take it further, and each one of them starts at an easier point than the one I started in.

When asked about her childhood, Sharon describes herself as "growing up with ideals." Both her parents were members of a socialist enterprise, a cooperative. Her father believed that "money is bad," worked very hard as a manager and a politician and believed in giving to the public, but not for money. Her mother, whom she describes as "very different" from her father, raised the children and earned money to support the family. Like Sharon, her father "was never home" but Sharon, who idealizes him, did not feel deprived because she felt loved:

> I think he is the most beautiful person in the world, until today, my father is the most beautiful person, of true giving I have ever met. My mother isn't good. She is more egotistic, much more. He was absent from the house a lot . . . but I knew that I was his flower, all my life. I knew that I was the love of his life. I did not feel the absence of a father, but my mother felt the absence of a husband. I don't remember feeling this absence. I knew he adored me . . . he thought I was beautiful and smart . . .

When asked to give a title for her life, Sharon said: "I would have done the same things again."

Questions for Discussion

1 Which of Sharon's skills, abilities and aspirations are typical? and how do these correspond to the essentials required in the high-tech sector?

2 Trace Sharon's hurdles and explain them in the context of women entrepreneurship in the high-tech sector and in competitive environments.

3 List the growth strategies used by Sharon; explain her choice in line with the contextual factors she encountered.

4 Trace Sharon's background and indicate the junctions that might have predicted that Sharon would choose entrepreneurship.

5 What is the role of social and emotional support and encouragement in Sharon's course of action? Do you think Sharon's business would have survived without this support? Explain.

6 How would you explain Sharon's parents' influence on her career choice?

Growth Strategies of Women Entrepreneurs in Technology-based Firms

Barbara J. Orser
Deloitte Chair in the Management of Growth Enterprises, Telfer School of Management, University of Ottawa, Ontario, Canada

Introduction

This article summarizes key lessons learned from a study of Canadian women business owners in the advanced technology sector. The full report, *Showcasing Women Entrepreneurs in Canada's Advanced Technology Sector,*[6] provides details about the strategies used to identify entrepreneurial opportunities and growth in advanced technology-based firms. While the strategies described in the report are not unique to women, the profiles may encourage other women to consider a career in Canadian advanced technology. This is important for several reasons. Technology-oriented and knowledge-intensive enterprises are engines of Canadian economic growth. Yet, compared to men, women are significantly underrepresented in most advanced technology sectors.[7] The proportion of women in certain technology-based professions is also dropping. Hence, the report and summary of lessons learned may motivate other women to capitalize on their technical, intellectual and entrepreneurial abilities. Here are several insights shared by the Presidents and CEOs of ten innovative advanced technology-based firms.

Lesson 1 Customer Relationships Drive Enterprise Growth

Academic studies and media about the advanced technology sectors have focused primarily on the commercialization of innovation, intellectual property (IP), and technology. While these are all important organizational assets, several women CEOs spoke about the economic value of client and supplier relationships. According to Dale Gantous (InGenius Group of Companies) reputation is a more important asset in long-term growth than technology. Likewise, Angela O'Leary of Nisha Technologies identified the will to grow and the ability to listen to customers as key drivers of growth. She also cited the instrumental role of clients in stimulating the growth of her firm's services portfolio. Isabelle Bettez (8D Technologies) spoke of the need to manage customers carefully and the benefits of transforming customers into strategic partners.

Firm growth is, therefore, an outcome of healthy customer relationships. These perspectives about the importance of customer relationships indicate a need to focus on market and customer outcomes, in addition to financial and technical performance.

Lesson 2 Access to Capital Does Not Limit Growth for Women in Technology

There is no single or right formula to finance innovation. Canadian women use a variety of financing models and types of capital to start and grow advanced technology firms. For most of the women profiled access to capital had not limited firm growth. Joanne Ball-Gautschi (Partner International Inc.) relied on retained earnings to grow her firm. Sharlyn Ayotte (T-Base Communications) and Tanya Shaw Weeks (Unique Solutions Design) secured external capital and spoke about the added-value external investors can bring (e.g., mentoring, networking, governance advice, and hands-on assistance). For some business owners, start-up entailed raising equity capital through angel syndicates and venture capitalists. Others relied on savings and love money (investment by family, friends, and colleagues). Securing start-up capital is not easy, particularly if the product is in an early stage of development, according to Cynthia Goh (Axela Inc. and ViveTM Nano). Cindy Gordon (Helix Commerce International Inc.) observed that venture capitalists have little interest in services firms. All business owners had established relationships with commercial lending institutions to finance their firms' ongoing operations.

These are important observations for several reasons. First, the media has suggested that lenders and investors discriminate against women. This assertion contradicts most systematic studies about gender and access to capital. What Canadian research has found is that borrowing experiences differ by size and sector of firm.[8] After allowing for these effects, compared to male business owners, women are significantly less likely to apply for capital (debt, leasing, supplier credit, and/or equity). For example, men are four times more likely to apply for equity (both angel and venture) capital compared to women. The primary reason women gave for not applying was that the "money was not needed." Second, the profiles suggest that it is the owners' assumptions and decision-making, rather than gender discrimination, which is associated with the capitalization of female-owned firms.

Lesson 3 Early Exporting Leads to Growth

Research has reported that international SMEs are the most productive, R&D intensive, and growth-oriented of all small businesses. Many of the businesses profiled were "born global" enterprises. Joanne Ball-Gautschi (Partner International Inc.), Tanya Shaw Weeks (Unique Solutions Design), and Joyce Groote (HoleysTM) demonstrate that Canadian women are launching global technology-based firms at or near inception. These women are taking advantage of new and inexpensive communication technologies, recognition of international market opportunities for small firms as well as Canadian trade agreements—all of which are helping to facilitate international business. Exporting is not, however, without challenges. Internal obstacles can include a lack of human and financial resources in addition to inadequate management knowledge and skill. Trade impediments, and costs, are reflected in: the challenges of finding local partners; obtaining foreign market intelligence; limited demand; time consuming and costly bureaucratic procedures and regulations; the added costs of operating abroad; the need to adapt products, packaging and services;

and the risks associated with foreign exchange, legislation, and politics. Canadian and international research has also documented that, on average, women-owned businesses are less likely to export compared to male-owned firms, regardless of sector.

While researchers are still not certain why women business owners are relatively less likely to export, the business owners profiled demonstrate that firm age and gender are not necessarily deterrents to launching new, rapid-growth global firms.

Lesson 4 Growth Reflects a Diversity of Skills

Technical expertise and credentials, such as engineering or computer science degrees, are not prerequisites to business ownership in the advanced technology sector. In some cases, women with management experience hired scientists and technicians to help create their firms' intellectual property. In other cases, women engineers and scientists hired professional managers to lead their firms. In almost every case study, success rested on evidence of both technical and management skills. As Cynthia Goh (Axela Inc. and ViveTM Nano) points out, what is required is the ability to work with a diverse team of experts, including leadership and communication skills. Lawyer and social entrepreneur Sue Van Der Hout (Girlphyte Inc.) also suggests that creativity is required to attract and retain consumers. These are important observations, for two reasons. First, compared to men, women are less likely to retain technical credentials or to bring technical experience to a business start-up. Yet, as the profiles demonstrate, women with different types of experience are nonetheless assuming leadership roles in the advanced technology sectors. Second, the ability to communicate with potential partners, employees, and clients is a prerequisite of entrepreneurial growth. In these ways, women business owners are attracting the management talent and scientific knowledge that is required to start and grow services and goods-producing businesses in the advanced technology sectors.

Lesson 5 Small is Not Always Beautiful

Many of the business owners spoke about a sense of accomplishment and the personal rewards of starting and managing a technology-based firm. But small business ownership is not always beautiful. Several business owners also spoke about the demands of business ownership. Candid comments included the need to be available—wherever and whenever needed, lack of owner compensation during start-up and the time commitments for work and travel. Several of the CEOs also cautioned "would-be" entrepreneurs not to underestimate the cost and time required to commercialize ideas (i.e., secure investment, build a market presence and generate revenue).

To overcome the demands of business ownership, women business leaders encouraged others to prioritize work/life balance by staying fit, remembering to have fun, using humour to dissipate stress, creating supportive networks, not letting others slow them down, and surrounding themselves with like-minded people.

Lesson 6 Alliances and Certification Can Offset the Liabilities of Newness and Size

Most of the women profiled were actively building collaborative relationships with other small- and large-sized firms. This strategy was used to offset the liabilities of newness and size such as limited market coverage, management "band width," and reputation. For example, to increase brand awareness among consumers, Tanya Shaw Weeks (Unique Solutions Design) established a co-branding relationship with a brand name pattern design firm. To further enhance her firm's credibility, Cindy Gordon (Helix Communications) obtained industry certification with several global software providers. Joanne Ball (Partners International) spoke about the importance of well-designed, non-confidential marketing material and non-disclosure agreements prior to approaching prospective partners. This requires undertaking, thorough due diligence, a learning process that helped the management team to better understand the market and to further clarify the firm's strategic position. Several of the women also spoke about the need to base relationships on mutual trust while remaining cautious about sharing intellectual property with clients and partners. Being clear early in negotiations about the firm's proprietary properties and differential advantages helps both parties understand the limits and opportunities of the relationship.

Lesson 7 Government Can Facilitate Growth

For some women business owners such as Angela O'Leary (Nisha Technologies) and Dale Gantous (InGenius Group of Companies), government is a key source of business and development opportunities. However, most case participants had not sought government. Only one business owner, Cynthia Goh (Axela Inc. and ViveTM Nano), obtained funding to develop commercial applications of technology that was created in an Ontario university. Cindy Goh spoke favorably about her experiences with the Ontario Centres of Excellence Market Readiness program. Two business owners benefited from foreign tax incentives in locating operations abroad. Conversely, one business owner described a government policy that significantly undermined her commercial operation, a decision that was undertaken without private sector consultation. These observations suggest that governments, at all levels, can do a yet better job of creating timely, relevant, and practical support services for women-owned advanced technology firms. For example, a section of the Industry Canada *Strategis* website should include case studies and research about gender-related challenges of enterprise growth. Industry Canada might also provide financial support to create cases and awards that recognize and enhance the visibility of successful women in the advanced technology sectors.

The business owners displayed a low level of awareness about government and related programs, suggesting the need for better coordination of programs across federal departments, provincial ministries, and regional economic development agencies. Program focus to support service providers in the advanced technology sector should be given additional consideration. Services are rarely the focus of technology support yet this sector is increasingly a source of Canadian economic prosperity and an area of economic activity in which women are disproportionately engaged. For example, Public Works and Government Services Canada (PWGSC) should be proactive in reaching out to women business owners through various SME training agencies and industry associations such as the Canadian Advanced Technology Alliance Women in Tech Forum. Members could then be alerted to pending requests for standing offers and supplier contract opportunities.

The profiles also suggest that initiatives that seek to stimulate investment in research and development must be linked to business start-up schemes and business registries. This will help to ensure that the owners of new firms are aware of available support services. As the profiles illustrate, governments must ensure that programs targeted to the advanced technology sector include women's participation, and that policy makers are alert and responsive to the evolving challenges of women business owners. Trade associations could also play a more active role in reporting to government about the experiences of women business owners in the advanced technology sectors. Several of these recommendations mirror Canadian studies which have reported on the need to better coordinate government programs to ensure firms are more aware of programs that facilitate cross-border movement of personnel and goods. As such, federal, provincial and municipal governments should monitor and report on SME program participation and impacts using gender-disaggregated data. Finally, the current government's focus on increasing productivity and innovation fails to consider gender influences that impact Canadian economic performance. This is a fundamental oversight and deterrent to enterprise growth.

Lesson 8 Attracting and Developing Talent is an Obstacle to Growth

A primary challenge for many women business leaders is to attract and retain talent. To ensure employees understand the nature and entrepreneurial culture of a firm, Joyce Groote (Holeys™) has worked with employees to create corporate value statements that specify the firm's entrepreneurial vision, performance expectations as well as the need for a solutions-oriented workplace environment. The profiles endorse the need to create a larger pool of workers. One means is to ensure that engineering, computer science, physics and other technical degree programs include mandatory entrepreneurship courses. Similarly, entrepreneurship courses should include curricula about the advanced technology sectors.

Lesson 9 Networking and Mentors Matter

Several business owners spoke about the importance of networks and mentors and how they proactively created opportunities to build social capital and support. Examples included establishing a syndicated network of angel investors, applying and "winning" an opportunity to be mentored through a regional talent competition, hosting peer-to-peer mentoring groups, long-distance mentoring with a high-profile female mentor, as well as attending trade association meetings. These are important observations, for several reasons. First, research has documented an association between mentoring and career advancement. The limited resources that typify small- to medium-sized firms imply that it is less likely that owners will be able to attend to mentoring issues. Second, it has been reported that women can face unique challenges in developing and maintaining effective mentoring relationships. Mentoring studies also report that the gender composition of the mentor/protégé dyad, type of mentoring (career versus psychosocial support), stage of the mentoring relationship, and the protégé's human capital are also relevant to career outcomes. For example, career support versus psychosocial support was seen to help women advance more than it did for men and that career support for women, from female mentors, was reported to be most useful. Women business owners are encouraged to proactively approach senior business owners and industry executives to establish mentoring relationships. Both the profiles and related research point to a role for trade associations in facilitating mentoring for women in the advanced technology sectors and to help identify one-on-one professional development opportunities for women.

Lesson 10 Multiple-use Applications Sustain Growth

Several women spoke about the importance of developing multiple-use technology platforms. This strategy served to insulate the firms from product failure and provided the means to beta test new technology applications and markets. In the services context, this lesson is described by Joanne Ball-Gautschi (Partner International) as having "several eggs and several baskets." Several women business owners spoke about the need to develop products and markets simultaneously. This is to ensure that emerging products are appropriate for new customers and that the firm secures new sources of revenue. The profiles also illustrate that Canadian women business owners are introducing ideas and affecting change with respect to the nature of advanced technology. Sharlyn Ayotte (T-Base

Communications) has helped to transform the market for braille and related services from a volunteer-based service delivery approach, to a technology-based, commercial delivery model. Joyce Groote (Holeys™) has introduced technology that is revolutionizing "the science of footwear." Cindy Gordon (Helix International Inc.) is building innovative "collaboration tools," technologies, and practices, some that are founded on her own academic research. These are just a few examples of the multiple ways in which Canadian women business owners are changing the face of the advanced technology sectors.

Final Observation: Technology May be Gender Neutral but the Industry is Not

Many, but not all, felt that the sector is not immune to gender-related challenges. For example, Joanne Ball-Gautschi is one of the few Canadian women entrepreneurs in the global defence and aerospace industries. She suggests that one reason for the absence of females in the sector is a lack of media coverage about women role models and that, compared to Europeans, Canadians are less progressive in supporting women's enterprise. Such observations are consistent with Canadian and international studies about women in the technology sector. A 2006 CATA WIT/Telfer School of Management study found gender-related career challenges remain.[9] Documented challenges included: perceived lack of credibility, credentials and confidence; misperceptions about ability; and lack of social capital and networking opportunities. The study suggests that men and women must take responsibility for the perceived gendering of occupational roles and organizational practices. Finally, some respondents to the study also expressed concerns about inappropriate and dismissive comments with respect to their performance or ability. Similarly, a recent survey conducted in the United Kingdom of women business owners operating in science, engineering, construction, and technology found that 40 percent of respondents attributed difficulties in starting a business to gender.[10] Perceived challenges included limited access to networks, assumptions that women are not as technically competent, and perceptions about conflicts between motherhood and entrepreneurship. Several United States-based studies have also examined career barriers in the technology sector. One study described youth-oriented hiring practices (where experience is not a valued asset), disrespect for women and a significant increase in age and sexism complaints lodged with the US Equal Opportunity Employment Commission.[11] Another typified the IT sector as: "masculine, white, and heterosexual, associated with hard programming, obsessive behaviour, and extensive working hours."[12] However, as this article illustrates, gender-related challenges do not stop talented and entrepreneurial women from creating and growing successful businesses in the advanced technology sectors.

Profiles of 10 Innovators in Canada's Advanced Technology Sector

Axela Incorporated and Vive™ Nano

> People talk about [the] disconnect between technology push and the market pull. I think it has to be a technology push meets market pull. We have to create wonderful new technology, but we also have to understand where the market is. And if it is not there, then it is not there.

Dr. Cynthia Goh: Scientist, Scholar, and Serial Entrepreneur

Cynthia Goh is Professor of Chemistry and Medical Science and Associate Director of the Institute for Optical Sciences at the University of Toronto. Her scientific innovations have led to an innovative medical diagnostics and drug discoveries platform. She is the co-founder of two Toronto-based firms, Axela Incorporated and Vive™ Nano. Both firms leverage scientific knowledge in the development on innovative products to assist researchers and industry partners. Axela Inc. (formerly Axela Biosensors) is recognized as a leading Canadian life science company. The firm's mission is to provide a simple and effective approach to understanding protein-protein interactions. Cindy Goh served as Chief Scientific Officer of Axela Inc. until 2004. Founded in 2006, Vive™ Nano is a Toronto-based firm that develops novel nanoparticle-based materials for a variety of fields such as catalysis and agricultural applications.

Girlphyte

> This is my passion. I'd like to be able to have an impact. I believe there is going to be a cultural shift. I think we are just dangling at the edge of a cultural shift in opportunities for women.

Susan Van Der Hout: Lawyer, Social Engineer, and Feminist Entrepreneur

Girlphyte Inc.'s founder and President Sue Van Der Hout is a former Bay Street tax litigator. Today, Sue Van Der Hout is leveraging her networks of women's organizations, technologists, media experts, and financial backers to develop an "interactive online engagement tool and profiling engine," initially targeted to women. This high-energy, social entrepreneur is convinced that women must utilize technology to help address gender differences in both the home and workplace. Her web-based technology is designed to facilitate an international dialogue among women about how they perceive, define, and achieve success.

InGenius Group

Running your own high-tech business is extremely fun. You have freedom to do things the way you want to do them. It is hard, but so is working for someone else. If you can rule your own destiny and make a living at the same time, it's really worth it.

Dale Gantous: Rocket Scientist, Communications Expert, and Turn-Around Entrepreneur

Dale Gantous is the Chief Executive Officer (CEO) of the InGenius Group of Companies. Based in Ottawa, InGenius People and InGenius Software provide software products and IT professional services to the federal government and to businesses worldwide. The InGenius Group of companies comprises two firms. InGenius People provides high quality IT professional services to the federal government. InGenius Software builds innovative, unified communications software for Voice over IP phone system customers around the globe.

The two businesses thrive together with common values that include pride in technical innovation, and belief that the only point of technical innovation is solving customers' problems, relieving their stress and thus making them happy. The following strategies have helped to build the company into a high performance global operation.

Nisha Technologies Inc.

In my business relationships and in making decisions, I am true to myself.

Angela O'Leary: Community Leader and Public Sector Entrepreneur

Angela O'Leary, President of Nisha Technologies Inc.'s Aboriginal business unit, manages a growing line of businesses while seeking out new partnerships, challenges, and opportunities. While working with Indian and Northern Affairs Canada, industry leaders and other stakeholders, Angela is also contributing her expertise to help determine how Aboriginal companies can benefit and move forward under the Procurement Strategy for Aboriginal Businesses program. She considers herself to be "entrepreneurial in nature" and is an avid believer in maintaining a balance between professional and personal life. Angela has over a decade of business development experience. Nisha Technologies supplies professional services, PCs, notebooks, work stations, and enterprise products to the federal government. O'Leary believes that her success is rooted in the ongoing monitoring of the federal government's $14 billion annual procurement spend, managing client and supplier expectations, keeping close to the customer as well as establishing strong partnerships.

Helix Commerce International Inc.

The heart of collaboration and innovation growth is trust and sense making!

Dr. Cindy Gordon: Transformation Change Architect, Author, and Serial Entrepreneur

Helix Commerce International Inc. specializes in collaboration commerce (c-commerce), next generation business models, and professional services that help clients build multi-dimensional relationships with customers, buyers, sellers, partners, and employees. Helix Commerce focuses on five core lines of business, leveraging knowledge from diverse disciplines that includes: customer capital, knowledge capital, human capital, digital capital and entrepreneurial capital all utilized to meet their clients' growth needs. Helix Commerce International Inc. (http://www.helixcommerce.com) operates three wholly-owned subsidiary operations: Helix Innovation Hive (http://stores.lulu.com/helixcommerce) specializes in publishing thought leadership and holding innovation conferences, Helix Talent (http://www.helixtalent.com) assists clients in attracting, retaining, and transitioning employees, Helix Virtual Worlds (www.helixvirtualworlds.com) advises on and develops virtual world experiences that enhance productivity through collaborative, socially stimulated digital 3D media and network marketing. Their clients are primarily Fortune 500 and mid-market firms in the advanced technology sectors.

Unique Solutions Design

Our goal is to scan millions around the world and help connect them with products and services that help enhance their life and fit their needs, bodies and lifestyle.

Tanya Shaw Weeks: Inventor and Born Global Entrepreneur

Founder and President Tanya Shaw Weeks positions Unique Solutions Design as the global connector of body measurement information. The firm's 3D scanning and measurement technology enables consumers to monitor body mass and fitness, find out what clothing size will fit them best and to order custom-made apparel from a growing list of clothing retailers. With a workforce of 32 employees, alliances with brand name suppliers and an acquisition strategy to ensure best-in-class innovation, this Halifax-based firm anticipates continued global growth. Underlying the success of Unique Solutions Design is a founder who understands the consumer mindset and holds other insights learned from experience as the past owner of a design and wardrobe-planning firm.

Partner International

We're making the world a smaller place.

Joanne Ball-Gautschi: Pioneer, Connector, and Dealmaker

Joanne Ball-Gautschi is the President of Partner International, a firm that develops business partnerships in the life sciences, pharmaceutical, aerospace, and defence sectors. Working directly with senior executives and embassies around the world, the firm deploys social capital to identify partners, facilitate introductions, negotiate deals and ultimately, build technology-based partnerships. Joanne started her career in radio, which was an experience that she believes provided valuable cross-sector learning and empathy for small business owners. Prior to launching Partner International, Joanne was vice-president of an American bio-technology firm. In 1999, Joanne launched Partner International in Halifax and Bern, Switzerland. She is also a Board member of the Nova Scotia Aerospace and Defence Association. Today, Joanne sees the world as her marketplace.

T-Base Communications

We are changing the story from dependence to independence.

Sharlyn Ayotte: Builder of Accessible Information Technologies for the Blind, Visually- and Hearing-Impaired

Success reflects Sharlyn Ayotte's tenacity, her desire to help others and her ability to create opportunities from misfortune. In 1976, Sharlyn was working within an information security firm when she lost her sight. Through this experience, she became convinced that all Canadians have the right to access information. When the federal government announced access-to-information legislation, she shifted focus from information security technology to creating accessible information. Today, T-Base Communications is a world leader in client solutions to transcribe printed information into braille, large print, audio, and secure online formats.

Holeys ™

Decide what you want to do in life and then act as if it is impossible to fail.

Joyce Groote: Biotechnologist, Footwear Scientist, and Owner of a Rapid-growth Enterprise

Holeys™ is a world leader in the use of injection foam molding technology. Holeys' first product was a popular colored foam clog. Today, Holeys™ designs and contract-manufactures lifestyle wear targeted at children, do-it-yourselfers, and duty professionals. With 6000 percent growth in 2006, Holeys ranked first on *Profit Magazine*'s Profit Hot 50 in 2007. Sustained growth entails new products, refined production processes, and investment in R&D focused on innovative and branded products. Joyce Groote's journey from biotechnologist to global businesswoman was unintentional. In 2004, opportunity came by way of a neighbor seeking advice about her home-based business that sold foam clogs. Within the year, a "shot-gun" agreement between the original owner and Joyce resulted in her purchasing Holeys™. Now President and CEO she manages a multi-million dollar enterprise that operates in over 40 countries. Prior to acquiring Holeys, Joyce's leadership skills were honed through 20 years of biotech experience, government regulatory and policy work, not-for-profit management and the establishment of BIOTECanada, helping start-up companies to "get up and running" operationally, and an investment network.

8D Technologies Inc.

Changing the world using technology is really a way to help achieve goals.

Isabelle Bettez: Visionary, Co-Founder, and Eco-Friendly Entrepreneur

Isabelle Bettez's vision to build a global enterprise was the outcome of trial and error. Founded in 1996, 8D Technologies Inc. is a world leader in the development of advanced, intelligent wireless, Machine-to-Machine (M2M), multi-function point of sale (POS) solutions. Its unique award-winning city parking system features 100 percent solar-powered wireless terminals that manage street parking and emerging municipal bike rental services, from a single network of user-friendly pay stations. The system can easily interconnect with public transit systems, answering the need for green, integrated solutions to control traffic congestion and pollution. POS terminals combine online payment with capacities for point of sale marketing (show tickets, rebate coupons, advertising, etc.) and information providing, in a totally autonomous solar device.

Questions for Discussion

Each of the lessons (e.g., strategies, practices) presented in this case study address different aspects of women entrepreneurs' ways of breaking barriers. The following questions address these lessons:

1   Select three lessons and discuss each of them separately with respect to its main message to women entrepreneurs on how to break through the barriers; then compare these messages and explain your conclusions.

2   Select three women entrepreneurs from the internet stories; provide the links to their websites. Discuss the "lessons" these women used to break through the barriers. Explain the differences between these women's strategies/practices.

3   Select three of the women innovators presented in this case study; for each, explain the main strategies/practices used to break through the barriers.

4   Select two different women innovators introduced in this case study; develop a plan for these women to break through the barriers and become even more successful; explain why you think that your plan will assist them.

Notes

1   At   http://www3.weforum.org/docs/WEF_Entrepreneurship_Report_2011. pdf; www.weforum.org

2   There are different approaches, as discussed in Chapter 9 on opportunity identification.

3   At http://www.fastcompany.com/magazine/132/the-most-influential-women-in-technology-the-entrepreneurs.html

4   Men and Women Entrepreneurs—Not that Different, at http://techcrunch. com/2010/10/10/men-and-women-entrepreneurs-not-that-different/ (October 10, 2010). Vivek Wadhwa is an entrepreneur turned academic. He is a Visiting Scholar at UC Berkeley, Senior Research Associate at Harvard Law School and Director of Research at the Center for Entrepreneurship and Research Commercialization at Duke University.

5   The author(s) of the case studies are fully and solely responsible for their content, phrasing consistency and flow, terminology, English proofing and reference lists.

6   To obtain the report *Showcasing Women Entrepreneurs in Canada's Advanced Technology Sector* contact Joanne Stanley, Canadian Advanced Technology Association Women in Tech (CATAWIT) Forum at jstanley@cata.ca.

7   Cukier, W. (2007). *Developing Tomorrow's Workforce Today*. Prepared on behalf of the Information and Communications Technology Council. Also see: Panteli, A. Stack, J., and Ramsay, H. (1999). "Gender and professional ethics in the IT industry" *Journal of Business Ethics*, October, 22(1): 51–61.

8   Orser, B.J., Riding, A.L., and Manley, K. (2006). "Women Entrepreneurs and Financial Capital," *Entrepreneurship Theory and Practice*, 30(5): 643–665.

9   Orser, B., Riding, A., Dathan, M., and Stanley, J. (2008). "Women in Advanced Technology: Examining the Influence of Role Orientation and Firm Structure on Perceived Gender Challenges," *Proceedings*, 5th Australia Graduate School of Entrepreneurship (AGSE) International Entrepreneurship Research Exchange, Melbourne.

10 Prowess. (2008). *Under the Microscope. Female Entrepreneurs in SECT Science, Engineering, Construction and Technology*. See: www.prowess.org.uk.

11 Xia A., and Kleiner, B. (2001). Discrimination in the computer industry. *Equal Opportunities International*, 20: 5–7.
12 Simard, C., Henderson, A., Gilmartin, S., Schiebinger, L., & Whitney, T. (2008). *Climbing the Technical Ladder: Obstacles and Solutions for Mid-level Women in Technology*. National Center for Women and Information Technology. Boulder: University of Colorado.

Concluding Remarks
The Fortitude of Women Entrepreneurs

This book is about women's entrepreneurial realm. It delineates the processes that women go through in the new venture creation, by thoroughly delving into their ecosystems, praising and acclaiming their exclusive experiences, challenges, motivations and dreams, while identifying their particular difficulties and barriers associated with turning an idea into a venture.

One predominant conclusion of this book refers to the quest for femininity and masculinity in the new venture creation. The concepts and models presented and discussed in this book, as well as the case studies and at-a-glance cases, reveal that the most successful and self-fulfilled profiles of women entrepreneurs are not those implementing exclusively feminine- or masculine-based styles to initiate and establish new ventures; rather, women who make use of competencies that are traditionally attributed to women, e.g., creativity, the ability to perform several activities simultaneously, keeping an open mind, tolerating novelty, focusing on the details, along with competencies attributed to men, such as focusing on the outcome, being target-oriented, implementing ideas rather than just dreaming them up—are more entrepreneurial and achieve more successes along the new venture creation process. The pivotal implication here is that women should retain their "feminine" strengths while being open to adopting "masculine" competencies that are known to be powerful in the new venture creation process. Renouncing their feminine competencies and adopting men's considered competencies to meet the "successful" masculine model of entrepreneurship is thus futile, because the masculine approach is only partially useful for a successful new venture creation process. Common sense would lead to the same conclusion regarding men's entrepreneurial world: they should maintain their strengths while being open to using more female-based competencies, to achieve the successful entrepreneurial profile.

Some other leading messages of this book address three main concepts—proactivity, empowerment, and acceptance and praise of diversity. This book is an endeavor to more accurately understand women's entrepreneurial world, to accept it, and to treat it as the standard rather than the exception, consequently allowing women to join forces as equals and to transform their ideas into viable, high-growth business ventures.

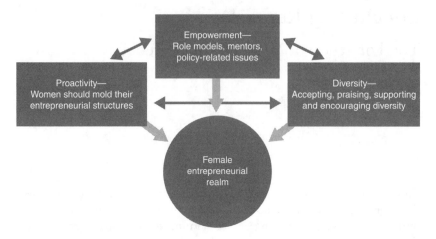

Figure C.1 The New Ground for Female Entrepreneurship.

The three main concepts of this book draw upon the frequently reiterated premise that women possess abilities and skills relevant to entrepreneurship, and as their most precious assets, these abilities and skills should be proactively exposed and exploited by women to pursue the entrepreneurial course. While research emphasizes the constraining factors on their entrepreneurial participation and success, e.g., women's educational and labor/market background, socialization, male domination of the market etc., this book aims to encourage women to take proactive measures targeted at eliminating or at least reducing the constraining impact of these hindrances on female entrepreneurship.

PROACTIVITY

Proactivity should be manifested all along women entrepreneurs' life course, from planning their entrepreneurial career, e.g., choosing educational tracks that they want and believe that they can be successful at, to selecting employment paths that match their skills and desires, maintaining their employability toward being promoted in their jobs, deepening their professional and business knowledge on an ongoing basis (Ajzen, 1991; Gundry & Welch, 2001; Kolvereid, 1996; Krueger & Carsrud, 1993). Proactivity at these stages, among others, would reduce the propensity of some women to follow stereotyped norms or satisfy gender-based, social expectations. Throughout the new venture creation process, proactivity should be manifested in struggling for their goals, including using creative means to accomplish those goals in the way that they visualize them. In short, women should concentrate on the "how" rather than on the "why," at least when they put their new ventures into practice.

Women entrepreneurs create businesses in different ecosystems worldwide, as exemplified by the various case studies presented in this book. While the underlying basis of the book is women entrepreneurs' heterogeneity and diversity, it nevertheless acknowledges the widespread, core hindrances in the female entrepreneurial realm, regardless of the woman's ecosystem. It is recommended that women entrepreneurs try to respond to these core hindrances in ways that match their specific needs, wishes and different entrepreneurial contexts.

This book is particularly attentive to women who have an entrepreneurial passion, yet avoid entrepreneurship, engage in limited forms of entrepreneurship, or restrict their entrepreneurial growth aspirations and actions. Female entrepreneurship cannot be fostered by simply convincing women to engage in entrepreneurial routines that are common among successful men entrepreneurs, or to follow a "generic success-solution" for entrepreneurs, as this would consist of enforcing a lifestyle that applies mainly to men or to the "generic entrepreneur," over a lifestyle that applies to women. Women and men are different, they go through different experiences and live in different ecosystems; they may even be stimulated by different incentives. Therefore, women should mold their entrepreneurial structures in a form that will best suit their own needs and interests.

This book calls for a reconceptualization of the traditional perceptions of female entrepreneurship by crafting, adjusting or merging various entrepreneurial forms and paths, for women and by women, which guarantee self-fulfillment, success and equality. For example, women set priorities that are compatible with their environments, attitudes, desires and needs; they juggle between these spheres and can accomplish their goals, in their own way and at their own pace. These may differ from the "ideal entrepreneurial type," yet they correspond to women's needs and desires. Men entrepreneurs would probably set different priorities, they may even experience frustration in following women's priorities. Such differences prove the relevance of the Latin saying "omnes viae Romam ducun"—"all roads lead to Rome":[1] different paths can lead to the same goal, and this is pertinent to the entrepreneurial realm. The following scenario illustrates this: a woman postpones a Skype meeting with potential investors because she has received a call from her child's school informing her that he/she is ill, and she is in a hurry to go and take care of her child. Does this automatically make her an unmotivated, non-achieving entrepreneur with twisted priorities? Will this necessarily make her an unsuccessful entrepreneur? The answer is no. Reflecting upon her behavior, she might even be more respected by the investors because in this particular case she exhibited strong family values, dedication and risk-taking (as she could have lost the investors' interest), which might then be echoed in her own business.

There is no one explicit type of successful entrepreneur, or one single means of accomplishing entrepreneurial goals. Women should be proactive and develop entrepreneurial structures and means that they can manage easily and effectively.

EMPOWERMENT

Empowerment is most relevant to women entrepreneurs, as it raises their self-confidence in their ability to initiate, create and run high-performing, new ventures. Empowerment is a multidimensional construct aimed at reflecting processes that foster individuals' internal strength, allowing them to gain or regain control of their lives, and increasing, or developing confidence in their capacity to act, implement and succeed, rather than attributing success to other people or to external conditions. Stemming from the concepts of "power"[2] and internal locus of control (Bandura, 1977; Mueller & Thomas, 2001; Shaver, 2004), empowerment addresses control and domination, and is used in this book to encourage women entrepreneurs to explore the extent to which they deem their entrepreneurial successes to be affected by their own decisions, actions and capabilities. In doing this, they can regain self-confidence in taking actions through their entrepreneurial course.

Empowerment can be transmitted to women entrepreneurs by others as well, for example, by significantly intensifying the magnitude of investments in women-led, entrepreneurial businesses; communicating women entrepreneurs' successes more frequently and more thoroughly in professional journals; inviting more women entrepreneurs to be on boards of directors. These actions, among others, could stay in the realm of "wishful thinking." This book takes a stand by proposing to intertwine empowerment with proactivity so that women will craft their own "empowerment format," to suit their natural heterogeneity and diversity. For example, some women may be empowered by being mentored in the process of their new venture creation; others by interacting with women who are role models, while yet others would favor being part of a significant network. Therefore, women should recognize the inner interests, needs and motivations that stimulate their entrepreneurial attitudes and actions, thus paving the way to the "empowerment format" that will fuel them with power and control over their businesses and lives, as well as with joy and fulfillment.

Role Models

Role models are a key factor in empowering women entrepreneurs. Role models are solid proof that dreams can be accomplished, as these are women who wanted to create new ventures and did not renounce their dreams, even when faced with barriers. Role models inspire by sharing their experiences and providing the motivation to take practical action to start a business. They have an energizing effect on women as their stories can sometime unleash deep-seated desires that these women had not found the courage to pursue, and had thus repressed.

Ms. Halla Tomasdottir,[3] the co-founder of Audur Capital, believes in values such as independence, risk awareness and emotional capital, among others. Her undertaking is aimed at bringing greater diversity, social responsibility and "feminine values" to the financial services industry. In a recent talk at TED, Ms. Tomasdottir revealed that the values she dissemi- nates and the awareness that she struggles to embed in the market appear to be taking hold. Ms. Tomasdottir's experiences provide a role model for success in business; e.g., according to Bloomber Businessweek,[4] October, 2011, she currently sits on the board of Reykjavik University, Veritas Capital hf. and the executive board of the Iceland Chamber of Commerce. Yet her success has been manifested in bringing "feminine values" to center stage in the male-dominated sectors. These achievements, combined with the stirring values upon which her business is founded, can empower women in the early stages of the new venture creation.

Raising the profile of role models nation- or worldwide is critical to boosting the visibility of existing female entrepreneurs, as they inspire women to enter into entrepreneurship with innovative and different approaches. Female role models should be sought, because women tend to absorb their spirit, derive and acquire relevant information and support from them, and then feel inspired to follow in their footsteps.

Female Entrepreneurs as Mentors

Different means of empowerment can be found in existing programs aimed at empowering women with their own strengths. These programs are governmental, public or private and address women entrepreneurs either globally, nationally, or locally, such as in a region or a city. Some programs are devoted to low-income women entrepreneurs, immigrants, ethnic women or women with disabilities; yet, the core of these programs is in establishing—for women, and by women (mentors)—entrepreneurial careers, by providing women with the necessary training, educational and personal resources that can lead to personal and economic empowerment.

One influential example is the European Commission's Ambassadors Network,[5] which is targeted to having successful entrepreneurs campaign in the field to inspire women of all ages to become entrepreneurs. Empowerment is focused on raising these women's confidence in their ability to create successful ventures. The woman ambassadors promote entrepreneurship among women across Europe by engaging and speaking to groups at schools, colleges and universities, to community groups and the media, as well as addressing conferences, business networks and employment initiatives.

Networking to Promote Women Entrepreneurs

A network for women that is targeted to responding to women entrepreneurs' needs and interests can encourage women to create their own businesses in various practical, social and emotionally related ways, such as by providing information on the market, competitors, potential unexploited niches, or know-how in starting a business (i.e., practical); partnering, sharing ideas or establishing trade relationships (i.e., practical and social); providing support and advising nascent women entrepreneurs (i.e., social, emotional).

Policy

Empowerment can be achieved by developing a straightforward policy for women entrepreneurs. Most countries are still lacking official gender-based statistics and documentation on women entrepreneurs, including data on the investments contributed to women-led businesses, rates of growth, mergers and acquisitions, among others. Policy-makers in many countries have accomplished a great deal in tackling the discrimination faced by women entrepreneurs, yet women still encounter hindrances, e.g., in accessing funding, information and business networks. Policies addressing these hindrances could minimize them greatly. To accomplish this, national bodies responsible for women entrepreneurs need to: research female entrepreneurship more thoroughly to understand these women's worlds; involve women in policy planning for female entrepreneurship; monitor policies that have already been implemented and adjust them according to their impact on success rates in female entrepreneurship. Female entrepreneurship can foster a country's wealth and should be rooted in any national policy developed for entrepreneurs. This would then create a higher, more positive public opinion of women entrepreneurs, such that certain factors that make entrepreneurship a less viable option for women, such as family–work imbalance, lack of role models and mentors, social stereotypes and lack of education in entrepreneurship skills, could be addressed at the national policy level.

Policy can empower women in addressing advocacy, providing a common hub of support services (e.g., best practices in female entrepreneurship, confronting contextual female-based barriers, raising the credibility of women entrepreneurs in science, high-technology and innovation-driven sectors, recommending measures to facilitate their access to financing, information, business networks, business training, etc.). Online resources are helpful to pull together the diverse entrepreneurship efforts, e.g., associations, projects, initiatives partnered with universities, education ministries and policy-makers, to promote female entrepreneurship.

The policy should be robust, to ensure that information and support services for women entrepreneurs be mainstreamed throughout the system to all stakeholders, by facilitating collaborations with already existing networks and organizations, constructing new collaborations, and enabling benchmarking, exchange of information and projects of common and promoting interests.

Implications for Education

The increasing desire in the development of educational programs in schools to encourage entrepreneurship seems to be neglecting the area of female entrepreneurship. The educational system is the backbone in designing perceptions about female entrepreneurship and in developing females' intentions, aspirations and self-confidence to become successful entrepreneurs. Yet the public education system in most countries is not particularly supportive of female entrepreneurship: it does not emphasize the value of female entrepreneurship, and only marginally cultivates an entrepreneurial culture and spirit that could embrace female entrepreneurship. Most public schools do not allocate many resources to identifying leading female students who possess entrepreneurial characteristics, in order to provide them with a suitable platform to develop their abilities. Moreover, schools do not deliberately provide opportunities to practice entrepreneurship, e.g., entrepreneurial thinking, innovation or creativity, under either formal curricular or extracurricular initiatives. Schools provide few occasions to meet with leading female entrepreneurs in order to place them center stage, appraise their contributions and educate young students that entrepreneurial success is not a function of gender. Furthermore, schools do not encourage female students to take classes in technology, sciences or computer sciences, thus possibly even suppressing the more scientific, innovative or entrepreneurial characteristics that some female students possess. Most schools largely disregard the differences between the genders' learning and working styles, thus implementing teaching practices that may apply to one group more than the other; as such, schools can actually inhibit female entrepreneurial intentions, as well as skills and networks (Aldrich & Baker, 2001; Katz, 2003; Peterman & Kennedy, 2003).

A propensity for entrepreneurship is commonly associated with values, attitudes, personal goals and personal traits that one might expect to see offered within formal education programs. Education should serve a preparatory function with regard to entrepreneurship, whereby the transfer of knowledge, and acquisition and development of relevant skills will increase female students' self-confidence in their ability to run successful entrepreneurial businesses. Schools should endeavor to create an environment that develops entrepreneurial abilities among students, regardless of gender, expose students to different entrepreneurial realms, provide them with opportunities to practice some entrepreneurial processes and educate them to accept diversity.

Accepting and Praising Diversity

The concept of diversity is at the center of a heated, worldwide debate: entrepreneurship, by definition, espouses diversity as one of its most significant strategic goals; yet, in the face of the hurdles tackled by women in the entrepreneurial realm, the prevalence of diversity in entrepreneurship becomes questionable. Diversity in entrepreneurship refers to differences in traits, capabilities, and resources that distinguish entrepreneurs, such as demographic characteristics, human capital, entrepreneurial resources, personal abilities, approaches and attitudes toward entrepreneurship, etc. However, differences often become synonymous with stereotypical views: attributes such as "gender," "feminine way of thinking," "female-oriented interests," among others, are then transformed into perceptions of women entrepreneurs' abilities and performance, regardless of the context, i.e., "inadequate ability to become an entrepreneur," "lack of entrepreneurial skills," or "limited chances of growing the business," confounding diversity in the entrepreneurial realm.

By accepting diversity, not only is the "stereotyped" group respected, but other groups which may have tackled similar or very different difficulties can benefit from the solution generated for the "stereotyped" group. For example, women entrepreneurs more than men are concerned with balancing time spent at the business and at home; in reassessing the employment conditions that can enable such a balance, men will benefit from the solution as well, and so can other groups, e.g., nascent entrepreneurs, employees in entrepreneurial businesses, managers of small and medium-size businesses.

Creativity, Innovation, Originality

Entrepreneurial businesses strive for resources such as creativity, innovation and originality to develop a sustainable, competitive advantage in the market. People possessing entrepreneurial thinking and spirit are therefore sought after (as partners, employees, consultants, outsourced assistance, etc.). Most businesses use the same "pool" to seek such resources, e.g., college students, head-hunted employees from leading corporations and consultants, and use identical means to foster those resources in the business, e.g., training programs, empowerment. Unintentionally, these activities can result in stifling creativity and innovation at the business level, thus eliminating the business's competitive advantages which have been based on these resources, as the sought-after creative/innovative people contribute identical intangible resources to the business: wherever creativity, innovation and originality become widespread and common, they cease to be creative and innovative, they become standard. Diversity is a key factor in enhancing creativity, innovation and originality in the business. People who have undergone different experiences can contribute to their business greatly by fueling it with new "flavors"—by sharing their experiences, acquainting others with the ecosystems they tackled, imparting their insights and thoughts, and reflecting jointly on the practical implications in line with the business's goals (in terms of product development, marketing, advertising, approaching new niches, etc.). Each of these "flavors" can serve as a stimulus for creativity, innovation and originality in the other people involved in the business, by either applying it in different contexts, merging it with existing processes, or developing new processes stimulated from the experience that has been shared or insights that have been imparted. The benefits for entrepreneurial businesses that encourage diversity are more pronounced than those obtained by established businesses, as the effect on the business processes pursued by any member in its early stages is particularly significant.

Encouraging gender diversity in the entrepreneurial realm means acknowledging that different businesses can generate sustainable competitiveness in the marketplace, by accepting, praising, supporting and encouraging internal and external diversity. Internal diversity refers to proactively encouraging different groups in the business, including gender groups, to produce ideas and solutions, or even identify the market's needs, through the prism of their different views and interpretations, thus introducing new ideas, views and higher potential innovation to the business. External diversity refers to accepting businesses led by women entrepreneurs into the market, treating them as routine, and respecting them. The potential advantages of joining forces are extremely lucrative for entrepreneurial businesses. Tahir, a scientist from Bangalore, India who founded an entrepreneurial business for the development of biological solutions for food hygiene presents a good example of this point. Tahir's business ran out of money after a substantial investment obtained three years prior. He was desperately searching for new financial sources for his venture when, while attending a conference in Europe, he met Kal (Kalaimagal), the founder of an internet-based business for pet health from New Delhi, India. Kal analyzed Tahir's business situation and suggested a co-operation on her blog, which turned out to be most beneficial for Tahir: he used the blog to report on the latest developments in food hygiene for pets, and this exposure assisted him in finding investors and partners for his venture. In Tahir's words, Kal had "shed new light regarding the business's situation . . . she gives totally different meanings than me to the same situations, and so she could come up with great ideas on how to solve them."

Communal Responsibility

Respecting diversity can intensify a general sense of responsibility and caring for other people, and can echo these both inward and outward. Applying responsibility inward can mean accepting women's views, thoughts and styles in the business, by respecting their priorities and their ways of thinking about and reflecting upon situations; considering women's ideas and solutions as equally valuable as those introduced by their male counterparts; encouraging brainstorming by the gender groups; publicly praising activities and initiatives taken to strengthen diversity in the business. Such spirit and practices fuel the business with a vigorous and dynamic atmosphere, promote stimulating relationships between women and men, and can result in new ideas, potential collaborations and future joint businesses, as well as new friendships and emotional support. Diversity can be implemented from the business outward via entrepreneurs' attentiveness to the shareholders' different views and approaches to their business's products, services or processes; respecting, as equals, the views of women entrepreneurs who run competing, complementary or investing businesses. These approaches will enable making the required adjustments, as well as spawning innovations in the market and producing new potential collaborations.

To demonstrate the role of diversity, and in honor of Mr. Steve Jobs who passed away in October 2011, this book ends on a celebratory note of optimism, change and respect for difference and diversity, echoed in the advertisement for Apple, "The Crazy Ones,"[6] in Mr. Jobs' voice.[7]

Here's to the crazy ones.

The misfits.

The rebels.

The troublemakers.

The round pegs in the square holes.

The ones who see things differently.

They're not fond of rules.

And they have no respect for the status quo.

You can quote them, disagree with them, glorify or vilify them.

About the only thing you can't do is ignore them.

Because they change things.

They push the human race forward.

And while some may see them as the crazy ones, we see genius. Because the people who are crazy enough to think they can change the world, are the ones who do.—Apple Inc.

NOTES

1 Appears in the form *Mille viae ducunt homines per saecula Romam* (A thousand roads lead men forever to Rome) in *Liber Parabolarum*, 591 (1175), by Alain de Lille.

2 Power relates to the ability to push others to do what we want, regardless of their own wishes or interests (Gerth & Mills, 1958).

3 At http://www.ted.com/speakers/halla_tomasdottir.html

4 At http://investing.businessweek.com/research/stocks/private/person.asp?person Id=78964619&privcapId=78878969&previousCapId=78878969&previousTitl e=Audur%20Capital

5 Supporting Women Entrepreneurs, at http://ec.europa.eu/enterprise/policies/ sme/promoting-entrepreneurship/women/ambassadors/index_en.htm

6 Apple's one-minute commercial, under the campaign of "Think different," featured black-and-white footage of 17 iconic 20th-century personalities, including Albert Einstein, Bob Dylan, Martin Luther King, Jr., John Lennon and Yoko Ono, Thomas Edison, Maria Callas, Mahatma Gandhi, Amelia Earhart, Martha Graham, and more. The text of the commercial was written by Rob Siltanen and Ken Segall. Originally: Here's to the crazy ones. The misfits. The rebels. The troublemakers. The round pegs in the square holes. The ones who see things differently. They're not fond of rules. And they have no respect for the status quo. You can quote them, disagree with them, glorify or vilify them. About the only thing you can't do is ignore them. Because they change things. They invent. They imagine. They heal. They explore. They create. They inspire. They push the human race forward. Maybe they have to be crazy. How else can you stare at an empty canvas and see a work of art? Or sit in silence and hear a song that's never been written? Or gaze at a red planet and see a laboratory on wheels? We make tools for these kinds of people. While some see them as the crazy ones, we see genius. Because the people who are crazy enough to think they can change the world, are the ones who do. (Wikipedia-http://en.wikipedia.org/wiki/Think_Different).

7 http://www.youtube.com/watch?v=8rwsuXHA7RA

References

Abir-Am, P. G. (2010). What's in a session? *History of Science Society Newsletter*, *35*(1), 24–25.

Acharya, M. (2001). *Efforts at promotion of women in Nepal*. Kathmandu: Friedrich Ebert Stiftung.

Achtenhagen, L., & Welter, F. (2007). Media discourse in entrepreneurship research. In H. Neergaard & J. P. Ulhoi (Eds.), *Handbook of qualitative methods in entrepreneurship research* (pp. 193–215). Cheltenham, UK: Edward Elgar.

Acs, A., & Dana, L. (2001). Contrasting two models of wealth creation. *Small Business Economics*, *16*, 63–74.

Acs, Z., & Szerb, L. (2007). Entrepreneurship, economic growth and public policy. *Small Business Economics*, *28*(2–3), 109–122.

Adler, P., & Kwon, S. (2002). Social capital: Prospects for a new concept. *Academy of Management Review*, *27*(1): 17–40.

Agars, M. D. (2004). Reconsidering the impact of gender stereotypes on the advancement of women in organizations. *Psychology of Women Quarterly*, *28*, 103–111.

Ahl, H. J. (1997). *Entrepreneurship research with a gender perspective: An overview of past research and suggestions for the future*. Paper presented at the 14th Nordic Conference on Business Studies, Bodö, Norway.

Ahl, H. J. (2002). The construction of the female entrepreneur as the other. In B. Czarniawska & H. Höpfl (Eds.), *Casting the other. The production and maintenance of inequalities in work organizations* (pp. 52–67). London: Routledge.

Ahl, H. (2006). Why research on women entrepreneurs needs new directions. *Entrepreneurship Theory and Practice*, *30*(5), 595–621.

Ahl, H. J., & Samuelsson, E. F. (2000). *Networking through empowerment and empowerment through networking* (Research report 2000-1). Jönköping: Jönköping International Business School.

Aidis, R., Welter, F., Smallbone, D., & Isakova, N. (2006). Female entrepreneurship in transition economies: The case of Lithuania and Ukraine. *Feminist Economics*, *12*, 631–646.

Ajzen, I. (1991). The theory of planned behavior. *Organizational Behavior and Human Decision Processes*, *50*(2), 179–211.

Ajzen, I., & Fishbein, M. (1977). Attitude-behavior relations: A theoretical analysis and review of empirical research. *Psychological Bulletin*, *84*, 888–918.

Ajzen, I., & Fishbein, M. (1980). *Understanding attitudes and predicting social behavior*. Englewood Cliffs, NJ: Prentice-Hall.

Albrecht, K., & Albrecht, S. (1987). *The creative composition.* Homewood, IL: Dow Jones-Irvin.

Aldrich, H. (1989). Networking among women entrepreneurs. In O. Hagan, C. Rivchun, & D. Sexton (Eds.), *Women-owned businesses* (pp. 103–132). New York, NY: Praeger.

Aldrich, H. E., & Baker, T. (2001). Learning and legitimacy: Entrepreneurial responses to constraints on the emergence of new populations and organizations. In C. Bird-Schoonhoven & E. Romanelli (Eds.), *The entrepreneurship dynamic: Origins of entrepreneurship and the evolution of industries.* Thousand Oaks, CA: Sage Publications.

Aldrich, H. E., & Ruef, M. (2006). *Organizations evolving* (2nd ed.). Thousand Oaks, CA: Sage.

Aldrich, H. E., Carter, N., & Ruef, M. (2002). With very little help from their friends: Gender and relational composition of nascent entrepreneurs' startup teams. In W. D. Bygrave, J. A. Hornaday, D. F. Muzyka, K. H. Vesper, & W. E. J. Wetzel (Eds.), *Frontiers of entrepreneurship research* (pp. 156–169). Boston, MA: Babson College.

Aldrich, H. E., & Wiedenmayer, G. (1993). From Traits to rates: An ecological perspective on organizational foundings. In J. A. Katz & R. H. Brockhaus Sr. (Eds.), *Advances in entrepreneurship, firm emergence, and growth* (pp. 145–195). Greenwich, CT: JAI Press.

Allen, E., Langowitz, N., & Minniti, M. (2007). *The 2006 Global Entrepreneurship Monitor special topic report: Women in entrepreneurship.* Babson Park, MA: Center for Women Leadership, Babson College.

Allen, I. E., Elam, A., Langowitz, N., & Dean, M. (2008). *2007 report on women and entrepreneurship.* Babson, MA: GEM and Global Entrepreneurship Research Association (GERA).

Alsos, G. A., & Kolvereid, L. (1998). The business gestation process of novice, serial and parallel business founders. *Entrepreneurship Theory and Practice, 22*(4), 101–114.

Alsos, G. A., & Ljunggren, E. (1998). Does the business start-up process differ by gender? A longitudinal study of nascent entrepreneurs. In P. D. Reynolds, W. D. Bygrave, S. Manigart, C. M. Mason, G. D. Meyer, N. M. Carter, & K. G. Shaver (Eds.), *Frontiers of entrepreneurial research* (pp. 137–151). Boston, MA: Babson College.

Alsos, A., Isaksen, E. J., & Ljunggren, E. (2006). New venture financing and subsequent business growth in men- and women-led businesses. *Entrepreneurship Theory and Practice, 30*(5), 667–686.

Alvarez, S. A., & Barney, J. B. (2007). Discovery and creation: Alternative theories of entrepreneurial action. *Strategic Entrepreneurship Journal, 1*(1–2), 11–26.

Alvarez, S., & Busenitz, L. (2001). The entrepreneurship of resource-based theory. *Journal of Management, 27*, 755–775.

Amabile, T. M. (1983). *The social psychology of creativity.* New York, NY: Springer-Verlag.

Amabile, T. (1988). A model of creativity and innovation in organizations. In B. M. Staw & L. L. Cummings (Eds.), *Research in organizational behavior* (vol. 10, pp. 123–167). Greenwich, CT: JAI Press.

Amabile, T., Conti, R., Coon, H., Lazenby, J., & Herron, M. (1996). Assessing the work environment for creativity. *Academy of Management Journal, 39,* 1154–1184.

Amit, R., & Schoemaker, P. J. H. (1993). Strategic assets and organizational rent. *Strategic Management Journal, 14*(1), 33–46.

Amit, R., & Muller, E. (1995). Push and pull entrepreneurship (two types based on motivation). *Journal of Small Business and Entrepreneurship, 12*(4), 64–80.

Anderson, A. R., & Miller, C. J. (2003). Class matters: Human and social capital in the entrepreneurial process. *Journal of Socio-Economics, 32,* 17–36.

Ang, S. H., & Hong, D. G. P. (2000). Entrepreneurial spirit among East Asian Chinese. *Thunderbird International Business Review, 42*(3), 285–309.

Anna, L., Chandler, G., Jansen, E., & Mero, N. (2000). Women business owners in traditional and nontraditional industries. *Journal of Business Venturing, 15*(3), 279–303.

Ansoff, I. (1965). *Corporate strategy.* New York, NY: McGraw-Hill.

Arbaugh, J., & Camp, M. (2000). Managing growth transitions: Theoretical perspectives and research directions. In D. Sexton & H. Landström (Eds.), *Handbook of entrepreneurship* (pp. 308–328). Oxford, UK: Blackwell.

Arbaugh, J. B., Camp, S. M., & Cox, L. W. (2005). A multi-country comparison of perceived environmental characteristics, industry effects, and performance in entrepreneurial firms. *Journal of Enterprising Culture, 13*(2), 105–126.

Arch, E. (1993). Risk-taking: A motivational basis for sex differences. *Psychological Reports, 73*(3), 6–11.

Archer, J., & Lloyd, B. (2002). *Sex and gender.* Boston, MA: Cambridge University Press.

Ardichvili, A., Cardozo, R., & Ray, S. (2003). A theory of entrepreneurial opportunity identification and development. *Journal of Business Venturing, 18*(1), 105–123.

Arenius, P., & Autio, E. (2006). Financing of small businesses: Are Mars and Venus more alike than different? *Venture Capital, 8*(2), 93–107.

Argyle, M. (1990). *The psychology of interpersonal behavior.* Harmondsworth, UK: Penguin.

Argyris, C. (1993). *Knowledge for action.* San Francisco, CA: Jossey-Bass.

Arthur, M. B., & Rousseau, D. M. (1996). *The boundaryless career: A new employment principle for a new organizational era.* New York, NY: Oxford University Press.

Ashkanasy, N. M., & Tse, B. (2000). Transformational leadership as management of emotion: A conceptual review. In N. M. Ashkanasy & C. E. Hartel (Eds.), *Emotions in the workplace: Research, theory, and practice* (pp. 3–18). Westport, CT: Quorum Books/Greenwood Publishing Group.

Autio, E., Keeley, R. H., Klofsten, M., & Ulfstedt, T. (1997). Entrepreneurial intent among students: Testing an intent model in Asia, Scandinavia and USA. Retrieved from http//: www.babson.edu/entrep/fer

Avolio, B. J. (2003). Examining the full range model of leadership: Looking back to transform forward. In D. Day & S. Zaccaro (Eds.), *Leadership development for transforming organizations: Growing leaders for tomorrow* (pp. 71–98). Mahwah, NJ: Lawrence Erlbaum Associates.

Avolio, B. J. (2005). *Leadership development in balance: Made/born*. Mahwah, NJ: Lawrence Erlbaum Associates.

Avolio, B. J., Gardner, W. L., Walumbwa, F. O., Luthans, F., & May, D. R. (2004). Unlocking the mask: A look at the process by which authentic leaders impact follower attitudes and behaviors. *The Leadership Quarterly, 15*, 801–823.

Avolio, B. J., & Luthans, F. (2006). *The high impact leader: moments matter in accelerating authentic leadership development*. New York, NY: McGraw-Hill.

Azmat, F. (2010). Exploring social responsibility of immigrant entrepreneurs: Do home country contextual factors play a role? *European Management Journal, 28*(5), 377–386.

Baas, M., De Dreu, C. K. W., & Nijstad, B. A. (2008). A meta-analysis of 25 years of mood-creativity research: Hedonic tone, activation, or regulatory focus? *Psychological Bulletin, 134*, 779–806.

Babcock, L., & Laschever, S. (2003). *Women don't ask: Negotiation and the gender divide*. Princeton, NJ: Princeton University Press.

Babcock, L., Laschever, S., Gelfand, M., & Small, D. (2003). Nice girls don't ask. *Harvard Business Review, 81*(10), 14–17.

Baer, J., & Kaufman, J. C. (2008). Gender differences in creativity. *Journal of Creative Behavior, 42*, 75–105.

Baker, T., Aldag, R., & Blair, E. (2003). *Gender and entrepreneurial opportunity evaluation*. Paper Presented at the 23rd Annual Babson Kauffman Entrepreneurship Research Conference, Babson College, Wellesley, MA.

Bales, R. F. (1950). *Interactionprocess analysis: A method for the study of small groups*. Cambridge, MA: Addison-Wesley.

Bandura, A. (1977). *Social learning theory*. Englewood Cliffs, NJ: Prentice-Hall.

Bandura, A. (2000). Cultivate self-efficacy for personal and organizational effectiveness. In E. A. Locke (Ed.), *Blackwell handbook of principles of organizational behavior* (pp. 120–136). Oxford, UK: Blackwell.

Barnett, R. C., & Hyde, J. S. (2001). Women, men, work and family: An expansionist theory. *The American Psychologist, 56*(10), 781–796.

Barney, J. B. (1986a). Organizational culture: Can it be a source of sustained competitive advantage? *Academy of Management Review, 11*(3), 656–665.

Barney, J. B. (1986b). Types of competition and the theory of strategy: toward an integrative framework. *Academy of Management Review, 11*, 791–800.

Barney, J. B. (1991). Firm resources and sustained competitive advantage. *Journal of Management, 17*(1), 99–120.

Barney, J. B. (2001). Resource-based theories of competitive advantage: A ten year retrospective on the resource-based view. *Journal of Management, 27*, 643–650.

Barney, J. B., & Hesterly, W. S. (2005). *Strategic management and competitive advantage: Concepts*. Upper Saddle River, NJ: Pearson Education, Inc.

Baron, R. A., Markman, G. D., & Hirsa, A. (2001). Perceptions of women and men as entrepreneurs: Evidence for differential effects of attributional augmenting. *Journal of Applied Psychology, 86*, 923–929.

Baron, R. A., & Tang, J. (2009). Entrepreneurs' social skills and new venture performance: Mediating mechanisms and cultural generality. *Journal of Management, 35*(2), 282–306.

Baron, R. A., & Tang, J. (2011). The role of entrepreneurs in firm-level innovation: Joint effects of positive affect, creativity, and environmental dynamism. *Journal of Business Venturing, 26*(1), 49–60.

Barrett, M. (1995). Feminist perspectives on learning for entrepreneurship: The view from small business. In W. D. Bygrave, B. J. Bird, S. Birley, N. C. Churchill, M. Hay, R. H. Keeley, & W. E. Wetzel, Jr. (Eds.), *Frontiers of entrepreneurial research* (pp. 323–336). Boston, MA: Babson College.

Barron, F., & Harrington, D. (1981). Creativity, intelligence, and personality. *Annual Review of Psychology, 32*, 439–476.

Bass, B.M., & Bass, R. (2008). *The Bass handbook of leadership: Theory, research, and managerial applications.* New York, NY: Free Press.

Bates, E., Thompson, M., & Vaile, C. (2003). *I am Diva: Every woman's guide to outrageous living.* New York, NY: Warner Books.

Baughn, C. C., Chua, B. L., & Neupert, K. E. (2006). The normative context for women's participation in entrepreneurship: A multicountry study. *Entrepreneurship Theory & Practice, 30*(5), 687–708.

Baum, J. R., Locke, E. A., & Kirkpatrick, S. A. (1998). A longitudinal study of the relation of vision and vision communication to venture growth in entrepreneurial firms. *Journal of Applied Psychology, 83*(1), 43–54.

Bay, D., & Daniel, H. (2003). The theory of trying and goal-directed behavior: The effect and moving up the hierarchy of goals. *Psychology and Marketing, 20*(8), 669–684.

Baysinger, B. D., & Hoskisson R. E. (1989). Diversification strategy and R&D intensity in large multi-product firms. *Academy of Management Journal, 32*, 310–332.

Beasley, C. (1999). *What is feminism? An introduction to feminist theory.* London: Sage.

Bechthold, K. (2006). Editor's message. *Mompreneur*, June. Retrieved from http://www.themompreneur.com/ (accessed October 27, 2006).

Begley, T. M., Tan, W. L., Larasati, A. B., Rab, A., & Zamora, E. (1997). The relationship between socio-cultural dimensions and interest in starting a business: A multi-country study. Retrieved from http//:www.babson.edu/entrep/fer/papers97/begley/beg.htm

Bellu, R. R. (1993). Task role motivation and attributional style as predictors of entrepreneurial performance: Female sample findings. *Entrepreneurship and Regional Development, 5*, 331–344.

Bennet, R., & Dann, S. (2000). The changing experience of Australian women entrepreneurs. *Gender, Work and Organization, 7*(2), 75–83.

Benschop, Y., & Brouns, M. (2003). Crumbling ivory towers: Academic organizing and its gender effects. *Gender, Work and Organization, 10*(2), 195–212.

Bentley, A. (2002). Inventing baby food: Gerber and the discourse of infancy in the United States. In W. J. Belasco & P. Scranton (Eds.), *Food nations: Selling taste in consumer societies* (pp. 92–113). New York, NY: Routledge.

Bhagat, R. S., Kedia, B. L., Harveston, P. D., & Triandis, H. C. (2002). Cultural variations in the cross-border transfer of organizational knowledge: An integrative framework. *Academy of Management Review, 27*(2), 204–221.

Bhave, M. (1994). A process model of entrepreneurial venture creation. *Journal of Business Venturing, 9*(2), 223–242.

Bhide, A. V. (2000). *The origin and evolution of new businesses.* New York, NY: Oxford University Press.

Bhide, A. V. (2000). *The origin and evolution of new businesses.* Oxford, UK: Oxford University Press.

Birch, D., Haggerty, A., & Parsons, W. (1993). *Who's creating jobs?* Boston, MA: Cognetics, Inc.

Bird, B. (1989). *Entrepreneurial behaviour.* Glenview, IL: Scott Foresman.

Bird, B., & Brush, C. (2002). A gendered perspective on organizational creation. *Entrepreneurship Theory & Practice, 26*(30), 41–65.

Birley, S. (1989). Female entrepreneurs: Are they really any different? *Journal of Small Business Management, 27*(1), 32–38.

Birley, S., Moss, C., & Saunders, P. (1987). Do women entrepreneurs require different training? *American Journal of Small Business, 12*(1), 27–35.

Boden, R., & Nucci, A. (2000). On the survival prospects of men's and women's new business ventures. *Journal of Business Venturing, 15*(4), 347–362.

Boling, S. E., & Boling, J. L. (1993). Creativity and birth order/sex differences in children. *Education, 114*(2), 224–226.

Bolton, B., & Thompson, J. (2000). *Entrepreneurs, talent, temperament, technique.* Oxford, UK: Butterworth Heinemann.

Bomani, E. (2007). *The dynamic Diva dollars—for women who aren't afraid to become millionaires.* Las Vegas, NV: Papyrus.

Bonnett, C., & Furnham, A. (1991). Who wants to be an entrepreneur? A study of adolescents interested in a Young Enterprise scheme. *Journal of Economic Psychology, 12*(3), 465–478.

Bourdieu, P. (1986). Forms of capital. In J. G. Richardson (Ed.), *Handbook of theory and research for the sociology of education* (pp. 241–260). Westport, CT: Greenwood Press.

Bowen, D. D., & Hisrich, R. D. (1986). The female entrepreneur: A career development perspective. *Academy of Management Review, 11*(2), 393–407.

Bower, A. (2005). Meet the mompreneurs. Retrieved from http://www.time.com/time/magazine/article/0,9171,1053667-1,00.html (accessed October 27, 2006).

Bower, J. L., & Christensen, C. M. (1995). Disruptive technologies: Catching the wave. *Harvard Business Review, 73*(1), 43–53.

Boyd, N. G., & Vozikis, G. S. (1994). The influence of self-efficacy on the development of entrepreneurial intentions and actions. *Entrepreneurship Theory and Practice, 18*(4), 63–77.

Bray, F. (1997). *Technology and gender: Fabrics of power in late Imperial China.* Berkeley and Los Angeles, CA: University of California Press.

Brazeal, D. V., Schenkel, M. T., & Azriel, J. A. (2008). Awakening the entrepreneurial spirit: Exploring the relationship between organizational factors and perceptions of entrepreneurial self-efficacy and desirability in a corporate setting. *New England Journal of Entrepreneurship, 11*(1), 9–25.

Bray, F. (2007). Gender and technology. *Annual Review of Anthropology, 36,* 37–53.

Brenner, O. C., Tomkiewicz, J., & Schein, V. (1989). The relationship between gender role stereotypes and requisite management characteristics revisited. *Academy of Management Journal, 2,* 662–669.

Brinckerhoff, P. (2000). *Social entrepreneurship: The art of mission-based venture development.* New York, NY: John Wiley and Sons.

Brindley, C. (2005). Barriers to women achieving their entrepreneurial growth: Women and risk. *International Journal of Entrepreneurial Behaviour & Research, 11*(2), 144–161.

Bristor, J. M., & Fischer, E. (1993). Feminist thought: Implications for consumer research. *Journal of Consumer Research*, *19*(4), 518–536.

Brockhaus, R. H. (1980). Risk-taking propensity of entrepreneurs. *Academy of Management Journal*, *23*(3), 509–520.

Brooks, A., & Valentine, N. (2006). If Martha were a nurse. *Nurse Leader*, *4*(5), 47–58.

Bruni, A., Gherardi, S., & Poggio, B. (2004a). Doing gender, doing entrepreneurship: An ethnographic account of intertwined practices. *Gender, Work and Organization*, *11*(4), 406–429.

Bruni, A., Gherardi, S., & Poggio, B. (2004b). Entrepreneur-mentality, gender and the study of women entrepreneurs. *Journal of Organizational Change Management*, *17*(3), 256–268.

Bruni, A., Gherardi, S., & Poggio, B. (2005). *Gender and entrepreneurship: An ethnographical approach*. London: Routledge.

Brush, C. G. (1992). Research on women business owners: Past trends, a new perspective and future directions. *Entrepreneurship Theory and Practice*, *16*, 5–30.

Brush, C. G. (2008). Pioneering strategies for entrepreneurial success. *Business Horizons*, *51*, 21–27.

Brush, C. G., & Hisrich, R. D. (2000). *Women-owned businesses: An exploratory study comparing factors affecting performance*. Working Paper Series 00-02. Washington, DC: Research Institute for Small & Emerging Business, Inc.

Brush, C. G., Carter, N. M., Gatewood, E. J., Greene, P. G., & Hart, M. (2001). *The Diana Project: Women small business owners and equity capital: the myths dispelled*. Kansas City, MO: Kauffman Center for Entrepreneurial Leadership. Retrieved from http:// www.kauffman.org/pdf/Diana_project.pdf (accessed December 16, 2008).

Brush, C. G., Carter, N. M., Gatewood, E. J., Greene, P. G., & Hart, M. M. (2002a). *Gatekeepers of venture growth*. Kansas City, MO: Kauffman Foundation.

Brush, C. G., Carter, N. M., Gatewood, E., Greene, P. G., & Hart, M. M. (2002b). The Diana project: Women business owners & equity capital: the myths dispelled. *Venture Capital Review*, *10*, 30–40.

Brush, C., Carter, N., Gatewood, E., Greene, P., & Hart, M. (2003). *Gatekeepers of venture growth: A Diana Project report on the role and participation of women in the venture capital industry*. Kansas City, MO: Kauffman Foundation.

Brush, C. G., Carter, N. M., Gatewood, E., Greene, P. G., & Hart, M. M. (2004). *Clearing the hurdles: Women building high growth businesses*. Upper Saddle River, NJ: Prentice-Hall.

Brush, C. G., Carter, N. M., Gatewood, E., Greene, P. G., & Hart, M. M. (Eds) (2006a). *Growth-oriented women entrepreneurs and their businesses: A global research perspective*. London: Edward Elgar.

Brush, C. G., Carter, N., Gatewood, E., Greene, P. G., & Hart, M. (2006b). *Women entrepreneurs: Classics and new directions*. Cheltenham, UK: Edward F. Elgar Publishing.

Brush, C. G., Carter, N., Gatewood, E., Greene, P. G., & Hart, M. (2006c). Women's entrepreneurship in the United States. In C. Brush, N. Carter, E. Gatewood, P. Greene, & M. Hart (Eds.), *Growth-oriented women entrepreneurs and their businesses* (pp. 184–202). Cheltenham, UK: Edward F. Elgar Publishing.

Brush, C., Carter, N., Gatewood, E., Greene, P., & Hart, M. (2006d). The use of bootstrapping by women entrepreneurs in positioning for growth. *Venture Capital*, 8(15), 15–31.

Brush, C. G., de Bruin, A., & Welter, F. (2009). A gender-aware framework for women's entrepreneurship. *International Journal of Gender and Entrepreneurship*, 1(1), 8–24.

Brush, C., de Bruin, A., Gatewood, E., & Henry, C. (2010). Introduction: Women entrepreneurs and growth. In C. Brush, A. de Bruin, E. Gatewood, & C. Henry (Eds.), *Women entrepreneurs and the global environment for growth: A research perspective* (pp. 1–16). Cheltenham, UK: Edward Elgar Publishing Limited.

Bunker, W. K., & Smith-Doerr, L. (2005). Gender and commercial science: Women's patenting in the life sciences. *Journal of Technology Transfer*, 30, 355–370.

Burns, J.M. (1978). *Leadership*. New York, NY: Harper and Row.

Burns, P. (2001). *Entrepreneurship and small business*. Basingstoke, UK: Palgrave.

Burns, T., & Stalker, G. M. (1994). *The management of innovation*. New York, NY: Oxford University Press.

Burns, L., & Lafrance, M. (2001). *Disruptive Divas: Feminism, identity and popular music*. London, UK: Taylor & Francis.

Burt, R. S. (2001). Structural holes versus network closure as social capital. In N. Lin, K. Cook, & R. S. Burt (Eds.), *Social capital: Theory and research* (pp. 31–56). New York, NY: De Gruyter.

Burt, R. S., Hogarth, R. M., & Michaud, C. (2000). The social capital of French and American managers. *Organization Science*, 11(2), 123–147.

Butler, J. (1990). *Gender trouble: Feminism and the subversion of identity*. London, UK: Routledge.

Buttner, E. (2001). Examining female entrepreneurs' management style: An application of a relational frame. *Journal of Business Ethics*, 29(3), 253–269.

Buttner, E. H., & Rosen, B. (1989). Funding new business ventures: Are decision makers biased against women entrepreneurs? *Journal of Business Venturing*, 4(4), 249–261.

Buttner, E. H., & Moore, D. P. (1997). Women's organizational exodus to entrepreneurship: Self-reported motivations and correlates with success. *Journal of Small Business Management*, 35(1), 34–46.

Bygrave, W. D., & Hofer, C. (1991). Theorizing about entrepreneurship. *Entrepreneurship Theory & Practice*, 16(2), 13–22.

Byrnes, J., Miller, D., & Schafer, W. (1999). Gender differences in risk taking: A meta-analysis. *Psychological Bulletin*, 125, 367–383.

Cable, D. M., & Shane, S. (1997). A prisoner's dilemma approach to entrepreneur-venture capitalist relationships. *Academy of Management Review*, 22(1), 142–176.

Calas, M., & Smircich, L. (1992). Using the "F" word: Feminist theories and the social consequences of organizational research. In A. Mills & P. Tancred (Eds.), *Gendering organizational analysis* (pp. 222–234). Newbury Park, CA: Sage Publications.

Calás, M. B., Smircich L., & Bourne, K. A. (2009). Extending the boundaries: Reframing "entrepreneurship as social change" through feminist perspectives. *Academy of Management Review*, 34(3), 552–569.

Campbell, K. (2005). Quilting a feminist map to guide the study of women entrepreneurs. In D. Hjorth & C. Steyaert (Eds.), *Narrative and discursive approaches in entrepreneurship* (pp. 194–209). Cheltenham, UK: Edward Elgar.

Cann, A., & Siegfried, W. D. (1990). Gender stereotypes and dimensions of effective leadership behavior. *Sex Roles, 23*, 413–419.

Carland, J. C., & Carland J. W. (1992). Managers, small business owners and entrepreneurs: The cognitive dimension. *Journal of Business and Entrepreneurship, 4*(2), 55–67.

Carland, J. C., & Carland, J. W. (2000). New venture creation model. *Journal of Business and Entrepreneurship, 12*(3), 29–48.

Carland, J. W., Hoy, F., Boulton, W. R., & Carland, J. C. (1984). Differentiating entrepreneurs from small business owners: A conceptualization. *Academy of Management Review, 9*(3), 354–359.

Carland, J. W., Hoy, F., Boulton, W. R., & Carland, J. A. (1988). Distinctions between entrepreneurial and small business ventures. *International Journal of Management, 5*(1), 98–103.

Carland, J. A., Carland, J. W., Ensley, M. D., & Stewart, W. H. (1994). The implications of cognition and learning styles for management education. *The Journal of Management Learning, 25*(3), 413–431.

Carland, J. C., Carland, J. W., & Stewart, W. H. (1996). Seeing what's not there: The enigma of entrepreneurship. *Journal of Small Business Strategy, 7*(1), 1–20.

Carli, L. L., & Eagly, A. H. (1999). Gender effects on influence and emergent leadership. In G. N. Powell (Ed.), *Handbook of gender & work* (pp. 203–222). Thousand Oaks, CA: Sage Publications.

Carpenter, G., & Nakamoto, K. (1990). Competitive strategies for late entry into a market with a dominant brand. *Management Science, 36*, 1268–1278.

Carsrud, A., Brännback, M., Elfving, J., & Brandt, K. (2009). Motivations: The entrepreneurial mind and behaviour. In A. Carsrud & M. Brännback (Eds.), *Understanding the entrepreneurial mind: Opening the black box* (pp. 141–166). Heidelberg: Springer.

Carter, N. M. (2003). The career reasons of nascent entrepreneurs. *Journal of Business Venturing, 18*(1), 13–39.

Carter, S. (1989). The dynamics of performance of female-owned entrepreneurial firms in London, Glasgow and Nottingham. *Journal of Organizational Change Management, 2*(3), 54–64.

Carter, S. (2000). Gender and enterprise. In S. Carter, & D. Jones-Evans (Eds.), *Enterprise and small business: Principles, practice and policy* (pp. 166–181). London, UK: Prentice-Hall.

Carter, S., & Cannon, T. (1992). *Women as entrepreneurs*. San Diego, CA: Academic Press Ltd.

Carter, N. M., & Allen, K. R. (1997). Size determinants of women owned SMEs: Choice or barriers to resources? *Entrepreneurship & Regional Development, 9*(3), 211–220.

Carter, S., & Rosa, P. (1998). The financing of male- and female-owned businesses. *Entrepreneurship and Regional Development, 10*, 225–241.

Carter, N. M., Williams, M., & Reynolds, P. D. (1997). Discontinuance among new firms in retail: The influence of initial resources, strategy and gender. *Journal of Business Venturing, 12*(2), 125–145.

Carter, S., Anderson, S., & Shaw, E. (2001). *Women's business ownership: A review of the academic, popular and internet literature: report to the Small Business Service, RR002/01*. London, UK: Small Business Service.

Carter, N. M., Brush, C. G., Greene, P. G., Gatewood, E., & Hart, M. M. (2003). Women entrepreneurs who break through to equity financing: The influence of human, social, and financial capital. *Venture Capital, 5*(1), 1–28.

Carter, N. M., Gartner, W. B., Shaver, K. G., Gatewood, E. J. (2003). The career reasons of nascent entrepreneurs. *Journal of Business Venturing, 18*(1): 13–39.

Carter, N. M., Gartner, W. B., & Shaver, K. G. (2004). Career reasons. In W. B. Gartner, K. G. Shaver, N. M. Carter, & P. D. Reynolds (Eds.), *Handbook of entrepreneurial dynamics: The process of business creation* (pp. 142–152). Thousand Oaks, CA: Sage Publications.

Carter, S., Shaw, E., Lam, W., & Wilson, F. (2007). Gender, entrepreneurship, and bank lending: The criteria and process used by bank loan officers in assessing allocations. *Entrepreneurship Theory and Practice, 31*(3), 427–444.

Castrogiovanni, G., Combs, J., & Justis, R. (2006). Resource scarcity and agency theory predictions concerning the continued use of franchising in multi-outlet networks. *Journal of Small Business Management, 44*(1), 27–44.

Cavalluzzo, K. S., & Cavalluzzo, L. C. (1998). Market structure and discrimination: The case of small businesses. *Journal of Money, Credit & Banking, 30*(4), 771–792.

Cavalluzzo, K. S., Cavalluzzo, L. C., & Wolken, J. D. (2002). Competition, small business financing, and discrimination: Evidence from a new survey. *Journal of Business, 75*(4), 641–679.

Chaganti, R. (1986). Management in women-owned enterprises. *Journal of Small Business Management, 24*(4), 19–29.

Chaganti, R., & Parasuraman, S. (1996). A study of the impacts of gender on business performance and management patterns in small businesses. *Entrepreneurship Theory & Practice, 21*(1), 73–89.

Chandler, G., Lyon, D., & DeTienne, D. (2005). *Antecedents and exploitation outcomes of opportunity identification processes.* Presented at the National Academy of Management Best Paper Proceedings. Honolulu, HI.

Charumathi, B. (1998). Women entrepreneur's challenges and prospects. In C. Swarajya Lakshmi (Ed.), *Development of women entrepreneurship in India: problems and prospects*. New Delhi, India: Discovery Publishing House.

Chen, M. H. (2007). Entrepreneurial leadership and new ventures: Creativity in entrepreneurial teams. *Creativity and Innovation Management, 16*(3), 239–249.

Chrisman, J. J., Carsrud, A. L., DeCastro, J., & Heron, L. (1990). A comparison of assistance needs of male and female pre-venture entrepreneurs. *Journal of Business Venturing, 5*(4), 235–248.

Churchill, N. C., & Lewis, V. L. (1983). The five stages of small business growth. *Harvard Business Review, 61*(3), 30–39.

Churchill, N., & Lewis, V. (1991). The five stages of small business growth. In W. Sahlman & H. Stevenson (Eds.), *The entrepreneurial venture* (pp. 263–276). Boston, MA: Harvard Business School.

Cliff, J. E. (1998). Does one size fit all? Exploring the relationship between attitudes towards growth, gender and business size. *Journal of Business Venturing, 13*(6), 523–542.

Cohen, D., & Prusak, L. (2001). *In good company: How social capital makes organizations work*. Cambridge, MA: Harvard Business School Press.

Cockburn, C., & Ormrod, S. (1993). *Gender and technology in the making*. London, UK: Sage Publications.

Coleman, J. S. (1988). Social capital in the creation of human capital. *The American Journal of Sociology*: Supplement, Organizations and institutions: Sociological and economic approaches to the analysis of social structure, *94*, 95–120.

Coleman, S. (2000). Access to capital and terms of credit. A comparison of men- and women-owned small businesses. *Journal of Small Business Management*, *30*(3), 37–52.

Coleman, S. (2002a). Characteristics and borrowing behavior of small, women-owned firms: Evidence from the 1998 survey of small business finances. *Journal of Business and Entrepreneurship*, *14* (2), 151–166.

Coleman, S. (2002b). Constraints faced by women small business owners: Evidence from the data. *Journal of Developmental Entrepreneurship*, *7*(2), 151–174.

Coleman, S., & Carsky, M. (1996). Financing small businesses: Strategies employed by women entrepreneurs. *The Journal of Applied Management and Entrepreneurship*, *3*(1), 28–42.

Coleman, S., & Robb, A. (2009). A comparison of new firm financing by gender: Evidence from the Kauffman firm survey data (February 20, 2009). Retrieved from http://ssrn.com/abstract=1260980

Colombo, M. G., & Piva, E. (2008). Strengths and weaknesses of academic start-ups: A conceptual model. *IEEE Transactions on Engineering Management*, *55*(1), 37–49.

Commission of the European Communities (2001). Annual report on equal opportunities for women and men in the European Union 2000. *Report from the Commission to the Council, The European Parliament, the Economic and Social Committee and the Committee of the Regions*. Brussels, Belgium: Commission of the European Communities.

Conger, J. A., & Kanungo, R. N. (1998). *Charismatic leadership in organizations*. Thousand Oaks, CA: Sage Publications.

Conner, K. R., & Prahalad, C. K. (1996). A resource-based theory of the firm: knowledge versus opportunism. *Organization Science*, *7*(5), 477–501.

Constantinidis, C., Cornet, A., & Asandei, S. (2006). Financing of women-owned ventures: The impact of gender and other owner- and firm-related variables. *Venture Capital*, *8*(2), 133–157.

Coplon, J. (1999). *The first time*. New York, NY: Pocket Books.

Coviello, N., & Jones, M. (2004). Methodological issues in international entrepreneurship research. *Journal of Business Venturing*, *19*(4), 485–508.

Covin, J. G., & Slevin, D. P. (1991). A conceptual model of entrepreneurship as firm behavior. *Entrepreneurship Theory and Practice*, *16*, 7–25.

Covin, T. J. (1994). Perceptions of family-owned firms: The impact of gender and educational level. *Journal of Small Business Management*, *32*(3), 29–39.

Csikszentmihalyi, M. (1996). *Creativity, flow and the psychology of discovery and invention*. New York, NY: Harper Collins.

Davidsson, P., & Honig, B. (2003). The role of social and human capital among nascent entrepreneurs. *Journal of Business Venturing*, *18*, 301–331.

Davis, G. (1989). Testing for creative potential. *Contemporary Educational Psychology*, *14*, 257–274.

De Bruin, A., Brush, C. G., & Welter, F. (2006). Introduction to the special issue: Towards building cumulative knowledge on women's entrepreneurship. *Entrepreneurship Theory and Practice*, *30*(5), 585–593.

De Bruin, A., Brush, C., & Welter, F. (2007). Advancing a framework for coherent research on women's entrepreneurship. *Entrepreneurship Theory and Practice*, *31*(3), 323–340.

Decarolis, D., & Deeds, D. L. (1999). The impact of stocks and flows of organizational knowledge on firm performance: An empirical investigation of the biotechnology industry. *Strategic Management Journal*, *20*, 953–968.

Dees, J., Emerson, J., & Economy, P. (2001). *Enterprising nonprofits: A toolkit for social entrepreneurs*. New York, NY: John Wiley and Sons.

DeFillippi, R. J., & Arthur, M. B. (1994). The boundaryless career: A competency-based perspective. *Journal of Organizational Behaviour*, *15*, 307–324.

Degryse, H., & van Cayseele, P. (2000). Relationship lending within a bank-based system: Evidence from European small business data. *Journal of Financial Intermediation*, *9*(1), 90–109.

Delmar, F., & Shane, S. (2002). What founders do: A longitudinal study of the start-up process. In W. D. Bygrave, E. Autio, C. G. Brush, P. Davidsson, P. G. Green, P. D. Reynolds, & H. J. Sapienza (Eds.), *Frontiers of entrepreneurship research* (pp. 632–645). Wellesley, MA: Babson College.

Delmar, F., & Wiklund, J. (2008). The effect of small business managers' growth motivation on firm growth: A longitudinal study. *Entrepreneurship Theory and Practice*, *32*(3), 437–457.

DeMartino, R., & Barbato, R. (2003). Differences between women and men MBA entrepreneurs: exploring family flexibility and wealth creation as career motivators. *Journal of Business Venturing*, *18*, 815–832.

Di Domenico, M., Haugh, H., & Tracey, P. (2010). Social bricolage: Theorizing social value creation in social enterprises. *Entrepreneurship Theory and Practice*, *34*(4), 681–703.

DeTienne, D., & Chandler, G. (2007). The role of human capital and gender in opportunity identification. *Entrepreneurship Theory and Practice*, *31*(3), 365–386.

Dillman, D. A. (2000). *Mail and internet surveys: The tailored design method*. New York, NY: Wiley.

Ding, W. W., Murray, F., & Stuart, T. E. (2006). Gender differences in patenting in the academic life sciences. *Science*, *313*, 665–667.

Ding, W. W., Murray, F., & Stuart, T. E. (2010). *From bench to board: Gender differences in university scientists' participation in commercial science*. Harvard Business School, Working Paper 11-014. Retrieved from http://www.hbs.edu/research/pdf/11-014.pdf

Dirks, K. T., & Ferrin, D. I. (2002). Trust in leadership: Meta-analytic findings and implications for research and practice. *Journal of Applied Psychology*, *87*, 611–628.

Domeisen, N. (2003). Canada releases report on women entrepreneurs. International Trade Centre, International Trade Forum. *Economics*, *28*, 239–255. Retrieved from http://www.liberal.parl.gc.ca/entrepreneur

Donckels, R., & Lambrecht, J. (1995). Networks and small business growth: An explanatory model. *Small Business Economics*, 7(4), 273–289.

Drucker, P. (1985). *Entrepreneurship and innovation: Practice and principles.* New York, NY: Harper Business.

Drucker, P. (2002). *Managing in the next society.* New York, NY: St. Martin's Press.

Dudek, S. Z., Strobel, M. G., & Runco, M. A. (1993). Cumulative and proximal influences of the social environment and children's creative potential. *Journal of Genetic Psychology*, 154(4), 487–500.

Dumas, C. (2001). Evaluating the outcomes of micro-enterprise training for low income women: A case study. *Journal of Developmental Entrepreneurship*, 6(2), 97–128.

Du Reitz, A., & Henrekson, M. (2000). Testing the female underperformance hypothesis. *Small Business Economics*, 14, 1–10.

Dyer, W. G., & Whetten, D. A. (2006). Family firms and social responsibility: Preliminary evidence from the S&P 500. *Entrepreneurship Theory and Practice*, 30(6), 785–802.

Eagly, A. H. (1987). *Sex differences in social behavior: A social-role interpretation.* Hillsdale, NJ: Erlbaum.

Eagly, A. H., & Johnson, B. T. (1990). Gender and leadership style: A meta-analysis. *Psychological Bulletin*, 108, 233–256.

Eagly, A. H., Karau, S. J., & Makhijani, M. G. (1995). Gender and the effectiveness of leaders: A meta-analysis. *Psychological Bulletin*, 117, 125–145.

Eagley, A. H., Johannesen-Schmidt, M. C., & van Engen, M. (2003). Transformational, transactional, and laissez-faire leadership styles: A meta-analysis comparing women and men. *Psychological Bulletin*, 129, 569–591.

Eckhardt, J., & Ciuchta, M. (2008). Selected variation: The population-level implications of multistage selection in entrepreneurship. *Strategic Entrepreneurship Journal*, 2(3), 209–224.

Edwards, J. R., & Rothbard, N. P. (2000). Mechanisms linking work and family: Clarifying the relationship between work and family constructs. *Academy of Management Review*, 25(1), 178–199.

Eggers, J. H., & Smilor, R. W. (1996). Leadership skills of entrepreneurs: Resolving paradoxes and enhancing the practices of entrepreneurial growth. In R.W. Smilor & D.L. Sexton (Eds.), *Leadership and entrepreneurship.* Westport, CT: Quorum Books.

Eisenhardt, K. M., & Martin, J. A. (2000). Dynamic capabilities: What are they? *Strategic Management Journal*, 21, 1105–1121.

Elam, A. B. (2008). *Gender and entrepreneurship: A multilevel theory and analysis.* Cheltenham, UK & Northampton, MA: Edward Elgar Publishing.

Etzkowitz, H., Kemelgor, C., & Uzzi, B. (2000). *Athena unbound: The advancement of women in science and technology.* Cambridge, MA: Cambridge University Press.

European Commission (2009). *Statistics and indicators on gender equality in science.* Retrieved from http://ec.europa.eu/research/science-society/document_library/pdf_06/she_figures_2009_en.pdf (accessed June 1, 2010).

Evald, M., Klyver, K., & Svendsen, S. (2006). The changing importance of the strength of ties throughout the entrepreneurial process. *Journal of Enterprising Culture*, 14(1), 1–26.

Fabowale, L., Orser, B., & Riding, A. (1995). Gender, structural factors, and credit terms between Canadian small businesses and financial institutions. *Entrepreneurship Theory and Practice, 19*(4), 41–65.

Fagenson, E. A. (1993). Personal value systems of men and women entrepreneurs versus managers. *Journal of Business Venturing, 8*, 409–430.

Fagenson, E. A., & Marcus, E. A. (1991). Perceptions of the sex-role stereotypic characteristics of entrepreneurs: Women's evaluations. *Entrepreneurship Theory and Practice, 15*(4), 33–47.

Fagenson-Eland, E., & Baugh, G. (2000). Career paths, networking, and mentoring. In D. Smith (Ed.), *Women at work—leadership for the next century* (pp. 145–161). Englewood Cliffs, NJ: Prentice Hall.

Fairlie, R. W. (2004). *Self-employed business ownership rates in the United States: 1979–2003.* U.S. Small Business Administration, Office of Advocacy, SBAHQ-04-M-0248.

Feingold, A. (1988). Cognitive gender differences are disappearing. *American Psychologist, 43*(2), 95–103.

Felstead, A., & Jewson, N. (2000). *In work, at home: Towards an understanding of homeworking.* London, UK: Routledge.

Festinger, L. (1957). *Theory of cognitive dissonance.* Stanford, CA: Stanford University Press.

Filion, L. J. (1989). Le développement d'une vision: un outil stratégique à maîtriser. *Gestion, 14*(3), 24–34.

Filion, L. J. (1990). L'intrapreneur: un visionnant. *Revue internationale des petites et moyennes organisations, PMO, 5*(1), 22–33.

Filion, L. J. (1991). Vision and relations: Elements for an entrepreneurial metamodel. *International Small Business Journal, 9*(2), 26–40.

Filion, L. J. (2004). D'employés à intrapreneurs. *Organisations et territoires, 13*(1), 21–32.

Filion, L. J. (2005). *Pour une vision inspirante en milieu scolaire* (2nd ed.). Québec, Canada: Les Presses Inter Universitaires.

Filion, L. J., & Ananou, C. (2010). *De l'intuition au projet d'entreprise.* Montréal, Canada: Transcontinental.

Fischer, E., & Reuber, A. R. (2011). Social interaction via new social media: How can interactions on Twitter affect effectual thinking and behavior? *Journal of Business Venturing, 26*(1), 1–18.

Fischer, E. M., Reuber, A. R., & Dyke, L. S. (1993). A theoretical overview and extension of research on sex, gender and entrepreneurship. *Journal of Business Venturing, 8*(2), 151–168.

Fleishman, E. A. (1973). Twenty years of consideration and structure. In E. A. Fleishman & J. G. Hunt (Eds.), *Current developments in the study of leadership* (pp. 1–40). Carbondale, IL: Southern Illinois University Press.

Forbes, D. P., Borchert, P. S., Zellmer-Bruhn, M. E., & Sapienza, H. J. (2006). Entrepreneurial team formation: An exploration of new member addition. *Entrepreneurship Theory and Practice, 30*(2), 225–248.

Foxall, G. R., & Hackett, P. M. W. (1994). Styles of managerial creativity: A comparison of adaption-innovation in the United Kingdom, Australia and the United States. *British Journal of Management, 5*, 85–100.

Franco, A., & Winqvist, K. (2002). *The entrepreneurial gap between women and men: Statistics in focus.* Brussels, Belgium: Eurostat.

Freud, S. (1976). *The complete psychological works of Sigmund Freud: The standard edition*. New York, NY: W.W. Norton & Co.

Frietsch, R., Haller, I., Funken-Vrohlings, M., & Grupp, H. (2009). Gender-specific patterns in patenting and publishing. *Research Policy*, *38*, 590–599.

Frone, M. R. (2003). Work-family balance. In J. C. Quick & L. E. Tetrick (Eds.), *Handbook of occupational health psychology* (pp. 143–162). Washington, DC: American Psychological Association.

Gannon, M. J. (1994). *Understanding global cultures: Metaphorical journeys through 17 countries*. Thousand Oaks, CA: Sage Publications.

Gartner, W. B. (1985). A conceptual framework for describing the phenomenon of new venture creation. *Academy of Management Review*, *10*(4), 696–706.

Gartner, W. (1988). "Who is an entrepreneur?" is the wrong question. *American Journal of Small Business*, *12*(4), 11–32.

Gartner, W. B., Shaver, K. G., Gatewood, E., & Katz, J. A. (1994). Finding the entrepreneur in entrepreneurship. *Entrepreneurship Theory and Practice*, *18*(3), 5–10.

Gatewood, E. J., Shaver, K. G., & Gartner, W. B. (1995). A longitudinal study of cognitive factors influencing start-up behaviors and success at venture creation. *Journal of Business Venturing*, *10*(5), 371–391.

Gatewood, E., Brush, C. G., Carter, N. M., Greene, P. G., & Hart, M. M. (2009). Diana: A symbol of women entrepreneurs' hunt for knowledge, money, and the rewards of entrepreneurship. *Small Business Economics*, *32*(2), 129–144.

George, J. M. (2000). Emotions and leadership: The role of emotional intelligence. *Human Relations*, *53*, 1027–1055.

Gerth, H. H., & Mills C. W. (1958). *From Max Weber: Essays in sociology*. New York, NY: Oxford University Press.

Gibb, A., & Davies, L. (1990). In pursuit of frameworks for the development of growth models of the small business. *International Small Business Journal*, *9*(1), 15–32.

Gillani, W. (2004). No policy framework to address women entrepreneurs. *Daily Times*. Retrieved 16 July, from http://www.dailytimes.com.pk

Granovetter, M. (1973). The strength of weak ties. *American Journal of Sociology*, *78*, 1360–1380.

Granovetter, M. (1983). The strength of weak ties: A network theory revisited. *Sociological Theory*, *1*(1), 201–233.

Grant, J. (1988). Women as managers: What can they offer to organizations? *Organizational Dynamics*, *16*(3), 56–63.

Greene, P. G., Brush, C. G., Hart, M. M., & Saparito, P. (2001). Patterns of venture capital funding: Is gender a factor? *Venture Capital*, *3*(1), 63–83.

Greene, P. G., Brush, C. G., & Gatewood, E. (2006). Perspectives on women entrepreneurs: Past findings and new directions in entrepreneurship. In M. Minniti (Ed.), *The engine of growth—Perspective Series* (Vol. 1). Westport, CT and London, UK: Praeger Publisher—Greenwood Publishing Group.

Greenhaus, J., & Beutell, N. (1985). Sources of conflict between work and family roles. *Academy of Management Review*, *10*, 76–88.

Greenhaus, J., & Powell, G. N. (2006). When work and families are allies: A theory of work-family enrichment. *Academy of Management Review*, *31*(1), 72–92.

Gundry, L., & Kickul, J. (1994). Building the creative organization. *Organizational Dynamics*, 22, 22–37.

Greve, A., & Salaff, J. (2003). Social networks and entrepreneurship. *Entrepreneurship Theory and Practice*, 28, 1–22.

Gundry, L. K., & Welsch, H. P. (2001). The ambitious entrepreneur: High growth strategies of women-owned enterprises. *Journal of Business Venturing*, 16(5), 453–470.

Gundry, L. K., Ben-Yoseph, M., & Posig, M. (2002). The status of women's entrepreneurship: Pathways to future entrepreneurship and development. *New England Journal of Entrepreneurship*, 5(1), 39–50.

Gupta, V. K., Turban, D. B., Wasti, S. A., & Sikdar, A. (2009). The role of gender stereotypes in perceptions of entrepreneurs and intentions to become an entrepreneur. *Entrepreneurship, Theory and Practice*, 33, 397–417.

Hackman, M. Z., Furniss, A. H., Hills, M. J., & Paterson, T. J. (1992). Perceptions of gender-role characteristics and transformational and transactional leadership behaviors. *Perceptual and Motor Skills*, 75, 311–319.

Haines, G., Orser, B., & Riding, A. (1999). Myths and realities: An empirical study of banks and the gender of small business clients. *Canadian Journal of Administrative Science*, 16(4), 291–307.

Hall, D. T. (1996). *The career is dead—long live the career*. San Francisco, CA: Jossey-Bass.

Hall, D. T. (2004). The protean career: A quarter century journey. *Journal of Vocational Behavior*, 65(1), 1–13.

Hall, J. A. (1985). Male and female nonverbal behavior. In A. W. Siegman & S. Feldstein (Eds.), *Multichannel integrations of nonverbal behavior* (pp. 195–225). Hillsdale, NJ: Erlbaum.

Hall, J. A. (1998). How big are nonverbal sex differences? The case of smiling and sensitivity to nonverbal cues. In D. J. Canary & K. Dindia (Eds.), *Sex differences and similarities in communication: Critical essays and empirical investigations of sex and gender in interaction* (pp. 155–177). Mahwah, NJ: Erlbaum.

Hamel, G. (1998). Strategy innovation and the quest for value. *Sloan Management Review*, 39(2), 7–14.

Hammond, M. M. (2007). *The Diva Principle: Secrets to divine inspiration for victorious attitude*. Eugene, OR: Harvest House Hill.

Hanks, S., Watson, C., Jansen, E., & Chandler, G. (1993). Tightening the life cycle construct: A taxonomic study of growth stage configurations in high-technology organizations. *Entrepreneurship Theory and Practice*, 18(2), 5–29.

Haraway, D. J. (1989). *Primate visions: Gender, race, and nature in the world of modern science*. New York, NY and London, UK: Routledge.

Haraway, D. J. (1997). *Feminism and technoscience*. New York, NY and London, UK: Routledge.

Harding, S. (1987). Is there a feminist method? In S. Harding (Ed.), *Feminism and methodology* (Introduction). Milton Keynes: Open University Press.

Harper, D. (2007). *Foundations of entrepreneurship and economic development*. London and New York: Routledge.

Harris, R., & Trainor, M. (1995). Innovations and R&D in Northern Ireland manufacturing: A Schumpeterian approach. *Regional Studies*, 29(7), 593–604.

Haugh, H. (2005). A research agenda for social entrepreneurship. *Social Enterprise Journal*, 1(1), 1–12.

Haynes, G. W., & Haynes, D. C. (1999). The debt structure of small business owned by women in 1987 and 1993. *Journal of Small Business Management*, 37(2), 1–19.

Hayton, J. C. (2005). Promoting corporate entrepreneurship through human resource management practices: A review of empirical research. *Human Resource Management Review*, 15(1), 21–41.

He, Z. L., & Wong, P. K. (2004). Exploration vs. exploitation: An empirical test of the ambidexterity hypothesis. *Organization Science*, 15(4), 481–494.

Hechavarria, D. M., & Reynolds, P. D. (2009). Cultural norms & business start-ups: The impact of national values on opportunity and necessity entrepreneurs. *International Entrepreneurship and Management Journal*, 5(4), 417–437.

Helfat, C. (1997). Know-how and asset complementarity and dynamic capability accumulation: The case of R&D. *Strategic Management Journal*, 18, 339–360.

Helfat, C. E., & Raubitscek, R. S. (2000). Product sequencing: Co-evolution of knowledge, capabilities and products. *Strategic Management Journal*, 21, 961–979.

Helfat, C. E., & Peteraf, M. A. (2003). The dynamic resource-based view. *Strategic Management Journal*, 24, 997–1010.

Helfat, C., Finkelstein, S., Mitchell, W., Peteraf, M. A., Singh, H., Teece, D. J., Winter, S. (2007a). *Dynamic capabilities: Understanding strategic change in organizations*. Oxford, UK: Blackwell.

Helfat, C. E., Finkelstein, S., Mitchell, W., Peteraf, M. A., Singh, H., Teece, D. J., & Winter, S. G. (2007b). Dynamic capabilities: Foundations. In C. E. Helfat, S. Finkelstein, W. Mitchell, M. A. Peteraf, H. Singh, D. J. Teece, & S. G. Winter (Eds.), *Dynamic capabilities: Understanding strategic change in organizations* (pp. 1–18). Malden, MA: Blackwell Publishing.

Helgeson, S. (1990). *The female advantage: Women's ways of leading*. New York, NY: Doubleday.

Hemphill, J. K., & Coons, A. E. (1957). Development of the Leader Behavior Description Questionnaire. In R. M. Stogdill & A. E. Coons (Eds.), *Leader behavior: Its description and measurement* (pp. 6–38). Columbus, OH: Ohio State University, Bureau of Business Research.

Henderson, R. M., & Clark, K. B. (1990). Architectural innovation: The reconfiguration of existing product technologies and the failure of established firms. *Administrative Science Quarterly*, 35, 9–30.

Henderson, R., & Robertson, M. (2000). Who wants to be an entrepreneur? Young adult attitudes to entrepreneurship as a career. *Career Development International*, 5(6), 279–287.

Henry, C., Hill, F., & Leitch, C. (2005). Entrepreneurship education and training: Can entrepreneurship be taught? *Journal of Education and Training*, 47(2), 98–111.

Hessels, J., van Gelderen, M., & Thurik, R. (2008). Entrepreneurial aspirations, motivations, and their drivers. *Small Business Economics*, 31(3), 323–339.

Hewlett, S. A. (2002). Executive women and the myth of having it all. *Harvard Business Review*, 80(4), 66–73.

Hewlett, S. A., & Luce, C. B. (2005). Off-ramps and on-ramps: Keeping talented women on the road to success. *Harvard Business Review*, 83(3), 43–54.

Hiebert, D., & Ley, D. (2003). Assimilation, cultural pluralism and social exclusion among ethnocultural groups in Vancouver. *Urban Geography*, 24(1), 16–44.

Hisrich, R. (1989). Women entrepreneurs: Problems and prescriptions for success in the future. In O. Hagan, C. Rivchun, & D. Sexton (Eds.), *Women-owned businesses* (pp. 3–32). New York, NY: Praeger.

Hisrich, R., & Brush, C. (1983). The women entrepreneur: Implications for family education and occupational experience. In J. A. Hornaday, J. A. Timmons, & K. H. Vesper (Eds.), *Frontiers of entrepreneurship research* (pp. 255–270). Wellesley, MA: Babson College.

Hisrich, R. D., & Brush, C. (1984). The woman entrepreneur: Management skills and business problems. *Journal of Small Business Management, 22*(1), 30–37.

Hisrich, R., & Brush, C. (1987). Women entrepreneurs, a longitudinal study. In N. D. Churchill, J. A. Hornaday, B. A. Kirchhoff, O. J. Krashner, & K. H. Vesper (Eds.), *Frontiers of entrepreneurship research* (pp. 187–199). Wellesley, MA: Babson College.

Hisrich, R., & Özturk, S. (1999). Women entrepreneurs in a developing economy. *Journal of Management Development, 18*(2), 114–124.

Hitt, M. A., & Ireland, R. D. (2002). The essence of strategic leadership: Managing human and social capital. *Journal of Leadership and Organizational Studies, 9*, 3–14.

Hitt, M. A., Bierman, L., Shimizu, K., & Kochhar, R. (2001). Direct and moderating effects of human capital on strategy and performance in professional service firms: A resource-based perspective. *Academy of Management Journal, 44*, 13–28.

Hitt, M. A., Clifford, P. G., Nixon, R. D., & Coyne, K. P. (1999). *Dynamic strategic resources: Development, diffusion & integration.* Chichester, UK: John Wiley & Sons.

Hitt, M. A., & Ireland, R. D. (2000). The intersection of entrepreneurship and strategic management research. In D. L. Sexton & H. Landstrom (Eds.), *Handbook of entrepreneurship* (pp. 45–63). Oxford: Blackwell Publishers.

Hodgetts, R., & Kuratko, D. (1995). *Effective small business management* (5th ed.). (pp. 32 and 56–60). Fort Worth, TX: The Dryden Press.

Hofstede, G. H. (1980). *Culture consequences: International differences in work-related values.* London, UK: Sage Publications.

Hofstede, G. H. (1991). *Cultures and organizations: Software of the mind.* London, UK: McGraw-Hill.

Hofstede, G. H., and Bond, M. H. (1988). The Confucian connection: From cultural roots to economic growth. *Organizational Dynamics, 16*(4), 4–21.

Hofstede, G., Noorderhaven, N. G., Thurik, A. R., Uhlaner, L. M., Wennekers, A. R. M., & Wildeman, R. E. (2004). Culture's role in entrepreneurship: Self-employment out of dissatisfaction. In T. E. Brown & J. Ulijn (Eds.), *Innovation, entrepreneurship and culture* (pp. 162–203). Cheltenham, UK: Edward F. Elgar Publishing.

Hofstede, G., Hofstede, G. J., & Minkov, M. (2010). *Cultures and organizations: Software of the mind* (3rd ed.). New York: McGraw-Hill.

Holliday, R., & Letherby, G. (1993). Happy families or poor relations? An exploration of familial analogies in the small firm. *International Small Business Journal, 11*(2), 54–63.

Holmquist, C., & Sundin, E. (1990). What's special about highly educated women entrepreneurs? *Entrepreneurship and Regional Development, 2*(1), 181–193.

Hoopes, D. G., & Postrel, S. (1999). Shared knowledge, "clitches" and product development performance. *Strategic Management Journal, 20*, 837–865.

Howell, J. M., & Higgins, C. A. (1990). Champions of technological innovation. *Administrative Science Quarterly, 35*, 317–341.

Hoy, F., McDougall, P., & Dsouza, D. (1992). Strategies and environments of high growth firms. In D. Sexton & J. Kasarda (Eds.), *The state of the art of entrepreneurship* (pp. 341–357). Boston, MA: PWS-Kent Publishing.

Hsu, D. H., Roberts, E. B., & Eesley, C. E. (2007). Entrepreneurs from technology-based companies: Evidence from MIT. *Research Policy, 36*(5), 768–788.

Hudgens, G. A., & Fatkin, L. T. (1985). Sex differences in risk taking: Repeated sessions on a computer simulated task. *Journal of Psychology, 119*(3), 197–206.

Hughes, A., & Storey, D. J. (1994). *Finance and the small firm*. London, UK and New York, NY: Routledge.

Hutchinson, L. R., & Skinner, N. F. (2007). Self-awareness and cognitive style: Relationships among adaption-innovation, self-monitoring, and self-consciousness. *Social Behavior and Personality, 35*(4), 551–560.

Ibarra, H., Kilduff, M., & Tsai, W. (2005). Zooming in and out: Connecting individuals and collectivities at the frontier. *Organization Science, 16*(4), 359–371.

Ingham, J. N. (1983). *Biographical dictionary of American business leaders*. Westport, CT: Greenwood Press.

Ireland, R. D., Hitt M. A., & Sirmon, D. G. (2003). A model of strategic entrepreneurship: The construct and its dimensions. *Journal of Management, 29*(6), 963–989.

Izyumov, A., & Razumnova, I. (2000). Women entrepreneurs in Russia: Learning to survive the market. *Journal of Developmental Entrepreneurship, 5*, 1–19.

Jacobs, J. A., & Winslow, S. E. (2004). The academic life course, time pressures and gender inequality. *Community, Work and Family, 7*, 143–161.

Jain, S., George, G., & Maltarich, M. (2009). Academic entrepreneurs: Investigating role identity modification of university scientists involved in commercial activity. *Research Policy, 38*(6), 922–935.

Jennings, D. (1994). *Multiple perspectives of entrepreneurship*. Cincinnati, OH: South-Western Publishing Company.

Jianakoplos, N., & Bernasek, A. (1998). Are women more risk averse? *Economic Inquiry, 36*, 620–630.

Johannisson, B., Ramírez-Pasillas, M., & Karlsson, G. (2002). The institutional embeddedness of local inter-firm networks: A leverage for business creation. *Entrepreneurship & Regional Development, 14*(4), 297–315.

Johnson, G., & Scholes, K. (2002). *Exploring corporate strategy*. London, UK: Financial Times-Prentice Hall.

Johnson, J., & Powell, P. (1994). Decision making, risk and gender: Are managers different? *British Journal of Management, 5*, 123–138.

Johnson, S., & Storey, D. J. (1993). Male and female entrepreneurs and their businesses. In S. Allen & C. Truman (Eds.), *Women in business: Perspectives on women entrepreneurs* (pp. 70–85). London, UK and New York, NY: Routledge.

Jones, C., & DeFillippi, R. (1996). Back to the future in film: Combining industry and self knowledge to meet the career challenges of the 21st Century. *Academy of Management Executive, 10*(4), 89–104.

Joyce, T., & Stivers, B. P. (1999). Knowledge and innovation: A classification of US and Canadian firms. *International Journal of Technology Management, 18,* 500–509.

Justis, R. T., & Judd, R. J. (2004). *Franchising.* Cincinnati, OH: Thomson Learning.

Kalleberg, A. L., & Leicht, K. T. (1991). Gender and organizational performance: Determinants of small business survival and success. *Academy of Management Journal, 34*(1), 136–161.

Kangasharju, A. (2000). Growth of the smallest: Determinants of small firm growth during strong macroeconomic fluctuations. *International Small Business Journal, 19*(1), 28–43.

Kanter, R. M. (1989). Swimming in newstreams: Mastering innovation dilemmas. *California Management Review, 31*(4), 45–69.

Kao, J. (1991). *Managing creativity.* Englewood Cliffs, NJ: Prentice-Hall.

Kariv, D. (2008). Managerial performance and business success: Gender differences in Canadian and Israeli entrepreneurs. *The Journal of Enterprising Communities: People and Places in the Global Economy (JEC), 2*(4), 300–331.

Kariv, D. (2010a). Profiling women business founders from opportunity and necessity orientations: A multi-national assessment. *International Journal of Transitions and Innovation Systems (IJTIS), 1*(1), 59–82.

Kariv, D. (2010b). The role of management strategies in business performance: Men and women entrepreneurs managing creativity and innovation. *International Journal of Entrepreneurship and Small Business, 9*(3), 243–264.

Kariv, D., Menzies, T., Brenner, G., & Filion, L. J. (2009). Ethnic entrepreneurs in Canada: Transnational networking and business success. *Entrepreneurship and Regional Development, 21*(3), 239–264.

Karp, H., Fuller, C., & Sirias, D. (2002). *Bridging the boomer-Xer gap.* Palo Alto, CA: Davies-Black.

Katila R., & Shane, S. (2005). When does lack of resources make new firms innovative? *Academy of Management Journal, 48*(5), 814–829.

Katz, J. A. (2003). The chronology and intellectual trajectory of American entrepreneurship education 1876–1999. *Journal of Business Venturing, 18,* 283–300.

Katz, D., & Kahn, R. L. (1978). *The social psychology of organizations* (2nd ed.). New York, NY: Wiley.

Katz, J. A., & Gartner, W. B. (1988). Properties of emerging organization. *Academy of Management Review, 13*(3), 429–441.

Kaufman, J. C. (2006). Self-reported differences in creativity by ethnicity and gender. *Applied Cognitive Psychology, 20,* 1065–1082.

Kaufman, J. C., Baer, J., Agars, M. D., & Loomis, D. (2010). Creativity stereotypes and the consensual assessment technique. *Creativity Research Journal, 22*(2), 200–205.

Kaufman, J. C., Niu, W., Sexton, J. D., & Cole, J. C. (2010). In the eye of the beholder: Differences across ethnicity and gender in evaluating creative work. *Journal of Applied Social Psychology, 40,* 496–511.

Kaufmann, G. (2004). Two kinds of creativity—but which ones? *Creativity and Innovation Management, 13*(3), 154–165.

Kaufmann, P. J. (1999). Franchising and the choice of self-employment. *Journal of Business Venturing, 14,* 345–362.

Kazanjian, R. K. (1988). Relation of dominant problems to stages growth in technology-based new ventures. *Academy of Management Journal, 31*(2), 257–279.

Kazanjian, R. K., & Drazin, R. (1990). A stage-contingent model of design and growth for technology based new ventures. *Journal of Business Venturing, 5*(3), 137–150.

Keh, H. T., Foo, M. D., & Lim B. C. (2002). Opportunity evaluation under risky conditions: The cognitive processes of entrepreneurs. *Entrepreneurship Theory and Practice, 27*(2), 125–148.

Kepler, E., & Shane, S. (2007). *Are male and female entrepreneurs really that different?* Report for the Office of Advocacy, the United States Small Business Administration. Online at: http://archive.sba.gov/advo/research/rs309tot.pdf

King, A., & Zeithaml, C. (2001). Competencies and firm performance: Examining the causal ambiguity paradox. *Strategic Management Journal, 22*(1), 75–99.

Kirton, M. J. (1976). Adaptors and innovators: A description and measure. *Journal of Applied Psychology, 61,* 622–629.

Kirton, M. J. (2003). *Adaption-innovation: In the context of diversity and change.* New York, NY: Routledge.

Kogan, N. (1974). Creativity and sex differences. *Journal of Creative Behavior, 8*(1), 1–14.

Kogut, B., & Zander, U. (1996). What firms do: Coordination, identify, and learning. *Organization Science, 7,* 502–518.

Koka, B. R., & Prescott, J. E. (2002). Strategic alliances as social capital: A multidimensional view. *Strategic Management Journal, 23*(9), 795–816.

Kolb, D., & Williams, J. (2003). *Everyday negotiation: Navigating the hidden agendas in bargaining.* Hoboken, NJ: Jossey-Bass.

Kolvereid, L. (1996). Prediction of employment status choice intentions. *Entrepreneurship Theory and Practice, 21*(1), 47–57.

Kon, Y., & Storey, D.J. (2003). A theory of discouraged borrowers. *Small Business Economics, 21*(1), 37–49.

Kor, Y. Y., Mahoney, J. T., & Michael, S. C. (2007). Resources, capabilities and entrepreneurial perceptions. *Journal of Management Studies, 44,* 1187–1212.

Kostova, T., & Roth, K. (2003). Social capital in multinational corporations and a micro-macro model of its formation. *Academy of Management Review, 28*(2), 297–317.

Krishnan, R., Martin, X., & Noorderhaven, N. G. (2006). When does trust matter to alliance performance? *Academy of Management Journal, 49,* 894–917.

Kristensson, P., Magnusson, P. R., & Matthing, J. (2002). Users as a hidden resource for creativity: Findings from an experimental study on user involvement. *Creativity and Innovation Management, 11*(1), 55–61.

Krueger, N. F. (2000). The cognitive infrastructure of opportunity emergence. *Entrepreneurship Theory and Practice, 24*(3), 5–23.

Krueger, N. F., & Brazeal, D. (1994). Entrepreneurial potential and potential entrepreneurs. *Entrepreneurship Theory and Practice, 18*(1), 5–21.

Krueger, N. F., & Carsrud, A. L. (1993). Entrepreneurial intentions: Applying the theory of planned behaviour. *Entrepreneurship and Regional Development, 5,* 315–330.

Krueger, N., Reilly, M., & Carsrud, A. L. (2000). Competing models of entrepreneurial intentions. *Journal of Business Venturing, 15*(5/6), 411–532.

Kuratko, D., & Hodgetts, R. (1998). *Entrepreneurship: A contemporary approach* (4th ed., pp. 16, 35, and 107–109). Fort Worth, TX: The Dryden Press.

Kwang, N. A., Ang, R. P., Ooi, B. L., Wong, S. S., Oei, T. P. S., & Leng, V. (2005). Do adaptors and innovators subscribe to opposing values? *Creativity Research Journal, 17*(2), 273–281.

Kylén, S. F., & Shani, A. B. (2002). Triggering creativity in teams: An exploratory investigation. *Creativity and Innovation Management, 11*(1), 17–30.

Lagoarde-Segot, T., & Lucey, B. M. (2005). *Financial contagion in emerging markets: Evidence from the Middle East and North Africa*. Retrieved from: http://ssrn.com/abstract=829604

Lambing, P., & Kuehl, C. (1997). In *Entrepreneurship* (pp. 12–13). Englewood Cliffs, NJ: Prentice-Hall, Inc.

Lancaster, L. C., & Stillman, D. (2002). *When generations collide: Who they are, why they clash, how to solve the generational puzzle at work*. New York, NY: Harperbusiness.

Langowitz, N., & Minniti, M. (2007). The entrepreneurial propensity of women. *Entrepreneurship Theory and Practice, 31*(3), 341–364.

Lau, S., & Li, W. L. (1996). Peer status and perceived creativity: Are popular children viewed by peers and teachers as creative? *Creativity Research Journal, 9*(4), 347–352.

Lauder, E. (1985). *Estee: A success story* (1st ed.). New York, NY: Random House.

Lawson, B., & Samson, D. (2001). Developing innovation capability in organizations: A dynamic capabilities approach. *International Journal of Innovation Management, 5*(3), 377–400.

Lechner, C., & Dowling, M. (2003). Firm networks: External relationships as source for the growth and competitiveness of entrepreneurial firms. *Entrepreneurship and Regional Development, 15*(1), 1–26.

Lee, S. M., & Peterson, S. J. (2000). Culture, entrepreneurial orientation, and global competitiveness. *Journal of World Business, 35*(4), 401–416.

Lee, R., & Jones, O. (2008). Networks, communication and learning during business start-up: The creation of cognitive social capital. *International Small Business Journal, 26*(5), 559–594.

Lee, C., Lee, K., & Pennings, J. M. (2001). Internal capabilities, external networks, and performance: A study on technology-based ventures. *Strategic Management Journal, 22*, 615–640.

Lee, S. M., Chang, D., & Lim, S. (2005). Impact of entrepreneurship education: A comparative study of the US and Korea. *The International Entrepreneurship and Management Journal, 1*, 27–43.

Leitch, C., & Hill, F. (2006). Women and the financing of entrepreneurial ventures: More pieces for the jigsaw puzzle. *Venture Capital, 8*(2), 159–182.

Leitch, C., Hill, F., & Neergaard, H. (2010). Entrepreneurial and business growth and the quest for a "comprehensive theory": Tilting at windmills? *Entrepreneurship Theory and Practice*: Special Issue on Growth, Guest Editorial, *34*, 249–260.

Leonard-Barton, D. (1992). Core capabilities and core rigidities: A paradox in managing new product development. *Strategic Management Journal, 13*, 111–125.

Leonard-Barton, D. (1995). *Wellsprings of knowledge: Building and sustaining the sources of innovation*. Boston, MA: Harvard Business School Press.

Lerner, M., & Almor, T. (2002). Relationships among strategic capabilities and the performance of women-owned small ventures. *Journal of Small Business Management*, 40(2), 90–125.

Levie, J., & Hart, M. (2009). *Global Entrepreneurship Monitor, United Kingdom 2009 monitoring report*. Birmingham, UK: Aston Business School.

Levin, L., Snyder, M., & Chapman, D. (1988). The interaction of experiential and situational factors and gender in a simulated risky decision-making task. *The Journal of Psychology*, 122(2), 173–181.

Lewin, K., & Lippitt, R. (1938). An experimental approach to the study of autocracy and democracy: A preliminary note. *Psychometry*, 1, 292–300.

Lichtenstein, B., & Brush, C. (2001). How do "resource bundles" develop and change in new ventures? A dynamic model and longitudinal exploration. *Entrepreneurship Theory and Practice*, 25(3), 37–59.

Lippa, R. A. (2002). *Gender, nature and nurture*. Mahwah, NJ: Lawrence Erlbaum.

Littunen, H. (2000). Entrepreneurship and the characteristics of the entrepreneurial personality. *International Journal of Entrepreneurial Behaviour & Research*, 6(6), 295–310.

Locke, E. A., & Latham, G. P. (2002). Building a practically useful theory of goal setting and task motivation. *American Psychologist*, 57, 705–717.

Loring, A. L. (1991). *Opening doors: The life and work of Joseph Schumpeter*. New Brunswick, NJ and London, UK: Transaction.

Loscocco, K. A., Robinson, J., Hall, R. H., & Allen, J. K. (1991). Gender and small business success: An inquiry into women's relative disadvantage. *Social Forces*, 70, 65–85.

Lowe, K. B., Kroeck, K. G., & Sivasubramaniam, N. (1996). Effectiveness correlates of transformational and transactional leadership: A meta-analytic review of the MLQ literature. *Leadership Quarterly*, 7, 385–425.

Luthans, F. (2002). Positive organizational behavior: Developing and managing psychological strengths. *Academy of Management Executive*, 16, 57–72.

Luthans, F., & Avolio, B. (2003). Authentic leadership: A positive development approach. In K. S. Cameron, J. E. Dutton, & R. E. Quinn (Eds.), *Positive organizational scholarship* (pp. 241–258). San Francisco, CA: Berrett-Koehler.

Lüthje, C., & Franke, N. (2003). The making of an entrepreneur: Testing a model of entrepreneurial intent among engineering students at MIT. *R&D Management*, 33(2), 135–147.

Luthans, F., & Youssef, C. M. (2004). Human, social, and now positive psychological capital management: Investing in people for competitive advantage. *Organizational Dynamics*, 33, 143–160.

Luthans, F., Youssef, C. M., & Avolio, B. J. (2007). *Psychological capital*. Oxford, UK: Oxford University Press.

Mahoney, J. T., & Pandian, J. R. (1992). The resource-based view within the conversation of strategic management. *Strategic Management Journal*, 13(5), 910–959.

Mainiero, L. A., & Sullivan, S. E. (2005). Kaleidoscope careers: An alternate explanation for the opt-out revolution. *The Academy of Management Executive*, 19(1), 106–123.

Makadok, R. (2001). Toward a synthesis of the resource-based and dynamic-capability views of rent creation. *Strategic Management Journal*, 22(5), 387–402.

Malach-Pines, A., & Schwartz, D. (2008). Now you see them, now you don't: Gender differences in entrepreneurship. *Journal of Managerial Psychology, 23*(7), 811–832.

Manolova, T. S., Manev, I. M., Carter, N. M., & Gyoshev, B. S. (2006). Breaking the family and friends' circle: Predictors of external financing usage among men and women entrepreneurs in a transitional economy. *Venture Capital, 8*(2), 109–132.

Manolova, T. S., Carter, M. N., Manev, I. M., & Gyoshev, B. S. (2007). The differential effect of men and women entrepreneurs' human capital and networking on growth expectancies in Bulgaria. *Entrepreneurship Theory and Practice, 31*(3), 407–426.

Marlow, S., & Strange, A. (1994). Female entrepreneurs—success by whose standards? In M. Tanton (Ed.), *Women in management: A developing presence* (pp. 172–184). London, UK: Routledge.

Marlow, S., & Patton, D. (2005). All credit to men? Entrepreneurship, finance, and gender. *Entrepreneurship Theory and Practice, 29*(6), 717–735.

Martin, C. A., & Tulgan, B. (2002). *Managing the generation mix.* Amherst, MA: HRD Press.

Maslow, A. (1946). A theory of human motivation. *Psycholgical Review, 50*, 370–396.

Masters, R. (1989). Study examining investors risk taking propensities. *Journal of Financial Planning, 2*(3), 151–155.

Masters, R., & Meier, R. (1988). Sex differences and risk-taking propensity of entrepreneurs. *Journal of Small Business Management, 26*(1), 31–35.

McGrath, G. R., & MacMillan, I. (2000). *The entrepreneurial mindset: Strategies for continuously creating opportunity in an age of uncertainty.* Boston, MA: Harvard Business School Press.

McGrath, R. G., MacMillan, I. C., & Scheinberg, S. (1992). Elitists, risk-takers, and ragged individualists? An exploratory analysis of cultural differences between entrepreneurs and non-entrepreneurs. *Journal of Business Venturing, 7*, 115–135.

McClelland, D. C. (1961). *The achieving society.* Princeton, NJ: Van Nostrand.

McClelland, D. C. (1987). Characteristics of successful entrepreneurs. *Journal of Creative Behavior, 21*, 219–233.

McClelland, E., Swail, J., Bell, J., & Ibbotson, P. (2005). Following the pathway of female entrepreneurs: A six country investigation. *International Journal of Entrepreneurial Behaviour & Research, 11*(2), 84–107.

McDougall, P., & Robinson, R. (1990). New venture strategies: An empirical identification of eight archetypes of competitive strategies for entry. *Strategic Management Journal, 11*, 537–554.

McKelvie, A., & Wiklund, J. (2010). Advancing firm growth research: A focus on growth mode instead of growth rate. *Entrepreneurship Theory and Practice, 34*, 261–288.

McMullen, J. S., & Shepherd, D. A. (2006). Entrepreneurial action and the role of uncertainty in the theory of the entrepreneur. *Academy of Management Review, 36*(1), 132–152.

Maysami, R. C., & Goby, V. P. (1999). Female small business owners in Singapore and elsewhere: A review of recent studies. *Journal of Small Business Management, 37*(2), 96–105.

Meneely, J., & Portillo, M. (2005). The adaptable mind in design: Relating personality, cognitive style, and creative performance. *Creativity Research Journal*, *17*(2), 155–166.

Menzies, T., Diochon, M., & Gasse, Y. (2004). Examining venture-related myths concerning women entrepreneurs. *Journal of Developmental Entrepreneurship*, *9*(2), 89–107.

Miller, C. (2010). Out of the loop in Silicon Valley. *New York Times*, 18 April 2010.

Minkov, M., & Hofstede, G. (2011). The evolution of Hofstede's doctrine. *Cross Cultural Management: An International Journal*, *18*(1), 10–20.

Minniti, M. (2009). Gender issues in entrepreneurship. *Foundations and Trends in Entrepreneurship*, *5*(7–8), 497–621.

Minniti, M., & Bygrave, W. D. (2003). *National entrepreneurship assessment: The United States of America 2003*. Executive Report. Wellesley, MA: Babson College.

Minniti, M., Allen, E. I., & Langowitz, N. (2005a). *Global Entrepreneurship Monitor (GEM) 2004 report on women and entrepreneurship*. Boston, MA: Babson College. Retrieved from http://www3.babson.edu/CWL/upload/GEMWomensReport_Mar82005.pdf

Minniti, M., Arenius P., & Langowitz, N. (2005b). *The 2004 Global Entrepreneurship Monitor special topic report: Women in entrepreneurship*. Babson Park, MA: Center for Women Leadership, Babson College.

Minniti, M., Allen, E. I., & Langowitz, N. (2006a). *Global Entrepreneurship Monitor (GEM) 2005 report on women and entrepreneurship*. Boston, MA: Babson College. Retrieved from http://cspot01.babson.edu/CWL/upload/GEM%20Womens%20Report.pdf

Minniti, M., Allen, E., & Langowitz, N. (2006b). *The 2005 Global Entrepreneurship Monitor special topic report: Women in entrepreneurship*. Babson Park, MA: Center for Women Leadership, Babson College.

Mintzberg, H. (1987). Crafting strategy. *Harvard Business Review*, *65*(4), 66–75.

Mirowski, P. (1994). Doing what comes naturally: Four metanarratives on what metaphors are for. In P. Mirowski (Ed.), *Natural images in economic thought* (pp. 3–19). Cambridge, MA: Cambridge University Press.

Mitchell, R. K., Busenitz, L., Lant, T., McDougall, P. P., Morse, E. A., & Smith, J. B. (2002). Toward a theory of entrepreneurial cognition: Rethinking the people side of entrepreneurship research. *Entrepreneurship Theory and Practice*, *27*(2), 93–104.

Mitra, R. (2002). The growth pattern of women-run enterprises: An empirical study in India. *Journal of Developmental Entrepreneurship*, *7*(2), 217–237.

Mitton, D. G. (1989). The complete entrepreneur. *Entrepreneurship Theory and Practice*, *13*(3), 9–20.

Moore, D. P. (1990). An examination of present research on the female entrepreneur: Suggested research strategies for the 1990s. *Journal of Business Ethics*, *9*(4/5), 275–281.

Moore, D. P., & Buttner, E. H. (1997). *Women entrepreneurs: Moving beyond the glass ceiling*. Thousand Oaks, CA: Sage.

Morris, M. H., Miyasaki, N. N., Watters, C. E., & Coombes, S. M. (2006). The dilemma of growth: Understanding venture size choices of women entrepreneurs. *Journal of Small Business Management*, *44*(2), 221–244.

Mosey, S., & Wright, M. (2007). From human capital to social capital: A longitudinal study of technology-based academic entrepreneurs. *Entrepreneurship Theory and Practice, 31*(6), 909–935.

Mueller, S. L., & Thomas, A. S. (2001). Culture and entrepreneurial potential: A nine country study of locus of control and innovativeness. *Journal of Business Venturing, 16*(1), 51–75.

Mullins, J. W., & Forlani, D. (2005). Missing the boat or sinking the boat: A study of new venture decision making. *Journal of Business Venturing, 20*, 47–69.

Nahapiet, J., & Ghoshal, S. (1998). Social capital, intellectual capital, and the organizational advantage. *The Academy of Management Review, 23*(2), 242–266.

Nahapiet, J., Gratton, L., & Rocha, H. (2005). Knowledge and relationships: when cooperation is the norm. *European Management Review, 2*, 3–14.

Napier, N. K., & Nilsson, M. (2006). The development of creative capabilities in and out of creative organizations: Three case studies. *Creativity and Innovation Management, 15*(3), 268–278.

Neergaard, H., Shaw, E., & Carter, S. (2005). The impact of gender, social capital and networks on business ownership: A research agenda. *International Journal of Entrepreneurial Behaviour & Research, 11*(5), 338–357.

Negrey, C., & Rausch, S. D. (2009). Creativity gaps and gender gaps: Women, men and place in the United States. *Gender, Place and Culture, 16*(5), 517–533.

Nelson, G. (1987). Information needs of female entrepreneurs. *Journal of Small Business Management, 25*(3), 38–44.

Nelson, R., & Winter, S. (1982). *An evolutionary theory of economic change.* Cambridge, MA: Belknap.

Netemeyer, R. G., Boles, J. S., & McMurrian, R. (1996). Development and validation of work-family conflict and family-work conflict scales. *Journal of Applied Psychology, 81*(4), 400–410.

Nicholls, A. (2006). Playing the field: A new approach to the meaning of social entrepreneurship. *Social Enterprise Journal, 2*(1), 1–5.

Nonaka, I. (1994). A dynamic theory of organizational knowledge creation. *Organization Science, 5*, 14–37.

Nowell, I. (1996). *Women who give away millions: Portraits of Canadian philanthropists.* Toronto, Ontario: Hounslow Press.

O'Gorman, C., & Terjesen, S. (2006). Financing the Celtic Tigress: Venture financing and informal investment in Ireland. *Venture Capital, 8*(1), 69–88.

Olin, T., & Wickenberg, J. (2001). Rule breaking in new product development—crime or necessity? *Creativity and Innovation Management, 10*, 15–25.

Orhan, M., & Scott, D. (2001). Why women enter into entrepreneurship: an explanatory model. *Women in Management Review, 16*(5), 232–243.

Orser, B., & Riding, A. L. (2003). *Estimating the impact of a gender-based training program.* Ottawa, Canada: Carleton University.

Orser, B., Riding, A., & Manley, K. (2006). Women entrepreneurs and financial capital. *Entrepreneurship Theory and Practice, 30*(4), 643–665.

Ostgaard, T., & Birley, S. (1995). New venture competitive strategies and their relation to growth. *Entrepreneurship & Regional Development, 7*(2), 119–141.

Parasuraman, S., & Simmers, C. A. (2001). Type of employment, work-family conflict and well-being: A comparative study. *Journal of Organizational Behavior, 22*, 551–568.

Park, S., & Bae, Z. T. (2004). New venture strategies in a developing country: Identifying a typology and examining growth patterns through case studies. *Journal of Business Venturing, 19*(1), 81–105.

Parnell, J. A., Crandall, W. R., & Menefee, M. (1995). Examining the impact of culture on entrepreneurial propensity: An empirical study of prospective American and Egyptian entrepreneurs. *Academy of Entrepreneurship Journal, 1*, 39–52.

Paxton, P. (1999). Is social capital declining in the United States? A multiple indicator assessment. *American Journal of Sociology, 105*, 88–127.

Pelkonen, A. (2003). Intermediary organizations and commercialization of academic research. *Vest, 16*(1), 47–77.

Pellegrino, E., & Reece, B. (1982). Perceived formation and operational problems encountered by female entrepreneurs in retail and service firms. *Journal of Small Business Management, 20*(2), 15–24.

Penrose, E. (1952). Biological analogies in the theory of the firm. *American Economic Revue, 42*, 804–819.

Penrose, E. (1953). Biological analogies in the theory of the firm: Rejoinder. *American Economic Revue, 43*(4) 603–609.

Penrose, E. (1959). *The theory of the growth of the firm*. Oxford, UK: Blackwell.

Penrose, E. T. (1959). *The theory of the growth of the firm*. New York, NY: Oxford University Press.

Peteraf, M. (1993). The cornerstone of competitive advantage: A resource-based view. *Strategic Management Journal, 14*, 179–191.

Peterman, N. E., & Kennedy, J. (2003). Enterprise education: Influencing students' perceptions of entrepreneurship. *Entrepreneurship Theory and Practice, 28*(2), 129–144.

Peters, T. (1997). *The circle of innovation: You can't shrink your way to greatness*. New York, NY: Alfred A. Knopf.

Petrides, V., & Furnham, A. (2000). Gender differences in measured and self-estimated trait emotional intelligence. *Sex Roles, 6*, 449–461.

Petterson, K. (2005). Masculine entrepreneurship—the Gnosjö discourse in a feminist perspective. In D. Hjorth & C. Steyaert (Eds.), *Narrative and discursive approaches in entrepreneurship* (pp. 177–193). Cheltenham, UK: Edward Elgar.

Petty, R., & Guthrie, J. (2000). Intellectual capital literature review: Measurement, reporting and management. *Journal of Intellectual Capital, 1*, 155–176.

Pfeffer, J., & Salancik, G. R. (1978). *The external control of organization*. New York, NY: Harper and Row Publishers.

Porter, M. (1980). *Competitive strategy*. New York, NY: Free Press.

Porter, M. (1985). *Competitive advantage*. New York, NY: Free Press.

Porter, M. E. (1990). *The competitive advantage of nations*. New York: Free Press.

Porter, M. E., Sachs, J. D., & McArthur, J. W. (2002). Competitiveness and stages of economic development. In M. E. Porter, J. D. Sachs, P. K. Cornelius, J. W. McArthur, & K. Schwab (Eds.), *The Global Competitiveness Report 2001–2002* (pp. 16–25). New York, NY: Oxford University Press.

Portes, A. (1998). Social capital: Its origins and applications in modern sociology. *Annual Review of Sociology, 24*, 1–24.

Powell, G. (1990). One more time: Do male and female managers differ? *Academy of Management Executive, 4*(3), 68–75.

Powell, M., & Ansic, D. (1997). Gender differences in risk behavior in financial decision making: An experimental analysis. *Journal of Economic Psychology*, *18*(6), 605–628.

Powell, G. N., & Butterfield, D. A. (2003). Gender, gender identity, and aspirations to top management. *Women in Management Review*, *18*(1/2), 88–97.

Powell, G. N., & Greenhaus, J. H. (2010). Sex, gender, and the work-to-family interface: Exploring negative and positive interdependencies. *Academy of Management Journal*, *53*(3), 513–534.

Prahalad, C. K., & Hamel, G. (1990). The core competence of the corporation. *Harvard Business Review*, *68*, 79–91.

Porter, M. (1985). *Competitive advantage*. New York, NY: Free Press.

Priem, R. L., & Butler, J. E. (2001). Is the resource-based "view" a useful perspective for strategic management research? *Academy of Management Review*, *26*(1), 22–40.

Putnam, L. L., & Kolb, D. M. (2000). Rethinking negotiation: Feminist views of communication and exchange. In P. Buzzanell (Ed.), *Organizational and management communication from feminist perspectives* (pp. 177–208). Thousand Oaks, CA: Sage.

Quinn, J. B. (2000). Outsourcing innovation: The new engine of growth. *Sloan Management Review*, *41*, 13–28.

Ragins, B. R., Townsend, B., & Mattis, M. (1998). Gender gap in the executive suite: CEOs and female executives report on breaking the glass ceiling. *The Academy of Management Executive*, *12*(1), 28–42.

Ranga, M., & Etzkowitz, H. (2010). Athena in the world of *Techne*: The gender dimension of technology, innovation and entrepreneurship. *Journal of Technology Management and Innovation*, *5*(1), 1–12.

Reis, T. (1999). *Unleashing new resources and entrepreneurship for the common good*. Battle Creek, MI: The W.K. Kellogg Foundation.

Renzulli, L. A., & Aldrich, H. (2005). Who can you turn to? Tie activation within core business discussion networks. *Social Forces*, *84*(1), 323–341.

Renzulli, L. A., Aldrich, H., & Moody, J. (2000). Family matters: Gender, networks, and entrepreneurial outcomes. *Social Forces*, *79*(2), 523–546.

Reynolds, P. (2000). National PSED of U.S. business startups: Background and methodology. In J. A. Katz (Ed.), *Advances in entrepreneurship, firm emergence, and growth* (vol. 4, pp. 153–227). Stamford, CT: JAI Press.

Reynolds, P. D. (2007). *Entrepreneurship in the United States: The future is now*. New York: Springer.

Reynolds, P. D., Bygrave, W. D., Autio, E., Cox, L. W., & Hay, M. (2002a). Global entrepreneurship monitor (GEM): Executive report. Wellesley, MA and Kansas City, MO: Babson College and Ewing Marion Kaufmann Foundation. Retrieved from http://www.gemconsortium.org

Reynolds, P. D., Carter, N. M., Gartner, W. B., Greene, P. G., & Cox, L. W. (2002b). *The entrepreneur next door. An executive summary of the panel study of entrepreneurial dynamics*. Kansas City, MO: Kauffman Center for Entrepreneurial Leadership.

Rickards, T., & Moger, S. (2006). Creative leaders: A decade of contributions from Creativity and Innovation Management Journal. *Creativity and Innovation Management*, *15*, 4–18.

Riding, A. L., & Swift, C. S. (1990). Women business owners and terms of credit: Some empirical findings of the Canadian experience. *Journal of Business Venturing, 5*(5), 327–340.

Riggio, R. E., & Friedman, H. S. (1986). Impression formation: The role of expressive behavior. *Journal of Personality and Social Psychology, 50,* 421–427.

Riverin, N., & Filion, L. J. (2005). *Global Entrepreneurship Monitor (GEM) Canadian national report 2005.* Retrieved from http://neumann.hec.ca/chaire.entrepreneuriat/Projets%20en%20cours/GEM/Articles/Rapp_GEM_2005_angl.pdf

Rhoades, L., Eisenberger, R., & Armeli, S. (2001). Affective commitment to the organization: The contribution of perceived organizational support. *Journal of Applied Psychology, 86,* 825–836.

Robb, A., & Coleman, S. (2009). *Characteristics of new firms: A comparison by gender.* Retrieved from http://ssrn.com/abstract=1352601 (March 3, 2009).

Robinson, D. A., Davidsson, P., van der Mescht, H., & Court, P. (2007). How entrepreneurs deal with ethical challenges—an application of the business ethics synergy star technique. *Journal of Business Ethics, 71,* 411–423.

Rosa, P., Hamilton, D., Carter, S., & Burns, H. (1994). The impact of gender on small business management: preliminary findings of a British study. *International Small Business Journal, 12*(3), 25–32.

Rosa, P., Carter, S., & Hamilton, D. (1996). Gender as a determinant of small business performance: Insights from a British study. *Small Business Economics, 8*(6), 463–478.

Rosener, J. (1990). Ways women lead. *Harvard Business Review, 68*(6), 119–125.

Ross, S. M., & Offermann, L. R. (1997). Transformational leaders: Measurement of personality attributes and work group performance. *Personality and Social Psychology Bulletin, 23,* 1086–1078.

Rosser, S. V. (2004). *The science glass ceiling: Academic women scientists and the struggle to succeed.* New York, NT: Routledge.

Rosser, S. V. (2006). Using the lenses of feminist theories to focus on women and technology. In M. F. Fox, D. G. Johnson, & S. V. Rosser (Eds.), *Women, gender and technology* (pp. 13–47). Champaign, IL: University of Illinois Press.

Rotefoss, B., & Kolvereid, L. (2005). Aspiring, nascent and fledgling entrepreneurs: An investigation of the business start-up process. *Entrepreneurship and Regional Development, 17*(2), 109–127.

Sandberg, B. (2007). Enthusiasm in the development of radical innovations. *Creativity and Innovation Management, 16*(3), 265–273.

Sarri, K., & Trihopoulou, A. (2005). Female entrepreneurs' personal characteristics and motivation: A review of the Greek situation. *Women in Management Review, 20*(1), 24–36.

Scarborough, N. M., & Zimmerer, T. W. (2000). *Effective small business management* (6th ed.). (p. 30). Englewood Cliffs, NJ: Prentice-Hall.

Scheinberg, S., & MacMillan, I. (1988). An 11 country study of motivations to start a business. In B. A. Kirchoff, W. A. Long, W. E. McMillan, K. H. Vesper, & W. E. Wetzel Jr. (Eds.), *Frontiers of entrepreneurship research* (pp. 669–684). Wellesley, MA: Babson College.

Scherr, F. C., Sugrue, T. F., & Ward, J. B. (1993). Financing the small firm start-up determinants of debt use. *Journal of Small Business Finance, 3*(1), 17–36.

Schilling, M. A. (2005). A "small-world" network model of cognitive insight. *Creativity Research Journal, 17*(2), 131–154.

Schon, D. D. (1987). *The reflective practitioner.* San Francisco, CA: Jossey-Bass.

Schubert, R., Brown, M., Gysler, M., & Brachinger, H. W. (1999). Financial decision-making: Are women really more risk-averse? *American Economic Review, 89*(2), 381–391.

Schulman, M. (2002). How we become moral. In C. R. Snyder & S. Lopez (Eds.), *Handbook of positive psychology* (pp. 499–512). Oxford, UK: Oxford University Press.

Schumpeter, J. A. (1939). *Business cycles: A theoretical, historical and statistical analysis of capitalist processes.* New York, NY: Macmillan.

Schumpeter, J. A. (1943). *Capitalism, socialism and democracy.* London, UK: Allen & Unwin.

Schumpeter, J. A. (1950). *Capitalism, socialism and democracy* (3rd ed.). London, UK: Allen and Unwin.

Schumpeter, J. A. (1954). *History of economic analysis.* New York, NY: Oxford University Press.

Schumpeter, J. A., & Clemence, R. V. (2004). *Essays: On entrepreneurs, innovations, business cycles, and the evolution of capitalism.* New Brunswick, NJ: Transaction Publishers.

Scott, C. E. (1986). Why more women are becoming entrepreneurs. *Journal of Small Business Management, 24*(4), 37–44.

Segal, G., Borgia, D., & Schoenfeld, J. (2005). The motivation to become an entrepreneur. *International Journal of Entrepreneurial Behaviour and Research, 11*(1), 42–57.

Senge, P. M. (1990). *The fifth discipline: The art and practice of the learning organization.* New York, NY: Doubleday Currency.

Senor, D., & Singer, S. (2009). *Start-up nation: The story of Israel's economic miracle.* New York, NY: Twelve Hachette Book Group.

Seth, J. N., & Ram, S. (1987). *Bringing innovation to market: How to break corporate and customer barriers.* New York, NY: John Wiley & Sons, Inc.

Severo, R., (2004). Estée Lauder, pursuer of beauty and cosmetics titan, dies at 97. *New York Times,* April 26, A1, B6.

Sexton, D. L., & Bowman, N. B. (1986). Validation of a personality index: Comparative psychological characteristics analysis of female entrepreneurs, managers, entrepreneurship students and business students. In R. Ronstadt, J. A. Hornaday, R. Peterson, & K. H. Vesper (Eds.), *Frontiers of entrepreneurship research* (pp. 40–51). Boston, MA: Babson College.

Sexton, D. L., & Bowman-Upton, N. (1990). Female and male entrepreneurs: Psychological characteristics and their role in gender related discrimination. *Journal of Business Venturing, 5*(1), 29–36.

Shabbir, A., & Gregorio, S. (1996). An examination of the relationship between women's personal goals and structural factors influencing their decisions to start a business: The case of Pakistan. *Journal of Business Venturing, 11,* 507–529.

Shane, S. (1992). Why do some societies invent more than others? *Journal of Business Venturing, 7,* 29–46.

Shane, S. (1993). Cultural influences on national rates of innovation. *Journal of Business Venturing, 8,* 59–73.

Shane, S., & Venkataraman, S. (2000). The promise of entrepreneurship as a field of research. *Academy of Management Review, 25*(1), 217–226.

Shane, S., & Cable, D. M. (2002). Network ties, reputation, and the financing of new ventures. *Management Science, 48*(3), 364–381.

Shane, S. A., Kolvereid, L., & Westhead, P. (1991). An exploratory examination of the reasons leading to new firm formation across country and gender. *Journal of Business Venturing, 6*(6), 431–446.

Shane, S., Locke, E. A., & Collins, C. (2003). Entrepreneurial motivation. *Human Resource Management Review, 13*(1), 257–279.

Shane, S. A., Venkataraman, S., & MacMillan, I. (1995). Cultural differences in innovation championing strategies. *Journal of Management, 21*(5), 931–952.

Sharpe, R. (2000). As leaders, women rule: New studies find that female managers outshine their male counterparts in almost every measure. *BusinessWeek, 3708*, 74–84.

Shaver, K. G. (2004). Attribution and locus of control. In W. B. Gartner, K. G. Shaver, N. M. Carter, & P. D. Reynolds (Eds.), *Handbook of entrepreneurial dynamics: The process of business creation.* Thousand Oaks, CA: Sage Publications.

Shaver, K. G., Gartner, W. B., Gatewood, E. J., & Vos, L. H. (1996). Psychological factors in success at getting into business. In P. D. Reynolds, S. Birley, J. E. Butler, W. D. Bygrave, P. Davidsson, W. B. Gartner, & P. P. McDougall (Eds.), *Frontiers of entrepreneurship research* (pp. 77–90). Boston, MA: Babson College.

Shaw, S., & Taylor, M. (1995). *Reinventing fundraising: Realizing the potential of women's philanthropy.* San Francisco, CA: Jossey-Bass Publishers.

Shepherd, D. A., & DeTienne, D. R. (2005). Prior knowledge, potential financial reward, and opportunity identification. *Entrepreneurship Theory and Practice, 29*, 91–112.

Shook, C. L., Priem, R. L., & McGee, J. E. (2003). Venture creation and the enterprising individual: A review and synthesis. *Journal of Management, 29*(3), 379–399.

Singh, R. P. (2001). A comment on developing the field of entrepreneurship through the study of opportunity recognition and exploitation. *Academy of Management Review, 26*(1), 10–12.

Singh, S. P., Reynolds, R. G., & Muhammad, S. (2001). A gender-based performance analysis of micro and small enterprises in Java, Indonesia. *Journal of Small Business Management, 39*(2), 174–182.

Skinner, N. F., & Drake, J. M. (2003). Behavioral implications of adaption-innovation: III. Adaption-innovation, achievement motivation, and academic performance. *Social Behavior and Personality, 31*(1), 101–106.

Smallbone, D., & Wyer, P. (2000). *Growth and development of the small firm.* London, UK: Pearson.

Smallbone, D., & Welter, F. (2001). The distinctiveness of entrepreneurship in transition economies. *Small Business Economics, 16*(4) , 249–262.

Smith, K. G., Collins, C. J., & Clark, K. D. (2005). Existing knowledge, knowledge creation capability, and the rate of new product introduction in high-technology firms. *Academy of Management Journal, 48*(2), 346–357.

Smith, R. (2009). The Diva storyline: An alternative social construction of female entrepreneurship. *International Journal of Gender and Entrepreneurship, 1*(2), 148–163.

Solow, R. (2007). Heavy thinker. Review of Prophet of innovation: Joseph Schumpeter and creative destruction, by Thomas K. McCraw. *The New Republic*, May, 21, 2007, 48–50.

Sonfield, M., Lussier, R., Corman, J., & McKinney, M. (2001). Gender comparisons in strategic decision-making: An empirical analysis of the entrepreneurial strategy matrix. *Journal of Small Business Management*, 39(2), 165–173.

Sonnert, G., & Holton, G. (2006). *Who succeeds in science? The gender dimension*. New Brunswick: Rutgers University Press.

Sosik, J. J. (2001). Self-other agreement on charismatic leadership. *Group and Organization Management*, 26, 484–511.

Sternberg, R. J., & Lubart, T. I. (1993). Investing in creativity. *Psychological Inquiry*, 4(3), 229–232.

Stevenson, L. A. (1986). Against all odds: The entrepreneurship of women. *Journal of Small Business Management*, 24(4), 30–36.

Stevenson, L. (1990). Some methodological problems associated with researching women entrepreneurs. *Journal of Business Ethics*, 9(4/5), 439–446.

Stevenson, H., Grousbeck, I., Roberts, M., & Bhide, A. (1999). *New business ventures and the entrepreneur* (5th ed.). Boston, MA: Irwin McGraw-Hill.

Still, L. V., & Guerin, C. D. (1991). Barriers facing self-employed women: The Australian experience. *Women in Management Review & Abstracts*, 6(6), 3–8.

Stinerock, R., Stern, B., & Solomon, M. (1991). Sex and money: Gender differences in the use of surrogate consumers for financial decision-making. *Journal of Professional Services Marketing*, 7(2), 167–182.

Storey, D. J. (1994). *Understanding the small business sector*. London, UK: Routledge.

Strohmeyer, R., & Tonoyan, V. (2005). Bridging the gender gap in employment growth: On the role of innovativeness and occupational segregation. *International Journal of Entrepreneurship & Innovation*, 6(4), 259–273.

Stuart, R., & Abetti, P. A. (1987). Start-up ventures: Towards the prediction of initial success. *Journal of Business Venturing*, 2(3), 215–230.

Suarez, F. F. (2004). Battles for technological dominance: An integrative framework. *Research Policy*, 33, 271–286.

Sullivan, S. E., & Arthur, M. (2006). The evolution of the boundaryless career concept: Examining physical and psychological mobility. *Journal of Vocational Behavior*, 69(1), 19–29.

Tan, J. (2008). Breaking the "Bamboo Curtain" and the "Glass Ceiling": The experience of women entrepreneurs in high-tech industries in an emerging market. *Journal of Business Ethics*, 80, 547–564.

Taniguchi, H. (2002). Determinants of women's entry into self-employment. *Social Science Quarterly*, 83(3), 875–894.

Taylor, D. W., Jones, O., & Boles, K. (2004). Building social capital through action learning: An insight into the entrepreneur. *Education & Training*, 46(5), 226–235.

Teece, D. (2007). Explicating dynamic capabilities: The nature and microfoundations of (sustainable) enterprise performance. *Strategic Management Journal*, 28(13), 1319–1350.

Teece, D., & Pisano, G. (1994). The dynamic capabilities of firms: An introduction. *Industrial and Corporate Change*, 3, 537–556.

Teece, D. J., Pisano, G., & Shuen, A. (1997). Dynamic capabilities and strategic management. *Strategic Management Journal, 18*(7), 509–533.

Tegano, D. W., & Moran, J. D. (1989). Sex differences in the original thinking of preschool and elementary school children. *Creativity Research Journal, 2*(1–2), 102–110.

Tesfaye, B. (1997). Patterns of formation and development of high-technology entrepreneurs. In D. Jones-Evans & M. Klofsten (Eds.), *Technology, innovation and enterprise—the European experience* (pp. 61–106). London, UK: Macmillan Press.

Thomas, A. S., & Mueller, S. L. (2001). A case for comparative entrepreneurship: Assessing the relevance of culture. *Journal of International Business Studies, 31*(2), 287–301.

Thurik, A. R., Carree, M., van Stel, A., & Audretsch, D. (2008). Does self-employment reduce unemployment? *Journal of Business Venturing, 23*(6), 673–686.

Thursby, J. G., & Thursby, M. C. (2005). Gender patterns of research and licensing activity of science and engineering faculty. *Journal of Technology Transfer, 30,* 343–353.

Tiger, L., & Calantone, R. J. (1998). The impact of market knowledge competence on the new product advantage: Conceptualization and empirical examination. *Journal of Marketing, 62,* 13–29.

Timmons, J. A. (1999). *New venture creation, entrepreneurship for the 21st century.* Boston, MA: Irwin McGraw-Hill.

Timmons, J., & Spinelli, S. (2004). *New venture creation: Entrepreneurship for the 21st century* (6th ed.). Irwin, NY: McGraw-Hill.

Tominc, P., & Rebernik, M. (2007). Growth aspirations and cultural support for entrepreneurship. A comparison of post-socialist countries. *Small Business Economics, 28,* 239–255.

Tulgan, B. (2000). *Managing Generation X: How to bring out the best in young talent* (rev. and updated ed.). New York, NY: W.W. Norton.

Tulgan, B. (2006). *Managing the generation mix* (2nd ed.). Amherst, MA: HRD Press.

Turker, D., Onvural, B., Kursunluoglu, E., & Pinar, C. (2005). Entrepreneurial propensity: A field study on the Turkish university students. *International Journal of Business, Economics and Management, 1*(3), 15–27.

Ucbasaran, D., Wright, M., & Westhead, P. (2003). A longitudinal study of habitual entrepreneurs: Starters and acquirers. *Entrepreneurship & Regional Development, 15*(3), 207–228.

Unger, J. M., Rauch, A., Frese, M., & Rosenbusch, N. (2011). The ambitious entrepreneur: High growth strategies of women-owned enterprises. *Journal of Business Venturing, 26*(3), 341–358.

Utsch, A., & Rauch, A. (2000). Innovativeness and initiative as mediators between achievement orientation and venture performance. *European Journal of Work and Organizational Psychology, 9*(1), 45–62.

Uzzi, B. (1996). The sources and consequences of embeddedness for the economic performance of organizations: The network effect. *American Sociological Review, 61*(4), 674–698.

Van Beveren, J. (2002). A model of knowledge acquisition that refocuses knowledge management. *Journal of Knowledge Management, 6*(1), 18–22.

Van de Ven, A. H., Hudson, R., & Schroeder, D. M. (1984). Designing new business startups: Entrepreneurial, organizational, and ecological considerations. *Journal of Management, 10*(1), 87–107.

Van Gelderen, M., Thurik, R., & Patel, P. (2011). Encountered problems and outcome status in nascent entrepreneurship. *Journal of Small Business Management, 49*(1), 71–91.

Van de Lippe, T., & van Dijk, L. (2002). Comparative research in women's employment. *Annual Review of Psychology, 28*, 221–242.

Veciana, J. M., Aponte, M., & Urbano, D. (2005). University attitudes to entrepreneurship: a two countries comparison. *International Journal of Entrepreneurship and Management, 1*(2), 165–182.

Venkataraman, S. (2003). Foreword. In S. Shane (Ed.), *A general theory of entrepreneurship. The individual-opportunity nexus* (pp. xi–xii). Northampton, MA: Edward Elgar.

Verheul, I., & Thurik, R. (2001). Start-up capital: Does gender matter? *Small Business Economics, 16*(4), 329–345.

Verheul, I., Risseeuw, P., & Bartelse, G. (2002). Gender differences in strategy and human resource management. *International Small Business Journal, 20*(4), 443–476.

Verheul, I., Uhlaner, L., & Thurik, R. (2005). Business accomplishments, gender, & entrepreneurial self-image. *Journal of Business Venturing, 20*(4), 483–528.

Verheul, I., Van Stel, A. J., & Thurik, A. R. (2006). Explaining female and male entrepreneurship across 29 countries. *Entrepreneurship and Regional Development, 18*, 151–183.

Vesper, K. H. (1990). *New venture strategies.* Englewood Cliffs: Prentice-Hall.

Vesper, C. (1996). *New venture experience* (revised ed.). Seattle, WA: Vector Books.

Vroom, V. H., & Yetton, P. W. (1973). *Leadership and decision-making.* Pittsburgh, PA: University of Pittsburgh Press.

Wajcman, J. (2007). From women and technology to gendered technoscience. *Information, Communication, and Society, 10*(3), 287–298.

Waddock, S. (2009). Pragmatic visionaries: Difference makers as social entrepreneurs. *Organizational Dynamics, 38*(4), 281–289.

Waldman, D. A., Ramirez, G. G., House, R. J., & Puranam, P. (2001). Does leadership matter? CEO leadership attributes and profitability under conditions of perceived environmental uncertainty. *Academy of Management Journal, 44*, 134–143.

Walker, E. A. (2003). Home-based businesses: Setting straight the urban myths. *Small Enterprise Research, 11*(2), 35–48.

Walker, D., & Joyner, B. (1999). Female entrepreneurship and the market process: Gender-based public policy considerations. *Journal of Developmental Entrepreneurship, 4*(2), 95–116.

Wallsten, S. J. (2000). The effects of government-industry R&D programs on private R&D: The case of the small business innovation research program. *Rand Journal of Economics, 31*(1), 82–100.

Wang, C. K., & Wong, P. K. (2004). Entrepreneurial interest of university students in Singapore. *Technovation, 24*(2), 163–172.

Wang, K. Y., & Casimir, G. (2007). How attitudes of leaders may enhance organizational creativity: Evidence from a Chinese study. *Creativity and Innovation Management, 16*(3), 229–238.

Ward, T. B. (2004). Cognition, creativity, and entrepreneurship. *Journal of Business Venturing, 19*, 173–188.

Watson, J. (2002). Comparing the performance of male- and female-controlled businesses: Relating outputs to inputs. *Entrepreneurship Theory and Practice, 26*(3), 91–100.

Weinzimmer, L. (2000). A replication and extension of organizational growth determinants. *Journal of Business Research, 48*(1), 35–41.

Welter, F. (2004). The environment for female entrepreneurship in Germany. *Journal of Small Business and Enterprise Development, 11*, 212–221.

Welter, F., Smallbone, D., Mirzakhalikova, D., Schakirova, N., & Maksudova, C. (2006). Women entrepreneurs between tradition and modernity—the case of Uzbekistan. In F. Welter, D. Smallbone, & N. Isakova (Eds.), *Enterprising women in transition economies* (pp. 45–66). Aldershot, UK: Ashgate.

Wennekers, S., & Thurik, R. (1999). Linking entrepreneurship and economic growth. *Small Business Economics, 13*, 27–55.

Wennekers, S., Uhlander, L. M., & Thurik, R. (2002). Entrepreneurship and its conditions: A macro perspective. *International Journal of Entrepreneurial Education, 1*(1) , 25–64.

Wennekers, S., Van Stel, A., Thurik, A. R., & Reynolds, P. (2005). Nascent entrepreneurship and the level of economic development. *Small Business Economics, 24*(3), 293–309.

Wennekers, S., Van Wennekers, A., Thurik, R., & Reynolds, P. (2005). Nascent entrepreneurship and the level of economic development. *Small Business Economics, 24*(3), 293–309.

Wernerfelt, B. (1984). A resource-based view of the firm. *Strategic Management Journal, 5*(2), 171–180.

Westhead, P. (2003). Comparing the performance of male- and female-controlled businesses. *Journal of Small Business and Enterprise Development, 10*(2), 217–224.

Westhead, P., & Wright, M. (1998). Novice, portfolio and serial founders: Are they different? *Journal of Business Venturing, 13*(3), 173–204.

White, B. (1995). The career development of successful women. *Women in Management Review, 10*(3), 4–15.

Winsor, R. D., & Ensher, E. A. (2002). Choices made in balancing work and family: Following two women on a 16-year journey. *Journal of Management, 9*(2), 218–231.

Winter, S. (2003). Understanding dynamic capabilities. *Strategic Management Journal, 24*(10), 991–995.

Wilson, F., Marlino, D., & Kickul, J. (2004). Our entrepreneurial future: Examining the diverse attitudes and motivations of teens across gender and ethnic identity. *Journal of Developmental Entrepreneurship, 9*(3), 177–197.

Wilson, F., Kickul, J., & Marlino, D. (2007). Gender, entrepreneurial self-efficacy, and entrepreneurial career intentions: Implications for entrepreneurship education. *Entrepreneurship Theory and Practice, 31*(3), 387–406.

Winborg, J., & Landström, H. (2001). Financial bootstrapping in small businesses: Examining small business managers' resource acquisition behaviour. *Journal of Business Venturing, 16*(3): 235–254.

Winter, S. G. (2003). Understanding dynamic capabilities. *Strategic Management Journal, 24*(10), 991–995.

Wong, S. (1988). *Emigrant entrepreneurs: Shanghai industrialists in Hong Kong.* Hong Kong: Oxford University Press.

Wood, R., & Bandura, A. (1989). Social cognitive theory of organizational management. *Academy of Management Review, 14*(1), 361–384.

Woodman, P., & Schoenfeldt, L. (1989). Individual differences in creativity: An interactionist perspective. In J. A. Glover, R. R. Ronning, & C. R. Reynolds (Eds.), *Handbook of creativity* (pp. 77–92). New York, NY: Plenum Press.

World Bank (1996) *World development report 1996: from plan to market.* New York: Oxford University Press. Retrieved from: http://www-wds.worldbank.org/external/default/WDSContentServer/WDSP/IB/1996/06/27/000009265_3961214181445/Rendered/PDF/multi0page.pdf

Wright, M., & Zahra, S. (2011). The other side of paradise: Examining the dark side of entrepreneurship. *Entrepreneurship Research Journal, 1*(3), 1–5.

Wu, L. (2007). Entrepreneurial resources, dynamic capabilities and start-up performance of Taiwan's high-tech firms. *Journal of Business Research, 60,* 549–555.

Wyer, M. (2001). *Women, science, and technology: A reader in feminist science studies.* London, UK: Routledge.

Xie, Y., & Shauman, K. A. (1998). Sex differences in research productivity: New evidence about an old puzzle. *American Sociological Review, 63*(6), 847–870.

Xie, Y., & Shauman, K. A. (2003). *Women in science: Career processes and outcomes.* Cambridge, MA: Harvard University Press.

Zahra, S. A., Sapienza, H. J., & Davidson, P. (2006). Entrepreneurship and dynamic capabilities: A review, model and research agenda. *Journal of Management Studies, 43*(4), 917–955.

Zahra, S., Gedajlovic, E., Neubaum, D., & Shulman, J. (2009). A typology of social entrepreneurs: Motives, search processes and ethical challenges. *Journal of Business Venturing, 24*(5), 519–532.

Zhao, H., & Seibert, S. E. (2006). The big five personality dimensions and entrepreneurial status: A meta-analytical review. *Journal of Applied Psychology, 91*(2), 259–271.

Zapalska, A. (1997). A profile of women entrepreneurs and enterprises in Poland. *Journal of Small Business Management, 35*(4), 76–82.

Zaslow, J. (2006). *Baby-boomer managers struggle with mentoring.* Retrieved from <http://www.careerjournal.com/columnists/movingon/20030606-moving on.html>

Zemke, R., Raines, C., & Filipczak, B. (2000). *Generations at work: Managing the clash of veterans, Boomers, Xers, and Nesters in your workplace.* New York, NY: American Management Association.

Zinkhan, G. M., & Karande, K. W. (1991). Cultural and gender differences in risk taking behavior among American and Spanish decision makers. *Journal of Social Psychology, 131*(5), 741–742.

Index

Numbers in **bold** indicate figures and tables

accelerating systems 206, 208
adaptors 329
Ahmed, B. 248–53
Akizawa, K. 489
Annan, K. 271
Archer, L. 289–90
Athena in the World of Techne:
The Gender Dimension of
Technology, Innovation and
Entrepreneurship 260
Audur Capital 523
avoiding entrepreneurial opportunities
330–1
Axela Inc. 512
Ayotte, S. 515

Baby-Boomers 426
BabyCenter 494
Ball-Gautschi, J. 515
Bangladesh: Village Pay Phone
Program (VPP) 221–8
Bar Shalom, A. 267
Beetles, A. 95
Bennett, J. 123
Bettez, I. 516
Bianchini, G. 494
Black Economic Empowerment (BEE)
391
Bliss Soy Cheese 400–4; customer
relationships 402–3; operations and
distribution 401–2; product
overview 400–1; soy in the Indian
context 403
Blurb 494
Boater 453
Bodén, M. 277; innovative
entrepreneur in a non-innovative
sector 278–9

boundaryless careers 407
Bourdieu, P. 202–3
Brazil 144–9; entrepreneur, wife
and mother 147–8; recyclable
materials 145; self employment
145–6; social enterprise 146–7;
work, family balance and social
entrepreneurship 144–5
Brazil, Russia, India and China (BRIC)
115–49; economies 121–2;
emerging markets 120–2; emerging
markets and female perspectives
122–4; gender participation in
entrepreneurial activity 122;
support systems 123–4
Brindley, C. 93
business: motivation 73–6; New
Venture Creation Process 74–5;
women entrepreneurs 75
business concept 176–7
business development 136
business growth 477; breaking
through the barriers 476–517;
and business life cycle 480–1;
business-related constraining
factors 485–6; case studies
498–517; constraining factors
483–7; contributing factors 487–8;
dilemma in female realm 482–3;
ecosystem-related constraining
factors 486–7; entrepreneur-related
constraining factors 484–5; gender
comparisons in some parameters of
business growth 483; going global
495–7; growth strategies 478–81;
growth strategies of women
entrepreneurs in technology-based
firms 504–17; innovators in

Canada's Advanced Technology Sector 512–16; Israeli high-tech woman entrepreneur 499–504; key factors in female-led business growth 484; main factors associated with businesses that go global 495–7; overcoming female-related hurdles 488–91; predominant frameworks for growth in the New Venture Creation Stages 481; two approaches to overcoming hurdles 490; understanding the meaning 477; women in the high-tech sector 492–4

business idea 169, 171–2; authority-driven statements 171–2; communicative style 171; expressive communication style 171; lateral thinking 171; questioning style 171

business strategies 172–3; creativity and innovation 172; finance 173; knowledge management 173; managing teams 173; marketing 173; networking 172–3; opportunity exploitation 172; self-management 173

Campbell, N. 459

Canadian Advanced Technology Alliance Women in Tech Forum 509

capability 197–9

capital acquisition 358–404; best practices from women entrepreneurs' 379–81; Bliss Soy Cheese 400–4; case studies 384–404; classification 369; debt loans and equity 362–4; gender differences in raising capital in the new venture creation stages 370–3; Gwendolyn Smith Iloani and Smith Whiley & Company 386–9; origins and impact 360; reasons that women and men use different strategies to raise initial capital 370–3; role of networking 374–8; role of resource-based theory in women's entrepreneurship 385–6; seeking capital 361–2; Smith Whiley & Company 385–6; sources of financing the venture 367; spiral dynamics of female capital raising and networking 377; what does the financial process entail? 359–61;

women and 364–9; women and the investors' community 381–3; Women Investment Portfolio Holdings (WIPHOLD) of South Africa 390–400

Chadi, H. 286

Chanel, C. 452–3

Cherie Blair Foundation 286

China: female entrepreneurship and economic reformation 128–33

civil organization of public interest 217–18

Cohen, R. 14

"comfort zone" 79

communal responsibility 527–8

competition 178–9

cooperative 429

core competencies: 211, 212; capability 197–9; case studies 214; female entrepreneurship ethics 210–13; illustration 199; networking and social capital 202–5; social capital "flip side" in the female realm 205–6; start-up and innovation in the third sector 214–21; starting a new venture 196–228; support system function/ malfunction in women entrepreneur 206–10; Village Pay Phone Program in Bangladesh 221–8; women entrepreneur competitive advantage 199–202

Coronilla 343–52; building the pasta business 346–8; Marta takes over and prepares for strategic change 348–9; Marta's turnaround plan 351–2; resistance from all sides 349–51; and the Willie family 345

creative teams 239

creativity 233–4; Alice Goh 253–7; among women entrepreneurs 234–6; Bushra Ahmed 248–53; case study 248–57; celebrating in the Female Entrepreneurial Realm 233–57; cultivating creative ideas 244–6; definition 234; factors involved 235; and gender 236–7; the "idea" 243; the idea in Venture Creation 245; ideas in the female entrepreneurial realm 243–4; and its functions in the female venture creation process 242; managing in the business 240; managing in women-led businesses 238–42;

psychological approach 237; social
messages 237–8; sociocultural
approach 237; taking practical
action 246–7
cultural influence 81–2

8D Technologies Inc. 516
decision making: pre-launching stages
168–9; process models 170
DentaLoop 454
discouraged borrowers 365
Diva phenomenon 458–61
Donovan, M.O. 453–4
dynamic capabilities (DC) 197, 213,
487; approach 19–20, 264; theory
234
Dynamic Services 429–33

eBay 446
economic reformation: China
128–33
education 56, 82–3
efficiency-driven stage 116, 117
Elion, G.B. 273
Ellison, J. 123
emerging markets: Brazil 144–9;
BRIC markets 120–2; BRIC
markets and female perspectives
122–4; case studies 127–8;
China 128–33; female Venture
Creation Process 115–49; India
139–44; macro level look into
transitional economies and
female entrepreneurship 118–20;
MENA countries 124–5; Russia
133–9; women entrepreneurial
perspective 125–7
emotional support 209
empowerment 522
entrepreneur cycle 14
entrepreneurial activity: women
perspective 125–7
entrepreneurial avenues multiplicity
412–17; activists 414;
breaktrough-ers 416; combinations
414–15; franchising 412–13;
non-profit undertakings 415–16;
partnerships 414; philanthropy
417; self-employment 413–14;
transforming hobbies into
ventures 415
entrepreneurial cycle 14–15
entrepreneurial ecosystem 116,
117–18, 159, 160, 162

entrepreneurial mindset 79–84;
cultural and social influences 81–2;
education 82–3; family influence
83; relevant experience 83; social
expectation and socialization 83–4
entrepreneurial motivation: case study
92; coaching/mentoring and
business support provision 109;
consultant and entrepreneurial
profiles 110; examination 103–7;
female entrepreneurial mindset
79–84; female entrepreneurship
72–110; marketing women 93–6;
motivation factors 104; necessity
and opportunity entrepreneurship
108; opportunity and necessity
76–9; profiling the necessity
entrepreneur 105–6; reflections on
the business support process 106–7;
start a business 73–6; women and
business support services 99–107;
work-family 84–90
entrepreneurial paths: career transition
and the new venture's life cycle 425;
case studies 427–38; common
ground of female and social
entrepreneurship 422; Corinne:
social entrepreneur from Réunion
Island 428–33; entrepreneurial
career changes 424–5; focusing and
leveraging 418; generations and
female entrepreneurship 425–7;
home-based entrepreneurship 410;
mompreneurship 408–10;
multiplicity in entrepreneurial
avenues 412–17; new career patterns
and female entrepreneurship 406–8;
preferred entrepreneurial avenue
417–20; social entrepreneurship
420–4; step-by-step technique 419;
stories of three female entrepreneurs
435–8; virtual entrepreneurship
411–12; of women entrepreneurs
405–38; women's entrepreneurs in
Russia 433–4
entrepreneurial revolution 6–7;
entrepreneurial realm 7
entrepreneurship: female realm 9;
know-how 201–2; support
structures 101–2, 102–3
entrepreneurship policy: France
99–101
environment cycle 15–16
Estée Lauder 293–5

ethics: female entrepreneurship 210–13; main concepts in entrepreneurship **212**
Etzkowitz, H. 260
European women 43
Evans, M. 287
external diversity 527
extrinsic motivation 73

factor-driven stage 116
Fake, C. 494
female entrepreneurs: as mentors 523
female entrepreneurship: accepting and praising diversity 526; Angles in Female Entrepreneurial Research **5**; area 7–9; around the globe 44–6; Brazil 144–9; business life cycle models 20–1; case studies 59–62, 127–8; case study 92; cases of Norway and Thailand 63–8; China 128–33; coaching/mentoring and business support provision **109**; communal responsibility 527–8; constraints and opportunities 41–68; consultant and entrepreneurial profiles **110**; creativity, innovation, originality 526–7; distinctiveness **8**; diversity 13–16; emerging BRIC markets 120–2; emerging BRIC markets and female perspectives 122–4; empowerment 522; entrepreneurial cycle **15**; entrepreneurial mindset 79–84; entrepreneurial revolution 6–7; entrepreneurs motivation 72–110; ethics 210–13; female entrepreneurs as mentors 523; fortitude 519–28; global sphere 16–18; implications for education 525; India 139–44; initial phases of new venture creation 1–37; international view 43–4; leadership 443–74; macro and micro perspectives in female venture creation 52–6; macro level look into transitional economies 118–20; Main Hurdles Reported at Work by Women **10**; manifestation in different ecosystems **17**; marketing women 93–7; MENA countries 124–5; motivation to start a business 73–6; necessity and opportunity entrepreneurship **108**; networking to promote women entrepreneurs 524; new ground **520**;

opportunity and necessity motivations 76–9; policy 524–5; proactivity 520–2; research directions 46–7; role models 522–3; Russia 133–9; sex and gender issues 51–2; socio-cultural heritage 58–62; theoretical feminist perspectives 47–51; theoretical framework **21**; Venture Creation Process in emerging markets 115–49; women and business support services 99–107; women entrepreneurial perspective 125–7; work-family 84–91
female-oriented mindset 79–84
female-oriented processes 164–9; accumulating networks 168; business visualization 165; communicating and collecting feedback 165–6; diffuse thinking 166; filtering ideas 165; generating ideas 165; pre-launch decision making 168–9; pre-launch steps in the new venture creation process **166, 167**; reflecting ideas 165; selling the concept 167–8
femininity: construction 50–1
feminism 47–8, 50–1
feminist empiricism 20, 48
feminist theory 20, 47–51; directions 48; femininity and masculinity construction 50–1; gender differences 49–50; gender similarities 48–9
Fields, D. 295–6
Flickr 494
Foster, C. 93
Fotheringham, T. T. 183–4
Foundation for Research in Community Health (FRCH) 141
France: entrepreneurship policy 99–101; female entrepreneurship 58–63; necessity entrepreneurship 99–107
franchising 412–13
Freud, S. 73
functional support 209–10

Gantous, D. 513
Gcabashe, N.C. 390
gender 77–9, 102–3, 211; issues in entrepreneurship 51–2; stereotyping 46
gender difference 9, 11–13, 45, 49–50, 56, 57, 118;

community and external
environment level 12–13;
individual level 11–12;
new venture level 12
gender diversity 527
gender gap 46, 118, 125
Gender-related Development Index
(GDI) 64
gender similarities 45, 48–9
general approach 491
Generation X-ers 426
Generation Y-ers 426
Gerber, D. 291
Girlphyte Inc. 512
Gittins, E. 494
"glass ceiling" 75, 76, 77, 79
global entrepreneurship 44–6;
female entrepreneurship around
the globe 45; micro and macro
perspectives and female
entrepreneurship 46
Global Entrepreneurship and the
Successful Growth Strategies of
Early-Stage Companies 478
Global Entrepreneurship Monitor
(GEM) 44–5, 58–9
GO TRY IT ON 287
Goh, A. 253–7; age of female
entrepreneur 256; business
acumen 254; business and
community work expansion 255;
business strategies 254–5;
difficulty in business as an
entrepreneur 255; education of
female entrepreneur 256;
entrepreneurship promotion by
the government 256; exchange rate
risk 255; female entrepreneurship
promotion by the government
256–7; long working hours 255;
marital status 256; self-employed
vs entrepreneur 256; sibling
influence 254
Goh, C. 512
Goh Teck Wah Company 253–4
Goldman-Sachs report 121
Goodfellow-Baikie, R. 184–6
Gordon, C. 514
Gordon, M. 321
grabbing entrepreneurial opportunities
331
Graham, B. N. 454
Greene, C. 272
Groote, J. 516

growth strategies: women
entrepreneurs in technology-based
firms 504–17
Gundolf, K. 58
Gupta, I. 292
Gupte, M. 139–42
Gwave consulting 321

Hammargren, M.-L. 280–1
Harris, L. 95
Helix Commerce International Inc.
514
Helix Innovation Hive 514
Helix Talent 514
Helix Virtual Worlds 514
Hewlett, S. A. 123
Hodgkin, D. 272
Holeys 515
home-based entrepreneurship 410
human capital 199–200
Hutchison, S. 368

idea 243; cultivating creative ideas
244–6; in the female
entrepreneurial realism 243–4
Iloani, G. S. 386–9
India: female entrepreneurship of
NGOs 139–44; non-profit
entrepreneurs 139–44
individual–environment effects 75
InGenius Group 513
inno-daptation 330
Innovate/Educate 328
innovation 214–21; barriers 268–72;
case studies 276–81; in the context
of female entrepreneurship 258–81;
entrepreneur 215–16; female view
of the barriers to innovation 270;
ideas and major social needs
216–17; innovation/adaptation
265–6; innovative entrepreneur in a
non-innovative sector 278–9;
inventions and breakthroughs
among women entrepreneurs 272–3;
leading empirical research in the
context of innovation-adaptation
266; macro perspective of
innovation process 261;
owner-manager in the high-tech
sector 280–1; resource-based view
on the quest for innovation 263–5;
risk-taking 273–5; role in the
female venture creation process
259–63; woman-led perspective of

innovation flow **262**; women as innovators **269**; women as innovators or adaptors 266–8; Women's Entrepreneurship in a Scandinavian Welfare State 276–81

innovation-driven stage 116, 117

innovators 329

Institutional Support System 217

Instituto Evoluir 214; creation, project implementation and recognition 218–19; genesis 217–18; project expansion and future preparation 219–21

internal diversity 527

international entrepreneurship 43–4; international look at female entrepreneurship and attitudes 44

International Montessori Association (IMA) 463

interview themes: 95–6; reasons for staying in marketing 96; responsibilities outside work 96; success definition 96; trigger events to starting the business 96; work role definition 96

intrinsic motivation 73

Inuit entrepreneurship 180–2; values and principles 181–2

Inukpuk, E. 182–3

investments 382

Ittinuar, L. 182–3

Jantelov 65

Jaouen, A. 58

Jen, S. 494

Jepsen, M. L. 494

Jobs, S. 528

Johnson, C. 290

Kaleidoscope Career Model (KCM) 407

Kevlar 273

Khatun, R. 223–4, 226

Khatun-Bagerhart, S. 225

Khatun-Chittagong, J. 226

Kilookas 297–310

Knight, M. 273

knowledge-based view (KBV) 264

Kretova, M. 133, 135–8

Kwolek, S. 272–3

Labour Force Survey (LFS) 93–4, 94, 97

Laos 189–93; calendar 191; infrastructure 189–90; Monks 191; small business sector 192–3; traditional beliefs 190; values 191–2; wats 191

LaPiere, C. S. 459–60

Lauder, E. 293–5

leadership 444; case studies 462–74; diva phenomenon 458–61; emotional skills and 457–8; entrepreneurs are leaders 444–5; and entrepreneurship in the female context 448; entwining the value of business with the staff's set of values, ethics and business ideologies 452; envisioning 450; expanding the value of the business 451–2; in female entrepreneurship 443–74; key roles of leader-founder 454–5; leader-founder and female new venture creation 456–7; leaders and investors in their fields 452–4; MADARA Cosmetics 469–74; Maria Montessori and her schools 462–8; role models 450–1; styles and gender 445–6; traits and skills of a leader 445; vision—the linking chain 450–2; women entrepreneurs and leaders 446–9

Learn/ Innovate 328

Learn/Acquire 328

Learn/Replicate 328

Li, V. C.D. 482

liberal feminist theory 20, 48–9

Liquid Paper 454

Luhabe, W. 390

macro level of analysis 53–4; main theme of female entrepreneurship 54; profiling women entrepreneurs in the new venture creation process **52**

MADARA Cosmetics 469–74

Mahila Sarvangeen Utkarsh Mandal (MASUM) 139–40, 142–3

male-oriented mindset 80, 81

management creativity 239

marketing business 93–6

marketing women 93–6; breakdown of marketing occupations by gender 94; context 93–4; SMEs overview 95; voices 95–6

Marques, C. 214–21

masculinity: construction 50–1

Mavin, S. 95, 97

Mayer, M. G. 272
Meebo 494
micro-enterprises 125
micro level of analysis 54–6; main
 theme of female entrepreneurship
 54; profiling women entrepreneurs
 in the new venture creation process
 52; two forces in female
 entrepreneurship realm 56
Middle East 43
Middle East and North Africa
 (MENA) 115–49, 124–5
Miller, C. 273
Millman, A. 383
mobile phone 223–5
Mojela, L. 390
mompreneurship 408–10
monetary motives 75
Montessori, M. 462–8; as entrepreneur
 466–8; family, early childhood and
 education 463–5; as physician and
 educator 465–6
motivation 215
Mrs. Fields Cookies 295–6
multiple female roles 86

necessity entrepreneurship: France
 99–107
necessity motivations 76–9, 118;
 entrepreneurship-micro perspective
 78; push–pull trade-off for women
 entrepreneurs 77
Nelson, N. 321
networking 202–5, 374–5; promotion
 of women entrepreneurs 524
new venture creation 1, 74–5; area of
 female entrepreneurship 1–37;
 Brazil 144–9; capability 197–9;
 case studies 127–8, 214; China
 128–33; core competencies
 196–228; emerging BRIC markets
 120–2; emerging BRIC markets
 and female perspectives 122–4;
 female entrepreneurship ethics
 210–13; female entrepreneurship in
 emerging markets 115–49; India
 139–44; macro and micro
 perspectives 52–6; macro level look
 into transitional economies and
 female entrepreneurship 118–20;
 MENA countries 124–5;
 motivations 74; networking and
 social capital 202–5; Russia
 133–9; social capital "flip side" in

the female realm 205–6; stage
 processes 158; start-up and
 innovation in the third sector
 214–21; support system function/
 malfunction in women entrepreneur
 206–10; Village Pay Phone
 Program in Bangladesh 221–8;
 vision 158–9; women entrepreneur
 competitive advantage 199–202;
 women entrepreneurial perspective
 125–7
Ning 494
Nisha Technologies Inc. 512
nongovernmental organizations
 (NGO): India 139–44
Norway 64–6; agent 64; structure
 64–6

objective form 160
O'Leary, A. 512
O'Mara, K. 292
opportunities and threat: objective
 form 160; pre-launching stages
 160–1; subjective form 160–1
opportunity exploitation 315–56;
 barriers and hurdles faced by women
 entrepreneurs 335; breaking down
 the risk barriers 337–40; case
 studies 343–56; characteristics
 318–19; Coronilla of Bolivia
 343–52; and gender 320;
 gendered style 319–21; grabbing
 opportunities 330–2; hurdles from
 environment 334; hurdles from
 women's choices 332, 334; hurdles
 typical to venture creation of
 women-led businesses 332–; Ines
 in Germany 352–6; innovators
 and adaptors in the opportunity-
 exploitation process 329–30;
 learning and innovating in shaping
 new opportunities 328–9; main
 hurdles reported by women
 entrepreneurs 333; networking and
 social capital 325–7; networks;
 locating investors; financial
 approach 326; new venture's life
 cycle, resources needed and the
 female view 322–4; opportunities
 and the business life cycle 321–4;
 overcoming women-related
 barriers 338; planning through a
 female perspective 336–7; process
 316–18; processes 328; social

capital 327–8; symbiotic hurdles that combine women's self-stratification and the public approach to women 334; women-related strategies 340–2
opportunity-hindering factors 77
opportunity motivations 76–9, 118; entrepreneurship-micro perspective 78; opportunity-hindering factors 77; push-pull trade-off for women entrepreneurs 77
Ovil-Brenner, H. 338

Palli Phone *see* Village Pay Phone Program (VPP)
Partner International 515
Patterson, N. 95, 97
Paul-Feni, T. 225
Penrose, E. 385
"Perestroika" 134
personal competencies 200–1
Pixel QI 494
planning 336
Porter, M. E. 116
pre-launching stages 156–9; decision making 168–9; leading models of the business life cycle 157; opportunities and threat 160–1
pre-venture stages 155–94; business challenges 177–8; case studies 174; challenges reflection 179–80; communicating the idea 169, 171–2; competition and supply chain problems 178–9; elders Lizzie Ittinuar and Elisipee Inukpuk 182–3; female-oriented processes 164–9; gaps 161–4; Inuit women entrepreneurs opportunities 180–2; Laos 189–93; Madame Sithonh enterprise 193–4; Madame Vongpackdy Sithonh 188–9; main entrepreneurial strategies in pre-launching stages 172; market niche and business concept 176–7; pre-launching stages 156–9; pre-launching stages and entrepreneurial strategies 172–3; pre-launching stages opportunities and threats 160–1; Robin Goodfellow-Baikie 184–6; staff hiring and moving manufacturing facilities 179; supply chain management in Sri Lanka 175;

Tara Tootoo Fotheringham 183–4; textile industry in Sri Lanka 175–6; woman's view 159–60
proactivity 520–2
professional support 209
protean careers 407
psychoanalytical feminist theory 49
psychological feminist 20
"pull" factors 76–7
pull–push model 76–7, 103
"push' factors 76–7

radical feminist 20, 49–50
Ranga, M. 260
Rashid, R. 123
Razoss 331
recyclable materials: Brazil 145
ReMain Eco Design and Consulting 292
research directions 46–7; female entrepreneurship in research 47; micro and macro business 46; simple process model 46
Resource-based Theory (RBT): role in women's entrepreneurship 385–6
resource-based view (RBV) 19, 197, 213, 234, 263, 487
Robinson, C. 297–311; animal care courses and show business 308–9; career path rich in experience 301–2; childhood marked by discipline and stability 300–1; Dr. Paul Guindon: teacher, guide and mentor 303; encountered obstacles 307–8; inspiring models 300; Kilookas 304–7; main elements of his Résumé 310; passion dating back to childhood 299; passion for animals 297–8; self-employment assistance to launch her business 304; working week **309**
role identities 84–5
role models 522–3
role theory 84–5
Ross, G. 331
Rottenberg, L. 292
Roy, M.-L.: architecture and fashion 28; case study 27–36; childhood 27–8; education 28–9; self-employment 30–1; spiritual fulfillment through self-employment 35–6; spirituality 32–4; urban planning and architecture 31–2;

working in male-dominated
profession 29–30
Rugina, Z. 470
Russia 133–9; business idea evolution
135; Deonis Complex emergence
and growth 135–8; female
entrepreneurship 133–4

Schaefer, G. 329
Schumpeter, J. A. 259
self-employment 94, 97, 413–14;
Brazil 145–6
self-fulfillment 75
Senge, P. 291, 292
Serobe, G. 390
sex: issues in entrepreneurship 51–2
Shaha-Dinajpur, D. 227
Sharkey, T. 494
Shi, X. 128–9
Simpson, S. 159
Sinha, R. 494
Sithonh, V. 188–9; enterprise 193–4;
entrepreneur 188; methodology
188–9
Six Apart 494
SlideShare 494
Smith Whiley, Inc. 386
Smith Whiley & Company 385–6
Snelgar, G. 391
SOCADECO 286
social capital 56, 202–5, 327–8;
avenues 203; characteristics 204;
"flip side" in the female realm
205–6
social constructionism 20, 50–1
social enterprise: Brazil 146–7
social entrepreneurship 420–4; Brazil
144–5; facilitators 423–4; human
capital 422; motivations 422;
opportunities 421–2
social expectation 83–4
social feminism 49
social feminist 20, 49
social influence 81–2
social networking 56
social role 55
socialization 83–4
socio-cultural heritage 58–62
Sri Lanka: supply chain management
175; textile industry 175–6
stage gaps 161–4; assistance 162;
emotional support 162; partnering
162; role models 162; team 162;

unexploited area of pre-venture
creation process 163
*Start-up Nation: The Story of Israel's
Economic Miracle* 327
Statistics Sweden 277
stepwise approach 489
subjective form 160–1
supply chain 178–9; Sri Lanka 175
support systems: 123–4, 126; female
entrepreneurial needs 207; function/
malfunction in women entrepreneur
206–10; support means for women
entrepreneurs 209
Sweden: innovations 276–81; women
as owner-managers 277–81;
women's entrepreneurship in
Scandinavian Welfare State 276–7

T-Base Communication 515
TechCrunch 494
technology-based firms: growth
strategies of women 504–17
telecommunications: Village Pay
Phone Program (VPP) 222–3
textile industry: Sri Lanka 175–6
Thailand 66–8; agent 66; politics 67;
society 67, 68; structure 66–8
The Big Hang-Up 453
The Ledger Check 453
The Zippity-Do 453–4
Thiel, P. 382
Thornton, G. 66
Tisenkopfa-Iltnere, L. 469
Tomasdottir, H. 523
traits 200–1, 211, 212
transactional leaders 446
transformational leaders 446
transition countries 118–20
transitional economies: macro level
118–20; necessity–opportunity
demonstrations at the country
level 119
Trott, M. 494

unemployment 100
Unique Solutions Design 514–15

valuable, rare, imperfectly inimitable
and nonsubstitutable (VRIN) 19,
197–8
Van Der Hout, S. 512
venture capital (VC) 363
Village Pay Phone Program (VPP):
benefits and restraints 225–8;

Grameen Bank Bangladesh 221–8; telecommunications 222–3; women's access and the mobile phone 223–5
virtual entrepreneurship 411–12
vision 158–9; are women more visionary than men? 289–91; case study 297–311; Chantale Robinson and Kilookas 297–311; communicating the vision 292–3; communication-based view 293; core component in the venture creation process 285; as driving force 293–6; entrepreneurship foundation 282–310; feminine vision and women visionaries 289; and gender 286–9; insight from Estée Lauder's and Debbie Fields' success stories 293–6; look into the vision as embedded in feminist theories 288; and mental models 291; separating idealistic and realistic aspects 284–6; in the venture creation process 283–4
Vive Nano 512

Wadhwa, V. 494
Watt-Cloutier, S. 181
Weeks, T. S. 514–15
Wheatley, D. 93
Wherry, E. 494
White Smoke 338
Whitman, M. 446
Whitney, E. 272
Wilie, M. 344
woman-led businesses 42
woman-oriented entrepreneurial path 43
women and business support services 99–107

Women Business Owners and Equity Capital: The Myths Dispelled 366
women entrepreneur: categories of relevant female/male traits 201; competitive advantage 199–202; human capital 199–200; know-how 201–2; support system function/malfunction 206–10; traits and personal competencies 200–1
Women Investment Portfolio Holdings (WIPHOLD) 390–400; case contributions to the women entrepreneurship agenda 399–400; de-listing of WIPHOLD 398–9; institutionalizing (1998 to 2002) 396–7; IPO results 395–6; pioneering women's empowerment 391–2; preparing for the IPO 393–5; raising capital and finding the first deals 392–3; taking stock (2003) 397–8
work-family balance 86, 92; brazil 144–5
work-family factors 75–6, 84–90; benefits of work–family balance 90; contradictory demands 85; leading work–family perspectives and their implications for entrepreneurship 87–9; women entrepreneurs need to do to cope with the work–family conflict 91; work–life conflict 85
work–family segmentation 85–6
World Economic Forum (WEF) 478

Yogurtini 321
Yonath, A. 272
Yu, Y. 130–1

zero-sum situation 361
Zhang, Y. 131–2
Zukerberg, M. 382